MINNESOTA

OTA

TA

Mississippi

IOWA

A

River

AS

MISSOURI

AHOMA

ARKANSAS

LOUISIANA

ATLANTIC

OCEAN

GULF OF

MEXICO

0   150   300 Miles

0   150   300 Km.

Ethel K. Smith Library

Wingate University
Wingate, North Carolina 28174

Encyclopedia
OF THE
AMERICAN WEST

Editorial Board

Encyclopedia

OF THE

AMERICAN WEST

Charles Phillips
Alan Axelrod

Editors

VOLUME 4

Macmillan Reference USA
Simon & Schuster Macmillan
New York

SIMON & SCHUSTER AND PRENTICE HALL INTERNATIONAL
London • Mexico City • New Delhi • Singapore • Sydney • Toronto

Copyright © 1996 by Simon & Schuster

Produced by ZENDA, INC., Nashville, Tennessee
    Design: Gore Studios, Inc.
    Proofreading and Index of Professions: John Reiman
    General Index: Alexa Selph

Simon & Schuster Macmillan
1633 Broadway, New York, NY 10019

PRINTED IN THE UNITED STATES OF AMERICA

printing number
  2 3 4 5 6 7 8 9 10

LIBRARY OF CONGRESS CATALOGING-IN-PUBLICATION DATA

Encyclopedia of the American West / Charles Phillips and Alan Axelrod, editors
        p   cm.
    Includes bibliographical references (p.   ) and index.
    ISBN 0-02-897495-6
    1. West (U.S.)—Encyclopedias.   I. Phillips, Charles, 1948–
    II. Axelrod, Alan, 1952–
    F591.E485 1996
    978—dc20   96-1685
                                                                        CIP

Continued from Volume 3

SANTA ANNA, ANTONIO LÓPEZ DE

A leader in the Mexican revolution against Spain and president of Mexico for eleven separate terms, Antonio López de Santa Anna y Perez (1794–1876) was born in Jalapa, Veracruz. At the age of sixteen, he joined the Fijo de Veracruz Regiment of the Royal Spanish Infantry and fought against Father Miguel Hidalgo's and Father José Maria Morello's movements for Mexican independence. In 1821, as the rebels' efforts met with success, Santa Anna switched sides and became an antimonarchist. He fought to end Spanish rule and joined Agustin de Iturbide, a self-appointed leader of the revolution. Soon after independence, Iturbide crowned himself Emperor Agustin I of Mexico.

The monarchy of Iturbide was burdened by excessive expenditures. Santa Anna took advantage of the prevailing discontent, betrayed Iturbide, and joined the Plan de Case Mata with thirty allies to overthrow the emperor. Over the next thirty-five years, more than thirty-six public figures served as president of Mexico.

In 1829, Santa Anna came to widespread public notice as the "hero of Tampico." King Ferdinand of Spain had attempted to regain his former dominion by landing an expeditionary force at Tampico. Poor military tactics and yellow fever had decimated the Spanish force, thus giving Santa Anna a victory. He returned to Mexico City, deposed President Vincente Guerrero, and installed Vice-President Anastasio Bustamante, who remained in power over the next three years.

In 1832, Santa Anna deposed Bustamante's unstable government and allowed a grateful country to elect him president. Santa Anna retired to his estate at Jalapa and allowed his vice-president, Gomez Farias, to manage the country. When Farias's ultra-liberal reforms provoked the ire of the Catholic church, landholders, and the military, Santa Anna returned to Mexico City to rescue the nation from impending doom. After forcing Farias to flee, he then ruled Mexico single-handedly.

In 1833, Santa Anna was reelected president. Two years later, after declaring Mexico unfit for democracy, he extended his presidential term to eight years, abolished the federal Constitution of 1824, and replaced it with a centralist seven-part charter, which became known as the Siete Leyes or the Constitution of 1836.

While the president's popularity in Mexico was declining, the political winds in Texas were changing. An insurrection had started as a result of the annulment of the Constitution of 1824 and the enactment of laws that abolished slavery in Mexico and closed Texas to further American settlement.

On March 2, 1836, while Santa Anna was poised at the ALAMO, Texans formally declared their independence and appointed DAVID GOUVENEUR BURNET president, LORENZO DE ZAVALA vice-president, and General SAM HOUSTON commander of the army. On March 6, after a prolonged siege, Santa Anna initiated the final assault on the Alamo and ordered that no survivors be taken alive.

Following his victory at the Alamo, Santa Anna learned that Colonel JAMES WALKER FANNIN, JR., had surrendered 365 men to General José Urrea at the Battle of Goliad. Santa Anna ordered the execution of all American prisoners in custody.

On April 21, Santa Anna was defeated and taken prisoner at the Battle of San Jacinto by the forces of General Sam Houston. Although many called for Santa Anna's execution, President Burnet allowed him to leave for Veracruz with the understanding that the Mexican Congress would ratify Texas's independence.

In 1847, during the UNITED STATES–MEXICAN WAR, Santa Anna donned his uniform once more, raised an army of twenty thousand, and attacked General ZACHARY TAYLOR at the Battle of Buena Vista. Shortly afterwards, he was defeated by the U.S. Army under General WINFIELD SCOTT at the Battle of Cerro Gordo.

Following a short, self-imposed exile, Santa Anna was recalled by the Conservatives of Mexico in 1853 and reappointed president.

To finance his grandiose schemes for Mexico, Santa Anna sold to the United States forty-five thousand square miles for $10 million (the GADSDEN PURCHASE). In 1855, he was overthrown by the Liberals and banished from Mexico. During his wide-ranging travels, including a trip to the United States, Santa Anna continued to hope for permission to return to Mexico. In 1874, he was allowed to return. Old and tired, he died in obscurity at the age of eighty-two.

—*Fred L. Koestler*

SEE ALSO: Texas Revolution

SUGGESTED READING:

Calcott, Wilfred Hardy. *Santa Anna: The Story of an Enigma Who Once Was Mexico.* Norman, Okla., 1936.

Santa Anna, Antonio Lopez de. *The Eagle: The Autobiography of Santa Anna.* Edited by Ann Fears Crawford. Trans. by Sam Guyler and Jaime Platon. Austin, Tex., 1967.

SANTA BARBARA, CALIFORNIA

Santa Barbara, California, lies ninety-seven miles northwest of Los Angeles along the Pacific Coast at the base of the Santa Ynéz Mountains and faces the Santa Barbara Channel. A city of some eighty-five thousand people, with almost three hundred thousand more living in the surrounding metropolitan area, Santa Barbara enjoys a mild—some say ideal—climate throughout the year, in part because it is protected to the south by the Santa Barbara Islands and to the north by the mountains. By the early twentieth century, Santa Barbara had come to depend on the tourist trade to bolster an economy based also on citrus crops, cattle, and oil.

Named for the patron saint of mariners by Sebastian Vizcano in 1602, Santa Barbara became the site of a presidio in 1782 and a mission in 1786. The tenth California mission, it was the first founded by Father Fermin de Lasuén, and it was a rather large one, housing some 250 Indians in its village and boasting an extensive waterworks. One of the better preserved of the early Franciscan efforts, the mission became the see of California's first bishop, Francisco Garcia Diego, after Mexico secularized the mission system in 1834. Later, the Franciscans used the mission as a college for novitiates. The mission had its trials. In 1824, its converts joined an Indian uprising and chased out the fathers and the local Spanish troops before fading back into the hills. Before the Franciscans could reoccupy the grounds, Mexico secularized them. In 1846, California's Governor PÍO DE JESUS PICO bought the buildings and the lands; that same year, JOHN CHARLES FRÉMONT raised the U.S. flag over the Santa Barbara presidio. In 1853, the Franciscans returned to set up their school.

Early Spanish padres and settlers developed Santa Barbara as a port and an agricultural market. The city itself was incorporated in 1850 but did not grow much until the arrival of the SOUTHERN PACIFIC RAILROAD, when local boosters began promoting the place as a seaside resort. In the wake of a 1925 earthquake that did substantial damage to the mission, the entire town was rebuilt in the mission-revival style that architect Bertram Goodhue made popular in southern California in the 1920s. The mission is now a museum; and the city, a haven of wealth and privilege, so dedicated to its architectural heritage that the adobe character of its buildings is preserved by law. The law reflects what Kevin Starr has called an architectural *anacapa*, or "mirage," a pleasing illusion based on a genteel metaphor about the Golden Days of Old California.

Before the American conquest of California in the late 1840s, Anglo traders had married into some of Santa Barbara's elite families, and the village itself, developing from both a presidio and a mission, had a healthy middle-class of mestizo artisans. And, even after the conquest, during the early days of Americanization, there had been considerable interaction between Anglo and Hispanic elements of the population. But the great drought of 1863 to 1864 weakened the cattle economy, and in the course of a decade, Hispanic Californians lost much of their land to Anglos. The once-flourishing Hispanic artisan class—carpenters, mechanics, irrigation workers, gardeners, skilled craftspeople of all kinds—began to migrate from the region in the face of the growing Anglo ownership and the Anglo mechanic class. By the mid-1870s, Santa Barbara was thoroughly Americanized, and the remaining Hispanics, especially the mestizos, were a racial minority confined to a barrio called Spanishtown.

Spanishtown, a run-down collection of ancient adobes, many one-room hovels, housed Santa Barbara's embattled Mexican American and Chinese American communities, doubling as the city's saloon and red-light district. Resembling Los Angeles's Sonoratown barrio, Spanishtown seemed particularly to irritate Santa Barbara's leading promoters who, Starr says, had determined not to be another Los Angeles, worshipping growth for growth's sake. Dedicated to the genteel myth of Old California, they were resentful that Spanishtown was not more picturesque, that its "Mexicans" dressed like Americans, that its residents added wooden expansions to their adobes, worked for a living, and wore what they could find. Meanwhile, by 1900, Santa Barbara had become one of the hotel capitals of the world as tourists poured into the seaside resort that boasted so much "historic charm." "The workers of Spanishtown," writes Starr, "were allowed to live so shabbily in the very heart of the city because the labor-intensive [tourist] hotels needed a conveniently located, inexpensive work force."

The 1925 earthquake changed all that. Not only did it make possible the complete architectural revamping of the town, it got rid of the unpicturesque slum at its heart. The *anacapa* the city produced gave the "solidity of physical fact" to Santa Barbara's genteel metaphor of Old California. In fact, says Starr, the pleasing illusion itself became the Santa Barbara alternative to all that Los Angeles offered through aggressive growth.

—Charles Phillips

SEE ALSO: Architecture: Urban Architecture

SUGGESTED READING:

Camarillo, Albert. *Chicanos In a Changing Society: From Mexican Pueblos to American Barrios, 1848–1930.* Cambridge, Mass., 1979.

Starr, Kevin. *Material Dreams: Southern California through the 1920s.* New York, 1990.

SANTA FE AND CHIHUAHUA TRAIL

The Santa Fe Trail, the major trade route between the United States east of the Mississippi and the American Southwest, developed after 1821, when newly independent Mexico encouraged a group of Missouri fur traders to establish commercial links with their SANTA FE outpost. Missouri's WILLIAM BECKNELL, while engaged in the "Indian" trade in the fall of 1821, learned from a company of Mexican soldiers out on the Southern Plains that Mexico had freed itself from Spanish domination and that he could expect a warm welcome in Santa Fe, the capital of New Mexico and long an entrepôt of Mexico's traffic with the Indians and the settlers on its northern frontiers. Becknell hastened to Santa Fe, disposed of what little he had with him in the way of trade goods at a tremendous profit, and return to Missouri flashing bags full of Mexican silver. The following summer, Becknell returned to Santa Fe with three wagonloads of goods for sale, this time avoiding the treacherous Raton Pass that had slowed him down the previous autumn and pioneering a route across the Cimarron Desert. Becknell was not the only one heading for Santa Fe—the GLENN-FOWLER EXPEDITION of 1821 to 1824 also blazed a trail to the trading center—but his mule-train trek through the desert, opening and marking out the main trail, earned him a place in American history textbooks as the "father of the Santa Fe Trade."

At Santa Fe, Becknell's trail joined the historic Chihuahua Trail, which, for centuries had been New Mexico's life line to the Mexican settlements below EL PASO and to Spain's colonial capital at Mexico City. Actually the northern segment of El Camino Real, the Royal Highway (or Road), blazed by JUAN DE OÑATE in the late sixteenth century, the Chihuahua Trail was host to wagon caravans and mule trains bringing vital supplies to Spanish colonials and Catholic missionaries on the frontier, as well as goods to trade with the Indians of the Southwest for buffalo hides, jerked meat, salt, and piñon nuts, which the traders could then sell in the mining towns of Chihuahua on the way back. Not infrequently, they also trafficked in Indian slaves to work the mines. From Santa Fe, the north terminus of the Camino Real, the trail ran south along the Rio Grande through such settlements as Bernalillo, Albuquerque, and Peralta to a westward bend at Socorro, and then across one hundred miles of desert to El Paso del Norte and south toward Chihuahua. Traders called the desert crossing "Jornada del Muerto," or "Deadman's March," but they kept making it anyway with their annual caravans, or *conductas*, the historical prototype of the wagon trains that trundled down the Santa Fe Trail in the nineteenth century. Although Mexico's new republican government declared, in 1821, that the Royal Highway would henceforth be called "Camino Constitucional," or the "Constitutional Highway," folks around Santa Fe continued to call the Chihuahua Trail the "Royal Road" well into the twentieth century.

By the mid-1820s, the Santa Fe trade was established and brisk, grossing for American traders two hundred thousand dollars or so a year, a fortune at the time and certainly enough to persuade Americans such as Missouri's U.S. Senator THOMAS HART BENTON that the Santa Fe Trail was worth protecting from the Indians. Comanches and Kiowas, attracted by the new traffic, had been raiding caravans frequently and posed a serious threat when Benton introduced a bill to Congress in 1825 for funding an official survey of the road and for purchasing the right of way from the Indians. Raids continued nevertheless, and until 1828, the U.S. Army escorted wagon trains across the plains. That year, however, Congress economized, and the Santa Fe traders were left to their own devices.

Almost immediately, it was clear that the effects of establishing the trade route reached even beyond its lucrative traffic and the American infiltration of New Mexico; it demonstrated that wagon travel across the arid plains was possible, which meant that migration to this part of the West was also feasible. The town of Franklin, from which the Santa Fe trade had begun, was entirely washed away by a Missouri River flood in 1828. Independence, Missouri, became headquarters for traders, who loaded their goods on Murphy wagons—built in St. Louis by the Murphy firm—three feet wide and sixteen feet long, with rear wheels five feet in diameter and shod with four-inch-thick iron tires. The wagons were pulled by three or four yokes of oxen or by teams of as many as one dozen mules, which fared better than oxen in the desert.

The first stop on the westward journey was Council Grove, some 150 miles distant. It was here that the traders would pause to organize into larger caravans; for beyond this point, Indian attacks and natural hazards made individual travel foolhardy. A caravan captain was elected by the assembled traders, together with four lieutenants in charge of the four columns into which the wagons were divided. Sergeants of the guard, whose job it was to oversee the nightly watches, were also appointed. The caravan then proceeded west from Council Grove at the rate of ten to fifteen miles a day. The men lived off the austere rations they carried until they hit buffalo country, where it was an easy matter to shoot a feast from among the vast herds. If Indians were present, the four wagon columns formed themselves into a hollow square and proceeded thus, a moving stockade fort. Rivers had to be forded, sheer cliffs negotiated, and quicksand—endemic to ARKANSAS RIVER country—had to be crossed. If the water was high in these areas of quagmire, the unwieldy wagons had to be caulked and floated across.

Then, there was the dreaded Cimarron Desert, fifty miles of waterless, treeless, lifeless sand that had to be traversed at the agonizing ten- or fifteen-mile-a-day rate. The expanse was navigated in much the same way as a seafarer navigates the trackless ocean—by compass. (In 1834, a caravan crossed in torrential rain, leaving wheel ruts that baked in the sun and lasted for years—an indelible trail marker.) Past the Cimarron River, the going got easier all the way into Santa Fe, where the caravans encountered obstacles of a different sort. Mexican customs officials were, at best, whimsical, and it was entirely up to them to assess import duties. Shrewd merchants smuggled in as much as possible, duty-free, but even the shrewdest had to pay duties on the bulk of their goods. The art was in figuring how much to bribe in order to avoid injury to profits. Customs negotiations often consumed weeks.

Despite the hardships, the Mexican tariffs, and the Mexican graft, the trade was extraordinarily profitable at first, until tariffs grew higher and Indian attacks increased in number and ferocity. It was Pawnee and Comanche attacks on the Santa Fe caravans that first touched off demands for aggressive American military intervention against the Indians of the Far West. In 1829, 170 infantry were dispatched under the command of Captain Bennet Riley to accompany the Santa Fe caravan to the Mexican border. When, six miles beyond the border, the caravan was attacked by Comanches, Riley charged across the boundary, but by then the men of the caravan had beaten off the attack themselves. Riley's men rode escort for two more days before returning to the American side of the Arkansas River to await the return of the Santa Fe traders.

The wait was not pleasant. Indians kept the encampment under continual siege; foot soldiers were easy pickings for mounted warriors. The beleaguered troops greeted the return of the caravan with jubilation, for it was escorted by five companies of Mexican cavalry. It was not until 1832 that the War Department dispatched mounted troops to escort the caravans. Not surprisingly, Mexican-American relations became increasingly strained. The Texas rebellion interrupted the trade, of course, but it resumed after the war for independence, and in 1844, JOSIAH GREGG—who had journeyed on a Santa Fe caravan in 1831—came out with his widely read and extremely popular book, *Commerce of the Prairies.* Capturing the romance of the caravans, Gregg made the Santa Fe trafficking seem as much an adventure as a serious, sometimes dangerous business. By the late 1820s, the Americans had captured an existing north-south commerce and turned it east-west as wagon trains from the United States replaced mule trains from Mexico. Now, the Americans were making the roads to Santa Fe a reason to capture New Mexico itself.

By 1840, the Mexican government, growing increasingly nervous over the penetration of their northern frontier, began to look askance at the Santa Fe trade and rue the day that had invited the Missourians down. In 1841, the new Republic of Texas, which itself had been ripped from Mexican hands by the Anglos, launched an abortive Texas–Santa Fe expedition to conquer New Mexico. Mexico passed laws to restrict the activities of the foreigners, but they seemed to have little effect. As the Mexican press grew shrill about Anglos on its borders, it became clear that little could be done, short of war, to ease Mexico's anxiety, and although some editors did, indeed, call for a preemptive attack, the government was not so foolish as to listen to them. That Mexico's fears were entirely justified was evident when war did come. General STEPHEN WATTS KEARNY marched immediately into Santa Fe and claimed the province for the United States. After the UNITED STATES–MEXICAN WAR, of course, all restrictions vanished, the army built forts along the trail to protect traders and pioneers, and various companies launched stagecoach and mail service. By 1855, the Santa Fe trade had reached $5 million annually. Traffic became especially heavy during the California gold rush and, again, during the CIVIL WAR, when New Mexico became a target for the Confederacy. The trail continued to serve as an avenue of trade until after 1878, when the Santa Fe Railroad, at last, surmounted the Raton Pass. Two years later, it reached Santa Fe itself, and the Santa Fe Trail faded into history.

—*Charles Phillips and Alan Axelrod*

SEE ALSO: Overland Freight

SUGGESTED READING:

Chalfant, William Y. *Dangerous Passage: The Santa Fe Trail and the Mexican War.* Norman, Okla., 1994.

Moorhead, Max L. *New Mexico's Royal Road: Trade and Travel on the Chihuahua Trail.* Norman, Okla., 1995.

Taylor, Morris F. *First Mail West, Stagecoach Lines on the Santa Fe Trail.* Albuquerque, N. Mex., 1971

Walker, Henry Pickering. *The Wagonmasters: High Plains Freighting from the Earliest Days of the Santa Fe Trail to 1880.* Norman, Okla., 1966.

SANTA FE, NEW MEXICO

Originally settled by Spanish farmers around 1607, Santa Fe was established as the center of the "kingdom of NEW MEXICO" in 1610 by Don Pedro de Peralta, the second governor of New Mexico, who wanted a capital that was centrally located, well watered, and uninhabited by Indians. "La Villa de Santa Fe," as it was called, received its name in honor of the campsite used by Ferdinand and Isabella when they sieged Granada during the reconquest of Spain. Situated at the base of the Sangre de Cristo Mountains on a stream that had plentiful trout and water supplemented by natural springs, Santa Fe fulfilled Peralta's criteria and allowed the Spanish government to aid the Franciscan missionaries who set out to convert Pueblo Indians conquered by the Spanish.

For its first seventy years, Santa Fe remained a small hamlet with scattered buildings made of mud brick and rock. The town's plaza consisted of a number of official buildings, including today's PALACE OF THE GOVERNORS. At the time, the plaza occupied a small incline on the north side of the Santa Fe River, while on the south side, a barrio (neighborhood) was inhabited by Indian carriers and servants. This area, named "Analco"—a Nahuatl term for "other side of the river"—was also home to the San Miguel mission built sometime around 1625.

In 1680, the Pueblo Indians, motivated by drought, disease, and mistreatment at the hands of their conquerors, united to overthrow the Spanish administration. For the next thirteen years, Santa Fe was occupied by Tewa and Tano Indians from the pueblos of Taos and Picuris. In 1693, Don DIEGO DE VARGAS led an expedition of settlers and soldiers to recapture Santa Fe. He camped outside the city on a site that is today Rosario Cemetery, named for a statue of "Our Lady of the Rosary, La Conquistadora," which the settlers carried with them and considered to be the patroness of the town.

After the reconquest, a new parish church, which would house "La Conquistadora," was completed in 1714. The north transept of the church still houses the old statue in what is today the cathedral. San Miguel, which had been burned, was rebuilt, but still Santa Fe did not grow.

That changed, however, when Mexico won its independence from Spain. The Mexican policy of opening its doors to trade encouraged United States citizens who visited the capital city to engage in trade. The Mexican policy, coupled with New Mexico's proximity to Missouri, gave rise to the Santa Fe Trail, which created a commercial marriage between north-central Mexico and the eastern United States. Santa Fe became the midpoint for most of the commerce. In addition, the fur-trapping industry peaked in the Rocky Mountains, and a good portion of the pelts were shipped to Missouri via Santa Fe.

Over the next thirty years, the town grew to more than four thousand inhabitants, a good portion of whom came from the United States. Throughout the summer, caravans arrived from the East to meet merchants from Mexico. As many as eighteen wagon trains entered Santa Fe each year, usually from June through October.

When the UNITED STATES–MEXICAN WAR broke out, the United States Army of the West quickly occupied Santa Fe, and the town suffered an influx of soldiers, who increased its population by almost half. With the end of the war, Santa Fe became a part of the United States and served as New Mexico's territorial capital until 1912. During these years, the Santa Fe Trail became a stagecoach route; the town was occupied for a brief period by Confederate troops during the CIVIL WAR; New Mexico Governor Lew Wallace finished his novel *Ben Hur*; the ATCHISON, TOPEKA, AND SANTA FE RAILROAD replaced the Santa Fe Trail; and a majority of THEODORE ROOSEVELT's rough riders were recruited and sworn in on the plaza in front of the Palace of the Governors.

"East Side of Plaza, Santa Fe," 1866. *Courtesy National Archives.*

After New Mexico became the forty-seventh state of the Union in 1912, Santa Fe and some of its neighboring cities became tourist destinations. A colony of artists and writers developed in the town. The original plaza had shrunk to half its size, and all the main roads were paved. During World War II, Santa Fe became the gathering point for all mail and people destined to work on the Manhattan Project that developed the atomic bomb in neighboring Los Alamos.

Santa Fe's elevation is seven thousand feet. It has a ski run, outdoor opera, chamber music festival, chorus, two colleges, and six museums. The population in the mid-1990s was sixty thousand, and its two major industries were tourism and state government. Santa Fe is the oldest capital city in the United States and still retains reflections of its long history in its town plan, streetscapes, and people.

—*Thomas E. Chávez*

SEE ALSO: Pueblo Revolt; Spanish and Mexican Settlement

SUGGESTED READING:
Horgan, Paul. *The Centuries of Santa Fe.* New York, 1956.
Noble, David Grant. *Santa Fe: History of an Ancient City.* Santa Fe, N. Mex., 1989.
Sherman, John. *Santa Fe: A Pictorial History.* Santa Fe, N. Mex., 1983.

SANTA FE RING

The Santa Fe Ring (or Land Grant Ring), a loose, often changing coalition of prominent men, dominated politics and much of the economic activity in the New Mexico Territory. The ring flourished during the 1870s and 1880s and is thought to have had considerable influence into the early 1900s.

Missouri lawyers Thomas Benton Catron and his mentor STEPHEN BENTON ELKINS were the dominant figures throughout the ring's existence. Elkins arrived in New Mexico in 1863 and rapidly climbed the ladder of political office. He settled in Santa Fe after 1865, about the time that Catron arrived in the territory. Both men were staunch Republicans, although Catron was regarded skeptically by some party members because of his former Democratic affiliations and his service in the Confederate army. Their activities and the history of the ring were inextricably intertwined.

Gilded Age thought and attitudes, introduced into New Mexico's unique milieu, produced the Santa Fe Ring. In this period, the notorious Tammany Hall ran

New York City, and comparable machines dominated other urban centers. Many industrialists and politicians cynically subverted economic, legal, and political systems for personal gain. They were typically audacious, shrewd, domineering, and insatiable. Their consciences were assuaged, if it were necessary, by the philosophy of "social Darwinism," which justified material profit regardless of conventional morality.

While some rings and machines collected dues, held public meetings, and maintained headquarters, the Santa Fe Ring did not. It was amorphous, and its membership changed constantly. A few historians deny that it even existed, but most agree both that it was a powerful force and that Catron was its central figure. His political influence was undeniably great (he became a U.S. senator when New Mexico attained statehood), and his landholdings were impressive. Elkins was an equally central figure while he lived in New Mexico, but he was rarely in the area after his terms as territorial delegate to Congress from 1873 to 1877. Although his political focus then moved to the East Coast (he served as U.S. senator from West Virginia from 1895 to 1911), he continued to pursue many enterprises in New Mexico, often behind the scenes and in close association with Catron. His interests included land transactions, mining, and railroads, among other projects.

From the late 1860s to 1885, most of New Mexico's governors were reportedly associated with the Santa Fe Ring, as were many land officers, legislators, and judges. Land grant manipulations—based on biased surveys, false evidence, and tortured legal interpretation—were the norm for the ring. People associated with the ring were charged with murder in connection with the Colfax County War and the MAXWELL LAND GRANT COMPANY, but no convictions were ever attained. The LINCOLN COUNTY WAR was another major incident in which the ring was allegedly involved.

Not all ring associates were Republicans. Charles Gildersleeve and Henry Waldo, prominent Democrats, clearly were associated with the ring at times. Their participation shows that party affiliations were weak and that ring associates frequently cooperated not only for political power but also in pursuit of land and other profitable enterprises. The ring's preeminence declined markedly after 1885, when a Democratic president was inaugurated and filled New Mexican patronage positions with members of his party.

—*John Porter Bloom*

SEE ALSO: City Government; Federal Government

SUGGESTED READING:
Lamar, Howard R. "The Santa Fe Ring." In *The Far Southwest, 1846–1912: A Territorial History.* New Haven, Conn., and London, 1966.

SATANK
(KIOWA)

Born in the Black Hills region of a mother who was part Sacree, Satank (ca. 1810–1871), sometimes called Sitting Bear, was a medicine man and leader of the Principal Dogs, or Ten Bravest, a Kiowa military society. He was instrumental in arranging peace between the Kiowas and the Cheyennes about 1840.

In 1867, Satank, KICKING BIRD, SATANTA, and Stumbling Bear represented the Kiowas at the Medicine Lodge Council. Three years later, Satank's son died during a raid in Texas. The father traveled to Texas, collected his son's bones in a bundle, and carried them on a second horse wherever he went.

Satank, with Satanta, BIG TREE, and other Kiowas attacked an army supply train on its way to Fort Richardson in northern Texas in 1871. Ironically, the group of some one hundred warriors earlier in the day had allowed WILLIAM TECUMSEH SHERMAN and his escorts to pass the same road unmolested. The attack on the train resulted in the death of eight of the twelve teamsters. The Kiowas looted the wagon contents and stole forty-one mules. One teamster made his way to the fort to report the attack.

Later, Chief Satanta boasted of the raid to Indian Agent Lawrie Tatum, who reported the skirmish to Sherman. Satank, Satanta, and Big Tree were arrested

Satank. Photograph by William S. Soule, ca. 1868–1871. *Courtesy National Archives.*

and prepared for transport to Texas to stand trial. On the way, Satank sat manacled and under heavy guard. He began singing his death song, managed to slip off his manacles, and attacked his guard. He was shot dead, and his body was returned to Fort Sill for burial. Satanta and Big Tree were tried and convicted for their part in the supply-wagon raid. Sentenced to die, their punishment was commuted, and they were released in 1873.

—*Patricia Hogan*

SEE ALSO: Medicine Lodge Treaty of 1867; Texas Frontier Indian Wars

SUGGESTED READING:
Mayhill, Mildred P. *The Kiowa*. Norman, Okla., 1962.

SATANTA
(KIOWA)

Elevated to the rank of chief in his twenties because of his fearlessness, Satanta (ca. 1807–1878) was bold and reckless on the hunt and in battle and arrogant and talkative in tribal councils. Successful in war against hostile tribes and white settlers in Texas, New Mexico, and Kansas during the 1840s through the 1860s, he was noted for his raids along the Texas frontier.

In the decade after the Civil War, Satanta led the Kiowas in a continuing campaign of war and diplomacy against the U.S. Army and the settlers. In 1867, while representing the Kiowas on a peace mission to Fort Larned, Kansas, he so impressed General W. S. Hancock with his sincerity that Hancock gave him an officer's uniform, which Satanta wore while raiding the post's corral a short time later.

Satanta was also an able diplomat in his representation of the tribes. He signed the treaties of Little Arkansas on October 18, 1865, and Medicine Lodge on October 21, 1867, and at the end of the council, he called for peace as "our mutual heritage." But he was unhappy with the reservation lands and soon led the tribes out of the reservation to war. Captured by troops under Major General PHILIP H. SHERIDAN after a winter campaign in 1868, Satanta was briefly imprisoned along with LONE WOLF but was freed when he promised to accept the reservation.

After Sheridan left the Indian Territory in 1869, Satanta and the Kiowas continued to raid in Texas and, in 1871, destroyed the Warren wagon train and killed seven teamsters in the Salt Creek Massacre. Arrested by WILLIAM TECUMSEH SHERMAN, Satanta and the chiefs BIG TREE and SATANK were taken to Jacksboro, Texas, for trial. Satank was killed trying to escape; the other two were tried and sentenced to death by hanging. The sentence was commuted to life imprisonment, and the two were paroled by Texas Governor E. J. Davis in 1873. Satanta resumed raiding within a few weeks. Recaptured, he was returned to prison in Huntsville, Texas. On October 11, 1878, he died after a fall from a window of the penitentiary hospital. According to different accounts, he was either pushed from the window or committed suicide because of depression brought on by prison.

—*Patrick H. Butler, III*

SEE ALSO: Medicine Lodge Treaty of 1867; Texas Frontier Indian Wars

SUGGESTED READING:
Mayhall, Mildred P. *The Kiowas*. Norman, Okla., 1962.

SAUK INDIANS

SEE: Native American Peoples: Peoples Removed from the East

SCALPING

No image of Indian warfare is better known among whites than scalping, or subject to more folklore, misunderstanding, and misrepresentation. Traditionally, whites have used the Native American practice of scalping as evidence of the Indians' incorrigible barbarity. Others, imbuing the ritual with special religious significance, have claimed that in taking a scalp, the attacker was releasing the "soul" or "spirit" of the slain. Still others have suggested that scalping was unknown among Indian tribes before Europeans arrived in numbers.

Scalping was, in fact, practiced by Native Americans before the arrival of Europeans. Several early explorers reported instances of the practice, among them Jacques Cartier in 1535, Hernando de Soto in 1540, and Tristan de Luna in 1559. Not all tribes, however, practiced scalping, and it spread generally from East to West with the migration of Eastern tribes and contact with whites, who had adopted the custom from Eastern Indians. While whites did not introduce scalping among native populations, they did contribute to the proliferation of the custom, both by pushing Eastern Indians westward and by example.

Scalping was not intended as a spiritual benefit to the victim; at least, there is no evidence to support such a claim. The act, in truth, was meant as an insult, and the scalp served as a battle trophy. Colonial and later authorities added a profit motive to the practice by offering scalp bounties, rewards paid for the scalps of "hostiles."

Different tribal groups practiced various methods of taking the scalp. Some tribes took the whole skin of the upper head, ears included; others removed only the crown. After Europeans introduced sharper, sturdier steel knives and hatchets, many tribes practiced a faster method of scalping, which involved grasping the forelock, making a single cut in the front of the head, and popping the "scalp lock" trophy out with a quick tug. As the scalp-lock method was an abbreviated technique for taking scalps, so the practice of scalping seems to have its origins in the first place as a substitute for decapitation. The scalp trophy stood for the head, even as the head represented the entire person of the victim. In some tribes of the Great Plains, decapitation persisted, and a severed head was considered a greater trophy than a scalp or scalp lock.

—*Alan Axelrod*

SEE ALSO: Native American Cultures: Warfare

Artist George Catlin's sketches of scalping. From *Illustrations of the Manners, Customs, and Condition of the North American Indians. Courtesy New York Public Library.*

SCHOOLCRAFT, HENRY ROWE

Henry Rowe Schoolcraft (1793–1864) became inextricably linked to that part of the American West known as the "Old Northwest" during the formative decades of the 1820s and 1830s due, in part, to the popularity of his published travel narratives and to his writings about Native American cultures. Born at Norman's Kill, in the Manor of Rensselaerswyck, a large tract of land near Albany, New York, he went west as a young man and traveled throughout the Great Lakes region with Lewis Cass, Michigan's territorial governor. The pinnacle of Schoolcraft's exploration career came when he located the source of the Mississippi River and named it Itasca Lake. In the 1830s, 1840s, and 1850s, he built his reputation as one of the nation's preeminent Indian experts by publishing books that portrayed the complexity of Native American cultures to the world's scientific community.

Schoolcraft spent more than twenty years observing Indian life and examining religions, cultural beliefs, child-rearing practices, and societal values. Working as an Indian agent, he was in close and prolonged contact with Ojibwas (Chippewas), Ottawas, Dakotas, and Potawatomis. But it was his 1823 marriage to a mixed-blood Ojibwa woman, Jane Johnston, that gave him access to Ojibwa society that few outsiders have ever enjoyed. Jane Schoolcraft explained the inner meanings of her culture to her husband, who observed but could not comprehend it without her assistance.

That immersion into the Native American world contributed to Schoolcraft's desire to create a massive multivolume manuscript recounting the history and conditions of the North American Indian tribes. The seemingly overwhelming task occupied Schoolcraft for more than five years. Completed in 1856, *Historical and Statistical Information Respecting the History, Conditions, and Prospects of the Indian Tribes of the United States* was published between 1851 and 1856 in six volumes by Philadelphia publisher Lippincott, Grambo and Company.

Schoolcraft had many interests, and his personality reflected many influences: attitudes acquired from his schoolmasters, methods assimilated from the scientists he met, and values appropriated from his family—especially his father. He was an ambitious youth who was quick to use any advantage presented to promote his own interests—an attitude contemporary biographers claim is often overlooked.

Despite all his failings and biases, Schoolcraft left a legacy as one of the nation's first scientific ethnographers. His writings on the Indian peoples of North

America are still consulted by many scholars interested in understanding the nineteenth-century Old Northwest. Schoolcraft left vivid descriptions of the environment and of the peoples—descriptions that give current researchers insight into a world that is gone forever.

Schoolcraft's fame and fortune faded as he grew older. When he died on December 10, 1864, in Washington, D.C., his widow did not have the money to pay for his burial. The funeral costs for the legendary explorer and Indian agent were paid by the United States government as an acknowledgment for his many years of service.

—*Duane P. Mosser*

SEE ALSO: Art: Surveys and Expeditions; Exploration and Science

SUGGESTED READING:

Bieder, Robert E. *Science Encounters the Indian, 1820–1880.* Norman, Okla., 1986.

Bremer, Richard C. *Indian Agent and Wilderness Scholar: The Life of Henry Rowe Schoolcraft.* Mount Pleasant, Mich., 1987.

Schoolcraft, Henry Rowe. *Narrative Journal of Travels from Detroit Northwest through the Great Chain of American Lakes to the Sources of the Mississippi River in the Year 1820.* Reprint. New York, 1970.

Warren, William. *History of the Ojibway People.* Reprint. St. Paul, Minn., 1984.

SCHOOL LIFE ON THE FRONTIER

Because schools on the mid-nineteenth-century frontier were entirely under local control, school life reflected the uncertainty and fluidity of isolated settlements. Before schools were established in a settlement, families taught their children at home and used as texts whatever books they owned, magazines, and newspapers covering cabin walls. As more families located in an area, subscription schools were formed. Teachers in these schools were paid by the families of students. Subscription schools were also established when public funds for a teacher's salary were exhausted. In these cases, enterprising teachers set up schools in frontier churches or private homes or sometimes in schoolhouses. When a frontier settlement decided to establish a public school, often as a way of attracting other settlers, community members elected a school board and constructed a one-room schoolhouse of local materials ranging from boards or logs to sod or adobe, and heated with a central stove.

Many communities were anxious to start schools. Just five weeks after Martha Boynton, a pioneer teacher from Massachusetts, arrived in Wisconsin's Wyoming Valley in 1850, the community built a frame school and furnished it with a blackboard and globe. Boynton opened the school to thirty-three scholars from age four to twenty.

Classroom activities on the frontier followed a general pattern. The teacher heard small groups recite while the other pupils worked math problems on slates or read from assorted texts. The teacher presented lessons from the Bible and introduced singing, poetry, spelling bees, and circle games like "Drop the Handkerchief." Through holding public recitations at the end of a term, the teacher helped develop community support for the school.

By the late nineteenth century, school life in new settlements became more stable as county superintendents of schools exercised more control over local schools. States passed school laws requiring minimum terms. Teachers attended summer institutes and became qualified to teach by passing examinations. Standard texts, including McGuffey's readers, were generally available. What did not change, however, was the one-room schoolhouse, often in an isolated location, attended by mixed ages, and taught by one teacher.

—*Polly Welts Kaufman*

SEE ALSO: Public Schools; Teachers on the Frontier

SUGGESTED READING:

Fuller, Wayne E. *The Old Country School: The Story of Rural Education in the Middle West.* Chicago, 1982.

Gulliford, Andrew. *America's Country Schools.* Washington, D.C., 1984.

Kaufman, Polly Welts. *Women Teachers on the Frontier.* New Haven, Conn., 1984.

SCHREYVOGEL, CHARLES

Artist Charles Schreyvogel (1861–1912) grew up in poverty on New York City's East Side and in Hoboken, New Jersey. As a youth he sketched constantly, learned to carved meerschaum and was eventually apprenticed to a die sinker and, later, a lithographer.

Between 1887 and 1890, he studied art in Munich under Carl Marr and Frank Kirchbach. After returning to the United States, he established a small studio in Hoboken, where he supplemented his income from lithography by producing portraits and landscapes, miniatures on ivory, and calendar illustrations.

Captivated by the West, Schreyvogel sketched performers at Buffalo Bill's Wild West show in New York before finally embarking on a long trip to the Indian

Charles Schreyvogel at work. *Courtesy National Cowboy Hall of Fame and Western Heritage Center.*

reservations and cattle ranges of Colorado and Arizona in 1893. He returned to Hoboken laden with Western artifacts and imaginative artistic compositions but found little market for his work until his canvas, *My Bunkie,* won top honors at the 1900 National Academy Exhibition.

Schreyvogel's success irritated FREDERIC REMINGTON, the premier purveyor of Western images of the period, who publicly criticized the upstart's depictions of the frontier army. In the heated controversy with Remington over the painting *Custer's Demand,* Schreyvogel's defenders included ELIZABETH CUSTER and President THEODORE ROOSEVELT.

Unlike many of his contemporaries in the Western field, Schreyvogel steadfastly refused to become an illustrator. Although his artistic production was relatively limited, photographic reproductions of his works, known as platinum prints, were widely published. The artist also experimented with sculpture, and at least two clay models were cast in bronze by Tiffany's after his untimely death in Hoboken from blood poisoning.

Today Schreyvogel's works adorn many important public and private collections including the Metropolitan Museum of Art, the THOMAS GILCREASE INSTITUTE, and the NATIONAL COWBOY HALL OF FAME AND WESTERN HERITAGE CENTER.

—*B. Byron Price*

SEE ALSO: Art: Western Art

SUGGESTED READING:
Horan, James D. *The Life and Art of Charles Schreyvogel: Painter-Historian of the Indian-Fighting Army of the American West.* New York, 1969.
Kobbé, Gustave. "A Painter of the Western Frontier." *The Cosmopolitan* 31 (October 1901): 563–573.
Schreyvogel, Charles. *My Bunkie and Others.* New York, 1909.
Taft, Robert. *Artists and Illustrators of the Old West, 1850–1900.* New York, 1953.

SCHULZE, TYE LEUNG

Tye Leung Schulze (1887–1972) was born in San Francisco, California, to Chinese immigrant parents who lived with their eight children and several other relatives in two overcrowded rooms in Chinatown. Her parents sent her to a Presbyterian school to learn English, but after her older sister ran away to escape an arranged marriage, the embarrassed parents decided to send twelve-year-old Tye Leung in her place. One of her teachers then placed her in the Presbyterian Mission Home under the care of its matron DONALDINA MACKENZIE CAMERON.

Remaining at the home for nine years, Tye Leung converted to Christianity and acted as Cameron's interpreter. In 1910, Cameron recommended her for a post as interpreter for Chinese immigrant women at the Angel Island Immigration Station. Having thus broken a race barrier in hiring, she went on to break others. In 1912, she became the first Chinese American woman to vote in a primary election. In 1913, she met her future husband, white immigration inspector Charles Schulze. Because of California's antimiscegenation law (which prohibited whites from marrying Asian Americans), they went to Vancouver, Washington, to get married; both then lost their jobs.

Tye Leung Schulze had four children. After working at several different jobs, she took one she would hold for twenty years, as night operator at the Chinatown telephone exchange. Her job, her connections, and her language skills allowed her to assist Chinese Americans by smoothing the way for them with lawyers, courts, and immigration officials. Her success in doing so made her widely respected in San Francisco's Chinatown.

—*Peggy Pascoe*

SUGGESTED READING:
Yung, Judy. *Chinese Women of America: A Pictorial History.* Seattle, Wash., 1986.

SCHURZ, CARL

Secretary of the interior under Rutherford B. Hayes, Carl Schurz (1829–1906) was born in Germany near the village of Liblar on the west bank of the Rhine, about fourteen miles southwest of Cologne. In 1852, after engaging in reform activities in Germany and living for a short time in Switzerland and England, Schurz immigrated to the United States. He first lived in Philadelphia but moved to Watertown, Wisconsin, in 1856. There, among his German neighbors, he took up the antislavery cause. Speaking as a stump orator, Schurz affiliated with the newly formed Republican party and encouraged his fellow GERMAN AMERICANS to do likewise. His antislavery endeavors led to his nomination for lieutenant-governor on the Republican ticket in 1857; he lost the election by a narrow margin.

Carl Schurz. *Editors' collection.*

After Abraham Lincoln's nomination as the candidate for president, Schurz campaigned energetically for the Republican throughout the Midwest and East and swung the German American vote to Lincoln. For his help, Schurz was rewarded with the office of minister plenipotentiary to Spain. In January 1862, he returned to the United States to accept a commission as brigadier general in the Union Army and to persuade Lincoln that an end to slavery should be the goal of the Civil War.

In 1868, while living in Missouri, Schurz won the nomination as the liberal Republican candidate for the United States Senate. The Missouri legislature elected him, and he took his seat on March 4, 1869, the day of Ulysses S. Grant's inauguration as president. Shortly thereafter, Schurz denounced the president's administration as corrupt and, in 1871, launched the Liberal Republican party with the intent of derailing Grant's bid for reelection in 1872. The Liberal Republican candidate (Horace Greeley) failed to defeat Grant, and Schurz decided not to seek a second term in the Senate. During the next presidential election, Schurz supported Governor Rutherford B. Hayes of Ohio. Hayes' election brought Schurz back to Washington in the position of secretary of the interior, again as a reward for securing the German American vote.

As secretary of the interior, Schurz administered the GENERAL LAND OFFICE, the Territories of the United

States, the UNITED STATES GEOLOGICAL SURVEY, the Entomological Survey, the national parks and forests, public buildings and grounds, and an assortment of bureaus including the BUREAU OF INDIAN AFFAIRS, Patents, Census, and Education. Schurz was an early preservationist. He called for laws to end wasteful lumbering, timber theft, homesteading on forest land, and setting fires on public lands. He also advocated the preservation of forest land and the natural environment by planting seedlings each year to protect soils and streams.

Schurz's interest in Native Americans was humanistic. Schurz believed that the United States should seek a peace with Indian tribes and argued that the Bureau of Indian Affairs should remain under his jurisdiction rather than be transferred to the War Department, as some officials were urging. His first approach was the consolidation of Native Americans in the Indian Territory. The forced removal of the Poncas from their Missouri River reservation in Nebraska to the Indian Territory, however, produced a public outcry in the East and forced him to abandon his large reservation policy. Schurz hoped to accomplish the assimilation of Native Americans by educating their children, at least through the elementary level, and by training them to become farmers and ranchers. The shift from day schools on reservations to industrial boarding schools, like the one established in 1879 by Captain RICHARD HENRY PRATT in Carlisle, Pennsylvania, was the hallmark of his approach to assimilation by means of education.

Schurz's efforts to improve the quality of Indian agents was a dismal failure. Under his administration of the Interior Department, agents were no longer appointed by the Christian churches as they had been under GRANT'S PEACE POLICY. Instead, appointments were made through political patronage, and many agents with no qualification or knowledge about the needs of Native Americans were appointed to serve as agents.

Upon leaving the cabinet in 1881, Schurz worked for the *New York Evening Post* in the early 1880s and for *Harper's Weekly* in the 1890s. He became president of the National Civil Service Reform League in 1892 and served for ten years in that office.

—*Henry E. Fritz and Marie L. Fritz*

SEE ALSO: Indian Schools; United States Forest Service; United States Indian Policy

SUGGESTED READING:

Fritz, Henry E. "The Board of Indian Commissioners and Ethnocentric Reform, 1878–1893." In *Indian-White Relations: A Persistent Paradox*. Edited by James F. Smith and Robert Kvasnicka. Washington, D.C., 1976.

———. *The Movement for Indian Assimilation, 1860–1890*. Philadelphia, 1963.

Fuess, Claude Moore. *Carl Schurz: Reformer*. New York, 1932.

Mardock, Robert W. *The Reformers and the American Indian*. Columbia, Mo., 1971.

Prucha, Francis Paul. *American Indian Policy in Crisis: Christian Reformers and the Indian, 1865–1900*. Norman, Okla., 1976.

Schafer, Joseph. *Carl Schurz: Militant Liberal*. Evansville, Wis., 1930.

SCOTT, DRED

SEE: *Dred Scott* Decision

SCOTT, WINFIELD

Born in Petersburg, Virginia, Winfield Scott (1786–1866) was a dominant figure in the U.S. Army for more than a half-century. He attended William and Mary and was admitted to the bar before joining the army as a captain of artillery in 1808 and starting service on the Louisiana frontier.

During the WAR OF 1812, Scott won fame at the battles of Chippewa and Lundy's Lane. He was commissioned a brigadier general and received brevet rank as major general, while being recognized with medals by both Congress and the state of Virginia. He remained in the army, studied tactics in Europe, and was appointed departmental commander while writing and publishing *Rules and Regulations for the Field Exercise and Maneuvers of Infantry,* which became a standard reference for the army until the CIVIL WAR. His emphasis on military formality and propriety earned him the nickname "Old Fuss and Feathers," but he was also one of the most effective officers in the army. In 1838, he supervised the removal of the Cherokee Indians from Georgia along the TRAIL OF TEARS. He was also active in the Seminole War.

In 1841, Scott was made commanding general of the army and organized the forces for the UNITED STATES–MEXICAN WAR. Originally denied a field command because of his Whig politics, Scott was given command of the force that captured Veracruz in 1847. Scott's planning for the campaign had won over Democrats who had previously opposed giving him command. Among the innovations he developed for the campaign were the first amphibious landing craft and the use of rockets.

During his campaign to capture Mexico City, Scott's troops were plagued by lack of transport. In addition, many of the troops, as short-term volunteers, left for the United States when their terms ended. Scott pushed his command inland and succeeded in capturing the Mexican capital, thus demonstrating a triumph of personal will that overcame all obstacles. During that campaign, his forces of eleven thousand were outnumbered almost three to one by the Mexican army.

Four years later, the Whigs nominated Scott for president, but he lost the election to Democrat Franklin Pierce.

With the coming of the Civil War, Scott attempted to organize the army to prevent secession. His "Anaconda Plan" relied on the occupation of the Mississippi and a blockade of the coast to force the South into submission. Scott called Robert E. Lee back from Texas in 1861 and attempted to persuade him to take command of the army. In November 1861, Scott retired to West Point, where he lived and wrote about his career until his death.

—*Patrick H. Butler, III*

SUGGESTED READING:
Smith, Arthur D. Howden. *Old Fuss and Feathers: The Life and Exploits of Lieutenant General Winfield Scott.* New York, 1937.

SEARS ROEBUCK AND COMPANY

SEE: Trade Catalogues

SEATTLE, WASHINGTON

Seattle, with a 1990 population of 516,259, is the largest city in the northwestern portion of the forty-eight contiguous states. Located on the eastern shore of Puget Sound, Seattle sits on an hourglass isthmus with the harbor, Elliott Bay, intruding on its western shore and Lake Washington lining the eastern. By 1851, several Anglo-American settlers were farming in the valley that is now in Seattle's south end. But the party led by brothers Arthur and David Denny that landed that November prompted the formal platting and development of a city.

After a bleak winter on an exposed southwestern point, Arthur Denny moved across Elliott Bay and secured a land claim in the area now known as Pioneer Square. Other early entrepreneurs included Henry Yesler, who built the first steam-powered sawmill on the Sound, and the gregarious David (Doc) Maynard, who started salmon packing, thus giving the town initial industries derived from local resources. Timber from Seattle's hillside and other Puget Sound sites was shipped to California. Denny, Yesler, Maynard, and additional arrivals enlarged the village as they platted districts, built houses and stores, started other small industries, and constructed a wharf.

As settlement crept north along the shoreline and east up a ridge, city fathers helped ensure the town's permanence when they secured the territorial university (now the University of Washington). A minor skirmish during the Indian Wars of the middle 1850s barely slowed the town's growth. After losing the original northwest railroad terminus to neighboring Tacoma, Seattle businessmen endeavored to build railroads on their own; these tracks barely reached the hinterlands, but they tapped valuable coal fields in Cascade Mountains foothills. After 1893, Seattle became the hub of JAMES J. HILL's Great Northern Railroad, and shipping by both land and sea increased. Meanwhile, a fire that destroyed the business district in June 1889 led civic leaders to enact stricter and more enlightened zoning and building codes and to reorganize the city's streets to allow wise expansion. In 1897, the sawmill town became the primary taking-off point for Alaska-Yukon gold-seekers.

As prosperity increased, the city regraded hills, filled marshy areas to allow for expansion, and annexed several adjacent communities. Between 1900 and 1910, Seattle's population mushroomed from 81,000 to 237,000, a population growth that solidified the city's position as the dominant metropolis of the Northwest. Such rapid growth and busy seaport surroundings contributed to a bawdy atmosphere and wide-open corruption that led to the recall of the mayor and the imprisonment of his police chief. Yet, there were cultural refinements as well and a series of social and political reforms. A municipally owned hydroelectric-power project and a street-railway system were developed early in the century. During World War I, shipbuilding increased to major proportions, but this was followed by a short-lived general strike in February 1919 that accentuated the city's reputation for radical labor activities. In the 1920s, the bustling economy slowed even as the city became increasingly amalgamated with national trends: downtown became a modern complex of department stores and office buildings, and the automobile hastened the growth of outlying areas.

World War II probably affected the city and its environs more than any other single event. Defense contracts, primarily in shipyards and in the rising Boeing Aircraft Company, permanently altered the economic status of the city, and military activities around Puget Sound mounted. War also saw the removal of nine thousand Japanese Americans, who were interned in distant camps; most later returned, some to hostile receptions. Following the war, Boeing continued to dominate Seattle's economy as it shifted from producing war planes to building commercial jets and aerospace products. Boeing became the principal employer on Puget Sound, at times employing one of every five workers engaged in manufacturing.

The postwar years saw Seattle's population hover at the half-million level as its suburban area, indeed the entire Puget Sound region, grew enormously. The city remains 75 percent Caucasian, most of whom are descendants of Scandinavians and other western Europeans.

Seattle has been notable for its racial diversity since Native Americans mingled among early white settlers. The city is named for a friendly Suquamish Duwamish chief whose people inhabited nearby fishing villages. However, relations between the various races have not always been smooth. During the winter of 1885 to 1886, some 350 Chinese, displaced from railroad construction, mining, and other labor tasks, were driven from the city in a demonstration of xenophobic sentiment. Many eventually returned, and various Asian populations give a distinctive ingredient to the local culture. Many African Americans, attracted by employment opportunities during and after World War II, moved to the city. New residents have arrived from various Asian and Pacific nations; Filipinos constitute the largest single group, and the Hispanic population is growing.

—*Charles P. LeWarne*

SUGGESTED READING:

Berner, Richard C. *Seattle in the 20th Century*. Vol. 1: *Seattle 1900–1920: From Boomtown, Urban Turbulence to Restoration*. Seattle, 1991; Vol. 2: *Seattle 1921–1940: From Boom to Bust*. Seattle, Wash., 1992.

Morgan, Murray. *Skid Road: An Informal Portrait of Seattle*. Rev. ed. Seattle, Wash., and London, 1982.

Sale, Roger. *Seattle Past to Present*. Seattle, Wash., and London, 1976.

SEGALE, SISTER BLANDINA

Missionary and teacher in Colorado and New Mexico, Rosa Maria Segale (1850–1941) was born near Genoa, Italy, and immigrated with her family to Cincinnati in 1854. She entered the novitiate of the Sisters of Charity at the age of sixteen and received the name Sister Blandina. In 1872, her superior sent her to teach in a public school in Trinidad, Colorado. Later she worked

Sister Blandina Segale. *Courtesy Albuquerque Museum.*

in Santa Fe and Albuquerque, New Mexico, where she taught and addressed a variety of community needs among Mexicans and Native Americans.

During her twenty-one years in the West, Segale kept a journal, which was published in 1932. The journal provides accounts of several dramatic episodes, such as her rescuing a prisoner from a lynch mob, negotiating with "BILLY THE KID" to prevent several murders, and enlisting the help of Native Americans to avert a contrived mining disaster. Less sensational but equally impressive was her success in generating community support for an elementary school, an industrial trade school for girls, and a hospital for miners and railroad workers. Her career is an exceptional example of the role of Catholic sisters as educators and community-builders.

—*Martha Smith, C.S.J.*

SEE ALSO: Catholics; Missions: Nineteenth-Century Missions to the Indians

SUGGESTED READING:

Segale, Blandina. *At the End of the Santa Fe Trail*. Milwaukee, Wis., 1932.

———. "If You Are Not Afraid, Neither Am I." In *So Much To Be Done*. Edited by Ruth B. Moynihan, Susan Armitage, and Chistiane Fischer Dichamp. Lincoln, Nebr., 1989.

SEGOVIA, JOSEPHA

SEE: Juanita of Downieville

SEGREGATION

Segregation in Housing and Public Facilities
Jeffrey M. Garcilazo

Segregation in Education
Charles Phillips

SEGREGATION IN HOUSING AND PUBLIC FACILITIES

Racial and ethnic segregation in housing, education, and public facilities in the West began with Spanish colonialism but expanded and changed both in scope and character after the Euro-American conquest of the Southwest in 1848. What is now the American West and Southwest was once part of the colonial empire of New Spain. In 1598, the JUAN DE OÑATE expedition, accompanied by neophyte Tlaxcala Indians (who assisted in the Aztec conquest of 1521), colonized the area near Santa Fe, New Mexico. As the colony was established, the Tlaxcalans were residentially marginalized from the main nucleus of the colony in a barrio, or ethnic enclave. This settlement represented the first European community marked by racial segregation in North America.

From this early moment, Indian servants and neophyte Pueblo Indians lived in their respective parts of town separated from white ecclesiastical and civil authorities of New Spain. Spaniards regarded Indian pueblos as crude and centers of "devil worship." The colonists thus clustered their homes in new Spanish towns. The rate by which this change took place varied from one region to the next. For example, Spain did not begin to colonize California Indians until 1767.

Perhaps the most dramatic changes occurred among the contacts between Spanish soldiers and Indian villages. As the soldiers employed Indian servants and captive slaves from nomadic Indian tribes in their homes and towns, casual and formal marriages created a new mestizo population. This new sector of New Mexican society was ancestrally Indian and only nominally Spanish in language and faith. Mestizos represented the largest sector of colonial society and signified a new cultural community, one incorporating both Indian and Spanish customs and living arrangements. On the other hand, many of the original Pueblo Indians remained in their traditional villages and maintained, to a large degree, their language and customs. The Acoma Pueblo, for example, is the oldest continuously occupied village in North America.

Colonial missions attempted to educate Indian and mestizo children, but the primary beneficiaries were the offspring of the wealthy. Even after the secularization of the missions in Mexico in 1821, instruction was typically performed by the religious or hispanophile authorities. Of course, other than home teaching, there was little alternative to church-controlled instruction. Spaniards also prohibited Indians from riding horses, the privilege of aristocracy.

With the exploration and conquest of Mexico's northern borderlands by the United States, culminating with the UNITED STATES–MEXICAN WAR (from 1846 to 1848), the residential segregation among people of Mexican background and other racial and ethnic groups began a slow but long-term transformation. Some historians refer to this process as *barriozation* or *ghettoizaton*. Essentially, this process happened in one of two ways. The first occurred in annexed parts of the Southwest when large numbers of Anglos arrived and established commerce and residences outside of preexisting Mexican settlements. Anglos regarded the Mexican pueblos as "foreign," "backward," and "undesirable." Thus, de facto segregation appeared when Anglos founded separate communities, which began a tradition by which whites separated themselves from Mexicans and other minorities, especially newly arriving Chinese workers. Ghettoization also effectively shifted the center of power and commerce from the old Mexican pueblos to the new "American" sections.

The second form of barriozation tended to occur in areas where there was no significantly large preexisting Mexican community. For example, mining and railroad camps throughout the West segregated workers ostensibly to minimize conflict between different national groups; but this form of segregation also helped minimize worker solidarity in a strike situation. In many cases, unless the mines were abandoned, these original housing units became the nucleus of permanent racial and ethnic enclaves. In TOPEKA, KANSAS, the Santa Fe Railroad imported Mexican track workers and provided empty boxcars to serve as their housing. The Mexican track workers referred to this community as "La Yarda" ("the Yard"). In Topeka, like other areas of the West, educational facilities, public swimming pools, restaurants, and even churches reinforced racial and ethnic segregation and other social boundaries. While European immigrants tended to "melt" into the dominant white communities over time, racial and ethnic working-class residents remained in de facto segregated housing through the twentieth century.

In some communities, Euro-American emigrants quickly surpassed the Mexican population, thereby making the Mexican community, once the majority, into a new minority population. For example, in Monterey, California, the gold rush spurred Anglo migration and reduced the Mexican majority to less than one-third of the population. In other areas, the growth of industrial mining precipitated an increase in population. The Mexican population of SAN JOSE, CALIFORNIA, for instance, grew from approximately seven hundred in 1846 to twelve hundred in 1870 as a result of an increased demand for labor.

While BARRIOS emerged largely from Anglos' preference to create their own "American" section, barrios or ghettos also reflected minorities' desire to maintain familiar customs and traditions. Indeed, these ethnic enclaves softened the sometimes harsh realities of the new Anglo-American regime, which, because of racial animosity, was often unfriendly and oppressive. People of Mexican origins (including some American Indians) could meet with friends and family and enjoy traditional cooking and public festivities. Ethnic communities also provided informational networks about jobs, lodging, religious ceremonies, and their own patriotic celebrations. Indeed, in the case of Mexican communities, many of these original Mexican settlements still stand and are quaintly referred to as "Pueblo Viejo" ("Old Town"). Like the segregation of African Americans in the South, residential segregation in the West continued informally throughout the twentieth century. However, in some places where racial and ethnic communities witnessed rapid growth, local white authorities attempted to formalize segregation in housing.

Perhaps the most obvious forms of segregation of public facilities were in the form of schools, public pools, parks, and recreational areas. In many small towns, authorities designated certain days of the week for white children's use of public swimming pools. Mexican, African American, and other nonwhite children were restricted to using the pool on the other days. Following the days on which nonwhite children used the facility, the pool was typically drained and refilled with fresh water.

While use of public parks was not prohibited, authorities in the West followed the postbellum pattern of racial segregation in the South. Ostensibly, authorities provided separate but equal facilities for minority communities. However, like all forms of segregation, enforcement varied among communities. Regardless of how enthusiastically segregation was enforced, racial and ethnic minorities clearly understood that whites viewed their presence in the white part of town with suspicion.

From the late nineteenth century onward, railroads generally provided separate restrooms and sleeping and dining facilities for whites and nonwhites. Railroads also maintained separate hospital facilities and cafeterias, usually in the basement, for their Mexican and black workers. In Texas and other parts of the Southwest, nonwhites could obtain restaurant service only from the back door. In many cases, minority cooks prepared food for the same eating establishments that refused them service. This pattern of segregation and racial discrimination continued well into the twentieth century and did not begin to break down until after World War II, when American minority servicemen returned from fighting fascism abroad.

In 1964, the California Real Estate Association sponsored Proposition 14, which guaranteed property-owners the right to sell, lease, or rent property to whomever they wanted. This legislation meant that they could discriminate against minorities. Voters passed the initiative by a margin of two to one, but the courts later ruled it unconstitutional. According to Western historian Richard White: "Proposition 14 symbolized the commitment of whites to confining, segregating, and controlling blacks [and other minorities] as strictly as possible."

Segregation in housing and public facilities in the West paralleled segregation in schools and other institutions. While segregation was preceded by a form of separation during the Spanish and Mexican periods, it expanded, in part, as a result of the conquest of Mexico and the competition for resources under American rule. Ultimately, all nonwhites in the West were subjected to some form of de facto segregation in public facilities and housing.

—*Jeffrey M. Garcilazo*

SUGGESTED READING:

Camarillo, Albert. *Chicanos in California: A History of Mexicans in California.* San Francisco, 1984.

Chan, Sucheng. *Asian Americans: An Interpretive History.* Boston, 1991.

De Leon, Arnoldo. *Mexican Americans in Texas: A Brief History.* Arlington Heights, Ill., 1993.

Garica, Mario T. *Desert Immigrants: The Mexicans of El Paso, 1880–1920.* New Haven, Conn., 1981.

Garcilazo, Jeffrey M. "Traqueros: Mexican Railroad Workers in the United States, 1871–1930." Ph.D. diss., University of California, Santa Barbara, 1995.

Griswold del Castillo, Richard. *The Los Angeles Barrio: A Social History.* Berkeley, Calif., 1979.

Gutierrez, Ramon. *When Jesus Came the Corn Mothers Went Away: Marriage, Sexuality, and Power in New Mexico, 1500–1846.* Stanford, Calif., 1991.

Meinig, D. W. *Southwest: Three Peoples in Geographical Change, 1600–1970.* New York, 1971.

Swadesh, Frances Leon. *Los Primeros Pobladores: Hispanic Americans of the Ute Frontier.* Lafayette, Ind., 1974.

Takaki, Ronald T. *Iron Cages: Race and Culture in 19th-Century America.* Seattle, Wash., 1979.

SEGREGATION IN EDUCATION

Segregated education is an issue more often associated with the history of the American South than of the West, one having to do more with the treatment of African Americans by the dominant Euro-American culture than with the treatment of ethnic and racial minorities—Native Americans, Hispanos, and Asians—more typically considered Western. Western schools, too, were segregated on the basis of race, as were other social institutions, although there were differences both in the West's society and in its educational system that were reflected as well in the issue of segregated education in the trans-Mississippi region.

Segregation, in general, was as real in most of the West (and, for that matter, in the North) as it was in the South, but in the South, it tended, starting after the Civil War, to be imposed by law, or *de jure* (Latin for "in law"), as lawyers called it, whereas in the West, it was more a result of income distribution, custom, and residential patterns, for which the Latin legal phrase is *de facto*, or "in fact." Southern whites and blacks lived close to each other, and segregation laws reinforced custom to ensure the races did not mix except as employer and employee. In the West, blacks did not live close to whites, and neither did Native Americans, Mexican Americans, or Asian Americans, who, since at least the mid-nineteenth century, had been excluded from the dominant society and confined to reservations, BARRIOS, CHINATOWNS, and Little Tokyos.

Another difference was that the South's major minority had been denied an education of any kind before the Civil War, whereas in the West, even those the Anglo-American population considered foreigners were afforded some kind of education or vocational training in Catholic missions and PAROCHIAL SCHOOLS, LANGUAGE SCHOOLS, and INDIAN SCHOOLS. A third difference was in the educational system itself. In the West, educational institutions—especially COLLEGES AND UNIVERSITIES—tended to be publicly funded, since laws governing territorial development, such as the NORTHWEST ORDINANCE and the Wisconsin Organic Act, provided for public education, as did the MORRILL ACT OF 1862, which established land-grant colleges. In the East, on the other hand, higher education and even grammar and secondary schools had first developed as private institutions, which tended to educate those who had

money. Poor white Southerners frequently were only marginally better educated than former slaves.

Education in the South, then, was officially and universally segregated, at the primary and secondary levels, *de jure;* in higher education, by virtue of class as well as race, sometimes more so by class. In the West, on the other hand, education was officially available for every citizen but was segregated by virtue of the location and type of schools. Although some locales passed segregation laws, in general, there was no need to do even that, and the West could pride itself that its schools were open to all, the poor (white) immigrant as well as the scion of a wealthy family. Indeed, when African Americans began to move into the trans-Mississippi region in greater, if still relatively small, numbers after the Civil War, voting against legal segregation, as historian Richard White says, with their feet only to find themselves subject to de facto segregation out West, they often challenged the Western states' traditional arrangements in ways that led communities to introduce segregation laws for the first time. Black pioneers moved West not only to provide for themselves a better material life, but also a better cultural and spiritual one, and they emphasized, especially, education, which had been denied them in the slave states. Schools districts often had allowed young black children to be taught alongside whites, when it was a matter of a child or two, whose family was known to the whole community; but when fifteen or twenty-five African Americans attended a school, white parents objected to their presence, and school districts responded by discriminating against the blacks.

California's school law of 1851, providing for the apportioning of school funds to communities proportionate to the number of resident children between eight and eighteen, apparently referred to all school-age children, regardless of color, and so included Mexican Americans, Indians, Asian Americans, and African Americans, as well as whites. In 1854, however, the first school for black children was set up at San Francisco's St. Cyprian African Methodist Episcopal Church, and in 1855, Section Eighteen of a legislative act provided for the counting of white children only and indicated that all others were to be excluded. Despite the call for enumerating white children, blacks had not actually been excluded by law. There was, in fact, a lack of uniformity in handling the admission of blacks to public schools in the state, and the San Francisco papers that year reported that the city's Board of Education was still undecided on what course to pursue. Some suggested building separate schools; others, simply allowing blacks to attend schools with whites; still others, giving part of the school fund to the black community to create its own schools. The debate continued, and most schools remained segregated de facto, while others admitted black students and other minorities. In 1886, the school law itself was revised to prohibit all school-age children of African, "Mongolion," or Indian descent from attending white schools unless they lived under the care of white persons. If ten parents of nonwhite children petitioned a district board, the board was forced to establish a school for them. If they could not be provided for in any other way, they could attend white schools if the white parents did not protest in writing.

Thus began a policy of separate but equal schooling in principle, segregation in practice. The statutes admitting Nevada to the Union, for example, provided for the education of white children only and ignored the plight of Nevada's Indian, black, and Chinese American minorities. Oregon legally restricted nonwhites from attending school as resolutely as any former slave state. In 1847, the Iowa General Assembly passed a regulation making state schools open and free to all "white persons" between the ages of five and twenty-five. In 1867, Colorado, still a territory, had a statute that decreed whenever there were fifteen or more "colored" children in any district, the board of directors, with the approval of the county school superintendent, might provide a separate school for them. In 1893, the Oklahoma Territory made provision for the separate education of white and black children. In some Western states, especially where racial minorities were small, nonwhite children attended white schools despite the state laws. In Iowa in 1850, for example, at least seventeen blacks attended school, and when steps were taken to remove them, the Iowa legislature exempted black property-owners from paying schools taxes. In Oregon, where as late as 1925, blacks made up less than 1 percent of the population, they were admitted into the schools after the passage of the Fifteenth Amendment in 1870 had conferred citizen status upon African Americans. Some minorities fought segregation in court, only to find the separate-but-equal rule reaffirmed, as in California's 1873 *Ward* v. *Flood*. In 1885, when San Francisco declared it would fire any principal who admitted a Chinese American child, John and Mary Tape sued the school board and won a place for their daughter in the white schools, but the Board of Education responded by setting up a separate school for Chinese American children.

Some Western states, especially those with small black populations, did not legally exclude African Americans—Montana, Wyoming, Washington, New Mexico, Idaho, Utah, North Dakota, South Dakota, and Nebraska, although de facto segregation often kept their schools free of other nonwhite children. Kansas, whose proslavery legislature in 1855 provided schools open to whites only and specifically excluded all other racial groups in the state at that time, modified the ruling to a separate-but-equal status in 1862, after Kansas had entered the Civil War on the side of the Union. Then, in 1867, when the North had won the war, the Kansas legislature passed a law forbidding any district board from refusing to admit any child into public school and then went a step further, in 1876, by declaring common schools equally free and accessible to all. Some communities in Kansas, however, got around the statutes by having the legislature pass "private laws" that allowed them to set up separate but equal facilities.

In general, between the end of the Civil War and the turn of the century, the claim of blacks and other minorities in the West to equality in education was opposed most strongly in areas with relatively large black populations; otherwise, de facto segregation was the rule until the U.S. Supreme Court's 1896 decision in *Plessy* v. *Ferguson* made separate but equal facilities the law of the land. For the Mexican American population of the Southwest, the separate-but-equal policy allowed communities to create a two-tiered education, one for white children who would go on to play a role in the dominant culture, and the other for Mexican Americans, who would be needed as a cheap but disciplined work force for those white children. Vocational and industrial education became the cornerstone of the curriculum for the West's so-called Mexican Schools. In EL PASO, TEXAS, for example, educators directed their efforts in the segregated Mexican schools to manual and domestic education so that their students could find employment in the city's semiskilled industries, which had a real need for such workers. Garment manufacturers worked with LOS ANGELES's Chamber of Commerce and the public school board to set up cooperative trade schools and to establish a policy emphasizing vocational training in segregated Mexican public schools. San Bernardino's barrio school also concentrated on vocational education. As in the South, Western schools might well be separate, but they were hardly equal, even when they were well funded, which was not often. When the Supreme Court, led by liberal Chief Justice Earl Warren of California, reversed the separate-but-equal law in the 1954 *Brown* v. *Board of Education of Topeka*, the West's de facto form of segregation would prove even more resistant to change than the de jure segregation of the South.

—*Charles Phillips*

SEE ALSO: Americanization Programs; *Tape* v. *Hurley*

SUGGESTED READING:
Barr, Alwyn. *Black Texas*. Austin, Tex., 1973.

Savage, W. Sherman. *Blacks in the West.* Westport, Conn., 1976.

Takaki, Ronald T., ed. *From Different Shores: Perspectives in Race and Ethnicity in America.* New York, 1987.

———. *Iron Cages: Race and Culture in 19th-Century America.* Seattle, 1979.

SELMAN, JOHN HENRY

Outlaw and lawman famous for the slaying of gunman JOHN WESLEY HARDIN, John Henry Selman (1839–1896) was born in Madison County, Arkansas. He joined the Confederate Army on December 15, 1861, and deserted in 1863. After moving to Shackelford County, Texas, he worked as a deputy for Sheriff John Larn in 1877. When vigilantes killed Larn in his own jail, Selman fled to Lincoln County, New Mexico, and organized a band of desperadoes known as "Selman's Scouts."

Selman later drifted to El Paso, Texas. There, on April 3, 1894, he killed former TEXAS RANGER Baz Outlaw in a brothel shootout. On August 19, 1895, he put three bullets into John Wesley Hardin. Later, Selman argued with U.S. Deputy Marshal George Scarborough alongside the Wigwam Saloon. Scarborough shot Selman four times, and the constable died from his wounds. He is buried in an unmarked grave in El Paso's Concordia Cemetery.

—*Leon C. Metz*

SEE ALSO: Gunfighters

SUGGESTED READING:

DeArment, Robert K. *George Scarborough: The Life and Death of a Lawman on the Closing Frontier.* Norman, Okla., 1992.

Metz, Leon Claire. *John Selman, Gunfighter.* Norman, Okla., 1980.

SEMINOLE INDIANS

SEE: Native American Peoples: Peoples Removed from the East

SEQUOYAH (MIXED CHEROKEE)

Sequoyah (ca. 1760–1843), also called George Gist or Guess, created a syllabary—in effect, a written language—for the Cherokees. Born near present-day Vonore, Tennessee, the child of a Cherokee mother, Wurteh, and a trader and Revolutionary soldier, Nathaniel Guess or Gist, Sequoyah was raised on farms in Tennessee and then near Willstown, Alabama. After suffering a severe leg injury in a hunting accident, he turned to drink but managed to recover and became a silversmith of considerable renown.

Beginning in 1809, Sequoyah began developing a written version of the Cherokee language. His principal aim in this project was to help prevent Cherokee culture from being swallowed whole by encroaching white America. He believed that the ability to record tribal laws, a constitution, and other agreements, in addition to publishing newspapers, would serve as a cultural bulwark. Sequoyah began by developing a pictographic system but, after compiling more than one thousand symbols, realized the futility of this approach. In a series of brilliant strokes, he reduced the Cherokee "alphabet" to two hundred symbols, finally winnowing it to eighty-six characters, through which all the different sounds of the language could be represented. This work was completed by 1821, despite the destruction of his notes and books in a fire set by Cherokees who suspected Sequoyah of practicing witchcraft. Sequoyah became the only person in history to create an alphabet (more properly, a syllabary, because the symbols represent whole syllables) single-handedly. (The 1821 date is generally accepted, although some Cherokee tradition dates the syllabary earlier. Elements of Cherokee tradition also hold that Sequoyah did not work alone on the project. However, all agree that the syllabary was accepted and popularized through his efforts.)

The Cherokee Council officially adopted the syllabary after 1822, and after portions of the Bible were translated into it in 1825, white missionaries supported the system as well. In 1828, the Cherokee tribe wrote its first constitution, and that same year, on February 21, Sequoyah participated in the publication of the *Cherokee Phoenix,* the tribe's first newspaper, printed entirely in Cherokee and edited by ELIAS BOUDINOT.

Sequoyah had emigrated to Pope Count, Arkansas, in 1818. In 1829, he and his family moved to the Indian Territory and settled in present-day Sequoya County, Oklahoma. He served as president of the Western Cherokees and was instrumental in uniting the tribe's Western and Eastern faction in the Cherokee Act of Union of 1839. In 1842, Sequoyah, then ailing, organized an expedition to find a lost band of Cherokees who had migrated to the West during the American Revolution. The search was based on a study of Indian speech patterns. Unfortunately, the scholar's health failed, and he died near San Fernando, Tamaulipas, Mexico.

In addition to naming Sequoya County after him, the state of Oklahoma commissioned a statue in his honor at the capitol. Stephen Endlicher, a Hungarian botanist, named the giant redwoods of the California coastal region after the great Cherokee linguist.

—*Alan Axelrod*

SUGGESTED READING:
Foreman, Grant. *Sequoyah*. Norman, Okla., 1938. Reprint. 1984.

SERRA, JUNÍPERO

Junípero Serra (1713–1784), born Miguel Serra, was known as the "apostle of California" for his missionary efforts in Alta California. He initiated the Spanish mission system that, at his death, included nine missions with forty-six hundred Indian residents.

Serra came from humble origins. Part of his family was descended from *conversos,* Jews who had been

The Mission of San Diego, the first of a chain of missions Father Serra established in California. *Courtesy Library of Congress.*

Junípero Serra. *Courtesy Library of Congress.*

forcibly converted to Roman Catholicism in 1492. Perhaps because of this heritage, and because of his small stature, the Franciscans delayed in admitting him to probationary status. At the age of sixteen, however, he was at last admitted at the town of Palma. A year later, in 1731, he took his formal vows and the name Junípero from one of the companions of Francis of Assisi, founder of the order.

Serra flourished in the religious environment and earned a reputation for oratory, piety, and intelligence. After advanced training, he won a teaching position in moral philosophy at Palma's Lullian University in 1744. Five years later, at the age of thirty-five, he became a missionary to the Indians of New Spain (Mexico). Serra labored tirelessly in the missions of the Sierra Gorda region of Querétaro for twenty years before leading the Franciscans into Alta California in 1769, at the age of fifty-five.

Serra served as first Father President of the system, which established nine successful missions: San Diego (1769), San Carlos Borromeo (1770), San Antonio (1771), San Gabriel (1771), San Luis Obispo (1772), San Francisco (1776), San Juan Capistrano (1776), Santa Clara (1777), and San Buenaventura (1782). These missions sought to bring Indians into Spanish society by converting them to Christianity and teaching them "civilized" European life styles. Indians were induced to leave their native cultures and then submerged in Spanish-Christian culture in an environment of European work and agriculture coupled with religious instruction. Serra loved the Indians but believed them to be of limited intelligence and subject to sin that necessitated correction. Legally, Franciscans stood as Spanish fathers to their Indian children, and disobedience, either civil or religious, was frequently corrected by corporal punishment, including flogging.

Because of Serra's success at mission building and his reputation for holiness, the bishop of Monterey, California, proposed him for sainthood in 1935. The slow process of canonization, the three-step sequence by which sainthood is conferred, began in 1985 when the pope proclaimed Serra "Venerable," meaning that he had lived a life of "heroic virtue" by church standards. Descendants of the Mission Indians and others protested his canonization by claiming that Serra abused Indians in the missions and destroyed native cultures. Serra's advocates pointed to his self-sacrifice and love of Indians and asked that he be judged by the standards of his day rather than by those of the present.

—*James A. Sandos*

SEE ALSO: Missions: Early Franciscan and Jesuit Missions

SUGGESTED READING:

Costo, Rupert, and Jeannette Henry Costo. *The Missions of California: A Legacy of Genocide.* San Francisco, 1987.

Geiger, Maynard J., O.F.M. *The Life and Times of Junípero Serra.* 2 vols. Washington, D.C., 1959.

Guest, Francis F., O.F.M. "Junípero Serra and His Approach to the Indians." *Southern California Quarterly* 67 (1985): 223–261.

Sandos, James A. "Junípero Serra's Canonization and the Historical Record." *American Historical Review* 93 (1988): 1253–1269.

SEVERANCE, CAROLINA MARIA SEYMOUR

Carolina Maria Seymour Severance (1820–1914) was a California social reformer and pioneer of the women's club movement. She was born in Canandaigua, New York, attended female seminaries and boarding schools in upstate New York, and then taught in a boarding school near Pittsburgh. In 1840, she was married to Theodoric Cordenio Severance, with whom she settled in Cleveland, Ohio. She raised a family of five children and shared with her husband a commitment to the cause of liberal social reform. The Severance home became a meeting place for abolitionists, writers, temperance advocates, feminists, and advocates of dietary reform. After breaking with Presbyterianism, the Severances formed their own church, the Independent Christian church, which was abolitionist in orientation and attracted liberal Christians. In her own views, Severance combined quasi-Unitarianism with an intense attraction to Spiritualism and a belief in the imminence of the Second Coming.

Severance worked closely with Frances Dana Gage in the cause of women's rights and presided over the first annual meeting of the Ohio Woman's Rights Association in 1853. In 1855, she and her family moved to Boston, where Severance became deeply involved in the city's intellectual, religious, and reformist community, especially in the cause of abolition.

After the Civil War, Severance lectured on "practical ethics" at a school for young ladies in Lexington, Massachusetts, and, in 1866, joined Susan B. Anthony's crusade to delete the word "male" from the proposed Fourteenth Amendment, thereby granting the vote to women. She broke with Anthony in 1869 by joining Lucy Stone in founding the independent American Woman Suffrage Association. During 1867 and 1868, Severance worked with others to create the New England Woman's Club, the first of the century's important and influential women's organizations.

The Severances left Boston for California in 1875 and settled in Los Angeles, where they founded the city's first Unitarian congregation, which soon became the focus of religious liberalism in the region. Severance became active in civic and educational pursuits. She formed the Los Angeles Free Kindergarten Association in 1885, which succeeded in integrating kindergarten education into the public-school system. In the meantime, the Unity Church, which she and her husband had established, had evolved into the Los Angeles Woman's Club by 1885. It was short lived, disbanding in 1888, and Severance next established the Friday Morning Club and served as its first president from 1891 to 1894. The club was a driving force behind such civic reform as the establishment of a juvenile-court system in Los Angeles and, ultimately, throughout California.

At the turn of the century, Severance became a prime mover in the California's WOMEN'S SUFFRAGE movement and was generally responsible for inculcating among southern California's women the liberal intellectual spirit of New England reform.

—*Alan Axelrod*

SEE ALSO: Women's Clubs and Organizations

SEYMOUR, SAMUEL

The English-born painter Samuel Seymour (fl. 1796–1823), one of the first of his profession to travel west of the Mississippi, worked variously as a scenic designer and landscape painter in Philadelphia and New

York City during the first quarter of the nineteenth century. He is known to have practiced engraving in Philadelphia as early as 1796. In 1810, he was elected an associate member of the Society of Artists in the United States, later the Columbian Society, and beginning in 1814, he exhibited regularly with this group.

With artist-naturalist TITIAN RAMSAY PEALE, Seymour accompanied Major STEPHEN HARRIMAN LONG's expedition to the Rocky Mountains from 1819 to 1820 as its official artist, assigned to paint landscapes and native portraits. Six of his Western views were reproduced in the report of the expedition prepared by botanist Edwin James in 1823. That year, Seymour accompanied Long on another excursion to the headwaters of the Mississippi River. An account of their trip was published in London in 1825 with five more of Seymour's pictures. Little else is known of Seymour's life or career, and original examples of his work are relatively scarce. His views of the Rocky Mountains, James's or Pikes Peak, and the valleys of the Missouri, Platte, and Arkansas rivers are thought to be the earliest paintings ever made from firsthand observations.

A number of Seymour's Western landscapes, or copies by Titian Peale, were exhibited at one time in Charles Willson Peale's museum in Philadelphia. A small group of water colors is preserved today in the Paul Mellon collection of Yale University's Beinecke Library. Another water color is owned by the Academy of Natural Sciences in Philadelphia.

—*David C. Hunt*

SEE ALSO: Art: Surveys and Expeditions

SUGGESTED READING:
Ewers, John C. *Artists of the Old West.* Garden City, N.Y., 1965.
Viola, Herman J. *Exploring the West.* Washington, D.C., 1987.

SHAWNEE TRAIL

SEE: Cattle Trails and Trail Driving

SHEEP AND SHEEP RANCHING

Domesticated sheep *(Ovis aries),* cud-chewing, ruminant animals closely related to goats, make up part of the genus *Ovis* of the cattle family, *Bovidae.* They arrived in America in 1493 when Christopher Columbus, on his second voyage to the New World, brought them to the Caribbean. Not long afterward, settlers carried sheep to the mainland where, in New Spain (Mexico), they multiplied and, by 1550, had become common and cheap.

In 1598, sheep accompanied JUAN DE OÑATE and his farmer-settlers to the upper Rio Grande, and later Spanish soldiers and missionaries drove them to Texas. The first sheep in the Southwest were *churros,* the common meat (or mutton) breed of Spain. Each animal yielded only a pound or two of coarse wool when sheared, but *churros* provided the economic foundation for Hispanic settlements.

Missionaries and Spanish settlers in New Mexico taught European methods of sheepherding to the Pueblo people. *Churros* thrived under their care, and after several decades, drovers moved thousands of them southward to markets in Chihuahua and Viscaya. Eventually, Navajo herdsmen made sheep raising a principal occupation in their communities. They annually sheared small amounts of wool and used the product to make coarse woolen blankets, woolen cloth, and clothes.

By 1727, in Texas, sheep numbered approximately 9,000 head. Missions in the San Antonio area earned funds through raising sheep. About mid-century, sheep raising increased along the Rio Grande below Laredo, with an estimated 13,000 animals grazing in 1757 near present-day McAllen.

As Spain expanded its holdings north of the Rio Grande, missionaries took sheep to Arizona, where the animals grazed at mission stations under the direction of Native American herders. In the late eighteenth century, Spanish settlers drove sheep to California.

The interest of the Spanish in sheep raising in the Southwest declined somewhat during the late eighteenth century. High taxes, orders to close the missions, and other factors were all responsible. In the early nineteenth century, settlers from the United States moved into Texas and expanded Spanish sheep ranching toward the Rio Grande. After the United States–Mexican War, Anglo-Americans claimed large stretches of grazing land in New Mexico and California. Mormons brought sheep to Utah, and ranchers carried sheep to mining camps in California and Nevada.

Breeds

In the nineteenth century, Euro-Americans introduced breeds that produced greater amounts of wool. The Spanish Merino, the foundation breed of all fine-wool sheep, and the Rambouillet were early favorites; the Saxon also became popular. Fine-wool breeds tend to be relatively small in size, angular in form, and less developed in meat conformation. Their skin has a tendency to fold, and their legs and sometimes their faces are covered with wool. In the Southwest and in California, farmers and ranchers bred Merinos and Rambouillets to *churros*.

Medium-wool breeds, such as the Southdown, Chevoit, Cotswald, Hampshire, Delaine, and Suffolk, moved westward with pioneers who bred them with *churros* and Merino-*churros* or Rambouillet-*churros*. Medium-wool breeds are noted more for meat production than for their wool, and their fleece weight is relatively low in comparison to their size.

Long-wool breeds, such as the Lincoln and Leicester, which have heavy fleeces and are notable for meat production, have been less important in the American West. Their wool is coarse and has been used mainly in the manufacture of carpets and coarse rugs. But ranchers bred them to Merinos and Rambouillets to produce the Corriedale breed, popular among Western sheep-raisers in the mid-twentieth century.

Environmental changes

Sheep, with cattle and horses, changed the Western environment. The first animals carried with them the seeds of European weeds and grasses that thrived under the conditions of close herding. As the European plant varieties spread, they competed with native grasses. Unable to recover adequately from the changed grazing patterns, native grasses tended to give way to the intruding species. Moreover, the European animals harbored diseases—anthrax, brucellosis, and tuberculosis—that had a negative impact on bisons, elks, deer, and other animals native to the grasslands of Western America. Overgrazing and poor ranch management destroyed the range and turned lush grassland into veritable deserts of scrub brush and barren waste. The common practice of herding one sheep per acre on arid lands proved too taxing for native grasses, and without natural fires to destroy moisture-robbing mesquite every three to five years or so, the brush grew unchecked in the Southwest.

The boom years

When the Civil War closed off their cotton sources, New England textile manufacturers adjusted their equipment to the manufacture of woolen cloth. Their demand for wool created a sheep boom that rivaled the Great Plains cattle kingdom. In the 1870s and 1880s, herders moved great flocks of sheep out of California and New Mexico to ranges in the Great Plains. Heavy promotion by Henry S. Randall, president of the National Wool Growers Association, and George Wilkins Kendall, a pioneer sheep rancher in Texas and prominent newspaperman in New Orleans, encouraged many people to try sheep ranching on the dry upland ranges of the West. Cattlemen, while not abandoning their bovine herds, invested in wool growing and opened their ranges to sheep. Easterners, many of whom had never been west of the Mississippi River, sunk large sums of money into flocks, leased range land, and hired herders. Prices for sheep and wool reached high levels in the 1880s, and sheep raising spread to all areas of the West. On many of the small operations, where sheep served as an adjunct to field crops, farmers kept sheep in pens close to the house by night and sent them to pastures by day. The farmers themselves performed all the duties associated with sheep raising.

During the boom, on larger operations, two important systems of sheep ranching emerged. In the *partido* system, sheep owners (*ricos*, merchants, or ranchers) hired *partidarios* (herders) to tend the sheep. The *partidario* usually paid about 20 percent of the annual wool and lamb crop back to the owner, and if losses to disease, wolves, and other hazards were not large, the *partidario* made a profit and could build his personal flock. The herders might be Native Americans, Mexican Americans, or English, Basque, Mexican, or German immigrants. Perhaps with a dog for help, most of these herders were responsible for 1,500 to 2,000 sheep and stayed with the animals throughout the year. The system allowed many penniless German, Basque, and English immigrants to establish fortunes in the Western sheep and wool industry.

The other system, used on the largest haciendas and Anglo-American ranches, established an organizational hierarchy. At the top was the *haciendaro* (owner) or, in his absence, a superintendent. Below him was the *mayordomo*, a man of long experience in sheep raising. He constantly rode the range to inspect the various sheep camps, noted the conditions of the sheep, and suggested changes of ranges. Below him were three *caporales*, who produced monthly reports, rode the range, and provided their camps and their subordinates with provisions from the ranch headquarters. They each directed the work of three vaqueros, who provided a monthly report to the *caporal* and delivered supplies and news to three *pastores* (herders). The *pastores*, the lowest in the hierarchy, each had charge of about 1,500 to 2,000 sheep, which they accompanied on foot by day and camped with at night; the *pastores* were usually assisted by a dog or two.

Anglo-Americans modified the system to suit their needs and changed some of the terms—*vaquero* became *rustler*, *pastore* became *herder*, and *mayordomo* became *foreman*. On the largest ranches, such as those of Dominicker Hart and Charles Callaghan, there might be as many as fifty herders, eighteen rustlers, and six *caporales*.

During the boom, the number of sheep in the United States increased almost threefold, from 22,471,280 in

1860 to 61,503,713 in 1900. Wool production likewise increased, from 60,264,913 pounds in 1860 to 276,991,812 pounds in 1900. The largest gains were made in the West, where Montana and Wyoming were the country's leading states in the production of sheep and wool in 1900.

The money to be made in sheep raising came from the wool crop rather than from meat. Accordingly, in the late nineteenth century, owners built flocks of fine-wool sheep and sought improved methods—which varied from state to state—for marketing the annual wool clip. They also pressured the federal government to protect the domestic harvest from foreign competition, and Congress responded with protective duties in 1867, 1883, and 1890. When the Wilson-Gorman tariff of 1894 allowed foreign wool to enter the United States duty-free, the bottom dropped out of wool prices, and the Western sheep boom ended.

The industry recovered at the beginning of the twentieth century, and during World War I, sheep raising expanded again. Owners introduced different breeds, such as the Suffolk, Delaine, and Hampshire, and tried new breeds, such as the Corriedale. In the 1930s, breeding experiments expanded widely, and on dry upland pastures characteristic of much of the West, the Debouillet breed, a cross of Delaines and Rambouillets, became popular. But the sheep industry continued to endure financial highs and lows, foreign competition, and struggles over adequate grazing land. To respond to these challenges, many of the most successful wool growers in the West combined sheep raising with other livestock operations. On the state level, wool growers organized efficient wool-marketing associations and joined the National Wool Growers Association, which moved its headquarters to Utah.

Top: After the Civil War, sheep ranching boomed on the Great Plains and throughout the West. Pictured here is a sheep ranch in New Mexico. *Courtesy National Cowboy Hall of Fame and Western Heritage Center.*

Bottom: A sheep ranch in Lake Basin near Billings, Montana. *Courtesy Montana Historical Society.*

Ranch operations

Sheep ranching included busy seasonal activity; lambing time was the busiest. Depending on geography and climate, owners bred range ewes for lambing between March and May. The herder, acting as a midwife, carefully watched over the ewes in his band, assisted with difficult births, and forced indifferent mothers to nurse their offspring. Tending to orphaned lambs or lambs born to "dry" ewes, the herder attempted to get the animals through their critical first weeks of life. Larger operations hired special crews, *hijadores* (lambers), composed of three or four men to assist during lambing season, a period one herder called a "month long hell of worry and toil."

Shearing was also cumbersome work, but for the herders, shearing time was the "social season" of sheep ranching—a time when they could enjoy the companionship of others. Before electrically powered equipment, itinerant shearing crews, working from dawn to dusk, completed their task in barns or in large pens covered with brush. Boys counted sheep and applied medicine to the wounds of any animal accidentally cut. Men tied up each fleece before they placed it in an eight- to ten-foot sack, which weighed about 360 pounds when filled. The shearers might work several days on large operations before moving to another ranch.

Other activities included castrating, marking, and docking. Castration produced better mutton and ensured that the ewes would be bred only to prize rams. In the nineteenth century, castration was accomplished by a worker who held the back of the male sheep against his own chest and gathered and elevated all four legs. Once he had cut the end of the scrotum, he pulled out both testicles and, with a knife or sharp tug, severed the cords. Marking was used for identification. Owners painted their marks on freshly shorn animals and earmarked the sheep with distinctive combinations of cuts and slashes. If a rancher used a slightly different mark each year, he could tell the age of his sheep. Docking, which involved cutting off all but two inches of the tail, improved sanitation and aided reproduction.

Perhaps the most significant development in the early twentieth century was the adoption of mesh-wire ("wolf-proof") fences. Standing about forty-eight inches in height with a six-inch mesh and extended between posts, woven wire fences reduced the need for herders. Sometimes a rancher stretched a strand of barbed wire along the ground to prevent coyotes from scratching under the fence; this practice cut losses from predators. Because such fences were expensive, however, ranchers were slow to adopt them.

By 1940, the number of Western sheepherders had declined sharply, and throughout the twentieth century, the number of sheep on Western ranches declined as well. But because the average weight of each animal's fleece continued to increase, annual wool production climbed until World War II. In 1943, the peak year, approximately 375 million pounds came from America's flocks, and Texas, Wyoming, and Montana represented the country's leading states in the production of sheep and wool.

In the last years of the twentieth century, wool production, although down significantly from its peak years, remained economically viable, and sheep ranchers in the West continued to experiment with new breeds to improve wool quality. Concerned with the loss of tariff protection and other incentives to aid their industry, ranchers paid greater attention to more efficient and scientific range management and nearly always raised their sheep alongside other livestock.

—*Paul H. Carlson*

SEE ALSO: Navajo Stock-Reduction Program

SUGGESTED READING:

Baxter, John O. *Las Carneradas: Sheep Trade in New Mexico, 1700–1860*. Albuquerque, N. Mex., 1987.

Call, Hughie. *Golden Fleece*. Boston, 1942.

Carlson, Paul H. *Texas Woollybacks: The Range Sheep and Goat Industry*. College Station, Tex., 1982.

Kupper, Winifred. *The Golden Hoof: The Story of the Sheep of the Southwest*. New York, 1945.

Lehmann, V. W. *Forgotten Legions: Sheep in the Rio Grande Plain of Texas*. El Paso, Tex., 1969.

McGregor, Alexander Campbell. *Counting Sheep: From Range to Agribusiness on the Columbia Plateau*. Seattle, Wash., 1982.

O'Neal, Bill. *Cattlemen vs. Sheepherders: Five Decades of Violence in the West*. Austin, Tex., 1989.

Paul, Virginia. *This Was Sheep Ranching: Yesterday and Today*. Seattle, Wash., 1976.

Reeve, Agnesa, ed. *My Dear Mollie: Love Letters of a Texas Sheep Rancher*. Dallas, Tex., 1990.

Wentworth, Edward N. *America's Sheep Trails: History, Personalities*. Ames, Iowa, 1948.

SHELDON, CHARLES MONROE

Author, newspaper editor, and preacher Charles Monroe Sheldon (1857–1946) was born in Wellsville, New York, the son of a Congregational minister. Sheldon attended Phillips Academy in Andover, Massachusetts, and graduated from Brown University in 1883. He studied at the Andover Theological Seminary and was ordained a Congregational minister in 1886. Two years later, he was assigned to the Center Congregational Church in Topeka, Kansas, where he would remain for the next thirty-one years.

Once in Topeka, Sheldon found attendance at his Sunday evening services distressingly low, so he scrapped the usual sermons and read his own short stories. Parishioners flocked to hear Sheldon's plainly stated homilies and maxims they could relate to. The underlying theme in all Sheldon's stories was to ask if Jesus would do the same in the same situation. The readings were so successful that, in 1897, Sheldon published them in book form. In this book, *In His Steps,* Sheldon challenged readers to live for one year as Jesus would live and to ask the question, "Is this what Jesus would do?" For the next sixty years, *In His Steps* was a best-selling volume in the United States, second only to the Bible. Some have estimated sales as high as twenty-five million copies, but even the more conservative estimates of eight million copies show that the book was one of the more popular in American publishing.

In the wake of this success, the editor of the *Topeka Daily Capital* invited Sheldon to edit the paper for one week and conduct it as Jesus would have. Sheldon did so; with every story on vice or crime, he offered an editorial and remedy. His work produced a dramatic—if temporary—increase in the paper's circulation. Sheldon later accepted the editor's post at the *Christian Herald*, where he became a staunch advocate of world peace.

—*Kurt Edward Kemper*

SHERIDAN, PHILIP H.

In the Indian Wars of the 1870s, Philip H. Sheridan (1831–1888) was the officer to whom WILLIAM TECUMSEH SHERMAN, then commander of the U.S. Army's Division of the Missouri, entrusted the execution of his "total-war" policy, developed during Sherman's March to Atlanta at the end of the Civil War. Born in New York and raised in Ohio, Sheridan entered West Point in 1848 but did not graduate until five years later because of a one-year suspension for fighting. He saw his first frontier duty in Texas and the Pacific Northwest, where he fought in the Yakima War. Sheridan then served the Union brilliantly in the CIVIL WAR, rose rapidly to the rank of major general, and became commander of the Army of the Potomac's cavalry division, which was instrumental in cutting off Robert E. Lee's Army of Northern Virginia and bringing about the surrender at Appomattox. After the war, Sheridan commanded the Division of the Gulf from 1865 to 1867 and was given command of the Fifth Military District, which encompassed Texas and Louisiana. He held this post for only six months before president Andrew Johnson, concluding that Sheridan applied the principles of Reconstruction too harshly, caused his transfer to the West, where he replaced General Winfield Scott Hancock as commander of the Department of the Missouri.

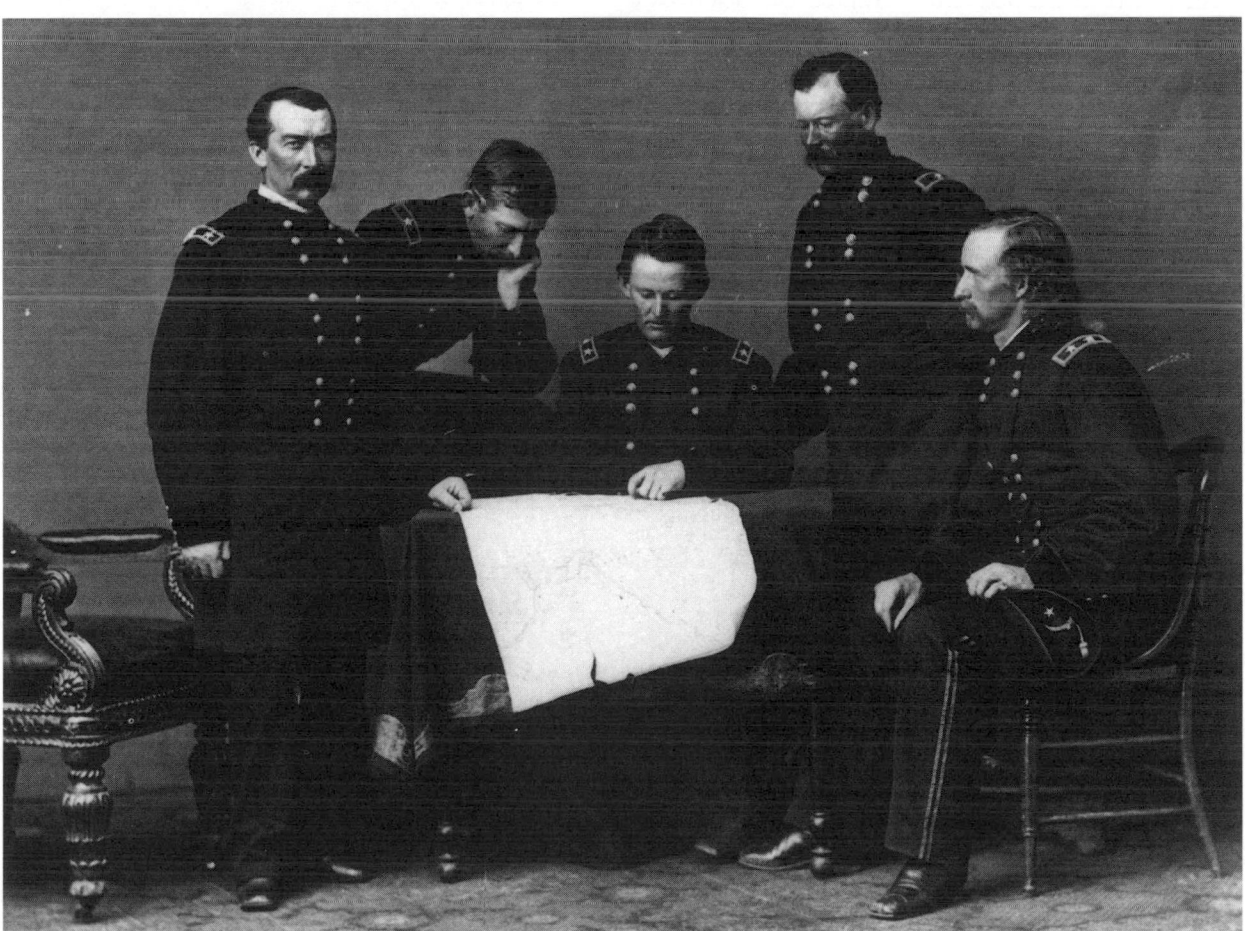

Philip H. Sheridan (far left) pictured with (left to right) James Forsyth, Wesley Merritt, Thomas Devin, and George Armstrong Custer. *Courtesy National Archives.*

During the Indian Wars, Sheridan was guided by Sherman's notion of total war—combat directed not against military objectives alone, but at the civilian population of the enemy as well, in order to destroy a people's very will to make war. In fact, Sheridan took Sherman's concept to an extreme by conducting a series of winter campaigns against the Cheyennes, beginning in 1868, with the aim of attacking Indians when they were most vulnerable. It was common practice among Indians to avoid fighting during the winter when food was usually in short supply and their maneuverability was limited. "These Indians required to be soundly whipped," Sheridan announced, "and the ringleaders in the present trouble hung, their ponies killed, and such destruction of their property as will make them very poor." What came to be called "Sheridan's Campaign" ended the Cheyenne warrior society, the Dog Soldiers, in western Kansas, and the Cheyenne "hostiles" retired to reservations after suffering losses to GEORGE ARMSTRONG CUSTER at Sweetwater Creek in the Texas Panhandle and along the Powder River in the Dakotas. But outside the brash and ambitious Custer, Sheridan's officers came to argue that such ruthless campaigns were almost as hard on the soldiers as they were on the Indians, although both Sherman and Ulysses S. Grant were heartened by the campaign.

Sheridan was promoted to lieutenant general in 1869 and given command of the Division of the Missouri when Sherman replaced Grant as general-in-chief of the army. Grant, of course, had become president of the United States. After campaigning in the Black Hills of the Dakotas from 1873 to 1874, against the Comanches, Kiowas, Southern Cheyennes, and Southern Arapahos in the Red River War from 1874 to 1875, and again against the Sioux in the Sioux War for the Black Hills from 1866 to 1877, Sheridan replaced Sherman as general-in-chief of the army in 1883. He then directed General GEORGE CROOK and, after him, NELSON APPLETON MILES, in the long struggle against the Apaches under GERONIMO. Sheridan was promoted to the rank of general of the army in 1888, the year in which he died.

—*Alan Axelrod*

SEE ALSO: Apache Wars; Central Plains Indian Wars; Sioux Wars; Texas Frontier Indian Wars.

SUGGESTED READING:

Axelrod, Alan. *Chronicle of the Indian Wars: From Colonial Times to Wounded Knee.* New York, 1993.

Hutton, Paul. *Phil Sheridan and His Army.* Lincoln, Nebr., 1985.

Utley, Robert M. *Frontier Regulars: The United States Army and the Indian, 1866–1890.* New York, 1973.

SHERMAN, WILLIAM TECUMSEH

Soldier William T. Sherman (1820–1891) was born in Lancaster, Ohio, the sixth child of Charles and Mary Hoyt Sherman. Left fatherless at the age of nine, "Cump" was reared in the home of the powerful Whig politician Thomas Ewing. After graduation from West Point Military Academy in 1840, Sherman was commissioned in the regular army. Sent to the Pacific Coast during the UNITED STATES–MEXICAN WAR, he observed and officially reported on the California gold rush. Marriage to Ewing's daughter Ellen, combined with bleak prospects in the army, led to his resignation in 1853 and entry into private business. As a banker in San Francisco and later as a lawyer in Leavenworth, Kansas, he became familiar with the West, but success eluded him. Only as superintendent of the Louisiana Military Seminary in Alexandria, Louisiana, from 1859 to 1861, did he achieve success and happiness as a civilian.

The CIVIL WAR brought Sherman fame and achievement. In the first months of the war, his hot temper and often bizarre statements and actions prompted widespread charges of mental instability and nearly cost him his commission. With the Vicksburg campaign of 1863, however, he hit his stride, in part because of his admiring partnership with Ulysses S. Grant and in part because of a growing understanding of the true nature of the Civil War. After the fall of Vicksburg, one triumph succeeded another, with the capture of Atlanta, the celebrated march to the sea, and the drive through the Carolinas. Sherman ended the Civil War second in public esteem only to Grant. When Grant became a full four-star general, Sherman became lieutenant general, the army's second soldier.

Sherman never lived farther west than St. Louis after the Civil War. The postwar years climaxed in the westward movement and the final wars between the U.S. Army and the Western Indians. First as commanding general of the Division of the Missouri (from 1866 to 1869), then as general-in-chief of the entire army (from 1869 to 1884), Sherman stamped his distinctive personality on the Western army. Ever solicitous of the regulars, he received in return their loyalty and respect.

Sherman's experiences in California and Kansas had convinced him that Americans must meet the West's challenges, populate its vast reaches, develop its rich potential, and make it a viable part of the nation. If Indians interfered with the process, they must be swept aside. He sympathized with them, but sentiment never governed his decisions or policies.

William Tecumseh Sherman. *Courtesy National Archives.*

As head of the Division of the Missouri, which included the Great Plains, Sherman oversaw the campaigns of 1866 to 1869 against the Great Plains tribes. With his subordinate, General Philip H. Sheridan, he emphasized the methods of "total war" that he had applied in his march through Georgia. Total war aimed at breaking the Indians' will to resist by destroying food, shelter, clothing, transportation, and other possessions.

During these years, Sherman also served as a member of the peace commission that negotiated the Fort Laramie and Medicine Lodge treaties. He never yielded his belief in military solutions to Indian difficulties, but political necessity forced him to go along with the peace attempts. When the treaties failed to bring peace, military methods regained favor.

Grant's election to the presidency in 1868 brought Sherman "the dreaded banishment to Washington." There he wore four stars and took his friend's place as general-in-chief of the army. Old conflicts over the position and authority of the general-in-chief in relation to the Secretary of War and the War Department staff, however, made his fifteen-year tenure frustrating and contentious. Controversy with Secretary of War William W. Belknap led to Sherman's virtual abdication when he moved his headquarters to St. Louis in 1874. The final years, back in Washington, were happier, but the underlying issues eluded solution. Even

so, he remained a venerated national hero and maintained his affectionate bonds with the regulars in the West.

Both on active duty and in retirement, Sherman basked constantly in public acclaim. Repeatedly he fended off pressures to run for the presidency. He wrote two volumes of memoirs and, with other veterans, refought the battles of the Civil War. He passed four years of retirement in St. Louis, then moved to New York City, where he died. He was buried in St. Louis.

—*Robert M. Utley*

SUGGESTED READING:

Athearn, Robert G. *William Tecumseh Sherman and the Settlement of the West.* Norman, Okla., 1956.

Marszalek, John F. *Sherman: A Soldier's Passion for Order.* New York, 1993.

Utley, Robert M. *Frontier Regulars: The United States Army and the Indian, 1866–1890.* New York, 1973.

Wooster, Robert. *The Military and United States Indian Policy, 1865–1903.* New Haven, Conn., 1988.

SHERMAN ANTI-TRUST ACT

An attempt by Congress to prevent gigantic business enterprises or "trusts" from overwhelming their competition, the Sherman Anti-Trust Act was passed by Congress in 1890. The law prohibited all combinations that restrained trade between states or with foreign nations. It applied as well to formal cartels and to any other type of agreement to fix prices, limit industrial output, share markets, or exclude competition. The law also made all attempts to monopolize any part of trade or commerce in the United States illegal.

Westerners had long advocated antitrust legislation, and both the Democrats and the Republicans placed the issue on their platforms in 1888. Reactions by farmers and labor were strong and may have contributed to the election of the Democrats in 1892. Rarely used against trusts in the decade after its passage, the law was instead aimed against trade unions. THEODORE ROOSEVELT was the first president to attempt vigorous enforcement of the law.

—*Patrick H. Butler, III*

SUGGESTED READING:

Hovenkamp, Herbert. *Federal Antitrust Policy: The Law of Competition and Its Practice.* St. Paul, Minn., 1994.

McCraw, Thomas K. *Prophets of Regulation.* Cambridge, Mass., 1984.

SHERMAN SILVER PURCHASE ACT OF 1890

A continuation of the debate over whether silver should be used, along with gold, to back the currency of the United States, the 1890 Sherman Silver Purchase Act called for the United States government to purchase and coin silver. Before 1873, the United States used a bimetallic standard (sixteen ounces of silver to one ounce of gold), but that year Congress dropped the silver dollar from its list of coins in circulation. The action was prudent because gold production was in decline, both in a relative and absolute sense, while silver production was on an increase. But in refusing to issue silver coins, the United States, in effect, adopted a tight monetary standard.

Southern farmers and debtors and Western silver miners favored the coinage of silver. The Sherman Silver Purchase Act was one of the ways in which silver advocates challenged the gold standard. The law expanded on an earlier measure—the BLAND-ALLISON ACT OF 1878—by allowing the U.S. Treasury to purchase nearly all silver produced in the United States and issue coins based on that purchase. The law was tied, however, to the market price of silver rather than to the sixteen to one ratio used before 1873. President Grover Cleveland blamed the 1890 act for the depression of 1893 and called Congress to a special session to abolish it. Repeal of the law helped polarize the Democratic party and contributed to the rise of WILLIAM JENNINGS BRYAN and the free-silver issue in the election of 1896.

—*Patrick H. Butler, III*

SEE ALSO: Currency and Silver as Western Political Issues

SHORT, LUKE

Cowboy, Indian trader, and army scout Luke Short (1854–1893) became a gambler and gunfighter later in life. Born in Mississippi, he moved with his family to Texas. As a teen-ager, he left the family's ranch and became a cowboy. In 1876, he went to Nebraska and sold whiskey to Sioux Indians near the Dakota line.

Next he served as both dispatch rider and civilian scout for the army during Northern Cheyenne Chief Dull Knife's raid in Kansas in 1878. Then he moved to Leadville, Colorado, where he probably had his first gunfight.

Showing up in Dodge City, he made friends with Wyatt Earp and BARTHOLOMEW (BAT) MASTERSON and dealt cards at the Long Branch Saloon. In 1881, Short was dealing at a saloon in Tombstone, Arizona, and there he killed Charles Storms over a card game.

Returning to Dodge City, Short purchased partial interest in the Long Branch and got involved in the "DODGE CITY WAR" of 1883. The conflict began when the city administration tried to tell Short how to run his business. After refusing to adhere to those regulations, Short had a gunfight with a policeman; neither was hurt. Forced out of Dodge City, a month later Short returned with Charlie Bassett, Bat Masterson and Wyatt Earp, members of the so-called "Dodge City Police Commission." An agreement was reached be-

Luke Short. *Courtesy Kansas State Historical Society.*

tween the two factions, and no blood was shed. After selling his interest in the saloon, Short moved to Fort Worth.

In 1887, he purchased a one-third interest in a Fort Worth saloon. A short time later, JIM COURTRIGHT, owner of a Fort Worth detective agency and former city marshal, demanded protection money from Short and his partner. Short refused to pay. A day after he sold his interest in the saloon, Short, accompanied by Bat Masterson, met Courtright in a Fort Worth saloon. Although Courtright pulled his gun first, Short shot Courtright five times, once in the heart. Short was later released on bond, and as the killing of Courtright was clearly self-defense, no trial was ever held.

In 1890, Short had a gunfight—his last—with Charles Wright over a gambling bet. Both were wounded and lived.

Suffering from dropsy, Short went to take the waters at Geuda Springs, Kansas, where he died.

—*Richard A. Van Orman*

SEE ALSO: Earp Brothers; Morning Star

SUGGESTED READING:

Cox, William R. *Luke Short And His Era.* Garden City, N.Y., 1961.

Masterson, W. B. *Famous Gunfighters of the Western Frontier.* Fort Davis, Tex., 1968.

Schoenberger, Dale T. *The Gunfighters.* Caldwell, Idaho, 1971.

SHORT BULL (SIOUX)

A Brulé medicine man, Short Bull (ca. 1847–1923) became one of the most ardent and well-known disciples of the GHOST DANCE. Together with KICKING BEAR, his brother-in-law, he joined an 1890 Lakota delegation to hear the prophet WOVOKA and then returned and taught the new religion. In November 1890, after the U.S. Army occupation of Rosebud reservation, Short Bull and his followers joined Oglala dancers at the Stronghold, north of Pine Ridge Agency, where they could dance in peace. He surrendered in January 1891 and was imprisoned at Fort Sheridan, Illinois. He then joined WILLIAM F. ("BUFFALO BILL") CODY's traveling Wild West show.

—*R. Eli Paul*

SUGGESTED READING:

Jensen, Richard E., R. Eli Paul, and John E. Carter. *Eyewitness at Wounded Knee.* Lincoln, Nebr., 1991.

Short Bull. *Courtesy Denver Public Library, Western History Department.*

SHOSHONE INDIANS

SEE: Native American Peoples: Peoples of the Great Basin, Peoples of the Great Plains

SIBLEY, HENRY HASTINGS

Soldier and Minnesota politician Henry Hastings Sibley (1811–1891) was born in Detroit and spent his early years as a fur trader for the AMERICAN FUR COMPANY. While still in his early twenties, he oversaw the firm's operations on the upper Mississippi River from Mendota located under the protective gaze of Fort Snelling. In 1848, Sibley headed to Washington, D.C., to secure territorial status for Minnesota, which he accomplished the following year. In 1851, Sibley negotiated a treaty to purchase of Sioux hunting grounds for $3 million. The land was needed to accommodate the tens of thousands of white settlers who migrated to the region in the 1850s.

Conflict between the Sioux and the settlers was brewing when Minnesota was admitted to the United States in 1858. Sibley became the state's first governor.

Henry Hastings Sibley. *Courtesy Whitney Gallery, Minnesota Historical Society.*

After retiring from the governorship, he assumed command of the state militia to respond to the Sioux uprising that began in August 1862. A man with no military experience, Sibley was slow to engage the Indians, but his defeat of LITTLE CROW on September 23, 1862, at Wood Lake ended the conflict. Intent on returning to private life, Sibley instead was named brigadier general of the U.S. Volunteers and led forces against Sioux warriors in the Dakota Territory in the summers of 1863 and 1864.

After his military career, Sibley participated in a variety of business, cultural, and civic organizations and served as president of the St. Paul Gas Light Company and of the St. Paul chamber of commerce and as chairman of the board of regents for the University of Minnesota.

—*Patricia Hogan*

SEE ALSO: Sioux Wars

SUGGESTED READING:
Oehler, C. M. *The Great Sioux Uprising.* New York, 1959.
Utley, Robert M. *The Last Days of the Sioux Nation.* New Haven, Conn., 1963.

West, Nathaniel. *The Ancestry, Life, and Times of Hon. Henry Hastings Sibley.* St. Paul, Minn., 1889.

SIBLEY, HENRY HOPKINS

Brigadier General Henry Hopkins Sibley (1816–1886), youngest son of Samuel Hopkins Sibley and Margaret I. McDonald, was born in Natchitoches, Louisiana. After attending the Grammar School of Miami University in Oxford, Ohio, he secured an appointment to West Point and graduated in 1838. Commissioned a second lieutenant in the Second Dragoons, he saw action in Florida in the Second Seminole War and fought in Mexico where he was breveted for heroism at Medellin near Veracruz. He spent five years on the Texas frontier, was in "Bleeding Kansas," and in the U.S. Army's expedition against the MORMONS in Utah from 1857 to 1858. Sent to the New Mexico Territory, Sibley was with Major EDWARD RICHARD SPRING CANBY during the unsuccessful 1860 Navajo campaign.

After resigning from the army in May 1861, Sibley went to Richmond where he persuaded Confederate President Jefferson Davis of the practicality of seizing the New Mexico Territory as a prelude to a Confederate conquest of Colorado and, eventually, California. Returning to Texas, Sibley assembled a brigade of Texans at San Antonio and set out along the Lower Military Road for Fort Bliss. Pushing up the Rio Grande, he was victorious at Valverde on February 21, 1862, but was turned back at Glorieta Pass near Sante Fe, in March 1862, and was forced to evacuate the territory. Sibley was widely blamed for the failure of the campaign because of his heavy drinking and his lack of leadership. He was court-martialed in Louisiana following the Battle of Bisland in 1863. Although acquitted, he was without a command for the remainder of the CIVIL WAR.

In 1869, he was recruited into the Egyptian army as a general but was expelled in 1873 because of drunkenness. Back in the United States, he wrote articles for *Frank Leslie's Illustrated Newspaper,* tutored students in French, and worked on several military inventions. Although well known at one time for the Sibley Tent and Stove, he died forgotten in Fredericksburg, Virginia.

—*Jerry Thompson*

SEE ALSO: Navajo Wars; Utah Expedition

SUGGESTED READING:
Hall, Martin H. *The Confederate Army of New Mexico.* Austin, Tex., 1978.
———. *Sibley's New Mexico Campaign.* Austin, Tex., 1960.
Thompson, Jerry. *Henry Hopkins Sibley: Confederate General of the West.* Natchitoches, La., 1987.

SIEBER, AL

Army scout Al Sieber (1844–1907) was born in the German Rhineland, immigrated with his family to the United States, and grew up in Lancaster, Pennsylvania. Not yet twenty years of age, he served in the Union Army during the Civil War and was wounded at the Battle of Gettysburg. Discharged in 1865, Sieber headed to southern Arizona. He became fluent in the Spanish language and the Athapascan tongue of the Apaches, knowledgeable about Apache war methods, and skilled as a tracker.

These talents earned Sieber an appointment as chief of civilian scouts for General GEORGE CROOK in 1870. Sieber, with TOM HORN as his assistant, headed a force made up of officers and Apache scouts from the San Carlos Reservation. Sieber's scouts led to the army's successful assault on the White Mountain Apaches at the Battle of Big Dry Wash on July 17, 1882.

When Apache chief GERONIMO broke out of the San Carlos Reservation in 1881, Sieber's advance party tracked him into Mexico and helped secure the surrender of about three hundred Apaches, including the chief himself. Geronimo fled the reservation again in 1885, and once more, Sieber followed in pursuit.

After Crook left his command in the Arizona Territory, Sieber scouted for Generals NELSON APPLETON MILES and OLIVER OTIS HOWARD. In 1887, Sieber was wounded in a ruckus with one of his own scouts, the APACHE KID, who, after deserting the scouts' corps turned killer.

Sieber retired as chief of scouts in 1890, having suffered, according to some accounts, twenty-nine gun, arrow, and knife wounds. He was killed in 1907 in a landslide while supervising a crew of Apache road-builders working near Roosevelt Dam.

—*Patricia Hogan*

SEE ALSO: Apache Wars; United States Army: Scouts

SUGGESTED READING:
Thrapp, Dan L. *Al Sieber: Chief of Scouts.* Norman, Okla., 1964.

SIERRA CLUB

In 1892, California naturalist JOHN MUIR merged a citizens' group, which he had organized to protect the Sierra Nevada from exploitation, with the Alpine Club, a small band of mountain-loving students at the University of California at Berkeley, to form the Sierra Club.

Muir's rationale in creating the organization was that those who enjoyed the wilderness would also show determination in fighting to protect it. The charter of the new club proclaimed a dedication to "exploring, enjoying, and rendering accessible the mountain regions of the Pacific Coast" as well as a commitment to enlist "the support and cooperation of the people and the government in preserving the forests and other features of the Sierra Nevada."

The Sierra Club's first major political action was to arrange the transfer of the Yosemite Valley from state to federal jurisdiction in 1906. Next, the club did legal battle with the city of San Francisco, which proposed to convert YOSEMITE NATIONAL PARK's Hetch Hetchy Valley to a reservoir. The club lost that lengthy struggle in 1913, and a year later, Muir died. He was succeeded as Sierra Club director by William E. Colby, a specialist in mining and forest law, who, between the world wars, led successful Sierra Club campaigns to enlarge Sequoia National Park, establish Kings Canyon National Park, and block logging in Washington's Olympic National Park.

Beginning in 1901, the Sierra Club sponsored annual High Trips in the mountains, which became increasingly popular. By 1973, club guides were leading approximately five thousands individuals on almost five hundred trips annually. As early as the 1950s, however, the charter mandate to render the mountains "accessible" began to conflict with the aim of preserving the wilderness. During that decade, the Sierra Club became increasingly critical of national policy with regard to outdoor recreation and successfully lobbied for the Outdoor Recreation Resources Review Act of 1958, which compelled public and private agencies to catalog park, wilderness, and wildlife resources and their recreational potential with an eye toward curbing overuse. Working with the Wilderness Society, the Sierra Club secured Congressional passage of the National Wilderness Act of 1964, which established a National Wilderness Preservation System.

The 1950s also saw the expansion of the club from an association of independent local chapters to a centrally directed national organization. David R. Brower, the first executive director of the newly constituted club, led a campaign to preserve Dinosaur National Monument against a BUREAU OF RECLAMATION dam project in 1952; between 1952 and 1954, Brower established Atlantic and Pacific Northwest club chapters. Beginning with the 1960 publication of naturalist-photographer Ansel Adams's *This Is the American Earth*, the club began its highly acclaimed—and highly profitable—Exhibit Format book series. The 1960s saw a steady increase in membership and political influence until 1966, when federal regulators determined to withdraw the organization's tax-exempt status. The resulting financial crisis fueled dissension within the organization. Gradually, during the 1970s, the downslide was halted. The Sierra Club resumed its leadership role in environmental battles, addressed such issues as the use of Alaskan lands, and expanded its scope to international environmental issues.

In the mid-1990s, the Sierra Club had three hundred thousand members in fifty-three chapters throughout the United States and Canada.

—*Alan Axelrod*

SEE ALSO: Hetch Hetchy Controversy

SUGGESTED READING:

Axelrod, Alan, and Charles Phillips. *The Environmentalist: A Biographical Dictionary from the 17th Century to the Present.* New York, 1993.

Cohen, Michael P. *The History of the Sierra Club, 1892–1970.* San Francisco, 1988.

Fox, Stephen. *John Muir and His Legacy: The American Conservation Movement.* Boston, 1981.

Jones, Holway R. . *John Muir and the Sierra Club: The Battle for Yosemite.* San Francisco, 1965.

Nash, Roderick. *Wilderness and the American Mind.* New Haven, Conn., 1967.

SILENTSPRING

SEE: Carson, Rachel Louise, and *Silent Spring*

SILVER ISSUE

SEE: Currency and Silver and Western Political Issues

SILVER KING, ARIZONA

SEE: Ghost Towns

SILVER MINING

The early history of silver MINING in the trans-Mississippi West was closely tied to that of GOLD MINING, since both were frequently found together. Sometimes discoveries of silver gave already existing mining camps and towns new life; other silver lodes became the basis for the booming of a camp, a town, or an entire region on its own. Indeed, silver combined far more readily with other minerals than gold did, but it was also harder to recognize for that reason: silver took on the various colorations of the metals with which it combined. In the COMSTOCK LODE, which, over the course of two decades, produced $105 million worth of silver, the white metal laced the gold that had led to a strike. In some parts of Colorado, ores containing silver and lead might be as black as tar; the rare, brittle, crystals that combined with silver and gave Telluride, Colorado, its name, tellurium, was silver-white. Silver ore could be yellow; it could be white or black or pale green; it came in shades of dark red and brown.

Prospecting for silver was even more difficult, however, because there was no convenient test for silver a miner could make in the field. There was only one sure test, treating an ore sample with nitric acid and hydrochloric acid. Both of them were dangerous to cart around in the rugged Rocky Mountains, so prospectors tended to pick up anything they thought might be silver and take it, eventually, to a professional assayer. Only then could they be sure they had enough to mine commercially, if they could remember where they had found it and keep others from getting to and staking the spot before them. Despite the difficulties, prospectors did make finds, some of them spectacular. Noah Kellogg, for example, claimed he stumbled across veins of silver-bearing ore along Idaho's Coeur d'Alene because his mule became fascinated by the sun rays reflecting off a vein of bright mineral. Like most prospectors, Kellogg was an accomplished liar. The ore he found was galena, a mixture of lead and silver, which turned a drab gray when exposed to light—it did *not* glisten in the sun. Nevertheless, the strike produced the bonanza Bunker Hill and Sullivan Mines, led to the founding of a boom town called Wardner, and yielded some $300 million in silver over the next sixty years.

Unlike gold, silver seldom occurred in easily mined placers. Exploiting silver finds effectively and profitably generally required the outlay of big capital necessary to dig out and refine underground ore. In other words, silver mining was, by and large, hard-rock mining. Indeed, the initial placer booms in California and Colorado proved deceptive, and at several points in Montana and all around the Great Basin, mining magnates and would-be magnates soon faced the task of freeing silver, and gold, too, from solid rock. The experiences of the Forty-niners were not much good to them, and the relative simplicity of the silver ores in the Comstock Lode were misleading. Many of the silver ores in the Rocky Mountains and the Great Basin were silver-lead, and silver-lead—no way around it—required smelting, which produced lead as a by-product. Shipping lead, a heavy metal, anywhere was not even thinkable before railroad transportation arrived in the area, and before the RAILROADS came there was no easy way to bring in the massive supplies, large amounts of fuel, and the big flumes needed for smelters. The Colorado lodes, once miners dug deep enough, also contained sulfides—tellurium, for example, shared many properties with sulphur. The miners called these "sulpherets," or "refractory," or "pyritic" ores. There was a reason peasants had long associated the smell of sulphur with the presence of the devil, and the deep veins of Colorado's hellish hard-rocking-mining days tended to burst into flames easily and kill all those who happened to be down the shaft.

In the 1860s and early 1870s, without the railroads, it made little sense to pour the placer profits already made into hard-rock mining, and the Western mining frontier went through a difficult transition. Then in the late 1870s, the economy of mining changed, and the time seemed right for investment. First, the railroads had arrived; second, other costs were more favorable because wages had been depressed in the hard times following the placer busts and interest rates were low; and third, there arrived on the scene professionally trained mining engineers from Europe and the East.

LEADVILLE, COLORADO, is a good example. In 1860, prospector Abe Lee struck gold in a valley ten thousand feet up the Rockies in the area around what would become Leadville. Lee found the placer gold in a stream flowing from the Mosquito Mountains, and the stream's gorge was dubbed California Gulch. The rush was soon on, and tents and crudely constructed buildings filled the narrow gorge for a mile along the stream down from Lee's find. Two years later, the gold ran out, the miners left their town without a backward glance, and the mining district was dead. Thirteen years later, a prospector named Will Stevens, possessed of an active imagination, tramped about the old diggings, became curious about the black sand and rock underlying the area, and decided to have a sample assayed. August R. Meyer, a European-trained mining engineer, was brought to California Gulch in 1876, and he correctly determined—and reported—that the stuff was a silver ore, or, to be more precise, that the lode was carbonate of lead containing two and one-half pounds of silver to the ton. Stevens and his friends, including Californian GEORGE HEARST, bought up all the idle claims they could find. Back home, Hearst raised the capital he needed to launch a hard-rock silver mine. By 1877, news had leaked, and a town mushroomed at the foot of the gulch. Called Leadville in honor of the silver-bearing lead carbonates, the place soon had not one but three railroads and became a great producer of silver, a major source of lead, and a center—and model—for effective smelting operations. In one twenty-four-hour period, one mine in Leadville pro-

duced $118,500. By 1880, Leadville had smelted and shipped $12 million in silver out of the district. Leadville's silver soon waned, and the town seemed headed once more for oblivion, but miners struck new deposits of copper and zinc, Leadville had the hard-rock mining capacity already at hand, and the town continued to prosper and make Hearst and his ilk incredibly rich.

This kind of thing went on all over the mountain West. Earlier, Eureka, Nevada, had produced a slightly lower output in silver and lead. The gold rush to Idaho's Coeur d'Alene region in the early 1880s led to the discovery of silver, lead, and zinc, and to the birth of yet another center of mining, ore treatment, and smelting of both base and precious metals. In BUTTE, MONTANA, the once penniless Irish immigrant MARCUS DALY persuaded three San Francisco tycoons, newly rich off hard-rock mining and including the veteran George Hearst, to back what they all thought was a silver mine, only to be informed by Daly, in 1882, that, it seemed, the Anaconda would not make its mark as a silver operation but as one of the richest copper mines in the world. Hard-rock silver mining served as a transition from the early days of placer mining to the industrial-mining period of the late 1880s and 1890s. And it was no accident that the areas with the big silver lodes—Leadville, Colorado, for example, or Coeur d'Alene in northern Idaho, or Tombstone and Bisbee in the Arizona Territory—also became the sites of major labor strife in the virtual class war that broke out late in the nineteenth century between miners and other migrant workers and the big, often self-made capitalists of the American West.

—*Charles Phillips*

SEE ALSO: Arizona Mining Strikes; Copper Mining; Industrial Workers of the World; Labor Movement; Lead Mining; Violence

SUGGESTED READING:

Brown. Ronald C. *Hard-Rock Miners: The Intermountain West, 1860–1920.* College Station, Tex., 1979.

Elliott, Russel R. *Nevada's Mining Boom: Toonpah, Goldfield, Ely.* Reno, Nev., 1966.

Fahey, John W. *The Ballyhoo Bonanza: Charles Sweeny and the Idaho Mines.* Seattle, Wash., 1971.

Greever, William. *Bonanza West: The Story of the Western Mining Rushes, 1848–1900.* Norman, Okla. 1963.

King, Joseph E. *A Mine to Make a Mine: Financing the Colorado Mining Industry, 1859–1902.* College Station, Tex., 1977.

Paul, Rodman W. *Mining Frontiers of the Far West, 1848–1880.* New York, 1963.

Peterson, Richard H. *The Bonanza Kings: The Social Origins and Business Behavior of Western Mining Entrepreneurs, 1870–1900.* Lincoln, Nebr., 1977.

Spence, Clark C. *British Investments and the American Mining Frontier, 1860–1901*. Ithaca, N.Y., 1958.

———. *Mining Engineers and the American West: The Lace-Boot Brigade, 1849–1933*. New Haven, Conn., 1970.

Wyman, Mark. *Hard-Rock Epic: Western Miners and the Industrial Revolution, 1860–1910*. Berkeley, Calif., 1979.

SILVER PLUME, COLORADO

SEE: Ghost Towns

SILVER REEF, UTAH

SEE: Ghost Towns

SILVERWORK

SEE: Native American Silverwork, Southwestern

SIMPSON, JERRY

A Populist agitator and congressman famed as "Sockless Jerry," Jerry Simpson (1842–1905) was born in New Brunswick, Canada. He received only a rudimentary education before leaving home to work for twenty-three years as a sailor and ultimately a captain on freighters on the Great Lakes. In 1879, he moved to Kansas, where he was, by turns, farmer, miller, rancher, and marshal of Medicine Lodge. Originally a Republican, Simpson turned to the reform politics of third parties. He ran unsuccessfully for the state legislature as a Greenbacker in 1886 and as a Union Labor nominee in 1888. In 1890, the new People's party (the Populists) nominated him for Congress, and in his homespun diatribes against corporate abuses, he articulated the swelling discontent of his rural constituents. An imprudent Republican effort to ridicule his style led to his being given the nickname "sockless" and solidified his popular support. With Democratic backing, he was elected to Congress and then reelected in 1892 and 1896. He lost two other races in 1894 and 1898.

In Congress, Simpson introduced few measures, but his quick wit and sharp tongue made him the leader of the Populist delegation. Beyond his commitment to HENRY GEORGE's plan for a single-tax, Simpson was rarely consistent in his reform beliefs. A persistent advocate of fusion—the joining of Democrats and Populists—in both state and national politics, he worked to secure Democratic cooperation even by undermining the reform objectives and candidates of POPULISM. Through such tactics to advance fusion (and himself), he often alienated other Populists and became embroiled in bitter personal and political quarrels. Following his 1898 defeat, Simpson briefly published a newspaper entitled *Jerry Simpson's Bayonet* and then retired from politics. For a time, he sold land in New Mexico for the Santa Fe Railroad he had previously attacked as a corrupt monopoly. His always poor health deteriorating, he returned to Kansas in 1905 and died in Wichita.

—*Peter H. Argersinger*

SUGGESTED READING:

Bicha, Karel D. "Jerry Simpson: Populist without Principle." *Journal of American History* 54 (1967): 291–306.

Diggs, Annie L. *The Story of Jerry Simpson*. Wichita, Kans., 1908.

SINCLAIR, UPTON

Upton Sinclair (1868–1968) well-known muckraker novelist, socialist, and unsuccessful candidate for CALIFORNIA governor, was born in Baltimore, Maryland. Early in his youth, Sinclair voraciously read the poets and prophets of social rebellion and developed close ties to socialists. His antiromantic bias and debunking passion are evident in his first novel, *Manassas* (1904), which bears comparison to Stephen Crane's classic *Red Badge of Courage*. His most celebrated book, *The Jungle* (1906), is an indictment of capitalist greed and disregard of the public welfare as manifested in the livestock and meat-packing industry. To be sure, most of the American public was indifferent or hostile to Sinclair's socialist message, but his nauseatingly graphic exposure of the unsanitary practices of the packing industry sent shock waves from the nation's grassroots to the corridors of power and sparked the passage of the national Pure Food and Drug Act of 1906.

Sinclair continued to act on his socialist philosophy—even experimenting with the establishment of a socialist commune—and continued to write as what President THEODORE ROOSEVELT had called a "muckraker" (the president adopted the term from John Bunyan's allegorical *Pilgrim's Progress*, in which a man uses a "muckrake" to sweep the filth around him, even as he remains unaware of the celestial glory overhead). Sinclair exposed the ills of American society, including venereal disease *(Damaged Goods,* 1913), mining monopolism *(King Coal,* 1917), the hypocrisy of mainstream journalism *(The Brass Check,* 1919), religious hypocrisy *(The Profits of Religion,* 1918, and *They*

Call Me Carpenter, 1922), and the shortcomings of American education *(The Goose-Step,* 1923, and *The Goslings,* 1924). In 1927, he probed the TEAPOT DOME scandal in *Oil!,* the story of Bunny Ross, the son of a big California oil man, who ultimately "betrays" his upbringing by siding with the workers his father exploits. A story of the Harding era, *Oil!* is replete with vivid images drawn from government corruption as well as a lurid portrait of southern California society, ranging from movie-star glamour to the hypocrisy of popular evangelism.

After *Oil!* Sinclair fictionalized the Sacco-Vanzetti case (*Boston,* 1928) and couched a defense of Prohibition in a 1931 novel entitled *The Wet Parade* (1931). In 1933, the novelist financed the publication of *Upton Sinclair Presents William Fox* (1933), an exposé of the Hollywood film industry, which no publisher would touch.

Sinclair unsuccessfully ran as the Democratic candidate for governor of California in 1934 on his EPIC (End Poverty in California) platform. In 1940, he published *World's End,* the first of a series of eleven novels devoted to Lanny Budd, a kind of superman and ultimate insider, the dynamic confidante of world leaders. The third Lanny Budd novel, *Dragon's Teeth* (1942), focused on Adolf Hitler's rise to power and won the 1943 Pulitzer Prize for fiction.

—*Alan Axelrod*

SEE ALSO: Progressivism; Socialism

SUGGESTED READING:
Bloodworth, William A., Jr. *Upton Sinclair.* New York, 1977.
Mitchell, Greg. *The Campaign of the Century.* New York, 1992.
Sinclair, Upton. *The Autobiography of Upton Sinclair.* New York, 1962.

Benjamin ("Pap") Singleton. *Courtesy Kansas State Historical Society.*

SINGLETON, BENJAMIN ("PAP")

Called the "father of the Exodus," Benjamin Singleton (1809–1892) was born in Nashville, Tennessee, into a life of slavery. He ran away frequently, only to be retrieved and then to run away again. After finally reaching Canada, Singleton returned to Detroit to help other slaves on the Underground Railroad. After the Civil War, he returned to Nashville, where he faced the hostility of embittered whites. When Reconstruction ended, AFRICAN AMERICANS lost their federal protection, and violence against blacks—some of it spawned by the new KU KLUX KLAN—escalated. Repressive laws and social customs made the lives of the freed black Americans hardly better than that of slaves.

Singleton first attempted to resettle blacks by forming the Edgefield Real Estate and Homestead Association, but whites refused to sell land to him. Singleton then decided to promote black migration to Kansas, the land of the near-mythical JOHN BROWN. Spending his meager savings, Singleton produced thousands of handbills and lithographs urging the migration to Kansas in the early 1870s. What resulted over the next several years was not so much a planned migration as an exodus from the South. Southern freedmen settled in Cherokee, Dunlap, Lyon, and Morris counties in Kansas. By 1880, the "EXODUSTERS," as they were called, had become so numerous that the U.S. Senate ordered an investigative hearing and called Singleton and other freedmen to testify. There, they reported horrifying experiences of ex-Confederates returning them to a condition of slavery and the Klan administering lynch law.

Although Singleton claimed in the hearings to be "the whole cause of the Kansas immigration," the exodus had no single leader. By the time of the hearings, the migration was essentially over. More than twenty thousand freedmen had fled the South, particularly Texas, Louisiana, and Mississippi. Many were unprepared for the cold winters in their new home; many others were unable to acquire land. By 1883, it was clear that the exodus had not delivered the hoped-for Promised Land. Singleton died nine years later in St. Louis.

—*Kurt Edward Kemper*

SUGGESTED READING:
Bontemps, Arna, and Jack Conroy. *Anyplace But Here.* New York, 1966.
Painter, Nell. *Exodusters: Black Migration to Kansas after Reconstruction.* Lawrence, Kans., 1976.

SIOUX INDIANS

SEE: Native American Peoples: Peoples of the Great Plains

SIOUX WARS

Northern Great Plains Sioux tribal forces, sometimes reinforced by Cheyennes, Arapahos, and others, waged war against non-Indians in defense of territory, natural resources, and cultural freedom beginning with the GRATTAN MASSACRE of 1854 and ending with an incident at Lightning Creek in 1903. The half century of sporadic conflict, the outcome of which depended on military acumen or the deployment of superior arms, included battles, tactical "massacres," and spontaneous "affairs" as well as unpremeditated military "incidents." Together, they composed one of the longest and most fateful armed confrontations between the United States and Native Americans in the country's history.

For more than half a century before the Grattan Massacre, a relationship of guarded suspicion prevailed between the United States and the tribes of the northern Great Plains. Federal employees, explorers, missionaries, and traders of good deportment were welcome across the region. Tribal members and non-Indian hunters harvested animal resources to the commercial advantage of white investors in hide- and fur-trading operations. Native Americans exchanged a part of their natural bounty and labor for manufactured items that improved their military proficiency, made their lives more convenient, and embellished their ceremonies and their arts.

Careful observers grew increasingly fearful that occasional clashes, such as the Arikara War of 1823, might escalate into widespread conflict. The depletion of wildlife by fur traders, accelerated by an attack on bison from professional hunters, threatened to diminish natural resources essential to tribal life. During the 1840s, overland travelers violated the boundaries of tribal lands without permission. Near mid-century, emigrants settled close to Indian communities and provoked cross-cultural conflicts.

By then, U.S. Army strategists, increasingly concerned about the potential for violence, had reversed the policy they had maintained. Since the establishment of Forts Snelling and Atkinson in 1819 and the treaty-making efforts of the Atkinson-O'Fallon Commission on the Yellowstone Expedition of 1825, army leaders had reduced their forces north of Kansas to accommodate military needs on the southern Great Plains. In 1848, however, federal troops built and occupied Fort Kearny and, in 1849, purchased FORT LARAMIE from traders to protect the migration of MORMONS and others traveling westward from Omaha along opposite sides of the Platte River basin.

The Treaty of Fort Laramie in 1851 arranged safe passage for overlanders through a procedure familiar to tribal leaders. Treaties, like those produced by the Atkinson-O'Fallon Commission, traditionally recognized the territorial claims negotiated among the tribes themselves for the privileges of passage or hunting. The Fort Laramie negotiations extended this intertribal diplomacy to accommodate non-Indians by producing a treaty that offered annuities as tolls for travel across Sioux, Cheyenne, and Arapaho country. For three years after the 1851 treaty, tribal soldiers allowed non-Indians to migrate unmolested until a misunderstanding provoked a bloody confrontation.

The Grattan Massacre and its consequences

In 1854, a party of Brulé and other Lakota soldiers might have perceived a lame cow, which accompanied a Mormon family, as fair game for a hunting party in need of food. Its Mormon owner took exception and reported a theft. Lieutenant J. L. Grattan sallied forth to arrest the Minneconjou soldier accused of putting the cow out of its misery. A spontaneous military affair—which the army called a "massacre"—ended in the death of the lieutenant and his entire unit, motivated the Brulés to raid other groups of non-Indians on the Oregon and Mormon trails, and initiated half a century of military conflict on the northern Great Plains.

General WILLIAM SELBY HARNEY appeared in 1855 with approximately one thousand men to assert the sovereignty of the United States government. After pun-

"Escapees during the Sioux uprising from Riggs and Williamson Missions, near the Upper Agency, August 21, 1862."
Photograph by Adrian Ebell. *Courtesy Minnesota Historical Society.*

ishing Lakotas by a victory in the Battle of Ash Hollow, Harney penetrated deeply into Sioux country as far as the decaying palisade at Fort Pierre, where he planned to station ten companies of infantry and cavalry. The following year, officially explaining the movement of troops as an abandonment of dilapidated facilities with limited access for steamboats, Harney retreated downstream on the Missouri River and established Fort Randall on a more advantageous site at the outer edge of Sioux country. A well-known natural tower marked a narrow point in the Missouri Valley where two networks of overland trails converged, where rushing water offered a suitable landing for steamers, and where an avenue of escape provided Harney's troops with a sense of security. At his new post, the general rattled a saber in the face of superior Lakota forces without much risk while he attempted to renegotiate the rights of passage for white emigrants. His efforts failed because the U.S. Senate declined to ratify the terms of the new understanding. At least by his presence, Harney contained further interruptions in traffic along the Platte for a time and offered protection for teams of surveyors under G. K. Warren and WILLIAM F. RAYNOLDS as they modified tribal trails into a map of suitable routes across Lakota land.

Would-be settlers arriving at the southeastern edge of Sioux country posed an even greater threat to the Native Americans. In 1851, federal negotiators made room for the settlers with treaties at Mendota and Traverse des Sioux. By 1855, the four tribes of Dakotas abandoned use and occupancy on some 20 million acres in southern Minnesota and northern Iowa and, in return, accepted annuity payments and agency services on reservation acreage along the upper Minnesota River valley.

Soils inhospitable to agriculture, bureaucratic mismanagement, and cultural misunderstanding between Dakota people and groups of U.S. citizens from the East, interspersed with immigrant peoples mainly of Scandinavian, German, Irish, and British descent, all contributed to a growing discord. In 1857, a Wahpekute Dakota named Inkpaduta, exiled from his tribe, led a tactical massacre of settlers at Spirit Lake in northwestern Iowa in retaliation for the hanging of his brother. He then terrorized Scandinavians near Jackson in southwestern Minnesota. To the chagrin of Captain James Starkey, who led Minnesota volunteers on a punitive expedition, white settlers showed little interest in retribution. "Such was the mixed character of the population at the time," wrote Starkey later on, "that a large proportion of the citizens were either by ties of consanguinity, or trading interest, allied to the Indians and their interests." Without the settlers' cooperation, there was little Starkey could do. Inkpaduta escaped with his party to die a natural death in Montana.

By 1857, there also was cross-cultural tension on the "Yankton Triangle," in the southeastern quadrant of present-day South Dakota, where Yankton tribal soldiers harassed settlers and speculators who trespassed on their lands. To prevent a war as much as to preserve a tribe with diminishing natural resources, the ranking leader STRUCK BY THE REE accompanied other tribal officials to Washington, D.C., where they affixed their marks or signatures to a treaty in 1858. By its terms, the Yankton people ceded to the United States the eastern half of the present-day state of South Dakota in return for four concessions: the retention of 430,000 acres as a reservation across the Missouri River from Fort Randall; a recognized claim to the sacred pipestone quarry in southwestern Minnesota; the establishment of an agency with a staff to support a transition into farming and ranching; and annuities payable over fifty years.

Uprising in Minnesota

As a result of the treaty, Yanktons alone among the Sioux never officially took up arms against the United States, but soon there was trouble at both ends of Sioux country. In 1861, the federal government—hampered by the extraordinary demands the American CIVIL WAR placed on its resources—failed to deliver on time the annuities due under the 1851 Dakota treaties. In a situation that called for the utmost diplomacy, the inexperienced U.S. agent for the Dakotas in Minnesota, Thomas J. Galbraith, bungled his response to the demands of hungry tribal members. Traders hoarded their wares, rather than providing Native Americans with the food and trade goods they needed to get through the winter but for which they could not (for the time being) pay, while Galbraith and his staff seemed willing to stand by and let the Indians starve. The traders' callousness and the agency's insensitivity to fundamental tribal needs precipitated a war.

Few conflicts in the history of Indian-white relations were more devastating than the one orchestrated by LITTLE CROW in Minnesota during 1862. Replete with battles, massacres, affairs, and incidents, the conflict demonstrated intercultural conflict beyond repair by appeasement and precipitously replaced an attitude of mutual suspicion with open hostility. "It is impossible to describe the bitter hatred, felt by nearly all [non-Indians]," the missionary Pond brothers later recalled, "toward every individual without exception, of the hated race. . . . Especially among those of foreign birth,

to be an Indian was to be a murderer, entitled to neither justice nor mercy." As many as 25,000 non-Indians fled out of fear, many never to return. Reports placed the casualties among those whites who remained at 490; the same reports claimed that 71 tribal members died (although there were probably more) and that 277 were taken prisoner.

Fighting ended after several months when Abraham Lincoln excused four units from Civil War duty to serve in the West. A northern Iowa brigade contained the Sioux War at the Minnesota boundary, while a volunteer force, the First Dakota Cavalry, protected southeastern Dakota territorial residents from attack. General HENRY HASTINGS SIBLEY assembled a militia force in Minnesota to expel Dakota people from the state. General ALFRED SULLY led a U.S. Army unit out of Sioux City to cooperate with Sibley in a pincer movement scheduled to close at Devil's Lake in North Dakota.

Sibley and Sully missed their rendezvous, but each accomplished his mission. Sibley cleared southern Minnesota and eastern Dakota Territory of tribal forces, driving most of them (with innocent tribal members) onto the Great Plains. Canadian traders estimated that as many as 2,500 Indians gathered around Hudson's Bay Company's Fort Garry on the Manitoba prairie and requested sanctuary. Sully led two expeditions up the Missouri River to establish U.S. military control as far west as Lakota country.

Minnesota non-Indians wanted retribution in blood, plus security against future attack, and federal officials responded to both demands. A military tribunal tried 307 tribal members, at a rate of 10 per day without legal counsel, preparation, witnesses, or adequate interpreters; convicted them of war crimes; and ordered their execution. Fortunately, President Lincoln's special agent, John George Nicolay, was in the area to prevent the collaboration of Ojibwa with Sioux forces as well as to negotiate the cession of Ojibwa land. At Nicolay's recommendation, Lincoln reduced the number scheduled for execution to 39, and officers on the scene accepted one additional change. Before a capacity crowd, evidently with music and lyrics about afterlife in the song "Lac qui Parle" to comfort them, 38 were hanged at Mankato. (Their bodies disappeared from shallow graves—suspiciously close to the residence of soon-to-be-famed physician William W. Mayo, near Le Sueur.) The remaining "war criminals" went by military escort with their families to Fort Davenport in northeastern Iowa, where they remained until a reunion with relocated Santees several years later.

More than 1,200 Mdewakantons and Wahpekutes traveled by steamboat down the Mississippi, up the Missouri River, to the Crow Creek (Fort Thompson) Agency, which had been established to receive them. A group of Winnebago people, caught on a Minnesota reservation, fled overland to the Crow Creek area. After more than 200 Santees perished from hunger, illness, and exposure, the Winnebagos established a new reservation on land relinquished by Omahas, and the Dakotas moved to their Santee Reservation in Nebraska.

Congress passed the Forfeiture Act on February 16, 1863, to protect non-Indians in Minnesota against future attack. Under the law, the four tribes of Dakotas lost all of their land claims and annuities as a penalty for war. Two Indian forces appeared shortly thereafter to create a demilitarized zone between Indian lands and lands held by the United States. Sisseton-Wahpeton Gabriel Renville's "Half Breed Scouts" patrolled between Fort Abercrombie and present-day Mellette, South Dakota; Yankton tribal scouts under General Sully ranged from Mellette to Yankton City on the Missouri River. Their duties were to prevent hostile Dakotas from returning to Minnesota or molesting settlers along the eastern side of the Dakota Territory and to provide places of surrender for innocent tribal refugees.

The epilogue to the war was a "trail of tears" that relocated Dakota people from Minnesota to five reservations in the United States and seven in Canada. In the 1880s, after small groups drifted back to their Minnesota homeland, Congress created five tiny reservations for occupancy by assignment. There they remained with little other federal assistance until the 1930s, when officials recognized them as members of four separate tribes on as many reservations comprising 3,389 acres for 556 residents, or 6.1 acres per capita.

Red Cloud's War

In 1865, any sympathy the United States or its military strategists might have felt for the anguish of the Dakota people vanished with the outbreak of RED CLOUD's War. Oglala Lakotas were incensed by a clear violation of the 1851 Fort Laramie Treaty. The federal government, seeking to link Omaha with Montana mining communities and to avoid the perils of steamboat transportation and tribal harassment along the Missouri River, authorized the construction of the BOZEMAN TRAIL. The trail cut across the heart of Lakota country where numerous tribes made their adjustment from reliance on bison to other species of large as well as smaller game.

An attack on federal forces north of Fort Phil Kearny in Wyoming was perceived by non-Indians as the FETTERMAN MASSACRE. On December 21, 1866, a tribal force inspired by CRAZY HORSE killed all 80 soldiers under Captain William Judd Fetterman and dismembered their bodies, surely to underscore the unbending determination of Lakota people to resist the encroachment of the Bozeman Trail. Subsequently, U.S. troops made heroic, symbolic gestures of defense in the so-called Hayfield and Wagon Box battles. At the latter, on Big Piney Creek, only 3 of 19 white soldiers died while repelling a force of Sioux, Cheyennes, and Arapahos estimated to include about 300 by a tribal observer, and as many as 3,000 by white reporters determined to demonstrate that the U.S. Army could stand against the western Sioux.

However the numbers may have been inflated, tribal forces were larger than those of the U.S. Army, and federal officials capitulated in 1868, signing a new Fort Laramie Treaty. They not only abandoned the Bozeman Trail but also recognized some 60 million acres west of the Missouri River as the Great Sioux Reservation, which would remain inviolate until three-fourths of the adult males in all of the signatory tribes authorized intrusion. Clearly, the Lakotas had triumphed, mounting a successful defense against unauthorized intruders that lasted for several years.

Sioux War for the Black Hills

In the 1870s, as surface deposits of gold disappeared in other parts of the West, individual prospectors ignored treaties to chase rumors of gold into the Black Hills. Several times, U.S. Army contingents expelled them, while twice investigative expeditions entered and estimated the quantity of gold: one led by GEORGE ARMSTRONG CUSTER, the other by geologist Walter P. Jenney with a military escort under Colonel Richard I. Dodge. Their reports suggested deposits in bonanza proportions, which lured a determined horde of new prospectors. President Ulysses S. Grant conferred with his generals and agreed to allow the illegal gold rush.

Tribal members assembled in numbers estimated as great as 30,000 to make a stand. They were known as "Sitting Bull people" because they rallied around a Hunkpapa Lakota soldier and spiritual leader whose unbending opposition to white intrusions had elevated him to regional fame. By the autumn of 1875, several U.S. agencies were in place to detach the tribes from each other, strip them of arms and ponies, and render them compliant to federal control. When, in the early months of 1876, SITTING BULL, the Oglala Crazy Horse, and other Lakota leaders resisted, a military showdown became inevitable.

Custer led one column in a three-pronged pincer movement similar to the one that had resulted in victory for the U.S. Army along the Washita River on the southern Great Plains. After Custer moved his contingent ahead of the others, a battle ensued that would be interpreted differently by non-Indian records and by tribal memory. White scholars, referring to their documents, claim that Custer surprised the Indian peoples. A brief stand-off collapsed when Crazy Horse led tribal soldiers to victory at the Battle of Little Bighorn, June 25–26, during which the more than 350 troops who accompanied Custer were killed and an unrecorded number of Native Americans died. Tribal memory holds that Sitting Bull knew precisely all of the movements of Custer's force, that by proficient strategy he lured Custer to an indefensible position, and that he then orchestrated the battle led by Crazy Horse, which annihilated the Seventh Cavalry.

Regardless of the interpretation, clearly the U.S. Army had once again been defeated. Tribal forces scattered in bands, however, attempting to survive without benefit of annuities and without sources for military supplies. They would have to face a much reinforced U.S. Army, funded by an indignant Congress, backed by industrial production, and blessed with efficient transportation. Most tribal members gave up their arms and ponies as they gathered around federal agencies. Crazy Horse surrendered at Fort Robinson in Nebraska and paid with his life. Seeking to prevent further bloodshed, Sitting Bull led a number estimated as great as 2,000 across the Canadian border to ask for sanctuary.

With tribal resistance diminishing, federal officials tried to negotiate the purchase of the Black Hills but to no avail. In clear violation of the 1868 Fort Laramie Treaty, Congress then expropriated the Black Hills and surrounding plains by an agreement approved on February 28, 1877. The Great Sioux Reservation shrank from 60 million to 21.7 million acres, on which the seven tribes of Lakotas plus Yanktonais, summoned to federal agencies, were told to prepare for reservation life.

With Sitting Bull in Canada, non-Indian Black Hills developers attempted to divide the Dakota Territory at the Missouri River, creating a new Lincoln Territory to the west. Although they failed, their efforts goaded territorial officials at Yankton City into organizing Pennington County and offering a full array of services at Rapid City. As the placer mining of individual prospectors gave way to the industrial mining of the great Homestake Lode, influential investors demanded better access to their mine than was offered by the cattle trails running north and south and by the rugged, dangerous wagon road running east to Fort Pierre, which was subject to the Bull Whackers Union's price-fixing. An obvious solution was a corridor eastward from Rapid City to Oacoma near the confluence of the White and the Missouri rivers.

Under political pressure, federal officials first tried to circumvent the requirement that three-fourths of all adult male Indians would have to agree to give up the corridor. They gathered the marks or signatures of band chiefs and other spokesmen in the tribes, but non-

Indian reformers objected, and the effort—exposed for the chicanery it was—failed. Federal officials then wrote an entirely new agreement and tried to entice the required numbers in all of the tribes to affix their marks or signatures to the new agreement.

Resistance in every tribe was determined and steady, yet official attention turned to Sitting Bull after his return from Canada in 1881. Federal officials placed their hopes in U.S. Agent JAMES MCLAUGHLIN, who transferred from Fort Totten to Standing Rock Agency with the charge of keeping Sitting Bull and his followers under control. McLaughlin approved frequent travel by the Hunkpapa leader to distant places and in his absence labored—unsuccessfully—with the likes of Pine Ridge Agent Valentine McGillicuddy to reduce the influence of Lakota traditionalists. The Indians' determination became obvious by 1887, when Lakota leaders initiated legal proceedings against the United States for the unconstitutional seizure of the Black Hills under the 1877 agreement. That determination grew increasingly intense as federal officials appeared on the reservations to gather the required number of signatures.

Federal records indicate that, under duress, 4,463 of 5,678 eligible tribal voters signed documents to open the coveted corridor between the Black Hills and the Missouri River. By the Agreement of March 2, 1889, the tract of 21.7 million acres remaining after the 1877 agreement shrank by 9 million acres, leaving only 12.7 million acres on six reservations.

The Lakota and Yanktonai people, who three times had been victorious against non-Indian troops and who had never been defeated by the army of the United States, were not about to suffer lightly the loss of nearly 79 percent of the Great Sioux Reservation by successive congressional agreements. More than ever, the burden of leadership fell on Sitting Bull. RED CLOUD resisted effectively, but peaceably, through diplomacy in defense of Oglala interests. HOLLOW HORN BEAR succeeded SPOTTED TAIL after the Brulé leader's death in 1881 and adopted a strategy similar to Red Cloud's. Lower Brulé and Crow Creek Lower Yanktonai leaders were preoccupied by problems of adjustment under a single agency at Fort Thompson. But Sitting Bull proclaimed his indignation from a home near his birthplace on the Grand River, surrounded by seven tribal enclaves heavily populated with peoples seething in anger, closely affiliated with other equally dissatisfied Lakotas around the Pine Ridge and Rosebud agencies.

Death of Sitting Bull and the Massacre at Wounded Knee

As tensions mounted, federal officials began to entertain the notion of removing the Hunkpapa leader to Fort Leavenworth. Sitting Bull hosted the mysterious GHOST DANCE, which non-Indians confused with a war dance, and remained extremely vocal in his resistance to the federal policy of acculturation. Agent McLaughlin (advised by his insightful spouse, the Mdewakanton Marie Buissant) tried to take control of the situation. He waved off an offer of negotiation by the flamboyant WILLIAM F. ("BUFFALO BILL") CODY, with whom Sitting Bull had traveled in Cody's Wild West show; made an agreement with military leaders to place federal troops in a backup role; and dispatched Captain Bull Head and his tribal police to arrest Sitting Bull. At sunrise on December 15, 1890, when the tribal police pulled Sitting Bull from his home, his supporters resisted the arrest. Shots were fired. Sitting Bull, a number of his followers, and some tribal policemen—Indians all—paid with their lives; already a legend, Sitting Bull became a Native American martyr.

Without a principal leader around whom to rally, Lakotas and some Yanktonais followed the ailing BIG FOOT. Tribal memory holds that his following headed for high country where, traditionally, Lakota and Yanktonai people had gone for protection and natural bounty. The Seventh Cavalry intercepted them, however, near Pine Ridge Agency at Wounded Knee.

On December 29, a large number of them perished at the WOUNDED KNEE MASSACRE. Official records indicated that 153 bodies were recovered the day after the attack, but reports varied regarding the total number dead. An official news organ developed by U.S. Agent John Brennan at the Oglala Indian Training School in Pine Ridge later contained estimates of 340 killed, including 100 tribal soldiers; and 370 casualties, including 120 with weapons. Tribal elders have recounted how survivors hid bodies in wood piles during the winter season and recovered them for burial in secrecy before a thaw came in the spring. Some called what happened that day a battle; others called it a massacre. Some claimed the tragedy was inadvertent; some said it came as a result of the medicine man Yellow Bird's signal to resist the troopers; still others blamed the Seventh Cavalry for attacking without provocation. The questions, still unresolved, are, in any case, moot. Whatever induced the Seventh Cavalry to fire on fleeing tribal members, the immediate effect of the slaughter was bitterness among all Native Americans as pronounced as that felt by Minnesota Dakota refugees after the 1862 war. Its historical consequence was to focus global attention on tragedy in the histories of all Native American tribes.

After Wounded Knee, agency employees labored to impose federal policies of acculturation on the several Lakota and Yanktonai reservations. James McLaughlin, who moved up the administrative ladder to the position of U.S. inspector, worked to accommodate both tribal and emigrant interests not only on the Great Plains, but also on reservations across the United States. Tribal members continued to hunt and fish, as always, mostly deer and antelope or smaller game.

Losses—and gains

A clash of arms between Lakota hunters from Pine Ridge Reservation and non-Indians of eastern Wyoming at Lightning Creek in 1903 was reported as "the Last Blood-Letting" in a long succession of Great Plains wars. Indeed, it was the terminal incident in half a century of northern Great Plains warfare.

Protracted resistance without defeat by Sioux people and some of their neighbors came at a high cost in casualties, anguish, and loss of land. But it was not without beneficial consequences as well. Their aggregate population never significantly diminished; on the contrary, by any method of calculation, it more than doubled over two centuries of contact with non-Indians. Especially in South Dakota, Lakotas, Nakotas, and Dakotas preserved a sanctuary for tribal traditions underground—10 percent of their prehistoric acreage compared to 3.5 percent by Great Plains tribes overall—and recently, they have nurtured ancient legacies into a cultural renaissance that has earned global recognition. They have carried their fight from victories in combat to litigation in federal courts. With some of their neighbors, Lakotas and Nakotas have refused more than $300 million in compensation for the illegal 1877 Agreement, unless the offer is enhanced by the return of Black Hills land to the control of the tribes. Despite the relinquishment of more than 90 percent of some 100 million acres in historical Sioux country, and even greater losses by most of the neighboring tribes, half a century of armed resistance to non-Indian intrusion was at the time effective and, more recently, has served to inspire a revival in tribalism.

But for peoples of tribal and non-Indian heritage alike, protracted warfare left great bitterness in its wake. More than a century after the Wounded Knee tragedy, social relations between citizens of the United States and the Native Americans of the northern Great Plains are still haunted by the aura of mutual suspicion that existed at the outbreak of the Sioux Wars.

—*Herbert T. Hoover*

SEE ALSO: Atkinson, Henry; Black Hills Gold Rush; Buffaloes; Homestake Mine; Little Bighorn, Battle of; Native American Peoples: Peoples of the Great Plains; Wild West Shows

SUGGESTED READING:
Ambrose, Stephen. *Crazy Horse and Custer: The Parallel Lives of Two American Warriors*. Garden City, N.Y., 1975.

Axelrod, Alan. *Chronicle of the Indian Wars: From Colonial Times to Wounded Knee.* New York, 1992.

Hassrick, Royal B. *The Sioux: Life and Customs of a Warrior Society.* Norman, Okla., 1964.

Hyde, George. *Red Cloud's Folk: A History of the Oglala Sioux Indians.* Norman, Okla., 1937.

———. *A Sioux Chronicle.* Norman, Okla., 1956.

———. *Spotted Tail's Folk: A History of the Brulé Sioux.* Norman, Okla., 1961.

Josephy, Alvin M., Jr. *The Civil War in the American West.* New York, 1991.

Lazarus, Edward. *Black Hills, White Justice: The Sioux Nation Versus the United States, 1775 to the Present.* New York, 1991.

Mooney, James. *The Ghost-Dance Religion and the Sioux Outbreak of 1890.* Washington, D.C., 1893. Reprint. 1965.

Oehler, C. M. *The Great Sioux Uprising.* New York, 1959.

Olson, James C. *Red Cloud and the Sioux Problem.* Lincoln, Nebr., 1965.

Parker, Watson. *Gold in the Black Hills.* Norman, Okla., 1966.

Utley, Robert M. *Frontier Regulars: The United States Army and the Indian, 1866–1890.* New York, 1973.

———. *Frontiersmen in Blue: The United States Army and the Indian, 1848–1865.* New York, 1967.

———. *The Lance and the Shield: The Life and Times of Sitting Bull.* New York, 1993.

———. *The Last Days of the Sioux Nation.* New Haven, Conn., 1963.

SIRINGO, CHARLES ANGELO

Charles Angelo Siringo (1855–1928), cowboy, detective, and author, popularized the romantic image of

Charles Angelo Siringo (right) pictured with cowboy actor William S. Hart. *Courtesy Kansas State Historical Society.*

the American cowboy. Born in Matagorda County, Texas, Siringo became a cowboy at the age of twelve. During the 1870s, he drove cattle to the Kansas railheads and often battled Indians and rustlers along the Chisholm Trail. In 1885, he published a colorful account of his experiences, *A Texas Cowboy, or Fifteen Years on the Hurricane Deck of a Spanish Pony,* which was the first cowboy autobiography.

Following the Haymarket bombing on May 4, 1886, Siringo joined PINKERTON NATIONAL DETECTIVE AGENCY in Chicago. Assigned to the agency's Denver office, "the cowboy detective" spent twenty-two years trailing criminals throughout the West and tracking suspects as far as Mexico City and Alaska. He pursued Harvey ("Kid Curry") Logan, a member of the notorious Hole in the Wall gang; infiltrated the Coeur d'Alene (Idaho) Miners' Union during labor unrest in 1892; and served as bodyguard for Pinkerton operative James McPharlan during the 1907 trial of WILLIAM D. ("BIG BILL") HAYWOOD of the WESTERN FEDERATION OF MINERS. Siringo's *A Cowboy Detective* (1912) recounted his career, but the Pinkerton Agency sued to enjoin him from using its name or revealing information acquired during his tenure there. Consequently, the book appeared with fictitious names.

In 1915, embittered by legal action, Siringo published a diatribe against the Pinkerton Agency entitled *Two Evil Isms,* which Pinkerton lawyers were able to suppress. Following brief service as a New Mexico Ranger, he produced *A Lone Star Cowboy* in 1919 and *History of Billy the Kid* in 1920. In 1927, his most polished effort, *Riata and Spurs,* appeared. The book was a combination of the best stories in *A Texas Cowboy* and *A Cowboy Detective.*

—*Roger Tuller*

SUGGESTED READING:

Pingenot, Ben E. *Siringo.* College Station, Tex., 1989.

Siringo, Charles A. *Riata and Spurs: The Story of a Lifetime Spent in the Saddle as Cowboy and Ranger.* Cambridge, Mass., 1927.

SITKA INDIANS

SEE: Native American Peoples: Peoples of the Pacific Northwest

SITTING BULL (SIOUX)

Sitting Bull (Tatanka-Iyotanka, 1831?–1890), a Hunkpapa Lakota Sioux chief, was probably born on the Grand River in present-day South Dakota. He counted his first coup at the age of fourteen, and thereafter, in warfare with enemy tribes, he accumulated a superior record that led to his designation, in 1857, as a tribal war chief. At the same time, he acquired a notable reputation as a holy man and master of the sacred mysteries and ceremonies of the Lakotas. His entire life was characterized by a profound spirituality, and many times he performed the sacrificial rites of the Sun Dance. As he assumed a commanding position among his people, Sitting Bull came to exemplify the four cardinal virtues of the Lakotas: bravery, fortitude, generosity, and wisdom. His name, fame, and finally his influence spread from his own Hunkpapa group to the other six Lakota tribes.

From Sitting Bull's earliest years, his people traded with whites at posts on the Missouri River. Not until the 1850s, however, did whites threaten the Hunkpapa world. Following the Minnesota Sioux uprising of 1862 and the discovery of gold in western Montana, the threat grew serious and immediate. The Lakotas were drawn into war with the United States. From 1863 to 1864, Sitting Bull and his warriors fought Generals HENRY HASTINGS SIBLEY and ALFRED SULLY in Dakota, and in 1865, they skirmished with columns of General PATRICK E. CONNOR in the Powder River country. Sitting Bull directed special venom against the military posts of the upper Missouri River, especially Forts Rice and Buford. He led a direct assault on each and, for five years, from 1865 to 1870, kept up a deadly harassment of Fort Buford.

The federal government's agents and policies divided the Hunkpapa and other Lakota tribes into factions. Some advocated accommodation; others, resistance. The Treaty of 1868, creating the Great Sioux Reservation in western Dakota, deepened the tribal division. Portions of each Lakota tribe settled on the reservation, while others remained in the buffalo ranges of the Powder and Yellowstone valleys.

Sitting Bull was the leading chief of these "nontreaty" Lakotas, whom government officials soon labeled "hostiles." A staunch foe of all government programs, he wanted no part of treaties, agents, rations, or any course that would interfere with the old life of following the buffalo and warring against enemy tribes. He and his friends designated him head chief of all the nontreaty Lakotas. For eight years, with the firm support of the Oglala war chief CRAZY HORSE, he held together a coalition of Lakota and Northern Cheyenne tribes that followed the old life in the buffalo ranges west and north of the Great Sioux Reservation.

Two white incursions roused the bitter ire of Sitting Bull's nontreaty bands. The first was the Northern Pacific Railroad, whose surveying parties, accompa-

Sitting Bull. *Courtesy National Cowboy Hall of Fame and Western Heritage Center.*

nied by military escorts, had to fight off Lakota and Cheyenne warriors led by Sitting Bull himself. The second outrage was the military exploration of the Black Hills by the Custer Expedition of 1874. The discovery of gold set off a rush to the hills, part of the Great Sioux Reservation and thus off limits to all whites. The Indians rebuffed government attempts to buy the area.

From the Black Hills dilemma sprang the Great Sioux War of 1876. If forced by military action to settle on the reservation, Sitting Bull's bands could be deprived of their independence and coerced into dropping their opposition to the cession of the Black Hills. The pretext for war lay in their continuing aggression against tribes friendly to the United States and scattered depredations against whites on the upper Yellowstone River. Both violated the Treaty of 1868, which Sitting Bull and his comrades had not signed.

On March 17, 1876, a military force attacked a village on Powder River, and Sitting Bull knew that the whites had declared war. The scattered bands drew together for self-defense and, bolstered by accessions from the reservation, made ready to fight. At the Battle of the Rosebud on June 17, they routed an army under General GEORGE CROOK. A week later, on June 25, they wiped out part of the Seventh Cavalry under Lieutenant Colonel GEORGE ARMSTRONG CUSTER at the Battle of Little Bighorn.

"Custer's Last Stand" on the Little Bighorn stunned and roused white Americans, and the government flooded the Sioux country with soldiers. Other battles were fought, and relentless military pressure through the winter caused most of the fugitives to surrender in the spring of 1877. Sitting Bull and others sought refuge in Canada.

Sitting Bull remained in Canada for five years. He got along well with the Queen's redcoats—the NORTH WEST MOUNTED POLICE. But the buffaloes were dwindling toward extinction, and food shortages led to hunger and finally even starvation. His ranks thinned by defections, on July 20, 1881, Sitting Bull surrendered at Fort Buford in the Dakota Territory.

After nearly two years as prisoners of war, Sitting Bull and his followers settled at Standing Rock Agency, Dakota Territory. There Agent JAMES MCLAUGHLIN sought to transform them into imitation whites—farmers, Christians, and American patriots. Sitting Bull resisted, and the two contended for the allegiance of the Hunkpapas for seven years. Sitting Bull vigorously contested the land agreement of 1889, which broke up the Great Sioux Reservation and opened nearly half of it to homesteaders. When this and other afflictions created a climate favorable to the GHOST DANCE religion, he emerged as the leading apostle of the doctrine at Standing Rock.

McLaughlin and the military authorities decided that Sitting Bull had to be removed from the reservation. On December 15, 1890, Indian police surrounded his cabin on the Grand River. His followers resisted, and in a bloody shootout, Sitting Bull and others were killed. His body was later buried in the military cemetery at Fort Yates, adjacent to Standing Rock Agency.

Today, Sitting Bull is remembered as one of the greatest of all Indian chieftains. He achieved distinction as a military, political, and spiritual leader as well as a man of great humanity. His inflexible resistance to the white advance, coupled with his refusal to compromise his principles, made him the most distinguished patriot of the Sioux but also eroded his power and led finally to his death.

—*Robert M. Utley*

SEE ALSO: Black Hills Gold Rush; Little Bighorn, Battle of; Montana Gold Rush; Sioux Wars

SUGGESTED READING:
Utley, Robert M. *The Lance and the Shield: The Life and Times of Sitting Bull.* New York, 1993.
Vestal, Stanley. *Sitting Bull, Champion of the Sioux.* Norman, Okla., 1957.

SLAUGHTER, CHRISTOPHER COLUMBUS

Texas cattleman, banker, and noted philanthropist, Christopher Columbus Slaughter (1837–1919) was born in Sabine County in the Republic of Texas. In the aftermath of the Civil War, he amassed a fortune by driving cattle over the Chisholm Trail from Texas to Kansas, and after the close of the Red River Indian War in 1874, he established the Long S, Runningwater, and Lazy S ranches in western Texas. By 1905, his holdings included ownership or lease of more than one million acres and forty thousand head of cattle.

Slaughter moved with his family across Texas and finally settled in Palo Pinto County in northern Texas in 1857 where the family engaged in stock raising. He served in a Texas Ranger militia company both before and during the Civil War.

In 1866, Slaughter, with his father and brothers, drove a small herd of cattle to Jefferson, Texas, where they netted a nice profit, and in 1868, they began driving cattle north to Kansas railheads. As railroads pushed into Texas, Slaughter developed his own breeding herds and, in 1877, began stocking large open-range pastures along the headwaters of the Colorado River in western Texas in Howard, Martin, Dawson, and Borden counties where he established the Long S Ranch.

After moving to Dallas in 1873, Slaughter founded three banks and invested in real estate. His philanthropy included contributions to Baptist schools and churches, especially Baylor University in Waco and Baylor Hospital in Dallas. He was also a founder of the Texas and Southwestern Cattle Raisers Association.

In 1884, Slaughter expanded his holdings by acquiring half-interest in the Circle Ranch in Lamb and Hale counties on the High Plains of northwestern Texas and, in 1890, acquired full control. In 1897, he started buying land to create another plains ranch, the Lazy S, located in Cochran and Hockley counties, and subsequently owned title to more than one-half million acres, making him one of the largest landholders in Texas.

Slaughter was among the first Texas cattlemen to make extensive use of barbed wire, windmills, and improved breeds of cattle. In 1899, he garnered national attention by purchasing a Hereford bull for an unprecedented five thousand dollars.

As railroads pushed into the Texas plains, Slaughter sold land to farmers as early as 1908, but most of his ranch holdings were still intact at his death in 1919. The Slaughter estate was divided ten ways among his heirs.

—*David J. Murrah*

See also: Cattle Industry

Suggested reading:
David J. Murrah. C. C. *Slaughter: Rancher, Banker, Baptist.* Austin, Tex., 1981.

SLAUGHTER, JOHN HORTON

Arizona "cattle king" and lawman John Horton Slaughter (1841–1922) was born in Sabine Parish, Louisiana, while his parents were en route from Mississippi to a new home in the Republic of Texas. His first four decades were spent in Texas, but after brief service with the Confederacy in the Civil War and with the Texas Rangers, Slaughter decided to make a new start in the Arizona Territory.

When Slaughter's first wife, Adeline, joined him in Phoenix in 1878, both she and their two small children had smallpox. Adeline died, but Slaughter nursed the children back to health. In 1879, he married Cora Viola Howell, and they eventually settled near the silver-mining boom town of Tombstone. In 1884, John and Viola Slaughter acquired the San Bernardino Ranch, a Mexican land grant straddling the United States–Mexican border east of present-day Douglas, Arizona. Slaughter used the numerous warm springs on the far-flung ranch and drilled several artesian wells. His holdings were second in size only to the Sierra Bonita Ranch of Colonel Henry Hooker near Tucson. Slaughter's *Z* brand was on cattle in both Arizona and Sonora.

Slaughter's reputation as a gunfighter preceded him from Texas and continued to grow during his tenure as sheriff of Cochise County. When he retired from office in 1890, it was said he left Cochise County "all washed, and rinsed, and hung out to dry." Slaughter brought many outlaws to justice; others, it was said, left the territory rather than face Slaughter's blazing gun.

In 1893, Slaughter built a commodious adobe ranch house just north of the international boundary and near the high promontory known from Spanish days as Mesa de la Avanzada. Situated near a large spring-fed pond that Slaughter had created and on the only road through the area, the ranch headquarters featured huge shade trees, orchards, and gardens. Slaughter used

John Horton Slaughter. *Courtesy Arizona Historical Society.*

Chinese and Mormon tenant farmers to cultivate some five hundred acres. In addition to two children by his first wife, he and Viola raised several foster children including Apache May, who was found during a military attack on an Apache ranchería in the Sierra Madre. At San Bernardino, the Slaughters kept open house for the steady stream of relatives, family friends, health-seekers, and visitors who enjoyed their oasis.

Slaughter was elected to the Arizona territorial legislature in 1906.

After Jesse Fisher, a family friend, was murdered in the ranch yard in a robbery in 1921, Slaughter and his wife moved to Douglas. He died in 1922, leaving his widow, a daughter, Addie Slaughter Greene, and four grandchildren.

—*Reba Wells Grandrud*

Suggested reading:
Erwin, Allen A. *The Southwest of John Horton Slaughter, 1841–1922: Pioneer Cattleman and Trail-driver of Texas, the Pecos, and Arizona and Sheriff of Tombstone.* Glendale, Calif., 1965.
Wells, Reba B. "Cora Viola Howell Slaughter: Southern Arizona Ranchwoman." *The Journal of Arizona History* (Winter 1989): 391–416.

SLAVERY

SEE: National Expansion: Slavery and National Expansion

SLAVERY AND INDENTURE IN THE SPANISH SOUTHWEST

Based on feudal traditions established during Spain's reconquest of the Iberian Peninsula, the *encomienda* (trusteeship) system emerged as a way in which the Crown could compensate the military nobility for the costs of conquest. The Crown delegated royal power to collect tribute from, and use the personal services of, the Crown's vassals; in turn, *encomenderos* (trust holders) were responsible for the physical and spiritual welfare of their charges and were required to bear arms in the Crown's defense. In the New World, the *encomienda* developed as a subterfuge for slavery and became the principal means of extracting wealth in the early colonies.

In 1493, during the conquest of the Americas, Pope Alexander VI made the Spanish Crown responsible for the spiritual and physical well-being of Native Americans and the ultimate beneficiary of their tribute and labor. This dual responsibility of paternalism and exploitation produced long-term tensions between the Crown and the nobility, between the Spanish state and the Catholic church, and between the Spanish explorers or colonists and Native Americans. In New Spain, the Crown distributed grants of *encomienda* to conquistadors, while attempting to prevent feudalistic control and abuse of Indian subjects. Accordingly, legal reforms throughout the sixteenth century reduced *encomienda* rights to tribute alone and restricted inheritance of these rights to three generations. But distance from the control of the Crown limited the effectiveness of such restraints.

After the Spanish established a colony in New Mexico in 1598, the *encomienda* system allowed *encomenderos* to coerce both goods and labor from the Pueblo Indians and put them at odds with Franciscan missionaries, who saw themselves as both protectors and beneficiaries of subject natives. Thirty-five *encomiendas* were established as rewards for the colonizers who accompanied JUAN DE OÑATE to New Mexico in 1598. The amount of these grants, varying according to the social status of the grantee, ranged from several entire pueblos to a part of one. For example, in 1662, don Francisco Gomez Robledo, the high status sargento mayor of the villa of Santa Fe, held the following encomienda titles: all of the Pueblo of Pecos, except for twenty-four houses held by Pedro Lucero de Godoy; two and one-half parts of the Pueblo of Taos; half of the Hopi Pueblo of Shongopovi; half of the Pueblo of Acoma, except for twenty houses; half of Pueblo of Abo; and all of the Pueblo of Tesuque.

The titles did not constitute land ownership; in fact, *encomenderos* were prohibited from living on the lands of their *encomiendas*. Eliminating the rights-to-labor element of *encomienda*, the reformist New Laws of 1542 had left only rights-to-tribute remaining to the *encomendero*. Since Pueblos could not pay the annual cash tribute of ten *reales* (1.25 pesos) per household, in-kind tribute was fixed at either a woven *manta* (cotton shirt) or a tanned hide and one *fanega* (1.5 bushels) of corn for each adult person. In practice, *encomenderos* used an alternative system, the *repartimiento* (labor appointment), to obtain a labor force by taking *criadas* (servants) into their homes and by requiring Pueblo men to work on the *estancias* (stock-raising lands).

The *repartimiento* allowed Spanish nobles and missionaries to levy Indian labor for planting, harvesting, and stock raising, as long as the draft did not exceed 2 percent of the population at any given time and the workers were paid a just wage. Again, because of New Mexico's distance from the Spanish Crown and the struggle for labor between missionaries and colonists, the *repartimiento* system fostered coercion and abuse of Pueblo men and women and acted as a severe drain on the Pueblo agricultural economy. Colonists and missionaries accused each other of withholding wages and physically abusing their charges.

As the colony struggled to survive, the Spanish turned to another institution, slavery, to augment their labor needs. The enslavement of Native Americans had also been abolished in the New Laws of 1542, except in those cases where captives were seized in "just wars," ostensibly rebellions against Spanish authority. In New Mexico, Spanish governors such as Juan de Eulate, who served from 1618 to 1625, and Luis de Rosas, who served from 1637 to 1641, captured supposedly hostile nomadic Apaches and sold them to mining operations in Nueva Vizcaya or retained them to work in *obrajes* (weaving workshops). Likewise, Franciscan missionaries made use of *rescate*, or the ransom of captives from heathen slavery, to purchase captives from other Indian groups and put them to work as indentured laborers in the mission fields and convents. That lesser citizens also participated in the trade is attested to in numerous government *bandos* (edicts) issued from Santa Fe that prohibited the purchase of heathen captives. In time, few Spanish homes were without at least one *indio de rescate*, who could be obtained for two horses and small trade goods and who would in theory work off the cost of his or her ransom during ten to twenty years of domestic service. In practice, this type of bondage ranged from familial incorporation to virtual slavery.

Suffering the effects of social and economic disruption, the Pueblo peoples united in 1680 to expel the Spanish from the colony. Although the Spanish returned in 1693, they did not reinstate the *encomienda* system. Instead, alternative forms of exploitation developed that would persist into the nineteenth century. After the PUEBLO REVOLT, the *repartimiento* was more carefully applied. Moreover, because socio-economic disruption and epidemic disease had severely reduced the Pueblo population, their adequacy as a labor source was lessened. By the 1750s, the *vecino* (Spanish citizen) population far outnumbered that of the Pueblos, and wage laborers came from the lower classes of colonial society. As a commercial sheep and wool industry developed from 1780 on, the *partido* system, or sheep raising on shares, became another major mode of labor organization. The peculiar brand of local slavery, based on captive seizure and sales, persisted into the 1870s after New Mexico had become a U.S. territory.
—*James Brooks*

SUGGESTED READING:

Brooks, James F. "'This Evil Extends Especially to the Feminine Sex': Captivity and Identity in New Mexico, 1700–1847." In *Writing the Range: Race, Class, and Culture in the Women's West*. Edited by Elizabeth Jameson and Susan Armitage. Norman, Okla., 1997.

Gutierrez, Ramon A. *When Jesus Came, the Corn Mothers Went Away: Marriage, Sexuality, and Power in New Mexico, 1500–1846*. Stanford, Calif., 1991.

Kessell, John L. *Kiva, Cross, and Crown: The Pecos Indians and New Mexico*. Albuquerque, N. Mex., 1987.

Swadesh, Frances Leon. *Los Primeros Pobladores: Hispanic America of the Ute Frontier*. Notre Dame, Ind., 1974.

SLOAT, JOHN DRAKE

Commander of U.S. naval forces in the Pacific at the start of the UNITED STATES–MEXICAN WAR, John D. Sloat (1781–1867) was the son of a Revolutionary War army officer. Born near Goshen, New York, Sloat entered the navy as a midshipman in 1800. He made one cruise to the West Indies, in the *President*. Discharged from the navy, he spent the next decade in the merchant service. He returned to the navy as a sailing master on January 10, 1812. He made one cruise, on the frigate *United States,* which captured the *Macedonian,* before his ship was blockaded for the rest of the War of 1812.

Sloat was commissioned a lieutenant on July 24, 1813. After the war, he served in the navy yard at New York from 1816 to 1820, in the Pacific from 1821 to 1822, and in the Caribbean from 1822 to 1823. He received his first command, the schooner *Grampus*, in 1823 and was promoted to master-commandant on March 21, 1826. He commanded the sloop *St. Louis* from 1828 to 1831 off Peru and was promoted to captain on February 9, 1837.

After serving in the navy yard at Portsmouth from 1840 to 1843, he received command of the Pacific Squadron in August 1844. The following year, he gathered the three frigates and four slopes under his command off Mazatlan, Mexico. His orders were to avoid any action that might cause friction with Mexico but, should war break out, to be ready to seize San Francisco and occupy or blockade other ports. Six months later, when word of war reached him, he sent one ship to San Francisco Bay and took the rest of his squadron to Monterey. Arriving there on July 2, 1846, he hesitated for five days before taking control of the customs house and proclaiming California an American territory.

On July 15, 1846, Commodore ROBERT F. STOCKTON arrived from Hawaii and, after conferring with Sloat, who had been ill for a number of months, took command first of forces ashore and then of the Pacific Squadron on July 29, 1846. Sloat returned to Washington via Panama. There, Secretary of the Navy George Bancroft praised his actions during the war; others criticized him for being too cautious and slow to act. After the United States–Mexican War, Sloat commanded the Norfolk Navy Yard and served with the Bureau of Construction and Repair. He retired from active duty on September 27, 1855.
—*James C. Bradford*

SUGGESTED READING:
Sherman, Edwin Allen. *The Life of the Late Rear-Admiral John Drake Sloat*. Oakland, Calif., 1902.

SMEDLEY, AGNES

Author, socialist, and foreign correspondent Agnes Smedley (1892?–1950) was born in Missouri. When she was a young girl, her family moved to southern Colorado, but the move did not much improve the family's circumstances. The family followed her father from coal mine to coal mine, and Smedley hired out for menial jobs more often than she attended classes. She did not complete grade school. After her mother's death, Smedley, at the age of sixteen, struck out on her own, learned stenography, and worked in Denver. She enrolled in the Normal School (teacher's college) in Tempe, Arizona, in 1911, married, and moved to southern California, where she took university classes at night and taught by day.

The marriage did not survive, and in 1916, Smedley moved on to New York City but not before she sampled the socialist ideas that were to have a lasting effect on her thinking and her writing. In 1919, she moved to Germany, where, for nine years, she undertook graduate work in oriental studies, taught English at the University of Berlin, became involved in India's struggle for independence, and increased the socialist activism she had begun in New York. An attempted suicide led her to psychoanalysis and to fiction writing. In 1927, she penned *Daughter of the Earth*, an autobiographical novel of the violent, hardscrabble life of a young woman coming of age in America's West and of women bound by social custom and economic necessity to the oppressive marriages characteristic of a capitalist system and a patriarchal order.

Smedley traveled to China as a correspondent for the *Frankfurter Zeitung* in 1928 and began a thirteen-year stint as a chronicler of the extraordinary political changes occurring in the country. Never a Communist herself, her writings reflected some sympathy for the cause, and at times, she collaborated with its leaders in the preparation of manifestos for the Western press and in the distribution of medical supplies and services. All the while, she published her observations. *Chinese Destinies* (1933) recorded Chinese life in the 1930s. *China's Red Army Marches* written from her travels with the army in some of its earliest campaigns appeared in 1934. In *The Great Road: The Life and Times of Chu Teh* (1956), she interviewed veterans of the Red Army's "Long March" in 1934 and 1935. *China Fights Back: An American Woman with the Eighth Route Army* (1938) documented the Red Army's resistance to Japan's 1937 invasion of China. Her most popular work, *Battle Cry of China* (1943) was written after her return to the United States following a bout of malaria and a gallbladder condition. Back in the United States, she continued to write and began a series of lectures and radio broadcasts. Her enthusiasm for China, however, continued into the late 1940s, even as Americans increasingly fretted over the communist takeover of China in 1949. That year, she was accused of complicity in a Soviet spy ring, and although the accusation was retracted, she fled to England. She died in a nursing home in 1950.

—*Patricia Hogan*

SUGGESTED READING:
Graulich, Melody. "Violence against Women: Power Dynamics in Literature of the Western Family." In *The Women's West*. Edited by Susan Armitage and Elizabeth Jameson. Norman. Okla., 1987.
Smedley, Agnes. *Battle Cry of China*. New York, 1943.
———. *Daughter of the Earth*. 1929. Reprint. Old Westbury, N.Y., 1976.

SMITH, ERWIN EVANS

Photographer Erwin Evans Smith (1886–1947), born in Honey Grove, Fannin County, Texas, developed an early love for cowboys and cameras. Intent on becoming a sculptor, he studied briefly at the Chicago Art Institute before entering the Boston Museum of Fine Arts in 1906.

Between 1905 and 1912, Smith spent summers photographing the great ranches of the Southwest, amassing several thousand negatives in the process. His photographs immediately achieved critical acclaim and appeared in *The Saturday Evening Post, Collier's* and other national magazines, often in tandem with articles and stories written by his traveling companion, George Pattullo. Smith's carefully chosen compositions helped both to document and to romanticize cowboy life.

After 1912, Smith abandoned his annual sojourns to the West and devoted himself instead to family ranching and farming operations. Publishers continued to demand his photographs as illustrations, nevertheless, and exhibits of his photography appeared at the Panama-Pacific Exposition in 1915 and the Texas Centennial in 1936. Smith died of cancer and was buried in Honey Grove.

—*B. Byron Price*

SUGGESTED READING:
Branda, Eldon S. "Portrait of the Cowboy as a Young Artist." *Southwestern Historical Quarterly* 71 (July 1967): 69–77.
Haley, J. Evetts. *Life on the Texas Range*. Austin, Tex., 1952.
Steger, Harry Peyton. "Photographing the Cowboy as He Disappears." *World's Work* 17 (January 1909): 11,111–11,124.

SMITH, HENRY NASH

SEE: Historiography, Western

SMITH, JEDEDIAH STRONG

Descended from Puritan stock, Bible-toting Jedediah Strong Smith (1799–1831) was a legend among MOUNTAIN MEN. His explorations contributed greatly to the geographical knowledge of the American West and helped arouse the interest of the U.S. government in California and the Oregon Country.

The sixth of fourteen children, Smith was born in Bainbridge, New York. In 1822, after joining WILLIAM HENRY ASHLEY and ANDREW HENRY's new fur company, Smith ascended the Missouri River and wintered on the Musselshell River in Montana. The following spring, Henry sent Smith down the Missouri to carry a message to Ashley. When the Arikara Indians attacked the Ashley party heading upriver and killed thirteen new recruits, Smith volunteered to make the dangerous trip back to Henry in order to bring down reinforcements. Later, he became captain of one of the companies involved in the Arikara Campaign.

With the coming of fall, Ashley and Henry decided to take an overland route to the Rockies, Smith led one of the brigades in search of furs. En route, a grizzly bear mauled Smith, resulting in numerous wounds to his head and face. One of his men, JAMES CLYMAN, sewed up the lacerations and reattached his ear. Thereafter, Smith wore his hair long to cover the scars.

After wintering with the friendly Crows in the Wind River Mountains in present-day Wyoming, Smith and his party, in the spring of 1824, crossed the Continental Divide, rediscovered South Pass, and recognized its significance as a gateway into the West. The following year, when Andrew Henry left the FUR TRADE, Smith became Ashley's partner. In July 1826, Smith, David E. Jackson, and William L. Sublette bought out Ashley. The new company, Smith, Jackson and Sublette, dominated the fur trade in the Rockies for the next four years.

Leaving his partners in the mountains, Smith made two trips to California. In 1826, he and his party went through present-day Utah and followed the Colorado River south to the Mojave villages in southwestern Arizona. Later, after crossing into California, Smith left his men encamped on the Stanislaus River while he, with two companions, made the tortuous trip across the Sierra Nevada and the Nevada and Utah deserts to attend the 1827 RENDEZVOUS at Bear Lake.

Following the rendezvous, Smith once more led a party of men to the Southwest. This time, the formerly friendly Mojave Indians attacked and killed ten of Smith's men. Because of problems with local Mexican authorities after the attack, Smith rejoined the men he had left the year before in California. The combined party traveled and trapped throughout northern California. After reaching the Pacific Ocean, the men worked their way up the Oregon coast, another first for an American, to the Umpqua River. There, the brigade was attacked by Indians on July 14, 1828. While Smith and three others escaped, fifteen men were massacred. The survivors made their way to FORT VANCOUVER, owned by the HUDSON'S BAY COMPANY.

After wintering at Fort Vancouver, Smith met his partner David Jackson near Flathead Lake in Montana, and together they traveled to the 1829 rendezvous at Pierre's Hole in eastern Idaho. During his final season in the trade, Smith contributed more financially to his firm than he had during the previous three years. Nevertheless, in 1839, the partners decided to abandon the fur trade in the Rockies.

Upon returning to Missouri, Smith, Jackson, and Sublette decided to enter the Santa Fe trade and bought a caravan to take to the Southwest in April 1831. At the age of thirty-two, while scouting alone for water, Smith was killed by a band of Comanche Indians on the Santa Fe Trail between the Arkansas and the Cimarron rivers.

—*Vivian Linford Talbot and Fred R. Gowans*

SUGGESTED READING:

Carter, Harvey L. "Jedediah Smith." In *The Mountain Men and the Fur Trade of the Far West.* Vol. 8, Edited by Leroy R. Hafen. Glendale, Calif., 1971.

Dale, Harrison. *The Ashley-Smith Explorations and the Discovery of Central Route to the Pacific, 1822–1829, with the Original Journals.* Cleveland, Ohio, 1918.

Morgan, Dale L. *Jedediah Smith and the Opening of the West.* Lincoln, Nebr., 1964.

Smith, Jedediah Strong. *The Southwest Expedition of Jedediah S. Smith: His Personal Account of the Journey to California, 1826–1827.* Glendale, Calif., 1977.

Sullivan, Maurice B. *Jedediah Smith, Trader, and Trail Breaker.* New York, 1936.

Weber, David J. *The California versus Jedediah Smith, 1826–1827: A New Cache of Documents.* Spokane, Wash., 1990.

SMITH, JOSEPH FIELDING

Born in Salt Lake City, Utah, a year before Mormon prophet BRIGHAM YOUNG's death, Joseph Fielding Smith (1876–1972) saw the CHURCH OF JESUS CHRIST OF LATTER-DAY SAINTS (commonly called MORMONS) grow from a small, persecuted sect in the Rocky Mountains into an international church.

Smith was born into a prestigious family in the Mormon church. His grandfather was the former Mormon church patriarch Hyrum Smith, and his great-uncle was the prophet JOSEPH SMITH, JR. Both men were murdered by a mob in Illinois in 1844. Smith's own father, Joseph F. Smith, was a member of the church hierarchy and eventually became the sixth president of the LDS church. The eldest of his father's forty-eight children, Joseph Fielding Smith was a studious young man who had a quiet, serious nature.

While growing up, Smith experienced the difficulties of having a father who practiced plural marriage. Joseph F. Smith married six women. After passage of the Edmunds Act of 1882, he was forced to go into hiding in order to avoid arrest and, at one point, spent seven years away from Salt Lake City. Joseph Fielding Smith took on the responsibilities of an adult at an early age because of his father's extended absences.

Smith, himself, married three times, and each of his wives preceded him in death. He was the father of eleven children and was caring and attentive. Because of his intense shyness, he was happiest when within the security of his own family.

In 1910, Smith's father called him to be an apostle for the Mormon church. As an apostle, Smith was one of a small hierarchy of men who directed the business of the church. During his more than sixty years in service, Smith saw the membership of the church grow from about 200,000 to more than 3,090,000.

Also during his ministry as an apostle, Smith distinguished himself as a scriptorian and scholar. An avid genealogist, he served as the president of the Genealogical Society of Utah. He also served for years as the church historian and published widely on aspects of Mormon doctrine and history.

Among Smith's better known publications were *Essentials in Church History* (1922) and his five-volume *Answers to Gospel Questions* (1957 to 1966). Another book he wrote was *Man: His Origin and Destiny* (1954) in which he attacked the theory of evolution and held to the literal interpretation of the creation as described in the scriptures. In this and his other writings, Smith demonstrated a conservatism that influenced his beliefs and teachings.

In January 1970, Smith became the tenth president of the LDS church and was viewed as a prophet by Mormons throughout the world. During his tenure as president, Smith oversaw the continued internationalization of the church, the professionalization of its historical department, the consolidation of publications, the restructuring of the Sunday school program and Church Education System, and the building of two new temples (places reserved for special rites of worship among Mormons).

—*Craig L. Foster*

SUGGESTED READING:

McConkie, Amelia, and Mark L. McConkie. "Joseph Fielding Smith." *Encyclopedia of Mormonism*. Vol. 3. Edited by Daniel H. Ludlow. New York, 1993.

McConkie, Joseph F. *True and Faithful: The Life Story of Joseph Fielding Smith*. Salt Lake City, 1971.

Smith, Joseph Fielding, Jr., and John J. Stewart. *The Life of Joseph Fielding Smith*. Salt Lake City, 1972.

West, Emerson Roy. *Profiles of the Presidents*. Salt Lake City, 1980.

SMITH, JOSEPH, JR.

Founder of Mormonism and first president of the CHURCH OF JESUS CHRIST OF LATTER-DAY SAINTS, Joseph Smith, Jr. (1805–1844), was born in Sharon, Vermont, the fourth of nine children. Forced to deal with the uncertainties of life in a lower-middle-class family, he moved with his family nine times throughout New England by the time he was eleven years old. His father, Joseph, Sr., moved the family once more in 1816 to Palmyra, New York, in the wake of his failure as a New England farmer and merchant.

Joseph, Jr., meanwhile, worked to supplement the family's meager income and received scant schooling. Working as a day laborer on various neighboring farms, he claimed to have the power to find buried treasure and hired himself out as a "money-digger."

In addition to economic uncertainty, Smith was unsettled by religion. Although his family was of New England stock, ancestors on both sides had long since rejected the basic tenets of Puritanism. His parents embraced "Christian primitivism." At the same time, however, Smith's mother and several other family members joined the Presbyterian church shortly after the family move to Palmyra. But his father held back, adhering instead to a set of mystical universalistic beliefs outside of any organized denomination and claiming to be influenced by divinely inspired dreams or revelations.

Despite the urgings of his mother, Smith did not join the Presbyterians and was, in fact, deeply distressed by the religious conflict within his family. He was confused about the correct source of religious authority, a situation further aggravated by the religious fervor of the Second Great Awakening, which swept through Palmyra and other parts of the so-called burned-over district of upstate New York during the early 1820s.

Deeply troubled, Smith sought divine guidance. He claimed to have experienced a vision in which he was told to join none of the existing religious denominations. According to Mormon belief, over the next several years, he experienced a number of other visions or divine manifestations, which culminated in his writing of the BOOK OF MORMON, allegedly translated from a set of golden plates long hidden within a hillside near his home. The *Book of Mormon*, completed in 1830, purported to be the sacred writings of three ancient American civilizations descended from a group of Israelites who had migrated from the Holy Land to the New World in 600 B.C. This work detailed their many conflicts and apostasies culminating in the destruction of the lighter-skinned Nephites by the darker-skinned Lamanites—the latter surviving group considered to be ancestors of the contemporary American Indians, according to Mormon belief.

The *Book of Mormon* served as the basis for a new church founded by Smith and a small group of his followers on April 6, 1830. Known ultimately as the Church of Jesus Christ of Latter-day Saints (or by its more common name, the Mormon church), the fledgling denomination grew rapidly. From a total church membership of 280 at the end of 1830, the number of adherents reached more than 680 by the end of 1831. Smith migrated from New York to the Midwest and formed two Mormon settlements—at Kirtland, Ohio (near Cleveland), where Smith maintained his principal residence with his wife, EMMA HALE (SMITH), whom he had married in January 1827; and at Independence, Missouri. By 1835, total Mormon church membership had climbed to 8,835, a thirteen-fold increase in just four years. And three years later, membership had doubled to 17,881. By the time of Smith's death in 1844, the MORMONS claimed some 26,000 members.

Several factors facilitated the growth of Mormonism. First, the message in Smith's writings, especially the *Book of Mormon*, struck a responsive cord among those Americans who were economically or religiously dispossessed. Smith's condemnation of the rich, most notably lawyers and merchants, found a ready audience among men and women of modest means and little education—specifically, those individuals "left behind" in a rapidly industrializing American society in which success was measured by materialistic acquisition through capitalistic individualism. Second, Mormonism's call for radical Christian reform—in particular, social and economic cooperation and the creation of an egalitarian society of "true believers" in preparation for the approaching millennium and Second Coming—appealed to those individuals dissatisfied with the current state of affairs. Finally, Smith himself, through his behavior and personality, contributed to the growth of Mormonism. He claimed divine powers as a "prophet, seer, and revelator," evident through a series of "revelations" given to his followers and ultimately published in a work of Mormon sacred scripture known as the *Doctrine and Covenants*. Smith, moreover, projected an imposing physical presence—six feet tall, muscular, and very handsome. He was a charismatic public speaker who presented himself as friendly, empathetic, and able to relate to even the most humble of his followers.

Despite Mormonism's appeal and related growth, or rather because of it, Smith and his followers encountered hostility from their non-Mormon neighbors. The Mormons were forced to flee first from upstate New York to Kirtland, Ohio, in early 1831; from Independence, Missouri, in July 1833; and from Kirtland, itself, in 1837. They made their way to northwestern Missouri by the late 1830s. But in Missouri, the Mormons found themselves in conflict, once more, with their non-Mormon neighbors—a conflict that escalated into open warfare. To make matters worse, Missouri's governor Liburn Boggs issued an "extermination order," calling for the expulsion of all Mormons from the state. During the Mormon-Missouri War from 1838 to 1839, Smith was jailed for five months and threatened with execution. He managed to escape in April 1839.

Smith fled to Illinois where he organized his followers into a new community at NAUVOO, located along the Mississippi River. Over the next five years under his guidance, Nauvoo grew and flourished, ultimately boasting a population of twelve thousand and rivaling Chicago as the state's largest community. Smith and his followers, however, found themselves in conflict once again with their non-Mormon neighbors due, in large measure, to the efforts of Smith and his followers to dominate, or at least, to influence state and local politics. Smith even projected himself into the national political arena by running for president of the United States in 1844 as an independent candidate. Meanwhile, he exerted significant political power on a local level as Nauvoo's mayor and commander of the Nauvoo Legion, the Mormons' own militia force.

Smith, moreover, generated further hostility through his implementation of certain controversial religious practices, the most provocative being polygamy. Smith took some fifty women as plural wives. The introduction of plural marriage caused deep divisions within Mormonism. A significant number of his Nauvoo-based followers broke away and formed a rival Mormon movement in the spring of 1844. When the dissidents began publishing a newspaper, the *Nauvoo Expositor,* which condemned Smith as a "fallen prophet," he ordered the destruction of its press as a "public nuisance." Smith was arrested by state authorities and incarcerated at nearby Carthage. But on June 27, 1844, he was murdered by members of an armed anti-Mormon mob, who had stormed the jail before the Mormon leader was brought to trial. Smith was just thirty-eight years old.

In the wake of Smith's death, the Mormon movement divided. The largest group followed BRIGHAM YOUNG, migrated to the Great Basin, and established Salt Lake City as its headquarters. A significant number of Mormons, however, refused to follow Young and remained in the Midwest. These dissidents formed a rival organization, known as the Reorganized Church of Jesus Christ of Latter Day Saints, which included Joseph Smith's immediate family—his widow Emma and her children. Smith's oldest son, Joseph, III, became its first president. The present-day headquarters of the Reorganized church is in Independence, Missouri.

—*Newell G. Bringhurst*

SEE ALSO: Church of Jesus Christ of Latter Day Saints, Reorganized; Polygamy: Polygamy among Mormons

SUGGESTED READING:
Brodie, Fawn M. *No Man Knows My History: The Life of Joseph Smith.* 2d ed., rev. and enlarged. New York, 1971.
Bushman, Richard L. *Joseph Smith and the Beginnings of Mormonism.* Urbana, Ill., 1984.
Hill, Donna. *Joseph Smith: The First Mormon.* New York, 1977.
Hill, Marvin S. *Quest for Refuge: The Mormon Flight from American Pluralism.* Salt Lake City, 1989.
Smith, Joseph, Jr. *History of the Church.* 7 vols. Edited by Brigham H. Roberts. Salt Lake City, 1932–1951.
Smith, Lucy Mack. *Biographical Sketches of Joseph Smith, The Prophet.* Liverpool, England, 1853.

SMITH, THOMAS JAMES ("BEAR RIVER TOM")

Thomas James Smith.
Courtesy Kansas State Historical Society.

Thomas James ("Bear River Tom") Smith (1830?–1870) was a peace officer and public official. While it is not known whether he was born in Ireland or in New York City, the historical record places him, in August 1868, at Green River, Wyoming, where he was a marshal. He was involved in the battles between railroad workers and vigilantes and police in Bear River, Wyoming, later that year. Smith also served as marshal of Wasatch, Utah. In the spring of 1869, he was elected mayor of Green River. On June 4, 1870, he became chief of police in Abilene, Kansas, where he was noted for enforcing city ordinances with his fists rather than with guns. He was killed in the line of duty as deputy sheriff of Dickinson County, Kansas, on November 2, 1870.

—*Joseph W. Snell*

SUGGESTED READING:
Miller, Nyle H., and Joseph W. Snell. *Why the West Was Wild.* Topeka, Kans., 1963.

SMOOT, REED

Reed Smoot (1862–1941) served as a Republican U.S. senator from 1903 until 1933. A native of Salt Lake City, Smoot also served as an Apostle in the CHURCH OF JESUS CHRIST OF LATTER-DAY SAINTS' (Mormon) ruling body. He became active in business affairs and achieved some notoriety as a banker. When the Utah legislature elected him to the Senate, Smoot became the focus of a lengthy series of Senate hearings designed to deny him a seat because of the LDS stand on polygamy.

Once seated, Smoot endeared himself to regular Republicans, who appreciated his business philosophy. During the 1920s, he sponsored legislation to lighten income-tax burdens on the wealthy as well as the Hawley-Smoot Bill to raise tariffs. This act cut off foreign trade and may have contributed to international depression. Defeated during the Democratic 1932 landslide, Smoot returned to his church work and died in St. Petersburg, Florida.

—*F. Ross Peterson*

SUGGESTED READING:
Jonas, Frank A. "Utah: The Different State." In *Politics of the American West.* Edited by Frank H. Jonas. Salt Lake City, 1968.
Merrill, Milton R. *Reed Smoot, Apostle in Politics.* Logan, Utah, 1990.

SMYTHE, WILLIAM E.

A popularizer of the "conquest of arid America," William E. Smythe (1861–1922) saw the Promised Land in the arid West. He preached the gospel of cooperative IRRIGATION as the salvation from land monopoly and as the technical means to dominate nature in the pursuit of progress. By 1900, Smythe had rallied Westerners behind his irrigation crusade, and his movement brought about vital support from the federal government for irrigation projects.

Born in Worcester, Massachusetts, Smythe grew up in a wealthy manufacturing family. After serving as an apprentice journalist, he departed New England for the West. In Kearney, Nebraska, he became editor and publisher of the newspaper *Expositor* in 1888. He experienced firsthand the effects of severe drought and visited the arid Southwest, where he witnessed the great utility of irrigation. On these visits, Smythe realized the potential of irrigation to save the West for individual progress and prosperity.

In 1891, Smythe organized and led the National Irrigation Congress, which met with representatives from every Western state in Salt Lake City. He also began publishing and editing the *Irrigation Age,* a clarion call to garner support for his ideas. In the 1880s, Smythe invested in irrigation colonies such as New Plymouth, Idaho, which floundered, and other experimental ventures in California such as Standish in Lassen County. While living there, Smythe wrote *The Conquest of Arid America* (1899).

As the vice-president of the California Water and Forest Association, Smythe worked to reform state water codes. In 1919, he held a position under Secretary of the Interior FRANKLIN KNIGHT LANE and directed a poorly administered soldiers' homestead colony. His last book, *City Homes on Country Lanes* (1921),

preached a back-to-the-land movement that had lost much of its popular support. Still, many writers have based their thinking about Western irrigation on Smythe's theories.

—*James E. Sherow*

SUGGESTED READING:

Carlson, Martin E. "William E. Smythe: Irrigation Crusader." *Journal of the West* 7 (1968): 41–47.

Lee, Lawrence B. "William Ellsworth Smythe and the Irrigation Movement: A Reconsideration." *Pacific Historical Review* 41 (1972): 289–311.

SNAKE RIVER

The main tributary of the Columbia River, the Snake River drains an area of 109,000 square-miles in Wyoming, Idaho, Oregon, and Washington, an area that

Snake River.

The Snake River, ca. 1868. Photograph by Timothy H. O'Sullivan. *Courtesy National Archives.*

The first of those explorers, indeed the first men of European descent to lay eyes on the Snake River, were WILLIAM CLARK and MERIWETHER LEWIS during their celebrated expedition, which reached the area sometime in the autumn of 1805. After exploring the Salmon River basin and floating down the Clearwater, Lewis and Clark followed the Snake River to the Columbia. They were, in turn, followed by American trappers and Canadian fur traders, among them ANDREW HENRY, who built Fort Henry in 1810 near today's St. Anthony, Idaho. Fort Henry was only the first of many trading posts along the Snake in the nineteenth century. The region became the haunt of the HUDSON'S BAY COMPANY agent PETER SKENE OGDEN and his Snake River Brigades, as well as what Howard Lamar has called part of an extended, immense frontier between two sovereign nations, the United States and Great Britain. In that century's rough equivalent of the twentieth century's "cold war," the American and Canadian traders competed with each other for beaver pelts and Indian alliances. The most important of the trading posts for the United States was perhaps FORT HALL, which not only became the rendezvous point for the FUR TRADE, but also a way station for emigrants moving along the OREGON TRAIL toward the Oregon Country's Willamette Valley. The later traffic more than the former trade turned the tide against the British in the Snake River basin and, more generally, in the Pacific Northwest.

Treaty negotiations between the United States and Great Britain led to the U.S. acquisition of Oregon in 1846. But, mainly because the Snake River Indian tribes did not much cotton to pioneers, permanent settlements in the basin failed to appear until the 1860s, when the federal government began gathering the Native Americans onto reservations. Around the same time, MORMONS out of Utah moved into the region to take advantage of the HOMESTEAD ACT OF 1862. Also in 1862, prospectors discovered gold near Boise, and miners rushed into the basin from California and Oregon. By 1864, Snake River communities were linked to Salt Lake City, The Dalles, Oregon, and Walla Walla, Washington, by stagecoach lines and mail service. The coming of the SOUTHERN PACIFIC RAILROAD in

represents not quite half the drainage (42 percent) of the entire Columbia River basin. The Snake's annual flow—3.7 million acre-feet—is about one-fifth that of the Columbia, however. Originating in YELLOWSTONE NATIONAL PARK, the Snake flows through Jackson Hole, Wyoming, before turning south and west into Idaho, where it runs northwestward toward its junction with Henry's Fork, its major headwater tributary. Arcing through the Snake River plain, running first southwest, then west, and ultimately northwest, the Snake cascades into the Grand Canyon at Snake Gorge. Created by the Snake as it cuts through the Rocky Mountains for more than one hundred miles along the Idaho-Oregon border, the gorge is one of the world's deepest. While flowing through the gorge, the Snake is fed by the waters of the Salmon River, its largest tributary, and the Clearwater River before veering west to empty into the Columbia. Rising among humid, but snow-covered peaks and flowing across the semiarid Columbia Plateau, the Snake was once described by a young U.S. Army engineer as belonging to a desolate region with few prospects for the future. Twentieth-century RECLAMATION programs would change that, and most visitors to the swath of green across modern-day Idaho would be hard-pressed to understand what he and the early explorers to the region had in mind when they called the area a wasteland.

1881 made it possible not only to reach the Snake River region, or to pass through it, but also to travel back and forth between points east and west, which brought increases in settlement.

After passing the NEWLANDS RECLAMATION ACT OF 1902, Congress authorized a number of projects aimed at developing the river's potential for IRRIGATION. It may be true, as Marc Reisner claims, that all the reclamation projects in the West only managed to change postage-stamp-size regions of the semiarid land green, but one of those stamps happened to cover the Snake River basin, whose future was ensured by reclamation. Inevitably, reclamation—as it did elsewhere in the West—led to controversies over whether to tap the immense potential for irrigation offered by the Snake and the Salmon, or whether to let such magnificently wild rivers run what was left of their natural courses. At the close of the twentieth century, the debate between environmentalists and developers, like the Snake River itself, sometimes still raged.

—*Charles Phillips*

SNAKES

SEE: Rattlesnakes

SNIVELY, JACOB

Republic of Texas army officer who led the ill-fated Snively Expedition against Mexican wagon trains, Jacob Snively (1809–1871) was probably born somewhere in Pennsylvania. The son of a German immigrant, the well-educated surveyor and engineer wandered to Texas in 1835, where he found work as a land surveyor for the Mexican government. He made Nacogdoches his home and was well respected by those who relied on his services, which eventually included work for private concerns in addition to the Mexican government. Extremely ambitious and adventurous, he took up a military career.

In March 1836, Snively joined the Republic of Texas army and ultimately rose to the rank of colonel of cavalry. He fought for the independence of Texas and was successively appointed paymaster general, secretary of war, adjutant, and inspector general. While holding the last position, he volunteered for a mission designed to attack Mexican wagon trains traveling across the New Mexico region, an area claimed as sovereign territory by the Republic of Texas. President SAM HOUSTON sanctioned Snively's proposal and encouraged him to engage in anti-Mexican banditry. The assignment became known as the Snively Expedition of 1843.

With 170 volunteers, he spent the next four months working his way along the Old Chihuahua Trail in search of the big Mexican train.

The expedition ended in disaster. A large number of his volunteers deserted, and Snively himself was finally disarmed and taken prisoner by U.S. Army Captain PHILIP ST. GEORGE COOKE, commanding officer of a company of 290 dragoons dispatched from Fort Leavenworth to protect Mexican trains and to prevent unauthorized military actions on United States soil.

In 1848, the expeditionary fiasco forgotten, Snively headed to California in search of gold. After a short stay in San Francisco, he moved to the Arizona Territory, where he resumed his former occupation as a surveyor. He was killed on March 18, 1871, by a band of Apache Indians.

—*Fred L. Koestler*

SNOW, ELIZA ROXCY

Leader of the RELIEF SOCIETY (LDS), the women's organization of the CHURCH OF JESUS CHRIST OF LATTER-DAY SAINTS, Eliza Roxcy Snow (1804–1887) was a spiritual, intellectual, and political leader of Mormon women.

Born in Massachusetts and raised in Ohio, she converted to Mormonism in 1835. In NAUVOO, ILLINOIS, she participated in the 1842 founding of the Relief Society and served in the holy ordinances of the temple the Latter-day Saints built there. A writer of poetry, published in newspapers and compiled in two volumes in 1856 and 1877, she was called "Zion's poetess" by JOSEPH SMITH, JR., the church's founding prophet. "O My Father," a poem she composed in 1845, was based on the Latter-day Saints' doctrine of the existence of a Mother as well as a Father in Heaven. Along with several of her other hymns, "O My Father" is still frequently sung in Mormon meetings.

Among the first to participate in polygamy, Snow was thirty-eight years old, in 1842, when she married Joseph Smith as a plural wife. After his death, she became wife to BRIGHAM YOUNG, Smith's successor as church leader. From 1852, when the practice was made public, until her death, Snow actively promoted polygamy among her contemporaries.

Snow arrived in Salt Lake Valley in 1847 with the second company of MORMONS to cross the plains from Illinois. During her early years in Utah she led literary and religious endeavors. The Polysophical Society, which she founded with her brother Lorenzo in 1854, provided a forum for poetry, music, rhetoric, and spiritual exercises. In 1872, she promoted and wrote for the *Woman's Exponent,* a twice-monthly newspaper by and for Latter-day Saint women. Her political activism, expressed through the press and other public platforms, not only found support among her women followers, but also led to the granting of suffrage to Utah women in 1870.

In addition to her occasional articles and two volumes of poetry, Snow published seven other books, among them a biography of her brother, a compilation of letters recording a journey to Europe and the Near East, and several children's Bible study manuals.

Gifted and charismatic, Snow blessed her sister Saints in religious exercises. She prophesied, spoke in tongues, and healed the sick. By the time of her death, "Sister Snow," or "Aunt Eliza," had become, and remains, the most revered woman among the Mormon faithful.

—Maureen Ursenbach Beecher

SUGGESTED READING:

Beecher, Maureen Ursenbach. *Eliza and Her Sisters.* Salt Lake City, 1990.

"Eliza R. Snow's Nauvoo Journal." Edited by Maureen Ursenbach Beecher. *Brigham Young University Studies* 15 (Summer 1975): 391–416.

SOCIAL BANDITRY

In the "Western Civil War of Incorporation," which Richard Maxwell Brown and Alan Trachtenberg have suggested characterized trans-Mississippi America after the Civil War, the West's common folk, and certainly its toiling classes, were frequently sympathetic to those whom, in less unsettled times, they might have considered outlaws or bandits or even brutal criminals and cold-blooded killers. Despite the fact that Jesse James, for example, seldom showed any remorse for killing anyone, including innocent bystanders, his murder by a treacherous member of his own gang was mourned widely not only in his home state of Missouri, but throughout the country. When Jesse's brother Frank James was tried twice for bank robbery, no jury of his peers could be found to convict him, regardless of the evidence presented. Similarly, when "BILLY THE KID," whom Robert M. Utley describes as a high-spirited, misplaced urban tough, was shot down by PATRICK FLOYD JARVIS (PAT) GARRETT, he became almost instantly a legendary hero rather than what he was: one of a number of hired guns in a sort of business range war. Among Mexican Americans, many bandits who fought the forces of Anglo LAW AND ORDER became cultural heroes: JOAQUIN MURIETA, JUAN NEPOMUCENO CORTINA, GREGORIO CORTEZ, even FRANCISCO ("PANCHO") VILLA. More was going on here than the ability of dime novelists like NED BUNTLINE to distort historical facts and tell a good story. For those on the losing side of the War of Incorporation, men such as Jesse James, "Billy the Kid," Joaquin Murieta, and Gregorio Cortez were as important for whom they opposed and what they represented as they were for what they did. Historian Eric Hobsbawm, in a formulation that has become classic among scholars, would call such men "social bandits" or "primitive rebels."

Classic social bandits, maintained Hobsbawm, were peasant outlaws regarded as criminals by the ruling class or the state but treated by common folk as heroes, champions, avengers, fighters for justice, maybe even liberators, but in any case men to be admired, helped, and supported. They appeared in every historical period and every place in the world—wherever a society was based on agriculture (including pastoral economies) and consisted mostly of peasants and landless workers who were ruled, oppressed, and exploited by someone else—lords, towns, governments, lawyers, even banks. "Such banditry tended to become epidemic," wrote Hobsbawm, "in times of pauperization and economic crisis." When rural society and village life was rent open by war, conquest, political breakdowns, or sudden changes in the administrative systems of which they formed small and remote parts, the social bandit appeared. Typically driven outside the law because of some personal act sanctioned by the local community but considered criminal by the distant state and its local authorities, the bandit remained a part of his community, even in a way represented it, and was certainly considered an honorable man within that community. Robin Hood was, of course, the archetypical social bandit, but so was the mostly legendary Joaquin Murieta, whose robberies and murders during gold-rush era became a form of communal protest for Mexican Americans against the oppressions of the mining industry and a racist United States.

Social bandits appeared all over the American West in the aftermath of the Civil War, when the federal government was committed to "reconstruction" politics and the rapid economic development of its Western colony from a largely precapitalistic, preindustrial society into a wide-open capitalistic one dominated by mostly extractive industries. Frank James was acquitted of crimes he certainly committed by a jury made up of "well-to-do thrifty farmers" who hated banks, RAILROADS, and Yankee social engineering, but the JAMES BROTHERS were not the only former rebel guerrillas to raid the robber barons. Others who had not served as Confederate guerillas—such as the bank robbers of the Doolin-Dalton gang in Oklahoma or the highwayman SAM BASS in Texas—garnered popular support in areas infected by social conflict where respect for the law had been eroded, if it had ever existed.

The *Ardmore State Herald,* for example, wrote about William (Bill) Doolin of the notorious Doolin-Dalton gang: "[He] is fully a romantic figure as Robin Hood ever cut." In the area where Doolin-Dalton gang's was active in the Oklahoma Territory, there was little love lost between the settlers and the U.S. marshals who represented the law. Not only did the farmers distrust the marshals, they considered them little better than criminals themselves. During the Oklahoma land rushes, the deputies used their offices to grab the best lands. Settlers—who saw themselves as a persecuted group of "poor defenseless claim holders"—insisted that the marshals arrested folks for minor crimes simply to collect fees they got for doing so. Like social outlaws everywhere, the Doolins and the Daltons depended on the local community, the "neighborhood," for their survival, and such community support gave them their ability to evade the law for years.

Often such desperadoes seemed hardly champions of the oppressed. Hobsbawm emphasized that social bandits were killers and thieves with little in the way of a conscious, social or otherwise, and, indeed, were almost always characterized by the excessive brutality of the VIOLENCE they employed to achieve their ends. Only occasionally, especially during the transition from precapitalist to capitalist economies, did the outlaws become quasi-revolutionary figures, which, in the Wild West, seemed better to fit the Hispanic outlaws than the Anglos. Banditry in California had its roots in the oppression of the Hispanics by vigilante violence, by the imposition of the FOREIGN MINERS' TAX OF 1850 and the expulsion of Mexicans from the mines, and by the land fraud that dispossessed native Californians of their homeland. Bandits appeared to prey on the miners, steal payrolls, rustle cattle. It was a Cherokee Indian gold miner-turned-journalist named JOHN RIDGE who fused the exploits of these numerous actual Mexican American bandits into the lone semimythic figure of Joaquin Murieta, transforming the social conflict that produced them into the adventures of a single man.

As Hobsbawm also pointed out, social banditry can occasionally create revolutionary conditions, but the social bandit himself is no revolutionary but usually, at best, a peasant rebel seeking revenge or plunder rather than permanent social change. Such, for example, was probably Juan Cortina.

In certain quarters of Texas, especially among the Mexican Americans, the TEXAS RANGERS enjoyed the kind of reputation the U.S. marshals enjoyed in Oklahoma. By the 1860s, the TEJANOS had come to see both state and local police forces as the hired agents of their Yankee oppressors. The Texas Rangers, who were organized initially to combat Indians and "Mexicans" and to patrol the Mexican border, frequently ambushed both Tejanos and Mexican immigrants by, according to scholar Richard White, intimidating, extorting, and ("legally") plundering them in the interests of the Anglo elite. Most whites dismissed the excesses of the rangers, but the Tejanos despised them and their associates in the local police. In 1859, in the overwhelmingly Hispanic South Texas, the thirty-five-year-old scion of a prominent Tejano family witnessed the brutal pistol-whipping of a drunken vaquero by Bob Spears, the sheriff of Brownsville. The witness's name was Juan Cortina, and he shot and killed the sheriff.

Cortina fled, but two months later, he was back with a band of sixty men. He broke all the Mexican American prisoners out of the Brownsville jail, looted the stores of the town's Anglo merchants, and executed four white men who were roaming about free after murdering a "Mexican." South Texas exploded into civil war, and Cortina and his followers did open battle with the Texas Rangers. When the rangers proved unable to capture the "bandit" during the course of what came to be called the "Cortina War," they slaughtered Mexicans and Mexican Americans indiscriminately throughout the region. Meanwhile, Cortina evaded for good not only the rangers, but also Mexican troops on the other side of the border.

Although outbreaks on such a scale would not recur, the tradition of the border bandit lingered on well into the twentieth century. The now famous Gregorio Cortez of Texas—when accused of horse theft in 1901—killed the sheriff sent to arrest him and took off on one of the West's most spectacular, if unsuccessful, horse chases, running against enormous odds in a flight that gained him the status of an Hispanic folk hero. And, of course, there was the Mexican revolutionary "Pancho" Villa, a social outlaw who came to define the very image of the "Mexican" bandit.

At length, Hobsbawm identified three main forms of social banditry: the noble robbers or Robin Hoods, the primitive resistance fighters or guerrillas, and the terrorists or avengers. Americans insisted on seeing the James brothers and the Doolin-Dalton gang as representatives of the first category, and Joaquin Murieta and Juan Cortina more comfortably fit the second. Certainly, the popular press of that day—and Hollywood movies since—portrayed William Bonney, "Billy the Kid," most often as a bandit avenger. If Hobsbawm is right, perhaps the popularity of such figures in the American West of the late nineteenth and early twentieth centuries is not unrelated to the very violent class-based confrontations taking place around the same time between the working-class members of such labor unions as the WESTERN FEDERATION OF MINERS and the INDUSTRIAL WORKERS OF THE WORLD (IWW) and the hired gunmen, strikebreaking toughs, and federal troops protecting the interests of big Western corporations. Perhaps many among the common people in the trans-Mississippi West of that period felt themselves less victimized by a small gangs of thieves than by the powerful men in the West who owned the banks, big businesses, and, especially, railroads. By this reading, in stealing from those the poor and the alienated felt to be robber barons, men such as Frank and Jesse James were—albeit symbolically—taking back the region for those who felt dispossessed in the War of Incorporation. In short, many ordinary working-class folk, at the time, may have been more comfortable with the romanticized image of out-and-out lawbreakers, who shared the rapacity and the daring of the millionaires, but who only wanted to rob them, not own them, lock, stock, and barrel.

—*Charles Phillips*

SEE ALSO: Dalton Gang; Doolin, William (Bill); Federal Marshals and Deputies; Film; Gunfighters; Labor Movement; Literature: Dime Novels

SUGGESTED READING:

Bold, Christine. *Selling the West: Popular Western Fiction, 1860 to 1960.* Bloomington, Ind., 1987.

Brown, Richard Maxwell. *No Duty to Retreat: Violence and Values in American History and Society.* New York, 1991.

Cawelti, John G. *The Six-Gun Mystique.* 2d rev. ed. Bowling Green, Ohio, 1984.

Denning, Mechanic Accents. *Dime Novels and Working-Class Culture in America.* London, 1987.

Hobsbawm, E. J. *Social Bandits and Primitive Rebels.* Glencoe, Ill., 1959.

Slotkin, Richard. *The Fatal Environment: The Myth of the Frontier in the Age of Industrialization, 1800–1890.* New York, 1985.

———. *Gunfighter Nation: The Myth of the Frontier in Twentieth-Century America.* New York, 1992.

Rosenbaum, Robert J. *Mexicano Resistance in the Southwest: "The Sacred Right of Self-Preservation."* Austin, Tex., 1981.

Tompkins, Jane. *West of Everything: The Inner Life of Westerns.* New York, 1992.

Trachtenberg, Alan. *The Incorporation of America: Culture and Society in the Gilded Age.* New York, 1982.

White, Richard. "Outlaw Gangs of the Middle Border: American Social Bandits." *Western Historical Quarterly* 12 (October 1981): 387–408.

SOCIALISM

Early utopian and communal socialism in America, such as that practiced and preached by Frances Wright, Robert Owen, and John Noyes, had given way in the face of rapidly rising heavy industries by the mid-nineteenth century to immigrant social-democrat and social-revolutionary movements and to another brand of socialism as well, ideologically driven, culturally focused, and highly intellectualized. After 1848, German immigrants and, toward the end of the century, Jewish immigrants, as well as a scattering of other former Europeans, gave a decided, if rough, Marxist cast to many American labor organizations, which they often had founded, to foreign-language newspapers, to mutual aid societies, and to numerous ethnic and cultural associations, especially in big cities and in small industrial towns. In St. Louis and San Francisco, but also in the hard-rock mining camps and towns of the Rocky Mountains and the Great Basin and in the upper Midwest and Texas, with heavy concentrations of Scandinavian and German immigrants, socialism took root, and the Socialist party found a constituency.

Given the ideological warfare of the twentieth century, it is important to remember that the same Karl Marx who someone like the twentieth century's Joseph McCarthy vilified, in the nineteenth century was a frequent contributor to the *New York Tribune* of Horace Greeley, and that the great debates between Marx and the French socialists over the nature of labor, capital, and productive value were followed in America's ethnic press by many literate and informed members of the immigrant working class. The American Socialist party combined a European ancestry in Owen, Charles Fourier, and Marx with characteristics uniquely American, including sometimes a fiery insistence on immediate, if not always practical, action.

At two points, at least, socialists had a major impact on nineteenth-century America. During the Great Railroad Strike of 1877, a few thousand socialists organized local strike committees, held rallies, distributed leaflets, and generally spread the strike across the country. In St. Louis, insurrectionary political leaders organized a general strike that, briefly, put them in charge of running the city under a strike committee or, as the sometimes hysterical mainstream press declaimed, "The Commune"—what mid-twentieth-century anticommunists would have called, just as inaccurately, a "soviet." When the American West was in the throes of what Richard Maxwell Brown and Alan Trachtenberg have called a "Civil War of Incorporation" during the mid-1880s, the working class attempted to secure an eight-hour workday and establish local labor unions and parties. Socialists—and some "revolutionary socialists," or anarchists, or syndicalists—frequently took a leading local and regional role in these attempts, especially in the West. The drive led big business and government to mount sometimes vicious counterattacks that bordered on class war or—

in the case of Chicago's Haymarket Square "Riot," following the 1886 national strike for an eight-hour workday—that crossed the border and became murderous repression.

In the waning decades of the nineteenth century, the greatest corporate power by far lay in the hands of the RAILROADS, which touched almost every aspect of economic life in the West. As a result, a hundred years ago, many assumed that Western politicians were the creatures of Eastern monied interests and that the West itself was a mere colony of Eastern capitalism, as have, to be honest, not a few historians since then. Even if the truth was more complex, even if conservative Western politicians and leaders, whom few dispute drew heavily on major vested outside interests, also found support among a range of local businessmen, wealthy farmers, and big ranchers, that simply made the socialists' point: they were, as Karl Marx pointed out, after all, a class, with a class interest in incorporating the West's wealth—mineral resources, grassy ranges, and stretches of timber. Just as the West's conservatives had local support, so did its liberals and radicals.

Agriculture set the tone of the West's political life in the 1890s, and farmers, big and small, constituted the largest social and economic group. Although they, like other Westerners, varied in their political beliefs, many of them came from liberal and socialist backgrounds in Scandinavia and Germany, and large numbers of them were attracted to the Farmers' Alliance, whose four million members contributed to the evolution of the People's (or Populist) party and POPULISM, the most powerful third-party movement in modern American history. Many among the region's middle class and business community chafed at the period's political ineptitude, which they simply considered "bad" government, and resented the arrogance, greed, and corruption they associated with the railroads, corporations, and unchecked wealth. They would ultimately tie themselves to the cause of PROGRESSIVISM, which inherited the mantle of reform from the Populist party after several electoral defeats led it to merge with the Democrats. Finally, the West was a hotbed of unionism, its working class attracted to socialism and strong regional unions, including four highly active and well-organized railroad brotherhoods.

All three groups, the agrarian Populists, the urban and suburban Progressives, and the industrial workers, shared a dislike of railroads and a distaste for industrialists, and all three, to some extent, wanted to socialize the railroads and utilities—the industrial workers and the Populists, through government ownership; the Progressives, through regulation. In general, then, as the events of the 1890s would demonstrate, Westerners were ready to revolt. As always in American politics, the revolt would have a regional cast, with the South and West allying against Eastern domination. Beginning with the Populist challenge, then spreading to socialist-influenced labor unrest, the revolt shook the nation and brought to power the more conservative Progressives, who restored some semblance of order by adopting the less radical of the Populists' reforms and by purging, as much as possible, the more radical socialism from American life.

In the 1890s, socialism itself was much affected by a second wave of American utopianism, which followed the publication of Edward Bellamy's novel *Looking Backward* (1888). Socialists organized hundreds of study circles or clubs that sought peaceful means to a classless society. This, along with the waning Populist movement, the catastrophic depression following the panic of 1893, and a growing disillusionment with corporate America's increasing control of nominally democratic institutions, gave rise to an education-minded political socialism among the native-born that both complemented and checked working-class immigrant Marxism and anarcho-syndicalism. After the Progressives, once they began to win elections, proved much more willing to listen to the managerial reforms proposed by the wealthier among their ranks than to entertain the class-based reforms of Populist unions, the West's small farmers and industrial (and often migrant) workers were attracted to socialist leaders such as Eugene V. Debs. A labor organizer who had created the American Railway Union, Debs led the 1894 Pullman strike and advocated an Americanized socialism that anticipated much New Deal legislation and the modern welfare state. The Progressive upper- and middle-class leaders, for all their talk of reform, looked down their noses at the poor and the immigrant, whom they often considered ignorant, criminal, or worse, seditious. The intellectuals of the Socialist party, which sprang into existence in 1901 with a membership of ten thousand when several socialist groups met and merged in Indianapolis, did not treat them as inferiors or aliens.

The Socialist party leader Daniel De Leon had come from the Socialist Labor party, founded back in 1877 when De Leon broke with the American Federation of Labor after it rejected political action. He, Debs, and WILLIAM D. ("BIG BILL") HAYWOOD were among the party members meeting with social radicals and Western labor-union members in Chicago in 1905 to form "one big union" called the INDUSTRIAL WORKERS OF THE WORLD (IWW). Dedicated to industrial rather than trade unionism, to broad class actions more than specific bread-and-butter issues, the IWW cut across various industries to organize workers as a whole. The WESTERN FEDERATION OF MINERS (WFM), which had been fighting pitched battles with company-hired gunmen in the Rocky Mountains, Great Basin, and Southwest, was the biggest union in the IWW, but Western migrant workers of all kinds constituted much of its membership. De Leon saw the new union as nothing less than the basis for a new civilization, one ready to install state-dominated political rule by the proletariat in the place of trade unions' purely functional economic cooperation with business. But he fell out with the more conservative leaders of the WFM, which the Socialists purged from the IWW, only to be purged themselves when De Leon, in turn, began to attack Western migrants as "bums" more interested in engaging directly in class warfare than in engineering an intellectually correct political takeover. Nevertheless, the Socialist party continued to wield tremendous influence within the Western working class.

Drawing support from rural radicals and urban labor, members of the Socialist party in the West gained some measure of power during the years before World War I. A surge of farm radicalism on the Southern Plains made Oklahoma perhaps the strongest Socialist party state in the nation. Although Oklahoma's population was scarcely 2 percent of the American total, it boasted 10 percent of the national Socialist party's membership. In 1906 and again in 1916, Oklahoma cast the highest vote percentages of all the states for Eugene Debs, the Socialist party's presidential candidate. Socialists won hundreds of legislative seats and elected numerous mayors throughout the West and, in 1911, nearly captured the mayoralty of Los Angeles. In 1912, Debs garnered nearly one million votes nationwide for his presidential candidacy. A Socialist party candidate for the U.S. Senate took 25 percent of Nevada's popular vote in 1914.

But the Socialists never bridged the gap between skilled and unskilled workers, and native-born whites, blacks, Mexican Americans, and immigrants. Unlike their European counterparts, whose more ethnically homogenous working class forged itself into a powerful modern political party, American Socialists offered only a philosophy of brotherhood and the resistance of this or that particular group at the edge of an all-powerful American capitalism. Because the exercise of that power in the West was so raw, the party enjoyed some success there, and especially by opposing America's entry into World War I—a popular position in the isolationist trans-Mississippi West—exercised its influence longer. But the rise of a new patriotic nationalism in World War I hurt the Socialist party. Many Western cities passed criminal-syndicalism laws, which, in effect, made it illegal for foreign-born workers to join unions or political parties advocating changes in government, and then began deporting, without trial,

immigrant members of the party. Western courts arrested, tried, and jailed as many Socialists as Western district attorneys could identify and found them guilty of treason, criminal conspiracy, sedition, or just about anything else they could come up with. The party itself split between those opposing the war and those supporting it. Debs was thrown in jail for his opposition to the war. After Debs died in 1926, Norman Thomas became the leading figure in the party, and he led a revival of the party's fortunes and socialism in general during the Great Depression. Socialist party candidate UPTON SINCLAIR captured the Democratic party nomination for governor of California during the state's primary election of 1934. Touting a plan he called "End Poverty in California" (EPIC), Sinclair mounted a legitimate threat to the Republicans, but his positions so frightened both Democrats and Republicans that they responded with vicious bipartisan opposition and defeated him. Neither Thomas nor those who followed him nor Sinclair ever approached the electoral popularity of Debs, and socialism never again held the kind of sway in the American West that it did early in the twentieth century.

—*Charles Phillips*

SEE ALSO: Agrarianism; Christian Socialism; Labor Movement

SUGGESTED READING:

Buhle, Paul. *Marxism in the United States: Remapping the History of the American Left.* London, 1987.

Burbank, Garin. *When Farmers Voted Red: The Gospel of Socialism in the Oklahoma Countryside, 1910–1924.* Westport, Conn., 1976.

Green, James R. *Grass-Roots Socialism: Radical Movements in the Southwest, 1895–1943.* Baton Rouge, La., 1978.

Schwantes, Carlos A. *Radical Heritage: Labor, Socialism, and Reform in Washington and British Columbia.* Seattle, Wash., 1979.

SOD HOUSES

If the great prairies of the West afforded little timber for house building, they nevertheless offered an abundance of another construction material: sod. The tough, root-bound earth—so stubbornly resistant to the settlers' plows—could readily be cut into remarkably sturdy bricks. However, a settler's first sod house was generally a quickly built and more or less temporary dugout or combination dugout and sod house. A site on the side of a hill or ravine was selected, and a hollow, which would serve as the rear and part of the side walls and roof, was dug out from it. The front portion of the house was closed off with sod bricks. To make the bricks, the ground was plowed, and from the furrows were cut bricks, customarily a yard long, from twelve to eighteen inches wide, and about three inches thick. They were laid into the walls just the way clay bricks were.

In most cases, the "half dugout" served for a season or two while the farm family established itself. It was generally replaced by a freestanding house—though a hill or rise might still serve as a rear wall—usually (though not always) of one room and perhaps as large as twenty by seventeen feet. A house this size called for furrowing a half-acre of sod to cut into bricks. The most expensive individual components of the house were the doors, windows, and their frames, which added five to ten dollars to the cost of the house. Only the more prosperous settlers could afford more than a single glass window. Many did not use glass at all, but sealed the window openings with blankets or buffalo robes.

Depending on the condition of the sod and the available vegetation, settlers often reinforced the walls with hickory stems, which they drove into the bricks like tie rods. Cracks in the bricks or the joints between them were easily filled with additional sod or clay. From an engineering point of view, the roof was more problematic. Settlers of meager means gathered brush, which they spread across rafters as an underlayment. Over this, they spread a layer of prairie grass, then a top layer of prairie sod, cut thinner than wall bricks and laid with the grass side down. Such crude roofs were leaky and required continual repair. Some settlers could afford lumber and tar paper in place of the brush and grass, but even with these materials, sod formed the top layer of the roof.

Interiors of sod houses varied widely. In many, the earthen walls were smoothed as much as possible with shovels and spades. If time and cash were available, plaster was applied to the interior walls. While some settlers actually constructed interior walls, most either contented themselves with the single common room or hung quilts or rag carpeting as room dividers. Furniture likewise varied widely, from family heirlooms brought from the East to crude crates and kegs.

The quality of life in a sod house was hardly luxurious. Made of dirt, "soddies" were impossible to keep very clean. Heavy rains and snow created discomfort and even danger: roofs leaked and walls oozed, and the roof was always in danger of collapsing. Even during dry spells, clumps of dirt and grass continually fell from the ceiling and walls, and many exasperated sod dwellers hung cheesecloth or umbrellas from the rafters to catch the fallout. Insects, snakes, and vermin were frequent house guests.

Although lacking in aesthetics and requiring frequent maintenance, sod houses did enjoy certain significant advantages. They were easily repaired, and the sod was an efficient insulating material from the cold of winter and the heat of summer. They withstood the onslaught of prairie winds, and they were virtually fireproof. Despite these qualities and a six- to eight-year life span, most settlers replaced sod houses with frame structures as soon as possible. Even then, the vacated "soddie" was not destroyed but recycled as a farm building or livestock shelter.

Sod houses first appeared in Kansas as early as the 1850s and proliferated on the Great Plains after the Homestead Act of 1862. Those of Custer County, Nebraska, were featured in nearly three thousand photographs by the homesteader-turned-photographer, SOLOMON D. BUTCHER, over a sixteen-year period beginning about 1882.

—*Alan Axelrod*

SUGGESTED READING:
Dick, Everett. *The Sod-House Frontier: 1854–1890.* Lincoln, Nebr., 1954.

SOIL CONSERVATION SERVICE

The Soil Conservation Service, an agency of the U.S. Department of Agriculture, assists individuals, state and local governments, and a wide variety of groups on resource problems and issues. Its employees, trained in several technical disciplines, work in field offices in cooperation with nearly three thousand conservation districts.

The Great Depression and resource problems—the DUST BOWL and widespread soil EROSION by water—gave HUGH HAMMOND BENNETT, a crusading soil scientist in the Department of Agriculture, an opportunity to demonstrate the value of soil and water conservation methods to America's farmers. Under Bennett's leadership, the Soil Erosion Service received $5 million in emergency employment funds and began operations on September 19, 1933, by establishing demonstration projects in areas plagued by erosion. The Soil Conservation Act of April 27, 1935, established the Soil Conservation Service as an agency in the Department of Agriculture and greatly expanded its operations and budget. During hearings on the bill, Bennett had used a dust storm passing over Washington to dramatic effect in urging congressmen to pass the bill.

Very soon, the Soil Conservation Service changed its method of operations from demonstration projects to working through locally organized and elected conservation districts. On February 27, 1937, President Franklin D. Roosevelt sent the Standard State Soil Conservation Districts Law to each governor and proposed that each state pass a law allowing the creation of conservation districts, which then could sign an agreement with the Department of Agriculture. Since then, nearly three thousand conservation districts have been organized and now cover most of the private land in the United States. Soil Conservation Service personnel work directly with these districts. While most districts are organized along county lines, some are based on other boundaries as in the case of Indian reservations.

The Department of Agriculture consolidated most of the activities related to technical assistance on land matters in the Soil Conservation Service. As a very decentralized agency, the service's programs, operations, and recommended conservation measures and practices are tailored to local conditions. In the West, the service worked with farmers on the efficient use of IRRIGATION water by concentrating on irrigation scheduling and matching irrigation needs to soil types and crop usage. Design of irrigation systems to limit erosion and salinity problems also became a service forte. Other conservation practices, such as use of cover crops in orchards and the use of wind strip cropping and stubble mulching, were promoted by the service in the West. The service also developed a range site and condition system, which is used in making range management recommendations to ranchers.

A prolonged drought returned to the Great Plains in the 1950s. Congress passed the Great Plains Conservation Program, which was based, in large part, on the Soil Conservation Service's experiences. Key elements of the program involved shifting land unsuitable for crops back to grazing and installing conservation practices for the farm and ranch lands of the area. Cooperating farmers and ranchers received financial and technical assistance, but they also signed long-term contracts obligating them to install and maintain conservation practices on the whole farm or ranch. These innovations have since become standard in other Soil Conservation Service programs.

An appropriations bill of May 17, 1935, approved funds for the Bureau of Agricultural Engineering in the Department of Agriculture to coordinate the collection of survey data on snow for use in forecasting water supply in the West. Employees of federal agencies, such as the Forest Service and the National Park Service, and state agencies trekked into the mountains with snow tubes to sample the snow pack so that water users in agriculture, industry, power generation, and recreation would have information on water supply in the summer. The information also helped forecast flooding. The program was transferred in to the Soil Conservation Service on July 1, 1939. Beginning in the 1970s, the service replaced much of the manual collecting system with SNOTEL, which uses meteorburst transmission technology to collect information from automated equipment located in the mountains. The instantaneous availability of information resulted in more accurate and timely forecasts.

While the Soil Conservation Service was best known for its work with farmers and ranchers, it also assisted other groups and many government entities. Under emergency authorities, it also assisted recovery from natural disasters such as floods, fires, mud slides, and earthquakes by clearing and restoring channels and reseeding burned areas and mud slides.

As part of the Department of Agriculture's reorganization in 1994, the Soil Conservation Service was renamed the Natural Resources Conservation Service.

—*J. Douglas Helms*

SUGGESTED READING:

Helms, Douglas. "Conserving the Plains: The Soil Conservation Service in the Great Plains. *Agricultural History* 64 (Spring 1990): 58–73.

———. "Snow Surveying Comes of Age in the West." *Proceedings of the Western Snow Conference*, 1992, 10–17.

Morgan, Robert J. *Governing Soil Conservation: Thirty Years of the New Decentralization*. Baltimore, 1965.

SOUTH DAKOTA

South Dakota ranks sixteenth in size among the fifty states, with boundaries that contain 77,166 square miles. Nicknamed the "Mount Rushmore State" after one of its more famous national monuments, it might better be called the "Land of Infinite Variety." South Dakota owes much more of its history to its varied terrain and its irregular climate, to the complexity of its government, and to its ethnic variety, than to the massive carvings of a few famous presidents.

Geography and climate

South Dakota's boundaries contain the geographic center of North America, located near Pierre (pronounced "peer"), the state capital named after the fur-trade magnate Pierre Chouteau, Jr., of St. Louis. At South Dakota's northeastern corner lies the only true divide on the continent. From lakes Traverse and Big Stone, water flows northward to Hudson's Bay and southward to the Gulf of Mexico. In all, the state boasts seven distinct geographic areas running from east to west: the Prairie Couteau (Hills); a luxuriant prairie;

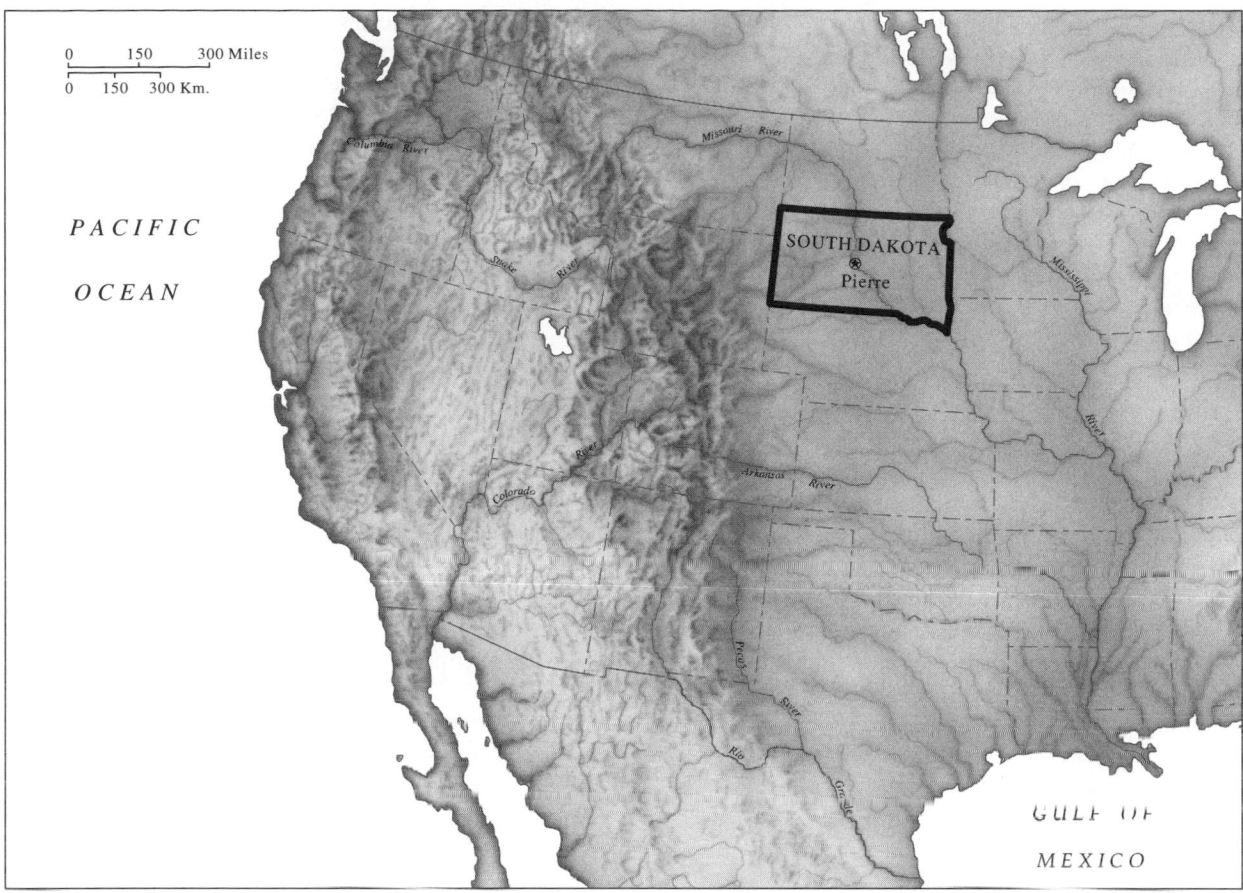

PACIFIC

OCEAN

the Missouri Couteau (Hills); the spacious Great Plains, which elevate to the Missouri Plateau; the fascinating Bad Lands; a substantial portion of the Sand Hills that extend southward into Nebraska; and the mysterious Black Hills. The Black Hills contain Harney Peak, the highest point in the United States east of the Rocky Mountains (7,242 feet above sea level); Bear Butte, a place of spiritual significance to many Native American tribes; and Homestake, a gold mine near Lead (pronounced "leed") that is the most productive in the Western Hemisphere.

Average annual rainfall ranges from twenty-six inches along South Dakota's eastern border to fewer than fourteen inches in the northwestern quarter of the state. Historically, droughts broken by periods of heavy precipitation have plagued an economy heavily dependent on crop and livestock production, creating wild fluctuations in production. The instability of South Dakota's topsoil, coupled with its dramatic swings in temperature, have long caused its streams to silt up and in springtime to jam with ice. As a consequence, the Missouri River and its eight major tributaries have produced great floods in South Dakota more devastating than any floods anywhere in the world, except

those that occur at about the same frequency and for similar reasons along Russia's Volga River on the opposite side of the globe.

History

The flags of several European powers and then of the United States have flown over present-day South Dakota, as the colonizing Western nations laid claim to land already occupied by Native Americans under prehistoric claim by a number of tribal governments. The Hapsburg Spanish first laid imperial claim to the area after 1493, then the Bourbon French in 1701, the Bourbon Spanish in 1762, the Napoleonic French in 1800, and the United States in 1803.

From prehistoric times, Sioux people and (until 1833) horticultural Arikaras claimed the area now called South Dakota. They selectively shared their resources with neighboring tribes on request by diplomats from other tribes. The abundance of fur and robe-bearing animals made present-day South Dakota the hub of a trading network under Pierre Chouteau, Jr.—a network extending from central Wisconsin to the Rocky Mountains. Tribal members and non-Indian hunters harvested animal resources to the commercial advantage of white investors. Native Americans exchanged a part of their natural bounty and labor for manufactured items that improved their military proficiency, made their lives more convenient, and embellished their ceremonial activities as well as their arts.

From the time THOMAS JEFFERSON bought the area from the French as part of the LOUISIANA PURCHASE until Congress organized it as part of the Dakota Territory in 1861, what we today call South Dakota was governed by federal officials who ran the Upper Missouri Agency in St. Louis. As the Louisiana Purchase lands were broken into territories, present-day South Dakota would appear, in turn, on territorial maps as an unsettled region of Indiana, Louisiana, and Missouri. In 1821, Congress reclassified the area as part of a vast Unorganized Territory until 1834, when the Unorganized Territory was divided along the Missouri River. That portion of South Dakota lying in what was called "East (Missouri) River" was at various times considered part of the Michigan, Wisconsin, Iowa, or Minnesota territories, although in the late 1840s and again between 1858 and 1861, it was once more officially designated as the Unorganized Territory. To make nominal matters worse, "West River" was Unorganized Territory from 1834 until 1854, when it was annexed to the Nebraska Territory without benefit of administration.

Beginning in 1820, the FUR TRADE gave rise to a service industry, operated along the Missouri River by mixed-bloods as well as non-Indians, known to outsiders as Steamboat Society or Missouri Valley Culture. This culture in turn encouraged settlement by non-Indians, a settlement met by prolonged tribal resistance. The Indians did not wish to relinquish their land, and nearly a half-century of conflict followed. The series of SIOUX WARS that began in the mid-nineteenth century were as agonizing and as important as any interracial confrontation in the history of America. The territorial encroachments of the Euro-Americans—first by overland travelers, then by gold prospectors, and finally by settlers—resulted in battles, massacres, spontaneous "affairs," and "incidents" that lasted from 1854 to 1903. Sioux soldiers soundly defeated U.S. troops on three occasions before the tragedy at Wounded Knee in 1890. Never were the Sioux defeated by the U.S. Army. Nevertheless, by 1889, they had surrendered approximately 72 percent of the acreage in the state.

From 1861 to 1889, the U.S. government called the areas of present-day South and North Dakota simply the Dakota Territory. Congress changed its boundaries on five occasions, sometimes to include Wyoming and a part of Nebraska. Federal officials resisted the territory's early attempts at statehood—despite a census in excess of the minimum requirement—because of its large Indian population. It was not until 1889 that a movement initiated in Yankton a decade earlier managed to overcome the partisan bickering and federal uneasiness and bring South Dakota into the Union together with North Dakota, Montana, and Washington under a single omnibus statehood act.

The protracted Indian warfare had by then turned the mutual suspicion of the fur-trade era into bitterness, if not hatred, on both sides. A century of peace has not quieted the tension between white citizens and tribal members, although attitudes today more closely resemble the aura of suspicion that existed until the 1860s. After statehood, tribal lands began rapidly to disappear; from a base of 14,030,770 acres in 1889, they shrank to 5,082,737 acres by 1985. Yet the population of the Sioux federation never substantially declined; in fact, it has multiplied since the earliest estimates by a factor of 2.65. Racial disharmony between tribal members and non-Indians in South Dakota is as pronounced as any in the United States.

Population

From the beginning, South Dakota's harsh environment restricted its population. When the Dakota Territory was formed in 1861, there were slightly more than 25,000 Native Americans and something fewer than 1,000 non-Indians living in present-day South Dakota. By the time South Dakota became a state, the population had grown to 328,808, and by 1930, it had reached 629,849. Most of the growth, of course, was attributable to immigration, as more than twenty-five ethnic groups came in two movements—one from northern and western Europe, another from southern and eastern Europe—and settled in enclaves. Most prominent among the immigrants were the Norwegians, Germans, Germans from Russia, Dutch, Irish, Swedes, Danes, Czechs, Mennonites, and Hutterites. Thereafter, an exodus—caused first by drought and depression in the 1930s, then by the lure of wartime employment in the 1940s—reduced the population to 589,702 in fifteen years. After 1945, there was a gradual increase to the approximately 700,000 recorded during the 1990 census (at least 10 percent of whom were of Native American heritage, mainly Sioux).

Thirteen of fourteen tribes in the federation named Sioux (by neighboring Ojibwas) are well represented in three cultural subdivisions. "Dakotas" belong to four tribes with the Anglicized names Medwakanton and Wahpekute (together called "Santee"), Sisseton, and Wahpeton. "Nakotas" are Yankton and Yanktonai. "Lakotas" include Oglala, Upper and Lower Brulé, Hunkpapa, Minneconjou, Sans Arc, Two Kettle, and Blackfoot Sioux.

"Hot Springs Hotel, South Dakota." Patrons greet the arrival of the stagecoaches at one of South Dakota's grand hotels, ca. 1899. Photograph by F. Jay Haynes. *Courtesy National Archives.*

Most of the Indians in South Dakota are enrolled on reservations: the Santees on Flandreau; Sissetons and Wahpetons on Lake Traverse; Yanktons on the Yankton; Lower Yanktonais on Crow Creek; Oglalas on Pine Ridge; Upper Brulés on Rosebud; Lower Brulés on Lower Brulé; Minneconjous, Sans Arcs, Two Kettles, and Blackfoot Sioux on Cheyenne River; and Hunkpapas, Upper Yanktonais, and Blackfoot Sioux on Standing Rock Reservation. Some members from all of the tribes also live full- or part-time in South Dakota's cities.

Most South Dakotans were classified as rural residents until 1960; since then, an increasing majority has been urban, with principal concentrations of population in Sioux Falls, Rapid City, Pierre, Aberdeen, and Yankton. Among non-Indians, the largest religious denomination is Lutheran, followed by Roman Catholicism. There are also large numbers of Episcopalians, Mennonites, Hutterites, Congregationalists, Presbyterians, and Methodists. Native Americans sustain on reservations a Sacred Pipe belief system, an incorporated Peyote religious network, and a modified Christian philosophy most prominently represented in Episcopal, Catholic, Presbyterian, and Congregational communities.

Government and politics

The thirteen Indian tribes assigned during the nineteenth century to South Dakota's nine reservations have rights of residence on and jurisdiction over the reserved lands—legal rights protected by treaty and by a trust vested in Congress by the U.S. Constitution. Each reservation group maintains a system of government and exercises sovereign powers subject to scrutiny only by the U.S. secretary of the interior. Separate from the non-Indian political system, there exists a constitution with bylaws to regulate the election or appointment of officials with executive, legislative, and judicial authority. These officials, serving tribal interests, operate an appellate judiciary, maintain law and order, perform numerous administrative functions, and promote economic developments to sustain ever-growing numbers of enrolled tribal members. Frequently, tribal officers have found themselves at odds with non-Indian officials about such matters as traffic regulation, taxation, school-board representation, social policies, and environmental management within reservation boundaries. Short of congressional remedies, confrontations have been resolved most often by litigation in federal courts or less frequently by "gentlemen's agreements" with federal approval. Certain land-allotment procedures and the Citizenship Act of 1924 made all Native Americans, regardless of their reservation status, eligible to participate in the politics of the state as well.

Non-Indian government evolved from a model based on the separation of powers, imported by politicians from states to the east. South Dakotans, from the start, defended local prerogatives, and Republicans—who founded a territorial Republican party in 1866—prevailed at all levels of state and local government. From statehood through the closing years of the twentieth century, Democrats, who first organized the South Dakota party in 1868, elected only four governors—in 1926, 1932, 1958, and 1970. In only three elections—1959, 1971, and 1993—did the Democrats gain a majority of seats in the state Senate at Pierre. Only once, between 1973 and 1975, did they gain equality with Republicans in the state House of Representatives. Until the 1960s, Republicans won three-fourths of all elections, with margins of victory ranging up to 92 percent.

Despite their predominance, South Dakota Republicans were not characteristically doctrinaire political conservatives. They were, however—especially during the late nineteenth century—frequently corrupt. Like most of America's Gilded Age Republicans, South Dakota's territorial Republicans were not immune to the charms of the spoils system, nor were they inclined to meddle in the affairs of businesses whose profits depended on public and governmental largesse. Doubling as ex officio superintendent of Indian affairs, Governor William Jayne looked away as U.S. Agent Walter Burleigh fraudulently raided the resources of Yankton tribal members. Governors John Burbank and John Pennington ignored corruption openly perpetrated by U.S. Agent Henry Livingston at Crow Creek Indian Agency.

Officials chosen by an electorate that was nearly 80 percent Republican, however, did change quickly under the reforms that began with the rise of frontier POPULISM and, by statehood, South Dakota Republicans had turned Progressive, supporting the government's involvement in economic affairs and service industries. Between 1917 and 1925, Progressive Republican governors PETER NORBECK and William McMaster, backed by a legislature enjoying popular support, marched steadily toward what many Republicans today might consider unabashed SOCIALISM. They purchased a coal mine. They opened a cement plant. They sold gasoline and lubricants. They offered crop insurance and created a "rural credits" state loan program for farmers and ranchers, which ultimately cost taxpayers almost $60 million after many of the loans went into default. The state of South Dakota still runs its cement plant and makes up to $10 million a year

from the enterprise. The state also operates several lodges and recreational facilities at a profit, and it shares receipts from a network of gambling operations.

Economy

Although separated by cultural heritage, governance, and economic interests, tribal members and non-Indians have shared a struggle for livelihood on South Dakota's 50 million acres.

Despite South Dakota's profitable public enterprises, state officials have long demonstrated an exaggerated commitment to fiscal conservatism. Since 1925, the cardinal rules of state finance have been an unwavering observance of a $100,000 constitutional restriction on general-obligation indebtedness; a guarded use of bonded indebtedness, arranged by constitutional amendment; and a budgetary restraint to preserve surplus funds in the treasury sufficient to deal with emergencies. Moreover, officials have repealed experimental income and personal-property taxes and raised revenues within the state mainly through levies on real estate, spending, and licensure. Such policies caused *Money Magazine* in 1992 to rank South Dakota the sixth most desirable state in terms of the low tax burden it put on individuals and corporations.

South Dakota could afford to be so fiscally conservative at home because it relied heavily on federal subsidies. The percentage of federal funds in allocations by state legislators grew from 20 percent in 1952 to 39.5 percent in 1992. The aggregate annual federal subsidy for agriculture and conservation reached its peak in 1991 at $436,180,886. Other forms of federal support included the purchase of materials and labor at such federal installations as the Strategic Air Command base near Rapid City and the Missouri River development facilities under the UNITED STATES ARMY CORPS OF ENGINEERS. Historically, voters grew to understand that conservative fiscal behavior among officials at Pierre depended on the election of senators and representatives to the U.S. Congress of liberal spending dispositions.

In fact, non-Indian South Dakotans have always relied more on federal funds than tribal members. True, from the end of the nineteenth century through 1920s, the U.S. government made "payments" to South Dakota's Native Americans through literally hundreds of thousands of vouchers issued by agency officials or through U.S. Treasury Department checks. But these legendary payments were not an example of some great federal beneficence; they represented proceeds from the sale of Indian land and individual Indian labor. After the land had been bought up, tribal members did receive New Deal support in the 1930s and Great Society "grants relief" during the 1960s, but no more—and with no greater preference—than the government extended to other groups in need. Since 1924, Indians have paid taxes on all incomes, expenditures, and properties (except restricted land), and some federal assistance has been provided to Indians who relocated from rural areas on the reservations to urban settings off reservation in search of education and employment. Tribal leaders shared with federal officials responsibility for the economic welfare of those who chose to remain on the reservations. Indians have made their livings primarily from farming, ranching, small business, craft work, public employment, community projects supported by grants, entitlements available to all U.S. citizens, and—more recently—casino gambling.

Although tribal members have in ways lived apart from non-Indians, they have in other ways participated in developments initiated by the state and its citizens to support a simple economy based primarily on farming and ranching, secondarily on tourism, and to a lesser extent on mining and service industries.

Social issues

Until the middle of the twentieth century, South Dakota's public officials concentrated mainly on such practical necessities as roads and schools. Transportation had always been a pressing need in South Dakota, and it was not until the "good roads" movement set the stage for federal matching funds—first under the Highway Act of 1916, then under the New Deal, and finally under the Highway Act of 1956—that the state managed to pull its roads out of the mud and get beyond the steamboats and railroads that remained the state's major means of transportation into the twentieth century. Education fared less well. By the early twentieth century, the state had developed three separate systems: an expensive public educational network from grade one to university; a system established by Christian denominations for white parishioners, which included primary schools, academies, and colleges; another created both by Christian denominations and by federal officials for Native Americans. These systems have proved resistant to reform. Although efforts beginning in the 1950s did manage to produce some moderate consolidations and a modicum of tribal control over some schools, South Dakota's educational system as a whole remained divided, inefficient, and costly.

Clearly, social issues in South Dakota are intimately related to its large Native American population. The "Americanization" of all immigrants except the Hutterites paralleled the forced acculturation of Native Americans for a century, but ancient legacies that survived mainly underground testified to the state's tenacious cultural complexity. A renaissance in ethnic expression took root in the 1960s and flourished across the state. Most noteworthy were the spiritual, ceremonial, linguistic, social, and artistic revivals on all tribal reservations, but a number of other—Mennonite, Dutch, Swedish, Norwegian, Czech, German, and Irish—celebrations, mostly annual, also began to mark the calendar.

National leaders

The list of South Dakotans who earned national and international recognition is illustrious and long. Native Americans include SITTING BULL, RED CLOUD, CRAZY HORSE, SPOTTED TAIL, HOLLOW HORN BEAR, BIG FOOT, public official Benjamin Reifel, artists Oscar Howe and John Saul, and cultural liaisons CHARLES EASTMAN and members of the Deloria family. Energetic politicians include U.S. Senators Peter Norbeck, KARL MUNDT, Francis Case, and Senator—and presidential candidate—George McGovern. The state's most prolific authors have been Ole Rolvaag, LAURA INGALLS WILDER, Frederick Manfred, and Herbert S. Schell. Distinguished women in addition to Wilder include Catholic Mothers Superior Joseph Butler, Raphael McCarthy, and Jerome Schmitt, and author and educator ELAINE GOODALE EASTMAN. Horticulturist Niels Ebbeson Hanson, prairie artist and World War I illustrator Harvey Dunn, and Nobel Prize winner Ernest O. Lawrence, inventor of the cyclotron, earned global recognition.

—Herbert T. Hoover

SEE ALSO: Chouteau Family; Federal Government; Progressivism

SUGGESTED READING:

Cash, Joseph H., and Herbert T. Hoover, eds. *To Be an Indian: An Oral History.* New York, 1971. Reprint. St. Paul, Minn., 1995.

Hoover, Herbert T., Carol Goss Hoover, and Elizabeth A. Simmons. *Bon Homme County History.* Freeman, S. Dak., 1994.

Hoover, Herbert T., and Karen P. Zimmerman. *South Dakota History: An Annotated Bibliography.* Westport, Conn., 1993.

Hoover, Herbert T., and Larry J. Zimmerman. *South Dakota Leaders.* Lanham, Md., 1989.

Schell, Herbert S. *History of South Dakota.* Lincoln, Nebr., 1975.

SOUTHERN PACIFIC RAILROAD

After the CENTRAL PACIFIC RAILROAD line was linked to the UNION PACIFIC RAILROAD to form the first transcontinental rail line, the industry's "Big Four"—COLLIS P. HUNTINGTON, CHARLES CROCKER, AMASA LELAND

STANFORD, and MARK HOPKINS—turned to the creation of the Southern Pacific Railroad. The company was actually chartered as a route from San Francisco to San Diego in 1865, four years before the driving of the Golden Spike. When the Big Four took control of the SP in 1870, its southern terminus was relocated to San Bernardino. The network was further enlarged in 1871 when Huntington and the others acquired the California Pacific, which linked Sacramento and San Francisco. By 1876, the Southern Pacific extended to Los Angeles and Mojave, and by the following year, the railroad controlled 85 percent of all trackage in CALIFORNIA and pushed eastward into Arizona as far as Yuma.

In 1877, the Southern Pacific went head to head with the TEXAS AND PACIFIC RAILROAD, which was planned as a route from El Paso to the sea. Seeking to outmaneuver the Texas and Pacific, Huntington, who had originally seen the SP as nothing more than a way to develop the Pacific end of the transcontinental railroad, pushed his road farther to the east, connecting with the Santa Fe at Deming, Arizona, thereby creating the nation's second transcontinental route. The SP then acquired a number of small railroads that gave it a direct route through to New Orleans. The New Orleans–California axis would define the Southern Pacific's principal extent.

The rapid and extensive development of the Southern Pacific was evidence of the Big Four's acumen and willingness to take risks. The new rail network was a great boon to the development of California; however, this "service" to the state was seen by many as exploitation of the worst kind. The many-branched route charged top dollar for freight, blocked potential competition at every turn, and earned the epithet of "the Octopus." In actuality, both assessments of the Southern Pacific were true. It contributed immeasurably to the state's growth, even as it held agricultural producers and handlers in a suffocating grip.

By the 1880s, popular outrage over the power of "the Octopus" prompted the formation of what was designed as a strong railroad commission. By then, however, the railroad had grown so influential that California politicians, including the railroad commissioners, tended to knuckle under to whatever the Southern Pacific required. For good measure, Huntington liberally bribed state legislators and proclaimed, "If you have to pay money to have the right thing done, it is only just and fair to do it."

The development of the Southern Pacific was thus characterized by a combination of financial daring, a wholehearted (but hardly selfless) commitment to the development of the state of California, acute financial acumen, ruthless energy, and a willingness to seize power at every turn. Not only were competing railroads repeatedly blocked, but competition from cheap ocean transport was dealt with by the acquisition of a steamship affiliate, the PACIFIC MAIL STEAMSHIP COMPANY, begun in 1874.

Despite popular resentment against it and despite its top-dollar rate structure, the Southern Pacific gave to California a rail network that rivaled those of Eastern regions in extent, efficiency, and quality of service. The Southern Pacific greatly accelerated the development of California, while proving tremendously profitable.

—Alan Axelrod

SUGGESTED READING:
Daggett, Stuart. *Chapters on the History of the Southern Pacific.* 1922. Reprint. Los Angeles, 1966.

SPALDING, HENRY HARMON AND ELIZA HART

Henry and Eliza Spalding were members of the first missionary party sent in 1836 by the AMERICAN BOARD OF COMMISSIONERS FOR FOREIGN MISSIONS (ABCFM) to convert the Indians of the Oregon Country.

Born in Berlin, Connecticut, to Martha and Levi Hart, Eliza Hart (1807–1851) moved with her family to a farm in Holland Patent, New York. There, she attended local schools and, like many other future missionary wives, attended a female academy and taught school. Deeply influenced by the evangelicalism of the Second Great Awakening, she joined the Presbyterian church in 1826. Several years later, at the suggestion of a friend, she began corresponding with Henry Harmon Spalding, who was preparing for a missionary career and was searching for a suitable female companion.

Henry Spalding's (1803–1874) background differed dramatically from Eliza's. He was born in Steuben County, New York. Illegitimate and desired by neither of his parents, he grew up in a foster family where he may have been physically abused. Despite poverty and limited education, he decided to pursue a career in the ministry. In 1825, he joined the Presbyterian church; several years later, he read a religious tract that prompted his decision to become a missionary. After he corresponded for a time with Eliza, the two married in 1833 and moved to Cincinnati where Henry attended Lane Theological Seminary. After Henry graduated and was ordained, the couple expected to become missionaries among the Osage Indians (in present-day Kansas). Fellow missionary Marcus Whitman, however, persuaded them to join his party, which was headed for Oregon.

Tensions between the Spaldings and the Whitmans emerged during the overland trip. Henry Spalding was impetuous, proud, and often difficult. His relations with the Whitmans were complicated by the fact that Marcus's wife, Narcissa, had refused Henry's marriage proposal years before. Eliza Spalding's piety and single-minded devotion to the missionary cause probably made Narcissa Whitman jealous. Not surprisingly, once in the Oregon Country, the families decided to open separate stations. The Whitmans went to work among the Cayuse Indians near present-day Walla Walla, Washington; the Spaldings set their Lapwai station among the Nez Percé Indians in present-day Idaho. Despite the distance between the families, differences remained and were fed by the Spaldings' initial success with the Nez Percé Indians. Henry was accused of having lowered church admission standards and of being too independent—charges that almost resulted the Spaldings' recall in 1842.

During the early years at Lapwai, both Eliza and Henry were zealous agents of Christ and American culture. Eliza taught school to as many as two hundred Nez Percés a day and coped imaginatively with language and cultural barriers by painting pictures of Bible stories to instruct her students. She encouraged her female charges to accept white middle-class gender roles and taught them to weave and spin and to dress in American clothes. Meanwhile, Henry learned the Nez Percé language, taught basic Christian ideas, and baptized several members of the tribe. Eventually, he translated parts of the Bible and hymns into the native language. He was an eager advocate of American-style agriculture and hoped to see the Nez Percés settle permanently as farmers.

By 1843, a house, a schoolhouse with weaving and spinning rooms, a meeting house, granary, workshop, printing office, grain mill and sawmill, and two guest houses attested to the hard work of the Spaldings and the Nez Percés alike. Yet many of the Nez Percés were disenchanted by the efforts to transform their culture. Several incidents of vandalism occurred, and by 1848, when angry Cayuse Indians murdered the Whitmans at Waiilatpu station, the Spaldings were depressed by tribal resistance and growing hostility. Nonetheless, when the Spaldings left the mission behind, they were not happy. Eliza wrote, "I have lost my home, my employment, and my people." She died three years later.

During the remaining years of his life, Henry Spalding publicized the work of the ABCFM missionaries and created a heroic image that his early biographer,

Clifford Drury, adopted. In recent years, however, historians have been more critical of missionaries and more sensitive to the Native American experience.

—*Julie Roy Jeffrey*

SEE ALSO: Missions: Nineteenth-Century Missions to the Indians; Protestants; Whitman, Marcus and Narcissa

SUGGESTED READING:
Dawson, Deborah Lynn. "'Laboring in My Savior's Vineyard': The Mission of Eliza Hart Spalding." Ph.D. diss., Bowling Green State University, 1988.
Drury, Clifford M. *Henry Harmon Spalding, Pioneer of Old Oregon.* Caldwell, Idaho, 1936.
Jeffrey, Julie Roy. *Converting the West: A Biography of Narcissa Whitman.* Norman, Okla., 1991.
Webster, Jonathan. "The Oregon Mission and the ABCFM." *Idaho Yesterdays* 31 (1987): 24–34.

SPANISH-AMERICAN WAR

SEE: National Expansion: The Imperial Impulse

SPANISH LAW

Spanish law prevailed in the West from the time the region was settled and was substantially unchanged by the transfer of ownership from Spain to Mexico. After the United States acquired the area, Spanish law remained in effect until specifically altered under American rule. Thus, until the mid-nineteenth century, the applicable law in Texas, New Mexico, Colorado, Arizona, and California was Spanish. Unlike American law, which follows English methods and models, Spanish law was based principally on the Roman system with some significant Visigothic and Moorish elements.

Spanish law relied on two types of legal practitioners: notaries, who prepared written documents (such as contracts, gifts, inventories, and powers of attorney), and pleaders, who represented clients before the courts. For a time in the mid-eighteenth century, there was one self-trained notary in Texas. At the end of the Mexican period in New Mexico and California, there were, for a short time, a qualified resident pleader and a trained judge, but during the rest of the Spanish and Mexican periods, law was applied without any other participation of resident lawyers. Governmental functionaries carried out the law, and the legal system operated among the settlers in accordance with Spanish customs and recollections from their Hispanic past. In the absence of professional lawyers to resolve disputes and to prepare documents involving property interests and agreements, governmental administrators, soldiers, and literate neighbors assisted their friends in accordance with Spanish traditions. When Hispano-Mexican administrators were removed from the region, only the legal traditions of the settlers remained.

With the shift to American sovereignty, the institutions of Spanish criminal law gave way almost totally to Anglo-American legal institutions with all the rights guaranteed by the United States Constitution. With respect to civil law, however, Americanization was much slower, and some Hispanic legal institutions are still preserved. During the 1820s and 1830s, the American colonists of Mexican Texas were accompanied by American lawyers who in the course of learning the local law acquired some attachment to certain Spanish legal rules. These lawyers were instrumental in perpetuating the Spanish civil rules in 1840 when Texas otherwise shifted to Anglo-American civil law. In New Mexico, the adoption of Anglo-American law occurred more gradually, but by the end of the nineteenth century, most Spanish legal institutions had been displaced. In California, the great migration of Americans caused a more radical shift to Anglo-American law in 1850. In Colorado and less markedly in Arizona, most Hispanic legal institutions disappeared soon after these regions were made territories of the United States in 1861 and 1863, respectively.

Aspects of the Spanish law of inheritance survived in the West more markedly than other rules of Spanish law. Among these rules, the COMMUNITY-PROPERTY law (by which spouses share equally in the gains of marriage) was the most notable survival. Community-property law has persisted in Louisiana, Texas, New Mexico, Arizona, California, and Nevada and has spread to Washington, Idaho, and Wisconsin. The rule has also affected the general law of the United States in prompting the federal government to allow joint income tax returns and marital deductions for purposes of federal estate and gift taxes.

Other remnants of Spanish law in the West are less notable. Although elements of Spanish civil procedural law tended to disappear sooner than rules of civil substantive law, Texas has preserved some Spanish concepts of judicial procedure. Because significant areas of Texas, New Mexico, Arizona, and California were the subject of land grants during the Spanish and Mexican periods, some aspects of land and water use continued to be controlled by the Spanish law in effect when the grant was made. Other rules of Spanish family law have also continued. Apart from these diffuse

survivals, the law of the West was wholly Americanized by the end of the nineteenth century.

—*Joseph W. McKnight*

SUGGESTED READING:

Cutter, Charles R. *The Legal Culture of Northern New Spain, 1700–1810.* Albuquerque, N. Mex., 1995.

McKnight. Joseph W. "Law without Lawyers on the Hispano-Mexican Frontier." *West Texas Historical Association Yearbook* 66 (1990) 51–65.

———. "Spanish Law for the Protection of Surviving Spouses in North America." *Anuario de Historia del Rerecho Español* 57 (1987): 365–406.

SPANISH AND MEXICAN TOWNS

From the early decades of the seventeenth century until the middle of the nineteenth century, the governments of, first, the Spanish empire and, then, Mexico developed towns along a frontier that stretched across the northern reaches of New Spain and Mexico from present-day Texas, through New Mexico and Arizona, and up the coast of California. In doing so, they laid the foundations for what would be come some of the trans-Mississippi West's largest cities—LOS ANGELES, SAN FRANCISCO, SAN JOSE, SAN DIEGO, ALBUQUERQUE, and SAN ANTONIO. Some of the Spanish and Mexican towns remained smaller, closer to their origins, but became historically significant as well, such as Sonoma, Monterey, SANTA FE, and Laredo.

The traditions upon which these towns were founded and built began with the arrival of Christopher Columbus in 1492. The first towns Columbus built in what Europe came to consider its New World did not survive, but Santo Domingo, founded in 1502, did. This Caribbean village was probably similar to the earlier towns; its construction indicates that, from the beginning, the Spaniards based their towns on the grid pattern of streets and plazas that was to characterize Spanish colonial urban design for some four hundred years. Those constructing the New World towns reported back to Spain. Later expeditions received directions on locating and building new communities. These directions grew more detailed and strict over time until Philip II, in 1573, codified all that had been learned and produced a set of building codes and colonial rules and regulations called the Law of the Indies and intended to dictate the establishment, construction, and administration of all future settlements in Spain's vast New World empire.

Some rules the colonial builders ignored; others they generally put into practice. Almost all Spanish settlements had a grid pattern of streets, a main plaza on which were located major, public buildings and subsidiary open spaces, grounds held in common surrounding the town, and a method of allotting land to settlers. The rules specified that founders of new towns should pick elevated sites for easy fortification that lay near fertile farms lands, pastures, and timber or other sources of fuel. The towns were built from the plazas outward, and the plazas were planned with an eye toward growth. In port cities, the plaza was near the harbor; inland, it lay at the center of town. The four corners of the plaza were supposed to face the four cardinal points of the compass, and they sometimes did. Plazas and main streets were supposed to, and often did, have porticos. The streets, too, were carefully planned to accommodate growth. The civil plaza, with a church, shops, merchant homes, and official residences, was designed to serve as the focal point of social, religious, and economic life. Most plans called for a customs house between the church and plaza. The rules specified two hospitals, one—for noncontagious diseases—next to the church, another—for contagious diseases—somewhere protected from disease-spreading winds. Slaughterhouses were supposed to be built down by the water or below the town. Generally, royal grants for settlement were square, five and one-quarter miles long on each side, and consisted of twenty-eight square miles. Elected councils and public officials had authority within the town, but not over its outlying farm lands, commons, or adjacent fields. The entire community, both its urban and agricultural sections, was called a *pueblo,* and less commonly in the American Southwest, at least, a *villa.* Local governments also managed tracts of lands called *propios,* which they rented to settlers. How closely such rules were followed depended on the size of the population, location, the skills of the builders, and, of course, historical events.

Spanish America consisted of more than civil communities, however. Two other kinds of communities played a major role in colonial settlement and dictated later developments under Mexican rule. Both of them, missions and presidios (or forts), were much more common than pueblos in the Southwest and probably more important. On the other hand, despite the fact that missions, presidios, and pueblos were established for different purposes and were constructed differently as well, the distinctions between them were not always maintained in practice. The typical mission complex stood in the middle of fields, orchards, and pastures, its buildings enclosed by an adobe wall. The wall created an interior quadrangle housing granaries, shops, crude Indian huts, and church-related and monastic structures. After Mexican independence, the missions were secularized and converted ultimately into civil communities. The Franciscans, who had steadfastly resisted attempts by Spanish liberals to secularize the missions, finally left, many of them precipitously, when Mexico took control. Chaos ensued in town construction, and many Mexican settlements that were formerly missions became architectural and social hodgepodges.

The presidios were built to protect the occupants of pueblos and missions from Indian attacks and invasions by other European imperialists. The pueblos and missions were expected to produce food and provisions for the presidio's troops and civilians to fill out the ranks when necessary. Presidios, unlike missions and pueblos, were not governed by the Law of the Indies, and their physical forms depended on the desires and personalities of their commanders. Normally walled compounds, the forts also attracted surrounding settlements of soldiers with families, houses, and farms of their own and settlers drawn to the security the fort offered. In the late eighteenth century, Spain further blurred the distinction between pueblos and presidios as a matter of policy and, in Texas, Arizona, New Mexico, and parts of California and northern Mexico, pointedly encouraged civilian settlement. Thus, the early military character of the forts changed over time, and combined garrison and municipal communities came into existence at such sites as Tubac, Arizona, San Diego, SANTA BARBARA, and Monterey in Alta California, and Goliad, Texas.

Missions, pueblos, and presidios resembled each other physically. They all functioned as colonizing outposts. When all three were in the same general area, the differences between them grew even more vague. Santa Fe, for example, was a villa, a presidio, and a religious center; at San Antonio, Texas, the presidio and pueblo stood side by side, while the mission lay a few dozen yards away across the river at San Antonio de Valero. In the San Francisco area, a presidio sat at the mouth of the Golden Gate. The mission lay a few miles away. Halfway between, a pueblo named Yerba Buena ("good herb") grew up on a cove off San Francisco Bay. Close together and intimately related, the three kinds of Spanish colonial settlements grew under the late empire and into the period of Mexican rule to be true towns, whose residents—villagers, soldiers, padres, Indian neophytes—engaged in social and spiritual intercourse and developed market and family relations. Anglo small towns also served as market and supply centers for outlying agricultural areas, but they had little of the kind of community, for better or worse, that was created in the Spanish and Mexican urban-agricultural complexes by their strictly defined social and political hierarchies, communal lands, shared religion, officially public spaces, planned construction, and, indeed, functional sociability.

—*Charles Phillips*

SEE ALSO: Barrios; City Planning; Urban West

SUGGESTED READING:

Reps, John W. *Cities of the American West: A History of Frontier Urban Planning.* Princeton, N.J., 1979.

———. *The Forgotten Frontier: Urban Planning in the American West before 1890.* Columbia, Mo., 1981.

Weber, David J. *The Spanish Frontier in North America.* New Haven, Conn., 1992.

SPANISH SETTLEMENT

Spanish expansion and settlement along the North American frontier of New Mexico, Arizona, Texas and California was a response to pressure from administrators in Mexico City and Spain reacting to competition from France, England, and Russia. Settlement was made difficult by factors of distance, lack of apparently exploitable resources, and resistance by the native populations. Settlement in the trans-Mississippi West by the Spanish followed four primary routes: the upper Rio Grande in the late sixteenth and seventeenth centuries with the establishment of New Mexico; expansion north in the 1690s from Sonora into what became southern Arizona; expansion across the lower Rio Grande into modern eastern Texas in the late seventeenth and eighteenth centuries; and expansion into California along the coast beginning in 1769.

The impulse driving Spanish expansion was mixed. While the original explorers of much of the modern Southwest followed the trail of ÁLVAR NÚÑEZ CABEZA DE VACA and FRANCISCO VÁSQUEZ DE CORONADO, permanent settlement was deferred until the end of the sixteenth century. In a burst of expansion, Spanish imperial authorities established settlements in New Mexico and Florida, in part to claim territory in the face of challenges from France and Britain, and briefly considered a settlement along the California coast to protect the Philippine trade with Mexico before Viceroy Montesclaros ended the scheme in the early seventeenth century.

First begun by JUAN DE OÑATE in 1598, New Mexican settlements proved to be difficult to develop. New Mexico's distance—more than eight hundred miles—from the existing Mexican mining frontier made settlement slow. In 1606, Oñate was removed from control of New Mexico and bankrupted by the costs of the privately funded colony. The future of New Mexico was in doubt. The apparent success of the Franciscan friars at converting the Pueblo Indians led the crown to support continued settlement despite the difficulties of distance and limited opportunities for temporal wealth. With crown support, which included a supply

caravan every three years, soldiers, and a civil establishment, New Mexico grew slowly over the course of the seventeenth century. By the time of the PUEBLO REVOLT in 1680, only about 3,000 individuals of at least partial European ancestry lived in New Mexico. At the same time, because of the impact of disease and starvation, the Pueblo Indian population had dropped from approximately 130,000 estimated in 1580 to approximately 17,000.

The Franciscans, whose activities gave impetus to New Mexico's survival, stationed about forty friars in the colony for most of the seventeenth century. The friars brought Roman Catholicism to the Indians, and because the friars believed that the only true Roman Catholic was one who lived like a Spaniard, they imposed European patterns of life, including language, diet, and education, on the Indians. Rather than establishing separate missions, they took advantage of the support of the soldiers to establish missions within the pueblos, using their base to educate the community and, in particular, to convert children. The zeal with which they worked to convert the Indians and eliminate their religion could be dangerous and caused resentments, which flared up in revolts and murder of priests a number of times before the 1680 revolt.

After the Pueblo Revolt, conditions in New Mexico gradually stabilized within the Pueblo-Spanish community. The Spanish officials recognized the need for tolerance and allowed Indian traditions to continue. The values of Hispanic and Indian cultures became mixed, as did the people, over the course of the eighteenth century. The hoped-for Christianization program slowly lost its zeal, while the Indian population continued to decline. By 1765, the non-Indian population of New Mexico was about 9,850, of whom 3,140 lived in the El Paso district, which grew as a trade and transportation center during the eighteenth century. At the same time, Hispanicized Pueblo Indians and detribalized Indians numbered about 10,500, of whom 1,600 lived near El Paso. The population of El Paso, itself, was 2,635, making it the largest urban center on the northern frontier, followed by Santa Fe with 2,324. Although the missions continued to exploit the Indians, the threat presented by the Navajos, Utes, Comanches, and Apaches forced the Spanish and Pueblos together.

Life in frontier New Mexico was relatively impoverished, although probably less so than elsewhere on the frontier. Trade with frontier tribes, combined with limited trade with Chihuahua, kept New Mexico poor and dependent on a barter economy rather than one based on currency. Because of New Mexico's distance from other European settlements, trade between New Mexico and the French or English was limited or nonexistent, despite some efforts by the French in the middle years of the century.

The preliminary moves towards settlement in present-day southern Arizona did not begin until 1692, when the Jesuit EUSEBIO FRANCISCO KINO visited the Pima Indian village of Bac in 1692. Efforts to establish a church were begun in 1700, but only in 1732 was a mission built, replaced by the existing structure of San Xavier del Bac in 1797. Originally a part of Nueva Vizcaya, the territory was included in the province of Sonora, established in 1734. By the late 1760s, the community adjacent to San Xavier del Bac included no more than 600 Hispanics living in the presidio of Tubac along the Santa Cruz River. Serving Pimas, the mission was run by a Jesuit until members of the order were withdrawn in 1773. Like New Mexico, the southern Arizona region was an impoverished frontier territory.

By the mid 1770s, in an effort to support the colonists in California, JUAN BAUTISTA DE ANZA, commander of Tubac presidio, sought to open a land route to the new settlements. Along with Father Francisco Garces and a small party, de Anza sought a trail to the Pacific Coast from Arizona in 1774. His venture, which led him over two thousand miles to Mission San Gabriel and Monterey and then returning to Tubac, marked him for future promotion. In 1776, de Anza led an overland expedition to establish a presidio on San Francisco Bay. In 1776, Father Garces sought a route from Sonora to Santa Fe and hoped to open a trail all the way to Monterey. Although he was stopped at the Zuni pueblos and forced to turn back, he effectively mapped the way for communication between California and New Mexico. Because of Indian resistance, however, de Anza's trail through Sonora was used instead. Efforts to court the Yuma Indians failed by 1780 as the pressure of the Spanish presence led to the destruction of Spanish settlements west of the Colorado and the death of Father Garces on June 17, 1781. Despite Spain's efforts to reassert control over the frontier, other demands on resources brought Spanish expansion on the Lower Colorado River and in upper Arizona to an end.

Although Baja California had been explored in 1533 by Fortun Jimenez, expansion into what is the present-day state of California was delayed for 164 years. From 1697 on, a chain of missions was established in Baja California, but the arid land discouraged expansion of settlements and forts. The Indian population declined from an estimated 40,000 in 1697 to about 7,000 by 1768. Meanwhile, José de Galvez, the inspector general of New Spain from 1765 to 1771 and secretary of the Indies in 1776, grew interested in the northern frontier of New Spain because of threats he perceived from Russia, in particular, as well as Brit-

ain and the Netherlands. One step to counter these threats was the establishment of a colony at Monterey Bay in California.

In Baja California, Galvez found two individuals, Gaspar de Portola and JUNÍPERO SERRA who were able to support his plans for California. Serra, a Franciscan, was part of the group that had replaced the Jesuits when they were removed from New Spain and had a zeal for missionary activity. In 1769, two parties left Baja California for San Diego Bay—one by land, the other by sea. Although both reached San Diego, only the land-based party under Portola could continue up the coast. After finding the anchorage at Monterey Bay not to his liking, Portola proceeded north to San Francisco Bay. With a resupply, Portola established settlements at Monterey and San Diego, but these were precarious, existing at the end of perilous land and sea supply lines and vulnerable to attack by hostile Indians. Although friendly at first, the Indians soon became hostile to the Spanish and, by 1775, attacked the San Diego mission. In the mid-1770s, the mission system slowly expanded, with the Spanish settlements adjacent to the missions, and reached San Francisco Bay in 1776. Efforts to explore the upper California coast at the direction of viceroy Antonio Maria de Bucareli were limited, although claims were established up to Nootka Sound. Hostile Yuma Indians, however, blocked the overland supply lines through Sonora, although the livestock that went up the supply lines before 1780 established cattle in California.

In 1776, Felipe de Neve became governor of California, based at Monterey. He followed a policy of making the settlements self-sufficient and encouraged civil settlements at San Jose and Los Angeles to supply produce and grain for the presidios. Civil authorities wanted the missions to be open to Hispanic settlers, but the Franciscans delayed secularizing the missions. Yet the missions did not develop into self-supporting communities, and the Indian populations they served declined as they did elsewhere.

In general, the Indian population of California declined from 300,000 in 1769 to about 200,000 in 1821; yet the population of the missions grew from 4,650 in 1784 to about 21,000 in 1821 as Indians from the interior came to the missions. The Hispanic settlement of California also grew slowly from 900 in 1790 to 1,800 in 1800 to 3,200 in 1821. By 1821, a majority of the Hispanic settlers were descended from immigrants who had arrived before 1782.

The fourth major thrust by the Spanish was settlement in what is now eastern Texas. During the 1680s, the French under SIEUR DE LA SALLE attempted to establish a settlement near Matamoros. Despite its failure due to internal struggles and Indian attacks, the settlement provoked the Spanish to move into Texas in an effort to stop French expansion from the Mississippi westward. The French threat, temporary though it was, forced the Spanish to act to defend what they perceived to be their territory. They selected the mission system as the vehicle for expansion and established missions under the leadership of Alonso de Leon and Father Damiean Mazanet along the upper Neches among the prosperous Caddo Indians. Mazanet did not want unruly soldiers at the new missions, and de Leon returned to Mexico with most of the troops. Epidemics among the Indians made them hostile, and missionaries were given the choice of withdrawal or death in 1693. They returned to the Rio Grande.

French efforts to establish trade and missions on the western edge of Louisiana at the Natchitoches villages by 1714 led the Spanish to occupy eastern Texas, first settling among the Hasinai and then just west of the French fort at Natchitoches. A governor, Martin de Alarcon, was appointed for Texas. In 1718, San Antonio was established as a villa, higher than a pueblo or village, but it did not immediately become the capital because of the French threat. To counter the threat, the governor settled in East Texas to support the struggling missions. In 1719, the Spanish temporarily pulled back to San Antonio until reinforced by the marques de Aguayo with about 500 men. By 1721, the Spanish were back in East Texas where they established a fort at Los Adaes, which served as capital until the French left Louisiana.

After the so-called War of Quadruple Alliances, Spanish trade with Louisiana, the initial reason for the move into Texas, gradually developed. Like the other frontier colonies, Texas was seen as an expensive defensive effort rather than as a source of wealth, and the communities of Texas stagnated for much of the eighteenth century. Missions established on the Texas frontier were precarious and threatened by the Comanches. In 1758, the San Saba mission, established only a year before, was destroyed, despite the presence of a fort nearby. In 1759, a punitive expedition was forced to retreat, after a defeat by the Indians, possibly with support from the French. The five missions established at San Antonio were the most successful but attracted relatively few Indians, perhaps only 1,000 by 1750.

San Antonio was settled by civilians from Tlacala with additional settlers from the Canary Islands supported by the crown. Without Indian labor, the small villa stagnated, although after 1749, the Apaches and Hispanics reached a peaceful agreement, reducing the Indian threat. Only in the 1770s, with the development of markets for cattle in Louisiana and of the mines in northern Mexico did San Antonio began to develop beyond a barter economy. The population grew slowly from 500 in 1731 to 1,190 by 1760 plus the Indians in the missions. In 1790, the population stood at 2,510.

The northern frontier of Mexico, in what is now the states of New Mexico, Texas, California, and Arizona, grew slowly and served primarily a defensive purpose. The economies were limited both by their structure, which limited trade with the outside, and by the relative lack of exploitable resources, such as mineral wealth. In the 1760s, the Spanish made an effort to rationalize the structure of the northern defenses under the direction of the marques de Rubi. The plan, later given voice in the Regulations of 1772, was a typical European reaction to the frontier rather than a reflection of the realities of settlement or geography. The plan, supported by José de Galvez, forced settlers to withdraw from east Texas, although they returned in 1774 to a new settlement, the town of Bucareli (and in 1779, with the threat from the Comanches, they moved east to the site of the mission of Nacogdoches). In 1776, as a part of the effort to provide structure to the frontier, Carlos III of Spain created the Comandancia General to govern and defend the frontier. Teodoro de Croix served as the first head of the Comandancia General from 1776 to 1783 and attempted to modify the Regulations of 1772 by restructuring the presidios. He also hoped to enlist Indian allies, but the pressures of the war with England, beginning in 1779, forced him on the defensive. In the Instructions of 1786, the Spanish policies shifted from the traditional emphasis on force when dealing with the Indians to one of trade, treaties, and toleration. This included the establishment of some Apache settlements. With peace developing in the late 1780s and the 1790s, the border communities began to develop and stabilize and improved their trade, particularly with the mining settlements in Chihuahua and Sonora. After 1810, with the growing revolution in Mexico, the frontier became more unstable, both because of the revolution itself and the presence of the Anglo-American traders on the frontier.

With the transfer of Louisiana back to France in 1802 and then to the new United States in 1803, the Spanish frontier faced a new threat in the land-hungry, ambitious citizens of the United States. Matters were made more complex for Spain with the occupation of the homeland during the Napoleonic Wars, which weakened the authority of the empire and damaged the colonial trade when the Spanish lost control of the seas. Given the lack of trade and centralized authority, the Spanish empire became vulnerable and, after 1814, with the abdication of King Joseph, saw the beginning of a series of revolutions that included the Mexican Revolution, which succeeded in 1821. The collapse of the Spanish empire led to the creation of the nation of Mexico and, in turn, provided to the

United States the opportunity for expansion, which climaxed in the TEXAS REVOLUTION of 1835 to 1836 and the UNITED STATES–MEXICAN WAR of 1846 to 1848, both of which brought most of the old Spanish northern frontier colonies into the United States.

—*Patrick H. Butler, III*

SEE ALSO: California Ranchos; Mexican Settlement; Missions: Early Jesuit and Franciscan

SUGGESTED READING:

Bolton, Herbert Eugene. *The Spanish Borderlands: A Chronicle of Old Florida and the Southwest.* New Haven, Conn., 1921.

Gutierrez, Ramon. *When Jesus Came, the Corn Mothers Went Away: Marriage, Sexuality, and Power in New Mexico, 1500–1846.* Stanford, Calif., 1991.

Weber, David J. *The Spanish Frontier in North America.* New Haven, Conn., 1992.

SPARKS-HARRELL CATTLE COMPANY, NEVADA

One of the great cattle operations of the Northwest, the Sparks-Harrell Cattle Company encompassed a large tract of southern Idaho. It became the public focus of the ongoing range warfare between cattlemen and sheepmen from 1895 to 1897, when an employee of the cattle company was convicted of having murdered sheepmen along the region's so-called dead line, which separated sheep country from cattle country.

Cattle baron John Sparks hired Jackson Lee ("Diamondfield" Jack) Davis, a cowboy and self-styled former diamond miner, to work as an "outside man," patrolling the "dead line" that formed the perimeter on the Sparks-Harrell spread through the middle of Cassia County, Idaho. Davis's assignment, for which he was paid fifty dollars a week (top money for a turn-of-the-century cowhand), was (in Sparks's words) to "keep the sheep back." He instructed Davis not to kill anyone but to "shoot to wound if necessary." Sparks pledged, however, that "if you have to kill, the company will stand behind you."

Davis set off to do his job and was soon involved in an armed exchange with some sheepmen. He then rode south into Nevada, boasting throughout the region about the shooting scrape. In the meantime, the bodies of two sheepherders were discovered, shot to death. "Diamondfield" Jack was accused of the murders, and a sheepmen's association offered a forty-six hundred dollar reward for his capture. In the vastness of the West, he was not apprehended until March 1897, when he was found in prison at Yuma, Arizona, serving time for assaulting a peace officer.

John Sparks hired a team of three prominent attorneys, including the famed John H. Hawley of Boise, to defend his employee, while the sheepmen also brought in an impressive team, including WILLIAM E. BORAH, who would later become a U.S. senator. The trial took place in Albion, the Cassia County seat and a bastion of sheep interests. Despite clearly suspect testimony, "Diamondfield" Jack was convicted and sentenced to hang. Hawley appealed. Just one week before the scheduled execution, James E. Bower, a Sparks-Harrell ranch superintendent, sent a deposition to the pardon board claiming that he and Jeff Gray, a local cowboy, had exchanged fire with the sheepherders. Gray also signed the deposition.

Despite the deposition, the pardon board yielded to pressure from the sheep interests and denied a pardon, but the U.S. Court of Appeals stayed "Diamondfield" Jack Davis's execution. In the meantime, Bower and Gray were tried for murder and acquitted on the grounds of self-defense. Davis remained in prison, even though two of the prosecutors wrote to the pardon board on his behalf and stated that they now believed him to be innocent. The greatest leniency the pardon board could muster was a commutation to a life sentence. However, in December 1902, "Diamondfield" Jack was granted a full pardon after having served five years in prison.

The notorious case is one of very few incidents in which cattle interests, rather than sheep interests, suffered at the hands of the legal system in the West.

—*Alan Axelrod*

SPEER, ROBERT WALTER

Mayor of Denver, Colorado, Robert Walter Speer (1855–1918) was born in Pennsylvania. He moved to Denver in 1878 to recover from tuberculosis. Elected Denver city clerk in 1884, he later secured appointment to the city's fire and police board and, in 1901, became president of the board of public works. After Denver won considerable freedom from state control in 1902, the city drafted a charter providing for a strong mayor. Speer, a Democrat, won the office in 1904 and 1908 with help from corporations and, according to charges by reformers, with the connivance of gamblers and saloonkeepers. Declining to run in 1912, he stayed out of office during the city's flirtation with commission government from 1913 to 1916, but voters returned him to power in 1916.

Speer's victories rested not only on his political machine but also on Denverites' appreciation of his efforts to transform their city from an undistinguished big town into an attractive metropolis. More than doubling park acreage, he created new parks such as Berkeley, which boasted the city's first public golf course, and Sloan's Lake. He purchased and cleared the land for the city's civic center, completed the municipal auditorium in time to host the 1908 Democratic convention, established a public bathhouse, promoted the planting of more than one hundred thousand trees, and beautified Cherry Creek. His love of animals prompted the fashioning of natural habitats at Denver's zoo. His fondness for the mountains sparked the acquisition of tens of thousands of acres for the city's mountain parks. By encouraging citizens to "give while you live," he secured numerous public memorials for the city. A one-hundred-thousand-dollar bequest from gambler Vaso Chucovich was intended for a monument to Speer but was diverted to fund a children's wing at Denver General Hospital. The city did honor Speer, however, by naming the boulevard flanking Cherry Creek for him. His wife Kate (born Kate A. Thrush), who outlived him by thirty-seven years, worked to publicize his memory.

Often at war with the traditional Denver press, Speer used the city-sponsored magazine *Municipal Facts* to tout his programs. When he died midway through his third term, the *Denver Post* admitted, "His vision was broad, his activities effective, forceful and unceasing. He was the creator of the 'city beautiful.'"

—*Stephen J. Leonard*

SUGGESTED READING:

Leonard, Stephen J., and Thomas J. Noel. *Denver: Mining Camp to Metropolis*. Niwot, Colo., 1990.

MacMechen, Edgar C., ed. *Robert W. Speer: A City Builder*. Denver, Colo., 1919.

SPOKAN INDIANS

SEE: Native American Peoples: Peoples of the Pacific Northwest

SPOTTED TAIL (SIOUX)

Spotted Tail (Sinte Galeska; 1823–1881), celebrated chief of the Brulé Sioux, was born along the banks of the White River in the southwestern part of what became the state of South Dakota. He was murdered on August 5, 1881, near his home on the Rosebud Reservation by CROW DOG, a long-time rival. Spotted Tail rose to leadership through the force of his personality, his family connections, and his bravery in battle, especially against the Pawnees. He was among the war-

Spotted Tail. *Courtesy National Archives.*

riors who led attacks on traders and travelers in the Platte Valley during the late 1840s. He was present at the Fort Laramie Council of 1851, called to try to bring peace to the Platte River Road, but he was not yet important enough to sign for his people. However, he assumed a position of increasing leadership among those who attacked the whites in defiance of the Treaty of 1851, and by the time the Brulés surrendered to General WILLIAM SELBY HARNEY in 1855, Spotted Tail was the tribe's most important war leader. By 1866, he was recognized as head chief of the Brulés.

Following the surrender to Harney, Spotted Tail, among others, was taken to Fort Leavenworth, where he was detained—although not actually imprisoned—for a year. This involuntary sojourn made Spotted Tail realize that the whites were so numerous, so powerful, and so well equipped that the Sioux could not possibly prevail against them. He came back to the Indian Country as a spokesman for peace and remained throughout his life the leading proponent among the Sioux of peace with the whites. This put him in direct competition with RED CLOUD and others who were calling for war with the whites. At the Fort Laramie peace conference of 1866, for example, when Red Cloud stormed out after the arrival of troops under Colonel Henry B. Carrington, Spotted Tail continued the negotiations and ultimately signed the treaty, which permitted a road through the Powder River country to the gold fields of Montana. (Actually, Spotted Tail had little interest in the Powder River country; he and his people preferred to hunt south of the Platte River.)

Although he steadfastly kept the peace, Spotted Tail retained the hope that his people would be permitted to continue to roam over their traditional hunting grounds and would not be forced to settle on a restricted reservation to make their living as farmers. Even though he yielded to what he knew was inevitable, he did so reluctantly. As a result, he frequently was characterized by officials as a "non-progressive."

After being located successively on the White River and the Missouri, Spotted Tail's people finally, in 1878, were established at what became their permanent agency on Rosebud Creek. There the government built for Spotted Tail a substantial frame house where he lived until he was murdered. With Spotted Tail's death, the Brulés lost their last great chief and one of the most skillful negotiators to emerge from among the Indians of the plains.

—*James C. Olson*

SUGGESTED READING:
Hyde, George E. *A Sioux Chronicle.* Norman, Okla., 1956.
———. *Spotted Tail's Folk.* Norman, Okla., 1961. Reprint. 1974.

SPRECKELS, CLAUS

A California sugar refiner and Hawaiian planter, Claus Spreckels (1828–1908) was born in Lamstedt, Germany. He came to the United States in 1846 and engaged in the grocery business in Charleston, South Carolina, New York City, and San Francisco, where he moved in 1856. He opened his first sugar refinery in 1863. By 1881, using technological innovations and business skill, the "sugar king" of California made his California Sugar Refinery the most modern refinery in America.

Spreckels's refineries depended on Hawaiian sugar cane. After ratification of the reciprocity treaty between the United States and HAWAII, he sailed to the islands in 1876 to establish his own sugar plantations. To obtain land leases and water rights, he allied himself with King David Kalakaua. In the decade after his arrival, Spreckels became the single largest sugar planter in Hawaii and created on Maui the Spreckelsville plantation, which he ran through his Hawaiian Commercial and Sugar Company. His plantations produced up to one-third of the entire crop, and through the factoring firm he established with William G. Irwin, Spreckels bought a substantial portion of the remaining crop.

Local planters resented Spreckels's alliance with the monarchy and eventually sought to oust him. Although he initially endorsed a plan to annex Hawaii to the United States after the Hawaiian Revolution of 1893, he soon actively opposed the plan. After annexation in 1898, the local firm of Alexander and Baldwin bought out Spreckels's company and took control of Spreckelsville plantation.

In California, Spreckels's interests also included investments in beet-sugar refineries, railroads, utilities, and trolleys. The last fifteen years of his life were marred by family warfare over the control of his companies. Nonetheless, the civic philanthropies and business interests of Spreckels and his children established the family as a dominant force in California.

—*John S. Whitehead*

SUGGESTED READING:
Adler, Jacob. *Claus Spreckels: The Sugar King in Hawaii.* Honolulu, Hawaii, 1966.
Kuykendall, Ralph S. *The Hawaiian Kingdom.* Vol. 3. Honolulu, Hawaii, 1967.

SPUR RANCH, TEXAS

The Spur Ranch was located on headwater tributaries of the Brazos River in the Texas counties of Dickens, Garza, Kent, and Crosby. In the 1880s, the ranch covered more than eight hundred thousand acres. Established in 1879 as a small open-range ranch by J. M. Hall, the Spur took its name from Hall's "road" or trail brand. Fort Worth bankers Alfred M. Britton and Spotswood W. Lomax subsequently acquired Hall's cattle with profits they had made in 1883 from their sale of the nearby Matador Ranch to Scottish investors.

In 1884, Lomax and Britton organized the Espuela Cattle Company, acquired title to nearly a half-million acres, and thus displaced approximately thirty open-range ranchers in the area. In 1885, Britton and Lomax sold the Espuela to British investors, who organized the Espuela Land and Cattle Company, Ltd. The venture sustained huge losses, due to extensive drought, and in 1906, the British investors sold the Espuela to a New York investment group, S. M. Swenson and Sons. Under Swenson control, the ranch continued to operate as the Spur, but much of the tillable land was sold when the new owners took an active role in town building and land colonization in the region around Spur, Texas. Only a remnant of the Spur Ranch remains in operation.

—*David J. Murrah*

SUGGESTED READING:
Holden, William Curry. *The Espuela Land and Cattle Company.* Austin, Tex., 1970.

SPURS

SEE: Cowboy Tools and Equipment

SQUAMISH INDIANS

SEE: Native American Peoples: Peoples of the Pacific Northwest

STAGECOACHES

Stagecoaches were vehicles, usually drawn by horses, that carried passengers, mail, and packages on scheduled runs over designated routes. The name was derived from *coach*, for an enclosed carriage and the procedure of traveling in *stages* between frequent stops.

Origin and design

American stagecoaches evolved from the English coach and four, which was introduced into the colonies in the late seventeenth century. Stagecoaching service, which had been instituted in all thirteen colonies by the time of the Revolutionary War, gravitated westward. Throughout the West, the Concord was the best-known stagecoach. Named after its place of manufacture—Concord, New Hampshire—the vehicle was produced by Abbot, Downing and Company. The firm completed its first vehicle in 1826. By the 1850s, the company employed three hundred men in a facility whose buildings occupied a four-acre site.

Standing eight feet high, the Concord coach was designed to withstand the rigors of rough trails. Its oval-shaped box was suspended from the axles by thick leather supports. This unique springless design caused the box to stay essentially level regardless of hilly terrain and gave passengers a gentle swaying motion. Built relatively low to the ground, the Concord was designed to negotiate sharp turns. Abbot and Downing, meticulous craftsmen, built Concords with only the finest seasoned woods. Particular care was paid to the construction of wheels and axles, but boxes were also built with attractiveness and durability in mind. Completed coaches, which sometimes weighed as much as twenty-five hundred pounds, often had red or green colored boxes with tawny wheels. They were lavishly upholstered with quality leather and cloth, and panels on the inside of the doors featured paintings of natural scenes or famous female entertainers. Those that carried mail had the insignia of "U.S. Mail" in prominent gold letters on the outside of the doors.

Concords were spacious and solidly built. As many as fifteen people could be carried in a single coach. The driver and guard occupied the front outside seat; the three inside seats had a capacity of nine passengers; and usually on short trips, another four could ride on the firm roof. Luggage and packages were stored in front and rear compartments called *boots*. Although the name "Concord" became nearly synonymous with the word *stagecoach*, there were rival products because Concords were costly; prices reached as high as fifteen hundred dollars per coach.

The Concord's principal competitors were Troy stagecoaches, manufactured in Troy, New York, and Celerity wagons, a type of mud wagon. Smaller than Concords, mud wagons were lightweight, narrow-wheeled, highly maneuverable vehicles particularly suited for fast driving or use on muddy and mountainous roads.

History

In the trans-Mississippi West, stagecoaching grew apace with settlement. Missouri's first regular stagecoach line was started in 1820, and during the next three decades, stagecoach companies began providing local and regional service in Iowa, Minnesota, and Texas. The greatest need for fast overland transportation over long distances was caused by the CALIFORNIA GOLD RUSH, which started in 1849. The overland California mail was first delivered by wagons over the central route that ran through the Platte River valley and South Pass. In 1857 James E. Birch, a founder and owner of the large California Stage Company, which had massive operations within that state, was awarded a federal-government contract to carry mail by stagecoach from San Antonio, Texas, to San Diego. Birch's biweekly service over the 1,500-mile route was supplanted the next year by the OVERLAND MAIL COMPANY, often called the Butterfield Overland Mail in recognition of JOHN BUTTERFIELD, its principal owner.

The Butterfield Mail was caught up in the bitter sectional controversy between the North and South. The postmaster general in the administration of President James E. Buchanan was sympathetic to the Southern cause. Consequently, he designated Memphis, Tennessee, and St. Louis, Missouri, as the starting points for the mail route, which converged at Fort Smith, Arkansas, and then ran southwestward across the Indian Territory and Texas to El Paso before following the arid Gila River route across Arizona. Butterfield's business on this 2,000-mile oxbow route was a business success. Nonetheless, it was ridiculed by Northerners who favored the central route.

After the outbreak of the Civil War, the Union government switched the Overland Mail Company's contract to the central route. Rather than attempt to use its own resources to provide a daily mail and passenger service from St. Joseph, Missouri, to Sacramento, the firm sublet portions of its nearly two-thousand-mile route to other carriers. The section east of Denver was managed by the Central Overland California and Pike's Peak Express Company (generally known as the COCPP), which had been formed by the freighting firm of RUSSELL, MAJORS AND WADDELL to provide stage-coaching to the recently opened Colorado gold fields. After Russell, Majors and Waddell declared bankruptcy with the failure of its vaunted PONY EXPRESS and other ventures, the COCPP was taken over by BEN HOLLADAY,

A Wells, Fargo and Company stagecoach. *Courtesy Wells Fargo Bank.*

one of its major creditors. Holladay, who gained fame as the "Stagecoach King," was a force in Western stagecoaching for five years. By 1864, the Holladay Overland Mail and Express Company controlled slightly more than 3,000 miles of stagecoach routes in the central region from the Missouri to Salt Lake City and the Pacific Northwest. Although he was awarded lucrative mail contracts, Holladay suffered heavy losses from Indian attacks. Consequently, in 1866, when the completion of the UNION PACIFIC RAILROAD was imminent, Holladay sold out to WELLS, FARGO AND COMPANY. Organized in New York in 1852 to exploit the business opportunities offered by the California gold rush, Wells Fargo had become California's major stagecoach firm by 1860. After purchasing Holladay's interest, Wells Fargo dominated stagecoaching throughout the West. As its longer lines were replaced by railroads, the company continued to provide local service into the twentieth century as feeder routes to railroads.

Trail life

Stagecoach lines maintained numerous "swing" and "home" stations along their routes. Swing stations, usually located 10 to 15 miles apart, were only relay points where the four- or six-horse teams were changed. The less frequent home stations, usually staffed by a manager and his family, offered a full range of services including meals, lodging, and blacksmithing. Four to six stages—the distances from station to station—composed a drive, the work distance of a driver. Ordinarily about 60 miles long, drives were the subunits of divisions, a distance of from 150 to 450 miles long,

that were administered by superintendents. Trail life could be arduous for passengers, who often traveled around the clock on express coaches at a speed of about 8 miles an hour.

Significance and contribution to folklore

The stagecoach was especially important in the development of the West because the region had a general lack of navigable rivers and because of the slow construction of a railroad network. Consequently, the stagecoach symbolized westward expansion more so than any other thing. Overland travelers—including the journalists and writers Samuel Bowles, Horace Greeley, and MARK TWAIN—helped ingrain the stagecoach image into American culture. With their vivid accounts of OVERLAND TRAVEL, they contributed to the nation's fascination with larger-than-life characters by describing the rigors of stagecoach travel and the exploits of such drivers as the legendary Hank Monk. Movie and television producers have contributed to stagecoach lore by prominently featuring stages in westerns. John Ford's 1939 movie *Stagecoach,* which portrayed a perilous trip in the hostile environment of the desert Southwest, has been widely hailed as a western classic.

—*William E. Lass*

SEE ALSO: Film: The Western; Pike's Peak Express Company

SUGGESTED READING:

Banning, William and Banning, George Hugh. *Six Horses*. New York, 1928.

Bowles, Samuel. *Across the Continent*. Springfield, Mass., 1865.

Greeley, Horace. *An Overland Journey from New York to San Francisco in the Summer of 1859*. New York, 1860.

Hungerford, Edward. *Wells Fargo: Advancing the American Frontier*. New York, 1949.

Twain, Mark. *Roughing It*. Hartford, Conn., 1872.

Winther, Oscar Osburn. *Via Western Express and Stagecoach*. Palo Alto, Calif., 1945.

STANFORD, AMASA LELAND

Leland Stanford (1824–1893), lawyer, merchant, and railroad tycoon, became the governor of California, a U.S. senator, and the founder of Stanford University. Born in Watervliet, New York, he briefly attended Cazenovia Seminary, read law in Albany, and was admitted to the New York bar in 1848. In 1850, he moved to Wisconsin, where he also practiced law. When his four brothers went to California during the gold rush, he and his wife decided to try to better their fortunes in the West.

The Stanford brothers opened several hardware stores in California's "motherlode country" and became prosperous merchants. Leland Stanford's first store was in Cold Springs, north of Sacramento. He also supplied miners throughout California's Sierra Nevada with vital necessities. While he never again practiced law, his legal knowledge helped him acquire valuable properties.

In Sacramento, Stanford combined business ventures with an interest in politics. In 1856, he helped organize the state's first Republican party. Five years later, he was elected governor of California. During the Civil War years, he turned his Sacramento home into the governor's mansion.

By 1863, Stanford was at the center of discussions concerning the building of a transcontinental railroad. That year, he was elected president of the CENTRAL PACIFIC RAILROAD Company, a post he held until his death. While he played only a small role in railroad construction, he used his considerable political skills to lobby for legislation—both federal and state—which favored his own company. Frequently, he and his associates (MARK HOPKINS, CHARLES CROCKER, and COLLIS P. HUNTINGTON) were accused of giving bribes to legislators in order to receive favors. Because of their success, their increasing wealth, and their unscrupulous business dealings, the four men came to be labeled "robber barons."

Also known as the "Big Four," Stanford and his partners built the western part of the nation's first transcontinental railroad with handsome government subsidies. In the process, they also gobbled up numerous small railroad companies and thereby eliminated competition. These lines were incorporated within the new SOUTHERN PACIFIC RAILROAD system, of which Stanford also became president.

By 1885, Stanford elbowed out a candidate for the U.S. Senate favored by his business associate, Collis P. Huntington, and himself was elected by California's Republican legislature amid talk of a possible bid for the presidency. Stanford and Huntington were not compatible, except superficially, and Huntington never forgave Stanford for thwarting his political ambitions.

Stanford somehow found time to dabble in a wide variety of interests outside of politics—horse breeding, motion pictures, farming and ranching, viniculture, the collection of art, and European travel. When the Stanfords' son suddenly died of typhoid fever in Florence, Italy, at the age of fifteen, the heartbroken couple decided to found a university in his name. They deeded their extensive Vina ranch and stock farm near Palo Alto to the new university. Stanford lived long enough to see the launching of the new institution in 1891. He died two years later at the age of sixty-nine.

—*Andrew Rolle*

SEE ALSO: Colleges and Universities; Railroads

SUGGESTED READING:

Bancroft, Hubert Howe. *History of the Life of Leland Stanford, A Character Study*. Oakland, Calif. Reprint. 1952.

Clark, George T. *Leland Stanford, War Governor of California, Railroad Builder, and Founder of Stanford University*. Stanford, Calif., 1931.

Lewis, Oscar. *The Big Four: The Story of Huntington, Stanford, Hopkins, and Crocker; and the Building of the Central Pacific Railroad*. New York, 1938.

Tutorow, Norman E. *Leland Stanford, Man of Many Careers*. Menlo Park, Calif., 1971.

STANFORD, JANE ELIZA LATHROP

Cofounder of Stanford University, Jane Eliza Lathrop Stanford (1828–1905) was educated at the Albany Female Academy and married AMASA LELAND STANFORD in 1851, a lawyer from Watervliet, New York. The couple settled in Port Washington, Wisconsin, where Leland Stanford set up a law practice. After fire destroyed his law offices, the family returned to Albany, where Jane Stanford remained while her husband went to California to establish a mercantile business in gold country. His fortunes restored—and, indeed, vastly grown—he brought his wife to Sacramento. He became California's governor in 1861 and one of the "Big Four" financial backers of the Central Pacific, the Western link of the transcontinental railroad. Through these ventures, Leland Stanford became a millionaire. Jane Stanford became a leading northern California philanthropic and social activist and contributed large sums to Sarah B. Cooper's San Francisco kindergartens and to other causes. With her husband's election to the U.S. Senate in 1885, she became a prominent Washington, D.C., hostess as well.

The Stanfords' only child, Leland, Jr., born in 1868, was the object of the couple's intense affection. He died of typhoid while the family was on a European tour in 1884, and the grief-stricken Stanfords resolved to establish a university in his memory. It was Jane Stanford who immersed herself most completely in planning the university that would be established on the Stanfords' seven-thousand-acre Palo Alto ranch. The school that would become Stanford University was opened as the Leland Stanford, Jr., University in October 1891.

Following the death of her husband in 1893, Jane Stanford was plagued by financial problems during a long, tangled, and bitter probate process. During this period, she used her own comparatively limited finances to sustain Stanford University. She also completed the university's endowment and deeded to its trustees one hundred thousand acres and $11 million in securities. She also proceeded with construction of the university's vast campus, and it was she who envisioned much of the university's beauty as an oasis of learning, aloof from the mundane realities of the rest of the world. Her dream was expensive, however, and building came at the expense of faculty salaries, which brought a crisis in morale. She also caused the dismissal of Edward A. Ross, a radical economist, from the faculty in 1900—an act that brought liberal condemnation upon her and the university. Under pressure, Stanford relinquished her considerable authority to the university's board of trustees. She left on a world tour, followed by a Pacific cruise undertaken to recover from accidental poisoning. She succumbed to a heart attack in Honolulu in 1905.

—Alan Axelrod

SEE ALSO: Colleges and Universities

STANLEY, JOHN MIX

Artist John Mix Stanley (1814–1872) was born in Canandaigua in western New York and was apprenticed in his teens to a coach-maker in Buffalo as a decorator of sideboards. Moving to Detroit, Michigan, in 1834, he worked as a sign painter until he met James Bowman, who gave Stanley his first lessons in portrait painting. Never long in one place over the next several years, Stanley made his living as an itinerant portraitist in Chicago, Philadelphia, Baltimore, and Troy, New York. In Washington, D.C., he worked briefly for a daguerreotypist and experimented with photography. In 1839, he visited Fort Snelling, Minnesota, and he ventured into the Indian Territory, now Oklahoma, to paint portraits among the various Native American groups in the area three years later. In 1846, he traveled to Santa Fe, New Mexico, and joined STEPHEN WATTS KEARNY's expedition to California. Assigned to WILLIAM HEMSLEY EMORY's topographical unit as a member of its scientific staff, Stanley prepared the botanical plates for Kearny's subsequent report to Congress. Stanley later visited the Oregon Territory and the Hawaiian Islands before returning to New York City in 1849 to prepare his work for exhibition in several Eastern cities.

In 1852, Stanley exhibited a large collection of his Western paintings at the Smithsonian Institution. The following year, he accompanied Isaac Stevens's survey of a northern route for the proposed transcontinental railroad. He returned to Washington in 1854 to assist in the publication of the lithographic plates illustrating Stevens's reports.

Stanley married in 1854. Ten years later, he moved back to Detroit, where he completed perhaps his best known painting, *The Trial of Red Jacket,* in 1868. Meanwhile, most of his Western collection at the Smithsonian was consumed by fire in January 1865. Another fire that year at P. T. Barnum's museum in New York City and yet another at Stanley's studio in Detroit in 1872 destroyed nearly everything he had produced relating to his experiences in the trans-Mississippi West.

One of the most widely traveled Western artists of his day, Stanley may have been the first to use a daguerreotype apparatus in the West for documentary purposes. He also produced at least two large, movable panoramas, both of which are now lost. Stanley is represented today by several chromolithographs. Original examples of his work survive at the Smithsonian Institution, the Buffalo Historical Society, the Detroit Institute of the Arts, the THOMAS GILCREASE INSTITUTE in Tulsa, Oklahoma, and the Stark Museum of Art in Orange, Texas. Four portraits of Hawaiian royalty by Stanley are preserved in the Bernice P. Bishop Museum in Honolulu.

—David C. Hunt

SEE ALSO: Art: Western Art, Surveys and Expeditions

SUGGESTED READING:

DeVoto, Bernard. *Across the Wide Missouri*. Boston, 1947.

Forbes, David. *Encounters with Paradise*. Honolulu, Hawaii, 1992.

Taft, Robert. *Artists and Illustrators of the Old West, 1850–1900*. New York, 1953.

Tyler, Ron., et al. *American Frontier Life: Early Western Paintings and Prints*. Fort Worth, Tex., 1987.

STARR, BELLE

Consort of outlaws, Belle Starr (1848–1889) was the "Outlaw Queen" of Missouri, the Indian Territory, and Texas. The legend of Belle Starr is extensive: she was a Confederate spy during the Civil War; she rode with WILLIAM CLARKE QUANTRILL's guerrillas and later with the James-Younger band; she was the lover of bandit Cole Younger who fathered her first child; she became the leader of her own band of desperadoes and murdered men, stole cattle and horses, and robbed banks, trains, and stagecoaches. For a century, she has reigned as the West's most famous female outlaw. Such myths have led more than one responsible scholar to conclude that Belle Starr was "one of the most extraordinary women in the history of the west."

Unfortunately, the real Belle Starr was no "Outlaw Queen." Extensive research by historian Glenn Shirley has revealed that none of the myths mentioned above is true and that Belle Starr's principal attribute was her propensity for marrying or living with desperadoes of the worst stripe.

She was born Myra Maybelle Shirley in Jasper County, Missouri. Her father, John Shirley, owned a hotel, livery stable, and blacksmith shop in Carthage, where young May, as she was called, grew up. Her parents gave her a good upbringing but could not quell a hot temper and restless spirit. She was educated at the Carthage Female Academy and loved to read and play the piano. The outbreak of the Civil War in 1861 tore Missouri and the Shirley family apart and ruined the family business. Her eldest brother, Bud, joined a band of rebel bushwhackers and was killed in 1864. The grief-stricken family moved south and settled near Dallas, Texas.

There, in 1866, May married Jim Reed, a former Confederate guerrilla. They had two children. May's younger brother, Ed Shirley, became a horse thief and was killed in Texas in 1868. Her husband took part in several robberies and was killed while resisting arrest in 1874. A few years later, May took up with Bruce Younger, a gambler, horse thief, and relative of Cole Younger. In 1880, she married Sam Starr, a Cherokee Indian thief, and settled in a cabin near the Canadian River west of Briartown in what is now Oklahoma. By then known as "Belle Starr," she was convicted, along with her husband, of stealing a neighbor's horse in 1883 and was sentenced to nine months in federal prison. In 1886, she was accused of horse theft and robbery but was acquitted of both charges. A few months later, Sam Starr was killed in a gunfight with an old enemy. Belle's final lover was Jim July, another Cherokee horse thief, fifteen years her junior. In 1889, she was killed during an ambush by a neighbor, Edgar Watson, a fugitive murderer from Florida.

Belle Starr often wore a six-shooter and seemed to revel in her local notoriety. She loved badmen and disliked women. She once said, "I had been estranged from the society of women, whom I thoroughly detest . . . I thought I would find it irksome to live in their midst." Her historical significance lies mainly in the enormous number of legends that have grown up around her name.

—*John Boessenecker*

SEE ALSO: Younger Brothers

SUGGESTED READING:

Shirley, Glenn. *Belle Starr and Her Times*. Norman, Okla., 1982.

STARR, HENRY

One-quarter Cherokee Indian, Henry Starr (1873–1921) was one of the West's most prolific bank robbers. Born near Fort Gibson, Indian Territory, he was related by marriage to Belle Starr. By the age of nineteen, he was the leader of a bandit gang, whose members robbed banks in Caney, Kansas, and Bentonville, Arkansas, and held up a train at Pryor Creek in the Indian Territory. He murdered a deputy U.S. marshal,

Henry Starr, just after being shot by Paul Curry at Stroud, Oklahoma, March 27, 1915. *Courtesy Western History Collections, University of Oklahoma Library.*

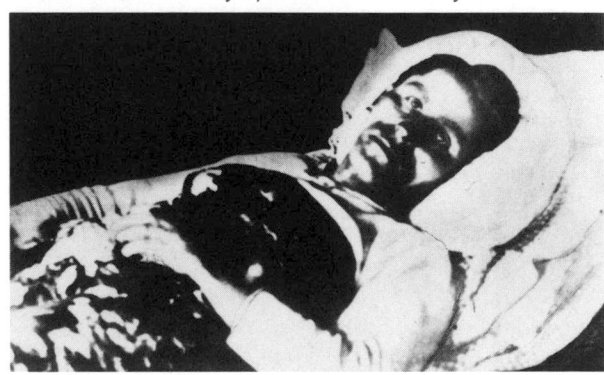

Floyd Wilson, who had attempted to arrest him. Captured and tried before Judge ISAAC CHARLES PARKER, Starr was twice sentenced to death. He successfully appealed and was finally sent to prison. Pardoned in 1903, he took up his old ways and was imprisoned in 1909 for robbing a bank in Colorado. Starr was paroled in 1913 but was then suspected of robbing a dozen more banks in Oklahoma. In 1915, he was shot while leading a double bank robbery at Stroud. Paroled after serving only four years, he produced a silent film, *A Debtor to the Law*. He was killed while robbing a bank in Harrison, Arkansas.

—*John Boessenecker*

SUGGESTED READING:

Shirley, Glenn. *Henry Starr: Last of the Real Badmen*. New York, 1965.

STEELE, SAMUEL BENFIELD

Commander of the NORTH WEST MOUNTED POLICE during the Yukon Gold Rush, Samuel Benfield Steele (1849–1919) helped develop the "Mounties" into a world-renown force.

Born in the province of Ontario, Steele joined the military at the age of seventeen, enlisting first in the local militia and then in the Ontario Rifles. While he was with this outfit, he served in the Red River Campaign of 1870 to 1871 against native Canadian tribes. In 1873, he was the first to enlist in the Royal Canadian Artillery, the first unit of the permanent Canadian Army. After serving as commander of Battery A in the RCA, Steele was named sergeant major of the newly formed North West Mounted Police.

Steele set out to mold the Mounties into a strong and efficient unit. During his first two years in command, he and his troops traveled almost two thousand miles, set up remote outposts, dealt with Indians, and mediated disputes between settlers and trappers. The Mounted Police enjoyed reasonably good relations with the native peoples of Canada and succeeded in maintaining law and order on the Canadian frontier.

In 1885, Steele was promoted to superintendent and commanded his own troops during the Northwest Rebellion that year. He was soon promoted to the rank of major. With the discovery of gold in the Yukon region in 1897, the federal government in Ottawa grew concerned about the kind of lawlessness and vigilantism that had characterized the mining towns of British Columbia and California. The government moved to establish authority, and the Mounties were quickly assigned to the region. Steele set up a governing struc-

ture that used the Mounted Police not only for enforcing law and order, but also as postal workers, tax collectors, and experts in Indians relations. Most visible, however, was the record Steele's men compiled for solving crimes. The Mounties could claim with some justification that "they always got their man."

—*Alan Axelrod*

STEFFENS, JOSEPH LINCOLN

Muckraking author Joseph Lincoln Steffens (1866–1936) was born in San Francisco, the son of an oil and paint dealer whose fortunes grew with the state. In 1887, the family moved into a house that would, in 1903, be sold to the state as the governor's mansion. Lincoln Steffens attended the University of California and was awarded a Ph.D. in 1889. He then went to Europe to study psychology with Wilhelm Wundt in Leipzig and with Jean-Martin Charcot in Paris.

Steffens returned to the United States and settled in New York City, where he worked as a newspaperman for nine years. In 1901, he became managing editor of *McClure's Magazine* but continued to work as a reporter and to focus on government issues and government corruption. In 1906, he moved on to the *American Magazine* and, two years later, became a free-lance writer and lecturer. His articles were published in *The Shame of the Cities* (1904), *The Struggle for Self Government* (1906), and *Upbuilders* (1909). His work had a sociological character that gave it the quality of a case study. Throughout his career, he allied himself to various reform movements.

While spending much of his professional life in the East, he always regarded himself as a Californian and a Westerner and, when the opportunity arose, wrote on Western subjects. He described himself as a central figure in the trial of James B. and John J. McNamara for bombing the *Los Angeles Times* building in 1910 and the trial of Clarence Darrow, the McNamara's attorney, for attempting to bribe a juror. Steffens also wrote a series of articles between 1906 and 1908 on such leaders as Judge BENJAMIN BARR LINDSEY, Rudolph Spreckels, and WILLIAM SIMON U'REN.

By 1914, his interest had turned to the international arena, and he traveled to Mexico, Europe, and Russia. He returned to the United States in 1927 and settled in Carmel, California, where he became an elder statesman in leftist literary circles. His *Autobiography,* published in 1931, brought him renewed acclaim, particularly among the left.

—*Patrick H. Butler, III*

STEGNER, WALLACE

Born in Lake Mills, Iowa, Wallace Stegner (1909–1993) was a prolific writer of popular histories of the American West and of novels set in the region. Stegner attended the University of Utah and the University of Iowa, from which he received a Ph.D. in English in 1935. From 1933 to 1945, he taught in various universities. He was appointed professor of English at Stanford University in 1945.

His first major book was a history of the Mormon experience entitled *Mormon Country* (1942). Like his subsequent historical nonfiction, *Mormon Country* focused on the "presentness" of the past by humanizing the figures and personalities portrayed. Other major works of nonfiction include *Beyond the Hundredth Meridian: John Wesley Powell and the Second Opening of the West* (1954), *The Gathering of Zion: The Story of the Mormon Trail* (1964), and *The Sound of Mountain Water* (1969).

Stegner is even better known for his fiction, the best known of which is *The Big Rock Candy Mountain* (1943), a generously proportioned account of a Norwegian family's struggle to create a home in the West during the early 1900s. The relatively late date of the novel's action contributes to the poignancy of the hero's story; Bo Mason is a pioneer born out of his time. Stegner's *The Preacher and the Slave* (1950), fictionalizes the life of legendary labor leader Joe Hill, and *Angle of Repose* (1971) imaginatively focuses on the life of Western novelist Mary Hallock Foote. For this novel, Stegner received the Pulitzer Prize. In 1977, he won the National Book Award for *The Spectator Bird* (1976), and his substantially autobiographical novel *Crossing to Safety* (1987) was warmly received.
—*Alan Axelrod*

Suggested reading:

Robinson, Forrest G., and Margaret G. Robinson. *Wallace Stegner*. Boston, 1977.

STEREOTYPES

STEREOTYPES IN POPULAR WESTERNS

Since the early years of the film industry, stereotypes, both male and female, have shaped the development of the western movie. Beginning with *The Great Train Robbery* in 1903, westerns have provided excitement and satisfaction based on clearly identifiable themes such as the triumph of good over evil, the coming of civilization, and the consequent closing of the frontier, all permeated with the image of the lone, laconic cowboy. As John Cawelti noted in *The Six-Gun Mystique,* the formula western that resulted centered around "an epic moment" of confrontation between the pioneer and the wilderness. The hero, who was squared off against nature and savages, represented civilization as did the homestead, ranch, and town. The heroine was often a spirited rancher's daughter or a refined Easterner who represented the moral fiber of the community as well as its susceptibility to danger. The final union of the hero and heroine in many westerns meant that the spiritual strength and physical durability of American society would continue. After World War II, however, westerns began to move away from this traditional form by exploring more complex, psychosocial themes. The John Wayne–style hero was joined by Clint Eastwood's brooding antihero as westerns attempted to reflect contemporary, and darker, issues.

Women have always played important roles in westerns, but the male hero has dominated the genre. Female roles reflected two basic stereotypes: the good woman-civilizer and the bad woman-prostitute. The rancher's wife, the army officer's lady, and the pioneer mother, as nurturers and civilizers, all served to soften the savagery of the West. Variations of the "bad woman" included the whore with a heart of gold, the bad woman turned good (usually through the love of a good man), the somewhat tarnished saloon singer, and the common prostitute. As the western has evolved over time, however, women have not enjoyed the breadth of character development granted the male hero.

Early westerns were shaped by the popularity of dime novels, Wild West shows, and the works of James Fenimore Cooper and Owen Wister. Wister's novel *The Virginian,* with its manly hero, his dramatic conflict with the villain, and his pursuit and winning of the heroine Molly Wood, fixed the image of the cowboy West in the popular imagination. During the silent-film era, roles for women were well defined and limited. In this period (1910 to 1930), westerns were often grand, sweeping spectacles that depicted the taming of the West through gunfights, cattle stampedes, Indian attacks, cavalry charges, gold and silver rushes, and innumerable saloon fights. These grand westerns used Victorian ideas that divided womanhood into either-or categories: good women or bad women.

Lillian Gish and Mae Marsh were two actresses who personified the Victorian-inspired heroine. In *The Battle of Elderbrush Gulch* (1913), the actresses played two young Eastern women who came to live in the West, encountered Indians on the warpath, and were rescued when the hero arrived with the cavalry. Such sexless and saintly images, however, were soon out of step with society with the coming the lively Jazz Age in the 1920s.

Although the addition of sound to film greatly enhanced the appeal of movies among the general public, women's voices (literally as well as figuratively) were not heard in dramatically different ways in the western. Variations on the traditional stereotypes continued, along with the addition of sex and comedy in the 1930s. In *Destry Rides Again* (1939), Marlene Dietrich played Frenchy, a saloon singer who managed to charm the hero (James Stewart) but later died in his arms. Mae West used her special brand of sexuality and humor to "get her man" (W. C. Fields) in *My Little Chickadee* in 1940 but was forced by the newly established Legion of Decency (known as the "Hayes Code") to soften the innuendoes and eliminate outright suggestive material.

Westerns, more than other genres, responded to the Hayes Code by adopting a more conventional format. This response triggered the rise of the B western with its emphasis on fighting cowboys, singing cowboys, and comic sidekicks. The 1940s and 1950s marked the heyday of the singing cowboys, especially GENE AUTRY and Roy Rogers, and their female counterparts, often played by Dale Evans, Jane Withers, and Gail Davies, among others. The heroine in the B film "horse operas" was usually a passive, permanent-waved civilizer whose main function was to provide motivation for the action; it was her ranch or cattle the villains coveted.

A variation on this role was the spunky ranchwoman who rode the range, handled the herd, and kept up with the cowboys while still maintaining her femininity. Barbara Stanwyck personified that heroine perhaps more than any other actress. Usually the heroine struggled to hold on to her ranch in the face of great odds and despite the loss of a father or husband. In *Cattle Queen of Montana* (1954), Stanwyck (with the help of government agent Ronald Reagan) brought to justice a gang of cattle rustlers. But winning back the herd also gained her a husband; she was thus allowed to continue the family dynasty according to prevailing cultural values.

Films made in the 1930s and 1940s frequently highlighted strong female roles and marked a high point for "women's films." Joan Crawford, Katherine Hepburn, Betty Davis, and Barbara Stanwyck all played forceful, dominant heroines in a period when women were central to family life and the work place. Yet, while women on the homefront were taking on new responsibilities and seeking more fulfilling film roles, American men wanted sex symbols in bathing suits and tight sweaters. The result, for women in film, was sexual exploitation, even in westerns. *The Outlaw* (1943, released in 1946) was an especially degrading film for Jane Russell; in the movie, she was raped, abused, and regarded primarily as a sex object for "BILLY THE KID." In *Duel in the Sun* (1946), Jennifer Jones played Pearl, a passionate mixed-blood who was torn between good and evil and who died in the hero's (Gregory Peck's) arms after a shootout. Those were only two of many movies made during the 1940s that treated sexuality in an exploitative and sensational manner.

Female roles in the films of Howard Hawks and John Ford, two directors highly regarded for their westerns, rarely strayed from the civilizer–saloon-singer stereotypes. Ford's heroines tended to be strong, supporting women who exemplified goodness and virtue: Cathy Downs in *My Darling Clementine* (1946) and Shirley Temple, Joanne Dru, and Maureen O'Hara in the John Ford–John Wayne trilogy *Fort Apache* (1948), *She Wore a Yellow Ribbon* (1949), and *Rio Grande* (1950). In *Stagecoach,* the 1939 classic that marked John Wayne's rescue from B westerns, Ford provided an important variant of the prostitute stereotype: the bad woman turned good. However, it was ultimately the hero's (John Wayne's) love for her that legitimized Dallas's (Claire Trevor's) presence in the stagecoach. Howard Hawks was less interested in portraying romantic love, yet his heroines embodied a strength and independence lacking in Ford's roles for women. Angie Dickinson in *Rio Bravo* (1959) played a tough, resilient saloon-singer–gambler who allowed John T. Chance (John Wayne) to pursue her but on her terms.

Two classic westerns made in the 1950s provided important but predictable roles for women. In *Shane* (1953), Jean Arthur played the traditional, loyal wife who, although she developed feelings for the drifter Shane, remained on the homestead and kept the family intact. *High Noon* (1952) had two strong heroines—the stereotypical fair-haired civilizer and wife, Amy Kane (played by Grace Kelly) and the exotic Mexican woman of questionable virtue, Helen Ramirez (played by Katy Jurado). Helen had been the lover of sheriff Will Kane (played by Gary Cooper) and understood why Will had to face down his killer. Amy was a Quaker whose belief in nonviolence prevented her from recognizing the code of honor that drove Will to the confrontation until Helen wisely advised her to "stand by her man." Helen, however, recognized that her own future depended on taking the noon train out of Hadleyville. At the last moment, Amy put aside her personal beliefs and ran to her husband's side, and the tainted woman left town. Both films had traditional endings befitting the moral climate of the 1950s: intact families and duty prevailed.

Social changes in the 1960s and 1970s triggered on-screen changes in two ways: the exclusion of women from the scene of action and the development of a new stereotype: the strong and determined "modern" woman. Three films starring Jane Fonda demonstrated the development of more complex roles for women: *Cat Ballou* (1964), *Comes a Horseman* (1978), and *The Electric Horseman* (1979). These films depicted the heroine in situations that required strength and independence. *Heartland*, a film made in 1979 by the Montana Women's Collective and funded by a grant from the National Endowment for the Humanities, provided a heroine historically closer to reality than offered by the typical Hollywood film. Based on the letters of Elinor Pruitt Stewart, a neither young nor beautiful heroine (played by Conchata Ferrell) traveled Denver to Green River, Wyoming, to serve as housekeeper for rancher Clyde Stewart (played by Rip Torn). They soon married (romance came later), and Stewart took out a homestead claim adjacent to her husband's property. Together, they battled the forces of nature and shared the work of ranching. Although the film garnered many awards, it did not do well at the box office.

The other noticeable change in the 1960s and 1970s reflected a diminished female presence while expanding the role of the male hero. In the near-absence of women, men developed relationships with nature (*Jeremiah Johnson*, 1972) and with other men (*Two Rode Together*, 1961; *Ride the High Country*, 1962; and *Long Riders*, 1980). *Butch Cassidy and the Sundance Kid* (1969) was the story of love between two men that sometimes included Sundance's girlfriend, Etta Place (played by Katherine Ross). Violence, often directed against women, was also a theme, as in the films of Sam Peckinpah (*The Wild Bunch*, 1969) and the "spaghetti" westerns starring Clint Eastwood (*A Fistful of Dollars, For a Few Dollars More*, and *The Good, the Bad, and the Ugly*). These films suggested that the era was not empathetic to the realities of women's lives and reflected society's uncertainty with women's changing social, political, and cultural roles.

In 1974, film critic Pauline Kael pronounced the western dead, although many would mark 1980, with

its disaster *Heaven's Gate*, as the year the genre went into decline. By the end of the 1980s, however, the popularity of the western had increased, and by the mid-1990s, it appeared to be enjoying yet another of its frequent booms, due in large part to the blockbuster success of Kevin Costner's *Dances with Wolves* (1990). When Clint Eastwood's *Unforgiven* won the Academy Award for Best Picture in 1992, the western was once again riding a wave of popularity. And while Costner's sensitive treatment of Native Americans and Eastwood's softening of the hero's hard-bitten determination to kill are commendable, women are still waiting for more fully developed, complex roles that not only parallel the role of the male hero but that also reflect the realities of women's lives.

—*Sandra Schackel*

SEE ALSO: Film: The Western; Literature: Dime Novels, The Western Novel; Motion Picture Industry; Rogers, Roy, and Dale Evans

SUGGESTED READING:
Cawelti, John. *The Six-Gun Mystique*. Bowling Green, Ky., 1971.
Fenin, George N., and William K. Everson. *The Western: From Silents to the Seventies*. Rev. ed. New York, 1973.
Haskell, Molly. *From Reverence to Rape: The Treatment of Women in the Movies*. New York, 1973.
Lenihan, John. *Showdown: Confronting Modern America in the Western Film*. Urbana, Ill., 1981.
Schackel, Sandra. "The Civilizer, the Saloon Singer, and Their Modern Sister." In *Shooting Stars: Heroes and Heroines of Western Film*. Edited by Archie McDonald. Bloomington, Ind., 1987.

STEREOTYPES OF NATIVE AMERICANS

Stereotypes are often defined as generalized misconceptions about a particular group of people. Many Euro-American stereotypes of Native Americans are deeply ingrained in American culture; most project negative and inaccurate images that serve to dehumanize Native Americans. Various segments of society perpetuate stereotypes, which can be found in art, literature, music, movies, television, advertisements, and sports.

Stereotypes of Native Americans range from the "noble" to "ignoble savage." The noble savage is the exotic, friendly, and aristocratic, whereas the ignoble savage is the wild, uncivilized, lustful, drunken, unintelligent, and bloodthirsty. The pattern can be seen quite clearly by looking first at stereotypes of Native American women.

Non-Indians have viewed native women in basically two categories: the "Indian princess" (noble) and the "squaw" (ignoble). With their first contact with

Native Americans, Europeans began forming stereotypes of Native American women. Europeans traditionally depicted the land, including continents, as female, and when Europeans came into contact with North and South America, they depicted these continents as feminine, native women. To emphasize contrasts, artists represented Europe as a "refined" woman based on European standards, but they represented America as naked, unrefined, and wild. Many early drawings and paintings portrayed native women as barbaric, savage, cannibalistic, strong, dominant, at times childlike, but always exotic. By the late eighteenth century, these images of Indian women began to change. After the American Revolution, Euro-Americans sought to establish their new sovereign status. Because they did not want the United States to be represented by the "childlike" or "savage" native woman, they changed the country's image to one of a "Roman goddess." Her body was covered with flowing robes, her skin was lightened, and she became a symbol for liberty. The Statue of Liberty exemplifies the Roman goddess figure.

Stereotypical images of native women exist concurrently. The stereotype of the Indian princess is found in the legendary tale of the rescue of John Smith by Pocahontas. The story goes that, in 1607, Chief Powhatan captured John Smith, one of the founders of Jamestown, and ordered his execution. Supposedly, Pocahontas dramatically threw her body over him, pled for his life, and saved him. From the Euro-American perspective, she became the European embodiment of the "good" Indian woman who allied herself with whites, rejected her native life, converted to Christianity, and served as an example for other natives to follow.

The Indian princess, who usually befriends a white man, flourishes in many western movies. The stereotype reduces native women to a childlike and submissive, one-dimensional being. The Indian princess image has also been used in advertising, such as box labels, medicinal remedies, and food products. Companies also exploit the image of Indian princess for gift items, including china plates and dolls.

The word *squaw*, on the other hand, carries degrading images. One image is that of native women who are willing sexual partners (conquests) of white men, who regard them as exotic sex symbols. Another image is that of a beast of burden or a drudge who does all of the work, while her Indian male partner is depicted as lazy.

Native men have also been subjected to stereotypes and inaccurate depictions. Art, literature, film, and other forms of media often portray native men as savages who attacked whites, including white women. Native men also captivate non-Indian imagination as

sexual objects; they are as lustful and exotic as their squaw counterparts. Both images appear in invented situations in which white men rush to protect their white women's virtue. Yet historical examinations of captivity narratives from the period of early European contact show that most Indian men did not threaten the virtue of white women. Instead, many tribes adopted white women into their society or used them for general household duties as any other captive was used in the seventeenth and eighteenth centuries.

Another stereotype of native men is that of the "noble savage," exemplified by the character Chingachgook in James Fenimore Cooper's novel *The Last of the Mohicans* (made into feature-length films in 1936 and 1992). Like the Indian princess, the noble savage earns the right to be noble because he assists and befriends whites and is the last of his tribe (the vanishing Indian image).

Indian men, in general, have been viewed as strong and fierce warriors. The Great Plains warrior, wearing a feather headdress, dominates popular American culture. Sports teams of the twentieth century continue to perpetuate this one-dimensional portrayal as evident in "Indian" mascots and team names.

All stereotypes of Native Americans are inventions of the non-Indian mind. They do not reflect the reality of native peoples and serve to dehumanize Native Americans.

—*Annette Reed Crum*

SEE ALSO: Literature: Indian Captivity Narratives

SUGGESTED READING:

Bataille, Gretchen M., and Charles L. P. Silet, eds. *The Pretend Indians: Images of the Native Americans in the Movies*. Ames, Iowa, 1980.

Berkhofer, Robert F., Jr. *The White Man's Indian*. New York, 1978.

Green, Rayna. "The Pocahontas Perplex: The Image of Indian Women in Popular Culture." *Massachusetts Review* 16 (Autumn 1975): 678–714.

McClung Fleming, E. "The American Image as Indian Princess, 1765–1783." *Winterthur Portfolio II* (1965).

Stedman, Raymond William. *Shadows of the Indian: Stereotypes in American Culture*. Norman, Okla., 1982.

STEREOTYPES OF MEXICANS

In the nineteenth century, Anglo-American visitors to the borderlands of the Southwest—today's California, Arizona, New Mexico, and Texas—depicted the Mexican residents of the region in unflattering and stereotypical terms. They described Mexicans as lazy, ignorant, bigoted, superstitious, cheating, thieving, cruel, and sinister and dismissed them as half-breeds and "greasers." Mexican women, they told one another, were temptresses— voluptuous, loose, immoral, "hot-blooded" señoritas. In the opinion of the Americans, depraved Mexicans were incapable of developing republican institutions and were even more unlikely to achieve material progress. Even the positive images some visitors and writers had of the Mexicans—that they were generous, hospitable, and sociable—were fed and formed by stereotypes: the Mexicans like to play games, hold parties, gamble, take siestas, dance fandagos, and, in general, live for the present, not the future. Mexicans, of course, had their own stereotypes about Yankees that were no more or less true, and there were, indeed, some customs, activities, and individual personalities to which the Anglo-American writers of such opinion could point for support of their unflattering portraits. But the truth is that the stereotypes the Anglo-Americans perpetrated had existed, in some measure, among English-speaking people before there was ever extensive contacts between Anglos and Mexicans. These stereotypes functioned to push the political agenda of the United States in the region during the mid-nineteenth century. Fed by American popular culture—particularly Hollywood movies—many of the stereotypes persist to the present day.

Many historians have pointed to the fact that since the seventeenth century, Americans quite regularly projected certain traits—particularly the potential for violence and a kind of blood lust—that they, as a people bent on expansion at the expense of others, sometimes exhibited. Thus, the Indians, the French in the Ohio Valley, the Spanish, and the Mexicans were cruel and barbarous and determined to exterminate American settlers encroaching on what they considered their lands. Southwestern scholar David J. Weber has suggested that the root of many stereotypes of Mexicans lay in the BLACK LEGEND that English colonists inherited from the British, who were competing with the Spanish for a worldwide empire. English-speaking Protestants, during the colonial period, believed that the Catholic Spanish government, which had launched the Inquisition and destroyed and looted the great Aztec and Inca civilizations of Central and South America, was authoritarian, corrupt, and decadent and that the Spanish themselves were bigoted, cruel, greedy, tyrannical, fanatical, treacherous, and, above all, lazy. The conquistadors, says Weber, were viewed as the "apotheosis of evil," and as evidence, English ideologues had the self-critical writings of the Spanish themselves, especially of the religious orders, who were, in some ways, colonializing competitors with the conquistadors. To recognize that English colonials used anti-Spanish sentiment to justify their own conquests does not diminish the horrors of what the Spanish actually did in the New World, but for the English, the Spanish were adventurers after treasure and easy living off the backs of enslaved Indians, not hard-working families looking for better homes as the English imagined themselves to be. Another source of American stereotypes for Mexicans, according to Weber, Arnoldo de Leon, and a number of others, was the racial mixture of the Mexican population. Color-conscious Anglo-Americans, for whom the presence of African slaves was fast becoming a determining factor in the history of their own country, nearly unanimously, says Weber, commented upon the dark skin of the "swarthy" Mexican mestizos who, they argued, inherited the worst qualities of both the Spaniards and the Indians.

Clapping eyes upon beautiful California, RICHARD HENRY DANA declared that in the hands of an enterprising people it could become a marvelous country, and that is the key: as Indian savagery justified taking native lands in order to bring Indians the benefits of civilization and as stupidity, animal lust, and beastliness justified enslaving black people for the benefit of a higher race, so Mexican laziness, decadence, cruelty, and indifference to progress justified taking the American Southwest, more than half of which was then part of the Republic of Mexico, in order for an enterprising and ambitious people to make good use of it. Stereotypes are almost always functional in this way for the dominant group. They offer as well a means to distinguish the "haves" from the "have nots," "us" from "them." Thus, the lustiness of Latinas helped ease the conscience of "white" men in the Mexican borderlands who took lovers and sometimes wives from an "inferior" stock, the way the much touted lasciviousness of Indian women justified the "country wives" of fur trappers and frontiersmen, and the animality of "Negresses" justified the clandestine visits of white slave owners to the slave quarters at night. Stereotypes, then, not only demonized Mexicans as enemies, which frequently occurs in times of war or social conflict, they also dehumanized them, and—as with African Americans in the post-Reconstruction South—"an astonishing number of Mexicans," to quote de Leon, "in the nineteenth century fell victim to lynch law and cold-blooded deaths at the hands of whites who regarded the killing of Mexicans as inconsequential."

The early nineteenth century, however, had no monopoly on the stereotyping of Mexicans and Mexican Americans. Especially as the American West became highly industrialized after the Civil War, American businessmen in the Southwest began to look to Mexico and the region's Mexican American population as a source of cheap labor, and they perpetuated the stereotype of the Mexican "peon" to justify the low wages and poor treatment of unskilled and migrant laborers.

With the outbreak of the Mexican Revolution of 1910, Mexican immigration into the United States reached historic proportions. In the 1920s, an alarmed middle class developed a highly nativist immigration policy, which also played on stereotypes of Mexicans, to deny the immigrants citizen status. Thus, while American businesses sought to employ "the Mexican" because "[he] is probably the most docile and gullible of all the immigrant arrivals that the United States has ever seen," they also argued that the wages of Mexican workers must be kept low because, like all "peons" they lived largely for the moment, took time off freely, had no dread of unemployment, and worked efficiently only when supervised. At the same time, politicians and restrictionists moved to keep these workers from immigrating permanently because they were not white, but mestizo, or of mixed Indian and Spanish ancestry and, therefore, could not be "assimilated" into mainstream America.

Up to and including 1920, the U.S. Census Bureau had always enumerated Mexican Americans and Mexican immigrants as part of the white population, making their situation analogous the Euro-Americans and to European immigrant groups. But as thousands of Mexican workers entered the United States in the 1920s, Albert Johnson, the powerful chairman of the House Immigration and Naturalization Committee, needing better statistics to make the case for restriction, persuaded Secretary of Commerce Robert P. Lamont to have his census director reclassify Mexicans in a separate racial category for the 1930 census. The government, says Mark Reisler, merely accepted the public's de facto perception of Mexicans, making Spanish-speaking people a "people of color" clearly subordinate, as were all people of color in the nation's hierarchy of races. In Texas and the Southwest, Anglos had long called those descended from the original European settlers of the region "Mexicans," not "Americans," despite the fact that the United States had granted many of their ancestors citizenship under the treaties following the UNITED STATES–MEXICAN WAR. Now, the bureaucratic term *Hispanic* referred to all Spanish-speaking peoples descended from Spain's New World conquerors. Their "Indian" origin was used to brand all Mexicans and Mexican American workers as peons, servile individuals fit to work cheaply in agriculture and construction, but the opposite of the rugged, self-reliant yeomen who had made the country prosperous and progressive. The Hispanic immigrant from the south, never the potential citizen, always the peon laborer, is a racial stereotype that still plagues the Southwest and America's immigration-policy apparatus.

Hispanic and *peon* were not the only stereotypes Mexican Americans continued to face in the twentieth century. Hollywood became enamored of the "hot-blooded" Latina and the half-crazed, senselessly cruel "bandito," an image that helped justify the United States's intervention in the Mexican Revolution in the first decade of the century. Even the large, extended families that were supposedly a standard fixture of Mexican and Mexican American culture became a kind of negative stereotype, since such families obviously prevented the effective assimilation of Hispanics into the mainstream. But as Richard Griswold del Castillo has pointed out, the notion is a false one, based on a faded historical reality, and the Hispanic family can be as fragmented, dysfunctional, or nuclear as any other. In the 1960s, many Mexican Americans launched a crusade against the continuing use of stereotypes to debase, dehumanize, and control their lives. But despite real gains made by the Chicano movement, Hispanic stereotypes continued to be a feature of American culture in the late twentieth century as anyone who watched television or attended movie theaters to see films about youth gangs and drug dealers could vouch for themselves. And such stereotypes continued to serve functional political purposes as was clear in the anti-immigrant referendums in California, the various get-tough policies of the U.S. border patrols, and the moves to slash social services for the poor, often based on notions of lazy, unambitious, violence-prone Mexicans with large and extended families they wished to sneak into the country to take advantage of the generous social benefits, medical-care programs, and wages available to "true Americans."

— *Charles Phillips*

SUGGESTED READING:

de Leon, Arnoldo. *They Call Them Greasers: Anglo Attitudes toward Mexicans in Texas, 1821–1900.* Austin, Tex., 1983.

Griswold del Castillo, Richard. *La Familia: Chicano Families in the Urban Southwest, 1848 to the Present.* Notre Dame, Ind., 1984.

Reisler, Mark. *By the Sweat of Their Brow: Mexican Immigrant Labor in the United States, 1900–1940.* Westport, Conn., 1976.

Weber, David J., ed. *New Spain's Far Northern Frontier: Essays on Spain in the American West, 1540–1821.* Albuquerque, N. Mex., 1979.

STEREOTYPES OF MORMONS

While MORMONS have always considered themselves sincere, honest, truth-seeking, and persecuted, outsiders have seen them and their church, the CHURCH OF JESUS CHRIST OF LATTER-DAY SAINTS, very differently. Some accounts by outsiders have been moderately complimentary, but from the church's origins in 1830, the standard picture was negative. Church founder and prophet JOSEPH SMITH, JR., and other leaders were panned as charlatans and demagogues, while their followers were described as deluded dupes. The religion itself was portrayed as patent nonsense, a disgrace to modern civilization, possible only because of the combination of the cleverness of the leaders and the gullibility of the uneducated.

In 1852, with the public announcement of the practice of polygamy, by which men took more than one wife at a time, those unfriendly to the Mormons had the ideal headline. Although only a minority of the Mormons practiced polygamy, it became the central trait by which they were identified. Attached to it in the public mind was a cluster of related negative images: the tyrannous, cruel husband; the lecherous, manipulative missionary; greedy, dictatorial leaders who profited from the system; oppressed women; and neglected children who were physically and mentally handicapped. Travel accounts, newspaper articles, and scores of cartoons purveyed these and other negative stereotypes of the Mormons. Among the novels including Mormons as titillating subjects were Metta Victoria Fuller's *Mormon Wives: A Narrative of Facts Stranger than Fiction* (1856) and MAX BRAND's *Bessie Baine: or, The Mormon's Victim: A Tale of Utah* (1876). After the official termination of polygamy in 1890, the negative stereotyping continued in cartoons, magazine articles, and such early movies as *Trapped by the Mormons* (1922).

In the twentieth century, especially since about 1930, the public image of the church as measured by content analysis of articles in periodicals has become far more positive. The church's public-affairs department has consciously promoted such positive aspects as the health benefits of the Mormon life style. The Tabernacle Choir has created a favorable impression among those who view it in concert or on television. As with blacks and Jews and others, however, negative stereotypes persist and are deliberately promoted by hate groups.

—*Davis Bitton*

SEE ALSO: Polygamy: Polygamy among Mormons

SUGGESTED READING:

Arrington, Leonard J., and Jon Haupt. "Intolerable Zion: The Image of Mormonism in Nineteenth Century American Literature." *Western Humanities Review* 22 (1968): 243–260.

Bunker, Gary L., and Davis Bitton. *The Mormon Graphic Image, 1834–1914.* Salt Lake City, 1983.

Nelson, Richard Alan. "From Antagonism to Acceptance: Mormons and the Silver Screen." *Dialogue: A Journal of Mormon Thought* 10 (1977): 58–69.

STEREOTYPES OF ASIANS

Negative and positive stereotypes have a serious impact on the socio-economic, cultural, and political lives of Asians in the United States and throughout the world. Stereotypes are used broadly to characterize Asian people and their communities in racial and cultural terms. Such generalizations often ignore, demean, and distort the rich culture and history of Asian individuals and communities.

In the 1800s, Asians were depicted as vermin, parasites, or invading hordes overtaking the shores of Anglo-America. Asian women were depicted as slaves and prostitutes, and Asian men as decadent and immoral, skulking in dark Chinatown alleys, frequenting brothels, smoking opium and gambling, and salivating lasciviously over white women. Fears were raised concerning the safety of white women.

For more than sixty-five years, the American entertainment media produced a range of inaccurate and limited portrayals of Asians—stereotypes that have become the staples of the popular American imagination. Asians are frequently represented as villains who are vicious, inscrutable, and sneaky.

On the other hand, there are the supposedly positive stereotypes of Asian people as obedient domestics, wise detectives, or deferential, nonthreatening sidekicks to the major Anglo male characters. Many cartoons, books, and films depict Asians as "natural" house boys, cooks, gardeners, and restaurant and laundry workers. However, because of institutional and attitudinal racism, Asians were often forced to find work in occupations such as laundry or domestic work—occupations that whites found undesirable. The Charlie Chan character, created by the writer Earl Derr Biggers, was portrayed in films as a wise, benevolent super-detective, who spoke in silly fortune-cookie aphorisms.

Asian women suffer from a variety of racist and sexist stereotypes in film and literature. Renee Tajima describes two basic types of female stereotypes: "the Lotus Blossom Baby (a.k.a. China Doll, Geisha Girl, shy Polynesian beauty) and the Dragon Lady." Anna May Wong, one of the few Asian actresses featured in early Hollywood films often played dragon-lady types—in the film *The Thief of Baghdad* (1924), for example. In *The World of Suzie Wong* (1960), Nancy Kwan portrayed a prostitute, bar girl, and mistress, who is in love with an Anglo-American. In *Flower Drum Song* (1961), Kwan played the manipulative femme fatale, while Miyoshi Umeki played the passive, subservient lotus-blossom–type character. That these stereotypes affect the daily lives of Asian women in America and abroad is evidenced by the thriving sex tourism and mail-order bride industries in Thailand, Korea, Hong Kong, the Philippines, and elsewhere. Asian women are perceived as docile, obedient, and exotic women, whose main purpose in life is to serve men's needs.

The image of Asian Americans as a "model minority" or "super minority" is another detrimental stereotype. Although it is true that Asian Americans have achieved a high level of educational attainment as well as financial and occupational success, the model-minority stereotype does not account for the experiences of all Asian American groups. There are serious consequences for Asian American individuals and for different racial or ethnic communities who believe the myth that Asian Americans are all natural achievers and success stories. The stereotype ignores the very real socio-economic problems confronted by many segments of the Asian American population, especially recent immigrants and refugees. Asian American students suffer greatly from personal and communal pressures to live up to the image of "super-achievers." At the same time, there are the backlash stereotypes of Asian Americans as computer nerds, as asocial math or science whizzes, or as invading hordes in academia—aliens who must be controlled by quota systems.

In broader terms, the model minority stereotype creates an environment of hostility, resentment, and violence against Asian Americans, who are held up as an example for other oppressed minorities to emulate. Such superficial comparisons fail to consider diverse socio economic and historical realities. In addition, the racist reactions of some Americans over the fluctuating political and economic relations between the United States and Asia have resulted in tragic incidents for Asian Americans, such as the internment of Japanese Americans during World War II. In another example, Vincent Chin, a young Chinese American, was brutally beaten to death in Detroit in 1982 by white men angry about the impact of the Japanese car industry on the U.S. economy.

—*Wendy Ho*

SEE ALSO: Chinese Americans; Japanese Americans

SUGGESTED READING:

Chan, Sucheng. *Asian Americans: An Interpretive History.* Twayne's Immigrant Heritage of America Series. Boston, Mass., 1991.

Daniels, Roger. *Asian America: Chinese and Japanese in the United States Since 1850.* Seattle, Wash., 1988.

Kim, Elaine. *Asian American Literature: An Introduction to the Writings and Their Social Context.* Philadelphia, 1982.

Tajima, Renee. "Lotus Blossoms Don't Bleed: Images of Asian Women." In *Making Waves: An Anthology of Writings by and about Asian American Women.* Edited by Diane Yen-Mei Wong and Asian Women United of California. Boston, 1989.

Takaki, Ronald. *Strangers from a Different Shore: A History of Asian Americans.* Boston, 1989.

STETSON, JOHN BATTERSON

Hat manufacturer John Batterson Stetson (1830–1906) was born in Orange, New Jersey, the son of a hatter. He pursued the trade of his father until he was afflicted with tuberculosis. Hoping to regain his health in the West, he moved to Saint Joseph, Missouri, in the late 1850s and found work in a brickyard. He eventually became part owner of the enterprise before a flood washed away his investment.

Rejected for Civil War service on account of his health, Stetson joined a party of prospectors bound for the gold fields of Colorado. During the trip, he fashioned a crude, high-crowned, broad-brimmed felt hat from beaver and rabbit fur. An eager teamster bought the protective headgear for five dollars.

Stetson returned to Philadelphia in 1865 and re-entered the hat trade. Discouraged with local prospects, he began replicating a refined version of the hat he had made in Colorado and sought a market for it in the Southwest.

Merchants eagerly embraced Stetson's new creation, christened "Boss of the Plains," and the flood of orders that followed forced him to abandon his tiny one-man shop for an expansive, modern factory erected in the suburbs of Philadelphia. In time, as many as ten thousand retailers handled Stetson's stylish yet durable creations, affectionately known in Western ranch country, as "John B.'s"

His factory was turning out two million hats at the time of his death at the age of seventy-six. Stetson used

The hat made and made famous by John B. Stetson. *Courtesy National Cowboy Hall of Fame and Western Heritage Center.*

part of his substantial fortune to endow DeLand Academy in Florida, renamed Stetson University, and served as president of its Board of Trustees.

—*B. Byron Price*

SUGGESTED READING:
Hubbard, Elbert. *John B. Stetson.* East Aurora, N.Y., 1912.
Nordyke, Lewis. "Boss of the Plains: The Story behind the 'Stetson.'" In *The Cowboy Reader.* Edited by Lon Tinkle and Allen Maxwell. New York, 1959.
"Stetson: Hat of the West." *Persimmon Hill* 8 (Winter 1979): 42–51.

STETSON HAT

SEE: Cowboy Outfits

STEUNENBERG, FRANK

Elected by the largest margin in Idaho gubernatorial history, Frank Steunenberg (1861–1905) served from 1893 to 1901. A native of Keokuk, Iowa, he moved to Idaho as a newspaperman only ten years before becoming the state's second governor. He attended Iowa State College, worked for years as a newspaper writer, and later bought the *Caldwell Tribune.*

Steunenberg's tenure as governor was characterized by labor violence and agriculture disputes. The 1890s saw massive labor unrest, and the mining districts of northern Idaho exploded continuously. Steunenberg pressed for convictions of labor organizers as well as for the conviction of J. L. Davis, a notorious hired gun for cattle ranchers. Harry Orchard, a militant union man, assassinated Steunenberg on December 30, 1905, at his Caldwell home.

—*F. Ross Peterson*

SUGGESTED READING:
Beal, Merrill D., and Merle W. Wells. *History of Idaho.* 3 vols. New York, 1959.
Wells, Merle. "Frank Steunenberg." In *Idaho's Governors.* Edited by Robert C. Sims and Hope A. Benedict. Boise, Idaho, 1992.

STEVENSON, MATILDA COXE

Ethnologist Matilda Coxe Stevenson (1850–1915) studied and wrote about the Zuni, Sia, and Hopi tribes of the Southwest. Born in Texas, Stevenson moved with her family to Washington, D.C., and attended Miss Anable's School in Philadelphia. In 1872, she married James Stevenson, a geologist with the U.S. Geological Survey. When the Bureau of Ethnology was founded, James Stevenson was transferred to the department to report on archaeological remains and specimens in the U.S. territories.

In 1879, Matilda Stevenson and her husband, along with FRANK HAMILTON CUSHING and J. K. Hillers, traveled to New Mexico on an anthropological expedition. Spending six months in the region, she instructed Zuni women in sanitation and selected as her first student a Zuni man-woman named We-wha, who so easily learned her regime of cleanliness that he became launderer for the expedition. Stevenson, meanwhile, discovered her own burning interest in anthropology. Three years later, she began working with the Hopis in Arizona, and over the next seven years, she conducted extensive field work among the two tribes. Earning the respect of the Zunis, she was, for a while, able to move freely among the tribe and gained access to secret religious rituals and ceremonies. Over the years, however, as some Native Americans grew wary of white culture, Stevenson was not as free to move among them as she had been in the early days of her studies.

Stevenson served as the first president of the Women's Anthropological Society, an organization founded in 1885. During the last years of her life, she lived near San Ildefonso, New Mexico, and continued her research, despite her failing health due to increased used of alcohol. She published extensively on the topic of Native Americans in the Southwest, notably *The Sia* (1894) and *The Zuni Indians* (1904). Her coverage of these tribes included legends, games, ethnobotany, and religion. She urged other anthropologists to undertake holistic studies of the Pueblo tribes before white culture dissipated their individuality. Her works remain standard references for scholars of the Southwest tribes.

—*Candace Floyd*

SUGGESTED READING:
Lurie, Nancy O. "Women in Early American Anthropology." In *Pioneers of American Anthropology.* Edited by June Helm. Seattle, Wash., 1966.

STEWART, WILLIAM M.

A United States senator from Nevada and staunch supporter of silver miners, William M. Stewart (1827–1909) was born in Galen, New York. In 1850, he moved to California, where he mined for gold, studied law, and entered politics. He served as district attorney in 1853 and as acting attorney general in 1854. In 1859, he moved to Nevada, where the huge deposits of gold and silver in the COMSTOCK LODE were creating excitement. Serving in the territorial legislature and the constitutional convention of 1863, he was elected U.S. senator on the Republican ticket in 1864. In the Senate, he constantly promoted the coinage of silver dollars by the U.S. government. After serving two terms, he moved to California to practice law. In 1886, he returned to Nevada and was again elected to the Senate, with the help of COLLIS P. HUNTINGTON of the Southern Pacific Railroad and the backing of the Silver League. Returning to the Republican party in 1900, he retired from the Senate in 1906 having served a total of five terms.

—*Candace Floyd*

SUGGESTED READING:
Glass, Mary Ellen. *Silver and Politics in Nevada, 1892–1902.* Reno, Nev., 1969.

STILLMAN, CHARLES

Merchant and founder of Brownsville, Texas, Charles Stillman (1810–18??) was born in Wethersfield, Connecticut, the son of Francis and Harriett Stillman. At the age of sixteen, he embarked on the ship *Albion* with his father for Matamoros, Mexico. In 1832, after learning some Spanish and mastering the complexities of dealing with the Mexican government, he opened a store in Matamoros, where he offered a variety of items to approximately three hundred foreign residents.

After the death of his father in 1838, Stillman continued his business with several different partners. He remained in Matamoros during the TEXAS REVOLUTION, during the years of the Republic of Texas, and during the UNITED STATES–MEXICAN WAR. In 1849, however, he moved to Texas. At the beginning of the United States's war with Mexico, General ZACHARY TAYLOR had erected a military post opposite Matamoros on the Texas side of the Rio Grande. The fort had been named Fort Texas and later was renamed Fort Brown in honor of Major Jacob Brown who had been killed in action nearby. At the end of the war, Stillman—or Don Carlos, as the Mexicans called him—recognized the commercial potential of the fort, negotiated the purchase of 4,676 acres of land next to the installation, and renamed the resulting town site Brownsville.

On August 17, 1849, Stillman married Elizabeth Pamela Goodrich, a Virginian, whom he had met during a visit to Wethersfield. He and his wife had six children.

—*Fred L. Koestler*

STOCK RAISING HOMESTEAD ACT OF 1916

The Stock Raising Homestead Act, also known as the Grazing Homestead Act, provided for homesteads of 640 acres of nonirrigable lands that contained no marketable timber and were valuable primarily for grazing and the production of forage crops. Mineral and coal rights were reserved by the government, as were watering places and related access ways. Improvements of $1.25 per acre were required for patent. Since eligible lands consisted of those on which 640 acres were "reasonably required" to support a family, the act was clearly restricted in its geographical applicability to the Rocky Mountain and Great Basin regions.

Introduced by Representative Harvey B. Fergusson of New Mexico and guided through Congress by Representative Edward T. Taylor of Colorado, the measure was a logical response to the growing back-to-the-land sentiment within the United States. It also represented the principle of use and commercial development of the public domain championed by THEODORE ROOSEVELT and Woodrow Wilson. The latter viewed the bill as conservation-oriented and signed it into law in the fall of 1916.

The West generally supported the bill but by no means unanimously. Many Westerners felt the only way to restore deteriorating range lands was through a leasing arrangement as proposed in an alternate bill sponsored by Representative William Kent of California. By the early 1930s, when the shortcomings of the Stock Raising Homestead Act had become apparent, the president and Congress initiated a radical change in land policy—away from disposal and toward leasing. The Stock Raising Homestead Act became, therefore, the nation's last general homestead act.

—*Stanford J. Layton*

SUGGESTED READING:
Gates, Paul W. *History of Public Land Law Development.* Washington, D.C., 1968.
Peffer, E. Louise. *The Closing of the Public Domain: Disposal and Reservation Policies, 1900–50.* Stanford, Calif., 1951.

STOCKTON, ROBERT F.

A career naval officer, Robert F. Stockton (1795–1866) gained national prominence in the American conquest of California from 1846 to 1847.

A descendant of a prominent New Jersey family, Stockton was born in Princeton. He attended Princeton

University, and in 1811, he was appointed midshipman. He gained recognition for bravery during the War of 1812. During the 1830s, he took an extended leave and became involved in business enterprises, such as the Delaware and Raritan Canal Company and the Camden and Amboy Railroad. New Jersey politics also interested him, and he eventually became a close associate of ANDREW JACKSON.

Stockton returned to active naval duty in 1838 with the rank of captain. In October 1845, as relations deteriorated between the United States and Mexico, he was ordered to reinforce the American Pacific Squadron. When he reached Monterey, California, in July 1846, he discovered that fighting had already begun. He then assumed command of all naval and land forces on the West Coast.

By August, Stockton had organized a civil and military government, headed by himself as territorial governor. In the early weeks of the conquest, it appeared that California could be controlled with little bloodshed, but by September the Californios (native-born Californians of Hispanic descent) had retaken all the towns of southern California with the exception of San Diego, which became Stockton's base of operations. In December 1846, his land forces rescued STEPHEN WATTS KEARNY's army, which had been surrounded by Mexicans at San Pasqual. With the assistance of JOHN CHARLES FRÉMONT's Bear Flaggers, Stockton's forces began to subdue the region. Following the final surrender of the Californios in Los Angeles in January 1847, Stockton appointed Frémont to serve as governor and departed for the East. His authoritarian conduct toward Mexicans, as well as his favoring of Frémont over Kearny, brought his leadership skills into question. In 1850, he resigned from the navy.

During the next decade, Stockton played an active role in national politics. Elected as a Democrat to the U.S. Senate from New Jersey in 1851, he soon embraced the views of the American party and was regarded as a possible presidential candidate. Just before the outbreak of the Civil War in 1861, Stockton was a delegate to the unsuccessful Peace Conference.

—Gerald Thompson

SUGGESTED READING:
Bayard, Samuel J. *A Sketch of the Life of Com. Robert F. Stockton.* New York, 1856.

STOUDENMIRE, DALLAS

Famous as the man-killing city marshal of El Paso, Texas, Dallas Stoudenmire (1855–1882) was born in Aberfoil, Macon County, Alabama. He served a brief stint in the Confederate Army before moving, about 1867, to Columbus, Texas, where he killed a few men. During the late 1870s, he was a city marshal in Socorro, New Mexico.

He became the town marshal of El Paso on April 11, 1881, and three days later, he engaged in the downtown "Four Dead in Five Seconds Gunfight." Three days after that, Bill Johnson, a former city marshal, tried to assassinate Stoudenmire with a shotgun but was instead shot dead on the city street.

By then, Stoudenmire was feuding with everybody: local politicians, the press, the TEXAS RANGERS. The city council called for his resignation, and the marshal complied. He then became a United States deputy marshal.

When saloon owner James Manning killed Samuel M. Cummings, Stoudenmire's brother-in-law, the marshal swore vengeance. The Stoudenmire-Manning feud came to a close on September 18, 1882, when James and Doc Manning killed the marshal during one of the most dramatic gunfights in Western history. The Mannings were acquitted of murder, and the local Masons shipped Stoudenmire's body to Columbus, Texas, for burial. He is buried in an unmarked grave near Alleyton, Texas.

—Leon C. Metz

SEE ALSO: Gunfighters

SUGGESTED READING:
Egloff, Fred R. *El Paso Lawman: G. W. Campbell.* College Station, Tex., 1982.
Metz, Leon C. *Dallas Stoudenmire: El Paso Marshal.* Norman, Okla., 1993.

STRAUSS, LEVI

Clothier Levi Strauss (1829–1902) was born Loeb Strauss in Buttenheim, Bavaria. After his father's death, he immigrated to the United States with his mother and two sisters in 1847. He joined two brothers already in the dry-goods business in New York City and became a traveling salesman in Kentucky. In 1850, he founded Levi Strauss and Company and, three years later, joined his brother-in-law, David Stern in a dry-goods business in San Francisco. There, Strauss began supplying miners with stout canvas, duck, and denim pants produced on the East Coast and shipped West by his brothers.

In 1872, Jacob Davis, a Nevada tailor and customer of Levi Strauss and Company, announced the invention of men's work trousers with pocket seams and other weak points reinforced with copper rivets.

Strauss assisted Davis in patenting the idea on May 20, 1873, and established a factory on Fremont Street to produce the improved "waist-high overalls" and later, work shirts, hunting coats, and a variety of other garments. Meanwhile, the company continued to wholesale an assortment of other dry goods from linens to corsets.

David Stern died in 1874, and with the waning of the nineteenth century, Strauss, a lifelong bachelor, gradually retired, leaving the daily operation of his company to his four nephews, the children of his sister Fanny and David Stern. In 1890, Strauss and the Stern incorporated the company.

Praised for his fairness and integrity in business, Strauss was a charter member and treasurer of the San Francisco Board of Trade. He also served as a director of the Nevada Bank, the Liverpool, London and Globe Insurance Company, and the San Francisco Gas and Electric Company. In 1874, he became a partner in the Mission and Pacific Woolen Mills, which provided fabric to Levi Strauss and Company.

A well-known philanthropist, Strauss supported many charities and endowed twenty-eight scholarships at the University of California at Berkeley in 1897. Bequests from Strauss's $6 million estate extended this benevolence, especially to orphans.

Strauss's death in San Francisco after a brief illness was widely mourned, and many local businesses closed during the funeral.

Strauss's nephews continued to operate and expand the company, despite the devastating earthquake and fire of 1906 that destroyed its factory and headquarters. The company eventually developed into the largest manufacturer of apparel in the world with sales in the 1980s reaching more than $2.5 billion annually.

—B. Byron Price

SUGGESTED READING:
Cray, Ed. Levi's. Boston, 1978.
Josephy Alvin M., Jr. "Those Pants that Levi Gave Us." American West 22 (July-August 1985): 30–37.
Levi Strauss and Company, San Francisco, California. Everyone Knows His First Name. San Francisco, n.d.

STRUCK BY THE REE (YANKTON)

Struck by the Ree, or Padaniapapi (ca. 1804–1888), should not be confused with Padaneapapi, an Upper Yanktonai (Ihanktuwala) band chief who translated his name "Strike the Ree." Padaniapapi first appeared in records when explorers MERIWETHER LEWIS and WILLIAM CLARK met a Yankton headman with an infant son. Out of respect, Clark reportedly wrapped the infant in an American flag and predicted his rise to leadership as a man of peace.

Tribal elders do not know what name he was given in infancy and explain the assignment of Padaniapapi in several ways. One is that during a skirmish with Padani (Arikara) soldiers, one of the Rees inflicted a wound that extended from his forehead well back on his scalp. Thereafter, he covered the scar either with a lock of hair or a fur hat and preferred to be recognized as "Struck by the Ree."

From the death of War Eagle in 1851 to his own death in 1888, Struck by the Ree was the principal leader and spokesman for the Yankton tribe and was at the front line of contact with non-Indians who entered the Dakotas. With unbending integrity and dazzling oratorical skills, he was mainly responsible for making his tribe the only tribe of Sioux who never officially took up arms against non-Indians. Struck by the Ree is also remembered for raising a force of tribal scouts that kept peoples of the two races at a distance from each other until tempers cooled during the 1862 Minnesota Sioux Uprising.

A faction of the tribe condemned and sometimes persecuted Struck by the Ree for his affable relationship with white people and open compliance with federal policies. Nevertheless, he is revered by tribal members as the greatest of Yankton leaders and is recognized in records as perhaps the most influential proponent for peace in all of Sioux country. His skill at diplomacy was comparable to that of other distinguished diplomats such as SPOTTED TAIL and HOLLOW HORN BEAR of the Brulés and RED CLOUD and AMERICAN HORSE of the Oglalas.

—Herbert T. Hoover

SUGGESTED READING:
Hoover, Herbert T. The Yankton Sioux. New York, 1988.

STUART, GRANVILLE

Known as "Mr. Montana," Granville Stuart (1834–1918) was born in Clarksburg, West Virginia. As a child, he moved with his family to Illinois and then to Iowa. In 1849, his father joined the gold rush to California; in 1853, he and his brother, James, followed. The brothers—and companion Reese Anderson—left California in 1857 and settled in Montana's Deer Lodge Valley. The next year at the mouth of Gold Creek, the three young men discovered gold. During the 1860s, the Stuarts engaged in mercantile trade, with outlets in several mining camps.

Granville Stuart, 1898. *Courtesy Montana Historical Society.*

After James Stuart died in 1873, Granville Stuart pursued freighting, mining, and banking in the Montana Territory. In 1879, he became a partner with SAMUEL THOMAS HAUSER and Andrew J. Davis in an extensive open-range cattle operation in central Montana—the DHS outfit. Stuart remained resident manager of the business, later known as the Pioneer Cattle Company, until 1888.

Stuart was instrumental in organizing the Montana Stock Growers Association in 1884 and served as its first president, as well as president of the Montana Board of Stock Commissioners. In 1884, he also directed a group of vigilantes—"Stuart's Stranglers"—against rustlers in central Montana.

An active Democrat, Stuart served in the territorial legislature in 1872, 1875, 1879, and 1883. In 1883, he became president of the Council (senate) and remained important in Democratic politics into the twentieth century. In 1894, he was appointed the U.S. ambassador to Paraguay and Uruguay, a position he held until 1898.

Returning to Montana, Stuart became director of the Butte Public Library and worked diligently to document the history of the Montana Territory. In 1917, the state legislature funded some of his research and writing. The product of Stuart's last years is the pivotal two-volume work, *Forty Years on the Frontier.*

—*David A. Walter*

SEE ALSO: Montana Gold Rush

SUGGESTED READING:

Kittredge, William, and Steven M. Krauzer. "'Mr. Montana' Revised: Another Look at Granville Stuart." *Montana: The Magazine of Western History* 36:4 (Autumn 1986): 14–23.

Reece, William S. "Granville Stuart of the DHS Ranch." *Montana: The Magazine of Western History* 31:3 (Summer 1981):14–17.

Remley, David. "'To Struggle against an Adverse Fate': Granville Stuart, Cowman." *Montana: The Magazine of Western History* 31:3 (Summer 1981): 28–41.

Stuart, Granville. *Forty Years on the Frontier, As Seen in the Journals and Reminiscences of Granville Stuart.* 2 vols. Edited by Paul C. Phillips. Cleveland, 1925.

STUDEBAKER, JOHN MOHLER

John Mohler Studebaker (1833–1917) was a partner in the Studebaker Brothers Manufacturing Company, which, through the manufacture of more than 750,000 wagons, carts, and carriages, played a large part in America's nineteenth-century westward movement. Born in Pennsylvania, Studebaker was one of five brothers, who all eventually entered the wagon-making business. As a young man, he struck out for the gold fields of California, where his experience as a blacksmith and wagon-maker earned him more money than his gold seeking. He always had plenty of work repairing the wagons and carts of the other gold prospectors.

When he returned East in the mid-1850s, Studebaker brought with him an appreciable amount of cash that he had earned during the gold rush. In the meantime, around 1852, two of his brothers, Clement and Henry, had organized the firm of H. and C. Studebaker near South Bend, Indiana. The company was well on its way to becoming a leading manufacturer of wagons when John Studebaker bought Henry's interest in the business in 1857.

In 1868, when another brother, Peter, joined the company, the three men reorganized the business under the name Studebaker Brothers Manufacturing Company. In 1870, a fifth brother, Jacob, joined the company, which had become the world's largest manufacturer of horse-drawn wagons and carts. When Clement died in 1901, John succeeded him as president of the company. He continued Clement's new focus on gasoline-powered automobiles, and the company manufactured it first automobile in 1901.

The Studebaker Corporation and the Packard Company merged operations in 1954, and the company continued to manufacture automobiles in the United States until 1963.

—*James A. Crutchfield*

SUGGESTED READING:
Longstreet, Stephen. *A Century on Wheels: The Story of Studebaker, A History, 1852–1952.* Westport, Conn., 1952. Reprint. 1970.

SUBLETTE BROTHERS

The Kentucky-born Sublette brothers' fame rests on their exploits as MOUNTAIN MEN—trappers and traders in the far Western FUR TRADE. The two eldest brothers, William Lewis (1799–1845) and Milton Green (1801–1837), the more famous of the five, were born in Somerset. They entered the fur trade as novice trappers in 1822 or 1823 in the employ of WILLIAM HENRY ASHLEY and ANDREW HENRY. Later as William Sublette prospered, he recruited his other brothers, Andrew Whitley (1808?–1853), also born in Somerset, and Solomon Perry (1812–1857) and Pinckney Whitley (1813?–1828), both born in Lincoln County. Pinckney's career was short-lived; he accompanied William to the 1827 Bear Lake RENDEZVOUS and then joined a trapping party led by Samuel Tulloch. En route to the Portneuf River, the party encountered hostile Blackfoot Indians, and in the ensuing skirmish, Pinckney and two other trappers were slain.

William and Milton Sublette were with the Ashley-Henry party that sustained heavy casualties in a bloody battle with the Arikara Indians on the upper Missouri in present-day South Dakota in 1823. The defeat forced the mountain men to find an alternative route. As a result, in 1824 a new trail was blazed across the plains from St. Joseph to the recently discovered South Pass, a route that would eventually be known as the OREGON TRAIL. In 1830, William was the first to take a wagon train along this route to the annual fur-trade rendezvous.

In 1826, William Sublette and two other trappers bought out Ashley and Henry. Over the next four years, Smith, Jackson, and Sublette, as the firm was styled, effectively expanded the perimeter of fur trapping. Smith undertook two trips to Mexican California in 1826 and 1827; the latter trip took him north to the Oregon Country where he wintered at FORT VANCOUVER, headquarters of the HUDSON'S BAY COMPANY. In 1830, the partners wrote an extensive report on their activities and sent it to Secretary of War Thomas Eaton. That same year, they sold their company to the ROCKY MOUNTAIN FUR COMPANY, in which Milton Sublette was one of five partners. Between 1830 and 1834, Milton

trapped in Blackfoot country on the Lewis Fork of the Columbia and in the vicinity of the Snake River forks before the Rocky Mountain Fur Company dissolved. He then joined two other friends in a new independent partnership, which was sold in 1836 to their arch rival, the AMERICAN FUR COMPANY. By this time, Milton was crippled from an 1826 wound from an Apache arrow that never quite healed. By 1835, the situation was so dire that his leg was amputated. He valiantly tried to carry on in the fur trade, but he died at Fort William (later Fort Laramie) in 1837.

In the meantime, William Sublette returned to the fur trade as a contractor in partnership with ROBERT CAMPBELL in 1832. At the same time, William also began to invest in real estate and other mercantile ventures, which brought him prosperity. His association with Campbell lasted until 1842. Thereafter, he managed his land holdings until he died from tuberculosis, an affliction that also troubled brothers Andrew and Solomon.

Andrew Sublette entered the fur trade in 1830 when he went to work for his brother William. In 1835, Andrew entered into a partnership with another longtime fur trader, PIERRE LOUIS VASQUEZ, and trapped in the vicinity of present-day Colorado before turning to farming in 1840. From 1844 to 1845, having become bored with farm life, he worked out of Bent's Fort. With the advent of the United States–Mexican War, he raised a company of men, first dubbed the "Oregon Batallion" and subsequently called "Sublette's Rangers." After his discharge from the army, he headed for the California gold fields in November 1848 but failed to strike it rich. He then moved to Los Angeles and was killed by a grizzly bear while hunting.

Solomon Sublette fared no better. He joined the fur trade in 1839 and for three years trapped between Santa Fe and Bent's Fort with little success. In 1844, he became an Indian trader before heading overland to California for a seven months' visit. During the United States–Mexican War, he carried dispatches for the army under a civilian contract. He then worked for the federal government as agent to the Sac and Fox Indians but resigned after seven months. He married in 1848 and settled down on the farm William had willed to him. He died of tuberculosis at the age of forty-two.

—*Doyce B. Nunis, Jr.*

SEE ALSO: Mountain Men

SUGGESTED READING:
Hafen, LeRoy R. *The Mountain Men and the Fur Trade of the Far West.* 10 vols. Glendale, Calif., 1965–1972. Biographical sketches for Andrew (vol. 8: 349–363), Milton

(vol. 4: 331–349), Pinckney (vol. 1: 373–375), Solomon (vol. 1: 377–389), and William (vol. 5: 347–359).

Nunis, Jr., Doyce B. *Andrew Sublette, Rocky Mountain Prince, 1808–1853.* Los Angeles, 1960.

Sunder, John E. *Bill Sublette, Mountain Man.* Norman, Okla., 1959.

SUFFRAGE

SEE: Women's Suffrage

SULLY, ALFRED

A United States Army officer honored for his Sioux campaigns, Alfred Sully (1821–1879) was the son of American painter Thomas Sully. Born in Philadelphia, Sully was a quiet man and a painter and draftsman in his own right. He graduated from West Point in 1841 and joined the Second Infantry at the end of the Seminole War.

In 1847, Sully took part in the bombardment of Veracruz, Mexico. After the United States–Mexican War, he was assigned to Benicia Barracks in California. He rose to the rank of captain in 1852, and the following year, he participated in the Rogue River War in Oregon.

Sully then transferred to Fort Ridgley, Minnesota, and accompanied his regiment to Fort Pierre in the Nebraska Territory in 1855 to join WILLIAM SELBY HARNEY's campaign against the Lakota Sioux. He spent three years on the Missouri River before returning to Fort Ridgley. Two years later, he campaigned against the Cheyenne.

Sully's leadership skills compensated for his limited combat experience when the CIVIL WAR began. He assumed command of the First Minnesota Volunteer Regiment in late 1861, fought in several battles in Virginia, and was honored for gallantry and meritorious service. Shortly thereafter, he was brevetted a colonel for his leadership in the battle of Malvern Hill. He fought with distinction at Antietam and was commissioned brigadier general of the volunteers. After the battles at Fredericksburg and Chancellorsville, Sully assumed command of the District of Iowa to fight the Dakota Indians in Minnesota.

Sully's Civil War record and Western experiences made him a logical choice for the post. He marched from Sioux City, Iowa, and on September 3, 1863, attacked the Dakotas under Inkpaduta at Whitestone Hill on the border between North and South Dakota. In the battle, more than 300 Indian men were killed; 250 women and children were taken prisoner; and Sully

Alfred Sully. *Courtesy Minnesota Historical Society.*

lost only 22 men. The following year, he attacked a combined Dakota and Lakota camp at Killdeer Mountain near Fort Union.

He reverted to his regular army rank in 1866 and discovered that the post–Civil War army assigned young officers with no experience in tribal warfare to lead campaigns. Bitter over this state of affairs, he moved to his last assignment as post commander at Fort Vancouver. He also investigated the FETTERMAN MASSACRE and assisted General OLIVER OTIS HOWARD in the CHIEF JOSEPH affair.

Sully's convincing victories over the Dakotas did not end the conflict between whites and the Great Plains Indians because American territorial expansion never abated. Reformers in the second half of the nineteenth century criticized him for being brutal in his campaigns against the Indians.

—*Richmond L. Clow*

SEE ALSO: Pacific Northwest Indian Wars; Sioux Wars

SUGGESTED READING:

Heitman, Francis B. *Historical Register and Dictionary of the United States Army.* Vol. 1. Washington, D.C., 1903.

Sully, Langdon. *No Tears for the General: The Life of Alfred Sully, 1821–1879.* Palo Alto, Calif., 1974.

Utley, Robert M. *Frontiersmen in Blue: The United States Army and the Indian, 1848–1865.* New York, 1967.

SUMNER, EDWIN V.

Born in Boston, Massachusetts, Edwin V. Sumner (1797–1862) began, in 1819, a military career that, for the most part, took place in the cavalry on the frontier. During the United States–Mexican War, Sumner served under Winfield Scott. At Cerro Gordo, a musket ball glanced off his ear, and from then on his nickname was "Bull Head." Impressed by the boom of his voice, those who served under him reportedly called him "Bull of the Woods."

Following peace with Mexico in 1848, Sumner took command of the Department of New Mexico, territory recently acquired in the war and occupied by a number of Native American tribes. For the region and its overland routes, Sumner devised a defense system that relied on the establishment of a string of forts. He first built Fort Union where the Cimarron branch of the Santa Fe Trail met the Mountain branch. Fort Defiance, located at the mouth of Canyon Bonito in the heart of Navajo country, was followed by Fort Conrad, Fort Fillmore, Fort Webster, and others. Although the details of Sumner's system changed over the decades, his plan for defending the region lasted some forty years.

Sumner had less success in the region's civil affairs. Friction between Sumner and New Mexico civil authorities developed over the soldier's aggressive meddling in territorial politics and his intolerance for interference from either New Mexico politicians or Bureau of Indian Affairs officials in matters of subduing the region's Indians. Fond of neither its people nor its climate, Sumner recommended, in 1852, that the United States abandon New Mexico altogether.

Sumner was appointed commander of Fort Leavenworth in Kansas in 1857, at a time of conflict between proslavery and Free-Soil settlers. In addition, the Cheyenne Indians, at the time, carried out raids against white travelers on the Southern Plains. In the summer of 1857, Sumner led an assault on the Cheyennes at Solomon River in Kansas. In the following year, he took charge of the Department of the West, encompassing lands between the Mississippi River and the Rockies Mountains (but excluding Texas and New Mexico). During the Civil War, Sumner attained the rank of major general.

—*Patricia Hogan*

Edwin V. Sumner. *Courtesy National Archives.*

SUSTAINED YIELD

Sustained yield is a production-oriented economic concept associated with the American conservation movement. In the late nineteenth century, wasteful methods of natural-resource exploitation and consumption drew criticism. GEORGE PERKINS MARSH in *Man and Nature* (1864) argued that civilization possessed the power to disrupt and destroy nature's resources, but it also possessed the intelligence to cooperate with nature and defend the resources on which civilization depended. Out of his argument grew the concept of "wise use" promoted by European-trained foresters B. E. Fernow and GIFFORD PINCHOT. Fernow suggested by using sustained-yield forestry techniques, the lumber industry should exploit only that amount of forest resources that could be replaced annually through regrowth and not delve into the capital base of the forest resources. He viewed a forest as an agricultural crop. But in the United States, mature forests came under the ax and the saw on a large scale. After the initial plundering harvest, however, sustained-yield forestry could be adopted. The policy appealed to large timber companies that could afford to slow the harvest and thus enjoy higher prices.

Sustained yield continues to reflect the principles of husbanding forest resources to protect their renewable potential in contrast to the depletion of resource mining. Its principle is at work in a wide variety of resource-management activities. The sustained-yield concept enters the twenty-first century redefined in light

The goal of sustained yield was to ensure a supply of lumber in spite of operations such as the mill pictured here. *Courtesy Bancroft Library.*

of the understanding and acceptance of the role of biodiversity in the forest ecosystem.

—*William D. Rowley*

SUGGESTED READING:
Steen, Harold K. *United States Forest Service: A History.* Seattle, Wash., 1976.
Williams, Michael. *Americans and Their Forests: A Historical Geography.* Cambridge, 1989.

SUTHERLAND, GEORGE

Utah jurist George Sutherland (1862-1942) was born in England. After immigrating to the United States, he became a leader in the Republican party in Utah, where he practiced constitutional law. He was elected to the first Utah state senate in 1896, to the U.S. House of Representatives in 1900, and to the U.S. Senate in 1905. Serving in the Senate until 1917, he was then appointed by President Warren G. Harding to serve as an associate justice on the Supreme Court, where he built a reputation as a strict and conservative interpreter of the Constitution. He was a member of the conservative minority in the "five-to-four" decisions that upheld New Deal measures.

—*S. George Ellsworth*

SUGGESTED READING:
Paschal, Joel. *Mr. Justice Sutherland, A Man against the State.* New York, 1951.

SUTRO, ADOLPH

Mining entrepreneur, public benefactor, and mayor of San Francisco, Adolph Sutro (1830–1898), an urbane millionaire Populist, was born in Aix-la-Chapelle of German Jewish parents. Immigrating in 1850 with his mother to New York City, he moved to California and became a merchant in San Francisco and Stockton. Beginning in the 1860s, Sutro, an engineer by training, organized the construction of a drainage and ventilation tunnel through the Sierra Nevada to the COMSTOCK LODE of Nevada. In the process, he became an inveterate foe of the Southern Pacific Railroad, which tried to thwart his venture, and a hero of the miners, who saw his tunnel as an attempt to bring safer working conditions to the mines. In 1879, Sutro sold his stock in the tunnel venture and invested in the undeveloped western lands of San Francisco; he became the city's largest landowner.

Not at all a California land baron, Sutro became, instead, the benevolent "king" of suburban San Francisco. Around his cliff-top mansion in Sutro Heights, overlooking the Pacific, he welcomed the public to his Sutro Gardens, a sculpture park and picnic grounds. In 1894, he completed the Sutro Baths, huge indoor swimming pools at the ocean's edge. He also collected rare books, made them available to scholars, and founded the Sutro Library. In 1893, he forced the Southern Pacific to lower its exorbitant fares on the streetcar line to Sutro Heights by constructing a parallel line. Because Sutro believed that the Southern Pacific was "the curse of our country and responsible for the evil condition of the Pacific Coast," he was a natural nominee of the Populists in the 1984 mayoral election. Because his powers under the old city charter were limited, he served primarily as a symbol of opposition to the political corruption attributed to the Southern Pacific. Although he did not run for a second term as mayor, he did increase the constituency in favor of political reform, which under the leadership of JAMES DUVAL PHELAN, was embodied in the new charter for the city in 1899.

—*Philip J. Ethington*

SUGGESTED READING:

Ethington, Philip J. *The Public City: The Political Construction of Urban Life in San Francisco, 1850–1900.* New York, 1994.

Stewart, Robert E., and Mary E. Stewart. *Adolph Sutro: A Biography.* Berkeley, Calif., 1962.

SUTTER, JOHN AUGUST

The first non-Indian to settle in the California interior, John (Johann) August Sutter (1803–1880) owned the sawmill where gold was first discovered in the region. He was born to Swiss parents in Kandern, Germany, near Basel, Switzerland. As a young man, he settled in Burgdorf, Switzerland. There, he married and became a dry-goods merchant, but his business failed. To avoid debtors' prison, Sutter abandoned his wife and five children and fled to America in 1834.

In 1835, Sutter was living on the Missouri frontier where he concocted a military background and adopted the title of captain. He made two commercial trips down the Santa Fe Trail and traded with the Shawnee and Delaware Indians, but these ventures failed. In 1838, he journeyed to California by a roundabout route through the Rocky Mountains to Oregon, the Sandwich Islands (Hawaii), and Alaska; he finally arrived in California in 1839.

The governor of California, which was then a part of Mexico, permitted Sutter to settle in the Sacramento Valley at the confluence of the American and Sacramento rivers. Although fur traders and trappers had visited the region since 1827, Sutter was the first non-Indian to settle there. Sutter's Fort became the center of an extensive pastoral and agricultural enterprise that Sutter called "New Helvetia." Indian laborers did most of the work in Sutter's fields, and he used every means at his disposal to get them to work including wage labor, debt peonage, and outright slavery. Sutter recruited an Indian army to control his labor force and to dominate the large Indian population in the California interior.

Overland emigrants proceeded to New Helvetia, and Sutter employed them in his shops and fields and helped them establish their own farms as well. By 1846, a substantial number of Americans had settled in the vicinity of New Helvetia. Sutter professed loyalty to the Mexican government, but the Americans resented Mexican rule and rebelled at the time of the UNITED STATES–MEXICAN WAR. Sutter eventually joined the American cause, and his fort became a center of American military operations during the conflict.

After the war, Sutter built a sawmill up the American River. There, in January 1848, his overseer, James Marshall, found gold and instigated the CALIFORNIA GOLD RUSH. The discovery could have made Sutter a rich man, but miners who rushed to the region overran his land, stole his livestock, and took advantage of his hospitality and gullibility. Sutter had always operated on the margins of financial ruin, and he could not keep up with the high-flying financial times of the 1850s. In 1865, he finally lost what remained of his vast California holdings and retired to Pennsylvania. Until he died, Sutter unsuccessfully petitioned the federal government to pay him for the losses he suffered during the war with Mexico and the gold rush.

—*Albert L. Hurtado*

SUGGESTED READING:

Dillon, Richard. *Fool's Gold: The Decline and Fall of Captain John Sutter of California.* New York, 1967.

Hurtado, Albert L. "Indians in Town and Country: The Nisenan Indians' Changing Economy and Society as Shown in John A. Sutter's 1856 Correspondence." *American Indian Culture and Research Journal* 12:2 (1988): 31–51.

Ottley, Allan R. *John A. Sutter's Last Days: The Bidwell Letters.* Sacramento, Calif., 1986.

Zollinger, James Peter. *Sutter: The Man and His Empire.* New York, 1939.

SUTTON-TAYLOR FEUD

The Sutton-Taylor feud erupted after the Civil War in South Texas. The Taylor clan of ranchers and farmers bitterly resented the Reconstruction authority imposed by such officials as William Sutton, DeWitt County deputy sheriff, and Jack Helm, who served as county sheriff and as one of four captains of the detested State Police. In November 1867, brothers Hays and "Doboy" (DuBois) Taylor killed two federal soldiers, the first casualties of the deadliest and longest blood feud in Texas.

During more than eight years of ambushes, street fights, and assassinations, Hays, Charley, Buck, Pitkin, Scrap, and Jim Taylor were slain, along with at least nine of their relatives and friends. Sutton and Helm rode at the head of two hundred "Regulators" who terrorized the countryside in the name of the law. But in 1873, Jim Taylor and JOHN WESLEY HARDIN, who was related by marriage to the Taylors, killed Helm in Albuquerque, Texas; and the next year, Jim and Bill Taylor shot to death William Sutton and a friend aboard a steamer in Indianola. The Suttons retaliated by lynching three members of the opposition, but the Taylors killed the new Sutton leader, Cuero City Marshal Rube Brown. Texas Ranger Captain LEANDER H. McNELLY and his company were ordered to intercede, but not even the redoubtable McNelly could stop the bloodletting. When Jim Taylor and two friends were killed late in 1875, the feud finally seemed to subside, although related shootings the next year brought in the Texas Rangers under Captain Lee Hall. Aside from countless skirmishes, there were numerous indictments through the years, and legal appeals dragged on for decades; the verdict in the final case was not reached until 1899.

—*Bill O'Neal*

SEE ALSO: Texas Rangers; Violence

SUGGESTED READING:

Sonnichsen, C. L. *I'll Die before I'll Run.* New York, 1951.

Sutton, Robert C., Jr. *The Sutton-Taylor Feud.* Quanah, Tex., 1974.

SWAN, ALEXANDER HAMILTON (ALEC)

Wyoming cattle rancher Alexander ("Alec") Hamilton Swan (1831–1905) was born in Greene County, Pennsylvania. He was a stockman-farmer in Ohio and Iowa from 1858 to 1873. In 1874, he, along with other family members, organized Swan Brothers and began to acquire ranches and herds along the Chugwater in Wyoming. During the 1870s, he served in the territorial legislature and chaired the Laramie County Board of Commissioners (forerunner of the Wyoming Stock Growers' Association). In the 1880s, Swan organized some twenty companies capitalized at $25 million. Four companies founded in 1883 document Swan's grasp of the CATTLE INDUSTRY from breeding to marketing: the Wyoming Hereford Association introduced purebred bulls to organized range breeding controlled by the WSGA; the South Omaha Land Syndicate and The Union Stockyards Company of Omaha provided stockyards, marketing, and slaughtering facilities; the Swan Land and Cattle Company, Ltd., acquired assets in cattle and land in Wyoming and sold them to a prestigious group of Edinburgh investors. As ranch manager, he purchased 500,000 acres of Union Pacific land and continuously consolidated ranch holdings. Capitalized at $3 million and owning thirty-two ranches, 577,120 acres, and 108,763 head of cattle, the "Two-Bar" was the second largest foreign-owned land and cattle company in America. Swan was discharged and sued by the owners in 1887, the year of the greatest climatic disaster and devastation of herds on record. That year, his own firm of Swan Brothers went into receivership. Swan then left Wyoming, and his later career is clouded.

—*Harmon Mothershead*

SUGGESTED READING:

Mothershead, Harmon Ross. *The Swan Land and Cattle Company, Ltd.* Norman, Okla., 1971.

Smith, Helen Huntington. "The Rise and Fall of Alec Swan." *The American West* 4 (August 1967): 21ff.

TABOR, HORACE AUSTIN WARNER

Horace Austin Warner Tabor (1830–1899), Colorado's renowned MINING man, was born in Holland, Vermont. No man in his day better typified what success in mining could accomplish for an individual. At the peak of his wealth and fame, in the 1870s and 1880s, Tabor's investments stretched throughout the West and the world and included mines, railroads, newspapers, real estate, and banks. His prestige and political power gained him a seat in the U.S. Senate. Colorado benefited from his enterprise and money; he was the first of the state's millionaires to reinvest his fortune at home. His fame and investments helped make Colorado one of the nation's leading mining states.

Like others, Tabor went to the West in 1855 to seek his fortune. Active in the Kansas Free-Soil movement, he tried farming without financial success. In 1859, he and his hard-working wife Augusta and son Maxey joined the Pikes Peak gold rush.

Between 1859 and 1876, Tabor followed Colorado's mining fortunes and became a businessman and mine investor rather than a working miner. In his late forties, he still sought the golden dream that brought so many people to the West. In 1876, R. G. Dun estimated his worth at fifteen thousand dollars.

That all changed with the discovery of LEADVILLE's silver bonanza. After grubstaking prospectors for years, Tabor finally hit his bonanza when two of his partners discovered the Little Pittsburg Mine. Tabor then purchased the Chrysolite and Matchless mines. His fortune soared to more than $7 million.

The mining investor and businessman then became an entrepreneur. He built lavish opera houses in Leadville and DENVER and the Tabor Block, which became one of Denver's finest, most modern office

Horace Austin Warner Tabor and Baby Doe Tabor. *Courtesy Colorado State Historical Society.*

buildings. He also emerged as a leading Colorado Republican politician and silver-issue spokesman. However, by the late 1880s, his investments had severely drained his fortune, and the crash of 1893 and subsequent depression furnished the final blow. In 1898, he was appointed Denver's postmaster, a position he held at his death.

The romantic and tragic story of Horace, Augusta, and his beautiful second wife Elizabeth "Baby Doe" Tabor evolved into a legend. The opera, *The Ballad of Baby Doe,* and many books tell the story.

—*Duane A. Smith*

SUGGESTED READING:
Smith, Duane A. *Horace Tabor: His Life and the Legend.* Niwot, Colo., 1989.

TALIAFERRO, LAWRENCE

Born to a prominent Virginia family in King George County, Lawrence Taliaferro (1794–1871) served as an agent at Fort Snelling to the Sioux and Ojibwa (Chippewa) Indians at a time when white encroachments on Indian lands strained relations among native tribes, white traders and settlers, and the federal government. After completing his studies with private tutors, Taliaferro enlisted in a volunteer unit at the outbreak of the War of 1812 and remained in the army when the war ended. He had been stationed at a number of frontier posts before President James Monroe, in 1819, appointed him Indian agent at Fort Snelling in present-day Minnesota.

Taliaferro executed his duties with an uncommon compassion for the native peoples and their cultures. He fought to protect their rights in treaty negotiations with the federal government and strove to protect them from the consequences of the white traders' liquor. He worked to keep peace among enemy tribes and often succeeded, for many tribes came to believe that "Iron Cutter," as the natives called him, was truly their friend.

For his many successes in dealing with the Indians, however, Taliaferro's tenure was difficult. He made enemies among white fur traders who ignored the laws he enforced and who agitated unsuccessfully for his removal. Often the government failed to deliver supplies not otherwise available on the remote frontier, and federal Indian policy changed frequently and in ways that he could not explain to the satisfaction of the Indians in his charge. In 1827, Taliaferro was forced to give up his care of the Ojibwa Indians when the War Department ordered them to move to the agency at Sault Saint Marie. His efforts at introducing agriculture to the Indians failed, and during the 1830s, he

could no longer keep various tribes at peace. Discouraged and disillusioned, he resigned in 1839, just after he had been appointed to a sixth term.

Taliaferro moved to Bedford, Pennsylvania, after 1840 and spent most of his time there until 1857, when he reentered the military and served in the quartermaster department in Kansas, Texas, and Pennsylvania. He retired in 1863.

The diaries that Taliaferro kept during the twenty years of service as an Indian agent offer insight into his integrity and valuable details about frontier life.

—*Patricia Hogan*

SUGGESTED READING:
Mardock, Robert W. *The Reformers and the American Indian.* Columbia, Mo., 1971.

TANAKA, MICHIKO

Michiko Tanaka is the pseudonym of a pioneer Japanese immigrant wife and mother whose struggle to survive and prevail was typical of many Issei (first generation) Japanese women in America. Tanaka's oral history was recorded by her daughter, anthropologist Akemi Kikumura, in *Through Harsh Winters: The Life of a Japanese Immigrant Woman.*

Tanaka, the third daughter of a well-established merchant family in Hiroshima, impetuously married an employee of her parents. "I had consented to marriage," she said, "because I had the dream of seeing America. I didn't care for him much . . . he didn't have much education. I could have married a real good person in Japan, but I wanted to see America and [her husband, Saburo] was a way to get there." In 1923, after selling her kimono and borrowing five hundred dollars, the couple sailed to America. "We decided to go for a short while, make enough money . . . then return home." But they never returned to Japan and eventually lost contact with relatives there. Saburo's penchant for gambling and drinking, their World War II evacuation to Arkansas, and his death in 1953 trapped Tanaka in a continuing struggle to keep the family intact while working at menial jobs. On May 15, 1980, after surviving fifty-seven years in America, with eleven children and twenty-two grandchildren, Michiko Tanaka became an American citizen.

—*Donald Teruo Hata, Jr., and Nadine Ishitani Hata*

SEE ALSO: Japanese Americans; Japanese Internment

SUGGESTED READING:
Kikumura, Akemi. *Through Harsh Winters: The Life of a Japanese Immigrant Woman.* Novato, Calif., 1980.

TANNER, JOHN

SEE: Literature: Indian Captivity Narratives

TAOS, NEW MEXICO

The name "Taos" generally refers to three settlements. Of them, the oldest is Taos Pueblo, a multistoried adobe dwelling that the Pueblo Indians have occupied since approximately the fourteenth century. Archaeological evidence indicates that prehistoric hunters and pit-house dwellers occupied the Taos valley even before the existing Pueblo structure was begun. The second settlement, Ranchos de Taos, is an agricultural village settled by the early Spanish. The third settlement, the modern town of Taos, is located between Taos Pueblo and Ranchos de Taos and was settled as Don Fernando de Taos in the latter years of the eighteenth century.

The first Spanish people to visit the area were members of FRANCISCO VÁSQUEZ DE CORONADO's expedition, which passed through the valley in 1540. When the Spanish colonized New Mexico in 1598, the Spanish governor, JUAN DE OÑATE, visited Taos and appointed a missionary priest to work among the Taos Indians. Some settlement of the valley by Spanish colonists took place in the mid-seventeenth century, but in 1680, the Indians of the Rio Grande pueblos rose up in a bloody revolt against their conquerors and drove all Europeans from the area. In the Taos valley, two priests were slain, some seventy settlers were reported killed, and the remaining Spanish fled down the Rio Grande to Mexico. The revolt was instigated by Popé, a San Juan Indian living at Taos Pueblo.

The Spanish reclaimed New Mexico in 1694, and resettlement of the valley followed. Mexico's declaration of independence from Spain in 1821 brought a change of sovereign authority over New Mexico but otherwise did little to change daily life in the valley. Of much greater consequence was the occupation of New Mexico by the United States in 1846. Local resentment of the Americans led to the Taos Rebellion of 1847, in which the new governor, Charles Bent, and many other Americans were killed. Seven Taos Indians were executed for their roles in the hostilities.

From approximately 1821 to 1846, Taos was the southern center of the Rocky Mountain FUR TRADE. The Turley Mill on the Rio Hondo became a prosperous trading establishment between 1830 and 1847 and provided plenty of "Taos lightning" from its distillery to enliven the annual rendezvous of the MOUNTAIN MEN.

In modern times, Taos has attracted artists, aesthetes, skiers, and summer tourists to enjoy its unique

The Taos Pueblo, the first settlement to bear the name, appears in this image of a 1910 celebration of San Geronimo Day. *Courtesy Museum of New Mexico.*

combination of cultural, historical, scenic, and recreational features. In recent years, TOURISM and small business have been the most dependable sources of income. Agriculture, once the major occupation of the valley people, continues on a small scale but has declined in economic importance. The area's mountains have at times supported significant mining activity.

The population of Taos valley—including Taos, Ranchos de Taos, and their outlying villages—in 1990 was 11,265, with approximately 1,200 additional residents at Taos Pueblo. Most notable today for its diverse arts community, the Taos County population of just over 22,000 consists of approximately 65 percent Hispanics, 7 percent Native Americans, and the remainder primarily non-Hispanic whites.

—*David L. Caffey*

SEE ALSO: Pueblo Revolt; United States–Mexican War

SUGGESTED READING:
Grant, Blanche C. *When Old Trails Were New: The Story of Taos.* New York, 1934.
Morrill, Claire. *Taos Mosaic: Portrait of a New Mexico Village.* Albuquerque, N. Mex., 1973.
Sherman, John. *Taos: A Pictorial History.* Santa Fe., N. Mex., 1990.

TAOS SCHOOL OF ARTISTS

From the last decades of the nineteenth century to the beginning of World War II, the small, northern New Mexico community of Taos became not only a center for Western art but also one of the focal points for regional artistic innovation in America. Euro-American painters working in Taos were challenged by the peoples, topography, light, and fertile traditions of both Indian and Hispanic art and culture.

Joseph Henry Sharp was the initial catalyst in the development of a community of artists at Taos. Born in Bridgeport, Ohio, he studied art in Cincinnati and Munich. In 1893, on a Western sketching trip, Sharp made his way to Taos and was immediately charmed by the artistic potential of this small village and pueblo. While in Paris in 1895, he described with great enthusiasm to Bert Greer Phillips and Ernest L. Blumenschein the uniqueness of northern New Mexico for artists. While continuing to travel extensively in the West, Sharp established himself in Taos after 1902 and bought a home there in 1909. Consumed by his art, Sharp painted seven days a week both in his studio and in the open air. His Taos paintings are quiet, poignant portrayals of a people living in harmony with their environment. A charter member of the Taos Society of Artists, Sharp encouraged the artists who were settling at Taos to follow their own artistic motivations.

The Taos Society of Artists was formed in 1914 to promote the painting and careers of the small colony of artists working there. In addition to Sharp, the society initially included Phillips, Blumenschein, O. E. Berninghaus, E. Irving Couse, and W. Herbert Dunton. Later, Walter Ufer and Victor Higgins became members, and still later, E. Martin Hennings, Catherine C. Critcher, and Kenneth M. Adams joined the group. The society neither promoted any specific school of painting or distinctive methodology nor issued any manifestoes about the social or political values of its paintings or advanced any theories about "modern art." The goal of the society was to advance good art, not a particular style of art, and to market the work of its members. The art of the society's members celebrated in a variety of evolving styles the beauty and grandeur of the mountains, deserts, and forests and the naturalness of the life of the Indians and Hispanics of this high valley. Their portraits and landscapes—romantic, exotic, representational, and uniquely Southwestern—always conveyed a love of the land and its peoples. Many of their works were romantically realistic while others were more romantically imaginative. Some were modern in style, technique, and execution while others were traditional and conservative. The artists were well trained, and most had studied abroad and were aware of the current movements in contemporary American and world art. The success of their works attracted other artists to the area and helped transform Taos into a significant force in the development of Western art. In 1927, the society was dissolved, for its members had become commercially successful and had found it increasingly difficult to participate in the exhibitions, activities, and traveling shows of the organization.

Seeking opportunities to promote TOURISM in the Southwest, the ATCHISON, TOPEKA AND SANTA FE RAILROAD became an early supporter of the Taos artists. Their paintings were reproduced annually on the railroad's calendars and advertisements and were displayed in depots and at Harvey hotels. The artists were given free transportation for themselves and for their paintings until such acts were prohibited by law. This relationship particularly aided Couse; from 1923 to 1936, twenty-three of his paintings appeared on the railroad's calendars.

During the Great Depression, the abundant opportunities the Taos artists once enjoyed evaporated. Some of them then participated in Works Project Administration (WPA) mural projects; others became portrait painters; and still others began to teach. The energy of this artistic community was further diminished by the deaths in 1936 of Couse, Dunton, and Ufer. After World War II, tastes changed, and modern art became the vogue. The tranquil Indian surrounded by golden aspens, a Hispanic worker with his sheep, or a sun-clothed landscape against an azure sky with women fetching water were no longer desired and were often criticized as being too sentimental and representational.

—*Phillip Drennon Thomas*

SEE ALSO: Art: Western Art

SUGGESTED READING:
Bickerstaff, Laura M. *Pioneer Artists of Taos.* Denver, 1955.
Broder, Patricia Janis. *Taos: A Painter's Dream.* Boston, 1980.
Coke, Van Deren. *Taos and Santa Fe: The Artist's Environment, 1882–1942.* Albuquerque, N. Mex., 1963.

TAPE V. HURLEY

In 1885, Joseph and Mary Tape, Chinese immigrants, filed a law suit against Jennie M. A. Hurley, principal of the Spring Valley School of San Francisco's public school system, her superintendent, A. J. Moulder, and the members of the San Francisco school board after Hurley barred the Tapes' daughter Mamie from attending classes.

Just prior to Mamie's attempt to enter the school, San Francisco's school board had issued resolutions stating that each school principal "is, hereby absolutely prohibited from admitting a Mongolian child of schoolable age, or otherwise, either male or female," into the school's classes. Failure to abide by the board's policy subjected the principals to immediate dismissal. When Mamie Tape appeared at the door of the Spring Valley School, Hurley followed board policy.

Mamie Tape's confrontation with the school board took place in a era when anti-Chinese sentiment ran rampant in California. Only three years before, the United States passed the Chinese Exclusion Act of 1882, which prohibited Chinese migrants from entering the United States. Having halted the influx of Chinese immigrants, white San Franciscans intended to keep CHINESE AMERICANS already in the country at a distance and certainly far away from their own children. San Franciscans and their school board did not care that Mamie, by virtue of being born in the United States, was an American citizen, nor that her parents, by law, paid taxes that supported the school system from which their child had been barred.

Mary Tape, mother of Mamie, was indignant at the board's treatment of her daughter. "May you Mr. Moulder," she wrote, "never be persecuted like the way you have persecuted little Mamie Tape! . . . I will let the world see sir What justice there is when it is govern by Race prejudice men!"

The Tapes' case on behalf of their daughter was presented before San Francisco Superior Court Judge Maguire, who ruled that the board could not deny Mamie Tape a place in the school. "Our Legislature has enacted that all children within the State shall have equal facilities for education so far as regards the right to attend the public schools."

The board appealed Maguire's ruling to the state's Supreme Court. In a unanimous decision presented by Judge J. R. Sharpstein, the court upheld Maguire's ruling. Mamie Tape was allowed to attend school.

The school board, in the end however, won. Rather than admit Mamie to Spring Valley School, it established a separate school for Asian students, in which Mamie was enrolled.

—*Patricia Hogan*

SEE ALSO: Chinese Exclusion; Segregation: Segregation in Education

SUGGESTED READING:

Low, Victor. *The Unimpressible Race: A Century of Educational Struggle by the Chinese in San Francisco.* San Francisco, 1982.

Yung, Judy. *Chinese Women of America: A Pictorial History.* Seattle, Wash., and London, 1986.

TARIFF POLICY

Historical background

The word *tariff*, which technically means the schedule of customs duties, or taxes, placed on commodities crossing a political border, is typically used interchangeably to mean those duties themselves. Customs duties or tariffs are frequently the most politically charged means of raising revenue at a government's disposal, since they almost always involve foreign as well as domestic policy. American tariffs have been used for a variety of reasons: to raise money to cover the costs of government, to force foreign powers to act as the United States government wants them to act, and especially to protect domestic goods from competition from outside the country.

Protective tariffs, and arguments about them, are as old as the American republic, but after the Civil War—particularly in the trans-Mississippi West—they took on a new importance and complexity. Since the days of HENRY CLAY's AMERICAN SYSTEM, Westerners had been ambivalent about high tariffs. Young industries in the Ohio Valley and the Old Northwest supported tariffs that protected them from foreign competition, while farmers generally complained about the high costs of basic goods such tariffs engendered. As long as tariffs could be used for internal improvements, which provided the transportation for farm goods to Eastern markets, farmers could be appeased with reasonably soft-money fiscal policies. They listened reluctantly to Clay, a Kentuckian, who explained to them that he was using protection to build a national economy.

The old Whig party had included not only protectionists such as Clay, but also such free-traders as Robert J. Walker, who would manage (with the backing, generally, of the trans-Appalachian West) to push tariff reform through Congress, resulting in the Walker Tariff Act of 1846 and the weakening of protectionism. The agrarian-based Democrats, dominated before the Civil War by the South's cotton planters, consistently opposed high tariffs. When the Whigs began to disintegrate during the mid-nineteenth-century sectional crisis, the new Republican party attracted a number of protectionist Whigs as well as antislavery Democrats and the recently arrived German and Scandinavian settlers in the Midwest. In favor of high tariffs and hard money from the start, the Republicans always counted among their ranks those who questioned the Republican commitment to protectionism.

During the Civil War, Republican administrations justified tariff bills on the grounds that the internal taxes made necessary to support the war effort put

American industries at a competitive disadvantage and that these industries needed protection to hold their own against foreign manufacturers. With the old opposition to high tariffs basically in rebellion, Congress passed a series of tariff acts that raised what had been modest duties on foreign goods of 18.6 percent in 1861 to an average of 40.3 percent in 1866. No Republican or Democrat ever admitted that these rates were anything but temporary, but at war's end, American industry, relieved of internal war taxes, quickly become accustomed to the high prices they had been charging and the big dividends and handsome profits made possible by the lack of competition from abroad. A strong protariff lobby sprang up, funded by big businesses, to ensure the protective tariffs remained in place. Both parties in Congress accepted protection on principle, even though they each faced strong dissent among their own constituents.

Tariff policy and the American West

Protective tariffs became a part of the nexus of business-government cooperation, founded during the war, that helped launch the post–Civil War industrial boom, a peacetime expansion of markets based on highly developed investment groups in the East and the exploitation of raw materials by rapidly developing extractive industries in the West. The new Western industries soon were calling for continued protective tariffs, and throughout the second half of the nineteenth century, Great Lakes and Pacific Northwest lumber lords, Michigan salt-mine magnates, Montana copper kings, and Great Plains cattle barons lined up behind the big farm-equipment firms in Chicago, Rock Island, Milwaukee, and Racine, the sugar-cane plantations in Louisiana, and the agribusinesses running sheep farms, dairy operations, or sugar-beet plantations on irrigated land in the Far West to make sure that Congress protected their "infant" industries.

Homesteaders, small farmers, and wage workers, who also trundled into the trans-Mississippi in the wake of the Civil War, grew increasingly distressed and pointed out that high tariffs meant high retail prices, that the outrageous profits produced by protected industries came straight out of the average consumer's pocket, and that the tariff was—in their phrase—"the mother of monopoly." In addition, they argued, the $100 million that the tariff produced each year in surplus revenues, which went directly into the U.S. treasury, kept needed currency out of circulation in tight-money times. The federal government typically spent the surpluses on pork-barrel appropriations that led to more Western development or simply reduced taxes on the luxuries purchased by the rich rather than lowering the tariff on basic necessities that produced the surplus in the first place.

Occasionally a president would take a stab at reform; Congress responded with legislative legerdemain that removed the bite of such efforts. Although the Tariff of 1870, for example, reduced duties on foreign coffee, tea, spices, and the like, it left untouched the protective duties on products that Americans produced. The tariff was lowered in 1872 but was restored almost immediately on the excuse that the panic of 1873 had hurt federal revenues. Democratic reform bills in 1876 and 1877 never made it out of committee. In 1883, President Chester A. Arthur vetoed a lavish pork-barrel appropriation for river and harbor improvements and suggested that the surplus revenues be used to reduce taxes and the high tariff, only to have Congress override his veto. Then in December 1887, President Grover Cleveland stood up to Congress in his state of the union address by denouncing high tariffs as unjust, inequitable, and absurd and by dismissing the notion that hundred-year-old industries could be called "infant" at all much less expect federal protection. In control of the House, the Democrats introduced tepid reform legislation; in control of the Senate, the Republicans killed it in committee. The deadlock made tariff reform the first clear-cut economic issue between the parties since Reconstruction.

The election of 1888

The 1888 presidential election, a contest between Cleveland and Republican candidate Benjamin Harrison from Indiana, was probably the most corrupt in the nation's history. Democrats called for tariff reform; Republicans dragged out the specter of free trade and said they were "uncompromisingly in favor of the American system of protection." Much of the Republican money was spent persuading Western farmers that they had a stake in high tariffs; the party flooded the region with tracts that invoked the fierce competition European farmers were ready to hand out to Americans if the protective shield of the tariff were dropped. Western agrarians grumbled, especially in Minnesota, but they were promised a free-silver bill in return for tariff support, and the Republicans hung on to the heartland. Despite Cleveland's stance on the tariff, he carried some manufacturing states, made gains in normally high-tariff states, and won the popular election by almost one hundred thousand votes. The Republicans bought the needed votes in the swing states to ensure a narrow victory in the electoral college, and afterward Harrison complained that he could not even name his own cabinet because party managers "had sold out every place to pay election expenses."

For the first time since 1875, the Republicans controlled the presidency and both houses of Congress. "Czar" Thomas Reed, Speaker of the House, appointed William McKinley, a high-tariff representative from Ohio, to the House Ways and Means Committee, and McKinley went to work fulfilling the party's campaign pledges of higher tariff rates. The McKinley Tariff Bill of 1890 did more that protect infant industries and discourage foreign competition; it created new industries and eliminated competition entirely. The massive surpluses into the treasury soon produced what became known as the "Billion-Dollar Congress." In quickly passed gimcrack bills, Congress doled out money as subsidies to steamship lines, pork-barrel construction for river and harbor improvements, and huge premiums for government-bond holders. Congress even returned to the Northern states every cent they had paid in federal taxes during the Civil War. By 1894, the money was spent, and the federal government would never again have a treasury-surplus "problem."

The Republicans did indeed pass the SHERMAN SILVER PURCHASE ACT OF 1890 as promised, but it proved to be a shifty piece of legislation that in the long run did little to solve currency problems or relieve farmers of their hard-money credit problems.

Politicians and big business flourished under the Harrison administration, but farmers and small businesses suffered. Farmers had to buy expensive farm equipment in markets protected by the tariff and sell their crops in unprotected markets worldwide. As a result, cotton and wheat prices, which had been declining steadily over two decades, plummeted. Cotton, averaging 15.1 cents per pound from 1870 to 1873, sold for 5 cents a pound between 1894 and 1898. During the same period, wheat fell from 106.7 to 63.3 cents a bushel and corn from 43 to 29.7 cents. And those were market prices, not what the farmer got paid. In 1889, for example, Kansas farmers got 10 cents a bushel for corn; some burned it for fuel instead of selling it for this price. Long before the McKinley Tariff Act, Western and Southern agrarians were already poised for a revolt, and their complaints had rung out increasingly in Granger halls and county courthouses in the two decades before 1890. Two years after the passage of the tariff, they met in St. Louis to form the Populist party, the most radical third party in American history.

As the Populist revolt led Westerners to line up behind the Democrats' WILLIAM JENNINGS BRYAN and inflationary free-sliver in the presidential election of 1896, McKinley ran on a slogan of "Peace, Prosperity, and Protectionism." He won by a landslide, carrying all the states to the west of the Missouri except California, Oregon, and North Dakota. It was obvious that despite considerable Populist sentiment in the trans-Mississippi West, especially in the Midwestern states, the region remained a bastion of Republicanism and the high tariff. The Dingley Tariff of 1897, which followed the election and was the highest in the country's history, raised duties on imported goods by an average of 57 percent. In response, foreign countries passed retaliatory tariffs, which hurt American exports, and the West supported a tariff reduction under the Payne-Aldrich Tariff of 1909. After World War I, when collapsing markets depressed agriculture severely once more, farmers—most of them now running much larger operations—also lined up behind protective-tariff walls. Indeed, both the Fordney-McCumber Act of 1922 and the Smoot-Hawley Act of 1930 took the names of congressmen from North Dakota, Michigan, Oregon, and Utah. The Smoot-Hawley Tariff, one of the most destructive pieces of legislation ever passed, triggered the trade war that led to a worldwide depression. Afterward, the United States generally embraced free trade, although occasionally even in the late twentieth century, "infant" industries such as computer manufacturing in California's Silicon Valley lobbied for protection against "unfair" foreign competition.

—*Charles Phillips*

SEE ALSO: Banking; Booms; Currency and Silver as Western Political Issues; Financial Panics; Populism

SUGGESTED READING:

McGuire, Robert A. "Economic Causes of Late Nineteenth Century Agrarian Unrest: New Evidence." *Journal of Economic History* 41 (December 1981): 835–851.

Pollack, Norman. *The Populist Response to Industrial America.* Cambridge, Mass., 1962.

Taussig, F. W. *The Tariff History of the United States.* New York, 1931. 8th ed. Reprint. 1967.

TAVERNIER, JULES

Painter and illustrator Jules Tavernier (1844–1889) immigrated to the United States from his native France in 1871 following a brief service in the Franco-Prussian War. He soon found employment in New York City as an illustrator for *Graphic* and *Harper's Weekly* magazines. In 1873, *Harper's* asked Tavernier to undertake a tour of the American West with fellow artist and expatriate Paul Frenzeny and sketch scenes and incidents along the route of their travels. *Harper's* publicized the trip in a campaign promoting the West with a series of articles illustrated by Frenzeny and Tavernier between 1873 and 1876.

Jules Tavernier, with Paul Frenzeny, traveled extensively throughout the West in 1873 for *Harper's Weekly*. The illustrations, such as those pictured here, appeared in magazine issues from 1873 to 1876. *Courtesy Patrick H. Butler, III.*

The two artists followed a circuitous route westward by rail and stagecoach through Nebraska, Kansas, the Indian Territory, Texas, and Colorado. Spending the winter in Denver, they arrived via the Union Pacific Railroad in San Francisco in the spring of 1874. Neither was anxious to return to the East. Both were elected to membership in San Francisco's Bohemian Club in 1874. Frenzeny eventually returned to New York City and continued to work for *Harper's* and other magazines. Tavernier sailed for the Hawaiian Islands in 1884 and settled in Honolulu, where he spent the last five years of his life.

Tavernier achieved a local celebrity in Hawaii for his dramatic landscapes, many of which featured volcanoes. Following a trip in 1885 to the island of Hawaii with artist Joseph Strong, Tavernier exhibited his sketches of the island in the Hawaiian Hotel in Honolulu at an opening attended by King Kalakaua, his ministers, and the resident diplomatic corps. A large album or folio of Tavernier's Hawaiian views was subsequently planned but was never published. A panoramic landscape measuring twelve by ninety feet was exhibited in Honolulu in 1886. Entitled *Hawaii's Wonder,* it has since been lost.

A number of the artist's Hawaiian landscapes are preserved today at the Honolulu Academy of Arts as well as in private collections. Several of his paintings of the American West also survive, but Tavernier is more often remembered today for the work he did with Frenzeny for *Harper's Weekly.*

—*David C. Hunt*

SEE ALSO: Art: Book and Magazine Illustration

SUGGESTED READING:
Taft, Robert. *Artists and Illustrators of the Old West, 1850–1900.* 1953. Reprint. Honolulu, Hawaii, 1992.

TAVERNS

SEE: Saloons

TAYLOR, GLEN HEARST

The son of itinerant preachers, Glen Hearst Taylor (1904–1984) was born in Portland, Oregon, and grew up in northern Idaho. As a teen-ager, he began traveling with vaudeville shows, and during the Great Depression, he and his family toured the West as a country band. The vagabond turned to politics in 1938 and ran in every open primary until he won a seat in the U.S. Senate in 1944.

Taylor distinguished himself as an excellent errand-boy senator, but foreign-policy issues preoccupied him. A critic of the Cold War, he opposed the Truman Doctrine, Marshall Plan, and NATO. Invited by HENRY AGARD WALLACE to be his running mate in the 1948 Progressive party ticket, Taylor accepted. In 1950, Taylor lost his bid for reelection in a vicious campaign in which the supporters of Joseph McCarthy attacked him as a communist sympathizer. Although he tried to regain his Senate seat in 1954 and 1956, he did not succeed. He died in Burlingame, California.

—F. Ross Peterson

SUGGESTED READING:

Neuberger, Richard. *They Never Go back to Pocatello*. Salem, Oreg., 1988.

Peterson, F. Ross. *Prophet without Honor: Glen H. Taylor and the Fight for American Liberalism*. Lexington, Ky., 1968.

Taylor, Glen H. *The Way It Was with Me*. Seacaucas, N.J., 1979.

TAYLOR, JOHN

The third president of the CHURCH OF JESUS CHRIST OF LATTER-DAY SAINTS, John Taylor (1808–1887) was born in England to James and Agnes Taylor. He was the only church president to be born outside of the United States.

As a young man, Taylor felt destined to spread the gospel of Jesus Christ and traveled in 1832 to Canada where he became a Methodist preacher. In 1836, he was introduced to Mormonism and joined the church shortly thereafter. With an enthusiasm that never seemed to wane during the next fifty years of his life, Taylor moved to Missouri to gather with the MORMONS. In 1838, he was selected to be one of the church's twelve apostles, one of the ruling bodies of the Mormon church. As an apostle, Taylor joined other church leaders in a mission to Great Britain, where he opened the Isle of Man and Ireland to Mormon missionary work. He eventually served four missions for the church, three of which took him to Europe. As a missionary to France, he published the BOOK OF MORMON in French.

During his ministry, Taylor gained a reputation as a powerful orator and writer. He edited a number of church newspapers and authored several works defending the Mormon church and its doctrines. He began practicing plural marriage at the request of JOSEPH SMITH, JR., the founder of Mormonism, and became a staunch defender not only of plural marriage but also of Joseph Smith. On June 27, 1844, Taylor was with Joseph Smith, his brother Hyrum Smith, and Willard Richards in the Carthage jail when the men were attacked by a mob, an event that resulted in the murders of the Smith brothers. Taylor, himself, was seriously wounded in the hip and leg and narrowly escaped death when a bullet hit and shattered the face of his pocket watch, which he wore over his left breast. For the rest of his life, he walked with a limp and suffered enduring pain.

After BRIGHAM YOUNG's death in 1877, Taylor succeeded him as leader of the church and officially became president of the church in 1880. During his administration as church president, the *Pearl of Great Price*, a combination of ancient and modern scripture, was canonized by the Mormons. The church also created churchwide programs for children and young women and continued a restructuring of church government begun under Brigham Young. Taylor was perhaps best known for his stubborn defiance of United States antipolygamy laws. He was the husband of seven wives and father of thirty-five children.

Taylor's personal motto was "The Kingdom of God or nothing." Because of his dedication to the church and its teachings, he could not and would not abandon plural marriage. His defiant stance cost him and other members of the church dearly. As a result of the antipolygamy legislation of the 1880s, Taylor was among many women and polygamous men who were forced into hiding in order to avoid arrest. He spent the last two years of his life hiding from law officials, as a reward of three hundred dollars had been placed on his head. He died in July 1887 while still in hiding.

—Craig L. Foster

SEE ALSO: Edmunds Act of 1882; Edmunds-Tucker Act of 1887; Polygamy: Polygamy among Mormons

SUGGESTED READING:

Taylor, Samuel W. *The Kingdom or Nothing: The Life of John Taylor, Militant Mormon*. New York, 1976.

West, Emerson Roy. *Profiles of the President*. Salt Lake City, 1980.

TAYLOR, NATHANIEL G.

A congressman from Tennessee and commissioner of Indian affairs, Nathaniel G. Taylor (1819–1887) was born in Happy Valley, Carter County, Tennessee. He received an education at Washington College in Tennessee and Princeton University. After graduating from Princeton in 1841, he was admitted to the Tennessee bar but decided to become a Methodist minister rather than practice law after his sister was struck and killed by lightning.

Being a man of the cloth did not prevent Taylor from getting involved in politics. Running as a Whig candidate from Tennessee in 1849 and 1853, he failed to win election to the United States Congress. After being named to serve the unexpired term of Brookins Campbell, who died in office, Taylor again ran for office in 1855 and again was defeated. In 1860, he joined the National Constitutional Union party and was chosen elector-at-large for the state of Tennessee. In 1865, he at last won a seat in Congress as a moderate Republican. Two years later, President Andrew Johnson appointed him commissioner of Indian affairs. Taylor's appointment was opposed by Secretary of the Interior Orville Browning, who preferred the appointment of Lewis Bogy. Browning tried to undercut Taylor's authority as commissioner by employing Bogy as a special commissioner at a salary higher than Taylor's own.

While in office, Taylor supported ideas that were by 1870 incorporated in GRANT'S PEACE POLICY, a plan to clear Western land for white settlement by driving hostile Indians onto reservations. There the Indians would be placed under the supervision of church-appointed agents, who would prepare young Indians for assimilation into white culture. Taylor's ideas concerning the use of persuasion rather than brute force to implement a permanent peace between white settlers and Native Americans led to the creation on July 20, 1867, of a peace commission, which he chaired.

Taylor spent much of his time as commissioner fighting to save the BUREAU OF INDIAN AFFAIRS from military dominance. In his annual report for 1868, he strongly expressed his opinion that the bureau should not be transferred to the War Department. It was not until the election of President Ulysses S. Grant, whose administration ultimately supported many of Taylor's ideas on Indian policy, that he felt the bureau was secure enough for him to retire. He left the office on April 25, 1869, and returned to Tennessee to farm, practice law, and preach. In 1880, however, he tried, in vain, to regain the position of commissioner.

—*Henry E. Fritz and Marie L. Fritz*

SEE ALSO: United States Indian Policy

SUGGESTED READING:
Fritz, Henry E. *The Movement for Indian Assimilation, 1860–1890*. Philadelphia, 1963.
Kvasnicka, Robert M., and Herman J. Viola, eds. *The Commissioners of Indian Affairs, 1824–1877*. Lincoln, Nebr., 1979.
Mardock, Robert W. *The Reformers and the American Indian*. Columbia, Mo., 1971.
Prucha, Francis Paul. *American Indian Policy in Crisis: Christian Reformers and the Indian, 1865–1900*. Norman, Okla., 1976.

TAYLOR, ZACHARY

Zachary Taylor (1784–1850), U.S. Army officer and twelfth president of the United States, was born near Montebello in Orange County, Virginia. Before the age of one, he moved with his family to Louisville, Kentucky. In 1806, with little formal education, Taylor embarked on a military career, which he pursued with few interruptions for the next forty-two years. During the War of 1812, he served under General William Henry Harrison and earned the U.S. Army's first brevet promotion (from captain to major).

In 1832, Taylor participated in BLACK HAWK'S WAR. During the Second Seminole War (from 1835 to 1842), he defeated the Seminoles at the Battle of Lake Okeechobee in 1837, a victory that garnered him another brevet promotion, this time to brigadier general. Earning the sobriquet "Old Rough and Ready," he spent the next two years attempting to force the Seminole War to a conclusion. Unsuccessful in his endeavors, Taylor asked for and received a reassignment and transfer to Baton Rouge. He purchased a plantation near Baton Rouge and another in Mississippi. In 1841, he commanded a military district with departmental headquarters at Fort Smith, Arkansas.

With the annexation of Texas by the United States in 1845, Taylor was ordered to protect American interests in the boundary dispute with Mexico. In March 1846, Taylor advanced from Corpus Christi to present-day Brownsville, Texas, where he erected Fort Texas across the Rio Grande from Mexican-held Matamoros. He won major victories over a numerically superior Mexican army at Palo Alto (on May 8, 1846) and Resaca de la Palma (on May 9, 1846), the first battles of the UNITED STATES–MEXICAN WAR. In August, with thirty-five hundred men, Taylor began his campaign to capture Monterrey, Mexico. In a six-day battle (from September 19 to 24), Taylor assaulted the city from front and rear. On September 25, the Mexican forces at Monterrey surrendered. Taylor granted the Mexicans an eight-week armistice, which infuriated President JAMES K. POLK, who thought the terms too lenient. By that time, Taylor suspected political sabotage by both Polk and Secretary of War William L. Marcy. His suspicions proved true when General of the Army WINFIELD SCOTT directed Taylor to relinquish command of most of his U.S. regulars for use in Scott's Veracruz invasion.

In February 1847, Taylor won a stunning victory over Mexican President ANTONIO LÓPEZ DE SANTA ANNA at the Battle of Buena Vista. Outnumbered by a four to one margin, Taylor's troops held steady and forced Santa Anna to retreat, thus ending the fighting in Mexico's northern regions. By then a national hero, Taylor won the Whig party's nomination and the 1848 presidential election.

As president, Taylor became embroiled in disputes with members of Congress over the admission of California and New Mexico as free states. Taylor's most notable achievement during his term in office was the signing of the Clayton-Bulwer Treaty with England. The treaty provided for dual control of any canal constructed across Central America. Taylor's last weeks in office were rocked with scandals involving cabinet members. While attending ceremonies for the laying of the cornerstone of the Washington Monument on July 4, 1850, Taylor suddenly took ill; he died on July 9 and was buried in his family's plot near Louisville, Kentucky. While Taylor was not a brilliant military strategist, his unpretentious dress and manners won him the loyal support of his troops.

—*Neil C. Mangum*

SUGGESTED READING:

Bauer, Jack K. *Zachary Taylor: Soldier, Planter, Statesman of the Old Southwest.* Baton Rouge, La., 1985.

Dyer, Brainerd. *Zachary Taylor.* New York, 1946.

Eisenhower, John S. D. *So Far from God: The U.S. War with Mexico 1846–1848.* New York, 1989.

Nichols, Edward J. *Zach Taylor's Little Army.* Garden City, N.Y., 1963.

TAYLOR GRAZING ACT

The Taylor Grazing Act, passed by Congress in June 1934, established districts to regulate the grazing of livestock on public lands in the West. Since the late 1880s, Western lands had been open to all and were abused by all. Over the opposition of conservationists, President HERBERT HOOVER proposed, from 1929 to 1932, to cede the public lands to the states, but the states refused because mineral rights were not included in the offer. Conservationists and other interests opposed a long-standing proposal to lease the lands to Western grazing interests. A combination of the Great Depression, a drought in the West, and an activist national administration under President Franklin D. Roosevelt provided favorable circumstances by 1933 for the extension of federal grazing regulations to the remainder of the public domain beyond those over which the UNITED STATES FOREST SERVICE already exerted regulations.

Few could agree on a plan for regulation, but the forest service offered an example of grazing oversight on its lands, and some of the cooperative benefits of local rancher agreements had been observed in experiments in the Mizpah-Pumpkin arrangement in Montana and in Custer County, Idaho. The provisions of the Taylor Grazing Act, unlike those of the Forest Service, adhered to the principle of local control of a federal policy. The central fixture was the local grazing district, which granted permits, agreed on the numbers of livestock to be grazed, set the time limits for grazing, and determined who would receive the permits. The Division of Grazing in the Department of the Interior enforced the regulations. A five-cent grazing fee per animal-unit-month (AUM) was imposed to help cover the costs of administering the program.

The act, introduced by Congressman Edward T. Taylor of Colorado, provided for grazing districts governed by a Grazing Advisory Board elected by all of the range users within a district. Not until after 1936 were all areas of the public grazing lands, beyond the originally stipulated eighty million acres, subject to district organization. Farrington R. Carpenter, trained at Harvard law school and a rancher from Hayden, Colorado, was the first director of the Division of Grazing until 1939, when the name of the agency was changed to the Grazing Service.

The local grazing boards, although technically advisory, in reality granted grazing permits to local stock operators based on their ownership of ranches, traditional use of the range, and water ownership. These factors worked to eliminate tramp sheepherders whose flocks often appeared early in the spring, consumed the best range, and then moved on to greener pastures. The boards also prevented the entry of new stock or start-up enterprises on the range. Personnel of both the Division of Grazing and later the Grazing Service were generally hired from the state in which they served. With so much emphasis on local control and the establishment of state advisory boards, the Taylor Grazing Act made the entire process of range regulation highly politicized. As a result, stock numbers often continued to exceed the ability of the range to support them. In disputes over administrative costs, which far surpassed original estimates, Congress abolished the Grazing Service in 1946 and replaced it with the BUREAU OF LAND MANAGEMENT, which continued many of the previous policies and traditions.

—*William D. Rowley*

SUGGESTED READING:

Calef, Wesley. *Private Grazing and Public Lands: Studies of the Local Management of the Taylor Act.* Chicago, 1960.

Clawson, Marion. *The Bureau of Land Management.* New York, 1971.

Foss, Philip O. *Politics and Grass.* Seattle, Wash., 1960.

Muhr, James, and Hanson R. Stuart. *Opportunity and Challenge: The Story of the BLM.* Washington, D.C., 1988.

Stout, Joe A. "Cattlemen, Conservationists, and the Taylor Grazing Act." *New Mexico Historical Review* 45 (1970): 311–332.

TEACHERS ON THE FRONTIER

Pioneer teachers in the mid-nineteenth century came primarily from two groups. One, made up of single women and men looking for opportunities in frontier schools, came from the East; the other, made up of sons and daughters, often in their teens, or mothers in local settlements, were already in the West. As the frontier territories turned into Western states, county superintendents exercised direction over local schools by

A male teacher and his students in a Kansas classroom. *Courtesy Kansas State Historical Society.*

qualifying teachers through examinations and trying to standardize the length of the school year. As a result, teachers began to attend institutes and new Western normal schools instead of preparing for teaching through informal methods.

As school terms lengthened and the cost of teacher training rose, men were less likely to choose teaching as a career, and young men who had seen teaching as a supplementary or temporary position before entering a profession left teaching behind. Young women, who had few other professional occupations open to them, increased their personal and financial investment in teaching and began to see themselves as professionals, even though many taught only during the interim between their schooling and marriage. In Iowa, for example, only 19 percent (23 of 124 teachers) in 1848 were women, but by 1865, this figure had risen to 65 percent. By 1870, in the ten north-central states, 56 percent of the teachers were women.

While men from the East generally found teaching positions in the West on their own or through collegial or ministerial networks, the first women pioneer teachers were sponsored by formal organizations or female seminaries. The Ipswich (Massachusetts) Female Seminary sent 57 women teachers to Ohio and the Mississippi Valley between 1835 and 1839. Mount Holyoke and Troy female seminaries also sponsored women as Western teachers generally in care of a minister. Women missionaries also started schools in the West. Nearly 300 Protestant women taught in missions serving the Five Civilized Tribes in the Indian Territory between 1820 and 1860, and religious communities of Catholic women established schools in the Washington Territory and on the northern Great Plains.

The most successful organization sending teachers to the West was the NATIONAL POPULAR EDUCATION BOARD, which sponsored nearly 600 single women from New England and upstate New York as pioneer teachers in the Mississippi Valley and Oregon between 1846 and 1857. The women were trained at six-week institutes and urged to discipline their students using moral suasion. When Ellen Lee, at the age of twenty, met fifty students between the ages of fourteen and twenty-two in a log school in a small Indiana settlement, the school board doubted that she could control them because a previous male teacher had failed. "I was allowed to take my course," she said, "and I gave them only one rule—do right & by awakening their consciences to a sense of right and wrong . . . I have succeeded much better."

Teachers were paid low salaries and were expected to board with one scholar's family after another. Several National Board teachers resisted this practice. In Illinois, Sarah Quick told the school directors that it "was not my duty to board around, and I would not do it." The National Board expected the teachers to receive a minimum of $150 for a school year in addition to board. When the new graded schools opened in Lafayette, Indiana, in 1854, Cynthia Bishop's salary was $300 for a school year without board.

In the late nineteenth century, daughters of pioneers took advantage of the new normal schools in the West. In Colorado, more than 90 percent of the 300 women who graduated from Colorado State Normal School in the decade after its establishment in 1891 found teaching jobs. Only 50 percent married within ten years of their graduation; the others chose careers over marriage.

The highest position Western educators could aspire to was school superintendent. Herbert Quick, who was whipped for talking out loud in the pioneer school he attended, saw his election to the position of county superintendent as his chance to become a county leader. Although men held the majority of these positions, especially in settled areas, many women also became county superintendents, especially in counties closer to frontier conditions. The first woman to be elected to the position was Julia Addington in Iowa in 1869. In California, nearly half of the county superintendents were women by 1900, but they were concentrated in the mountainous northern counties.

In southern Minnesota's Blue Earth County, Sarah Christie Stevens was elected superintendent of schools in 1890. For a salary of $1,000 a year, she visited 137 ungraded district schools, more than half located on open prairies subject to winter storms. She examined and certified teachers and pressed for improvements in schools. One third of her county's teachers left their schools after only one year; most were not high-school graduates. Men, who made up 27 percent of the teachers in her county, were paid $35.82 a month and women $26.35 a month. As she rode horseback alone over the prairies through sparsely settled territory to her schools, Stevens continued the traditions of the first pioneer teachers.

—*Polly Welts Kaufman*

SEE ALSO: Colleges and Universities; Public Schools

SUGGESTED READING:

Christie, Jean. "Sarah Christie Stevens, Schoolwoman." *Minnesota History* 48 (1982): 245–254.

Cordier, Mary Hurlbut. *Schoolwomen of the Prairies and Plains: Personal Narratives from Iowa, Kansas, and Nebraska, 1860s to 1920s.* Albuquerque, N. Mex., 1992.

Fuller, Wayne E. *The Old Country School: The Story of Rural Education in the Middle West.* Chicago, 1982.

Kaufman, Polly Welts. *Women Teachers on the Frontier.* New Haven, Conn., 1984.

An 1895 image of a teacher with her students in front of a sod schoolhouse in Woods County, Oklahoma Territory. *Courtesy National Archives.*

McMillan, Ethel. "Women Teachers in Oklahoma, 1820–1860." *Chronicles of Oklahoma* 27 (1949): 2–32.

Underwood, Kathleen. "The Pace of Their Own Lives: Teacher Training and the Life Course of Western Women." *Pacific Historical Review* 55 (1986): 513–530.

TEAPOT DOME

Control and use of the naval oil reserves at Teapot Dome, Wyoming, and Elk Hills, California, became the center of a scandal that rocked the Warren G. Harding administration in 1922 and 1923. After ALBERT B. FALL, a rancher and Republican senator from New Mexico between 1912 and 1921, became secretary of the interior, he urged that control of the oil reserves be transferred from the Navy Department to the Department of the Interior. Secretary of the Navy Edwin Denby did so in the fall of 1921, despite some criticism from Congress.

In the spring of 1922, Fall secretly arranged for two firms to lease the rights to these fields. The first was the Teapot Dome Field, which was granted to Harry Sinclair's Mammoth Oil Company on April 7, 1922. EDWARD LAURENCE DOHENY, president of Pan American Petroleum Company and a long-time friend of Fall, got the rights to the Elk Hills and Buena Vista Hills reserves in California. At the time the leases were signed, Doheny gave Fall a one-hundred-thousand-dollar unsecured, interest-free loan, and Sinclair gave Fall more than three hundred thousand dollars in government bonds and cash.

As rumors of the secret leases circulated in Washington during the spring of 1923, President Harding began to worry about the state of his loosely run administration. The rumors are believed to have been a factor leading to his death on August 2, 1923. After Harding's death, the Senate Public Lands Committee, led by Senator Thomas J. Walsh of Montana, launched an investigation of the leases in October 1923. The investigation revealed the bribes given to Fall by Doheny and Sinclair. On February 8, 1924, in a joint resolution from the House and Senate, Congress agreed to sue to cancel the leases. In 1927, the Supreme Court ruled the leases fraudulent and the transfer of the oil reserves from the Navy Department to the Department of the Interior illegal.

In the aftermath, Fall, Doheny, and Sinclair were tried for conspiracy to defraud the government but were acquitted. Sinclair spent six and a half months in jail for contempt of the Senate and jury tampering, and Fall paid a large fine and spent a year in prison after being convicted for bribery in 1931. Neither Denby nor Harding was implicated in the case.

The scandal became the symbol for the corruption of the Harding administration, also tainted by fraudulent transactions in the Veterans Administration and Justice Department and by the president's extramarital affairs with Nan Britton and Carrie Phillips. Moreover, the Teapot Dome scandal seemed to reflect what many saw as the decay in the country's morals during the excesses of the Prohibition era. The impact of the scandal on the Republican party's national dominance during the 1920s, however, was minimal.

The term "Teapot Dome" became synonymous with scandal and political corruption in the American vocabulary. During the 1924 New York gubernatorial campaign between Al Smith and Colonel Theodore Roosevelt, Jr., Eleanor Roosevelt used the scandal against her cousin. In her vigorous efforts to support Smith, she followed "Ted" Roosevelt around the state in a car with a teapot mounted on top, unfairly implying that, as assistant secretary of the Navy under Harding, he had been involved in the scandal.

Strait-laced Calvin Coolidge, who had been Harding's vice-president, was elected in his own right in 1924 and, given his demeanor, was not tainted by the story that dominated the headlines for much of the campaign year.

—Patrick H. Butler, III

SUGGESTED READING:
Murray, Robert K. *The Harding Era.* Minneapolis, Minn., 1969.
Noggle, Burt. *Teapot Dome: Oil and Politics in the 1920s.* Baton Rouge, La., 1962.

TEATRO VILLALONGÍN (COMPAÑÍA HERNÁNDEZ-VILLALONGÍN)

Encouraged by the growth of the port cities and the facility of travel and communications, itinerant Hispanic theatrical troupes had become resident repertory companies in California by the mid-nineteenth century. In Texas, Hispanic theater developed at a somewhat slower pace. By the end of the nineteenth century, there were approximately ten Mexican drama companies touring northern Mexico and venturing into Texas for performances in halls and open-air market plazas. When the railroads extended north into Texas, some of these companies and many others not only established regular circuits that ran from Laredo to San Antonio and El Paso but also set down roots and became repertory companies in Texas cities. The Compañía Hernández-Villalongín was one of the first companies to establish itself in San Antonio by renting performance halls and performing by subscription.

As early as 1900, the Hernández-Villalongín company had performed in San Antonio at the opening of a new opera house. By 1910, the company seems to have become a resident in San Antonio with its rental of the Teatro Aurora, a simple hall over a print shop on South Santa Rosa Avenue. Included in the troupe's repertoire were nineteenth-century historical dramas and melodramas such as *Don Juan Tenorio*. By the time the Mexican Revolution of 1910 precipitated the flood of economic and political refugees into San Antonio, the company was well placed to provide melodrama to mixed audiences of workers and professionals thirsty for the artistic works in the Spanish language and the culture of their homeland.

In 1912, the company was invited to perform at the inauguration of Teatro Zaragoza, San Antonio's first large theater (the remodeled Dixie Theater) created specifically for the Hispanic community. During the latter years of the decade, the company performed frequently at the San Fernando Cathedral auditorium under the name of Gran Compañía Lírico Dramática de Carlos Villalongín, a name change that reflected its productions of *zarzuelas* and other lyric genres. Throughout the later 1910s and the 1920s, the company performed at other halls and theaters around town, including the Sociedad de la Unión, an association of San Antonio mutual-aid societies.

The Great Depression brought difficult times for Hispanic theater in the Southwest. The Villalongín family weathered the storm by joining forces with director and impresario Manuel Cotera and performing in his company in San Antonio and throughout central Texas and the Rio Grande Valley throughout the 1930s and 1940s. The company and its patriarch in Texas, Carlos Villalongín, represented the first generation of a Texas theatrical family whose members remain active on stage and in the media today.

—*Nicolás Kanellos*

SUGGESTED READING:

Kanellos, Nicolás. *A History of Hispanic Theater in the United States, Origins to 1940.* Austin, Tex., 1990.

TECUMSEH (SHAWNEE)

Born into one of the twelve Algonquian-speaking tribes called "Shawnee," Tecumseh (ca. 1768–1813) became the best-known Indian leader of his day to the American public and, aside from the Sioux Chief SITTING BULL, arguably the best-known in history. Born in Ohio, perhaps around Springfield, Tecumseh was the older brother of a Shawnee shaman named Tenskwatawa, frequently called by whites "the Prophet." As a young man, Tecumseh fought with distinction in the forty-year Algonquian resistance against Euro-American incursions in the Ohio Valley and the Old Northwest—a conflict that began with the French and Indian War, included Pontiac's Rebellion, and ended with the victory of "Mad" Anthony Wayne at the Battle of Fallen Timbers in 1794. Both Tecumseh's father and his two older brothers were killed during the long struggle, and following Fallen Timbers, an embittered Tecumseh moved west to present-day Indiana, although he returned regularly to the Ohio Valley to hunt. During the last five years of the eighteenth century and into the first few years of the nineteenth, he earned the admiration, respect, even affection of not only the Indians but also whites, for his veracity and for his opposition to the traditional Algonquian practices of captive torture and ritual cannibalism. Among the tribes of the Old Northwest, he quickly became a one-man political power who consciously modeled himself on Pontiac.

After the defeat of the Old Northwest tribes was finalized in the Treaty of Greenville in 1795, the trans-Appalachian frontier remained relatively peaceful, and an encouraged President THOMAS JEFFERSON directed the governor of the Indiana Territory, William Henry Harrison, to obtain "legal" title to as much Indian land as possible in preparation for further white expansion into the West. Harrison, who made no effort to ensure that he dealt with legitimate tribal representatives, ac-quired seventy million acres in less than three years by a series of questionable treaties, resulting in growing dissension among the tribes. Tecumseh, a persuasive and charismatic leader of remarkable strategic acumen, realized that, while his tribe could not survive a prolonged peace that ushered in thousands of new settlers, his people were not powerful enough alone to endure a prolonged war.

Tecumseh and Tenskwatawa worked closely together. Tenskwatawa claimed inspiration from the Great Spirit, preached a mixture of Shaker-influenced doctrine and traditional beliefs, and called on Indians to cleanse themselves of the unclean white race. His visions attracted recruits to the transtribal alliance that Tecumseh had begun to put together in 1805. In 1807, Tecumseh established headquarters for the alliance at the abandoned site of Fort Greenville on Indiana's Tippecanoe River, which quickly became known to the whites—who considered Tenskwatawa, not Tecumseh, the leader of the new "religious" movement—as Prophet's Town. Using the threat of war to intimidate Governor Harrison and to buy time while he traveled in 1811 throughout the Ohio country and beyond—west to the Sioux and south to the land of the Chickasaws, Choctaws, and Creeks—Tecumseh preached the need for an Indian confederation stretching from the Great Lakes to the Gulf of Mexico. Only as a unified, sovereign state, Tecumseh reasoned, could the Native Americans resist displacement or absorption and death as a people.

While Tecumseh was gone, Tenskwatawa managed to embroil the Ohio Valley tribes that had already joined the alliance into a disastrous battle at Tippecanoe. The Shawnees, Delawares, Miamis, Potawatomis, Ottawas, Winnebagos, Ojibwas (Chippewas), and Wyandots, angry at Harrison's treaties and defiantly ensconced at the old fort where Tecumseh had placed them, were joined by Black Hawk's Sac (Sauk) and Fox (Mesquakie) before Harrison mustered his troops, attacked, and soundly defeated them. The Prophet was discredited. When Tecumseh returned from his largely unsuccessful recruiting expedition in the South, he joined in the public rebuke of his brother. After the Battle of Tippecanoe, the Potawatomi, Winnebago, and Sac and Fox Indians, though shaken, remained loyal to Tecumseh's confederacy. Wyandot followers of the militant Chief Roundhead likewise adhered to the cause. But among the Delaware, Miami, and even Shawnee tribes, there were wholesale defections. The alliance began to crumble.

At this crisis point, however, the United States and Great Britain commenced the War of 1812. Tecumseh, who had sought the support of the British in Canada in 1810, only to be rebuffed, now eagerly embraced an alliance with England against the Americans. Initially, the alliance went well for the Indians. In the course of the war's first year, some four thousand Americans were either killed or captured, while combined British and Indian casualties numbered around five hundred. Yet even the Indian victories were pyrrhic, and their losses—homes burned, crops destroyed, populations displaced—were grim. By the second year, the British in the West had experienced a number of reverses, and the Indians' alliance with them began to disintegrate. As the British evacuated the territory, Tecumseh grew desperate. He persuaded the British to take a stand against the American army at Moravian Town on the north bank of the Thames River.

In a battle especially distinguished by the brilliant performance of a Kentucky mounted regiment under Colonel Richard Mentor Johnson, William Henry Harrison defeated the combined British and Indian forces at the Battle of the Thames on October 5, 1813. The Americans never found Tecumseh's body. Some say grieving warriors bore him off the field and gave him a secret burial, so even the site of his grave is a mystery. No one knows who killed him. But he was dead, and there would be no confederate Indian state in the American West. In fact, by the time Richard Johnson became vice-president of the United States under Martin Van Buren, Kentucky, Ohio, Indiana, Illinois, and Michigan were no longer even be considered the real American West. Those running his political campaign in the election of 1836 claimed Johnson had felled the great warrior, but he would never confirm it. On the day Tecumseh died, vengeful frontiersmen jumped on the body of a fallen warrior they thought to be the great Shawnee sachem, stripped the skin from his body, and cut it into strips. Later, in some of the fashionable shops in Washington, D.C., Americans could buy imitations of these "Tecumseh Razor Strops."

Dying with Tecumseh was the last credible hope the Native Americans had of containing land-hungry Americans east of the Mississippi. All barriers to migration into the trans-Mississippi had, in effect, been removed. It was only a matter of years before the tribes themselves would also be removed across the river.

—*Charles Phillips*

SEE ALSO: Black Hawk's War

SUGGESTED READING:
Edmunds, R. David. *Tecumseh and the Quest for Indian Leadership*. Boston, 1984.
Gilbert, Bil. *God Gave Us This Country: Tekamthi and the First American Civil War*. New York, 1989.
Tucker, Glenn. *Tecumseh: Vision of Glory*. New York, 1955.

TEJANOS

Although Spain laid claim to Texas in the early sixteenth century, Spaniards did not establish permanent settlements there until French threats from Louisiana in the 1680s and early 1700s compelled them to do so. In 1716, Spanish colonizers established Nacogdoches; in 1718, they founded SAN ANTONIO; and in 1721, they settled Goliad. As a colonial outpost of what was then called "New Spain," Texas was under the administration of a governor whose responsibility it was to carry out imperial policy and to see to the region's protection. In 1810, elements from among the Mexican settlers in Texas, or Tejano, population of approximately 3,500 joined efforts to overthrow Spanish rule in Mexico, and in 1821, Texas became part of the new republic of Mexico.

As settlers and common folks from Mexico trekked toward Texas, they brought with them the language, Catholic religion, foods, social institutions, and various material accouterments of Hispanic civilization. They formed an identity in Texas that combined cultural understandings with traits necessary for survival in the hinterlands. Tejanos thus became used to self-reliance, ruggedness, and a certain egalitarianism that distinguished them from their compatriots in the interior.

Between 1821 and 1836, Texas existed as a section within the state of Coahuila. For many Tejanos, the arrangement left much to be desired, for it meant unequal representation for them in the legislature. Nonetheless, the more elite elements in the province persuaded the state government during the 1820s to enact a colonization program that would permit Anglo-Americans to immigrate into Texas. Rancheros and other entrepreneurs hoped to form an alliance with the new arrivals; together, Mexicans and Anglos would transform the region into a capitalist success.

But Anglos, assisted by some elements within the Tejano population dissatisfied with Mexican rule, launched a successful independence movement in 1836. From then on, the Tejano community—which grew to more than 160,000 people by 1900—lived under the political domination of Anglo-Americans, who devised a variety of mechanisms to dilute any power Mexican Americans might muster. Through devious means, Anglos weakened the old elites immediately after the Civil War. Through violence, they kept the masses at bay. Since the Tejanos were generally beholden to some rancher or merchant for their livelihood, Anglos artfully managed their vote, thus dictating the outcome of issues and the result of political campaigns. Under Anglo-American rule, Tejanos were politically disfranchised, having little determination on matters of justice, education, and community improvement.

Despite their general powerlessness, Tejanos did assert themselves politically. Prominent political figures included JOSÉ ANTONIO NAVARRO and Santos Benavides, both legislators, the former from San Antonio and the latter from Laredo. Tejanos also joined political clubs and factions, campaigned for political candidates—both Tejano and Anglo—and, in South Texas and the El Paso Valley particularly, won elections to various local posts. Additionally, they took stands on numerous issues of regional and national importance.

Tejanos used their association with Anglo employers, church groups, political figures, and other intermediaries to acquaint themselves with the Anglo society, and throughout the nineteenth century, a good portion of the Tejano community transferred allegiance to the United States. Tejanos functioned as a bicultural people and integrated themselves into the American economy, joined fledgling labor societies, paid heed to American traditions and holidays, and otherwise took an interest in the affairs of their country of residence. At the same time, Mexico's contribution to Tejano society survived in a number of ways: through their native tongue, religious and folkloric beliefs, foods, feast days, and nationalist sentiments.

From the beginning of their settlement in Texas, most Mexican Americans made their living as common laborers, relying primarily on ranch and farm work. Many had worked the range, and they continued doing so for Anglo ranchers after 1836. As commercial farming began replacing ranching in the 1880s, however, many Tejanos became migratory farm laborers.

In the towns, Tejanos generally earned their livelihood as unskilled workers. Few rose above poverty. Instead, they lived in segregated, poverty-stricken sections (BARRIOS) of Anglo towns, did without sanitary facilities, and endured the vagaries of the weather, disease, and the indifference of white society.

But there did exist an elite element, that, despite the problems encountered after the Texas war for independence, persisted throughout the nineteenth century. This cohort was composed of a few tenacious ranch owners who managed to ward off disaster, enterprising merchants, local political officials, and some professionals. Actually, the middle class made up only a small segment of the entire Tejano population.

—*Arnoldo De León*

SEE ALSO: Mexican Settlement

SUGGESTED READING:
Chipman, Donald. *Spanish Texas, 1519–1821.* Austin, Tex., 1992.

De León, Arnoldo. *Mexican Americans in Texas: A Brief History.* Arlington Heights, Ill., 1993.
Montejano, David. *Anglos and Mexicans in the Making of Texas, 1836–1986.* Austin, Tex., 1987.
Rocha, Rodolfo. "The Tejano Experience." In *The Texas Heritage.* 2d ed. Edited by Ben H. Procter and Archie P. McDonald. Arlington Heights, Ill., 1992.

TELEGRAPH

The completion of the first successful telegraph line by Samuel F. B. Morse in 1844 set the stage for a communications revolution that would play an important role in the growth and unification of the United States and, in particular, the West, during the nineteenth century. Critical to the success of the new system was the development of the Morse code, a simple system of dots and dashes that could translate the alphabet and numerals into signals transmitted by electrical impulses. Requiring only wire, poles, and a small amount of equipment, the system was inexpensive, and many entrepreneurs rushed to establish telegraph companies.

By the 1850s, the many small enterprises began to coalesce, and efforts were mounted in both California and Missouri to create regional systems with the potential for developing a transcontinental line. At the same time, telegraph companies in Texas and other Western states also began to tie cities together and to reach towards the national network.

The first California company was the California State Telegraph Company, which linked San Francisco with San Jose, Stockton, Sacramento, and Marysville. The lines of other companies established in California during the mid-1850s linked San Francisco to Los Angeles by 1860. Meanwhile, the California legislature offered six thousand dollars a year to the first company to connect California to the East with an additional four-thousand-dollar annual subsidy for a second line to back up the first in case of loss of service.

In Missouri, a line connected St. Louis to Kansas City through Boonville along the banks of the Missouri River. At the same time, a line was started in Memphis with the goal of reaching Los Angeles along the route of the Overland Mail Company. Regional service in Texas began in 1854 with the creation of the Texas and Red River Telegraph Company, which operated lines from Marshall, Texas, to Shreveport and New Orleans, Louisiana. In 1856, the Texas and New Orleans Telegraph Company began construction to link San Antonio, Austin, and Galveston with New Orleans, but service was not completed until 1862.

As construction crews string telegraph lines across the plains, a Pony Express rider, probably unaware that the telegraph will put him out of business, offers greetings. *Courtesy Library of Congress.*

On June 16, 1860, Congress passed the Pacific Telegraph Act, authorizing forty thousand dollars a year for ten years to any company constructing a telegraph system from Missouri to San Francisco. Jeptha H. Wade consolidated the California telegraph companies into the Overland Telegraph Company, which pushed a line east from Carson City, Nevada, to Salt Lake along the Pony Express route. In 1851, a number of smaller systems merged to form the Mississippi Valley Printing Telegraph Company. In 1856, the company's name was changed to Western Union Telegraph Company, suggesting the goal of a system linking East and West. A number of lines pushed west from Missouri, including the Missouri and Western Telegraph Company and Western Union's Pacific Telegraph Company under Hiram Sibley and Edward Creighton. The Pacific Telegraph Company by-passed Denver when the city refused to buy twenty-thousand-dollars worth of stock and went instead through Laramie and South Pass.

Supply and maintenance was a problem throughout construction, since equipment for the California line had to be shipped by sea around Cape Horn. Moving timber for poles across the treeless plains was equally difficult for the lines coming from the East. These obstacles and others, including Indian raids and resistance by the Mormons who did not want to lose their isolation, were overcome, and the first service was initiated on October 24, 1861, when the lines were connected in Salt Lake City. STEPHEN J. FIELD, chief justice of California, sent the first message to President Abraham Lincoln, reaffirming California's loyalty to the Union.

While development slowed during the Civil War, the telegraph network grew rapidly in the late 1860s and 1870s along with the expansion into the West by railroads and settlers. Wherever a rail line was built, the telegraph soon followed. Army posts across the West were linked together by wire in the 1870s.

The telegraph network tied the West together and brought the newly settled regions into contact with the rest of the United States. The system made possible the rapid communication of business, political, and cultural information. Every community served by the telegraph had a newspaper to give citizens immediate access to all the information that came across the wire from the entire world. Isolation that typified life in the pre–Civil War West quickly disappeared with the coming of the telegraph line.

—*Patrick H. Butler, III*

SUGGESTED READING:

Thompson, Robert L. *Wiring a Continent: The History of the Telegraph Industry in the United States, 1832–1866.* Princeton, N.J., 1947.

TELEVISION WESTERNS

SEE: Radio and Television Westerns

TELLER, HENRY M.

A U.S. senator from Colorado and an articulate champion of Western interests, Henry M. Teller (1830–1914) was born in Alleghany County, New York. He headed west as a young lawyer, first to Illinois for three years, then to Central City, Colorado, in 1861. He served as a major general in the Union militia and fortified Denver against threatened Indian attacks. After the war, he built a lucrative law practice that represented mining corporations, served as president of the Colorado Central Railroad, and dabbled in territorial politics.

When Colorado joined the Union in 1876, Teller was sent to the U.S. Senate. In 1882, he resigned to become President Chester A. Arthur's secretary of the interior, but he returned to the Senate in 1885 and remained there for four terms, during which he became known for his impassioned speeches on the causes he supported, including Cuban independence from Spain, women's suffrage, federal regulation of big business, tax reform, and Western reclamation projects.

Teller's party affiliations during his four terms revealed his evolving political sensibilities. In two terms, he served as a Republican. By his third term, he had broken from the Republicans over the party's endorsement of the gold standard, allied himself with the Silver Republican party, and briefly garnered support as a presidential candidate in 1896. By his fourth term, he was a Democrat. He left the Senate in 1909 and died in Denver five years later.

—*Patricia Hogan*

SUGGESTED READING:

Ellis, Elmer. *Henry Moore Teller: Defender of the West.* Caldwell, Idaho, 1941.

TEMPERANCE AND PROHIBITION

Since the late eighteenth century, Americans have occasionally banded together to try to persuade, cajole, or force other Americans to quit drinking. Such temperance movements have been cyclical, much like American religious revivals, and they have usually appealed to evangelical, middle-class, native-born American Protestants.

A prohibition meeting takes place in Bismarck Grove, Kansas, in 1878. *Courtesy Kansas State Historical Society.*

In the two decades before the Civil War, temperance movements had some effect in reducing the amount of liquor Americans drank, which from colonial times had been prodigious. By the 1840s, middle-class Americans no longer automatically entertained guests with a drink as they had in the previous century, and a country intent on developing its industry had begun to demand discipline among its work force by banning the once frequent practice of drinking during special breaks on the job.

Alcohol consumption, however, began to increase again after the mid-nineteenth century with the coming of German, Irish, and other immigrants, whose drinking habits were European and who tended to congregate in saloons after work to socialize and discuss politics. In fact, by the late nineteenth century, saloons had become immigrant political institutions, homes of city bosses and political mechanics who found work for their ethnic kin in return for political loyalty and votes on election day. Prohibition, the heir to the temperance movement, took on a nativist cast and was often associated with progressive campaigns against corruption and "bossism": an attempt by middle-class Protestants, whose social and political dominance was threatened by Catholic immigrants, urbanization, and industrialization, to preserve the status quo.

By the 1870s, the temperance movement had become associated with women's reform as well. In part, this had to do with the real threat that male drunkards posed for their wives and children; since by common law, men controlled not only their own property but that of their wives, they could literally drink the family into destitution, and tales of wayward drunkards who physically abused their mates became standard fare in temperance tracts and at temperance meetings, where all present were urged to take the pledge and become a "T(temperance)-Totaler." But the prominence of women—and mostly middle-class women, whose husbands did not drink away their livelihoods or, for the most part, beat their wives—in the temperance movement of the late nineteenth century had also to do with a century's worth of social, economic, and ideological developments.

As American society grew more industrial, it developed what historians call the "doctrine of separate spheres," the notion that a man's world was in the work place and a woman's at home, but that both were important to family life. Male and female patterns of drinking began to diverge, as men did their social drinking outside the home and women, especially middle-class women, aspired to "true womanhood," which meant that while they were more delicate than men, they were also more morally refined. Once considered weak and immoral as a sex, they were now viewed as passionless and proper. It was their duty to see to the moral education and refinement of future generations, to use their roles as mothers to set good examples for their children and as ladies for their employees and less fortunate neighbors. With such a charge, most middle-class women quit drinking altogether. When cheap immigrant labor provided middle-class families with domestics to handle the household drudgery, these morally upright women expanded their duties from managing households to participating in charitable work in the community and, eventually, to taking up social issues such as suffrage and temperance.

On December 23, 1873, a Harvard-educated temperance advocate trained in homeopathic medicine, Dr. Diocletion Lewis, gave a temperance lecture in Hillsboro, Ohio. Entitled "The Duty of Christian Women in the Cause of Temperance," the speech inspired local women to do as he said his mother had done when she was at wit's end over his father's drinking: invade saloons and shops that sold alcoholic beverages and persuade the owners to quit trafficking in drink. Throughout the winter, women in other towns followed their example, and after the *New York Times* picked up the story, thousands of women in hundreds of communities organized into groups that invaded saloons and demanded pledges from bartenders, prayed, sang hymns, marched on the streets outside bars and drugstores, formed picket lines to prevent beverage deliveries, took down the names of patrons who ignored them, and held mass temperance meetings. The short-lived Women's Temperance Crusade gave birth to the WOMAN'S CHRISTIAN TEMPERANCE UNION, which, under the leadership of Frances Willard, became the major vehicle for prohibition over the next two decades. Willard and others spread the organization into the South and West where it became associated with the whole gamut of agrarian and radical Western reforms, from suffrage to the free coinage of silver. By 1890, more than half the counties in America contained WCTU organizations, and a Prohibition party had been formed to take the fight to the ballot box. Republicans uneasily adopted prohibition as a cause, while Democrats—outside the South—opposed it. And in the West, the prohibitionists achieved the reformers' first major victory.

In 1878, Kansas voters passed an amendment to the state's constitution prohibiting the importation, sale,

A poster announcing a 1917 gathering of the Anti-Saloon League. *Courtesy the Strong Museum.*

Townspeople gathered to watch prohibitionists attack a Kansas saloon. *Courtesy Kansas State Historical Society.*

women's temperance organizations, the Anti-Saloon League limited itself to one issue, prohibition, and would back any candidate, accept any proposal, support any group that advanced the cause in any fashion. The prototype of modern political-pressure groups, the first league was formed in 1893 and became national in 1895, when the Ohio group merged with a similar organization in Washington, D.C. The league depended not on volunteers but on paid staff, mostly recruited from Protestant churches, and its general council and legislative superintendent, Wayne B. Wheeler, actually wrote the Volstead Act. Although league members used any argument to advance their cause, they concentrated not on individual drinkers or domestic issues but on propaganda about the massive influence of the liquor "interests" in American and especially big-city politics and on economic arguments that claimed intemperance hurt worker productivity and that saloon districts discouraged urban growth. Knowing that for emerging manufacturers confronting workers with traditional drinking habits prohibition seemed a way to instill discipline for machine production, the league pitched its message to businessmen; John D. Rockefeller, for example, was an early and substantial patron.

Social changes affecting various trans-Mississippi states made the West receptive to the league's proselytizing. In the late nineteenth century, those living on the mining frontier were mostly young, transient men working intermittently at jobs under the direction of a labor boss, and mining towns and camps were flush with SALOONS filled with drinkers. But by 1900, irrigation and dryland farming had allowed states such as Colorado and Idaho to attract a fresh wave of farmers and their families from older Midwestern states. The new arrivals from Kansas and Iowa, which had already passed prohibition laws, underwrote the growth of an expanding agriculture by raising potatoes or sugar beets for market, a kind of work that required planning and discipline. Meanwhile, mining communities, whose members once dominated the economy and the politics of the states, stagnated as commercial agriculture prospered. The Irish and Europeans who worked as miners continued their traditional drinking habits, and

and manufacture of liquor, and three other trans-Mississippi states—Iowa, North Dakota, and South Dakota—soon adopted the "Kansas plan." The battle bore all the hallmarks of ethnic conflict that distinguished local-option fights in the East. Catholics, Germans (both Lutheran and Catholic), the Irish, eastern Europeans, the working class, urbanites, and those Western counties where a disproportionate number of residents were male tended to vote against such amendments. Evangelical Protestant farmers tended to support them. Prohibition was a domestic issue and a small-town and rural issue, all arenas in which the effects of excessive drinking tended to be most obvious. Also in the four Western prohibition states, rural communities dominated the state houses. In states like California, with large urban and cosmopolitan populations, and in states with primarily hard-drinking young male work forces, prohibition did not fare so well. In fact, South Dakota soon thought better of its decision and repealed its amendment in 1906. Almost as quickly as it had arisen, Western temperance seemed to have run its course.

But then, the turn of the century witnessed the birth of the Anti-Saloon League. Prohibition party gatherings could have easily been mistaken for revivals, but not so Anti-Saloon League meetings: they were all business. Like the Women's Temperance Crusade, the Anti-Saloon League began in Ohio, but unlike the when conflicts broke out between workers and bosses, the prohibitionists blamed the class hostility on the saloons that served as gathering places for workingmen. In 1892, for example, after the bloody battles between miners and the private armies of the mine owners at Couer d'Alene, Idaho, a Prohibition party organizer declared that prohibition would have prevented the entire incident.

The Anti-Saloon League and other prohibitionists pointed to the growing incidence of radical protest from such organizations as the INDUSTRIAL WORKERS OF THE WORLD (IWW) and argued that it spread in step with liquor consumption. Blaming working-class drinking for industrial conflict was disingenuous at best, since almost all unions—including the IWW—insisted that their members remain sober, and many required a pledge to this effect in order to become a member. But middle-class voters accepted the link between drinking and labor militancy because they did not wish to face the true sources of the disorder, while unions and workers were hostile to the Anti-Saloon League not for its anti-alcohol message but for diverting attention from pressing issues of wealth and power. Industrialists, on the other hand, supported the league for just this reason, and most league leaders were members of the Republican party. The result was that farmers and their wives voted rural areas dry under local-option laws in order to protect their families from—and impose their sober, Protestant, American values and work habits on—a "foreign" working class while their native-born allies in the urban middle class voted their states dry to restore the order they believed was being disrupted by slum-dwelling, alien anarchists. Once again, small towns proved the seedbed for the struggles over liquor, and nativism was its engine of growth.

The new wave of Progressive reform hit in the West around 1907, when Oklahoma entered the Union with a prohibition clause written into its state constitution. During 1914, Arizona, Colorado, Oregon, and Washington all voted dry. While California voters rejected prohibition, many rural locales banned the manufacture and sale of alcohol under local-option laws. Idaho, Montana, Nevada, Texas, and Idaho also enacted some type of prohibition. Indeed, the Progressive West had become a bastion of prohibition even before the United States ratified the Eighteenth Amendment in 1919, and the entire nation became dry.

Prohibition went into effect in 1920, the year the U.S. Census documented that for the first time the number of people living in American cities had surpassed those living in rural areas. And in those cities, industrialization was ushering in yet another change. In an economy that was producing more goods than it could sell, one that relied increasingly on advertising to foster new needs and create fresh markets for its surplus, pleasure-seeking became an approved pastime. The Broadway Club life that developed from the cabarets of the 1890s was attracting young middle- and upper-class urbanites, who mixed with mobsters in a modern culture that exalted consumption and display rather than industry and thrift, valued self-expression and individuality rather than sacrifice and family, and found fulfillment in leisure rather than work. In Hollywood, California, a new industry began to produce movies that extolled glamour and sophistication on the silver screen for a mass audience. Los Angeles real-estate promoters were soon pushing a carefree existence under the sun in a town by the beach. In the modern West, the industrialization that the temperance reformers had historically embraced was proving corrosive to the Victorian values that had once seemed themselves so modern. Even before the Great Depression brought to office the Democrats who repealed the Eighteenth Amendment in 1933, prohibitionists were losing all the ground it had taken them more than a century to gain, except in areas in the rural South and Midwest, where dry laws would linger on in spots well into the second half of the twentieth century.

—*Charles Phillips*

SEE ALSO: Populism; Progressivism

SUGGESTED READING:
Blocker, Jack S., Jr. *American Temperance Movements: Cycles of Reform.* Boston, 1989.
———. *"Give to the Winds Thy Fear": The Women's Temperance Crusade, 1973–1874.* Westport, Conn., 1985.
Bordin, Ruth. *Women and Temperance: The Quest for Power and Liberty, 1873–1900.* Philadelphia, 1981. Reprint. New Brunswick, N.J., 1990.
Kerr, K. Austin. *Organized for Prohibition: A New History of the Anti-Saloon League.* New Haven, Conn., 1985.
West, Elliott. *The Saloon on the Rocky Mountain Mining Frontier.* Lincoln, Nebr., 1979.

TEN BEARS (COMANCHE)

Ten Bears (1792–1872) was a Comanche of the Yamparika band. His Comanche name was Parra-Wa-Samen, and he was also known as Ten Elks. Ten Bears acquired an early reputation as a brave and aggressive warrior. Later in life, he concluded that resistance to the advance of Euro-American settlement was futile, and he became an advocate of peace. He was chosen in 1863 as a tribal delegate to speak in Washington, D.C., for Comanche interests. In 1865, he represented

Ten Bears (Comanche).
Courtesy National Archives.

the tribe at the Little Arkansas Council, held in Kansas, and two years later, he spoke at the Medicine Lodge Council, also in Kansas. During the last year of his life, he returned to Washington, D.C., with TOSAWI, spokesman for the Peneteka Comanches, and delegates from other tribes.

Ten Bears was highly respected in the nation's capital, but he was reviled by many of members of his tribe and band. Despite Ten Bears's efforts at peace, many Yamparika Comanches joined QUANAH PARKER during the Red River War (1874 to 1875), just two years after Ten Bears's death.

—Alan Axelrod

"TEN-GALLON" HAT

SEE: Cowboy Outfits

TENSKWATAWA

SEE: Tecumseh

TERRITORIAL GOVERNMENT

Origin of the territorial system

The earliest territorial ordinance was drafted by THOMAS JEFFERSON in order to rationalize the transition of newly acquired regions into statehood. The 1784 ordinance provided for approximately sixteen territories to be established northwest of the Ohio River, with self-government to be increased in proportion to the increase in population. The following year, a new land ordinance created a system of federal land sale based on one-square-mile survey lots (called "sections"), thirty-six of which made up a township. As early as the 1785 ordinance, one of every thirty-six sections was set aside to finance public education within the township. Two years later, the NORTHWEST ORDINANCE

evolved from this scheme and provided government for the Northwest Territory and laid the foundation for subsequent territorial governments farther west.

The Northwest Ordinance retained the section- and township-survey scheme. It empowered the president to appoint a territorial governor, a secretary, and three judges. These administrators were charged with creating laws for their territory by adopting and adapting laws from existing states. The Northwest Ordinance also spelled out the orderly transition from territory to state. When a territory attained a population of at least five thousand white adult males, it was empowered to elect the lower house of a bicameral legislature. Appointment of members to the upper house was reserved to the president of the United States. Together, the legislative houses would elect a single, nonvoting delegate to represent the territory in the U.S. Congress. Only after a territory's population had reached sixty thousand could the territory apply for statehood.

The Old Northwest

The first U.S. territory, the Northwest Territory was established in 1788. Arthur St. Clair, the first territorial governor, established two important precedents. First, he established the principle of liberally modifying existing state laws adopted for use by the territory. Second, he defined his office to included a de facto function as superintendent of Indian affairs.

In 1798, the population of the Northwest Territory warranted election of a legislature, and in 1800, the Indiana Territory was created, encompassing all of the Northwest Territory, except for Ohio, which applied for statehood and was admitted in 1803.

White's precedents

The territory south of the Ohio was administered according to the provisions and precedents established by the Northwest Ordinance, except that slavery was permitted. By the time the territory was created, Kentucky had achieved a sufficient population to gain admission as a state without passing through the territory stage. However, the large region ceded to the federal government by North Carolina—the region that would become the state of Tennessee—first became the Southwest Territory in 1790, administered by Governor WILLIAM BLOUNT. It was the first territory actually to send a delegate to Congress, James White, who established the precedents for moving Congress toward admitting a territory into statehood. The procedure White originated included the passage by Congress of an enabling act, directing the territorial governor to take a census and call an election for a constitutional convention; popular ratification of the constitution and election of state offices; congressional approval of the state constitution; and congressional passage and presidential signature of an act of admission, followed by the seating of the new state's congressional delegation.

Federal supervision

Supervision of territorial governments was initially entrusted to the U.S. Department of State. After 1873, authority was passed to the Department of the Interior. However, the first stage prescribed by the Northwest Ordinance, in which all administrative officials were appointed by the president, was abandoned in 1817, when the Territory of Alabama was created simultaneously with a legislature to govern it. After 1836, when the Wisconsin Territory was created, all subsequent territories were governed by popularly elected legislatures. However, the president continued to appoint territorial governors, secretaries, and judges. The governor could veto legislation, and Congress could, if necessary, override both the territorial legislature and the governor.

With sweeping responsibility but relatively limited authority, territorial governors were obliged to cooperate with many federal agencies—the army, the Post Office, the General Land Office, and others.

Effectiveness of the territorial system

The longevity of the territorial system attests to its general effectiveness. In all, thirty-one states were territories or parts of territories before being admitted to the Union. Although territories were permitted an increased degree of democratic government by the first third of the nineteenth century, they were ultimately subject to federal authority. That the system worked as well as it did may have been the product of good faith on the part of governors, legislators, Congress, and presidents as much as it was the result of legal design.

All of the territories contiguous to the United States had been admitted as states by 1912, and Alaska and Hawaii by 1959. Puerto Rico, a U.S. territory since the Spanish-American War, did not pass into statehood, but became a commonwealth in 1952 and is the most autonomous of all U.S. territories, past or present. Territories are currently administered by the Office of Territorial and International Affairs of the Department of the Interior and include Guam, American Samoa, the Virgin Islands, the Commonwealth of the Northern Mariana Islands, and the Trust Territory of the Pacific Islands, which encompasses the Marshall Islands, Palau, and Micronesia (the Trust Territory Islands are administered by the United States under United Nations trusteeship—a unique arrangement unforeseen in the eighteenth and nineteenth centuries).

—*Alan Axelrod*

TERRITORIAL LAW AND COURTS

Determined by Congress in the organic acts establishing the territories, territorial courts followed the pattern established in the NORTHWEST ORDINANCE of 1787. The territories had a supreme court, with justices appointed by the president, and inferior courts, whose nature and extent were determined by the territorial legislatures. The structure most common to the territories of the West was the county court and the justice of the peace. The 1836 Wisconsin Organic Act called for justices of the peace to dispense local justice, a circuit court to hear first appeals, and a territorial supreme court to hear final appeals; Congress followed this pattern in establishing future courts.

The justice of the peace was responsible for administering laws at the county level. Typically social, economic, and political leaders of their communities, justices of the peace had limited jurisdiction. They could hear civil suits involving amounts of less than one thousand dollars, nonfelony cases, and cases of special jurisdictions created by the legislatures, such as contested elections, city-ordinance violations, and the like. The nature and extent of their jurisdiction depended on territorial legislation.

Intermediate trial or appellate courts also varied by territory. Decisions could be appealed to the territorial supreme court. Originally, territorial supreme court justices staffed appellate trial courts. This changed, however, because the justice who had origi-

This illustration, entitled *Execution of Robbers*, shows a military firing squad meting out justice. Before the establishment of territorial governments, the military took responsibility for law and order. *Courtesy Library of Congress.*

nally heard the case at the appellate-court level was then asked, at the supreme-court level, to review his decision. Territories created county courts as well as specialized courts such as probate courts, recorders courts, and police courts. The courts with specialized jurisdiction addressed obvious local needs for judicial action without resort to county-level action. Further, they were easily accessible in terms of time, distance, and expense.

The territorial supreme court was the highest appellate court of the territory. Patronage was clearly a substantial factor in the appointments of justices by the president. The justices of the territorial supreme courts in the West generally were young lawyers with records of political activity; few had substantial legal reputations prior to appointment, and most had modest social-class positions. Using the appointment for subsequent gain in position, some territorial justices were on the bench a very short time. Others made a career of judging and continued on the bench after the territory became a state. Still others were famous in legal circles of their time. WILLIS VAN DEVENTER of Wyoming was elevated to the U.S. Supreme Court, and MOSES HALLETT became one of Colorado's most noted jurists on the state and federal bench. Although the people on the bench varied, the quality of justice in the territories generally was of high quality.

The development of law in the West came substantially from the territorial courts dealing with subject matter seldom considered in the courts of the East and Midwest. Justices of the territorial supreme courts frequently looked to the works of the California Supreme Court, but they gave equal weight to the experiences of their own territories.

The territorial courts produced a record of decisions that had continuity with the traditions of the East. English common law was the rule of decision in the East, except in Louisiana, and territorial legislators made it the rule of decision in the West. The statutes that adopted English common law provided, however, that it was the rule of decision for the territory only to the extent that it was applicable. Lawmakers recognized that the West was different and that the experience of the American people differed from that of the English. In Utah and New Mexico, lawmakers did not adopt English common law. The Mormon-dominated legislature in Utah rejected English common law because it did not recognize the legality of polygamy then practiced among the faithful. In New Mexico, the territorial legislature refused to adopt English common law because it outlawed the practice of peonage, a condition of servitude compelling people to perform labor in order to pay off debts. Both territories eventually yielded. A federal campaign against polygamy and the

Mormons resulted in a change in official church policy, and in New Mexico, Congress moved to ban the practice of peonage.

The territorial courts in the West faced challenges never addressed in Eastern courts. In the mid-nineteenth century, the discovery of gold and silver in the West set off both a great movement of populations and an expansion of law. MINING law came from the grassroots of the industry, the mining camp. People gathering to exploit the soil, rivers, and mountains of the West came together to write down the rules of the mining industry. These rules were known as "local mining district regulations." For every mining district, there was a set of regulations. In this case, Westerners created law to govern behavior before the institutions of the law had a chance to respond to the new challenge. Territorial legislatures first validated by statute the work of the local mining district and then passed more general statutes setting out what would be required of mining districts subsequently making regulations. Congress responded in a similar fashion with the Mining Law of 1866, which validated the local mining district regulations, and then with the MINING LAW OF 1872, which set out some of the national rules for miners on the public domain. Territorial courts were soon required to interpret these rules and apply English common law to a new industry. The record of decisions at the territorial appellate level substantially influenced later decisions of state and federal courts.

WATER law was another area in which the territorial courts and legislatures displayed creativity. Miners and farmers attempting to exploit the arid regions of the West found that the scarcity of water required changes in law. Miners put their legal thinking to paper in the local mining district regulations and gave first comers the right to use water to the extent of their initial appropriation. Farmers saw the necessity of irrigation on the rich soil of the West made barren by lack of moisture. Miners, farmers, and other water users went to court to make law for their respective interests. The water law that emerged was the law of prior appropriation. This law states basically that the first appropriator of water has a right to the beneficial use of the amount of water first appropriated. This was far different from the English common law based on riparian rights that held that the owner of the bank of the stream has a right to the reasonable use of the water and that owners of land upstream could not unreasonably diminish the quantity or quality of water. The important difference between the two concepts revolved around use. By English common law, the riparian owner could use water for any purpose and do so inefficiently. By Western territorial law, the prior appropriator was held to beneficial use and a higher level of efficiency as agricultural research improved knowledge of water requirements of soils and crops. As the demands of urbanization and industrialization increased water use, the beneficial-use requirement made clear the advantages of prior-appropriation law.

Territorial courts and legislatures dealt with a wide array of less spectacular elements of territorial life. In their first sessions, lawmakers had to adopt codes of civil and criminal law. Many territorial legislatures created statutes every session and made law one step at a time. Others, like the Arizona legislature, created a commission to write a comprehensive law code for the territory. Still others, like the legislatures in Montana and the Dakotas, looked to the Field Code of New York and California for guidance in creating a legislative code system. Courts interpreted the handiwork of the legislatures and used English common law to fill in where gaps and need existed.

Territorial law also provided for transactions in a market economy. Courts used the familiar law of property and contract to decide cases arising from marketplace agreements. Here the law of the West was much like the law of the East. There were exceptions, of course, like mining partnerships. Unlike partnership law in the East, Western mining law held that a mining partner could assign his interest without the consent of his partners. In Western law, the death of a partner did not dissolve the partnership; rather death brought the heirs in as partners. Mining partners had no implied power to execute a promissory note or to draw or accept a bill of exchange in the name of the partnership. Territorial courts interpreted the law to maintain the entity of the mining partnership to give it continuity for the exploitation of mineral wealth.

Territorial law responded to the demands of mining labor with protective labor legislation. In Montana and Colorado, mine unions lobbied legislatures to pass statutes that provided some safety regulation of the mines. Territorial courts followed familiar paths when employees were injured on the job in mines or railroad yards. The courts followed the law of "fellow servant," which held that an injured employee could not recover damages from his or her employer if the cause of injury was the negligence of a fellow servant on the job. As time and cases worked against the rule, the courts changed. Passing wrongful-death statutes, the legislatures reversed the rule of English common law that a cause of action died with the plaintiff and gave the plaintiff's heir access to the courts. Safe-place and safe-tool statutes further protected workers, and territorial courts generally supported the trend to employer liability for injury on the job.

Territorial law for crimes was borrowed from the East and molded by the experience of the West. The standard designations of felony and misdemeanor graced the territorial penal codes. Cities had the authority to create municipal violations in their codes. Over time, territorial legislatures criminalized behavior—such as breaking irrigation works—that civil penalties had not deterred. Early statutes provided for the death penalty for a substantial array of crimes, including crimes against property, such as the theft of horses or cattle. The territorial courts heard many of these capital cases and followed a common nineteenth-century line of reasoning that accorded the people, as represented by their legislatures, the authority to determine punishment.

An Idaho case demonstrated the territorial courts' adherence to the traditions of the common law. A gang of three musicians killed a traveling tinker. Apprehended, they were brought to the bar of justice where their attorney argued that the alleged act did not constitute a crime. Congress had failed to carry over the law of Washington in the Organic Act for Idaho, and the alleged act had occurred in the Idaho Territory before the territorial legislature had met and passed a penal code. It followed that since Congress had not provided for a penal code and Idaho had not yet done so, the act of killing was not a crime. The territorial supreme court agreed and dismissed the accused. The American common-law tradition held that unless an act is declared to be criminal by law, a court had no authority to criminalize the act.

—*Gordon Morris Bakken*

SEE ALSO: Kearny Code; Law and Order, Spanish Law

SUGGESTED READING:
Bakken, Gordon Morris. *The Development of Law on the Rocky Mountain Frontier.* Westport, Conn., 1983.
Brown, Richard Maxwell. *Strain of Violence.* New York, 1975.
Friedman, Lawrence M. *A History of American Law.* 2d ed. New York, 1985.
Pisani, Donald J. *To Reclaim a Divided West.* Albuquerque, N. Mex., 1992.
Reid, John Phillip. *Law for the Elephant.* San Marino, Calif., 1980.
Wunder, John R. *Inferior Courts, Superior Justice.* Westport, Conn., 1979.

TERRY, ALFRED HOWE

Major General Alfred Howe Terry (1827–1890) was born in Hartford, Connecticut, attended Yale, and then became clerk of the Supreme Court of Connecticut. While working in this job, he raised a volunteer regiment in 1860 and became its colonel. He distinguished himself in battle and command during the Civil War.

One of the few volunteer officers to remain in the service, he was promoted to brigadier general of the regular army in 1865.

At the end of the Civil War, Terry's career shifted briefly to the West when he was given command of the Department of Dakota in 1866. During this period, he expanded the military presence in the department with a series of new forts to protect the trails and surround the Sioux territory. He served as a military representative to the peace commission that established the Medicine Lodge and Fort Laramie treaties. In 1869, he was transferred to South Carolina but returned to Dakota in 1872.

Terry was in command of the Dakota Territory during the critical years of Indian fighting. He had disagreed with GEORGE ARMSTRONG CUSTER over the Black Hill's expedition in 1872 and 1873 but eventually allowed his subordinate to return to the command of the Seventh Cavalry for the Little Bighorn campaign. He accepted criticism of his action in silence but continued to prosecute the war against the Sioux while supervising the inquiry that followed the Battle of Little Bighorn. By 1877, his troops had subdued the Sioux. That year, he headed an unsuccessful mission to Canada designed to persuade SITTING BULL to return to the United States in peace.

Terry remained in command of the Dakota Territory until 1886. Promoted to major general, he was then given command of the Military Division of Missouri. He retired on disability in 1888.

—*Patrick H. Butler, III*

SEE ALSO: Little Bighorn, Battle of; Medicine Lodge Treaty of 1867

SUGGESTED READING:

Bailey, John W. *Pacifying the Plains: General Alfred Terry and the Decline of the Sioux, 1866–1890.* Westport, Conn., 1979.

Utley, Robert. *Frontier Regulars: The United States Army and the Indian, 1866–1891.* New York, 1973.

Willert, James, ed. *The Terry Letters.* La Mirada, Calif., 1980.

TEXAS

The state of Texas has been under six different flags (Spain, France, Mexico, Texas, the United States, and

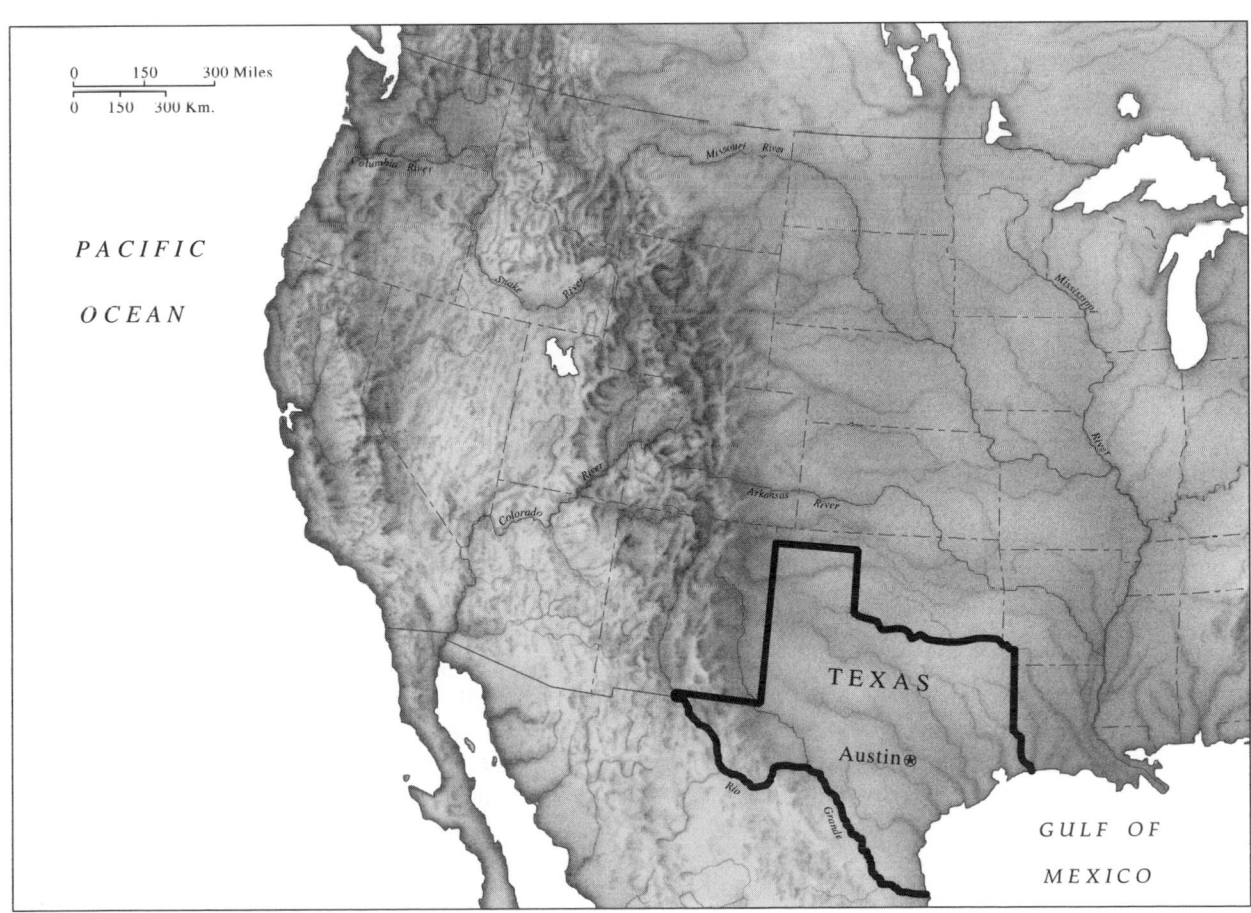

The possibility of Texas entering the Union prompted a cartoon depicting Sam Houston and Stephen Fuller Austin in the boat, proannexation advocate James K. Polk on the river bank, and those who opposed annexation, led by Henry Clay, pulling the Texas boat away from American soil. *Courtesy Library of Congress.*

the Confederacy) and is the one state in the continental United States to have been an independent republic with diplomatic recognition from the United States, Britain, and France. The "Lone Star State" nickname is derived from the flag designed for the Republic of Texas in 1838 and used today as the state flag, which bears a single star in a blue field. The Spanish named the territory Texas, a derivation of the Hasinai Caddo Indian word *Taychas* meaning "friend or ally." For many, the word *Texas* inspires visions of the westering experience, the cattle culture, and the frontier. In the nineteenth century, settlers wrote "GTT" (meaning "gone to Texas") on the doors of their abandoned homes in the East. John Steinbeck observed, "Texas is a state of mind, Texas is an obsession. Above all, Texas is a nation in every sense of the word."

Texas is located at the middle of the southern border of the United States. Austin in central Texas has served as the capital since 1839 when Texas was a republic. The second largest state, it covers 266,807 square miles of land and water. The greatest north-south distance of the state is 801 miles and the greatest

east-west distance is 773 miles. The population of Texas in 1990 was 16,986,510, making it the third largest state in terms of population. The people of Texas are diverse and are becoming increasingly urbanized. In 1990, 60.6 percent of the population was Anglo; 11.6 percent, black; and 25.2 percent, Hispanic with the remaining 2.2 percent from other ethnic groups. In all, twenty-two identifiable ethnic groups are represented among the state's population. By 1990, the urban population had increased from 79.5 percent in 1980 to 80.3 percent. Only 1.1 percent of the population lived on farms. Overall, the growth in Texas population continued, a pattern unbroken since the state entered the Union.

Although the cowboy tradition remains essential to modern Texas, the state is a sophisticated entity. The economic interests, ranging from the high technology of the Johnson Space Center to traditional ranches and farms, includes heavy and light industry; extractive industries such as oil, coal, sulfur, and timber; cattle, sheep, and goat ranching; cotton, citrus, grain, and truck farms; and tourism based on both natural and historical attractions. The state supports a variety of cultural and educational institutions including more than 400 museums, almost 150 institutions of higher learning, major symphonies and dance companies in the larger cities, a strong tradition of popular music centered in Austin, and a variety of activities reflecting the diversity of the state's past and present.

While the image of Texas as a rural state remains strong, large cities have grown up across the state. Three cities—HOUSTON, DALLAS, and SAN ANTONIO—are among the ten largest in the United States. Other major urban centers with populations over 200,000 include Austin, Beaumont–Port Arthur, Brownsville-Harlingen, EL PASO, Fort Worth–Arlington, Killeen-Temple, Lubbock, and McAllen-Edinburg-Mission. The growth of the cities has been a twentieth-century phenomenon, reflecting the changes in the economy and the population. Today, Texas has twenty-seven major metropolitan areas, more than any other state.

Geography

The boundaries of Texas are defined primarily by water. The RIO GRANDE, between El Paso and the Gulf of Mexico, separates Texas from Mexico. To the southeast, from the mouth of the Rio Grande north to the mouth of the Sabine, the Gulf Coast borders the state. The Sabine River forms the boundary between Texas and Louisiana. A short boundary line separates Texas from Arkansas. On the north, the Red River divides Texas and Oklahoma. The Panhandle, surrounded by Oklahoma and New Mexico, and the northern border between trans-Pecos Texas and New Mexico are defined by political boundaries.

Although often depicted as desert or rolling plains, the geography of Texas falls into four primary regions, essentially a series of steps ascending from east to west, rising to 4,600 feet on the Great Plains and to 8,751 feet at Guadalupe Peak in far West Texas, which is a part of the Rocky Mountains. The fertile and densely populated Coastal Plain, between the Gulf Coast and the Balcones fault line, includes major agricultural areas along the coast and the lower Rio Grande Valley. Rising to a height of almost 1,000 feet, the coastal plain ends at the Balcones escarpment, a geological formation marked on the map by the location of the cities of Dallas, Waco, Austin, and San Antonio. To the west of the fault lies the Hill Country, consisting of the two regions—the Edwards Plateau in the south and the North-central Plains in the north on the southern edge of the Great Plains. At the western edge of the North-central Plains rises the Caprock Escarpment, which marks the beginning of the High Plains; and farther to the south and west lies the most rugged part of the state—the trans-Pecos region, the southern end of the Rocky Mountain chain. West of the Balcones fault, the climate becomes semiarid and arid, more typical of the Hollywood image of the state.

Six major river systems, most having their headwaters in the western part of the state, cross the Coastal Plains. However, because the terrain remains relatively flat, the rivers run shallow and slow, making navigation difficult. Houston, the greatest port in the state and the third largest in the United States, achieved its prominence only because of the conversion of Buffalo Bayou, a small stream emptying into Galveston Bay, into a ship canal in the early twentieth century. Before then, maritime trade entered the state through a series of small ports on the Gulf Coast with shallow harbors.

Given Texas's scale, generalizations about the weather are almost meaningless. The Coastal Plain, particular in the northeast, experiences heavy rains—almost forty-five inches a year—and enjoys an average temperature of about 70° F at Houston, while the Panhandle averages about 60° F and less than twenty inches of rain. The variety of climate is matched by a wide variety of plant and animal life. East Texas was built on the LUMBER INDUSTRY, based on varieties of pine, while farther south, the Coastal Plain supports a variety of agricultural activities. In western Texas, the limited rainfall supports grasses appropriate to GRAZING animals from the buffaloes to cattle. Despite averages, in any season and in any part of the state, weather may change rapidly, from the "blue northers" in the winter when temperatures drop as much as fifty degrees in one hour, to tornadoes and hurricanes, which appear in the spring and summer and bring massive destruction by winds and floods.

Native Americans

The first Paleo-Indians appeared in far western Texas about fifteen thousand years ago. They were hunters associated with the Clovis and Folsom cultures. With the changing climate at the end of the Ice Age, natives began to supplement hunting with AGRICULTURE.

The Indians in Texas at the time of European contact fall into four different groups. All appear to have lived in cultures less developed than the Indians to the south in Mexico and to the east in lower Louisiana but benefited from these cultures. In the east lived the forest dwelling Caddo Indians, who blended to the south with the Atakapas and Karankawas on the coast and were related to the mound-builders in Louisiana. In South Texas, the Jumanos were farmers, who cooperated most easily with the Spanish but went into decline because of droughts in the early sixteenth century. The Apaches, the most warlike of the tribes, lived in the far west. After the arrival of the Spanish, the Comanches pushed into West Texas from the mountains when they acquired HORSES. For the most part, the eastern and southern Indians did some farming, although they still relied on hunting. The Wichita tribes in Central Texas appear to have served as mediators between the other major cultural groups, although they were not as settled as the Caddos and the Jumanos.

Spanish and French exploration

Alonso Alvarez de Pineda led the first Europeans into Texas and explored the Texas coast at the mouth of the Rio Grande (originally the Rio de las Palmas) in 1519 and 1520. Spaniards returned to Texas in 1528 as survivors of the PÁNFILO DE NARVÁEZ expedition on the Gulf Coast. Attempting to reach Mexico on rafts, expedition members were swept ashore on the island of Mulhado, probably today's GALVESTON. Only four, led by ÁLVAR NÚÑEZ CABEZA DE VACA, survived shipwreck, enslavement by Indians, and the environment to reach Mexico. One, a black Moroccan slave named Esteban, remained in Mexico and led an expedition under FRAY MARCOS DE NIZA in search of Cíbola, the seven cities of gold. This expedition reported that a Zuni pueblo, seen at a distance, might be one of the cities. Expeditions under FRANCISCO VÁSQUEZ DE CORONADO and Hernando de Soto crossed Texas in search of gold but could report only that the area was suitable for agriculture. JUAN DE OÑATE explored the upper Rio Grande at the end of the seventeenth century and opened settlements in El Paso and Isleta as well as Santa Fe.

The Spanish sent parties into Texas during the seventeenth century. The notable but short-lived efforts by Father Juan Domingues de Mendoza and Father Nicholas Lopez helped the Jumano Indians along the San Saba deal with the Apaches in 1683. Although the fathers sought to return to Texas, the arrival of the French led the Spanish in other directions to counter French activities.

The French began to explore territory claimed by the Spanish in 1682 along the lower Mississippi and Arkansas. René Robert Cavelier, SIEUR DE LA SALLE, led an expedition down the Mississippi to the Gulf. La Salle returned to France but, two years later, led a sea expedition in search of the mouth of the Mississippi. He landed at Matagorda Bay to establish an ill-fated settlement that ended in death for all but a few.

Spanish settlement

La Salle's expedition, plus permanent French settlement in Louisiana, led the Spanish to establish missions and settlements in Texas. The French, using bases in Louisiana, supplied the Indians with arms, and in 1758, one Spanish military expedition under Colonel Diego Ortiz de Parilla, sent to punish the Comanches for destroying the mission at San Saba, was defeated and almost wiped out by Wichitas armed by the French. Although military campaigns could not defeat the Indians, the diseases carried by the Spanish and French decimated the eastern tribes, easing Spanish expansion during the eighteenth century.

The Spanish settled eastern Texas by establishing a series of missions tied together by El Camino Real, which ran from Laredo on the Rio Grande to Nacogdoches at the Louisiana border. The missions were supplemented by permanent communities, particularly on the Bexar River at what became San Antonio. Established in 1718 as a part of the province of Coahuila, the community slowly grew as a center for the missions and other settlers. It was given a boost in 1731 with the arrival of fifty-nine settlers from the Canary Islands who created the first legally recognized government for the city. At the same time, the Spanish position on the upper Rio Grande between El Paso and Santa Fe, which predates Jamestown, expanded to account for most Spanish settlement during the seventeenth and eighteenth centuries. Even the PUEBLO REVOLT of 1683, which forced the Spanish out of Santa Fe, did not dislodge them from El Paso.

Despite pressures from the Comanches and from the French, Spanish settlements in eastern Texas continued to grow. In 1763, with the cession of Louisiana to the Spanish through the Treaty of Paris, the Spanish position in Texas seemed to be secure. After the American Revolution, a new threat to the Spanish Texas appeared.

Texas was on the fringes of the American rebellion. Its settlers drove cattle along the coast to New Orleans to supply the American cause and, through the alliance between Spain and France, to oppose the British. The end of the Revolution extended the new nation to the eastern banks of the Mississippi, and the young United States viewed the Spanish possessions with an eye towards conquest and expansion. The example of revolution against a European imperial state emboldened dissatisfied Spanish colonists to aspire to independence. In 1803, after the Spanish had ceded Louisiana back to France, Napoleon sold the Louisiana Territory to the United States. Americans claimed all territory between the Sabine and the Rio Grande as a part of the purchase but, through the 1819 ADAMS-ONIS TREATY, accepted the Sabine River as the border between New Spain and the United States. Many Americans, including ANDREW JACKSON, had ambitions of NATIONAL EXPANSION into the Texas territory.

Mexican Revolution

As the Spanish empire declined in the early nineteenth century, Napoleon invaded Spain, and American colonists throughout the empire began to think of separation and revolution. The Mexican Revolution began in 1809 and brought Spanish rule to an end in 1821.

Between 1811 and 1821, a series of abortive revolutionary outbreaks occurred in Texas. ANTONIO LÓPEZ DE SANTA ANNA came to Texas for the first time as a junior officer in the forces that put down the 1811 revolutionaries. Filibusters from the United States joined Hispanic Texans in a series of rebellions between 1815 and 1821.

Recognizing the threat from Indians to the sparsely occupied lands of Texas, the Spanish government initiated a system of empresario grants, in which land was granted to individuals in return for bringing new settlers to Texas. The first of the EMPRESARIOS was MOSES AUSTIN, a businessman impoverished by the depression and panic of 1819, who applied for a grant in 1820 and 1821. He died shortly after receiving the grant, but his son, STEPHEN FULLER AUSTIN, took up the grant, renegotiated it with the newly installed Mexican authorities, and brought settlers to Texas. The first of several empresario grants, the Austin colony attracted settlers from the United States. Other empresario colonies were established along the coast, and settlement of Texas expanded rapidly in the 1820s and early 1830s.

By 1832, there were an estimated twenty thousand Anglo-Americans in Texas in addition to residents of Hispanic descent.

The Texas Revolution

Between 1832 and 1835, unrest in Texas grew, despite efforts by both the Mexican government and Stephen Austin to ameliorate the situation. Armed conflict between Texans and the Mexican authorities began at Gonzales in the fall of 1835, and the TEXAS REVOLUTION, one of several outbreaks against the central government of Mexico in the mid-1830s, followed. Despite an invasion by a Mexican army under Santa Anna in the late winter and spring of 1836 and the disastrous defeats at Goliad and the ALAMO, forces under SAM HOUSTON defeated and captured Mexican units and confirmed the independence of Texas. Leadership of the new nation was shared by Anglos and Hispanics, but power remained with the Anglos.

The republic

Although annexation of Texas by the United States had been contemplated for years and appears to have been a part of the policies of the Jackson presidency, union did not immediately follow the victory at San Jacinto. Commander of the army Sam Houston was elected the first president of the Republic of Texas and took office in the newly established capital city of Houston. He was followed as president by MIRABEAU B.

LAMAR, a bitter critic of Houston. Houston served as the third president and led efforts for annexation. He was succeeded by ANSON JONES, who oversaw annexation.

During the era of the republic, life in Texas was chaotic. Texas grew rapidly, from an estimated population of 40,000 in 1836 to over 120,000 in 1846, including 40,000 slaves, who worked on the coastal cotton plantations. Although the new nation attracted citizens who could leave their debts behind while acquiring land, it had almost no revenue. Jacksonian Democrats controlled the policies of the new nation and opposed financial policies, including extensive taxation, which might have brought stability to the economy. Although recognized by France and Britain, the republic had to offer only the limited trade of its one major export crop, cotton, with few resources to sustain itself. The republic always suffered under pressure from the frontier Indians, who raided Victoria in 1840, and the Mexicans, who invaded Texas in 1842, captured San Antonio, and threatened the new capital at Austin before withdrawing. The Texans' response, in the form of the Mier Expedition, ended in disaster, as did the invasion of New Mexico, an invasion that was an effort to confirm Texas's claim to the upper Rio Grande.

The new republic never settled on a clear Indian policy. Houston attempted to reconcile Texans with the Indians, but his successor, Lamar, initiated military campaigns against both friendly and hostile tribes. Lamar took advantage of the incomplete capitol building and pressure from frontier settlers to move the capital from Houston to the small central Texas settlement of Waterloo, which was renamed Austin.

The United States deferred annexation, despite evidence that Texans wanted to join the Union. First delayed because of potential diplomatic problems between Mexico and the United States, annexation was opposed by abolitionists because slavery was legal in Texas. Diplomatic negotiations continued through the early 1840s. The U.S. Congress voted to annex Texas in 1845, following the election of Democrat presidential candidate JAMES K. POLK, who had campaigned for it. Under the terms of the agreement, Texas was recognized as a state and retained its public lands and its debt. Despite efforts by Britain and France to block annexation, the voters of Texas approved it in the fall of 1845, and the process was completed in 1846.

Statehood

With statehood came war with Mexico over the boundary lands between the Nueces and the Rio Grande. An army under ZACHARY TAYLOR was sent to the border. The Battle of Palo Alto in the Nueces Strip initiated war with Mexico, which had not recognized

In truth and in legend, the cattle industry has been closely associated with Texas. The May 2, 1874, issue of *Harper's Weekly* featured a number of Frenzeny and Travenier illustrations of the cattle industry in Texas. *Courtesy Patrick H. Butler, III.*

the independence of Texas and viewed it as a province in rebellion. The U.S. victory not only confirmed its control over Texas but also extended that control over much of the Southwest to the West Coast.

Texas reorganized its government at a constitutional convention presided over by Thomas Jefferson Rusk. J. Pinckney Henderson was elected the first governor, and Rusk and Sam Houston were elected to the U.S. Senate.

After the UNITED STATES–MEXICAN WAR ended, Texas laid claim to territory in New Mexico and Colorado, but eventually, the COMPROMISE OF 1850 resolved disputes over the land in question by paying Texas $10 million from the U.S. Treasury to settle the state's debt. During this period, the rapid expansion of Texas, particularly along the Gulf Coast, continued with the population growing from 300,000 in 1850 to more than 600,000 in 1860, mostly from the South. One-fifth were slaves. San Antonio, with 8,000 residents, and Galveston, with 4,000, were the only major urban centers in the state.

Migration from the South contributed to the growing proslavery settlement in Texas and set the stage for secession from the United States in 1861. The Southern sympathizers settled on the Gulf Coast, where they expanded the slave-owning cotton economy. Cattle ranching was growing in importance, particularly in South Texas and the Hill Country.

Texas benefited from an influx of European settlers, particularly Germans, who settled in Central Texas during the 1840s and 1850s. Unlike many Texans, some Europeans were Unionist in sympathy, their natural allegiance to their new nation reinforced by the efforts of the army to protect the frontier from continuing Indian raids. When the pro-Union Sam Houston was elected governor in 1860, many believed that Texas might side with the North. Nevertheless, in 1861, Texas seceded, and Houston was forced to resign as governor because he would not swear allegiance to the Confederacy.

The Civil War

Texas's primary role in the CIVIL WAR was as a supplier of troops to battlefields across the South and as the center of the trans-Mississippi Confederacy. Texas cotton, sold to Europe, contributed to the economy of the Confederacy. After the Union blockaded the coast, Texas smuggled cotton across the Rio Grande to Mexico for shipment to world markets. During most of the war, the state saw little fighting except for the capture of El Paso and raids along the Gulf Coast. Rebels persecuted Texas Unionists, primarily GERMAN AMERICANS, some of whom were executed during the war under the rules of martial law.

Although the war disrupted the Texas economy and many men died in the armies of the South, the state suffered less physical damage than most of the Confederacy, and the economy recovered quickly. While cotton continued to be important for East Texas, ranching grew in South and Central Texas, and cattlemen rounded up Texas longhorns, who had multiplied dramatically during the Civil War, and drove them to railheads to the north beginning in 1866. In East Texas, lumbermen began to exploit the vast pine forests, and before 1900, lumber was the largest industry in the state. Also, RAILROADS expanded to serve both the cotton and cattle markets, and Texas was quickly connected to the national railways. During this period, cities in North-central Texas, particularly Dallas and Fort Worth, grew into transportation and business centers.

During Reconstruction, Texas was occupied by the largest concentration of troops in the South, in part because of the size of the state, in part due to the Indian threat, and in part due to the efforts to force the French to withdraw from Mexico. The new constitution Texas wrote in 1876 to end Reconstruction, with many amendments, continues to serve as the constitution of Texas.

During the late 1860s and 1870s, under the protection of the army, settlement expanded into western Texas and pushed the Indians back. The campaigns of RANALD SLIDELL MACKENZIE from 1871 to 1874 forced the Indians off the Llano Estacado and set the stage for the continued growth on the frontier, first ranching and, later, farming. At the same time, buffalo herds, which had flourished on the plains, were wiped out, and whites brought in cattle to graze on the plains. Texas saw the birth of huge ranching operations, including the XIT RANCH, the SPUR RANCH, the Spade Ranch, and others. Some of the ranches were owned by Texans; others were owned by investors from the East and from Europe. As the CATTLE INDUSTRY expanded, long drives became commonplace until the coming of railroads in the 1880s and 1890s.

During the last third of the century, Texas continued to grow, but its economy remained controlled by outside interests. Capital needed for railroads, ranches, cotton gins, lumber mills, and other industries came from beyond the state's borders. The Texas economy produced raw materials for market rather than finished goods. In essence, although the state grew, it retained a colonial economy, vulnerable to outside forces and subject to the whims of the capital markets in the East and in Europe.

As a legacy of the Civil War and Reconstruction, Democrats dominated Texas politics. Texans also resented outside economic forces. Government in Texas was limited, both by the prevailing conservative phi-

The Texas state capitol in Austin was built by the Capitol Freehold Syndicate in exchange for the three million acres of land in West Texas that made up the XIT Ranch. *Courtesy Patrick H. Butler, III.*

losophy and by the lack of economic resources. During the 1890s, the Populist party appeared as an active force in Texas politics. Leaders of the Democratic party, particularly Governor JAMES STEPHEN (JIM) HOGG, were able to tap into the Populist sentiment, bringing it into the Democratic fold. The state enthusiastically supported WILLIAM JENNINGS BRYAN in his 1896 and 1900 presidential campaigns.

Twentieth-century Texas

As the new century began, the population of Texas expanded to the three million mark. A series of events combined to change the state. In 1900, the Galveston storm killed more than six thousand people and weakened what had been a major commercial center and port. Following the storm, Texas converted Houston into a major port city, safe from the hurricanes that pounded Galveston.

Between 1910 and 1920, Mexican immigration, which had begun as early as 1890, peaked due to the Mexican Revolution. Although there had always been a substantial Mexican community in San Antonio and along the border, the new migrants moved into cities such as Houston and Dallas and reshaped their social, economic, and political landscapes.

While cotton, ranching, and timber had been the mainstays of the Texas economy, the Lucas gusher, brought in at Spindletop near Beaumont in East Texas in the 1920s, opened the oil boom in Texas. The OIL AND GAS INDUSTRY transformed not only the Texas economy, but those of the nation and world. Although the oil business quickly became international, many of the corporations made their headquarters in Houston and Dallas, and the income from oil provided capital that led to other changes in Texas. The wildcatter, a speculator who drilled his own wells in search of oil, quickly joined the cowboy in the Texas pantheon of mythic figures.

Houston benefited perhaps more than any other city from the oil boom. Oil was more easily transported out of the newly developed Houston Ship Channel to the world than from Beaumont, and Houston bankers, led by Jesse Jones, provided the money needed for development of the drilling industry, refineries, transportation companies, and all the spin-offs of the oil industry. Heavy industry soon developed along the Houston ship channel and expanded elsewhere in Texas. In 1923, the first air conditioning was installed in Houston, and this modern convenience contributed to the growth that made the city the largest in Texas by 1930. Not until the 1980s, when Arab oil embargoes changed the structure of the business, did Texans seek to diversify the oil-driven economy.

Oil money also helped the University of Texas and Texas A & M to expand. It supported art collections, symphonies, museums, and other cultural institutions. With the new money, oil barons demanded high-priced material goods, and stores such as Nieman Marcus and Sakowitz sprang up to meet these demands.

Because of oil, Texas has yet to impose a state income tax, although in the 1980s, with the oil bust and the decline in oil values, the possibility of instituting such a tax was considered seriously. Meanwhile, Texas remained close to the bottom of the list of states in terms of support for social services and education.

The resources of Texas in the twentieth century contributed to the rise in influence of Texas politicians, particularly within the Democratic party. In 1932, during the Depression, the Democrats captured the presidency, and JOHN NANCE GARNER, former Speaker of the House of Representatives, became vice-president. Other Texans followed Garner into the national limelight, including Speaker of the House SAMUEL TALIAFERRO RAYBURN, Vice-President and President LYNDON B. JOHNSON, and Speaker of the House Jim Wright. With its large number of electoral votes and substantial blocks of campaign financing, Texas has been courted by both sides in presidential politics. President John F. Kennedy was courting voters in Dallas on November 22, 1963, when he was assassinated. The growth of the air and space industry in Texas, including the Johnson Space Center, was the result of the influence of Texas Democratic power.

While the Democratic party dominated state and national elections for more than half the century, many Texans became disenchanted with the national Democratic party in the 1950s, voted for Dwight D.

Eisenhower in presidential elections, and began a movement that, by the late 1970s, saw Republicans in office, such as Bill Clements, who in 1978 became the first Republican governor since Reconstruction, and George Bush, a U.S. representative from Texas before he was vice-president, then president of the United States.

For much of the century, oil drove an economy that suffered few reversals. In 1983, the decline in oil prices, combined with a BANKING system that had relied heavily on oil values to support loans, weakened the Texas economy. Savings and loan institutions and banks came close to collapsing as capital fled Texas. During the 1990s, the Texas economy entered a period of recovery and diversity.

At the end of the century, although the image of Texas was still tied to the myth of the cowboy and the wildcatter, the state had changed dramatically. Minority groups, particularly Hispanics and blacks, challenged political leadership in the state. Traditionally Democratic groups joined the Republican party. The economy grew more diversified. Although Texas continued to grow, changes in the political and economic climate made the future less certain for a state that has attempted to combine and resolve the tensions between the interests of diehard individualists and booming big business.

—*Patrick H. Butler, III, and Ron Tyler*

SEE ALSO: Agrarianism; Aircraft Industry; Camino Real, El; Cíbola, Seven Cities of; Louisiana Purchase; Missions: Early Franciscan and Jesuit; Populism; Progressivism; Pecos River; Spanish Settlement; Texas Frontier Indian Wars

SUGGESTED READING:

McDonald, Archie P. *Texas: All Hail the Mighty State.* Austin, Tex., 1983.

McComb, David G. *Texas: A Modern History.* Austin, Tex., 1989.

Meinig, D. W. *Imperial Texas: An Interpretive Essay in Cultural Geography.* Austin, Tex., 1969.

TEXAS ANNEXATION

SEE: National Expansion: Texas and National Expansion

TEXAS FEVER

Also known as cattle tick fever, splenic fever, or red water fever, Texas fever was a tick-born parasitic disease that killed thousands of cattle in the late nineteenth century. With the expansion of the beef industry and the cattle drives of the West in the mid-nineteenth century, longhorn and hybrid cattle being driven north and west out of Texas brought with them a deadly heritage. Due to years of built-up immunities, Texas cattle were made them ill but were not killed by the disease; however, the newly exposed herds in places such as Colorado, Kansas, and Missouri were devastated.

The disease caused a high fever, hence the name, as well as the destruction of red blood cells, bloating of the spleen, and the engorgement of the liver. Thousands of otherwise healthy cattle were stricken by the disease. Although it was quickly determined that the Texas cattle were the culprits, no one knew what caused the disease, how to treat it, or how to prevent it. Faced with no other alternative, ranchers quarantined Texas cattle from the rest of the Northern Plains states, thus effectively placing an embargo on the largest cattle-producing state in the union. Before the cause or cure could be discovered, the quarantine helped bring about the demise of the open range.

Beginning in the 1884, the Department of Agriculture ordered a study, led by Theobald Smith, of the disease. In 1893, he published his results, positively identifying the tick as the carrier of the disease. However, eliminating the common tick on the Great Plains in an open-air industry like cattle ranching seemed impossible. The quarantines proved immensely successful, although they severely hindered the industry. Undaunted, the Department of Agriculture formed the Bureau of Animal Industry, and in 1897 at Fort Worth, Texas, bureau personnel experimented with dipping cattle in a crude mineral-oil bath. Although it was time consuming to dip entire herds, cattle dipping was quickly embraced by all the states. Dipping stations mushroomed, and by the end of the nineteenth century, the quarantines were either abolished altogether or proved negligible. The BAI continued to tinker with the dipping formula and, in 1911, found a satisfactory mix of mineral oil and arsenic that all but eradicated the disease. Weaker strains of the disease were found to respond to an inoculation developed in 1926, but it was not as effective as dipping. By 1928, Texas fever had been eradicated, removing the shadow it cast over the Texas CATTLE INDUSTRY, but only after the days of the open range.

—*Kurt Edward Kemper*

SUGGESTED READING:

Schlebecker, John T. *Cattle Raising on the Plains, 1900–1961.* Lincoln, Nebr., 1963.

Smith, E. E. *Life on the Texas Range.* Austin, Tex., 1952.

TEXAS FRONTIER INDIAN WARS

Upon annexing Texas in 1845, the United States government inherited many of the former Lone Star republic's disputes with a variety of Indian tribes. For years, Indians had resisted efforts by the Spanish, Mexicans, and Texans to establish military superiority or to forcibly remove them from the region. Periodic efforts to establish treaties or reservations in Texas proved largely futile, and the wars between Indians and non-Indians continued for four decades after annexation.

In North Texas, the most powerful tribes included the Comanches, estimated in 1849 to number about twenty thousand, and the Kiowas, believed to number some fifteen hundred persons. To the west and the south were the Lipans and Mescalero Apaches, believed to number roughly five hundred and fifteen hundred, respectively. Divided into numerous small bands, neither the Lipans nor the Mescalero Apaches had much political structure; nonetheless, their mounted warriors were determined to prevent outside intrusions into the Southern Plains. Warfare, raiding, and the quest for plunder were crucial to their cultures. For generations, the tribes had ranged across the Southern Plains and often struck deep into Mexico. Seeking protection against the raids, the Mexican government had encouraged several Kickapoo bands to move south of the Rio Grande. The enmity between the Kickapoos and the Texans, however, soon led to open warfare between these two peoples as well.

To confront the tribes in Texas, the United States Army relied on a combination of fixed posts, small patrols, and sporadic punitive campaigns. Before the CIVIL WAR, the regulars constructed a double line of forts in a huge arc across central Texas and the lower Rio Grande Valley. Posts were also built along the roads to El Paso. Despite a strong federal presence (during the mid-1850s, nearly one-quarter of the entire United States Army was stationed in Texas), the violence between Indians and non-Indians continued. Hampered by shortages of mounted troops, a lack of formal doctrine applicable to Western conditions, and the skillful hit-and-run tactics of the Indians, the bluecoats failed to crush the tribes, although Texas-based expeditions into the Indian territory in 1858 did manage to destroy a Comanche village at Rush Spring.

Unsympathetic to the Indians and anxious to push farther west, Texans listed the FEDERAL GOVERNMENT's supposed lack of attention to Western needs as one of their reasons for seceding from the Union. Soon, however, Texas clashed with the Confederacy over the same issue. The state wanted to use more of its troops for defense against the Indians; the Confederacy wanted to employ the Texans against Union forces. In the wake of the regular army's withdrawal, many non-Indian settlers "forted up" in small blockhouses, but the combination of local, state, and Confederate units offered only incomplete protection. In October 1864, several hundred Comanches launched a particularly devastating raid into Young County's Elm Creek settlements. The following January, six hundred Kickapoos en route from the Indian Territory to Mexico routed state and Confederate troops at Dove Creek.

After the Civil War, United States troops reoccupied Texas and initially concentrated on duties associated with Reconstruction rather than on wars against the Indians. Once the state accepted federal authority, regulars returned to the frontiers and extended their posts as settlers and buffalo hunters poured farther west. The tribes found their old raiding grounds and their nomadic life styles increasingly endangered. They struck back with a series of raids; during one Kiowa raid near Fort Richardson in 1871, Commanding General WILLIAM TECUMSEH SHERMAN, there to inspect the troops, was nearly killed.

To overwhelm resistance in northern Texas, the army launched several expeditions into the Texas Panhandle and the Indian Territory. Texas-based troops played a vital role in the Southern Plains operations in 1868 and 1869, and Colonel RANALD SLIDELL MACKENZIE disrupted the trade between Plains Indians and illegal Comanchero traders in 1872 by destroying a large Kotsoteka Comanche village near McClellan Creek. In 1874 and 1875, Mackenzie and other regulars from Texas garrisons also participated in the Red River War, which crushed the military power of the Southern Plains tribes.

Texans continually complained about Indian and bandit attacks from Mexico. In 1859 and 1860, the army had attempted, without success, to crush resistance led by JUAN NEPOMUCENO CORTINA. During the 1870s, state units, known as Texas Rangers, aggressively patrolled the Rio Grande region. The rangers secured several small victories but enraged many with their seemingly indiscriminate attacks against all Indians and Mexicans. In 1873, acting upon the verbal instructions of Lieutenant General PHILIP H. SHERIDAN, Mackenzie splashed across the river and burned a Kickapoo village near Remolino, Mexico. Supported by Brigadier General Edward O. C. Ord, the commander of the Department of Texas, small detachments of regulars again crossed the Rio Grande in 1875 and 1876. The following year, Lieutenant Colonel William R. Shafter led yet another column into Mexico; in 1878, Mackenzie returned with the biggest expedition to date. The army's incursions prompted vigorous protests from

Mexico, and armed clashes between the soldiers of the two nations were narrowly avoided. The U.S. punitive expeditions did, however, spur Mexico to initiate offensive operations in Coahuila against the Lipans, Mescaleros, and Kickapoos.

The final large-scale campaigns in Texas occurred in the trans-Pecos region, where the army had long sought to fend off Apache raids from New Mexico and Mexico against immigrants and travelers. When active pursuits proved fruitless, Colonel BENJAMIN HENRY GRIERSON opted instead to garrison the region's water holes in 1880. Confused by Grierson's strategy and bloodied in several skirmishes, VICTORIO and his followers abandoned Texas for Mexico, where he was killed by Mexican troops.

Several very different cultures engaged in the ruthless struggle for military supremacy throughout much of southern, western, and northern Texas. Indian tribes opposing the federal government were forced either into Mexico or onto reservations north of the Red River. Decisive battlefield actions were rare; the federal government's triumph was much more attributable to the grueling pursuits conducted by the UNITED STATES ARMY, the destruction of the Southern Plains buffalo herds, and the relentless occupation of the regions by non-Indian settlers.

—*Robert Wooster*

SEE ALSO: Central Plains Indian Wars; Native American Peoples: Peoples of the Great Plains

SUGGESTED READING:

Hamilton, Allen Lee. *Sentinel of the Southern Plains: Fort Richardson and the Northwest Texas Frontier 1866–1878.* Fort Worth, Tex., 1988.

Smith, David Paul. *Frontier Defense in the Civil War: Texas' Rangers and Rebels.* College Station, Tex., 1992.

Utley, Robert M. *Frontiersmen in Blue: The United States Army and the Indian, 1848–1865.* New York, 1967.

Wooster, Robert. "The Army and the Politics of Expansion: Texas and the Southwestern Borderlands, 1870–1886." *Southwestern Historical Quarterly* 93 (1989): 151–68.

———. *Soldiers, Sutlers, and Settlers: Garrison Life on the Texas Frontier.* College Station, Tex., 1987.

TEXAS AND PACIFIC RAILROAD

The Texas and Pacific Railroad never directly fulfilled the "Pacific" promise of its name. Except for its terminus in Texarkana, Arkansas, its right of way lies entirely within the state of Texas, and it extends no closer to the Pacific Ocean than El Paso. The line's other major points include Houston, San Antonio, Dallas, and Fort Worth.

Chartered in 1857, the Texas and Pacific began with twenty-three miles of track linking Swanson's Landing (on Caddo Lake) to the town of Marshall. In the early 1870s, Thomas Alexander Scott, president of the Pennsylvania Railroad, took over the Texas and Pacific. He wanted to make it the central link in a true Atlantic-to-Pacific railroad. Scott's plan was to build the Texas and Pacific east to St. Louis, the western terminus of the Pennsylvania Railroad, and to extend the railroad westward to California. The Texas and Pacific accordingly expanded—within Texas—but Scott was foiled by a combination of the financial panic of 1873, the explosion of the CRÉDIT MOBILIER OF AMERICA scandal during that same year, and the aggressiveness of COLLIS P. HUNTINGTON, whose SOUTHERN PACIFIC RAILROAD effectively checked the westward progress of the Texas and Pacific at El Paso. Scott, discouraged and broken in health, stepped down from the Texas and Pacific in 1880. He died the following year. Nominally operating as an independent railroad, the Texas and Pacific came under the effective control of JAY GOULD's Missouri Pacific in 1882.

—*Alan Axelrod*

TEXAS RANGERS

In 1823, only two years after the first Anglo-American settlement in Texas, empresario STEPHEN FULLER AUSTIN hired ten experienced frontiersmen, called the Rangers, for a punitive expedition against the Indians. But not until November 24, 1835, did Texas lawmakers create a force known as the Texas Rangers. The organization had a complement of 56 men in three companies, each commanded by a captain and two lieutenants. Their immediate superior and leader had the rank of major and was subject to the commander in chief of the regular army. He was, in turn, responsible for enlisting recruits, enforcing rules, and applying discipline. Officers received the same pay as U.S. dragoons, and privates earned $1.25 per day; however, they supplied their own mounts, equipment, arms, and rations.

The rangers did not fare especially well at first. During the TEXAS REVOLUTION, while serving as scouts and couriers, they carried out a number of drudgelike tasks. As settlers fled east to escape advancing Mexican armies after the fall of the ALAMO on March 6, 1836, the rangers retrieved cattle, convoyed refugees, and destroyed produce or equipment left behind. In fact, during the Battle of San Jacinto on April 21, they were on "escort" duty, much to their chagrin. Their

A group of Texas Rangers photographed with their weapons. *Courtesy Texas State Library.*

situation did not improve appreciably over the next two years in the republic era because President SAM HOUSTON favored government economy and promoted friendly relations with the Indians.

In December 1838, MIRABEAU B. LAMAR succeeded to the presidency and immediately changed the frontier policies of the republic as well as the role of the rangers. The Texas Congress allowed him to recruit eight companies of mounted volunteers and maintain a company of 56 rangers and, a month later, to provide for five similar companies in central and southern Texas. Over the next three years, the rangers waged numerous battles. The most notable were the Cherokee War in East Texas in July 1838, the Council House Fight at San Antonio against the Comanches in March 1840, and the Battle of Plum Creek (near present-day Lockhart) against one thousand Comanche warriors in August 1840.

Sam Houston, upon being reelected to the presidency in December 1841, realized that ranger companies were the least expensive and the most effective way to protect the frontier. Under Captain JOHN (JACK) COFFEE HAYS, 150 rangers helped drive two Mexican armies out of San Antonio in 1842 and protected Texans against Indian attacks over the next three years. Hays also initiated ranger traditions and esprit de corps by recruiting and training a tough contingent of men

skilled in frontier warfare. Out of Hays's command arose such famous ranger captains as Ben and Henry McCulloch, Samuel H. Walker, W. A. A. ("Big Foot") Wallace, and Richard Addison (Ad) Gillespie.

With the coming of statehood and the UNITED STATES–MEXICAN WAR in 1846, the rangers achieved worldwide fame as an effective fighting force. After acquitting themselves admirably during the battles of Palo Alto and Resaca de la Palma on May 8 and 9, 1846, the rangers became General ZACHARY TAYLOR's eyes and ears. Superbly mounted, armed to the teeth with a large assortment of weapons, and obviously at home in the desert wastes of northeastern Mexico, they found the most practical route for the American army to Monterrey. Then late in September, the rangers rashly set the tempo and style of Taylor's successful storming of the city. Although furloughed in October after a brief armistice, they returned to active duty early in 1847 in time to provide Taylor enough military information to help win the Battle of Buena Vista in February.

In March 1847, the theater of war shifted. The American army under General WINFIELD SCOTT landed at Vera Cruz and quickly muscled its way into the Valley of Mexico. For the next five months, the rangers under Jack Hays and Samuel Walker figured prominently in American victories. In fact, so ruthless were they against Mexican guerrillas and so lethal the results that a hostile, but fearful, populace appropriately called them "Los Diablos Tejanos" (the Texas Devils).

With the end of the war with Mexico, the United States assumed responsibility for protecting the Texas frontier; therefore the rangers had no official function. The organization lost its famous captains as well as the nucleus of its frontier defenders. But with the appointment of John S. ("Rip") Ford as senior captain in January 1858, the rangers briefly upheld their fighting traditions. Late in the spring, they moved north of the Red River to "chastise" a large band of "hostiles" and, in the process, killed the noted Comanche chief Iron Jacket. Then in March 1859, Ford and his men were assigned to the Brownsville area, where, together with the U.S. Army, they experienced only limited success against "the Red Robber of the Rio Grande," General JUAN NEPOMUCENO CORTINA.

For fourteen years after this campaign, the rangers ceased to be either significant or effective. With the coming of the Civil War in 1861, they rushed individually—rather than in companies—to Confederate colors. Although the Eighth Texas Cavalry was known as Terry's Texas Rangers, its founder Benjamin F. Terry was never a member of the state organization nor did he necessarily recruit experienced fighters. To protect its frontiers, the state had to rely on young boys, old men, or rejects from Confederate conscription. Then, during Reconstruction, either the U.S. Army or Republican Governor E. J. Davis's State Police were responsible for carrying out such duties, but with little or no success.

In 1874, the Democrats returned to power in the state—and so did the rangers. The legislature created two military groups to deal with the badmen overrunning the state, the Indians ravaging the western frontier, and the Mexican bandits pillaging and murdering along the Rio Grande. The first was the Special Force of Rangers under Captain LEANDER H. MCNELLY. During 1874, he and his men helped curb lawlessness engendered by the deadly SUTTON-TAYLOR FEUD in Dewitt County. Then in the spring of 1875, they moved into the Nueces Strip (between Corpus Christi and the Rio Grande) and, after eight months of fighting, restored order, if not peace, to the area. In 1875, the special force enhanced its fearful reputation by stacking twelve dead rustlers "like cordwood" in the Brownsville square; McNelly also precipitated Las Cuevas War, in which he violated international law by crossing the Rio Grande, attacking Mexican nationals, and retrieving stolen American cattle.

The second military unit created by the Democrats in 1874 was designated the Frontier Battalion. Composed of six companies (with 75 rangers in each) under Major John B. Jones, the battalion participated in fifteen Indian battles in 1874 and, together with the U.S. Cavalry, destroyed the power of the fierce Comanches and Kiowas by the end of 1875. In much the same time frame, the battalion also thinned out more than three thousand Texas desperadoes such as bank robber SAM BASS and notorious gunfighter JOHN WESLEY HARDIN.

For the next three decades, their prominence and prestige waning, the rangers retreated before the onslaught of civilization. They occasionally intercepted Mexican and Indian marauders along the Rio Grande, contended with cattle thieves, especially in the Big Bend country and the Panhandle, and, at times, protected blacks from white lynch mobs. By 1900, critics of the rangers urged that they be curtailed, if not completely abandoned. As a result, in 1901, the legislature cut the force to four companies, each headed by a captain who could recruit no more than 20 men. Only because of the leadership of such captains as J. A. Brooks, W. J. (Bill) McDonald, J. H. Rogers, and John R. Hughes were the rangers able to maintain their existence and traditions during the lean years of the 1890s and early 1900s.

Violence and brutality soon increased along the Rio Grande, where the rangers continued to participate in numerous bloody brush fights with Mexican nationals. In 1910, a revolution against Mexican President Porfirio Díaz unsettled the populace on both sides of the border. Then in 1914, with the coming of World War I, problems in the border country focused on Mexican nationalism, German intrigue and sabotage, and American draft dodgers. In 1916, FRANCISCO ("PANCHO") VILLA's raid on Columbus, New Mexico, intensified already harsh feelings between the two countries. The rangers, along with hundreds of "special" rangers appointed by Texas governors, killed approximately five thousand Hispanics between 1914 and 1919—and therein lay both scandal and embarrassment.

In January 1919, at the insistence of Representative J. T. Canales of Brownsville, the Texas legislature overhauled the force in order to restore public confidence. During the next two months, sordid stories of ranger brutality, debauchery, and injustice emerged. State lawmakers decided to maintain four companies but reduce the number of recruits from 20 to 15 per unit. To attract men of high moral character, they instituted more competitive salaries, but with minimal expense accounts. They also established specific procedures for citizen complaints against any ranger wrongdoing.

Leander H. McNelly, a captain of the Texas Rangers. *Courtesy Texas State Library.*

After these reforms, the force performed well during the 1920s. With the enactment of Prohibition, the Rangers patrolled the Rio Grande against tequila smugglers and cattle rustlers; they protected federal inspectors from harm in the so-called tick war in East Texas; they prevented both individual injury and property damage in labor disputes and Ku Klux Klan demonstrations; and, increasingly, they tamed the lawless oil boom towns of Miranda City, Desdemona, Mexia, Wink, and Borger.

With the Great Depression of 1929, the state legislature slashed budgets, and the ranger complement never exceeded 45. In the fall of 1932, the rangers made a grave political error: they openly supported Governor Ross Sterling against Miriam A. ("Ma") Ferguson in the Democratic primary. After Ferguson was elected and took office in January 1933, she fired 44 rangers. The legislature then slashed salaries and budgets and then further reduced the force to 32. Texas then became a haven for such criminals as Raymond Hamilton, George ("Machine Gun") Kelly, and Clyde Barrow and Bonnie Parker.

In 1935, however, James V. Allred became governor; his platform called for better law enforcement. The legislature created the Texas Department of Public Safety (DPS). A three-person Public Safety Commission was responsible for selecting a director and an assistant director, who, in turn, oversaw three basic units: the Texas Rangers, the Highway Patrol, and a modern scientific crime laboratory and detection center known as the Headquarters Division. The rangers became an important part of a much larger law enforcement team. Their basic structure remained intact—five companies—but changes occurred in hiring and promotion procedures.

For several years, the rangers were apprehensive about their future because of leadership changes in the Department of Public Safety. In September 1938, with the appointment of Homer Garrison, Jr., as the new director, the rangers regained their status as a "crack" law enforcement body. Over the next thirty years, they became the plain-clothes detectives of the DPS. They also expanded to six companies with an overall complement of 45 men in 1941, 51 in 1947, and 62 in 1961. They were actually a rural constabulary, with most of the officers stationed in small Texas towns.

During the Garrison era, the rangers operated at peak performance. In World War II, they rounded up enemy aliens and instructed civilians and local police in the latest defense techniques to protect plants, dams, factories, and industries from sabotage, while carrying out their regular duties. In the 1950s, they investigated more than eight thousand cases annually. And in the 1960s, their case load increased because of the civil-rights movement and the emergence of a more populous, urban state.

With the death of Garrison in 1968, the Department of Public Safety commissioners again reorganized and redefined the ranger guidelines. Wilson E. Speir, Garrison's successor, expanded the force to 73 men in 1969, 82 in 1971, 88 in 1974, and 94 in 1975. The rangers were highly trained and better equipped. The DPS provided them with high-powered cars equipped with the latest radio equipment as well as with a large array of sophisticated weapons and defensive armor. And the state began paying better salaries and providing more benefits.

As a result, the rangers have evolved into the elite of Texas law enforcement. Training has intensified; the weaponry and crime-detection equipment have become even more sophisticated. The legislature enlarged the overall complement to 99 officers (including two women) in September 1993 , then to 104 in September 1995, with increased salaries and benefits.

—*Ben Procter*

SUGGESTED READING:

Procter, Ben. *Just One Riot: Episodes of Texas Rangers in the 20th Century.* Austin, Tex., 1991.

Webb, Walter Prescott. *The Texas Rangers: A Century of Frontier Defense.* Austin, Tex., 1965.

TEXAS REVOLUTION

Long before the Texas Revolution of 1835 to 1836, Spanish Texas was a hotbed of unrest. Concerned about U.S. intentions after ANDREW JACKSON had handed Spanish Florida to the expansion-minded democracy to the north in 1819, Spanish authorities fell back on their ages-old policy of trying to use America's westwardly migrating settlers both as a barrier to Indian raiders and to block U.S. expansion into Spain's North American holdings by creating the empresario system, a system quixotically aimed at making settlers into loyal subjects of the crown. Not only did the EMPRESARIOS, however, bring potential settlers to the region, they helped fan the unrest among colonial Mexicans against Madrid, an unrest that ultimately resulted in Mexico's independence in 1821.

The colonization policy of the new Mexican republic closely followed that of Spain. The Mexican Colonization Law of 1824 guaranteed land, security, and exemption from taxes for four years to foreign settlers. Except that it required foreigners to pledge allegiance to Mexico, the revolutionary government placed few restrictions on immigrants. In many ways, the Mexican immigration policy resembled that of the United States; it was intended to encourage economic growth and open new markets. In the long run, Mexico hoped to dilute the dangerous concentration of Americans in Texas by recruiting other foreigners, mostly from Europe, but until then it had little choice but to come to terms with the three thousand Americans who by 1823 were already living as illegal aliens in the Mexican state of Coahuila y Texas. The new law was equal parts appeasement and co-option, an attempt to win the Americans' loyalty by making them landowners with a stake in the future and fortunes of the Republic of Mexico.

The Americans brought to Coahuila y Texas by STEPHEN FULLER AUSTIN and other empresarios came from the hardscrabble farms of Kentucky, the cotton plantations of Georgia, the swampy battlefields of Florida, and the wilds of Missouri. They destabilized the new United States–Mexican borderlands with their disputatious political habits, their land hunger, their racial hatreds, and their propensity for hair-trigger violence. While they also realized Mexico's hopes and revitalized the provincial economy, they nevertheless gave its officials pause: the new settlers may have called themselves citizens of Mexico, but they obviously still considered themselves to be Americans. Conflict between these "Texians" and Mexico took root from the very beginning.

The short-lived FREDONIA REBELLION, which broke out in 1826 when the Mexican government revoked a few land grants held by local troublemakers without notice, was typical. Texans saw it as an example of arbitrary rule; Mexicans, as yet another gesture in the U.S. scheme to take Mexico's northern provinces. This impression was confirmed when President John Quincy Adams offered to buy Texas—all of it—for $1 million. The offer was declined. When Andrew Jackson upped the ante to $5 million, Mexico turned down that offer as well. Jackson replaced his negotiator and minister to Mexico, Joel R. Poinsett, with someone considerably less scrupulous. On behalf of President Jackson, ANTHONY BUTLER attempted bribery and usury (forcing on the Mexicans an unpayable loan with Texas as collateral) and advocated the use of force if necessary.

Reasons for rebellion

Such diplomacy only inflamed the situation in Texas, as it was perhaps intended to do. Historians have long debated the ultimate causes of the conflict that led to the Texas Revolution. Some have blamed religion. Most of the Texas settlers were Southern Protestants; the Mexican government sanctioned Catholicism as a matter of national policy and nominally prohibited public worship by any non-Catholic sect.

But in Texas, as in the other border provinces, the Catholic hierarchy could barely minister to its own flock, and neither Mexico nor Rome spent much time trying to impose the state religion on Texans. In fact, Mexico in 1834 guaranteed that "no person shall be molested for religious or political opinions provided the public order is not disturbed." Whatever else Texans might have wanted to fight for, there was no reason to fight for freedom of religion. Other historians have pointed to slavery as a cause. Some Texas settlers brought slaves with them to work the land and made it clear they would require more; the Mexican government proposed gradual but absolute emancipation in Texas and had already abolished slavery throughout the rest of Mexico. But by 1829, Mexico compromised and granted Texas a presidential exemption from the decree abolishing slavery; Mexico's handling of its slave owners could hardly be used as an example of its persecution of Texans.

The Texans also sought free trade with the United States, and they reacted with hostility to Mexican taxes and restrictions; they—along with many TEJANOS—took to smuggling. Like Texas, other frontier states within Mexico, including California, the Yucatan, and New Mexico, supported the federalist structure of Mexico and opposed the move by the centralists during the late 1820s and early 1830s to place all power in the hands of Mexico City. They had numerous grievances—some justifiable, some petty—against the slow, cumbersome, and arbitrary Mexican legal system, and all of them complained about their lack of autonomy. Only the Texans, however, seemed to be pushing for what amounted to an American republic within Mexico. The Texans simply saw themselves as racially, morally, and politically superior to the Mexicans, whom they regarded as slow, indolent, and priest-ridden. There smoldered within the Texans a powerful resentment at having to answer to the authority of such people. From the perspective of the United States, Mexico was young, corrupt, and unstable; Texas was nearby; despite considerable domestic opposition, Andrew Jackson's America (where market forces were stimulating the rapid growth of the cotton kingdom) wanted it; inferior to United States, Mexico did not deserve to keep it.

Mexico was not unaware of the problem. The popular Mexican press mercilessly caricatured the unwelcome "Anglo-Saxons." In 1827, the Mexican government, worried about the expansionist intentions of the United States, sent a commission under General Manuel de Mier y Teran into Texas to investigate the influx of Americans. When the commission visited San Felipe de Austin, the heart of Austin's colony, one of Teran's party noted: "In my judgment the spark that will start the conflagration that will deprive us of Texas, will start from this colony."

By 1830, some 7,000 Norte Americanos in Coahuila y Texas outnumbered the Mexicans by more than two to one. On April 6 of that year, seeking to stave off the American "menace," Mexico enacted legislation augmenting the number and size of garrisons in the province and aimed at stopping U.S. immigration into Texas while increasing immigration from European countries. The new laws—which "closed" the border to Americans, canceled empresario contracts, and prohibited the introduction of slavery—failed miserably. They halted *legal* immigration, but anybody could cross the long border illegally and at will. In 1833, Mexico again began admitting Americans. The fever to rush to Texas raged. By 1835, Texas had a population of only 3,500 Mexicans and some 30,000 Americans. There were almost as many American slaves, 3,000, in Mexico's Texas as there were Mexicans.

Gone to Texas

Many in this latest wave of Texans went by the acronym GTT for the words "gone to Texas" that they scrawled across notes or chalked on log-cabin doors when they pulled up stakes and migrated west. Traveling with them were lawyers and land speculators, who knew that a "free" Texas would be an enriching Texas. And as Mexico drifted in the 1830s toward civil war between liberal federalists and conservatives who wanted to centralize control in Mexico City, a Texas independent of Mexico seemed ever more possible. Texas malcontents split into war and peace parties, the latter headed by Stephen Austin, the former organized by the new up-and-comers and consisting mostly of GTTs, whom the more "respectable" early settlers called "War Dogs" or "Crazy-orians."

There were mob uprisings all over East Texas in the early 1830s, and war with Mexico loomed just as Mexico faced a revolt by ANTONIO LÓPEZ DE SANTA ANNA and his federalist forces. In his first bid for power, Santa Anna hoped to overthrow Anastasia Bustamente's xenophobic and anti-American government. Austin and the majority of Texans were not prepared for out-and-out rebellion. In mid-1832, SAM HOUSTON arrived in Texas, possibly as an unofficial agent of Andrew Jackson. Certainly, Jackson suggested that Houston, who had just weathered a scandalous trial in Washington, D.C., go to Texas and gave him five hundred dollars, a passport, and instructions for some kind of confidential mission, if only to look over the situation. Within six months, Houston was the head of Texas's volunteer army and deeply engaged in its political maelstrom.

Austin negotiated peace and pledged the Texans' support for General Santa Anna, who was at the time still professing his liberalism. When Santa Anna emerged victorious, Texans felt they deserved favor for having supported his cause. It seemed a good time to present to the new president the grievances of the province, which included a petition for separate statehood within the Mexican Republic.

A Texas constitutional convention had met in 1833; the Texans had reiterated their grievances; Houston had drafted the state constitution; Austin now carried the document to Mexico City. There for some five months, he attempted to see Santa Anna. When he finally did gain an audience, the president expressed willingness to remedy all grievances except for the statehood demand. Still, it was more than Austin had expected, and he began his journey back to Texas—only to be arrested at Saltillo, returned to Mexico City, and imprisoned for a letter he wrote urging Texas statehood. He spent the next two years in jail.

In 1835, Austin, an embittered man broken in health, returned to Texas. During his two-year absence, the War Dogs had strengthened their position. In June 1835, thirty Texans forced the small garrison and customhouse at Anáhuac to surrender, and although communities throughout Texas disavowed the revolt, Texas did not turn the rebels over to Mexico City. Santa Anna, meanwhile, had turned brutal, repudiating all of his previous liberal policies and proclaiming himself dictator of a centralized Mexico; worst of all in the eyes of Texas slave holders, he threatened to enforce Mexico's ban on the "peculiar institution." Having decided that force was all the Texans understood, Santa Anna sent additional troops north at the end of 1835 to pacify the frontier. This time even Austin was in no mood or position to mediate. He, too, counseled revolt. Austin urged his fellow settlers to "Americanize" Texas and bring the territory under the U.S. flag. He invited Americans to come to Texas "passports or no passports," "each man with his rifle." Violence was inevitable, he declared: "War is our only recourse. There is no other remedy."

The insurrection begins

No doubt Texas, with its overwhelmingly Anglo population, was sooner or later bound to break away from Mexico, but as it happened, the movement toward armed insurrection began in 1835, led by Sam Houston and heartily applauded by two prominent Mexico City radicals, one of them the liberal former vice-president Gomez ("Furioso") Farias whom Santa Anna had banished to the north the year before. The event that precipitated the insurrection occurred on October 2, 1835, when the Mexican cavalry crossed the Rio Grande and demanded the surrender of a cannon in Gonzales. The Americanos quickly forged a small army and chased the Mexican force southward. Next, Austin himself led a force of 500 against San Antonio, where most of the retreating Mexican army, under General Martín Perfecto de Cós, had taken refuge. The Texans mounted a siege in November. That same month, representatives of the twelve American communities of Texas convened to decide just what the territory was fighting for: independence or a return to Mexico under the 1824 constitution. The vote was solidly against independence. A provisional government was created; its goal was to appeal to Mexican liberals to unite against Santa Anna so that Texas might rejoin a constitutionally governed Mexico.

Not immediately declaring independence did garner the Texans some Tejano support, but most Tejanos—and Mexican liberals, in general—distrusted the Americans, and with good reason. Already the Texans had sent a delegation, including Austin, to Washington to test Andrew Jackson's reaction to the possible annexation of Texas by the United States. Meanwhile, life for the ragtag army of siege was becoming increasingly miserable during a bitter winter. When their temporary commander decided to withdraw to winter quarters at Gonzales, frontiersman Ben Milam challenged volunteers to attack the city with the cry "Who will go with old Ben Milam?" On December 5, 300 Texans, their patience exhausted, forced their way into San Antonio. They fought the Mexican troops in the town's streets, and General Cós retreated with some 1,100 troops into the garrison's barracks and armory at the ALAMO. The Texans brought their cannon to bear against the Alamo's walls, and Cós finally surrendered. After taking the Alamo, the Texans began to repair the fort so that the converted mission could be effectively defended.

Meanwhile, Sam Houston and Henry Smith, governor of Texas, were urging independence and warning that reprisal from Santa Anna himself was inevitable. But land speculators—men such as Dr. James Grant—feared that titles to the huge tracts of land they had amassed by bribing the corrupt Coahuila y Texas legislature were as likely to be nullified by an independent Texas as by Santa Anna's centralized government, and they persuaded a legislative council to dispatch a force to Matamoros, a Mexican town located at the mouth of the Rio Grande and known as a stronghold of liberals opposed to Santa Anna. By seizing Matamoros and uniting with the liberals, Grant and his cohorts hoped to inflame sentiment throughout Mexico for a revival of the old federalist system established by the constitution of 1824, thus creating a government friendly to their real-estate claims.

But the mission, led by JAMES WALKER FANNIN, JR., bogged down by indecision and divisive elements within his command, never reached Matamoros. Ultimately, Fannin holed up in the fort at Goliad as Sam Houston had asked him to do from the start. As Houston suspected, Santa Anna was on his way north to punish the rebels personally. He had begun gathering an army at San Luis Potosi, the traditional spot from which Mexico had organized and outfitted expeditions to Texas. In January 1836, surrounded by his splendid entourage and closely followed by his mounted staff and army, Santa Anna marched out.

About that time back in San Felipe de Austin, Sam Houston told Governor Smith that unless the new constitutional convention, set for the coming spring, laid solid groundwork for a strong government, "the country must be lost." The news he had received from the Alamo on January 16 was not encouraging. Lieutenant Colonel James Clinton Neill, the garrison's commander, wrote to Houston that his men were tired, had not been paid, and were talking of going home to the United States. Houston himself did not wish to defend the Alamo. Even repaired and modified with firing platforms, it was a poor excuse for a fortress. He had always believed San Antonio and the Alamo were too far away from San Felipe de Austin to be defended successfully. Far better for the outnumbered Texans to fight a guerrilla war against Santa Anna in the countryside familiar to volunteers.

The news from Goliad also was bad. Fannin was threatening to strip the fort of men, munitions, and transport to launch the expedition on Matamoros. That meant the interior of Texas would lay exposed to Santa Anna. Houston decided to concentrate what strength he had left sixty miles east of San Antonio at Gonzales. He dispatched JAMES (JIM) BOWIE to Neill in San Antonio with orders to remove the Alamo's guns, blow up the fortress, and abandon it. Meanwhile, Houston and two others had been commissioned by the Consultation to visit the Texas Cherokees in East Texas and negotiate with Cherokee leader Duwali and others a treaty that would ensure the Indians' neutrality in the coming fight. Houston and John Forbes entered into these negotiations on February 22, 1836; on February 23, they had their treaty. This meant, however, that Houston was absent from the scene when the Alamo came under attack.

Siege of the Alamo

When Bowie reached San Antonio, he did not enforce Houston's orders. He and Neill decided that the Alamo was the major obstacle to any Mexican advance and resolved not to "be driven from the post of honor" in defending it. Meanwhile Santa Anna was approach-

William H. Hiddle's *Surrender of Santa Anna*, 1886, depicts a wounded Sam Houston offering Santa Anna a seat. *Courtesy Texas State Library.*

ing the Rio Grande, where he was to join General Joaquin Ramirez y Sesma, who had originally gone north to reinforce Cós. When Santa Anna crossed into Texas, he showed up at San Antonio de Bexar with about 2,000 troops fit for duty. At the Alamo, Neill and Bowie, with little more than a hundred men, a quarter of them regulars, the rest volunteers, were appealing for reinforcements. Fannin turned a deaf ear to the pleas, as he was still contemplating the Matamoros objective from his loosely organized camp at Goliad. Another commander did bring aid, however, in the form of two dozen men: Colonel WILLIAM BARRET TRAVIS, a GTT and early leader of the Texas war faction. Then on February 8, DAVID (DAVEY) CROCKETT arrived, leading a dozen men from Tennessee and seeking to revive a moribund political career in the states by joining the Texans.

By February 11, 1835, Neill had left the Alamo, and command had passed into the hands of Jim Bowie and William Travis. Five days later, Santa Anna began his march up from the Rio Grande. Bowie and Travis had about 150 men to hold the Alamo. Travis had ample warning of the Mexicans' advance, but he did

not believe the rumors; he was sure Santa Anna would wait until spring to march his army through the barren country south of San Antonio. By that time, Texas and the world would have answered Travis's repeated pleas for aid. But on February 25, the vanguard of Santa Anna's army entered San Antonio. Some 25 noncombatants, mostly women and children, took refuge in the Alamo, and the siege began as a red flag was raised from a church steeple. It signified Santa Anna's intention to show no mercy, to take no prisoners. Travis responded by firing a cannon.

Bowie was more cautious. Hearing a cavalry bugle, he took it as a signal that the Mexicans wished to parley. Bowie sent a messenger to Santa Anna and offered surrender on the condition that the defenders would be granted what the Texans had allowed General Cós and his men at the Alamo in December: freedom to return to their homes unharmed. Santa Anna demanded unconditional surrender. Meanwhile, Bowie had become increasingly ill and had been injured in an accident while placing a cannon. Unable to stand, he was confined to his cot. Travis, during a lull after the first twenty-four hours of bombardment, wrote a dispatch "To the People of Texas & all Americans in the world," appealing again for reinforcements and promising "Victory or Death." One band of 25 men did finally materialize in San Antonio to reinforce the Alamo; they came from the militia at Gonzales, where Houston had gathered his forces; and they came against his orders.

After a week of unrelenting Mexican bombardment, not a single Texan had been killed in the Alamo, while Texas grapeshot and sharpshooters took their toll on Santa Anna's troops—although his army was augmented daily by the arrival of additional units. Within the fort, the defenders busied themselves with the endless task of shoring up walls crumbling under cannon fire. The bombardment finally stopped. The Texans waited. Santa Anna deployed some 1,800 soldiers for the final attack. They rushed the fortress just before daybreak on Sunday, March 6, 1835.

It was a clumsy attack that resulted in huge casualties, but in the end, sheer numbers prevailed. In a frenzy, Santa Anna's army began to pour over the Alamo walls. The fighting was hand to hand in the open plaza of the compound. To some of the Mexicans at the time, as to Texas schoolchildren ever since, the Texans, who had survived eleven days of fierce bombardment, seemed larger than life. By 6:30 on the morning of the sixth, it was quiet at the Alamo. The battle had taken ninety minutes. Santa Anna paid dearly to reclaim the useless, once-abandoned, tumbled-down old Franciscan mission: 600 of his men, fully a third of his army, and all but a handfull of the Texans lay dead in the crisp early morning light.

Santa Anna spared the women and children in the fort, charging one of them, Susannah Dickerson, with the task of telling all of Texas what had happened at the Alamo and warning that the same would befall any others who remained in revolt. Davey Crockett and other prisoners who had surrendered were executed on Santa Anna's orders. Santa Anna had unwittingly provided the Republic of Texas invaluable martyrs to the cause. Three days earlier, the constitutional convention in San Felipe de Austin had finally given Sam Houston what he wanted: a declaration of independence. Santa Anna now handed Houston the new republic's battle cry: "Remember the Alamo!"

The war for independence

The fall of the Alamo unnerved Colonel James Fannin. He grew no calmer when Sam Houston ordered him to destroy Goliad's fort and retreat. Following delays marked by Fannin's indecisiveness, on March 18, the volunteers slipped off into a thick fog after burning Goliad to the ground. Fannin's 400 men had so overloaded their horses, mules, and carts that when they reached the steep banks of the San Antonio River,

they were unable cross without off-loading and then packing up again on the opposite shore.

The additional delay allowed a force of 1,400 men under General José Urrea to surround Fannin and his troops on the open river plain. Fannin pulled his wagons into a hollow rectangle, from behind which his men stood off the Mexicans for two days, but during the fighting, Fannin was wounded. On March 20, amid the wrecked wagons, the dead oxen, and the thirst of exhaustion, the men began discussing surrender. Fannin capitulated, much to the relief of the majority of his men. Six days later, Santa Anna ordered his general to execute all the rebels.

Santa Anna firmly believed he had broken the back of the Texas resistance, and at first he appeared to be right. Texans panicked. In what became known as the "Runaway Scrape," thousands—men, women, and children—bolted east for the border as the Mexican army continued its steady advance. The provisional government fled with them. Amid the refugee hysteria, there was clearly anger over the disasters at the Alamo and at Goliad and certainly a desire for revenge. Houston turned the panic and the passion to advantage, using them to forge an army. He talked about the value of strategic retreat. He assured his men that he was playing for time in order to build strength. Most of all, he constantly drilled those he enlisted, hoping at last to train an effective fighting force. It took a month, but on April 20, with an army grown to some 800 troops, Houston felt ready to turn and make a stand.

Santa Anna was camped with about 700 men on an open prairie west of the San Jacinto River just off Galveston Bay. Houston took up position and set the next day for his attack. At the last minute, Santa Anna was joined by reinforcements that swelled his ranks, but unphased, Houston ordered an assault. The Battle of San Jacinto lasted eighteen minutes. The massacre of Santa Anna's fleeing troops afterward took hours. When it was over, Houston's troops had slaughtered 630 Mexican soldiers, more than all the Texans who had died at the Alamo and Goliad put together.

Santa Anna, captured while disguised as a common soldier and trying to escape after the fighting had stopped, assumed he would be executed. But Houston, instead, forced Santa Anna to sign the "treaty" of Velasco. In exchange for his life, Santa Anna ordered all Mexican soldiers to leave Texas and recognized his former province as an independent republic. Signed under duress, the treaty was nevertheless generally recognized abroad, although Mexico, under new leadership, immediately repudiated the document. Not really knowing what to do with him, the Texans imprisoned Santa Anna for two months before dispatching him to Washington. There, Andrew Jackson treated Santa

Anna courteously and received him as a head of state on January 19, 1837. As Jackson's guest, Santa Anna discussed the state of affairs in Texas, and the two men agreed to disagree on Mexico's recognition of Texas as an independent republic before Jackson sent him on his way to Vera Cruz under naval escort.

That same year, Sam Houston was elected the first president of the Republic of Texas.

—*Charles Phillips*

SUGGESTED READING:

Barr, Alwyn. *Texans in Revolt: The Battle for San Antonio, 1835.* Austin, Tex., 1990.

Casteneda, Carlos E. *The Mexican Side of the Texas Revolution.* Dallas, Tex., 1928.

Connor, Seymour V. *Adventure in Glory.* Austin, Tex., 1965.

de la Peña, José Enriqué. *With Santa Anna in Texas: A Personal Narrative of the Revolution.* Trans. by Armen Perry. College Station, Tex., 1975.

Everett, Diana. *The Texas Cherokees: A People between Two Fires.* Norman, Okla., 1990.

Hardin, Stephen L. *Texian Iliad: A Military History of the Texas Revolution, 1835–1836.* Austin, Tex., 1994.

Houston, Andrew Jackson. *Texas Independence.* Houston, Tex., 1938.

Lack, Paul D. *The Texas Revolutionary Experience: A Political and Social History, 1835–1856.* College Station, Tex., 1992.

Long, Jeff. *Duel of Eagles: The Mexican and U.S. Fight for the Alamo.* New York, 1990.

McDonald, Archie P. *Texas: All Hail the Mighty State.* Austin, Tex., 1983.

McComb, David G. *Texas: A Modern History.* Austin, Tex., 1989.

Meinig, D. W. *Imperial Texas: An Interpretive Essay in Cultural Geography.* Austin, Tex., 1969.

Merk, Frederick. *Slavery and Annexation of Texas.* New York, 1972.

Reichstein, Andreas. *Rise of the Lone Star.* College Station, Tex., 1989.

Weber, David J. *The Mexican Frontier, 1821–1846: The American Southwest under Mexico.* Albuquerque, N. Mex., 1982.

Wisehart, M. K. *Sam Houston: American Giant.* Washington, D.C., 1962.

THEATER

Historical Overview
   Misha Berson

Ethnic Theater
   Vicki L. Ruiz

Hispanic Theater
   F. Arturo Rosales

HISTORICAL OVERVIEW

In 1815, Samuel Drake, a New York actor-manager, undertook the first theatrical tour of towns in Tennessee, Kentucky, and Ohio. Drake and his troupe were among the first thespians to bring professional drama to the American West. As outposts swelled into cities, and cities into metropolises, Western theatrical entertainment expanded into a booming, highly competitive enterprise. The cultural and financial impact of live theater diminished in the twentieth century as Americans grew beguiled with the mass-media pastimes of movies, radio, and television. But even today, theater continues to make a vibrant contribution to the cultural fabric of the West.

Although plays were staged in the New England colonies as early as 1700, the spread of theater was held in check by Puritan admonitions and legal statutes against it. As religious opposition eased, theater impresarios established permanent playhouses in Philadelphia (Southwark Theatre, 1776), Charleston (Dock Street Playhouse, 1735), Boston (Federal Street Theatre, 1794), and New York (Park Theatre, 1798). More slowly, drama extended into the regions beyond the Eastern seaboard. James H. Caldwell founded the first English-speaking theater in New Orleans in 1819, and Noah Ludlow and Sol Smith followed suit in St. Louis in 1835. But the proliferation did not begin in earnest until the mass westward migrations of the mid-1800s.

In 1847, J. B. Rice erected the first Chicago playhouse; when it burned three years later, it was promptly rebuilt and was quickly joined by the McVicker's Theatre, Hooley's Theatre, and other venues. The 1849 gold rush brought droves of speculators and fortune-seekers to the burgeoning California city of San Francisco; and an impresario named Thomas Maguire opened the Jenny Lind Theatre in 1850 to provide entertainment for the new pioneers. Twice the Jenny Lind burned down, and twice Maguire replaced it. He also managed a half dozen of San Francisco's subsequent playhouses, and he made a fortune touring theater to the Sierra Nevada mining camps.

Utah had its first drama venue, the Salt Lake Theatre, in 1862, and Seattle opened one soon afterwards. Meanwhile, impresario John Langrishe carved out his own Western touring route, sending actors into the booming Rocky Mountain settlements of Denver, Helena, Cheyenne, and Deadwood. By the beginning of the Civil War, every sizable Western town boasted at least one entertainment hall and usually more.

These early Western stages were typically erected by businessmen and run by performers of English birth or descent who headed up "stock" acting companies. Even before railroad travel was possible, the great the-

The Salt Lake Theater, in the 1890s. *Courtesy Denver Public Library, Western History Department.*

ater celebrities of the day—Edmund Kean, Edwin Booth, and LOLA MONTEZ—were attracted by wages much higher than in the East and went West to guest-star in theatrical productions. Theater bills changed nightly and offered a potpourri of the era's favorite attractions: Shakespearean plays, grand operas, minstrel revues, frontier American drama, and, by the late nineteenth century, splashy vaudeville shows. Tickets were as cheap as ten cents and as high as five dollars; in the relaxed social climate, high-rolling mining moguls mingled in the lobby with common laborers.

Transcontinental railway service radically changed the regional nature of entertainment and shrunk the number of theaters. By the early 1900s, syndicates based in Chicago and New York dominated Western drama by controlling the largest playhouses and by sending out stars and entire companies on lengthy commercial tours. Hollywood dealt another blow in the 1910s and 1920s, when many Western auditoriums were converted into movie houses.

Although the larger remaining venues featured mostly imported fluff from New York, quasi-professional "little theaters" sprang up in the 1910s to introduce the plays of Henrik Ibsen, George Bernard Shaw, Eugene O'Neill, and other important writers. Serious new drama also got a boost during the era of the Great Depression, thanks to the establishment of government-sponsored Federal Theatre Project units in San Francisco, Los Angeles, Seattle, Dallas, and other Western cities from 1936 to 1939.

A new burst of activity in serious Western theater erupted after World War II. In 1947, Margo Jones founded the nonprofit Theatre '47 in Dallas, and Nina Vance opened Houston's Alley Theatre. Over the next three decades, with help from the government and private contributors, nearly every other major Western

city built its own municipal playhouse, dedicated to resident professional drama.

Many of the companies are still thriving, for example, the Seattle Repertory Theatre (1963), the Mark Taper Forum in Los Angeles (1967), San Francisco's American Conservatory Theatre (1967), and Denver Center Theatre (1979). Along with the remaining Broadway touring houses scattered around the region and a bevy of smaller professional and community theaters, Western drama today is diverse and plentiful.

—Misha Berson

SUGGESTED READING:

Berson, Misha. *The San Francisco Stage: From Gold Rush to Golden Spike, 1849–1869.* San Francisco, 1989.

Toll, Robert C. *On with the Show: The First Century of Show Business in America.* New York, 1976.

Wilmeth, Don B., and Tice L. Miller, ed. *Cambridge Guide to American Theatre.* New York, 1993.

Zeigler, Joseph Wesley. *Regional Theatre: The Revolutionary Stage.* Minneapolis, Minn., 1977.

ETHNIC THEATER

Ethnic theater in the West has strengthened cultural identity among its patrons. From a lavish theatrical palace in San Francisco's Chinatown to *carpas* (traveling circuses) arriving for a short stint in Mexican BARRIOS to community *O-bon* festivals among Japanese Americans, music and drama have played important roles in the building of communities. Segregated from the white population, Asians and Mexicans lived in their own neighborhoods where they sustained a high level of group identity. Although subject to prejudice and economic stratification, they organized themselves for political, economic, and cultural ends. In 1852, for example, the first Chinese play was performed in San Francisco. Twenty-seven years later, an elaborate three-story theater was constructed in Chinatown. With a capacity of twenty-five hundred people, the theater featured dramas and operas. According to historian Judy Yung, women could attend events at the theater, but only if they sat in a separate section.

Although many urban barrios maintained theaters (the earliest established in the 1840s in Los Angeles), traveling drama troupes evoked much excitement in Mexican communities. Ostensibly the most well-known, the Hernández-Villalongín Dramatic Company performed on both sides of the United States–Mexico border at the turn of the century. The company presented productions as varied as *La Llorona* (the Mexican weeping woman) to *La cabaña de Tom (Uncle Tom's Cabin)* in facilities as varied as opera houses to makeshift stages.

Historian Richard Griswold del Castillo asserts that the morality plays performed by Mexican thespians reinforced the parameters of acceptable behavior among Mexican Americans. Although the troupes did not survive the Great Depression, broadsides for *carpas* can still be spotted in Mexican communities. Today contemporary drama groups, such as the East-West Players and Teatro Campesino, bring ethnic theater to wide-ranging audiences.

—*Vicki L. Ruiz*

SEE ALSO: Teatro Villalongín (Compañía Hernández-Villalongín)

SUGGESTED READING:

Griswold del Castillo, Richard. *La Familia: The Mexican American Family in the Urban Southwest*. Notre Dame, Ind., 1984.

Kanellos, Nicolás. *A History of Hispanic Theatre in the United States: Origins to 1940*. Houston, Tex., 1990.

Matsumoto, Valerie. *Farming the Home Place*. Ithaca, N.Y., 1993.

Takaki, Ronald. *Strangers from a Different Shore: A History of Asian Americans*. Boston, 1989.

Yung, Judy. *Chinese Women of America: A Pictorial History*. San Francisco, 1986.

HISPANIC THEATER

Spanish-language theater, for more than four centuries, has functioned both as art and entertainment. The first dramas in the West were performed by Hispanic pioneers in New Mexico in 1558. These Christmas *pastorales* (shepherd's plays) captivated audiences and reinforced their Catholic faith. Today, such traditions continue in the form of *matachines,* who use Native American dance during Holy Week to reenact the betrayal of Judas or the battles between Christians and Moors.

In the nineteenth century, *cuadros* (troupes) of Spanish and Mexican actors toured northern Mexico and gold-rush California—the latter area provided a lucrative market. Typical fare were *Siglo de Oro* (seventeenth-century classical theater) and contemporary drama. To accommodate the art form, a number of Hispanic theater houses were built in San Francisco to entertain all audiences, regardless of ethnicity. A well-known group making its home in the Bay Area during that time was Gerado López del Castillo's *Compania Español.*

More than one million Mexicans crossed the border between 1890 and 1930 to work in rapidly expanding mining and commercial agriculture. Familiar with live drama and finding themselves in a hostile and alien land, they were hungry for reflections of their culture on the stage. Many new theater houses were built in Texas, California, and Arizona. Los Angeles

and San Antonio, where major immigrant *colonias* were established, became cultural centers rivaling Spanish American cities. Palatial houses attracted famous theater groups like that of Virginia Fábregas, a world-renowned actress.

To the *colonias* in smaller towns went more compact ensembles known as *carpas*. The entertainers, performing as clowns, acrobats, and actors, presented short didactic comedy skits. An important part of live entertainment were circuses. As in theater, the early circuses in the West were Hispanic. *El Circo Habana* and *El Circo Escalante* traveled the Southwest and set up their tents until everyone for miles had seen the shows. Much of the entertainment was in Spanish and attracted large audiences. Consequently, plays or circuses became central to fundraisers for political causes.

Political theater emanating from the Chicano movement of the late 1960s spawned sophisticated entertainment that reached large audiences. Luis Valdes's *Teatro Campesino,* which started as a corollary to Cesar Chávez's farm-worker union, has been the training ground for many mainstream Hispanic actors, and Luis Valdez himself is a well-known film producer.

—*F. Arturo Rosales*

SEE ALSO: Teatro Villalongín (Compañía Hernández-Villalongín)

SUGGESTED READING:

Garza, Roberto J., ed. *Contemporary Chicano Theatre.* Notre Dame, Ind., 1976.

Kanellos, Nicolás. *A History of Hispanic Theatre in the United States: Origins to 1940.* Austin, Tex., 1990.

THEOSOPHICAL SOCIETY

Founded by Russian seer Helena Petrovna Blavatsky in 1875, the Theosophical Society eventually spread to Point Loma, California, where it maintained headquarters from 1897 to 1942. Blavatsky's writings, *Isis Unveiled* (1877) and *Secret Doctrine* (1888), became the movement's basic texts. Theosophy (Greek for "divine wisdom") did not claim to be a new religion but attempted to identify elements common to the world's great religions and philosophies, which were augmented by speculative thought, mystical insights, and occult studies. Without an anthropomorphic deity, theosophists believed that all life is part of a Universal Being. Strongly inspired by Eastern thought, theosophical doctrine encompasses the concepts of karma, reincarnation, and universal brotherhood.

After Blavatsky's death in London in 1891, differences of approach and teaching divided the theosophists. One group, headed by Annie Besant, maintained

The Theosophical Society on Point Loma in San Diego featured the Homestead and Aryan Temple of Peace. *Courtesy San Diego Historical Society.*

headquarters in Adyar, India. In 1897, the second group, under the leadership of KATHERINE AUGUSTA TINGLEY, established its international headquarters on Point Loma, overlooking San Diego Bay. Eventually, the site grew to more than five hundred acres and included several large structures, a temple, and numerous cottages. There Tingley established her School for the Revival of the Lost Mysteries of Antiquity, later renamed the Raja Yoga Academy, which developed a full academic curriculum augmented by esoteric studies. Tingley also established smaller theosophical schools in Cuba, England, Germany, Holland, and Sweden.

Tingley's reform agenda included helping orphans and "unfortunate" women, abolishing capital punishment, working toward the compatibility of all races and economic levels, and banning vivisection (the dissection of living animals in scientific research). In 1902, the New York Society for the Prevention of Cruelty to Children tried to stop Cuban orphans from relocating to Point Loma. The society claimed that children at Lomaland (as it came to be called) were ill-treated and subject to immoral activities, but U.S. and Cuban officials invited to inspect the school cleared it of all charges.

The activities at Lomaland included education, agricultural experimentation, and an extensive publishing operation. Residents produced many of their own necessities, including much of their clothing and food. Lomaland horticulturists made significant advances in the introduction and adaptation of various plant species to the West. The Theosophical Press developed the first keyboard allowing the printing of Sanskrit with a linotype.

Tingley strongly advocated cultural pursuits such as music, dance, drama, literature, and art as a way to awaken spirituality. The first open-air Greek theater in America was constructed at Lomaland in 1901.

Among the many talented people Tingley attracted to Point Loma were Maya scholar William Gates, art historian Osvald Siren, Welsh poet Kenneth Morris, novelist Talbot Mundy, and artists Reginald Machell, Maurice Braun, and Edith White.

Tingley died in 1929 from injuries sustained in an automobile accident in Europe. Gottfried de Purucker assumed leadership of the organization. He published many books on theosophical concepts and made attempts at a reconciliation with the other theosophical groups. A deteriorating financial situation and structures that no longer met safety codes made it impossible for the group to remain at Point Loma. In 1942, Purucker moved the operation to Covina, California. The headquarters moved to its present location in Pasadena, California, in 1950, where it continues to carry out the objectives of the Theosophical Society.

—*Bruce Kamerling*

SUGGESTED READING:
Greenwalt, Emmett A. *California Utopia: Point Loma, 1897–1942.* San Diego, Calif., 1978.

THOMAS, ELBERT D.

A professor and U.S. senator from Utah, Elbert D. Thomas (1883–1953) was born in Salt Lake City. After a five-year church mission to Japan, he joined the staff of the University of Utah in 1922 and taught Greek, Latin, political science, and Asian history for the next twenty years. In 1932, he defeated REED SMOOT for the U.S. Senate and was reelected in 1938 and 1944. In the Senate, he involved himself in legislation dealing with labor, federal aid to education, military affairs, and foreign relations. In 1951, President Harry S Truman appointed him high commissioner of the United States Trust Territories of the Pacific.

—*S. George Ellsworth*

THOMAS, HENRY ANDREW ("HECK")

Western lawman Henry Andrew ("Heck") Thomas (1850–1912) was one of the famous "three guardsman" of Oklahoma; the others were his close friends WILLIAM MATTHEW TILGHMAN, Jr., and CHRISTIAN (CHRIS) MADSEN. Born in Georgia, Thomas, at the age of twelve, served as a courier in his uncle's Confederate Army brigade. At the age of eighteen, he was appointed a police officer in Atlanta and helped quell the Bush Arbor riot of 1868. Later he worked as a messenger for the Texas Express Company.

Henry Andrew ("Heck") Thomas. *Courtesy University of Oklahoma, Western History Collections.*

In 1878, when the notorious SAM BASS gang stopped his train near Dallas, Thomas was wounded, but he outwitted the bandits by hiding twenty-two thousand dollars in the stove of the express car. In 1885, as a private detective, Thomas and another officer tracked down and killed two outlaws, Jim and Pink Lee. The next year, he was appointed a deputy U.S. marshal for the federal court of "Hanging Judge" ISAAC CHARLES PARKER in Fort Smith, Arkansas. Thomas quickly became Parker's best officer, bringing in more wanted men than any other marshal in the Indian Territory, over which Parker's court had jurisdiction. Thomas shot and wounded the Cherokee Indian outlaw Ned Christie and was himself badly wounded in a pitched gunfight with a band of moonshiners in the Creek Nation. During the 1890s, Thomas played a major role in pursuing and breaking up the DALTON GANG. His greatest exploit took place in Lawson in the Oklahoma Territory, on August 24, 1896, when he shot and killed bandit chieftain WILLIAM (BILL) DOOLIN in a close-quarters gun duel. Thomas was chief of police of the rowdy boom town of Lawton, Oklahoma, from 1902 to 1909, when failing health cost him the office.

Although only fifty-nine years old, Thomas was gray and bent from the rugged, stressful life he had led. To support his family, he secured an appointment as a deputy marshal, but two years later, plagued by old wounds, he died.

—*John Boessenecker*

SUGGESTED READING:
Shirley, Glenn. *Heck Thomas: Frontier Marshal.* New York, 1962.

THOMAS GILCREASE INSTITUTE

Founded by Thomas Gilcrease, the Thomas Gilcrease Institute of American History and Art reflects the founder's interest in the history of the Western Hemisphere, specifically the nineteenth-century American West. The art collection is composed of more than ten thousand paintings, drawings, prints, and sculptures. The library collection includes almost one hundred thousand manuscripts, rare books, photographs, and maps. The artifact collection—primarily American Indian material—contains more than 250,000 objects.

Little of Gilcrease's early life provides insight into his later role as a visionary collector of Americana. The eldest of fourteen children, Gilcrease grew up in the Creek Nation in the Indian Territory. Upon the dissolution of the Indian Nations in 1906, Gilcrease's American Indian heritage entitled him to ownership of 160 acres of land. The allotted land was located about twenty miles south of Tulsa and later proved to be situated on one of the most profitable oil fields in Oklahoma. Gilcrease founded the Gilcrease Oil Company in 1922. By the late 1930s, he began collecting material related to American history and art.

To exhibit his immense collection, Gilcrease opened a museum on the grounds of his Tulsa estate in 1949. By the early 1950s, faced with debts yet desiring to maintain the collection intact, he began to search for an entity to purchase it. In 1954, citizens of Tulsa supported a bond issue to retire Gilcrease's debts and acquire the collection. Gilcrease committed oil revenues to the city of Tulsa until the income equalled the amount of the original bond funds, a goal attained in the early 1980s.

—*Sarah Erwin*

SUGGESTED READING:
Milstein, David R. *Thomas Gilcrease.* San Antonio, Tex., 1969.
Myers, Fred. *Thomas Gilcrease and His National Treasure.* Tulsa, Okla., 1987.

THOMPSON, BENJAMIN F.

Gunfighter, saloonkeeper, and peace officer Ben Thompson (1842–1884) was born in Knottingly, England. In 1851, his family moved to Austin, Texas. In 1858 and again in 1859, he wounded fellow teen-agers with a shotgun in individual confrontations, and the following year, he shot antagonists in two more altercations. At the outbreak of the Civil War, Thompson joined the Confederate Army and served in Texas, New Mexico, and Louisiana. He also found time to gamble,

Benjamin F. Thompson. *Courtesy Texas State Library.*

smuggle whiskey, engage in another shooting scrape, and marry Catherine Moore, the daughter of a prosperous Austin family.

During the Reconstruction years, Thompson inevitably clashed with the occupation soldiers, and after a shooting, he was jailed in Austin. He escaped to Mexico and received a commission in the forces of the Emperor Maximilian, killed a policeman in a Matamoros duel, and then returned to Austin to gamble and operate a saloon. He wounded his brother-in-law, threatened to shoot a justice of the peace, and was sentenced to a prison term. Upon his release in 1870, he moved to Kansas and operated the famous Bull's Head Saloon in rowdy ABILENE. He shifted his gambling activities to another Kansas cattle town, Ellsworth, where his brother Billy drunkenly killed Sheriff C. B. Whitney.

Back in Austin, Thompson celebrated Christmas in 1876 with a saloon fight, killing the owner and severely wounding the bartender. Although infamous as a gunfighter, Thompson generously supported numerous orphans, and in 1881, he won election as city marshal of Austin. Perhaps because of his fearsome reputation, he proved to be an excellent peace officer. But in 1882, a long feud climaxed with Jack Harris, part owner of San Antonio's most notorious night spot, where Thompson fatally wounded Harris. Foolishly, Thompson returned to the dive two years later with fellow gunman JOHN KING FISHER. A quarrel broke out with Harris's former partners and friends, and Thompson and Fisher were shot to death, with nine and thirteen wounds, respectively.

—*Bill O'Neal*

SEE ALSO: Gunfighters; Violence

SUGGESTED READING:

Paine, Lauran. *Texas Ben Thompson.* Los Angeles, 1966.
Schoenberger, Dale T. *The Gunfighters.* Caldwell, Idaho, 1971.
Streeter, Floyd B. *Ben Thompson, Man with a Gun.* New York, 1957.

THOMPSON, DAVID

Canada's premier explorer and surveyor in the pre-Confederation period, David Thompson (1770–1857) was born in London, England. Apprenticed to the HUDSON'S BAY COMPANY as a clerk at the age of fourteen, Thompson was sent to Rupert's Land in 1784 and rapidly acquired a practical, working knowledge of the northern FUR TRADE and Indian languages and customs. During the winter of 1789 to 1790, while recovering from a broken leg, he formally studied surveying and spent the next few years investigating an alternative route to Lake Athabasca through Reindeer Lake in present-day northern Saskatchewan.

Although Thompson was appointed surveyor of the Hudson's Bay Company in May 1794, he chafed under the company's pedestrian leadership and joined its rival, the Montreal-based North West Company, three years later. His first assignment (from 1797 to 1798), as a consequence of Jay's Treaty, was to chart the location of the forty-ninth parallel and the position of the North West Company's posts and major rivers in northwestern Ontario and southern Manitoba; during this exploratory work, he traveled to the Mandan and Hidatsa villages on the Missouri River and identified the headwaters of the Mississippi River. In the early 1800s, he turned his attention westward and explored the North Saskatchewan River into the Rocky Mountains and present-day central British Columbia. His most famous trip was in 1811 when he was ordered to travel overland to the mouth of the Columbia River, only to find JOHN JACOB ASTOR's Pacific Fur Company already there. Thompson thereafter tried to limit American activity in the area and, in doing so, completed his survey of the Columbia River.

Thompson retired to Quebec in 1812 but continued his mapping work, in particular the surveying of the international boundary, under the terms of the Treaty of Ghent, from the St. Lawrence River to Lake of the Woods. During his final years, while living in poverty, he began work on an autobiography. Poor health, however, prevented him from completing the manuscript, and it was not until the early twentieth century that the man and his accomplishments were commemorated through the publication of his writings.

—*W. A. Waiser*

SUGGESTED READING:
Ronda, J. R. *Astoria and Empire*. Lincoln, Nebr., 1990.
Thomson, D. W. *Man and Meridians*. Vol. 1. Ottawa, Ont., 1975.
Tyrrell, J. B., ed. *David Thompson's Narrative*. Toronto, Ont., 1916.
Wood, W. R., and T. D. Thiessen, eds. *Early Fur Trade on the Northern Plains*. Norman, Okla., 1985.

THOMPSON, ERA BELL

The daughter of African American settlers in North Dakota, Era Bell Thompson (1905–1986) achieved renown as a writer. Born in Des Moines, Iowa, she moved with her parents, Mary Logan and Stewart Calvin (Tony) Thompson, to Driscoll, North Dakota, in 1914 to escape urban problems, including a lack of job opportunities for Thompson's three brothers.

The granddaughter of a former slave, Thompson looked forward to living in a West full of possibilities, including kind treatment from other migrants. She later explained that during the early settlement period, neighbors were indeed helpful to each other and often brought supplies or delivered mail. She also recalled that, although in the Driscoll Township school in 1914 she and her brother "were the first bona fide Negro children" the teacher and students had ever seen, she soon overcame their curiosity.

In 1919, after her mother's death from a stroke, her father relocated the family on a farm near Sterling. The following year, the Thompsons moved to Bismarck, a city that proved inhospitable to its nineteen African American inhabitants. Thompson cut classes to escape comments about "thick-skulled" black slaves, avoided sitting by school bus windows because people outside stared at her, and shunned movie theaters, where ushers insisted that she sit in the balcony.

After graduating in 1924 from Bismarck High School, she enrolled in a commercial course in Mandan. The following fall, she attended the University of North Dakota in Grand Forks. There she worked for room and board, excelled in women's track events, and wrote for the student newspaper. In 1927, a case of pleurisy forced her to withdraw and return to Mandan.

Thompson soon moved to Chicago, where in 1928, for the first time in her life, she encountered thousands of AFRICAN AMERICANS: "All around me now were colored people, lots and lots of colored people." She took a position with a black magazine and discovered such figures of the Harlem Renaissance as Langston Hughes and W. E. B. DuBois. She returned home to settle her father's estate after his death in 1928, graduated from Morningside College in Sioux City, Iowa, in 1933, and worked as a domestic servant and part-time writer in Chicago during the 1930s and early 1940s.

The turning point came in 1945 when Thompson applied for a Newberry Library Fellowship to write a book about North Dakota and the committee asked her to write instead an autobiography. The result was *American Daughter,* published by the University of Chicago Press in 1946. Shortly afterward, Thompson joined the staff of a new African American magazine, *Ebony,* founded in 1945. For the next three decades, in editorials and articles, Thompson examined intraracial adoption, revealed the personalities of such African Americans as Martin Luther King, Jr., and Mahalia Jackson, and published *Africa, Land of My Fathers* (1954) based on her experiences in eighteen

African countries. Numerous honors, including North Dakota's Roughrider Award in 1976 and an honorary doctorate from the University of North Dakota in 1978, came her way as well.

Thompson died in Chicago on December 30, 1986. Both her life and writings offer insight into the ebb and flow of racial attitudes in the American West. She worked against prejudice throughout her life, but her very choices raise questions about the West's long-standing reputation as a land of opportunity for all.

Although in *American Daughter* she wrote optimistically that "the chasm is growing narrower," she stated in 1982 that "recently, the chasm has widened." Thompson's observations suggest that racial interaction provides a key not only to understanding the Western past, but the Western present and future as well.

—*Glenda Riley*

SUGGESTED READING:

Anderson, Kathie Ryckman. "Era Bell Thompson: A North Dakota Daughter." *North Dakota History* 49 (Fall 1982): 11–18.

Riley, Glenda. "American Daughters: Black Women in the West." *Montana: The Magazine of Western History* 38 (Spring 1988): 14–27.

Thompson, Era Bell. *American Daughter.* Reprint. St. Paul, Minn., 1986.

Henry David Thoreau. Editor's collection.

THOREAU, HENRY DAVID

Essayist, poet, naturalist, and philosopher Henry David Thoreau (1817–1862) was born in Concord, Massachusetts, where he wrote his masterpiece of transcendentalism, *Walden* (1854), an account of the two years he lived in a rude cabin he built himself along Walden Pond. Spending a night in jail for refusing to pay taxes to support either slavery or the United States–Mexican War, Thoreau became known to future generations as an advocate of civil liberties for the essay he produced on the experience entitled "Civil Disobedience" (1849). Thoreau's thoughts on human nature and the wilderness had an impact on subsequent American notions of the West. Arguing that no man should be completely civilized, he celebrated the freedom that the idea of the West represented as a metaphor. "Eastward I go only by force," he wrote in a oft quoted passage, "but westward I go free." A thoroughly American figure whose beliefs and attitudes, even in their inconsistencies, came to typify the temperament most people associate with Westerners, Thoreau believed that government best that governed least and that the ideal government was no government at all. He also, however, ignored his laissez-faire ideas in practice and called on the state to support the arts, education, good roads, crime prevention, and wildlife conservation. Seldom leaving New England, Thoreau died in his home town a relatively obscure local eccentric who had published two books, *A Week on the Concord and Merrimack Rivers* (1849) and *Walden,* both long out of print at the time of his death.

—*Charles Phillips*

SUGGESTED READING:

Paul, Sherman. *The Shores of America: Thoreau's Inward Exploration.* Cambridge, Mass., 1959.

THORPE, THOMAS BANGS

Writer and artist Thomas Bangs Thorpe (1815–1878) was a humorist of the Old Southwest. Born in Massachusetts, Thorpe grew up in New York and attended Wesleyan University in Connecticut but withdrew due to ill health. To improve his health, he moved south— to Louisiana—where he lived from 1837 to 1854. He returned to New York City in 1854 and remained a resident until his death.

Thorpe began his artistic training as a teen-ager in New York City. Apprenticed to the artist John Quidor, Thorpe exhibited his paintings at the American Academy in 1833. Realizing that he would not be successful as a painter, he turned to writing and newspaper work. His first short story, "Tim Owen, the Bee-Hunter," was published in 1839; his most famous story, "The Big Bear of Arkansas," in 1841.

During the United States–Mexican War, Thorpe traveled with ZACHARY TAYLOR's army. From his experiences in the war, he wrote *Our Army on the Rio Grande* (1846) and *Our Army at Monterrey* (1847). A collection of war stories, *The Taylor Anecdote Book,* was published in 1848. In 1854, he turned to writing fiction and published his one novel, *The Master's House: A Tale of Southern Life.* His real talent, however, lay in the short story—nature pictures, anecdotes of Southern life, hunting stories, and tall tales. Extensively published in periodicals, some of his short stories were collected in *The Mysteries of the Backwood* (1846) and *The Hive of "The Bee-Hunter"* (1854).

—*Candace Floyd*

SUGGESTED READING:
Thorpe, Thomas Bangs. *A New Collection of Thomas Bangs Thorpe's Sketches of the Old Southwest.* Edited and with a critical introduction and textual commentary by David C. Estes. Baton Rouge, La., 1989.

TIBBLES, SUSETTE LAFLESCHE

Indian reform lecturer Susette LaFlesche Tibbles (1854–1903) was born on the Omaha reservation in Nebraska, the eldest daughter of "progressive" Omaha Chief Joseph LaFlesche and his wife Mary Gale. Educated at the Presbyterian mission school on the reservation and at the Elizabeth Institute for Young Ladies in New Jersey, she later obtained a post as assistant teacher in the government school on the reservation.

Her claim to fame, however, resulted from her challenge to one of the saddest examples of U.S. government exploitation of the Indians. Eager to confine all Indians to reservations, government officials had thoughtlessly transferred Ponca Indian lands to their enemies, the Sioux, and then had forcibly removed the Poncas to the unfamiliar Indian Territory (in present-day Oklahoma). After a third of the tribe died there, Ponca Chief Standing Bear led a desperate group of his followers back to their homeland only to be ar-

rested and ordered to return to the Indian Territory. In hopes of stopping removals and raising money for legal efforts to protect the Poncas, Thomas Tibbles, a journalist in Omaha, Nebraska, arranged to take Standing Bear on a speaking tour of Eastern cities. LaFlesche, who accompanied them ostensibly as Standing Bear's interpreter, became a strong voice for Indian reform in her own right. LaFlesche, known to fascinated audiences as "Bright Eyes," and Standing Bear fanned the flames of outrage that attracted influential Easterners, including HELEN HUNT JACKSON and ALICE CUNNINGHAM FLETCHER, to the cause of Indian reform.

In 1881, LaFlesche married Tibbles, and for the next several years the two continued to bring the message of Indian reform to audiences in the Northeast and in England and to U.S. congressional committees in Washington, D.C. They lent considerable support to the allotment policy proposed by Senator HENRY LAURENS DAWES, whose DAWES ACT, a major shift in U.S. Indian policy, was enacted in 1887.

In later years, Susette LaFlesche Tibbles lived in Lincoln, Nebraska, where she wrote and illustrated children's stories and contributed editorials to her husband's Populist newspaper. In 1902, she moved to her allotment near Bancroft, Nebraska, where she died in 1903, at the age of forty-nine.

—*Peggy Pascoe*

SUGGESTED READING:
Crary, Margaret. *Susette LaFlesche: Voice of the Omaha Indians.* New York, 1973.
Wilson, Dorothy. *Bright Eyes: The Story of Susette LaFlesche, an Omaha Indian.* New York, 1974.

TILGHMAN, WILLIAM MATTHEW, JR.

William Matthew Tilghman, Jr. (1854–1924), was one of the preeminent professional lawmen of the West. Born in Iowa and raised in Kansas, he became a buffalo hunter on the plains at the age of sixteen. In five years, he killed some twelve thousand bisons and had many narrow escapes from hostile Indians. The experience made him tough and resourceful but cost him his brother, who was killed by a Cheyenne war party. Tilghman settled in Dodge City, ran a saloon, scouted for the army, and, in 1884, was appointed a deputy sheriff. He was a friend of such notables as Wyatt Earp and BARTHOLOMEW (BAT) MASTERSON and served as marshal of Dodge City until 1886. He maintained a good record as a lawman, although in 1888, he shot and killed a childhood friend, Ed Prather, in self-defense.

William Matthew Tilghman, Jr. *Courtesy University of Oklahoma, Western History Collections.*

In 1889, he joined the land rush to the Oklahoma Territory. There he achieved his greatest fame as deputy U.S. marshal, city marshal of Perry, sheriff of Lincoln County, and chief of police of Oklahoma City. He was kind and gentlemanly but a terror to the criminal. Perhaps his greatest feat was his single-handed capture of the bandit leader WILLIAM (BILL) DOOLIN in a bathhouse at Eureka Springs, Arkansas, in 1896.

In retirement, Tilghman produced a silent film, *The Passing of the Oklahoma Outlaws,* and from 1915 to 1920, he showed it around the country. In a scene suited to fiction, the governor of Oklahoma in 1924 asked the old lawman to tame the corrupt oil boomtown of Cromwell. There, at the age of seventy, Tilghman was killed while arresting a drunken Prohibition agent.

—*John Boessenecker*

SUGGESTED READING:
Shirley, Glenn. *Guardian of the Law: The Life and Times of William Matthew Tilghman.* Austin, Tex., 1988.

TILLAMOOK INDIANS

SEE: Native American Peoples: Peoples of the Pacific Northwest

TIMBER CULTURE ACT OF 1873

The Timber Culture Act of 1873 was part of the movement to settle the West with individual farmers. Similar to the HOMESTEAD ACT OF 1862, the Timber Culture Act granted a single quarter-section of land (160 acres) to any head of a family who planted and maintained forty acres of trees for ten years. Preindustrial farmers were dependent on wood for much of their material culture. Many believed that forests brought rain, and planting trees on the plains provided the basis for increased settlement. It also allowed people who homesteaded marginal land to acquire more than the 160 acres they could claim under the Homestead Act. The Timber Culture Act reflected the prevailing wisdom of its time, much of which has since been proved erroneous.

—*Hal Rothman*

SEE ALSO: Land Policy

SUGGESTED READING:
Robbins, Roy M. *Our Landed Heritage.* 2d ed., rev. Lincoln, Nebr., 1976.

TIMBER AND STONE ACT OF 1878

The Timber and Stone Act of 1878 was one of the many pieces of legislation that followed the HOMESTEAD ACT OF 1862 in attempting to help Americans acquire federal land at little or no cost. The act permitted settlers to purchase 160 acres of nonagricultural land, but they could only use its products for their personal needs. This illustrated an important dilemma in federal LAND POLICY. Americans assumed that agriculture was the best use of Western land; in many cases, the assumption was fallacious. Much of the West was poorly suited to farming, and large areas covered with timber had obvious other uses. Particularly in timbered areas of Washington, Oregon, and northern California, the temptation to subvert the law was great. At the instruction of timber companies, people filed homestead claims that they did not intend to patent, allowed timber companies to cut the lands, and abandoned them.

Although the Timber and Stone Act of 1878 was supposed to help homesteaders meet their needs on what was increasingly recognized as marginal land, in reality the law became a tool through which timber companies were able to get greater quantities of federal timber in defiance of the intent and letter of the law. The law stood as an illustration of the problems of applying the values of an industrial society in an agrarian framework. Like the Homestead Act, the Timber and Stone Act of 1878 showed that assumptions about the nature of Western land and Western economies had not yet responded to the changes caused by the process of industrialization.

—*Hal Rothman*

SUGGESTED READING:
Robbins, Roy M. *Our Landed Heritage.* 2d ed., rev. Lincoln, Nebr., 1976.

TINGLEY, CLYDE

New Mexico Governor Clyde Tingley (1883–1960) was born in Ohio. After working at construction on a railroad and building parts for airplane engines for the Wright brothers, he moved to Albuquerque, New Mexico, where he quickly became involved in local politics. He was elected city alderman in 1916 and mayor of Albuquerque the following year. From 1917 until his retirement from public service in 1954, Tingley was considered the undisputed ruler of city hall. Both in 1928 and 1932, Tingley served the Democratic National Convention as a delegate. This exposure helped him secure the Democratic nomination for governor in 1934. He narrowly defeated his challenger by fewer than seven thousand votes.

During the Great Depression, a third of the state's population was on federal assistance. Tingley established the New Mexico Relief and Security Authority to help people find jobs in federal work programs. He easily won reelection in 1936. State law required him to step down after his second term, and he returned to the mayor's office in Albuquerque and served the city in various capacities until 1954.

—*Kurt Edward Kemper*

TINGLEY, KATHERINE AUGUSTA

A leader in the American theosophical movement, Katherine Augusta Tingley (1847–1929) was one of three children born to James P. L. and Susan Chase

Katherine Augusta Tingley. *Courtesy San Diego Historical Society.*

Westcott in Newburg, Massachusetts. As a young girl, Tingley was attracted by the esoteric nature of her grandfather's Masonic teachings. In 1867, she left a convent school to marry the first of her three husbands.

In the 1880s and 1890s, Tingley founded several charitable organization dedicated to helping prisons and hospitals. She staged spiritualistic readings and dramatic recitals to fund her charity work. In 1892, she became associated with William Quan Judge, a proponent of theosophy, whose believers practiced a philosophically oriented religion based on mystical insights, occult study, and Far Eastern teachings. In 1895, Judge organized the THEOSOPHICAL SOCIETY of America, which Tingley headed after his death the next year.

In 1896, Tingley embarked on a world tour to popularize her version of theosophy and attract converts. On arriving in California from Australia in 1897, she acquired Point Loma overlooking San Diego Bay. She opened her headquarters there in 1900 and began developing one of the nation's most successful utopian settlements. The six-hundred-member community, which included an innovative educational program and the Theosophical University, was also a cultural center offering musical programs and classical theater.

Financial constraints, doctrinal disputes among the believers, and Tingley's own forceful personality militated against the community's continued success. After her death following an automobile accident in Germany, the Point Loma community declined. In 1942, it moved to Covina, California and then to Pasadena in 1951, where it still continues.

—*Gloria Ricci Lothrop*

SUGGESTED READING:

Greenwalt, Emmet A. *A California Utopias: Point Loma, 1897–1942.* San Diego, Calif., 1978.

TLATSKANAI INDIANS

SEE: Native American Peoples: Peoples of the Pacific Northwest

TLINGIT INDIANS

SEE: Native American Peoples: Peoples of the Alaska, Peoples of the Pacific Northwest

TODD, JOHN BLAIR SMITH

As a soldier, trader, land speculator, Indian-treaty negotiator, and politician, John Blair Smith Todd (1814–1872) gained renown in the upper Missouri River region from his arrival in 1855 until his death. Born in Lexington, Kentucky, Todd moved with his family to Illinois. He was appointed to the U.S. Military Academy and graduated in 1837. As a lieutenant, he then accompanied General WINFIELD SCOTT during the Seminole War in Florida and worked as a recruiting officer. After his promotion to the rank of captain, he helped relocate Eastern tribes to the Indian Territory (Oklahoma) from 1843 to 1846 and then served under Scott in his invasion of Veracruz during the UNITED STATES–MEXICAN WAR. In 1855, Todd participated in General WILLIAM SELBY HARNEY's retaliation for the GRATTAN MASSACRE against Lakota Sioux Indians at the Blue Water fight.

In 1856, Todd resigned his commission to become a trader at Fort Randall. He formed a partnership with another former army officer, D. M. Frost, and together they established a general store at Sioux City, the gateway for river traffic into the upper Missouri River region. Todd and Frost expanded their business to include trading posts at strategic places on the "Yankton Triangle" of land between the Big Sioux and Missouri rivers, with a main post along the lower James River.

At Fort Randall, Todd held discussions with Yankton tribal leaders who controlled the Triangle. Working with mixed-blood Charles F. Picotte, he accompanied head chief STRUCK BY THE REE and fourteen other Yankton leaders to Washington, D.C. By treaty on April 19, 1858, the Yanktons ceded 11 million acres to the United States in return for recognized claim to a 430,000-acre reservation, retention of their pipestone quarry site in southwestern Minnesota, an agency staff to help with adjustment to reservation life, and $1.6 million payable as annuities over fifty years.

In anticipation of opening the Triangle, Todd expanded his trading network, encouraged settlement, and entered public life. Collaborating with Frost, he drafted a petition for territorial government, approved by President JAMES BUCHANAN on March 2, 1861. Todd was a cousin of Mary Todd Lincoln, and his family relationship to the new president, Abraham Lincoln, enhanced his political appeal. Todd was elected territorial delegate to Congress as a Democrat in 1861. Reelected in 1862, he ran again but lost in 1864.

Todd served through turbulent times as a congressman without distinction. His term was interrupted by duty during the Civil War as the commander of a unit from Tennessee. He helped organize the territorial Democratic party and served a term in the lower house of the territorial legislature from 1867 to 1869.

—*Herbert T. Hoover*

SUGGESTED READING:

Hoover, Herbert T. "John Blair Smith Todd." In *Bon Homme County History.* Freeman, S.D., 1994.

Todd, John Blair Smith. "The Harney Expedition against the Sioux: The Journal of Captain John B. S. Todd." *Nebraska History* 43: 2 (1962): 89–130.

TOLOWA INDIANS

SEE: Native American Peoples: Peoples of the Pacific Northwest

TOMBSTONE, ARIZONA

SEE: Mining: Mining Camps and Towns; O.K. Corral, Gunfight at

TONTO BASIN WAR

SEE: Graham-Tewkesbury Feud

TOOHOOLHOOLZOTE (NEZ PERCÉ)

A spokesman and leader in the Nez Percé War, Toohoolhoolzote (ca. 1810–1877), whose name means "sound," lived along the Snake River near the mouth of the Salmon River in Idaho, an area ceded to the United States by the Treaty of 1863. Among the chiefs who refused to sign the treaty, Toohoolhoolzote held traditional Nez Percé beliefs, fostered their perpetuation, and avidly participated in the "dreamer cult" of the Wanapam religious leader Smohalla. He served as spokesman for the Lower Nez Percé bands in 1876, when United States officials pressed for enforcement of the 1863 treaty. When he refused to yield and vacate the ceded lands, he was jailed in 1877 by General OLIVER OTIS HOWARD. He was released after other "nontreaty" Nez Percés finally agreed to the treaty terms.

The treaty caused great discontent among many of the Nez Percés, especially the younger warriors. In June 1877, some Nez Percés killed four whites who were notorious for their ill treatment of Indians. Despite the efforts of Young Joseph (CHIEF JOSEPH the Younger), who had risen to a position of influence following the death of his father, war broke out. Toohoolhoolzote and Chief Joseph led their band of nontreaty Nez Percés on an epic flight from U.S. Army forces. Toohoolhoolzote was instrumental in the Indian victory at the Battle of Clearwater River on July 11, 1877. He was killed in the final battle of the Nez Percé War, at Bear Paw Mountain, on September 30, 1877.

—Alan Axelrod

TOPEKA, KANSAS

Topeka, Kansas, was founded on December 5, 1854, by "Free-Soil" men (men who opposed Kansas's ad-

An emigrant wagon train passes through Topeka in 1879. *Courtesy Kansas State Historical Society.*

mission to the United States as a slave state) near an Oregon Trail crossing of the Kansas River and adjacent to the Potawatomi Reserve. Among the founders were CHARLES ROBINSON, the state's first governor, and Cyrus K. Holliday, first president of the Santa Fe Railroad.

Topeka served as the capital of the extralegal free-state government during the territorial period and became the state capital in 1861. The city's importance as a rail center, as the seat of state and county government, and as a wholesale distribution point furthered its development following the Civil War. Washburn College (now Washburn University) opened there in 1865, and the public-school system began the same year.

During a land boom in the 1880s, several outlying towns sprang up and were soon connected to the city by street-railway systems. The suburbs had become part of Topeka by 1926, but several retained their names and distinctive characteristics as neighborhoods.

Topeka's first settlers were from the East and the Midwest. They were joined, primarily in the 1870s and 1880s, by Swedes, Germans, and Germans from Russia. Although several blacks were early residents, much larger numbers came from the South in 1879 and 1880. Mexicans, the last major immigrant group, were recruited as laborers by the railroads and came to Topeka early in the twentieth century. Descendants of immigrant groups continue to sponsor annual celebrations of their heritage.

Topeka's school system received national attention in 1954, when the U.S. Supreme Court decided the famous case *Brown* v. *Board of Education of Topeka*. In this decision, the Supreme Court struck down the practice of "separate but equal" schools for black students.

The city's population fluctuated between 30,000 and 35,000 from 1880 to 1900 and reached 64,120 in 1930. Remaining reasonably static until after World War II, the population increased to 119,883 by 1990.

Topeka has been hit by three major disasters—the Kansas River floods in 1903 and 1951 and a devastating tornado in 1966. Urban renewal, a movement of population and retail business away from the city center, and industrial development have altered the city's landscape and shifted segments of its population. A major medical center, Topeka is home to the Menninger Foundation and Clinic, which pioneered changes in the treatment of the mentally ill.

—Robert W. Richmond

SUGGESTED READING:
Bird, Roy D., and Douglas W. Wallace. *Witness of the Times: A History of Shawnee County.* Topeka, Kans., 1976.
Giles, F. W. *Thirty Years in Topeka, 1854–1884.* Topeka, Kans., 1886.

TOPOGRAPHICAL ENGINEERS

SEE: Corps of Topographical Engineers

TOSAWI (COMANCHE)

Chief of the Penetaka Comanche band, Tosawi, whose birth and death dates are unknown, was a leader of Comanche raiders during the early Comanche Wars, but he agreed to the terms of the MEDICINE LODGE TREATY OF 1867. In November 1868, forces under the command of GEORGE ARMSTRONG CUSTER brutally routed BLACK KETTLE's band of Cheyennes at the Battle of Washita. In response, Tosawi was the first Comanche leader to surrender at Fort Cobb in the Indian Territory. He approached General PHILIP H. SHERIDAN and announced, "Tosawi, good Indian." The general replied, "The only good Indians I ever saw were dead," which popular lore has translated into one of the most terrible clichés of the so-called Wild West: "The only good Indian is a dead Indian."

Tosawi was among the Comanche delegates who traveled to Washington, D.C., for an 1872 conference.

—*Alan Axelrod*

TOURISM

When the first European, Spanish explorer García López de Cárdenas, encountered the Grand Canyon in the 1540s, it was just a large hole in his way. Only the values of an industrial society with the resources to support travel and leisure have made it into an attraction to which millions flock each year. In this paradox are the roots of Western tourism. Its attractions—natural, historical, and otherwise—have only the meaning ascribed to them by culture.

The first tourists in the West were European nobles who came to see the sights of this new and different world in the first half of the nineteenth century. Some of these travelers, such as Prince Maximilian of Wied-Neuwied, whose 1833 party included artist KARL (OR CARL) BODMER, also collected ethnographic information, but most simply told tales of their adventures. Before the application of industrial-era technology to the vast landscapes of the West, tourism was a dangerous and expensive proposition left to the rich and foolhardy.

The RAILROADS that crossed the West in the last half of the nineteenth century made tourism available to a wider range of people. Although still overwhelmingly

Top: Women and children on Minerva Terrace, Yosemite National Park, September 8, 1888. Photograph by F. Jay Haynes. *Courtesy Montana Historical Society, Haynes Foundation Collection.*

Bottom: Dressed in their finery, a group of men, women, and children picnic in the wilds of Idaho. *Courtesy State Historical Society of Idaho.*

affluent, the tourists who came West did not have to endure the harsh realities of Western life. Instead, they could ride in a relatively comfortable railroad car and trek to more remote places by horse or wagon if they chose.

As railroads began to promote the features of the West, the new tourist industry mushroomed. Its economic dimension attracted the interest of American industry, while the wonders of the West touched the pulse of the nation. National parks, staples of early tourism, followed, in no small part as a result of the efforts of American railroads. Nathaniel Pitt "National Park" Langford worked closely with FERDINAND VANDEVEER HAYDEN and the Northern Pacific Railroad

Railroads promoted the beaches of California as tourist destinations. The success of their endeavors is apparent in these images of "Tent City" at San Diego's Del Coronado resort hotel. Patrons who could not afford the luxury hotel's accommodations took tents on the beach. *Courtesy San Diego Historical Society.*

as the ATCHISON, TOPEKA AND SANTA FE (AT&SF) built tracks across the Southwest, tourism proliferated.

The creation of amenities played an important part in the growth of Western tourism. The Fred Harvey Company in particular offered a level of service that superseded individualized enterprises. The company presented travelers with the meals, lodging, and later tours and other experiences that turned roughing it into "roughing it with style." Affiliated with the AT&SF, the Harvey company capitalized on such disparate features as the railroad's advertising—including the collection of lantern slides made available at the turn of the twentieth century—and the construction of HOTELS, such as the El Tovar on the rim of the Grand Canyon in 1904. The increase in traffic spurred by such innovations made passenger travel more affordable and increasingly desirable as prices dropped and more Americans became caught up in the cultural swirl of "See America First."

With the creation of the NATIONAL PARK SERVICE in 1916 and the appointment of millionaire STEPHEN TYNG MATHER as its first head, Western tourism jumped to new heights. Mather's favorite axiom was that "scenery is a hollow enjoyment to a tourist who sets out in the morning after an indigestible breakfast and a fitful sleep on an impossible bed." He worked to improve services at national park areas, thus ensuring a rise in quality across the West as visitors became accustomed to more than the haphazard offerings of the past.

By the 1920s, tourism was in the process of democratization, as more and more members of a larger and larger middle class sought to see the wonders of the nation. Railroads had ceased to be the only way to see the West; highways had become increasingly common as Western states developed infrastructures that not incidentally catered to the traveling public. A national park-to-park highway, connecting the major national parks from the Grand Canyon to Yellowstone and Yosemite, was planned and partially created. The construction of Route 66 as a national highway from Chicago to Santa Monica began in 1926 and was completed in 1938, adding hundreds of thousands of new visitors in each of the subsequent years. With the combination of New Deal programs that improved facili-

to ensure the establishment of YELLOWSTONE NATIONAL PARK in 1872. The Northern Pacific promoted the park with enthusiasm, particularly after its rails reached Yellowstone in 1883.

The relationship between national parks and railroads was strong and was strengthened by a surge of cultural nationalism that came to fruition in the last decade of the nineteenth century. Highlighted by the work of writers such as CHARLES FLETCHER LUMMIS, whose *Tramp across the Country* imprinted the features of the American West on the national mind, Americans began to sense the value of the natural and cultural heritage of their continent. When railroads such ties and infrastructure at national parks and forests, by the end of the 1930s, there were corridors of the West that depended on tourist travel for the basis of the local and regional economies.

During the 1930s, the range of tourism began to become more broad. W. Averill Harriman created the ski resort of Sun Valley, Idaho, as way to transport more people on his UNION PACIFIC RAILROAD. It was far enough from major Western cities and arterial roads that potential skiers had to travel on the railroad, and in the aftermath of the 1932 Winter Olympics in Lake Placid, New York, Americans became captivated with this previously European sport. Harriman recognized a market waiting to be served and met its needs.

Also during that decade, the National Park Service began to be involved in recreational tourism. Although few of the first areas it developed were in the West, planning and experimentation laid the basis for the many Western national recreation areas established beginning in the 1950s.

The modern West includes other forms of tourism as well: mass-market entertainment tourism, such as Disneyland and Knott's Berry Farm, and the combination of gaming and national entertainment spectacle that is LAS VEGAS. A staple of the Western economy, tourism creates corridors of prosperity at major destinations and along primary transportation routes. In an increasingly technical and specialized economy, tourism is one of the few industries that allows unskilled workers opportunity and offers incentive to small entrepreneurs. The combination of its features and its development have made the West into America's playground.

—*Hal Rothman*

SEE ALSO: Harvey, Ford Ferguson; Harvey Girls

SUGGESTED READING:
Pomeroy, Earl. *In Search of the Golden West.* New York, 1957.

TOWNLEY, ARTHUR CHARLES (A. C.)

A. C. Townley (1880–1959) founded the NONPARTISAN LEAGUE, a grassroots socialist organization that spread from North Dakota into twelve other Midwestern states in the early twentieth century. Born in Brown's Valley, Minnesota, Townley moved to western North Dakota and began farming at the age of twenty-seven. Unsuccessful in that venture, he went bankrupt, joined the Socialist party, and worked as a party organizer in the western counties. In 1915, he formed the Nonpartisan League and devised a platform that called for rural credit banks, tax exemptions for farm improvements, and state ownership of terminal elevators, flour mills, packing houses, and cold-storage plants.

From February 1915 until June 1916, Townley traveled through the state converting audiences to his political beliefs. Recruiting employees among former Socialist party staff members, he established a headquarters in Fargo. In 1915, the league secured control of the North Dakota House of Representatives; by the winter of that year, it had 28,000 members. Townley then started spreading his philosophy by organizing a National Nonpartisan League. By 1918, the league boasted more than 188,000 members—mainly in the Dakotas, Montana, and Minnesota—and a staff of five hundred speakers and organizers. The expanded league called for full employment, a democratic world government, public works for the unemployed, federal ownership of public transportation and communications, steeply graduated income and inheritance taxes, women's suffrage, and the repeal of wartime laws restraining civil rights.

In the 1917 special election in North Dakota, the league's candidate for U.S. Congress, John M. Baer, was elected. The following year, league candidates won all the state offices in North Dakota (except for superintendent of public instruction) and control of both houses of the legislature.

The league's power in North Dakota started to wane in 1921 when one of its most prominent members, Governor Lynn J. Frazier, was removed from his seat on the Industrial Commission, established by the legislature to manage state business enterprises. The league's reputation suffered when Townley was convicted of conspiring to discourage enlistments during World War I. He resigned from the league presidency in 1922 and led a life of obscurity until the early 1950s when he ran in North Dakota as a third-party candidate for U.S. Senate and was defeated.

—*Candace Floyd*

SEE ALSO: Socialism

SUGGESTED READING:
Morlan, Robert L. *Political Prairie Fire: The Nonpartisan League, 1915–1922.* Minneapolis, Minn., 1955.

TOYPURINA (GABRIELINO)

Leader of a short-lived rebellion against the Spanish priests of the San Gabriel Mission in 1785, Toypurina (fl. 1780s) was believed to possess spiritual powers that would help the Gabrielino Indians throw off their Spanish overlords.

The Gabrielino Indians of the San Gabriel Mission, located near present-day Los Angeles, California, chafed under the harsh rule of Spanish officials and religious leaders bent on making the native peoples good Christians and dutiful subjects of the Spanish Crown. In 1785, the shaman Toypurina, with her apprentice Nicholas José, planned an uprising and convinced the Gabrielinos of six villages to unite in an assault on the mission. The villagers joined the cause, confident that Toypurina's spiritual powers would conquer the mission's inhabitants. Gathering on October 25, 1785, the Gabrielinos stormed the mission. The priests and soldiers within, however, did not succumb to Toypurina's powers. In fact, they had been forewarned of the plot and were lying in wait for their attackers. The Gabrielinos, including Toypurina and José, were quickly overcome and arrested.

At her trial, Toypurina spoke eloquently of the Gabrielino culture and traditions her people had been forced to give up and lamented the loss of her peoples' lands: "I hate the padres," she exclaimed, "and all of you for living here on my native soil." But the Spanish were unmoved. The participants of the attack were convicted and flogged. José was imprisoned in the presidio at San Diego. Toypurina's punishment was particularly cruel. She, who so valued the Gabrielino way of life that she was willing to risk mortal combat, was exiled from her people to the San Carlos Mission in northern California.

—Patricia Hogan

TRADE CATALOGUES

While the origins of mail-order catalogues in the United States dates to the colonial period, the expansion into the trans-Mississippi West gave these catalogues a life that continues to this day. In addition to the general-merchandise books produced by Montgomery Ward and Sears, Roebuck, there were thousands of catalogues for all types of goods from sewing notions to furniture to houses to vehicles to tools and equipment. While some, particularly the "wish books" or general-merchandise catalogues, were sent directly to homes all over the West, other specialized catalogues were sent to local merchants, who used them to place special orders for their customers. With a mix of specialized catalogues, any merchant could order merchandise to be shipped by wagon and, later, by rail to the purchasers. While the specialized catalogues were welcomed by local merchants, the general-merchandise catalogues sent directly to the consumer were, on occasion, confiscated and destroyed to protect local businesses from competition.

Montgomery Ward was the first great national general-merchandise catalogue house. With capital of twenty-four hundred dollars, Aaron Montgomery Ward, a former storekeeper, organized a mail-order firm with George R. Thorne, his brother-in-law, in 1872. Having the endorsement of the Grange movement and offering its wares at low prices compared to most local merchants, the CHICAGO-based company expanded rapidly. Taking advantage of the growth of the railroads and the development of large rotary presses for catalogue production, the company reached across the Midwest and West.

In 1886, Richard Sears, a former telegrapher and station agent, organized his first mail-order enterprise, selling watches to other station agents. He quickly expanded his business and brought in Alvah Roebuck as a partner in 1887. Over the next few years, he moved his operations between Chicago and Minneapolis and back again, setting up distribution companies and then selling them. In 1887, he issued his first catalogue, primarily watches and jewelry. In 1893, he finally established the firm of Sears, Roebuck and Company and began to produce more extensive general-merchandise catalogues from his headquarters in Chicago. By 1895, the book had reached 507 pages and included a great variety of merchandise. Using a variety of advertising ploys, Sears expanded rapidly, overtaking Montgomery Ward by 1900. Sears operated on a cash-on-delivery basis in the early years but moved away from the practice in the early twentieth century. In 1906, to counter the regional distribution centers established by Ward, Sears moved into the same field with a center in Dallas, Texas. Although other Sears regional centers were established, only the Texas branch lasted. By the 1920s, the appearance of the automobile and the suburban shopping centers led the firm to move into distribution through stores, but the mail-order catalogue remained an important part of the operation until 1993, when it was terminated.

The catalogues, particularly those with general merchandise, were the "wish books" of the West, and they offered the customer almost anything imaginable. Taking advantage of new techniques in mass printing, new strategies for advertising, and the distribution network of the railroads, the catalogues were an important agency in bringing the products of industrial America to every corner of the United States and, in doing so, helped break the isolation of the Great Plains. They reshaped the consumer market and established the culture of consumption for the twentieth century.

—Patrick H. Butler, III

SUGGESTED READING:

Emmet, Boris, ed. *Unabridged Facsimile: Montgomery Ward and Co. Catalogue No. 57.* Spring and Summer 1895. New York, 1969.

Emmet, Boris, and John E. Jeuck. *Catalogues and Counters: A History of Sears, Roebuck and Company.* Chicago, 1950.

Schlereth, Thomas J. *Artifacts and the American Past.* Nashville, Tenn., 1980.

TRADE ROUTES

Waterways were the first major trade routes in the East, but west of the Mississippi, streams were fewer, and even the largest rivers flowed sluggishly most of the year. OVERLAND TRAVEL was the primary means of traversing the vast distances of the Western plains, mountains, and deserts, and many of the early routes followed animal trails. Instinctively, most large animals, especially buffaloes, follow the line of least resistance. Indians came to use animal routes in trading with other tribes, and when the Anglo-Americans arrived, they followed them or trade routes that had been established by the Spanish. The early Spanish routes included the Jornada del Muerto, running from Santa Fe to Albuquerque and El Paso; the OLD SPANISH TRAIL between Santa Fe and Southern California; and El Camino Real in Alta California.

The earliest major overland route used by Euro-Americans was the SANTA FE AND CHIHUAHUA TRAIL. WILLIAM BECKNELL blazed the route in opening trade between Missouri and Santa Fe in 1821, and the following year, he took the first wagon to Santa Fe over the route. In 1825, Congress funded a survey to mark the trail to Santa Fe, and by the early 1830s, Missouri merchants had entered the Santa Fe trade. A principal wagon-freighting firm was RUSSELL, MAJORS AND WADDELL, founded in 1854 to haul military supplies to Fort Riley, Kansas, and Fort Union, New Mexico, near the end of the Santa Fe Trail. Until the railroad arrived in Santa Fe in 1880, the Santa Fe Trail was a major commercial wagon route.

Another major overland route was the OREGON TRAIL, also called the California Trail and the Central Overland Road. First used by fur traders beginning in 1811, it became a principal emigrant route in about 1840. On the eastern end, it originated at several points along the Missouri River including Council Bluffs, Nebraska City, St. Joseph, Atchison, Fort Leavenworth, and West Port (Kansas City). The many branches came together and led to Fort Phil Kearny, FORT LARAMIE, and over South Pass. The trail then divided with one branch leading to Salt Lake City and on to Sacramento and the other to FORT HALL and northwest to Oregon. Although primarily an emigrant route, wagon freighters also traversed portions of it from the middle 1840s until the arrival of RAILROADS in the region.

During the 1850s into the 1860s, two routes were established to transport furs and buffalo hides from the Dakota and Manitoba prairies to St. Paul, Minnesota. The routes linked Pembina, a town on the Red River just south of the Canadian border, to St. Paul. The western leg was called the Red River Trail, while the eastern leg was called the Pembina Cart Trail. Two-wheeled carts, each pulled by a horse or ox and carrying up to a thousand pounds, traversed these routes.

Gold discoveries in the West required the establishment of new trade routes. In California, the routes linked the major river towns of Stockton, Sacramento, and Marysville with gold-mining camps. After the Comstock Lode was discovered in Virginia City, Nevada, a major wagon-freighting road was established between Sacramento and Virginia City over the rugged Sierra Nevada. The discovery of gold in Colorado in 1859 led to the establishment of the Leavenworth and Pikes Peak Express Road and the Smoky Hill Road linking trading centers on the Missouri River to Denver and nearby gold camps. Gold discoveries in western Montana during the early 1860s led to the establishment of at least four wagon-freighting routes to supply the mining camps. The shortest ran from FORT BENTON on the Missouri River southwest to Helena and on south and west to Bannock and Virginia City. Another route ran from Salt Lake City to Fort Hall, Idaho, crossing Monida Pass and Big Hole Basin to the Montana gold fields. A third route was Mullan Road, named for Captain John Mullan and built as a military route by the government in 1860. The route ran between Fort Benton and Walla Walla, Washington. The western portion from Walla Walla was used by wagon freighters to supply the Montana gold fields. The BOZEMAN TRAIL, opened in 1865, was the fourth route and linked the Central Overland Road to Bozeman, Virginia City, and the Montana gold fields. The Diamond "R," Garrison and Wyatt, and E. G. McClay and Company became prominent wagon-freighting firms in Montana.

By 1865, the principal wagon-freighting routes in the West were those emanating from the important river towns of Atchison, Kansas; Omaha and Nebraska City, Nebraska; St. Joseph, Missouri; Memphis, Tennessee; St. Paul, Minnesota; and Fort Benton in the Montana Territory. Other important routes began in river towns in the Far West, including Sacramento, California, and Portland, Oregon.

The overland trade routes of the nineteenth century, perhaps more than any other factor, shaped the course of settlement and economic development in the West. They not only provided access for emigrants wanting to settle in the West, but they were also the life lines that supplied the isolated settlements of the plains, desert, and mountains. The overland trade routes were abandoned with the arrival of the railroads, which displaced the wagon freighters and their slow moving wagons that had crisscrossed the West.

—*David Dary*

SEE ALSO: California Overland Trails; Camino Real, El; Pike's Peak Express Company; Red River Carts

SUGGESTED READING:

Dary, David. *Entrepreneurs of the Old West*. New York, 1986.

Walker, Henry Pickering. *The Wagonmasters: High Plains Freighting from the Earliest Days of the Santa Fe Trail to 1880*. Norman, Okla., 1966.

Winther, Oscar O. *The Transportation Frontier: Trans-Mississippi West 1865–1890*. New York, 1964.

TRADING POSTS

SEE: Fur Trade

TRAIL DRIVING

SEE: Cattle Trails and Trail Driving

TRAIL OF TEARS

The legal victory scored by the Cherokees in the 1832 Supreme Court case of WORCESTER v. STATE OF GEORGIA, whereby Georgia's systematic persecution of the tribe was declared unconstitutional, proved hollow. President ANDREW JACKSON refused to enforce the decision of the court and insisted that the Cherokees' only relief was to be found in their acceptance of removal to the Indian Territory. On December 29, 1835, federal negotiators concluded the Treaty of New Echota with representatives of a small minority of the Cherokees. This faction—representative of perhaps only one thousand of the seventeen thousand tribal members—sold seven million acres of Cherokee land and agreed to removal westward within three years.

The majority party of the Cherokee tribe—the so-called National party—repudiated the treaty. President Jackson responded by forbidding the party to hold meetings to discuss the treaty or alternatives to it. Jackson informed the party's leader, JOHN ROSS, that the United States would recognize no Cherokee government until removal had been completed. Moreover, the president warned, any attempt to resist removal would be met by force. Brigadier General JOHN ELLIS WOOL embellished this warning in no uncertain terms; he declared that any recalcitrant Cherokees would be "hunted up and dragged from your lurking places and hurried to the West."

Undeterred, John Ross and the National party campaigned through 1835 to 1838 to expose the fraud and injustice of the New Echota Treaty. During this period, too, the state of Georgia and others were hard at work to ensure that the Indians would be swindled out of the removal funds guaranteed them by the treaty. When the 1838 deadline for removal came and went, with only about two thousand Cherokees settled in the Indian Territory, Jackson's successor, Martin Van Buren, replaced Wool with Major General WINFIELD SCOTT as commander in charge of removal. Scott approached the mission aggressively and with vigor, dispatching his troops to round up the Cherokee and herd them into stockades, which had been hastily constructed to confine the Indians in preparation for the forced march to the West. Although a minority managed to hide in the mountains, some fifteen thousand Cherokees were penned into the stockades, where they suffered from disease and exposure during the long hot summer of 1838.

With the coming of fall and winter, the march of approximately twelve hundred miles to Arkansas and the Indian Territory began. The Indians—men, women, and children—endured hunger and devastating disease (primarily dysentery and cholera, the two great plagues of Western travelers), as well as the abuse and cruelty of their soldier-escorts. Of the fifteen thousand Cherokees who made the journey, some four thousand perished on the trail or within a short time of settling in the Indian Territory. The Trail of Tears stands to this day as a symbol of the worst aspects of Indian-white relations in the United States. Many years after he made the journey, an old Cherokee recalled:

Long time we travel on way to new land. People feel bad when they leave Old Nation. Womens cry and made sad wails. Children cry and many men cry, and all look sad like when friends die, but they say nothing and just put heads down and keep on go towards West. Many days pass and people die very much.

—*Alan Axelrod*

Robert Lindreux's *Trail of Tears. Courtesy Woolaroc Museum.*

SEE ALSO: Native American Peoples: Peoples Removed from the East

SUGGESTED READING:

Ehle, John. *Trail of Tears: The Rise and Fall of the Cherokee Nation.* New York, 1988

Fleischmann, Glen. *The Cherokee Removal, 1838.* New York, 1971.

King, Duane. *The Cherokee Indian Nation: A Troubled History.* Knoxville, Tenn., 1979.

Satz, Ronald N. *American Indian Policy in the Jacksonian Era.* Lincoln, Nebr., 1975.

TRAILS

SEE: Bozeman Trail; California Overland Trails; Camino Real, El; Cattle Trails and Trail Driving; Goodnight-Loving Trail; Mormon Trail; Oregon Trail; Overland Travel; Santa Fe and Chihuahua Trail; Trade Routes; Trail of Tears

TRANSCONTINENTAL RAILROAD SURVEYS

Frémont's survey

ASA WHITNEY, a New Yorker engaged in the China trade, proposed to Congress the first serious scheme for a transcontinental railroad. He wanted the United States to sell him nearly eighty million acres at sixteen cents per acre, from lake Michigan to the Columbia River, crossing the Rockies over South Pass. Whitney's plan was to resell parcels of the land to settlers and farmers, thereby financing the railroad as it pushed farther and farther West. Moreover, by selling the land along the right of way, he would also generate customers for the railroad. The scheme caught the public fancy, and Whitney gained the endorsement of seventeen state legislatures.

Whitney's idea also set Missouri Senator THOMAS HART BENTON to thinking about a transcontinental railroad—with its Eastern terminus not in Chicago (as

Whitney planned), but in St. Louis, the chief city of the Senator's home state. Benton disposed of Whitney's proposal by attacking it on the grounds of private ownership, and then in 1848, he persuaded Congress to fund a railroad survey led by his son-in-law, JOHN CHARLES FRÉMONT.

Frémont had ample experience as a railroad surveyor, having plotted a line from Charleston to Cincinnati. However, his conviction that he could find a pass over the Continental Divide by approximately following the thirty-eighth parallel was wishful thinking. Moreover, Frémont was bent on proving that the Divide route was an all-weather trail. He, therefore, deliberately set out to cross it in the dead of winter. The result was that he and his party of thirty-five were stranded in a Rocky Mountain blizzard. Ten men froze or starved to death before charitable Ute Indians came to the rescue. Despite that disaster, Frémont declared that the "result was entirely satisfactory . . . neither the snow of winter nor the mountain ranges were obstacles in the way of a road."

Benton believed him. He proposed the route to the Senate, which wisely balked because the senator could produce no detailed information concerning grades and curves. By that time, the U.S. Army was proposing a route of its own, a route roughly along the thirty-fifth parallel, through the territory newly won from Mexico. The result was years of fruitless argument until, in 1853, Congress authorized Secretary of War Jefferson Davis to conduct detailed surveys of the "principal routes to the Pacific."

Jefferson Davis's plan

With the nation drifting toward civil war, increasingly bitter North-South sectionalism presented as many political difficulties to the transcontinental railroad as topographical obstacles. A northerly route would set the seal on the perpetual economic superiority of the North, whereas a southerly route would greatly strengthen the South. Davis, the future president of the Confederacy, devised a scheme to promote the choice of the Southern Trail, not by making sure that the route figured prominently in the list of proposed surveys, but by dropping it from the list entirely. He reasoned that results from surveying the other routes would probably be as inconclusive as the results Frémont had obtained and that, therefore, the proposal for the unsurveyed southern route would win by default. Accordingly, Davis dispatched parties to survey routes between the forty-ninth and forty-seventh parallels, from the Great Lakes to Puget Sound; south of that, to survey the route Benton favored; farther south, a trail along the thirty-fifth parallel, from Fort Smith, Arkansas, to Albuquerque, New Mexico, to the region of present-day Los Angeles. Another party was commissioned to survey California's San Joaquin Valley for passes that could join the thirty-fifth parallel route with the Southern Trail. Only after those surveys were under way did Congress insist that Davis add the Southern Trail to the list of routes to be surveyed. The secretary's critics argued that the Southern Trail lacked timber for construction and did not lead to a viable pass through the Rocky Mountains.

A nineteenth-century lithograph of a railroad survey team at work. *Courtesy Library of Congress.*

In truth, Congress had doomed the surveys to virtual uselessness. After so many years of indecision and lack of direction, Congress was eager to move the project along and, therefore, imposed a ten-month deadline on the surveys. The deadline ensured that the surveys would be essentially superficial, lacking the precise data on grades and curves that Congress had branded a fatal shortcoming of the Frémont survey.

The Stevens survey

Isaac Stevens, the young, brash, and vigorous territorial governor of Washington, led the northernmost survey, from the Great Lakes to Puget Sound. He set off from St. Paul, Minnesota, west to Puget Sound while Lieutenant George B. McClellan probed the Cascade Range for viable passes. Ever the promoter, Stevens ended the survey by singing the praises of the northern route. He declared that a railroad could be built along the route for no more than $96 million. Furthermore, he concluded, the prospect of winter snow did not present "the slightest impediment to the passage of railroad trains." Congress and the public, well aware of Stevens's position as a governor in the Pacific Northwest, viewed his findings with great skepticism.

The Gunnison thirty-eight parallel survey

The survey of Benton's favorite route, westward along the thirty-eight parallel, produced far more conclusive results. The survey party, led by Captain John W. Gunnison, was attacked by Paiutes on the Sevier River in Utah, with the loss of eight men. At the time, it was the worst defeat the U.S. Army had suffered in the West, and many thought the Mormons had instigated it. (More likely, the attack was an act of revenge for the killing of a Paiute the previous month.) Although Lieutenant E. G. Beckwith assumed command of the survivors and led them successfully through Weber Canyon in the Uinta Mountains, then across the Great Basin and to a pair of viable passes over the northern Sierra Nevada, the fate of Gunnison persuaded politicians that Indian hostility along the so-called Buffalo Trail was a hazard too great not only for building, but for running a railroad.

The Whipple thirty-fifth parallel survey

Lieutenant Amiel Weeks Whipple encountered few problems surveying the thirty-fifth parallel route, much of which had been explored before. While the passage was easy and the trail feasible, Whipple concluded that building costs would amount to $169 million—a prohibitively large figure, especially when compared to Stevens's estimate of $96 million. Only later, after the thirty-fifth parallel route had been set aside, would it be discovered that Whipple was a better surveyor than

accountant. He had made an error in addition. The true estimate was closer to what Stevens had submitted for the Northern Trail.

The Pope-Parke thirty-second parallel survey

With the other routes discounted by Congress due to cost or Indian hostility, the southerly route Davis had favored was left. Captain John Pope led the survey party that trekked west from Fort Washita, and Lieutenant John G. Parke led a party east from Fort Yuma. The pair submitted an enthusiastic report about the route, and Secretary Davis was all too eager to second their enthusiasm. Through a preliminary report issued in 1855, Davis recommended the Southern Trail route to Congress. The single obstacle he admitted was the fact that part of the route lay below the Mexican border. To overcome that problem, Davis urged the GADSDEN PURCHASE so that the boundary could be readjusted and the necessary land acquired.

The value of the surveys

In the end, none of the surveys was used to build the transcontinental railroad, and none of the proposed routes was followed. The Union Pacific–Central Pacific essentially followed the forty-first parallel, a route that was not included in the surveys because it had been explored at various times in the past.

The surveys were valuable nevertheless. Although they were superficial in terms of providing the precise engineering data required to build a railroad, the final reports, published between 1856 and 1861, included a rich assortment of data collected by competent scientists concerning Western soil, climate, geology, and animal and plant life. Moreover, about a dozen artists accompanied the surveys and created images of the West that excited politicians and the public alike. William P. Blake, Albert H. Campbell, James G. Cooper, RICHARD HOVENDON KERN, Charles Koppel, Heinrich Möllhuasen, Carl Schuchard, Gustav Sohon, JOHN MIX STANLEY, John C. Tidball, and John J. Young were among the most prominent artists who created a significant body of work as a result of the transcontinental railroad surveys.

—*Alan Axelrod*

SEE ALSO: Art: Surveys and Expeditions; Central Pacific Railroad; Union Pacific Railroad

SUGGESTED READING:

Albright, George Leslie. *Official Explorations for Pacific Railroads, 1853–1855*. Berkeley, Calif., 1921.

Goetzmann, William H. *Army Exploration in the American West, 1803–1863*. New Haven, Conn., 1966.

TRANSCONTINENTAL TREATY

SEE: Adams-Onis Treaty

TRANSPORTATION

SEE: Adams Express Company; American System; Atchison, Topeka and Santa Fe Railroad; Bullwhackers; Burlington Northern Railroad; Central Pacific Railroad; Chicago, Milwaukee, St. Paul and Pacific Railroad; Conestoga Wagons; Crédit Mobilier of America; Denver and Rio Grande Railway Company; Federal Government; Handcart Companies; Oregon Steam Navigation Company; Overland Freight; Overland Mail Company; Pacific Mail Steamship Company; Pike's Peak Express; Pony Express; Railroads; Red River Carts; River Transportation; Roads and Highways; Russell, Majors and Waddell; Southern Pacific Railroad; Stagecoaches; Texas and Pacific Railroad; Trade Routes; Union Pacific Railroad; Y X Company

TRAPPERS

When American fur traders began to exploit the vast fur resources of the Louisiana Purchase after the War of 1812, beaver was the fur of choice. It was obvious to entrepreneurs such as WILLIAM HENRY ASHLEY that men who used steel traps and operated on a mass-production basis could best exploit the beaver supply. From the hundreds of young men arriving in Missouri from the Southern highlands and the Ohio Valley, the fur companies recruited trappers who became the MOUNTAIN MEN of the Western FUR TRADE.

Few Indians living in the region were trappers, and they had no background in obtaining beaver pelts as a source of livelihood. The prime beaver resources were in Western mountain streams, but the Indians of these areas hunted deer, elk, and buffaloes for subsistence.

While the majority of the beaver brigade men were trappers, about 20 to 25 percent worked as horse guards, camp keepers, or workers who skinned animals, stretched the skins, and packed them for carrying or shipment. The number of men in the beaver brigades in the Rocky Mountains has been estimated at one thousand in the period from 1830 to 1832. To this should be added a substantial number of the six hundred men employed by the HUDSON'S BAY COMPANY in Oregon and probably two hundred people trapping in New Mexico and the Southwest. Osborne Russell, an astute observer, estimated that there were six hundred trappers from the AMERICAN FUR COMPANY and the ROCKY MOUNTAIN FUR COMPANY at the RENDEZVOUS in 1834.

Wages were minimal for the risks involved. The very best leader of a trapping party might earn sixteen hundred or seventeen hundred dollars a year. An East-

The business of trapping lasted long after the time that beavers had all been hunted. Here, a trapper and his sons from Brown's Basin in the Arizona Territory pose beside their hunting animals in 1908. *Courtesy National Archives.*

ern observer who considered going into the business said a good hunter could average 120 skins a year and could be hired for four hundred dollars a year; most of the remuneration, however, was in the form of goods and supplies. Free trappers, men who were not affiliated with a particular fur company, were paid a maximum of five dollars a skin. Most trappers spent their entire earnings at the rendezvous and saved nothing.

Intermarriage between trappers and Indian women was fairly frequent, although lasting relationships were difficult. The ordinary trapper moved frequently, and many Indian women were deeply attached to their relatives. On the other hand, trappers were generous with little luxuries and accorded attention to their mates. The arrangement of most marriages included expensive presents for the father—presents that had to be purchased at the rendezvous. There are a number of examples of lifetime relationships where trappers—including JOSEPH LAFAYETTE MEEK, JAMES (JIM) BRIDGER, James Bordeaux, Lucien Fontenelle, PETER SKENE OGDEN, and Andrew Drips—raised families with their Indian wives.

Always in search of new trapping grounds and suitable travel routes, the trappers were superb explorers of every nook and cranny of the West. Their achievements have made them folk heroes, and thousands of modern mountain men try to emulate their dress, skills, and equipment. For many people, the mountain trapper is the symbol of the Western fur trade.

—*Charles E. Hanson, Jr.*

SUGGESTED READING:

Ross, Marvin C. *The West of Alfred Jacob Miller (1837)*. Norman, Okla., 1968.

Wishart, David J. *The Fur Trade of the American West*. Lincoln, Nebr., 1979.

Young, F. G., ed. *Sources of the History of Oregon*. Vol. 1, Parts 3-6. Eugene, Oreg., 1899.

TRAVELERS' GUIDEBOOKS

SEE: Emigrant Guidebooks

TRAVIS, WILLIAM BARRET

Commander of the ALAMO during the TEXAS REVOLUTION against Mexico, William Barret Travis was born in Edgefield District, now Saluda County, South Carolina. He moved with his family to south-central Alabama in 1818 at the urging of family patriarch Alexander Travis, an itinerant Baptist preacher. Travis's Uncle Alex founded Sparta, Alabama, and provided for his education there and in Monroeville. Travis taught school, studied law in the office of Judge James Dellet, opened a newspaper office, and married Rosanna Cato before he was twenty years of age. To them was born a son, Charles Edward, and a daughter, Susan Isabella. Before their daughter's birth, however, Travis left his family in 1831 and relocated in Anahuac, Texas, then a part of Mexico, where he opened a law office in partnership with Patrick Jack.

Travis became the focus of the Disturbance of 1832 in Anahuac. As the attorney for a U.S. citizen seeking the return of runaway slaves from a Mexican army commander, Travis offended authorities and was arrested. Armed men gathered to force his release, and although the incident ended without bloodshed, it led to further disturbances in Nacogdoches and Velaso and played a part in the coming of the Texas fight for independence.

Following his release, Travis moved to San Felipe de Austin, the nerve center of colonial Texas. He became secretary of the *ayuntamiento* (local government council) and continued to practice law. His diary provides evidence of a prosperous practice and a rich social life. While still married and in correspondence with his wife over custody of his son, he became engaged to Rebecca Cummins of Mill Creek. He gambled and drank spirits but apparently did neither to excess. He was noted as fastidious dresser.

Travis became involved in the "War party," an unorganized but determined group of men who resisted the centralists in Mexican politics. When the government dispatched Captain Antonio Tenorio to garrison Anahuac once more and to collect tariffs, Travis led a group that captured Tenorio's men and escorted the captured Mexicans to San Antonio. Branded an outlaw by General Martín Perfecto de Cós, military commander of the northern Mexican provinces, and unpopular with "Peace party" advocates, Travis begged for time to explain himself. Events of the revolution, which he had spurred, kept Travis from ever publishing an apologia.

Cós came to San Antonio and began to confiscate arms. Resistance at Gonzales produced the "Army of the People," led by STEPHEN FULLER AUSTIN. The army besieged Cós in San Antonio, and Travis served as a scout during the fall of 1835. When a convention met in San Felipe to prepare for war, Travis accepted the rank of lieutenant colonel of cavalry forces under interim Governor Henry Smith. Travis recruited men and led them to the command of Colonel James C. Neill in San Antonio. Shortly after Travis arrived, Neill obtained a furlough, leaving Travis in command of the garrison.

With Travis in San Antonio were fewer than fifty army regulars plus about one hundred volunteers who acknowledged only the leadership of JAMES BOWIE. Mexican President ANTONIO LÓPEZ DE SANTA ANNA besieged the Alamo. Following a thirteen-day siege, during which approximately thirty more Texans joined the defenders, Santa Anna stormed the Alamo. Travis died early in the fighting from a single bullet wound in the head. He was twenty-six years of age.

—*Archie P. McDonald*

SUGGESTED READING:
Davis, Robert E., ed. The *Diary of William Barret Travis, August 30, 1833–June 26, 1834.* Waco, Tex., 1967.
McDonald, Archie P. *Travis.* 2d ed. Austin, Tex., 1991.

TRIST, NICHOLAS

Nicholas Trist (1800–1874) is best known as the man who negotiated the Treaty of Guadalupe Hildago for the United States, thus formally ending the UNITED STATES–MEXICAN WAR. His political career as a diplomat was ruined, however, because he had concluded the negotiations without official authorization.

Born in Charlottesville, Virginia, Trist attended West Point. Failing to graduate from the military academy, he continued his education by working in THOMAS JEFFERSON's law office. He obtained a job as a clerk in the State Department in 1829. Four years later, he was given a post as American consul in Havana, Cuba, where he served until July 1841. When JAMES K. POLK was elected president in 1846, he appointed Trist to be the U.S. plenipotentiary to Mexico to negotiate a treaty.

In Mexico, Trist had problems not only with his health but also with the commanding general WINFIELD SCOTT. In meetings with his Mexican counterparts, Trist granted concessions that angered the administration. Polk recalled Trist, but when he received his notification, he ignored it. He believed that a satisfactory peace would be jeopardized by his leaving Mexico. On February 2, 1848, he and the Mexican representatives signed a treaty that satisfied his original instructions.

The U.S. Senate subsequently ratified the treaty. After the war, Trist worked in his legal practice and tried to get the government to pay him for his earlier work. In 1870, he was named postmaster in Alexandria, Virginia.

—*Richard Griswold del Castillo*

SUGGESTED READING:
Chamberlain, Eugene K. *Nicholas Trist and Baja California.* Berkeley, Calif., 1963.

Drexler, Robert W. *Guilty of Making Peace: A Biography of Nicholas P. Trist.* Lanham, Md., 1991.

TRUMAN, HARRY S

President Harry S Truman (1884–1972) was born in Lamar, Missouri, and lived nearly all of his life on the southwestern edge of the Midwest. After growing up in Independence, a city he often honored for its role in the opening of the West, and working in and around Kansas City, he served in France during World War I. Backed by the Pendergast machine, he embarked on a political career in the 1920s and was elected to the Jackson County (Missouri) court where he distinguished himself as a road builder. He was elected to the U.S. Senate in 1934. After nearly losing his bid for reelection in 1940, he gained fame as chairman of a wartime investigating committee. That work, plus his ability to get along with all factions in his party, led to his selection for the vice-presidency in 1944 and his rise to the presidency after Franklin D. Roosevelt died.

As president, Truman achieved significance chiefly for decisions in foreign affairs, including the use of atomic bombs against Japan, the establishment of the policy of containing communism, and the intervention in the Korean War. Although less successful in domestic matters, he did promote reform in race relations, military spending, public power, and reclamation. These programs contributed to the development of the West and helped him carry the region in the 1948 election. While he won a surprising victory in the presidential contest, he was not widely popular during his White House years. Nevertheless, he became highly regarded as a national leader after his death.

—*Richard S. Kirkendall*

SUGGESTED READING:
Kirkendall, Richard S., ed. *The Truman Encyclopedia.* Boston, 1989.
McCullough, David. *Truman.* New York, 1992.

TUCSON, ARIZONA

In 1776, in the Santa Cruz River valley on the northern frontier of New Spain, Spanish troops established the military post of Tucson. The presence of soldiers fostered local settlement, and in time, the presidio became a walled village surrounded by fields of crops and livestock herds. The troops, civilians, and Pima

Indians protected the community, and in the 1780s, it began to enjoy an era of growth and prosperity that lasted until the 1820s.

In the years following Mexico's independence from Spain, peaceful Apaches joined hostile Apaches in making life more dangerous for residents of Tucson. In 1846, matters grew worse when war broke out between the United States and Mexico. U.S. troops, meeting no resistance, entered Tucson, but the town remained a part of Mexico until the GADSDEN PURCHASE in 1854.

In the late 1850s, Anglos joined Mexicans in Tucson, and the town became the supply depot and distribution point for area forts, farms, ranches, and mines. Tucson attracted its share of troublemakers, but the most critical problem proved to be the disruption caused by the CIVIL WAR. Union forces occupied the town, and after the war, their continued presence inhibited the Apache threat; Tucson once again became the service center for area civilians and soldiers.

The seat of Pima County, Tucson became the capital of the Arizona Territory in 1867. It lost that distinction to Prescott in 1877, but as a commercial center, it continued to grow and prosper. In 1880, the SOUTHERN PACIFIC RAILROAD arrived, and Tucson became the largest city between San Antonio and Los Angeles.

Tucson's economy declined during the 1880s. With the end of the APACHE WARS, U.S. troops left the area, and the town lost the lucrative military trade. At the same time, the collapse of the silver boom in Tombstone and other nearby mining districts hurt Tucson's economy, and periodic droughts and floods limited stock raising and agricultural production in the area.

During the 1890s, the city enjoyed a mild business revival as it continued to be the urban hub of a sizable region. Tucson's reputation as a health mecca and winter resort grew, as did its reputation as a service center for area interests, notably copper mines, cotton farms, and cattle ranches. By the 1920s, Tucson booster organizations advertised the city as "The Sunshine Center of Arizona" and as "The Athens of Arizona," the latter because of the growing University of Arizona.

Over the years, relations between Anglos and Mexicans deteriorated, and the ratio of Mexicans to Anglos in Tucson declined. In 1878, about 67 percent of the inhabitants were of Mexican descent. Between 1900 and 1910, the Anglos gained a numerical advantage. By 1930, Mexican Americans composed only 31 percent of the total. As more Anglos arrived in the city, Mexican Americans remained in the older neighborhoods south of the railroad tracks.

The population of the city rose from 13,193 in 1910, to 20,292 in 1920, to 32,506 in 1930. During and after World War II, however, Tucson experienced unprecedented growth and development.

—*Bradford Luckingham*

SUGGESTED READING:

Bufkin, Don. "From Mud Village to Modern Metropolis: The Urbanization of Tucson." *Journal of Arizona History* 22 (Spring 1981): 63–98.

Luckingham, Bradford. *The Urban Southwest: A Profile History of Albuquerque, El Paso, Phoenix, and Tucson.* El Paso, Tex., 1982.

Naylor, Thomas H., Charles W. Polzer, and Thomas E. Sheridan. *Tucson: A Short History.* Tucson, Ariz., 1986.

Sonnichsen, C. L. *Tucson: The Life and Times of an American City.* Norman, Okla., 1982.

TUMBLEWEED

Russian thistle *(Salsola australis),* sometimes called saltwort, Russian cactus, and wind witch, but better known in the American West as tumbleweed, was accidentally introduced to South Dakota in 1877 by German Russian immigrant farmers. Edible forage for cattle and sheep in its early stages of growth, tumbleweed dries out as it matures and breaks away from its roots at the end of the growing season. Drifting easily with the wind, scattering its seeds in process, the round-top plant spreads rapidly throughout prairie and plains regions of the West.

Considered a noxious weed by most farmers and ranchers, the sharp-spine thistle posed a danger to livestock, robbed the range and crops of water, and choked out more desirable plants. The durable stalks of the weed sometimes damaged mowing and threshing machinery. Attempts to control the spread of this hearty annual through cultivation and burning enjoyed only mixed success.

In the twentieth century, the singing group Sons of the Pioneers paid romantic homage to the wayward thistle in the classic song "Tumbling Tumbleweeds."

—*B. Byron Price*

SUGGESTED READING:

Blevins, Winfred. *Dictionary of the American West.* New York, 1994.

Hoy, James, and Thomas Isern. *Plains Folk.* Norman, Okla., 1987.

TUNSTALL, JOHN H.

SEE: Lincoln County War

Frederick Jackson Turner. *Courtesy Huntington Library.*

TURNER, FREDERICK JACKSON

Frederick Jackson Turner (1861–1932) was the most renowned historian of the American frontier and author of the famous frontier thesis, which is still debated by scholars more than a century after it was first presented. Born in Portage, Wisconsin, Turner earned a bachelor's degree in 1884 from the University of Wisconsin and completed a master's degree in 1888. Later that year, he enrolled in the history doctoral program at the Johns Hopkins University. There, Turner was introduced to the germ theory of historical development (which found the origins of American institutions in medieval German systems) by Herbert Baxter Adams. In 1889, Turner returned to the University of Wisconsin, and in 1890, he received his doctorate.

In 1891, Turner published an important essay, "The Significance of History." Noting that "each age writes the history of the past anew with reference to the conditions uppermost in its own time," he provided an early example of what would later come to be known as the new history. Two years later, in 1893, he delivered his most renowned paper, "The Significance of the Frontier in American History." The frontier thesis was a reaction against Adams's germ theory. Turner was seeking the roots of American democratic institutions in American soil. He found in the frontier the source of American democracy, nationalism, and individualism. For all of the frontier's beneficial influence, Turner also noted negative effects, such as excessive and unrestrained individualism. Still, in the essay Turner worried about whether America could retain its democratic institutions without the frontier.

By the beginning of the twentieth century, Turner had developed a national reputation in academic circles. He assumed the presidency of the American Historical Association in 1909 and, in 1910, moved from Wisconsin to Harvard University. At Harvard, he developed his sectional thesis, presented in its fullest form in "The Significance of the Section in American History" (1925). While he pointed to the dangers of sectional tensions and rivalries within the country, he also viewed sectional differences as an important antidote to the force of national homogenization. The sectional thesis was quite complicated, and scholars have comprehended it less well and discussed it less eagerly than the frontier thesis.

Turner retired from Harvard in 1924 and returned to Wisconsin. In 1927, he took the position of research associate at the Huntington Library in Pasadena, California, where he remained until his death. During his life, he completed a book of essays, *The Frontier in American History* (1920) and a short monograph, *Rise of the New West, 1819–1829* (1906). Another essay collection, *The Significance of Sections in American History,* appeared in 1933 and received the Pulitzer Prize. Turner's other posthumously published work, *The United States, 1830–1850: The Nation and Its Sections* (1935) had to be completed by others; "the book" had been a source of frustration to Turner for much of his life. He was not the nation's most productive historian when measured merely in numbers of books. However, the influence of Turner's essays, particularly the frontier thesis, and his inspired teaching ensured that his impact on both Western and national history would be acute and long lasting.

—*David M. Wrobel*

SEE ALSO: Frontier: Frontier Thesis; Huntington Library, Art Collections, and Botanical Gardens

SUGGESTED READING:

Billington, Ray Allen. *Frederick Jackson Turner: Historian, Scholar, Teacher.* New York, 1973.

Faragher, John Mack, ed. *Rereading Frederick Jackson Turner: "The Significance of the Frontier in American History" and Other Essays.* New York, 1994.

Jacobs, Wilbur. *On Turner's Trail: 100 Years of Writing Western History.* Lawrence, Kans., 1994.

Ridge, Martin, ed. *History, Frontier, and Section: Three Essays by Frederick Jackson Turner.* Albuquerque, N. Mex., 1993.

Steiner, Michael C. "Frederick Jackson Turner and Western Regionalism." In *Writing Western History: Essays on Major Western Historians.* Edited by Richard W. Etulain. Albuquerque, N. Mex., 1991.

TUTTLE, DANIEL SYLVESTER

The first Episcopal bishop in Montana, Daniel Sylvester Tuttle (1837–1923) was born in Windham, New York. He entered the Episcopal academy at Delhi in 1850, graduated from Columbia College in 1857, and graduated from the General Theological Seminary in 1862. In 1866, just three years after entering the priesthood, he was elected missionary bishop to Montana.

Tuttle's task was daunting. His responsibilities were spread over Montana, Idaho, and Utah, an area of some 340,000 square miles that included only 155,000 people.

A majority of those in Utah were Mormons; of the rest, only three were Episcopalians. Tuttle's tenure in the West was marked by two things: the growth of the church and constant, though amicable competition with the Mormons. During his first trip to Salt Lake City, Tuttle visited Mormon leader BRIGHAM YOUNG and immediately disliked his moral countenance. Although he later referred to Young as "unscrupulous," Tuttle was generally careful to preach the positives of Christianity rather than to denigrate Mormonism.

Utah aside, Tuttle's chief responsibility was in Montana. He worked to bring order and civility to the numerous mining camps and nascent towns, where every other building was a saloon. One mark of his success was that Montana was set aside as its own jurisdiction in 1880. When he accepted the bishopric of Missouri in 1886, Tuttle left a region with two parishes, thirteen missions, and a thousand communicants.

        —Kurt Edward Kemper

SUGGESTED READING:

Addison, James Thayer. *The Episcopal Church in the United States, 1789–1931.* Hamden, Conn., 1969.

TWAIN, MARK (CLEMENS, SAMUEL LANGHORNE)

Samuel Langhorne Clemens (1835–1910) made his chosen pseudonym, Mark Twain, one of the most famous names not only in American literature, but in literature worldwide. Born in Florida, Missouri, he was raised in the Mississippi River town of Hannibal, Missouri, became a printer's apprentice, and then, in 1847, joined his brother Orion's *Hannibal Journal.* From 1853 to 1857, Twain traveled and worked as a newspaper correspondent and a printer in New York, Philadelphia, St. Louis, and Cincinnati. However, his consuming ambition, since boyhood, had been to become a Mississippi steamboat pilot. Moving to New Orleans in 1857, he apprenticed to a veteran pilot and worked in the trade until the Civil War blockades brought an end to river commerce. After an abortive stint as a Confederate soldier, Twain traveled in 1861 by stagecoach to Carson City, Nevada, with his brother Orion, who had secured a federal appointment as territorial secretary. Twain made desultory and wholly unsuccessful attempts at silver and gold mining before resuming his journalistic career as a correspondent for the *Virginia City Territorial Enterprise.* It was for this newspaper that he began writing humorous sketches of Western life, at first under the pseudonym "Josh," but then, in 1863, under "Mark Twain," a name he borrowed from the call of a Mississippi steamboat leadsman signifying a depth of two fathoms, safe water for a steamboat.

Having achieved a measure of local renown, Twain went to San Francisco in 1864 and gained national notice with his 1865 story "The Celebrated Jumping Frog of Calaveras County," a humorous tale that captured the gritty realities of life in a California gold-mining camp. The following year, he sailed to Hawaii as a correspondent for the *Sacramento Union.* His experiences in that exotic locale also furnished him with material for his first public lecture, which launched a long and spectacularly successful career as a public speaker. During an 1867 tour of the Mediterranean and the Holy Land, Twain provided letters to the *San Francisco Alta California,* letters that he reworked into book form in 1869 as *The Innocents Abroad.* This literary venture created an instant international sensation.

Twain married Olivia Langdon of Elmira, New York, in 1870, purchased an interest in the *Buffalo Express,* served as its editor, and then moved to Hartford, Connecticut. There, in 1871, he turned from journalism to "serious" literature as a full-time pursuit. In 1872, he published *Roughing It,* a remarkable and engaging account of his years in the West. He took a different tack the following year with *The Gilded Age* (cowritten with Charles Dudley Warner), a satire of the quick-wealth schemes and general political chicanery that characterized the era. So influential was this book that its title has served ever since to describe the boom-and-bust 1870s.

In 1875, Twain published *Sketches, New and Old* (1875) and *Tom Sawyer*, which subsequent generations have treasured as the idyll of a rural Midwestern American boyhood. A European tour in 1878 and 1879 yielded *A Tramp Abroad* (1880) and *The Prince and the Pauper* (1882), the author's first historical novel. He turned to history again with his satirical allegory *Connecticut Yankee in King Arthur's Court* (1889) and with *Personal Recollections of Joan of Arc* (1896), a turgid and humorless novel that he often stubbornly insisted was his finest work. In 1883, he expanded his earlier *Old Times on the Mississippi* into *Life on the Mississippi*, a detailed account of the river region. Wealthy enough at this time to acquire his own publishing firm, he established Charles L. Webster and Co. and published *Adventures of Huckleberry Finn* in 1884. Intended as a kind of sequel to the enormously popular *Tom Sawyer*, the new novel far surpassed the earlier work—and, indeed, was a quantum leap beyond anything Twain had written before. Many years later, Ernest Hemingway would sum up the work's significance by declaring that "All modern American literature comes from one book . . . *Huckleberry Finn*. . . . It's the best book we've had. . . . There was nothing before. There has been nothing so good since." Combining humor, humanity, and unflinching insight with Twain's extraordinary ear for the sound, pitch, and cadence of local speech, *Huckleberry Finn* explores—through the sensibility of a good-hearted and delightfully "uncivilized" eleven-year-old boy—the promise and brutality of life in the rural Midwest as the nation stood on the brink of Civil War.

Despite his tremendous success as an author, unwise investments plunged Twain into debt. He moved to Europe in 1891 after completing *The American Claimant* (1892). In 1894, his publishing company failed, and the Paige typesetting machine, in which he had invested heavily, was eclipsed by Ottmar Mergenthaler's linotype. Declaring bankruptcy, Twain nevertheless vowed to repay his creditors. He worked feverishly, turning out work after work, commercially profitable, though often of inferior literary quality, including *The Tragedy of Pudd'nhead Wilson* (1894), *Tom Sawyer Abroad* (1894), and *Tom Sawyer, Detective* (1896). He also launched a whirlwind, worldwide lecture tour in 1895, which he subsequently described in *Following the Equator* (1897).

The new books, and especially the tour, allowed Twain to repay his creditors and rebuild his fortune. However, the deaths of his eldest daughter in 1896 and his wife in 1904, as well as the epilepsy and mental deterioration of his youngest daughter, plunged him into a bitterness and despair evident in his writings of the late 1890s and 1900s. The long short story "The Man That Corrupted Hadleyburg" (1898) and *What Is Man?* (1906) are blistering reflections on human nature. Other late works, many of which Twain himself chose not to publish, also embody the pessimism of his declining years. But it is for his good-humored works of Western "local color," for *Tom Sawyer*, and, above all, for *Adventures of Huckleberry Finn* that Mark Twain will always be remembered.

—Alan Axelrod

SEE ALSO: Humor; Literature; Magazines and Newspapers

SUGGESTED READING:

Bridgman, Richard. *Traveling with Mark Twain*. Berkeley, Calif., 1987.
Brooks, Van Wyck. *The Ordeal of Mark Twain*. Rev. ed. 1933. Reprint. New York, 1977.
DeVoto, Bernard. *Mark Twain's America*. 1932. Reprint. Boston, 1952.
Kaplan, Justin. *Mark Twain and His World*. New York, 1974.
———. *Mr. Clemens and Mark Twain*. New York, 1966.
Steinbrink, Jeffrey. *Getting To Be Mark Twain*. Berkeley, Calif., 1991.

TYLER, JOHN

The tenth president of the United States and a proponent of the annexation of Texas, John Tyler (1790–1862) entered politics early and remained politically active for the rest of his life. He was elected to the Virginia House of Delegates at the age of twenty-one and later served in the House of Representatives, as Virginia's governor, and in the U.S. Senate. In the Senate, his activism on states' rights led him to oppose the imperial presidency of ANDREW JACKSON. His convictions earned him the support of the nascent Whig party but the censure of his own Democratic party. The Whigs selected Tyler to serve as William Henry Harrison's running mate in the 1840 presidential election. Harrison was elected but died thirty-one days into his term, making room for Tyler, the first to ascend to the presidency without being elected.

The Democrats refused to recognize Tyler as president, and the Whigs abandoned him when he twice vetoed a bill establishing the third national bank. Undaunted, Tyler pressed his primary goal, the annexation of TEXAS. Slavery in Texas caused many to oppose annexation, but Tyler feared that if the United States did not act at once, Great Britain would annex Texas, thus hindering further Westward expansion. A Treaty of Annexation was concluded in 1844, but the

Senate refused to ratify it. Instead, Tyler forced through both houses a resolution of admittance, requiring only a simple majority rather than the usual two-thirds, on his last day in office.

Tyler was elected to serve in the Confederate Congress but died on January 18, 1862, before he could be sworn in.

—*Kurt Edward Kemper*

SEE ALSO: National Expansion

SUGGESTED READING:
Chitwood, Oliver Perry. *John Tyler: Champion of the Old South*. New York, 1967.

UMATILLA INDIANS

SEE: Native American Peoples: Peoples of the Pacific Northwest

UNION LABOR PARTY, SAN FRANCISCO

PROGRESSIVISM was a national reform movement that transcended political party but not social class. Despite the fact that Progressives claimed to abhor class consciousness and sought to attract votes from union members, American labor never trusted Progressivism as a movement nor much liked Progressive leaders, upper and middle-class reformers who tended to look with nativist disdain on immigrants (who made up much of the working class) and who were openly hostile to such working-class institutions as SALOONS and political clubs. SAN FRANCISCO, a bastion of unionism in the late nineteenth century, offered a textbook example of the uneasy relationship between the unions and Progressivism, both of which sought to change American social and political institutions.

The city was the setting of the first major Progressive crusade in California, led by JAMES DUVAL PHELAN, a reform Democrat and a Catholic, who fought against municipal corruption and political machines in order to bring "good government" to San Francisco. Phelan thought that, since his reforms would "give employment to labor and circulate money," he should attract workers to his cause. When the unions did, in fact, back Phelan for office, the new mayor and his rich Progressive friends excluded union leaders from the highest level of city politics, and when the Teamsters Union went on strike in 1901—forcing twenty thousand out of work and tying up two hundred ships in San Francisco Bay—Phelan clashed head on with organized labor. The mayor was bitterly attacked by

labor leaders Mike Casey, head of the Teamsters Union, and Father Peter Yorke for calling out special police, the National Guard, and strikebreakers. The sight of these forces escorting nonunion teamsters and their wagons through the streets made it quite clear to the rank and file that Phelan was a loyal member of his own class and a traitor to his fellow Irish Catholics. Realizing that the mayor's union sympathies were limited, the city's workers deserted the Progressives, and the BUILDING TRADES COUNCIL organized its member unions into the Union Labor party.

The Union Labor party did not, however, abandon the crusade for change in city government. In fact, its stated goals differed from those of the Progressives only in its commitment to the closed shop, in the number of workers and union leaders it nominated for office, and in the political inexperience of its leaders. That the party, given the initial power vacuum in its leadership, came to be dominated by Boss ABRAHAM (ABE) RUEF, who himself was subsidized by the SOUTHERN PACIFIC RAILROAD, which certainly was no friend to labor, only underscored the ironies of the class conflict the politicians tried to deny existed. When it came down to brass tacks, San Francisco labor preferred a machine run by a lawyer from the city's mercantile elite and backed by the capitalist bosses of the Southern Pacific to a reform Democratic millionaire who ordered out the police to protect scabs. The strike destroyed Phelan's political career for more than a decade. Humiliated by his failure to negotiate a settlement in the teamster's strike, Phelan resigned from office. He stood by helplessly as Ruef's hand-picked Union Labor party choice for mayor, Eugene ("Handsome Gene") Schmitz, came to power. Schmitz was an Irish German orchestra leader, head of the musician's union, Ruef's friend and former business associate, and an ideal candidate for a coalition of workers and small businessmen.

In many ways, Ruef did not resemble any other big city political "boss." University educated, polished, tastefully dressed, sensitive to culture and the arts,

Ruef's finesse extended to the bribes that passed through his hands in discreetly unmarked envelopes from businessmen seeking franchises to the relevant city officials and from the owners of the city's "French restaurants" (fancy brothels serving exquisite cuisine on the first floor and less legitimate delights on the floors above) to the police. One-half million dollars or so of the money found its way into Ruef's pockets during the exchanges, but both Ruef and Schmitz shared their graft with working-class officeholders, and although union leaders once again found themselves excluded from the high councils of CITY GOVERNMENT, Schmitz's immense popularity with the city's workers protected the party from internal reform. While Phelan, shunted into political retirement, plotted his revenge, both Progressives and conservatives denounced the Union Labor party as a machine, much overestimating its powers. Ruef never exercised the kind of control some city bosses—such as TOM PENDERGAST in Kansas City—enjoyed, and when Progressive leaders and conservative businessmen combined to attack the Union Labor party in 1906 and 1907, the machine quickly crumbled. With help from an ambitious attorney—FRANCIS JOSEPH HENEY—backed by Los Angeles good-government reformers and by President THEODORE ROOSEVELT, Schmitz was convicted of corruption and Ruef, who testified against him, fell from power. The utility corporation executives who paid the bribes, however, remained untouched.

With Ruef and Schmitz out of the picture, union leaders at last took control of the Union Labor party. They turned it into a political wing of the powerful Building Trades Council and other city unions, which in turn led to the Union Labor party's return to power in 1909 when Patrick McCarthy, an Irish carpenter from county Limerick and president of the Building Trades Council, became San Francisco's mayor. In power, the Union Labor party floundered. Fearful of pushing a radical social agenda that would alienate its craft-union workers and middle-class supporters, it fell into disrepute with its working-class constituency, a disenchanted lot who saw the party, at best, as ineffective. That gave the Progressives an opening, and the party was pretty much co-opted by the state legislature controlled by Governor HIRAM WARREN JOHNSON. Among the range of Progressive reform measures the legislature passed between 1911 and 1913 were such items as a workingman's compensation act, an eight-hour workday law, a child-labor law, and a factory inspection act. Somewhat surprised by such victories for organized labor, workers who had tended to vote against Progressives began throwing their support to reform Republicans. When Progressive JAMES ROLPH replaced McCarthy as mayor of San Francisco, it be-

came clear the reformers had learned their lesson. Rolph, unlike Phelan, wholeheartedly supported the unions and campaigned for the closed shop.

—Charles Phillips

SEE ALSO: City Planning; Labor Movement

SUGGESTED READING:
Issel, William, and Robert W. Cherny. San Francisco, 1865–1832: Politics, Power, and Urban Development. Berkeley, Calif., 1986.
Kazin, Michael. Barons of Labor: The San Francisco Building Trades and Union Power in the Progressive Era. Urbana, Ill., 1987.
Starr, Kevin. Inventing the Dream: California through the Progressive Era. New York, 1985.

UNION PACIFIC RAILROAD

Perhaps the most famous name in American railroading, the Union Pacific started at Omaha, Nebraska, and was built 1,006 miles westward to PROMONTORY SUMMIT, Utah, where, on May 10, 1869, it joined the CENTRAL PACIFIC RAILROAD, which had been extended eastward from Sacramento, California.

Construction of a transcontinental railroad had been the subject of discussion for many years, but it was not until the South left the Union that Congress finally acted, pushing through the Pacific Railroad Act of July 1, 1862, which authorized the Central Pacific and the Union Pacific. The act granted each company four hundred feet of right of way through public lands and ten alternate square-mile sections of public land for each mile of track laid. In addition to this bonanza, loans of sixteen thousand dollars to forty-eight thousand dollars (depending on the terrain) per track mile were also available as a first mortgage on the railroad. In 1865, Congress doubled the land grant and made the financial subsidy a second lien on the property. Original plans called for the two railroads to meet at a specified point along the California-Nevada line; however, in 1866, Congress again amended the original legislation to allow the Central Pacific to advance eastward as far as necessary to meet the Union Pacific. With lucrative land grants hanging in the balance, the convergence of the two companies' lines was then transformed into a race.

While the Central Pacific confronted the more formidable geographical obstacles to construction, the Union Pacific also had to overcome challenging logistical difficulties, including the mass transportation of ballast material and crosstie lumber for construction across the treeless plains. Construction crews were also harassed by Plains Indians, mainly because white hunters were slaughtering prodigious numbers of buffaloes to feed the construction crews. In all, the Union Pacific laid 1,086 miles of track, compared to the Central Pacific's 689 miles.

Perhaps more formidable than the physical obstacles to completion were the financial scandals that accompanied the project. The most important and best known of the scandals involved CRÉDIT MOBILIER OF AMERICA, formed by the financial backers of the Union Pacific to finance construction. Standing to profit from construction and construction loans, manipulators padded the already staggering construction bills, thus leaving the fledgling railroad in great debt. After the scheme was exposed, the railroad went into receivership in 1893 and was reorganized four years later under the leadership of EDWARD HENRY HARRIMAN. It was Harriman, more than any other individual, who was most responsible for improving and standardizing operations of the Union Pacific. He made it a lean and profitable enterprise, which participated in, even as it contributed to, the economic development of the West.

Under Harriman's direction, the Union Pacific became a holding company for the securities of the other transportation companies he controlled. The Union Pacific proper expanded into thirteen Western states and extended from Council Bluffs, Iowa, outward to two Pacific terminuses—Portland in the Northwest and Los Angeles in the Southwest. In 1982, the railroad merged with the Missouri Pacific and the Western Pacific as the Union Pacific System. Today, the Union Pacific System is headquartered in Bethlehem, Pennsylvania.

While the first transcontinental line was opening the Great Plains, three other railroads were pushing toward the West Coast. By 1883, the SOUTHERN PACIFIC RAILROAD had connected New Orleans and Los Angeles, the Santa Fe ran between Chicago and southern California via Albuquerque, and the Northern Pacific extended from Duluth to Portland.

—*Alan Axelrod*

SEE ALSO: Railroad Land Grants; Railroads

SUGGESTED READING:

Fogel, Robert William. *The Union Pacific Railroad: A Case in Premature Enterprise*. Baltimore, 1960.

Kleo, Maury. *Union Pacific*. Garden City, New York, 1990.

McCague, James. *Moguls and Ironmen: The Story of the First Transcontinental Railroad*. New York, 1964.

White, Henry K. *History of the Union Pacific Railway*. Clifton, N.J., 1973.

UNITED ORDER OF ENOCH

The United Order of Enoch (known commonly as the United Order) was a communal economic-reform program launched by BRIGHAM YOUNG in Mormon-populated areas of the West in 1874. Some 221 United Orders were organized between 1874 and 1893. Most did not endure past 1874, although one was not formally disbanded until 1900.

Immediate practical circumstances and long-term ideology led Young to found the United Order. With the 1869 completion of the transcontinental railroad, the Great Basin became more fully integrated into the national economy. Railroads brought in a flood of more efficiently produced goods, thus causing dozens of small mills and factories operated by the MORMONS to close. The panic of 1893 was felt severely in those parts of Utah near mining districts that were more integrated into national markets. Young believed the United Order would mitigate these changes, strengthen the local economy, and preserve its independence.

Moreover, the Mormon prophet, then in his seventies, had long hoped to complete the agenda set forth by the founding prophet of Mormonism, JOSEPH SMITH, JR. Smith's ideology and the historical experience of the Mormons had created a society that was highly unified socially. But Smith had also intended for the Latter-day Saints to be united economically. Beginning in 1831, he announced the Law of Consecration and Stewardship, a communal economic order modeled on his vision of the ancient biblical city of Enoch. He called one branch of this program the "United Order." Consecration and Stewardship was largely abandoned by 1834, but forty years later, Young adapted Smith's language and aims in an effort to complete his predecessor's agenda. Launching the United Order of Enoch, Young traveled throughout Utah to urge every Mormon village to organize its production and consumption communally.

Young insisted that membership in United Order was to be voluntary. Moreover, he proposed no uniform program, but asked members of each community to implement whatever measures they could agree on that would lead them towards economic unity. The result was uncertainty and divisiveness, as church members debated what form their United Order should take.

Brigham City, sixty miles north of Salt Lake City, already had a cooperative that was so successful that Edward Bellamy visited there in 1886 while writing *Looking Backward* (1888). Townspeople owned the enterprise, worked in its various branches for wages, and received dividends as stockholders. In 1874, they responded to Young's initiative by simply changing the name of the Brigham City Mercantile and Manufacturing Association to the Brigham City United Order. In southern Utah, however, one group, committed to a more fully communal program, broke away from its parent community of Mt. Carmel in order to found

Orderville, where all goods were owned jointly, members worked under direction of a United Order board of directors, and families took meals together and shared profits equally.

These two extreme forms of the United Order—one a joint-stock company arrangement that hardly touched personal lives and property, the other a full-blown commune—were successful and enduring. Nearly all others were abandoned as soon as it was clear that the stress and divisiveness of trying to implement them tore at the social unity the Mormons so highly prized.

The United Order was implemented in founding colonies along the Little Colorado River in 1876 and in Cave Valley in Chihuahua, Mexico, in 1893. But Young's death in 1877 and federal hostility towards Mormon communalism caused subsequent leaders to back away from further implementation. The last, the United Order of Orderville, was officially disincorporated in 1900.

—*Dean L. May*

See also: Church of Jesus Christ of Latter-day Saints

Suggested reading:
Allen, Edward J. *The Second United Order among the Mormons.* New York, 1936.
Arrington, Leonard J., Feramorz Y. Fox, and Dean L. May. *Building the City of God: Community and Cooperation among the Mormons.* 2d ed. Urbana and Chicago, Ill., 1992.
De Pillis, Mario S. "The Development of Mormon 'Communitarianism,' 1826–1846." Ph.D. diss., Yale University, 1960.

UNITED STATES ARMY

Organization
Robert Wooster

Composition
Robert Wooster

Military Life on the Frontier
Sherry L. Smith

Volunteers and Militia
Charles Phillips

Scouts
Dan L. Thrapp

Strategy and Tactics
Robert Wooster

Arms and Equipment
Patrick H. Butler, III

Supplies and Logistics
Darlis A. Miller

Women and the Western Army
Sherry L. Smith

ORGANIZATION

On June 2, 1784, the Confederation Congress discharged the old Continental Army, except for 80 men needed to guard two military arsenals. The following day, however, Congress authorized a 700-man First American Regiment to protect American interests along the young confederation's western and northern frontiers. As eventually stipulated by the Militia Act of May 8, 1792, state militias were to supplement the small standing force in case of emergency. Ignominious defeats at the hands of several Indian tribes in Ohio, however, led to the creation of a 5,000-man Legion of the United States, which, in 1794, defeated an Indian coalition at the Battle of Fallen Timbers in the Northwest Territory.

Despite this success, Congress abolished the Legion in 1796 and left in place a smaller United States Army. But frontier demands for a military presence continued; by 1804, the regular army's 2,732 officers and men were stationed in 43 posts. More than two-thirds of the regulars were posted on or near the frontier. During the War of 1812, Congress authorized the regular army to increase to more than 62,000. Actual numbers, however, never approached this figure. Shortly after the war's close, Congress reduced the army to 10,000 enlisted men, divided into eight regiments of infantry, one rifle regiment, one regiment of light artillery, and an artillery corps. Considered by the national legislature to be too expensive, the mounted contingents were abolished entirely.

Secretary of War John Caldwell Calhoun proposed sweeping reforms during his tenure in the War Department from 1817 to 1825. Calhoun strengthened the various staff departments and bureaus created during the War of 1812 and supported the creation of the office of commanding general in 1821. In response to a congressional directive to reduce the regular force to 6,000 enlisted men, Calhoun proposed an "expansible army," whose skeletal units could be quickly increased in time of war. But Congress rejected Calhoun's plan and instead authorized a peak strength of 6,183 men and officers divided into seven infantry and four artillery regiments.

Increasing frontier duties led to several structural changes in the regular army over the next three decades. In 1833, Congress created the First Dragoon Regiment; almost immediately, the regiment was dispatched to present-day Oklahoma. Another regiment was established three years later. The outbreak of the Second Seminole War and continuing disputes with England in 1838 led Congress to allow existing artillery and infantry companies to enroll additional enlisted men, to create four new artillery companies along with a new infantry regiment, and to establish a separate CORPS OF TOPOGRAPHICAL ENGINEERS. In promoting Western development through a series of surveys, the latter organization loomed particularly important in the West until abolished as a separate agency in 1863. The Regiment of Mounted Riflemen, authorized specifically to help protect Western emigrant routes, was added in 1846.

At the close of the UNITED STATES–MEXICAN WAR, the regular army reverted to its peacetime organization of four artillery, eight infantry, and three mounted regiments. Recognizing that recent territorial acquisitions had increased the army's frontier duties, President Millard Fillmore authorized the army to increase to nearly 14,000 in 1850. As Western demands for military assistance grew, Congress created two new infantry and two new cavalry regiments in 1855, thus expanding the standing army to about 18,000.

Most regular units were transferred to the East during the CIVIL WAR, and their places on the frontiers were temporarily assumed by state volunteers. After the Civil War, Congress authorized a 54,000-man regular army, divided into ten cavalry, forty-five infantry, and five artillery regiments. Two cavalry and four infantry regiments were reserved for black enlisted personnel. Up to 1,000 Indian scouts could also be enlisted. In 1869, however, Congress eliminated twenty infantry regiments and left in place twenty-three white and two black regiments. Congress limited the number of enlisted men to 30,000 the next year and reduced the effective ceiling to 25,000 enlisted personnel in 1874 by restricting recruiting funds. With minor modifications, that figure remained constant until 1898.

Although between 10 and 25 percent of the army guarded military arsenals and Atlantic Coast fortifications, most soldiers served on the nation's southern, western, and northern frontiers. For most men, frontier forts were the focus of their army lives. Except at those positions boasting regimental, departmental, or divisional headquarters, the senior line officer on station served as commander. The number of posts proliferated in response to local demands for a military presence; in 1843, the army garrisoned 50 posts, but by 1857, it occupied 138. After the Civil War, the figure often approached 200. Denouncing the inefficiencies caused by the abundance of one- or two-company forts, military officials scrambled to concentrate reserves at some central position. During the 1830s and 1840s, Jefferson Barracks, Missouri, proved a favorite

In 1874, Brigadier General Frank Wheaton, standing in the center with the white plume on his hat, posed with officers and members of their families at Fort Walla Walla, Washington. *Courtesy National Archives.*

choice for the reserve force; after the Civil War, Fort Davis, Texas, and Fort Leavenworth, Kansas, were often suggested for a similar purpose.

But concentrating large numbers of regulars at any one point was extremely difficult, as local demands for a military presence and the limited size of the federal government forced the army to assume a variety of quasi-military tasks. Soldiers frequently worked as common laborers in constructing military posts, roads, and telegraph lines. In the wake of the increasingly violent struggles in Kansas over slavery, thousands of bluecoats were dispatched to that territory in 1855 and 1856. The following year, a large regular column occupied Utah during the UTAH EXPEDITION. Nearly 40 percent of the army was stationed in the South during the height of Reconstruction; countless other regulars guarded national parks, assisted civilians affected by natural disasters, and escorted or conducted scientific expeditions and observations.

Except during the War of 1812, the United States–Mexican War, and the Civil War, the regiment remained the army's basic organizational unit. Commanded by a colonel, the regimental staff included one lieutenant colonel, as many as three majors, a handful of junior officers (usually on temporary assignment), and a few enlisted men. Infantry regiments included ten companies; after 1865, cavalry and artillery regiments each boasted twelve troops or batteries, respectively. Regiments stationed on the frontier might number as many as 900.

Most regiments, however, were never collected at a single point. By necessity, then, the company served as the basic tactical unit. A captain commanded the

The U.S. Army was always short of funds adequate for its mission in the West. A Thomas Nast illustration for an 1874 issue of *Harper's Weekly* suggests the difficulty the military faced. *Courtesy Patrick H. Butler, III.*

company and was assisted by one first and one second lieutenant and a varying number of noncommissioned officers. Official company size varied according to time and service branch but generally numbered between 50 and 85. Desertion, sickness, death, leaves of absence, and temporary duty assignments left companies chronically short of men. In March 1853, for example, five companies of the Eighth Infantry were posted at Fort Chadbourne, Texas. Had these units been filled to their maximum allowable limits, the garrison would have boasted some 400 men. But company rolls listed only 15 officers and 225 enlisted men; of these, 12 officers and 77 men were away from the post on detached service or leave. Arrest, sickness, and extra duty claimed another 69 regulars. Thus the five infantry companies could, in reality, muster only 3 officers and 79 men for field service.

Among infantry regiments, the shortages of manpower became worse in late 1876 when Congress, in the wake of the debacle at the Battle of Little Bighorn, allowed the enrollment of an additional 2,500 enlisted cavalrymen without raising the 25,000 cap on the army as a whole. To raise the authorized number of mounted troops, the army cut the number of enlisted men per infantry company to 37. Allowing for normal effects of desertion, extra duty, and temporary assignments, infantry companies often had fewer than 30 men until the 1880s.

Indian auxiliaries frequently supplemented the regulars. Indian scouts almost inevitably accompanied successful field columns, and during the 1870s and 1880s, General GEORGE CROOK deployed expeditions composed almost entirely of white officers and Indian auxiliaries. During the last two decades of the century, Indian policemen also enforced order on numerous reservations. In 1890, seeking to further the cause of assimilation, the army enlisted one company of Indians as regular soldiers in several regiments, only to abandon the idea completely by 1897.

Individual states and territories also furnished troops on a sporadic basis. Thousands of volunteers served in frontier operations during the War of 1812; BLACK HAWK'S WAR; the forcible removal of Creeks, Cherokees, and Seminoles from the Southern states; the war against Mexico; and the Civil War. Oregonians and Californians participated in numerous campaigns against the Indians of their respective regions. Various state units, often called "Rangers," patrolled the Lone Star state; a battalion of Kansas Volunteer cavalry served during the army's 1867 operations against the Southern Plains Indians. Praised by their local legislatures and congressional delegations, the volunteers were generally scorned by the regulars, who believed them to be undisciplined and expensive.

To administer the nation's military needs, the War Department divided the country geographically. Following the War of 1812, the structure included two divisions—North and South—which were each carved into several numbered departments. In 1821, the nation was reorganized into the Eastern and Western Departments, each commanded by a brevet major general. In 1837, the newly renamed Eastern and Western Divisions were subdivided into numbered departments. Major changes came again in 1853, when the old divisions were scrapped in favor of the separate Departments of the East, New Mexico, Pacific, Texas, and West. New departments—Florida, the Platte, Utah, and Oregon—were added as events demanded. The three brigadier generals of the line chose the largest commands, and the other posts fell to regular colonels acting in their brevet ranks.

After 1865, the administrative structure was frequently adjusted to allow major generals to command divisions and brigadier generals to head departments. The Division of the Atlantic administered the area east of the Mississippi River. The Division of the Missouri—including the Departments of the Missouri, the Platte, Dakota, and sometimes Texas—served as the largest and most important command; its territory encompassed Minnesota, Illinois, Iowa, Kansas, Missouri, the Indian Territory, Texas, and the territories of Dakota, Montana, Utah, Nebraska, Colorado, and New Mexico. Normally composed of the lands west of the Continental Divide and subdivided into the Departments of the Columbia, California, and Arizona, the Division of the Pacific became the second-most important frontier command. When a situation required special attention, sections of departments were further subdivided into districts, which were usually commanded by a colonel.

Through much of the nineteenth century, the army's command structure remained a festering sore. The problem began at the top, as the office of commanding general created a potential rival to the secretary of the War Department. Constitutionally, the president served as commander in chief of the nation's armed forces. But did the secretary of war, acting as the president's civilian deputy, actually command the army, or did the commanding general, who served as the nation's ranking army officer? In practice, much depended on personalities. As commanding general from 1821 to 1828, Major General Jacob Brown was largely compliant to the wishes of the secretaries of war; Alexander Macomb, who served as commanding general from 1828 to 1841, sought to regain direct control over the various bureaus. Having claimed seniority, Winfield Scott routinely refused to obey Macomb's orders; during his own term as commanding general from 1841 to 1861, Scott also contested the authority of Secretary of War Jefferson Davis.

During the Civil War, President Abraham Lincoln gave Ulysses S. Grant, commanding general from 1864 to 1869, nearly unlimited powers, but as president, Grant effectively limited the independence of Commanding General William Tecumseh Sherman, who held that post from 1869 to 1883. To protest his lack of real authority, Sherman moved his headquarters to St. Louis in 1874 and returned two years later only after the forced resignation of Secretary of War William W. Belknap. As commanding general from 1883 to 1888, Philip H. Sheridan unsuccessfully sought to wrest effective control over the army from Secretary of War Robert T. Lincoln. Commanding General John M. Schofield, who served from 1888 to 1895, regained effective if informal influence by using his office in a nonthreatening advisory role. Schofield's successor, the talented if ambitious Nelson Appleton Miles, who served from 1895 to 1903, squandered most of the goodwill engendered by his predecessor, and upon Miles's resignation, the office of commanding general itself was finally abolished in favor of a chief of staff.

During the 1880s and 1890s, the army used Indian policemen to enforce law and order on a number of reservations. Red Tomahawk, a Yanktonai Sioux, was one of the Indian lawmen at Standing Rock Reservation. He may have fired the shot that killed Sitting Bull just before the Wounded Knee Massacre. *Courtesy National Archives.*

An elaborate system of staff bureaus and departments further complicated the command structure. To resolve the logistical fiascoes that had plagued the army during the War of 1812 and to ensure that the secretary of war had direct access to military specialists, the heads of the staff departments carved out independent fiefdoms nearly free of the commanding general's authority. These staff departments eventually included the Adjutant General's Office, the Inspector General's Department, the Judge-Advocate-General's Office, the Quartermaster's Department, the Subsistence Department, the Ordnance Department, the Corps of Engineers, the Medical Department, the Signal Bureau, and the Pay Department. Possessing relatively small staffs in Washington, these bureaus nonetheless exerted enormous political influence. Their officers and temporary appointees, stationed in department and division headquarters and at every military post, were responsible not to their immediate military superiors but to their staff chiefs.

In addition to serving as a major area of contention between commanding generals and secretaries of war, the command structure strained relations between line and staff. Officers assigned to the bureaus resented any interference from commissioned personnel who had less specialized knowledge or experience; line officers charged that their staff rivals dominated choice postings and operated with little regard for the needs of soldiers in the field. Assignments to staff bureaus became nearly permanent. Although several secretaries of war and commanding generals tried to establish a system for rotating line and staff personnel, Congress, acting largely at the behest of the powerful staff chiefs, blocked such legislation.

Slow promotion further damaged morale. Promotion came according to seniority—in the regiment through the rank of captain, and in the service branches through the rank of colonel. Generals were, with some exceptions, typically appointed according to seniority as well. The relative youth of the regular officer corps after the War of 1812 and the Civil War meant that a captain could expect to wait at least two decades before he was promoted to major. In 1890, Congress began to reform the system to allow for promotion by seniority within the service branch as a whole rather than within simply the individual regiment. Congressional reforms also required that candidates up for promotion to the junior grades pass physical and professional competency exams.

The common use of brevets also fueled much controversy. These temporary ranks provided a convenient means of recognizing meritorious service and allowed officers to hold positions otherwise reserved for higher ranks. Brevet ranks also created enormous confusion and jealousy. A lieutenant assigned to a position according to his brevet rank of major, for example, might outrank a regular captain who had no brevet appointments. Civil War honors made the problem even more acute; by 1869, more than 1,000 officers had one or more brevets, with no fewer than 138 boasting a brevet major generalship. By contrast, only 5 officers held the regular rank of major general. In 1890, Congress authorized the awarding of brevets for service against the Indians.

Organized more for convenience than to meet the demands of realities in the field, the nineteenth-century regular army was hamstrung from within and without by administrative and professional rivalries. For its part, Congress was willing to employ the regulars for a variety of military and quasi-military tasks but proved reluctant to reform the army's administration or to fund the military adequately. Army officials, by the same token, often seemed consumed by personal jealousies and by their desires to expand their own reputations. Given those organizational faults, however, the regulars managed to complete their Western assignments remarkably well, a success in large part due to the growing sense of professionalism evident among junior officers.

—*Robert Wooster*

SUGGESTED READING:

Coffman, Edward M. *The Old Army: A Portrait of the American Army in Peacetime, 1784–1898*. New York, 1986.

Prucha, Francis Paul. *The Sword of the Republic: The United States Army on the Frontier, 1783–1846*. New York, 1969.

Thian, Raphael P., comp. *Notes Illustrating the Military Geography of the United States 1813–1880*. 1881. Reprint. Austin, Tex., 1979.

Utley, Robert M. *Frontier Regulars: The United States Army and the Indian, 1866–1891*. New York, 1973.

———. *Frontiersmen in Blue: The United States Army and the Indian, 1848–1865*. New York, 1967.

Weigley, Russell Frank. *History of the United States Army*. New York, 1973.

Wooster, Robert. *The Military and United States Indian Policy, 1865–1903*. New Haven, Conn., 1988.

COMPOSITION

In response to problems stemming from the Indian Wars and Britain's refusal to abandon holdings in the Old Northwest, the Confederation Congress authorized the creation of a 700-man standing army in 1784. Although these troops were supposed to come from Pennsylvania, New York, New Jersey, and Connecticut, in reality Pennsylvanians dominated this force. Subsequent threats led the United States to increase the regular force from a national recruiting pool; by 1801, the officer corps included 115 men from the Middle Atlantic states, 55 from New England, and 54 from the Old South. Ten officers represented what was then the West (Kentucky, Tennessee, Mississippi, and the Northwest Territory), and 11 were foreign-born. Studies of enlisted men from 1799 to 1819 suggest that, like its Continental Army predecessor, the regular army included large numbers of men from less fortunate economic circumstances—42 percent were illiterate, and more than 15 percent were foreign-born. Enlistees averaged about 26 years of age.

Although army officials believed that American-born farm boys would make the best soldiers, the overwhelming majority of soldiers before the Civil War were recruited in cities along the northern Atlantic Coast. Recruiting in the Deep South was unproductive; in 1840, for example, only 4 men signed up at the army's stations in South Carolina and Louisiana, while 1,444 joined the army in New York alone. A study of recruits between 1839 and 1855 revealed that less than 15 percent listed farming as their occupation. Immigrants, who had composed about one-quarter of the army during the 1820s, outnumbered native-born recruits by more than two to one by the 1850s. The majority of foreign-born soldiers came from Ireland; perhaps another 20 percent came from the German states. Illiteracy rates gradually declined during the antebellum period, with only 25 percent of recruits from 1850 to 1859 unable to sign their names.

While regulations on enlistments varied, applicants were supposed to be sober white males, between the ages of 21 and 35, who could speak English and stood at least five feet three inches tall. Married men were required to secure special permission from army headquarters. In most years, the army rejected about one-third of applicants. When fewer recruits were needed, however, a much higher percentage might be refused. A study of 1852 figures revealed that recruiting officers accepted only 2,726 of 16,064 applicants. Twenty-four percent of those who failed were minors, 18 percent could not speak English, 15 percent were intemperate, 13 percent were too small, and 8 percent had varicose veins.

Between 1815 and 1860, 2,999 officers received commissions. Of these, 58.7 percent were graduates of the United States Military Academy. Slightly more than 38 percent were appointed from civil life; well over half of these men were commissioned during the UNITED STATES–MEXICAN WAR or in 1855 and 1856, when the army created four new regiments. Of the 97 officers promoted from the ranks, 69 secured their positions during the war with Mexico. In general, slightly less than 60 percent of officers in the army at any one time had been born in Northern states. By 1856, nearly 36 percent of the officers held appointments in infantry regiments. The remainder were divided, roughly equally, among staff, cavalry, and artillery. That same year, 714 of the 982 active duty officers were West Point graduates.

The political views of antebellum soldiers remain clouded. Anecdotal evidence, however, suggests that, during the 1850s, many officers expressed sympathy for the Democratic party, which to many seemed the more moderate of the national parties. Indeed, secession badly divided the officer corps; more than one in four officers resigned their commissions. Enlisted personnel, on the other hand, shared no such divided loyalties. Of the 15,000 enlisted men on the eve of the CIVIL WAR, only 26 were reported to have deserted and joined the Confederate Army.

The reductions in force after the Civil War most seriously affected the officer corps, as the thousands of men holding volunteer commissions could not possibly be transferred en masse to the regular establishment. Applicants for regular commissions were thus required to have Civil War experience and to pass an examination. Regulations prohibited former Confederates from consideration; vacancies were also proportioned by state or territory according to the number of volunteers each had provided during the war. Thirty-eight percent of available commissions went to officers from New York, Pennsylvania, and Ohio.

Additional reductions during the late 1860s and early 1870s left slightly more than 2,100 officers in the regular army, a figure that remained stable until the Spanish American War. Of the 3,598 commissions issued between 1865 and 1898, 1,360 went to former volunteer officers. The United States Military Academy filled 76.4 percent of the available vacancies after 1867. Civil appointees claimed 13.6 percent of the commissions, with former rankers filling the remaining slots. About 40 percent of the latter were foreign-born. Three of the line officers were black. The army also became a more permanent career choice for commissioned officers. While only slightly more than 50 percent of the 1830 to 1839 graduates of West Point remained in the service, more than 80 percent of West Point graduates from 1870 to 1879 made the army their career.

By reserving four regiments (six before consolidation in 1869) exclusively for black enlisted men, Congress dramatically altered the post–Civil War army's racial composition. Drawing most of their recruits from Civil War volunteer units, the black regular regiments initially included a sizeable number of Southern-born soldiers. Concerted efforts to recruit blacks from border states or the North in later years, however, shifted

Four regiments in the army were reserved for African American soldiers. They boasted an exemplary combat record in wars against Indians, and their desertion rate was lower than that of white troops. The artist Frederic Remington paid the Buffalo Soldiers homage in *Captain Dodge's Colored Troops to the Rescue. Courtesy Library of Congress.*

the balance away from the Deep South. Some white officers complained about the higher rates of illiteracy among black enlisted personnel, but the combat record of those regiments during the wars against the Indians was exemplary. Reenlistment rates in the black regiments were also higher than among white units.

Perhaps even more important was the low rate of desertion among black troops. A chronic problem for the regular army throughout the nineteenth century, desertion rates usually averaged about 15 percent annually. In some areas, such as California during the 1848 to 1850 gold rush, more regulars deserted than remained at their posts. Black troops, however, deserted considerably less frequently. In the 1890s, armywide annual desertion rates fell significantly below 10 percent, after Secretary of War Redfield Proctor and Commanding General John M. Schofield persuaded Congress to make a concerted effort to improve army food, reform military justice, withhold a portion of every soldier's pay until his discharge, and reduce the term of enlistment from five to three years.

In the years immediately following the Civil War, immigrants continued to dominate the enlisted ranks. From 1865 to 1874, for example, more than half of all recruits were foreign-born, with Ireland alone producing more than 20 percent. The German states contributed another 12 percent. Recruiting continued to be most fruitful in the North; in 1880, New York (21.1 percent) and Pennsylvania (14 percent) contributed the most native-born recruits; only 3 percent of enlisted personnel were from the Deep South. During the 1880s, the percentage of foreign-born soldiers declined, and

by the early 1890s, immigrants composed only about one-third of enlistees. The act of August 1, 1894, in which Congress required that all first-time enlistees either be citizens or declare their intent to become so, further reduced the numbers of foreign-born to roughly 25 percent of all those who enlisted.

A comprehensive study of soldiers in 1890 found that the average soldier stood five feet seven inches tall, weighed 153 pounds, and was 30.3 years old. As had been the case before the Civil War, relatively few farmers joined the regular army. In 1880, for example, fewer than 10 percent of recruits classified themselves as farmers, while nearly 30 percent listed their occupation as laborer. During times of economic depression, such as 1873 to 1874 and 1893 to 1894, army service increased in popularity as a means of employment, and recruiters were able to be more selective. The 1894 economic collapse, combined with the tighter rules of 1894, meant that only 17 percent of applicants were accepted that year.

Little is known of the collective religious beliefs of nineteenth-century American soldiers, and from 1818 to 1838, there were no designated chaplains. In 1838, Congress provided funds for chaplains at fifteen army bases; three years later, church attendance was made mandatory for several years despite the absence of designated clergymen from most military posts. After the Civil War, thirty posts had chaplains, as did each of the army's four black regiments. Episcopalian chaplains were most numerous, especially before the Civil War. Considering the large numbers of Irish among enlisted men, Catholics were seriously underrepresented among the clergymen; of the 125 regular chaplains

After the Civil War, more than half of the U.S. Army's recruits were foreign-born, and immigrants from the German states produced 12 percent of the troops. Towards the end of the century, Fort Keogh in Montana had its own German Singing Society, performing here at an open air songfest in 1894. *Courtesy National Archives.*

appointed between 1865 and 1897, only 7 were Catholic priests. Five blacks held positions as postwar chaplains.

The regular army thus represented a broad spectrum of American society. Upward mobility, as evidenced in the numbers of enlisted men who received commissions, was unlikely yet possible. Throughout the nineteenth century, immigrants composed a significant proportion of the regulars. Language deficiencies and educational limitations of the enlisted men often forced officers to do more routine army paperwork, but fewer foreign-born troops seem to have deserted or to have been forced from the service through courts-martial than their native-born counterparts. Likewise, black regulars deserted infrequently and proved fine soldiers; although segregated army life after 1865 was not without its difficulties and racial barriers, the military remained a respected career choice among the black community at large.

—Robert Wooster

SUGGESTED READING:

Coffman, Edward M. *The Old Army: A Portrait of the American Army in Peacetime, 1784–1898.* New York, 1986.

Utley, Robert M. *Frontier Regulars: The United States Army and the Indian, 1866–1891.* New York, 1973.

————. *Frontiersmen in Blue: The United States Army and the Indian, 1848–1865.* New York, 1967.

Weigley, Russell Frank. *History of the United States Army.* New York, 1967.

Wooster, Robert. *Soldiers, Sutlers, and Settlers: Garrison Life on the Texas Frontier.* College Station, Tex., 1987.

MILITARY LIFE ON THE FRONTIER

In 1885, an Eastern woman, assuming the entire army disbanded at the close of the CIVIL WAR, expressed surprise at meeting an army colonel. Her ignorance of the army's duties in the West, both before and after the Civil War, was not uncommon. Many Americans never gave a thought to soldiers' efforts to maintain peace and order as their countrymen and women expanded the national boundaries and displaced American Indians in the process. Occasionally army actions made headlines and penetrated national consciousness, such as GEORGE ARMSTRONG CUSTER's 1876 defeat at the hands of Sioux and Cheyenne warriors at the Battle of Little Bighorn. Otherwise, the army in the West toiled in obscurity.

Military life at the edges of Euro-American settlement was characterized not only by isolation but also by periods of hard physical labor, boring garrison routine, and sporadic campaigns with moments of danger. For the most part, the military served as a frontier

A view of the corral and surrounding area at Camp Apache in the Arizona Territory, 1877. *Courtesy National Archives.*

constabulary—policing the interactions between Indians and Euro-Americans, sometimes removing Euro-American trespassers from Indian lands, and more often launching military expeditions against natives who refused to acquiesce to government demands for land cessions and an end to raiding. The government located army posts all across the American West as a defense system to protect overland routes and settlements. Soldiers devoted much more time to constructing and maintaining these frontier forts than to fighting Indians.

Most men enlisted in the army because they needed work. Economic motives overshadowed all others among native-born as well as foreign-born recruits. In other cases, men enlisted to escaped their troubled pasts or to seek adventure in the West.

In signing an enlistment paper, a man agreed to serve five years. The base pay in the years following the Civil War was $13 per month for privates, $15 for corporals, $17 for sergeants, and $22 dollars for first sergeants. In addition, soldiers could expect increments of an additional dollar per month for their third, fourth, and fifth year of service. The government also provided soldiers with food, clothing, shelter, medical care, and transportation as part of the salary. Army service provided a man with a good deal of security. The salary earned in the military, along with the amenities (crude as they often were) of service, meant that a soldier's income and economic status compared favorably to that of other American workers.

Military life was not a life of luxury, however. The kind of shelter soldiers could expect depended on their assigned post. Undeveloped garrisons offered tents or adobe huts with straw mattresses and blankets. In

Before 1862, the U.S. Army provided each soldier a ration of whiskey. The practice was discontinued, and soldiers then had to pay for their liquor. These soldiers, pictured in about 1890, purchased their drinks at the canteen at Fort Keogh, Montana. *Courtesy National Archives.*

other forts, soldiers lived in poorly constructed wood buildings, which stopped neither wind nor cold weather. Established posts had more substantial barracks with rows of either single iron bedsteads or, in some cases, double bunk beds where soldiers would have to sleep in pairs. Clearly, privacy was not a government priority in creating housing for its soldiers.

The enlisted man's diet offered little variety. Bread, salt pork or beef, coffee, mush, beans, and sugar served as normal fare. Christmas dinner might include such "delicacies" as boiled beef, potatoes, and cabbage. In the summer, enlisted men enjoyed healthier fare. Posts sometimes had gardens, which provided fresh vegetables, and during military campaigns, soldiers could enhance their meals with fish or game. For much of the nineteenth century, the army provided no cooks. Instead, a soldier from the ranks would be detailed for ten days at a time to serve as cook. The cooks received no extra pay, nor was the job particularly respected. For all these reasons, enlisted men often spent a part of their pay on special treats, such as a can of peaches, to add to their normal diet. Until 1862, the army provided a ration of whiskey to every soldier. Once that practice ended, soldiers' pay often found its way into the pockets of whiskey peddlers.

One enlisted man called his fellow soldiers "armed laborers." Construction and maintenance of forts required much of the troopers' time. In fact, garrisons seemed to be in a perpetual state of constructing, maintaining, and even moving. Men posted at northern sites spent much time on logging details and gathering wood to construct buildings and stoke fireplaces. Forts in more temperate climates offered gardening, farming, and animal-tending chores. Oddly, soldiers received

very little military training either when newly recruited or once assigned to post. Systematic marksmanship drill was noteworthy for its relative absence all across the West. On the other hand, all garrisons did use guard duty as a form of training. Cavalrymen received slightly more training than infantrymen, especially regarding the care of their horses. Officers required each man to groom and feed his own horse. The man who fed himself before his animal could expect chastisement and even punishment.

Western garrisons, situated far from population centers, underscored the physical and psychological isolation of the military. Seclusion forced soldiers to devise their own leisure-time activities. GAMBLING, drinking and "womanizing" at nearby "hog ranches," along with hunting, fishing, swimming, and racing horses occupied some of the men. Others played checkers, card games, billiards, and bowling (the latter in more developed posts). Many forts maintained libraries where soldiers could find books and periodicals to read. Sometimes enlisted men organized dances, theatrical performances ranging from skits to the classics, and musical presentations. A few men joined singing or debating societies, temperance groups, and Masonic lodges. After the Civil War, baseball became something of a sensation at army posts. Competition between black and white regiment teams and community clubs

Within the army, there was much variety in the punishments meted out for offenses. A soldier of the Eighth Infantry faces execution at Prescott, Arizona, in 1877. His crime was not recorded. *Courtesy National Archives.*

followed, and in some cases, the desire to win led several posts to field racially integrated teams.

The army in the West was an authoritarian system, with military justice designed to maintain discipline. Soldiers had few legal rights, and commanding officers exercised tremendous discretionary powers over the men. This situation led to some instances of officers abusing enlisted men, either verbally or physically. Further, officers stood in judgment at court-martial proceedings. A garrison court-martial called for three officers, and a general court martial required between five and thirteen officers. Few of these men were lawyers. Finally, no guidelines matched punishments to crimes; as a result, there was much variation in punishment.

The majority of discipline cases involved drunkenness, but soldiers could face court-martial for other minor infractions—talking out of turn, failing to salute an officer, cursing one's horse, or having a dirty rifle. Typical punishments for lesser infractions were fines and confinement in the guardhouse, the latter being a particularly terrible punishment for jails were often dark, filthy places. Acts of violence, including murder, sometimes occurred. In murder cases, military law required the defendant be tried in civil court.

Desertion was a constant problem. In the 1850s, the desertion rate reached about 20 percent, but after the Civil War it increased to 30 percent. During the years of the California gold rush, the army found it especially difficult to deter deserters; in those days, a man could make more money in one day at the gold mines than he could in a month of military service. Beyond the attractions of civilian life, some soldiers deserted because of the crowded and overall unpleasant conditions in barracks, poor food, absence of a consistent system of justice, and lack of opportunity to rise to commissioned officer rank. African American soldiers, however, deserted their ranks much less often than their white brothers-in-arms. This meant they either were more content than white soldiers or, more likely, saw fewer opportunities for economic advancement outside the military.

Usually, the army did not actively pursue deserters. If authorities recaptured a deserter or he turned himself in, however, he could expect severe punishment. Before 1861, men found guilty of desertion might be flogged. They could also have an ear cropped, be branded with a "D" under their arm, be confined in a "black hole," or be put to work wearing a ball and chain. After the Civil War, the military justice system sentenced deserters to two to five years of hard labor in a military prison, issued a dishonorable discharge, and forfeited the soldiers' pay and allowance. Because the American public did not hold the army in high esteem, desertion from its ranks did not carry the stigma it would acquire in the twentieth century. In fact, many civilians helped deserters escape (although a few took advantage of rewards by turning in deserters for payment).

The opportunity to rise from the position of enlisted man to the rank of commissioned officer was slim indeed. The Civil War and the reorganization of the regular army in its immediate aftermath provided the best chance for enlisted men and noncommissioned officers to realize promotion. In fact, an 1867 law required that one-fourth of all second lieutenants be drawn from enlisted ranks. That proved to be a unique opportunity, however. Especially between 1867 and 1890, most officers faced frustrations in bettering their positions. More than 42 percent of the officers who served between the Civil War and the Spanish-American War received their commissions in the first two years after Appomattox. This meant a whole generation of men saw little hope of advancement.

If officers shared frustrations about the prospects for advancement, other things divided them. In the antebellum period, about 73 percent of the officers were educated at the U.S. Military Academy at West Point. This changed after the Civil War, when many men with distinguished war records remained in the military and sought commissions. Also under the 1867 law, some officers, including some foreign-born, were commissioned from the ranks. Although few of the foreign-born officers ever rose beyond the rank of captain, their presence underscored the regional and ethnic diversity of officers. By the end of the nineteenth century, however, West Pointers reasserted their dominance and composed about 60 percent of the officer corps. That number included three African American cadets who joined black regiments in the 1870s and 1880s.

Officers, who were mostly from middle-class backgrounds, usually had much more education than the typical soldier. Education, social and economic class, and the "military caste system," which emphasized difference in status, all reinforced the gap between officer and enlisted man. On the frontier, practical aspects of life reinforced the differences. Officers' quarters at more established posts included duplexes, houses, or at least private apartments in shared quarters. Although the army made no official provision for officers' wives or families to join them in the West, the housing situation of the officers made that prospect more inviting. Enlisted men and noncommissioned officers, on the other hand, were not allowed to have families join them (with a few exceptions).

While at their posts, officers' food was more varied and appetizing. Some had servants to cook meals for them and their families. Special occasions brought distinctive delicacies such as champagne and oysters. Yet officers shared a degree of tedium with enlisted man. Guard details, parades, general and garrison courts-martial, drills, and recitations in tactics occupied the time of frontier officers while in post. Their leisure activities did not differ significantly from those of enlisted men, although the caste system meant they usually pursued these endeavors with men of their own class.

When troops went out in the field, they spent a good deal of time searching for an enemy and marching over vast stretches of country. Commanders launched the majority of campaigns in spring, summer, and fall, but some of the most important campaigns took place in the winter. Commanding officers planned large-scale campaigns, but often the men were

When on field expeditions or searching for an enemy, army troops camped as best they could. Pictured here is General George Crook's headquarters in the field at Whitewood, Dakota Territory, on 1876. The tents have been improvised from wagon frames during Crook's Black Hills expedition. *Courtesy National Archives.*

called to participate in local outbreaks of hostilities between Indians and whites. Between 1865 and 1890, the army listed one thousand engagements and the loss of 948 officers and men. It did not keep records of Indian deaths.

During the expeditions, troopers usually averaged twenty miles per day. On the move before daybreak, soldiers found campsites by afternoon to allow sufficient light for setting up camp, looking after horses, and other chores. An infantryman would carry about fifty pounds of equipment and materials, including extra shoes and clothes, a knapsack, rations, and ammunition. A cavalryman would also have accoutrements for his horse, but the animal carried everything rather than the man. During winter campaigns, soldiers also carried wool overcoats and headgear or possibly buffalo coats and overshoes. Campaign cuisine consisted of hard tack, bacon, and coffee. Occasionally hunting excursions added fresh meat. Harsh climates challenged soldiers' stamina, whether they endured the heat of Arizona's summers or the frigid cold of Montana's and Wyoming's winters. After periods of prolonged field service, most soldiers welcomed the relative comforts of their posts.

Military men spent more time looking for Indians than fighting them. Further, most Indians in the West preferred guerrilla warfare to set-piece battles. Both army and Indian preferred to use the element of surprise whether they fought skirmishes or full-scale battles. Neither Indians nor enlisted men were particularly adept at marksmanship, but bullets found their human targets on enough occasions to make the Indian Wars a costly ordeal for both sides. The excitement of battle and the loss of comrades, regardless of rank, could lower caste barriers, at least temporarily, as soldiers confronted the horrible costs of warfare.

The men who joined the Western army looking for adventure soon realized it was a life of hardship, isolation, and sometimes danger. Mostly forgotten by their Eastern countrymen, soldiers asked for little

recognition and received less. They represented the military arm of an expanding nation. Few doubted the necessity of the army's efforts, but few lauded them for the adversities they endured in the course of subduing Indians' resistance to Euro-American settlement.
—*Sherry L. Smith*

SUGGESTED READING:

Coffman, Edward M. *The Old Army: A Portrait of the American Army in Peacetime, 1784–1898.* New York, 1986.

Hutton, Paul Andrew, ed. *Soldiers West: Biographies from the Military Frontier.* Lincoln, Nebr., 1987.

Knight, Oliver. *Life and Manners in the Frontier Army.* Norman, Okla., 1978.

Leckie, William H. *The Buffalo Soldiers: A Narrative of the Negro Cavalry in the West.* Norman, Okla., 1967.

Porter, Joseph C. *Paper Medicine Man: John Gregory Bourke and the American West.* Norman, Okla., 1986.

Rickey, Don. *Forty Miles a Day on Beans and Hay.* Norman, Okla., 1963.

Smith, Sherry L. *Sagebrush Soldier: Private William Earl Smith's View of the Sioux War of 1876.* Norman, Okla., 1989.

———. *The View from Officers' Row: Army Perceptions of Western Indians.* Tucson, Ariz., 1990.

Utley, Robert M. *Frontier Regulars: The United States Army and the Indian, 1866–1891.* New York, 1973.

———. *Frontiersmen in Blue: The United States Army and the Indian, 1848–1865.* New York, 1967.

———, ed. *Life in Custer's Cavalry: Diaries and Letters of Albert and Jennie Barnitz, 1867–1868.* New Haven, Conn., 1977.

VOLUNTEERS AND MILITIA

From the earliest days of the American republic, the United States had expressed a faith in civilian soldiers and a distrust of standing armies. Despite the fact that experience demonstrated again and again the superiority of the regular army, this revolutionary heritage continued to characterize the United States military in the nineteenth century. Indeed, the U.S. Constitution itself not only made the army responsible to executive and legislative branches of the government but also divided military power between the federal government's regular army and the states' militia system. Militias were seldom well organized; they lacked discipline; and they received only rudimentary training, all of which made them unsuitable for long, offensive campaigns. Rarely were they effective except in response to immediate threats, and they tended to lose their heads in frontier conditions where their attitudes and their very lives were attuned to the local situation. The regular army, however, tended to maintain a more professional calm. For that reason, the regular army,

however small, was more effective in providing protection in the outposts of the Far West, and its ranks were usually swelled by militias and volunteer units only during times of crisis.

When simmering hostility exploded into bellicose action, as during the UNITED STATES–MEXICAN WAR, for example, volunteer units could spring up quite quickly, and the army had little choice, given its traditionally tiny size but to rely on such units. Within hours of President JAMES K. POLK's announcement of war, volunteers around the country—except in reluctant New England—were rushing to the colors in the tens of thousands. In New York City, posters proclaimed, "Mexico or Death!" and "Ho, For the Halls of Montezuma!" City streets echoed with the pounding of drums, the piping of fifes, and the tramp of marching feet. In Indiana, Lew Wallace raised a company in three days simply by marching through Indianapolis and holding high a sign that read, "For Mexico: Fall In!" Ohio, home of considerable antiwar sentiment, nevertheless sent three thousand native sons to the front in less than two weeks. North Carolina tripled its quota, and Tennessee responded to a call for twenty-eight hundred men by sending thirty thousand, while those left behind tried desperately to buy their way in. The volunteers were not all motivated by patriotism or a sense of MANIFEST DESTINY. Privately, recruiters promised the adventure-hungry and the desperate "roast beef, two dollars a day, plenty of whiskey, golden Jesuses, and pretty Mexican girls." They swept into Mexico, most of them Southerners, by steamboats out into the Gulf and down to Point Isabel or to ZACHARY TAYLOR's advance position at Camargo seventy miles farther west.

Typically, army regulars were not pleased with what they saw as the arrival of an undisciplined mob. The young Captain Ulysses S. Grant wrote home:

> Since we have been in Matamoros, a great many murders have been committed. Some of the volunteers and about all the Texans seem to think it perfectly right to impose on the people of a conquered city to any extent, and even to murder them where the act can be covered by dark. And how much they seem to enjoy acts of violence too!

The first volunteers to arrive in Mexico in 1846 had been virtually useless. They were enlisted for six months, some for only three, and by the time most of them got to Point Isabel or Camargo, it was time to go home. Twelve-monthers came whooping into camp beginning in July. A Texas colonel thought the Tennessee men were worse than Russian Cossacks, but Zachary Taylor—like Grant—believed the Texans to be the worst, "too licentious to do much good." When they weren't physically assaulting Mexicans, they fought each other—or the regulars. They defied their officers. They helped their friends escape from the guardhouse. The slave holders among them expected the foreign-born regulars to wait on them. They cursed the pay, the food, the dysentery. Some of them, like the "Volunteers of Kentucky," wore full beards, tricornered hats, and hip boots faced with red morocco leather; others came in all shades of gray, green, yellow, pink, blue-and-white trimmed with red, calling themselves "Guards," "Rifles," "Killers," "Gunmen," "Blues," and "Grays."

Perhaps the wildest of them were indeed the volunteers from Texas, three regiments that were led by the state's governor, J. Pinckney Henderson, among them the frontier patrols called the TEXAS RANGERS. Long-haired, bearded, mustachioed at a time most men, especially soldiers, went clean shaven, they wore wide-brimmed slouch hats not unlike Mexican sombreros and sported a belt of pistols at their waists, much favoring the new Colt revolvers they would make famous. Unwashed and no strangers to lice, they regarded bathing as a "foppish affectation." To a man, they hated the Mexicans. By no means were all of them old Indian-fighters or former Texas revolutionaries. They included among their ranks doctors, lawyers, educators, engineers, professional men, and college-educated men. But they were good horsemen, and courageous, if hard-souled.

George Meade, who carefully censored his own letters home, said the volunteers were "full of mutiny. . . . They have killed five or six innocent people walking in the street, for no other object than their own amusement. . . . They rob and steal the cattle and corn of the poor farmers." WINFIELD SCOTT, still back in Washington, later admitted privately that American soldiers were committing "atrocities to make Heaven weep and every American of Christian morals blush for his country. Murder, robbery and rape of mothers and daughters in the presence of tied-up males of the families have been common all along the Rio Grande." Mexican priests denounced the volunteers in a local newspaper as "the horde of banditti, of drunkards, of fornicators . . . vandals vomited from hell, monsters who bid defiance to the laws of nature . . . shameless, daring, ignorant, ragged, bad-smelling, long-bearded men with hats turned up at the brim, thirsty with the desire to appropriate our riches and our beautiful damsels."

The Texas Rangers sneered at the protests of first General Taylor, then later General-in-Chief Winfield Scott, derisively nicknaming the latter "Ol' Fuss 'n' Feathers." Early on and to his credit, Taylor refused to accept any more volunteers from Texas, but he found he could hardly do without the services of the Texas Rangers. He had been favorably impressed by Sam Walker and his men in his two actions against Arista. He wanted the Texas Rangers with him as he planned to attack Monterrey, the capital of Nuevo Leon, on his way to Mexico City. And the exploits of the Missouri Volunteers under ALEXANDER WILLIAM DONIPHAN became legendary after the war, accomplishments that many considered remarkable precisely because Doniphan himself was so casual an officer who cared little for military discipline or order.

Although on a different scale than during the war in Mexico, the situation proved similar throughout the nineteenth-century trans-Mississippi West. Indian troubles spurred militias into action or spawned volunteer groups. Local populations might be proud of their fighting men, but the army had little respect for them, dreaded the trouble they might cause, and found their unruliness, their motives, and their zeal unsavory and counterproductive in many military situations, especially in dealing with the always volatile and delicate situations involving Native Americans. With the outbreak of the CIVIL WAR, the regulars were withdrawn from the frontier, and the government had little choice but to rely on volunteer units and state militiamen to man the posts and guard the roads. They managed to turn back the Confederate invasion of New Mexico and to fight effectively against Confederate regular and guerrilla forces in Missouri, Arkansas, Kansas, and the Indian Territory. Volunteers, too, faced the Western Indian tribes as hostilities developed later in the war. A group of Confederates, called "Galvanized Yankees," who agreed to serve in the West rather than remain in Yankee prisons, also fought Indians on the Northern Plains.

As always, the volunteer regiments in the West varied greatly in quality. Some fled at the first sign of real fighting. Some, like those in the California Column in New Mexico proved to be a well-disciplined, hard-fighting asset. And some, as during the Mexico conflict, were guilty of murder and outright atrocities. Artillery troops along the Oregon Trail used passing Indians for target practice. It was volunteers under the command of Colonel JOHN M. CHIVINGTON who in an attack on a Cheyenne village in 1864 perpetrated the SAND CREEK MASSACRE that so shocked the entire nation with its brutality. Not untypical of many volunteer actions, the attack provoked retaliatory—and quite damaging—raids by the Indians, with whom the regular army was at length forced to deal.

In the case of the Texas Rangers, a group of fighting men developed from a volunteer military unit into a self-defense outfit within the state and gained legal status as a supra-jurisdictional police force. Although the Texas Rangers became legendary heroes among many of the state's Anglo population, they did not truly shed the vigilante patina of many volunteer units for many years. They were openly hostile toward the Hispanic populations of Texas—an almost institutional racism that had its roots in the unit's Indian-fighting and revolutionary origins. Texas Rangers in particular, but also some U.S. Army troops working with them, not only battled Mexican Texans and Mexican bandits and, later, revolutionaries along the Texas border with Mexico, they also cooperated with land speculators to coerce Tejano villagers to sign over their lands and, in general, kept the TEJANOS "in line." While whites readily excused the rangers' excesses, the Tejanos despised them and regarded them not as lawmen but as an armed force designed to intimidate and plunder Hispanics in the interest of an Anglo elite. Other frontier volunteer forces, such as the Arizona Rangers, evolved along the lines of the Texas Rangers from a Mexican and Indian-fighting outfit to a self-defense and border patrol unit to an official law-enforcement force, although few if any lasted beyond the frontier conditions that gave birth to them, much less grew into the fairly conventional state police force that the Texas Rangers are today.

—*Charles Phillips*

SUGGESTED READING:

Brown, D. Alexander. *The Galvanized Yankees*. Urbana, Ill. 1963.

Eisenhower, John S. D. *So Far from God: The War with Mexico, 1846–1848*. New York, 1989.

Utley, Robert. *Frontiersmen in Blue: The United States Army, 1848–1865*. Lincoln, Nebr. 1967.

Webb, Walter Prescott. *The Texas Rangers: A Century of Frontier Defense*. Boston, 1935.

Weigley, Russell. *A History of the United States Army*. New York, 1973.

SCOUTS

Scouts, guides, and native auxiliaries were crucial to the U.S. Army in the West. No combat officer could neglect their employment, and their role was proven even in the New England colonies during King Philip's War from 1675 to 1676. Douglas Edward Leach, historian of the war, wrote that "the English soldiers showed themselves to be almost helpless in the face of Indian forest tactics, until they began to take friendly Indians with them as scouts."

In the struggles between the French and the English, the former made more extensive use of Indian allies, although in the Revolutionary War and the WAR OF 1812, the British used Indian auxiliaries more than the Americans. The employment of Indian scouts was not without its hazards, however. The 1690 siege of Fort Loyal, Maine, was terminated when the French commander solemnly swore quarter for the defenders who filed out in surrender only to be slaughtered by the Abenaki allies of the French. An analogous situation occurred in 1780 at the Kentucky fort of Ruddle's Station, where British Captain Henry Bird offered the defenders quarter, but when they surrendered, the Shawnee auxiliaries overwhelmed Bird's opposition and massacred many whites.

Western commanders at first tried to use white scouts—tough frontiersmen such as Simon, James, and George Girty who worked extensively for the British. Some white scouts (such as the Wetzels, Samuel Brady, Thady Kelley, and Simon Kenton), however, proved to be as hard to control as the Indian auxiliaries. Some white scouts had been captured and raised by the Indians and were knowledgeable about native ways. Others were some mixture of white and Native American.

The North brothers, Frank and Luther, enlisted, organized, and managed effectively the Pawnee Scouts—irregulars on the Great Plains from 1865 to 1877. Frank North had learned some Pawnee language and enlisted a company of one hundred Indians in January 1865. His scouts accompanied Brigadier General PATRICK E. CONNOR's three-pronged expedition into the upper Plains. On August 23, 1865, the Pawnees killed thirty-four Sioux and Cheyennes. They later guided Connor to an Arapaho village, which the U.S. troops captured, and they subsequently saved one element of the Connor expedition—lost and in desperate straits—from starvation. On March 1, 1867, Frank North, as a major, enlisted 200 Pawnees in a battalion of scouts, with Luther North as captain of one company. These valuable fighters helped Major Eugene Asa Carr gain a victory over the Cheyennes on July 11, 1869. Frank North was credited by some with killing Tall Bull, a Cheyenne chief.

The Pawnee Scouts were phased out before 1876, but 100 were reenlisted after GEORGE ARMSTRONG CUSTER's disastrous defeat at the Battle of Little Bighorn. The Pawnee Scouts performed valiantly on the Great Plains and took part in RANALD SLIDELL MACKENZIE's victory over the Cheyennes on November 25 and 26, 1876. On May 1, 1877, the Pawnee Scouts were finally mustered out of the army.

In 1866, Congress had approved "An Act to Increase and Fix the Military Peace Establishment." Empowering the president to "enlist and employ in the territories and Indian country a force of Indians, not to exceed 1,000, to act as scouts," the law called for the scouts to be paid about thirteen dollars a month—the same wage as given cavalry soldiers. While 1,000 Indian scout positions had been approved, army authorities limited enrollment to 300. The scouts were

Bloody Knife served as a scout to George Armstrong Custer on his Yellowstone Expedition. This image was taken by William R. Pywell in 1873. *Courtesy National Archives.*

parceled out among several military divisions and departments, and commanders jockeyed for their share.

Between the CIVIL WAR and the end of the Indian Wars, several Indian tribes supplied scouts for significant military operations. General GEORGE CROOK used Crow, Shoshone, Sioux, and Arapaho scouts on the upper Plains. Custer employed principally Arikaras (Rees), including the famous Bloody Knife. Custer also depended on mixed-blood scouts such as Minton (Mitch) Bouyer, who along with Bloody Knife perished in the Little Bighorn fight. Scouts were used in the Modoc War in northern California and in battles against the Paiutes of eastern Oregon and Nevada. Army units were severely handicapped by the lack of scouts in the Nez Percé campaign of 1877 and the Red River War on the Southern Plains from 1874 to 1875.

Along the Rio Grande in the 1870s, Colonel Ranald Slidell Mackenzie enlisted Seminoles for use as a sort of transition element between the

Pawnee Scouts and Crook's Apaches. Never numbering more than 50 at a time, the Seminoles operated almost as freely in Mexico (illegally, of course) as in Texas against Lipan and Mescalero Apaches and Kickapoos.

It was in the Southwest that Apache Indians were found to be indispensable as scouts. They attained their highest development and performed their ultimate service under Crook. Elsewhere in the West, commanders almost always enlisted as scouts men from bands inimical to those they were to fight. In Apacheria, however, Crook believed in enlisting Apaches to fight Apaches—not those of one band to fight another, but Apaches of a particular grouping to fight their own people. In Crook's view, the Apache scouts could fight better against their own people than could anyone else.

When Crook took command in Arizona in 1871, he sent out small commands, each accompanied by scouts and civilian chiefs of scouts. During his second Southwestern tour from 1882 to 1886, he perfected his system still further. He sometimes sent scouts into Mexico to seek information. Sometimes they operated alone, or again with white scout chiefs such as AL SIEBER.

Three outstanding operations illustrate the effectiveness of the Apache scouts. During the spring of 1880, VICTORIO, a Mimbres Apache of New Mexico, proved himself a redoubtable, elusive foe, repeatedly defeating army units. In May of that year, Henry Kinney Parker, a leathery chief of scouts, took his men to hunt down Victorio. Parker soon learned from his scouts that Victorio had retreated to a narrow canyon. Parker's

Apache scouts with an army officer and an interpreter. Some observers commented that it took the U.S. Army twenty-four years to learn that "only an Apache can catch an Apache." *Courtesy Arizona Historical Society.*

Apache Indian scouts were indispensable to the U.S. Army. The Apache scouts pictured here are engaged in drilling exercises with rifles at Fort Wingate, New Mexico. *Courtesy National Archives.*

men surrounded Victorio's camp and opened fire. They killed about thirty of Victorio's band, and wounded several others, including Victorio himself. Nearly out of ammunition, Parker sent a courier to his commanding officer to ask for more ammunition and reinforcements; neither was forthcoming, and he was forced to withdraw. While inconclusive, his feat was the only triumph over Victorio in this country during a long and grueling campaign. His success was due to the Apache scouts and to his own resourcefulness.

A second campaign using scouts effectively took place in the spring of 1883. General Crook decided to send an expedition into the nearly unexplored Sierra Madre of northern Mexico to contact several hundred Indians and persuade them to return to the San Carlos Reservation in Arizona. He knew he could never take a white column alone into Mexico, so he composed his expedition of forty-two cavalry men and 193 Apache scouts under Al Sieber. Crook's expedition marched into Mexico for six weeks. When he returned to Arizona, his mission had been successful, due to the loyalty and singular abilities of his scouts, who had not only located the enemy Indians, but had bested them in a single engagement.

A third successful use of Indian scouts was the GERONIMO campaign. On the very brink of success against Geronimo, a scheming bootlegger plied the Indians with whiskey and told them of the indignities that awaited them at the San Carlos Reservation. Geronimo and most of his followers retreated to the mountains. Crook was criticized by his superiors for his dependence on Indian scouts, and General NELSON APPLETON MILES was named to succeed him. Miles was instructed to use regular soldiers in bringing the campaign to a close. He was unsuccessful. His troops became exhausted in the Mexico mountains and could not locate Geronimo and his followers. After months of exasperation, Miles turned to Indian scouts. He sent Charles B. Gatewood, scout officer, out with 2 Chiricahua scouts—Kayitah and Martine—into Mexico. The scouts soon picked up Geronimo's trail, located his camps, and arranged for Gatewood to talk with the war leader. The result was the final surrender of Geronimo and the end of the organized APACHE WARS in the Southwest.

—*Dan L. Thrapp*

SUGGESTED READING:

Dunlay, Thomas E. *Wolves for the Blue Soldiers: Indian Scouts and Auxiliaries with the United States Army, 1860–90.* Lincoln, Nebr., 1982.

Downey, Fairfax, and J. N. Jacobsen. *The Red-Bluecoats: The Indian Scouts.* Fort Collins, Colo., 1973.

Thrapp, Dan L. *Al Sieber: Chief of Scouts.* Norman, Okla., 1964.

———. *General Crook and the Sierra Madre Adventure.* Norman, Okla., 1972.

STRATEGY AND TACTICS

Throughout the nineteenth century, the United States Army was called upon to explore, patrol, and police the trans-Mississippi West. Fundamental to the military's attempts to accomplish these tasks was the widespread acceptance of the idea of Indian inferiority and of the belief that the United States government, in order to further the causes of civilization and orderly expansion, had the right to remove Indian tribes from lands desired by non-Indian settlers. Economic and political constraints, however, weighed heavily on the army's Western experiences. Limited appropriations, stemming in part from traditional fears that a large military threatened democracy, restricted the size and composition of the standing army. The use of regular troops in a variety of quasi-military duties, especially during Reconstruction, further limited strategic options. And on several occasions, the Department of the Interior prevented the army from launching punitive expeditions against Indians. Real and alleged massacres of Indians further reinforced suspicions about the judgment and trustworthiness of the regular force.

A wide variety of Indian tribes lived west of the Mississippi River. Those posing the greatest military threat, however, usually followed nomadic life styles. Whether living in prairie, plains, mountain, or desert environments, they often fought in small bands and avoided combat except when circumstances seemed most favorable or when their homes and families were threatened. Using the terrain to its fullest advantage, they could be fiercely effective individual fighters, although their loose political and social organization usually prevented them from undertaking collective action for extended periods of time.

Within the United States Army, strategic and tactical development was haphazard. No systematic attempts were made to institutionalize policy making or planning. The few army personnel interested in developing military doctrine concentrated on methods applicable against enemies who fought in the traditional, European style. High-level analysis instead concentrated on discovering the means by which the regular army could most effectively oversee the American West and ensure the supreme authority of the FEDERAL GOVERNMENT.

During the early nineteenth century, Secretary of War JOHN CALDWELL CALHOUN had an unusually keen interest in outlining a rational blueprint for occupying the trans-Mississippi West. Calhoun tried, unsuccessfully, to create an "expansible" army, which could be quickly increased in size during an emergency. While most of his contemporaries focused rather narrowly on the routes and costs of building military roads to connect the army's Western garrisons, Calhoun unfolded aggressive plans for establishing military posts well ahead of non-Indian settlement. In so doing, he hoped to check British trade with Indians as well as to dominate the regions along the Missouri, Arkansas, and Red rivers.

But as the army pushed farther west, officials found themselves in a difficult balancing act. The West was too large, and the army too small. The regulars held scores of remote posts, many of which had been selected according to political demands or local convenience rather than to a predesigned, logical plan. Typically, the Western FORTS included a rambling collection of buildings assembled around an open parade ground rather than any walled defensive structures. Although Indians rarely attacked the forts, each garrison could still do little more than hold its own position. Rather than parceling out units to tiny garrisons, some officials hoped to concentrate a reserve force at a point like Jefferson Barracks, Missouri, to be deployed when conditions necessitated. Competing demands by the occupants of various regions, however, rarely allowed effective concentration.

Throughout the 1830s and early 1840s, military operations were predicated on the idea of a permanent Indian frontier beyond which white settlers would not venture. As Eastern tribes were removed to lands west of the Mississippi River, the army wanted to establish a defensive line to separate Indians from whites. During his tenure as secretary of war from 1831 to 1836, Lewis Cass argued that a north-south military road, stretching from Texas to the Michigan Territory and buttressed by military posts and active patrols, would form an effective barrier against Indian incursions. Secretary of War Joel R. Poinsett, who succeeded Cass in 1837 and served until 1841, disagreed with Cass's north-south road and argued that communications should run perpendicular to rather than parallel to the frontier. Still, the concept that some permanent Indian frontier might be established remained the cornerstone of military policy.

Others stressed the need for greater mobility, particularly as the army confronted the mounted tribes of the Great Plains. During the mid-1830s, Congress thus created two regiments of dragoons; it added another mounted regiment in 1846 and two more in 1855. Although the dragoons helped escort the growing overland trade with Santa Fe, the army needed to do more than merely establish fixed posts if it was to be successful at establishing peace. Several mounted expeditions ventured into the Southern Plains and the upper Mississippi Valley during the mid-1830s; Colonel STEPHEN WATTS KEARNY led 250 dragoons into the Rocky Mountains in 1845. Kearny and a variety of other observers, including General-in-Chief WINFIELD SCOTT and Indian agent Thomas Fitzpatrick, argued that such endeavors should become standard practice. Proponents of the roving patrols thought that army columns should periodically sweep the Plains to visit the various tribes and induce them to accept government treaties.

Increasing use of the overland trails to Oregon, the annexation of Texas, and the acquisition of new lands in the Treaty of Guadalupe Hidalgo (1848) rendered any notion of a permanent Indian frontier obsolete. The army's greatest obstacles usually came in finding the Indians and forcing them to fight. But in the face of continuing budgetary pressures and the transfer of the Office of Indian Affairs from the War Department to the newly created Department of the Interior in 1849, the army's task was frustrating. In 1852, a discouraged Secretary of War Charles Conrad even supported one officer's suggestion that the federal government buy all the property in New Mexico, encourage every resident to move, and abandon the territory to the Indians or Mexico. Conrad's proposal won little support but did suggest that traditional defensive measures had failed.

Secretary of War Jefferson Davis, during his tenure from 1853 to 1857, sought to energize the army's Western policies. Davis realized that better systems of transportation and communication were critical to effective military operations. Such improvements would reduce the high costs of equipping and supplying frontier garrisons and would allow the army to shift its forces to meet regional threats. Davis championed a transcontinental railroad, encouraged the construction of new military roads, and introduced CAMELS into the American West as beasts of burden. He also persuaded Congress to increase the maximum legal strength of the standing army from fourteen thousand to eighteen thousand.

One of few planners to compare the U.S. Army's experiences in the West with those of other nations, Secretary Davis patterned his Western policies upon the French experience in Algeria. He envisioned several new Western Indian reservations, and to enforce government policy, he concluded that roving columns should indeed replace the more traditional fixed-post garrisons. In September 1855, Colonel WILLIAM SELBY HARNEY's column of dragoons, infantry, and artillery attacked and routed a large Brulé Sioux village near Blue Water Creek, Nebraska. Nearly two years later, Colonel EDWIN V. SUMNER led a dramatic cavalry charge that scattered several hundred Cheyenne warriors along the Solomon River in Kansas. Captain Earl Van Dorn destroyed a Comanche village at Rush Spring in the Indian Territory in 1858. Active attempts to force or persuade tribes to move to reservations were also undertaken in Washington, Oregon, Texas, and New Mexico.

With the outbreak of the CIVIL WAR, the United States government transferred most of the regulars from frontier duty to the East. Western states and territories thus turned to volunteer units to replace the regular army. Violence between Indians and non-Indians increased as the volunteers sought to destroy the Indians' military power. Combining winter campaigns with relentless field operations, Colonel PATRICK E. CONNOR defeated the Utes, Shoshones, and Bannocks of Utah and Nevada. In New Mexico, General JAMES H. CARLETON and Colonel CHRISTOPHER HOUSTON ("KIT") CARSON conducted resolute strikes that penetrated the homelands of the Navajos and Mescalero Apaches, crushed their will to resist, and forced them onto Bosque Redondo reservations. Elsewhere, open warfare spread throughout the Great Plains; in an effort to unify disjointed federal efforts, General JOHN POPE was assigned control of a huge new administrative command, the Division of the Missouri, in late 1864. Pope planned a series of coordinated offensives for the spring and summer of 1865, but demands that the military cut costs and government peace initiatives reduced the size and scope of his projected campaigns.

After the Civil War, Congress once again slashed the size of the regular army and limited the total number of enlisted personnel to twenty-five thousand by 1874. Ten mounted, twenty-five infantry, and five artillery regiments formed the regular force. Protection for railroad construction received high priority, and General WILLIAM TECUMSEH SHERMAN, commander of the key Division of the Missouri and later the entire army, hoped to create an Indian-free belt between the Arkansas and Platte rivers. Attempting to force the issue using traditional means, General Winfield S. Hancock led a large expeditionary force west from Fort Riley, Kansas, in 1867.

When HANCOCK'S CAMPAIGN failed to bring about a peace, General PHILIP H. SHERIDAN, Sherman's trusted subordinate, undertook a more elaborate offensive during the late fall of 1868. Those Indians who did not assemble at a designated point were declared hostile. Army columns from Colorado, Kansas, and New Mexico operated nearly independently of one another and converged against suspected Southern Cheyenne, Arapaho, Comanche, and Kiowa haunts. Supplemented by substantial numbers of Indian auxiliaries, the army stalked the tribes throughout the winter, when the lack of forage reduced the Indians' mobility. Harassed, exhausted, and trapped between the army's formations, several Indian bands agreed to move to reservations.

In 1874, Sheridan launched another major offensive against the Southern Plains peoples. Five columns from Texas, the Indian Territory, Kansas, and New

Mexico converged on Indian villages near the headwaters of the Red River. Once again, field commanders moved as circumstances demanded rather than according to a predetermined plan. This time, however, Sheridan opted not to wait until the winter months because a delay might give Interior Department officials time to intervene and stop the attack. As was often the case, decisive battlefield encounters proved rare during the Red River War. But the relentless pursuits continued through the following spring and broke the military power of the Southern Plains tribes.

To the north, Sioux and Northern Cheyennes also challenged further intrusions by whites into their lands. With the successful conclusion of the Red River War, the discovery of gold in the Black Hills, and the determination to expand the Northern Pacific Railroad, the army took punitive action in early 1876. Because heavy snows and frigid weather had limited the success of initial winter campaigns, it was late spring before troops from the Departments of Dakota and the Platte renewed the offensive. From experience, field commanders assumed that large numbers of Indians would not remain together for any extended period of time and would avoid combat except when conditions seemed favorable. By surprising the tribes in their villages, dividing one's command, and encircling the Indians, however, an ambitious officer might bring about a decisive engagement.

This time, however, the large coalition of Sioux and Northern Cheyennes assembled in southern Montana were more than willing to fight. After turning back one army column at the Battle of the Rosebud, the tribes annihilated Lieutenant Colonel GEORGE ARMSTRONG CUSTER's command at the Battle of Little Bighorn. For the remainder of the fall, army columns swept the Northern Plains. Most successful were Colonel NELSON APPLETON MILES's infantrymen, who, from their base at the Tongue River Cantonment in the Montana Territory (later Fort Keogh), won skirmishes against several Sioux and Northern Cheyenne bands. By late spring 1877, most of the Northern Plains tribes had either moved to government reservations or fled north into Canada.

In subsequent victories over CHIEF JOSEPH and the Nez Percés, the Bannocks, and the Sheepeaters, the army used traditional methods—relentless pursuit and attacks against Indian villages. The final challenge to the federal government's military supremacy on the Northern Plains came in late 1890, when many Northern Cheyennes and Sioux left their reservations during the GHOST DANCE outbreak. Orchestrating the army's response, Miles mixed overwhelming force, attacks on Indian dependents and possessions, the rigors of winter campaigning, and diplomacy to force the disaffected peoples to return to their reservations.

Conditions along the Mexican border posed different challenges. For years, Indians, bandits, and revolutionary groups had crossed the border with impunity. Taking his cue from Sheridan's verbal instructions, Colonel RANALD SLIDELL MACKENZIE, much of his Fourth Cavalry Regiment, and dozens of Indian scouts splashed across the Rio Grande in 1873 and destroyed several Indian villages near Remolino, Mexico. Regular troops crossed the river on several occasions following Mackenzie's first raid; from 1877 to 1880, the U.S. Army did so in accord with presidential orders, which authorized troops to enter Mexico when in hot pursuit of raiders. Although the army encountered relatively few Indians during its cross-border expeditions, the troops did pressure Mexico into launching several of its own strikes against tribes in Coahuila.

In the Pacific Northwest, several tribes had challenged the government during the 1850s. In several 1858 engagements unusual for the willingness shown by the tribes to engage in formal combat, Colonel George Wright had crushed many of the mountain peoples. After the Civil War, Lieutenant Colonel GEORGE CROOK carved out a reputation as an innovative campaigner in a series of punishing operations in Oregon. By enrolling swarms of Indian auxiliaries on the federal payroll, using mules to carry supplies, and—regardless of terrain or climate—relentlessly pursuing tribes defined as hostile, Crook wore down his opponents.

In Arizona, New Mexico, and western Texas, the hit-and-run tactics practiced by relatively small numbers of Apaches had long bedeviled the regulars. Although operations during the mid-1850s had temporarily forced a few groups onto reservations, long pursuits conducted by traditional regular forces usually proved fruitless. Adopting new methods in 1880, Colonel BENJAMIN HENRY GRIERSON, commander of troops in the trans-Pecos region of Texas, had some success by stationing his men at strategic water holes. Rather than wasting his men and animals in fruitless treks across the arid region, Grierson simply allowed the enemy to come to him.

But even the energetic Crook failed to bring peace to the far Southwest. During his two terms as chief of the Department of Arizona, Crook outfitted small commands of officers and Apache auxiliaries rather than organizing cumbersome regular columns. He also took great pains to secure the cooperation of Mexican officials. But as depredations attributed to Indians continued, Sheridan, who had succeeded Sherman as commanding general in 1883, demanded that Crook depend more on his regulars. With great fanfare, Crook's replacement, Nelson Miles, pronounced that regular troops and non-Apache scouts would assume the brunt of the campaigning. But the chases quickly exhausted the regulars. Only after several months of difficult campaigning and the reintroduction of Crook's methods was resistance crushed in 1886.

During initial encounters with the regulars, Indians had been at times surprised by the long-ranged shoulder weapons and artillery pieces carried by the bluecoats. Although limited to a single shot, the succession of standard-issue weapons—the .69 caliber Model 1842 percussion musket, the .58 caliber Model 1855 rifle and rifle-musket, and the .45 Model 1873 Springfield rifles and carbines—had been fairly reliable and served the army well. Light artillery pieces, often referred to as "mountain howitzers," effectively supplemented the firepower of some army columns but tended to slow pursuits. Several models of repeating pistols, widely introduced among mounted troops during the early 1850s, gave cavalrymen a greater volume of firepower for close-range encounters.

Experience made tribes wary of engaging the regulars in open combat. Sometimes hampered by the lack of modern firearms and ammunition, Indian warriors tended to favor repeating weapons when they could get them. Hit-and-run raids, ambushes, and skirmishing became increasingly typical during the latter half of the nineteenth century. Both sides, however, often directed attacks against the homes and property of their enemy; during the sudden strikes, casualties included a high proportion of noncombatants.

Although it had spent the good part of a century on the trans-Mississippi frontiers, the United States Army developed neither strategic nor tactical policies applicable to Western conditions. Successful operations resulted from individual initiative, trial-and-error, and experience rather than from the adherence to official doctrine. Particularly after the Civil War, experienced commanders almost invariably employed large numbers of Indian auxiliaries. From several different directions, army columns converged on Indian villages. Even when tribes avoided battle, the psychological effects of long, relentless pursuits, sometimes undertaken during the winter months and often conducted by foot soldiers, wore down the Indians' will to resist. In the end, the fiercely independent tribes had been overwhelmed by a government whose superior resources and decades-long determination to conquer the American West they never fully recognized.

—*Robert Wooster*

SUGGESTED READING:

Coffman, Edward M. *The Old Army: A Portrait of the American Army in Peacetime, 1784–1898.* New York, 1986.

Hutton, Paul Andrew. *Phil Sheridan and His Army.* Lincoln, Nebr., 1985.

Prucha, Francis Paul. *The Sword of the Republic: The United States Army on the Frontier, 1783–1846.* New York, 1969.

Utley, Robert M. *Frontier Regulars: The United States Army and the Indian, 1866–1891.* New York, 1973.

———. *Frontiersmen in Blue: The United States Army and the Indian, 1848–1865.* New York, 1967.

Weigley, Russell Frank. *The American Way of War: A History of United States Military Strategy and Policy.* New York, 1973.

Wooster, Robert. *The Military and United States Indian Policy, 1865–1903.* New Haven, 1988.

———. "Military Strategy in the Southwest, 1848–1860." *Military History of Texas and the Southwest* 15 (1979): 5–15.

ARMS AND EQUIPMENT

In the years following the Civil War, the United States Army returned to the conservatism that had marked its policy of acquiring new weapons and equipment before the war. With warehouses full of surplus equipment, the army had enough supplies to last almost a generation. Despite the needs of an army that was fighting a guerrilla war against Native Americans in the West with its extremes of weather and terrain, changes in the army's equipment occurred slowly.

The war did lead the army to a reconsider the standard longarms issued to the infantry and army regiments. Breech-loading arms and metallic cartridges became available to the regular units shortly after the Civil War. This equipment's effectiveness in combat was dramatic. By 1867, the army had adopted the Allin Conversion Springfield, a modification of the famed wartime muzzle-loading musket. The new design was equipped with a breech mechanism that permitted the use of metallic cartridges. The pieces were, in the words of General Ulysses S. Grant, "simple, strong, accurate, and not apt to get out of order." Although minor improvements were made, infantry units used the weapon for seven years.

Rather than a rifle, cavalry units required a carbine, which was not so easily standardized. The Civil War demonstrated the utility of a variety of repeater models, including the seven-shot Spencer, as well as the single-shot Sharps. In 1872, the army convened a board under General ALFRED HOWE TERRY to evaluate the available weapons and, after testing more than a hundred pieces, selected a carbine version of the Allin Conversion Springfield, along with the rifle version for infantry use. These two weapons became the standard issue, with some improvement, for the next two decades. Gradually, the army came to prefer single-shot long weapons, which became standardized after 1872, over repeating rifles.

During the army review supervised by Terry, the Colt 1872 army revolver, the "Peacemaker," was the overwhelming favorite handgun, and it soon became the standard issue. The army purchased thirteen thousand single-action, .45 caliber pistols and about a thousand more each year through 1891. Sabers were also available, although the weapon was rarely used in the field.

Although soldiers were able to surprise the Indians with the new weapons in early engagements, such as the Wagon Box and Hayfield fights, the tribes also began to acquire new weapons. Despite some difficulty in obtaining ammunition and repeating rifles, such as the Winchester seven-shot repeating carbine, enough Indians obtained the new weapons to have an impact on the tactics of the war. At the Battle of Little Bighorn, the Indians carried Spencers and Winchesters, as well as more traditional weapons, while GEORGE ARMSTRONG CUSTER's command was equipped with the Springfield carbine, which jammed at times during the battle. Throughout the 1870s and 1880s, however, the Ordnance Department continued to reject requests by such commanders as Colonel RANALD SLIDELL MACKENZIE to obtain repeating rifles for their troops in the aftermath of the Little Bighorn fiasco. The Ordnance Department rejected the Winchester because its range was one hundred yards less than that of the Springfield, and it had half the penetrating power of the Springfield.

The army did have access to a variety of cannon, which were used in many of the campaigns. In addition to the twelve-pounder mountain howitzer, a pre–Civil War weapon, the army began to use breech-loading, rifled steel cannon and Gatling guns. Of these, the Hotchkiss "mountain gun," a 1.65 inch, two-pounder rifled steel cannon was the most popular. It could be taken almost anywhere on its wheeled carriage and provided rapid, effective fire at ranges up to four thousand yards.

While the Gatling gun, with a rate of fire of 350 rounds per minute, appeared to offer advantages in the West, it had many problems. The range of the weapon was comparable only to that of the rifle, and it was difficult to tell where the bullets were hitting. The black-powder cartridges left a residue that often fouled the guns, and the rate of fire led to overheating. In addition, the piece was cumbersome in the field, and commanders often chose to leave it behind, as Custer did in the Little Bighorn campaign.

With army warehouses bulging in 1866, the uniforms and field equipment of the frontier soldier were Civil War surplus. The dark blue blouse and light blue trousers were trimmed with the color of the wearer's arm of service (red for artillery; yellow for cavalry; blue for infantry). The uniform was not well adapted to frontier service and, to the annoyance of the quartermaster general, was the source of constant complaint. The "Kossuth" hat—with its high-crown, turned-up brim, and feathers—was of little use and the kepi, derived from French models, was poorly made and often ill-fitting. The uniforms were often poorly cut and required extensive alterations by individual soldiers. Because of the cheap cloth used, the uniforms wore out quickly. Moreover, the single weight of uniform was ill-suited to the extremes of cold and heat that characterized the frontier. The stock of Civil War uniforms was not exhausted until about 1880, but when some sizes were in short supply, the army revised uniform regulations in 1872. The dress uniform, influenced by Prussian designs, was markedly changed. Cavalry and artillery soldiers wore a spiked helmet decorated with a large metal eagle and a horsehair plume of the color of the arm. Infantry soldiers wore shakos with blue plumes for officers and blue pompons for enlisted men. In 1881, the shakos were replaced with spiked helmets carrying white plumes. The dress uniforms, particularly for officers, were a vision of gold cords, tassels, epaulettes, and brass buttons, while the simple undress blouse had five buttons and falling collar. Although the army made improvements to the kepi, it still provided little protection from the heat and was difficult to wear. Other types were tried, but the service issues proved unsuitable, and almost any type of hat except the service issue was worn in the field. The uniforms worn when campaigning were characterized by variety rather than regularity. To ease the wear in the saddle, pants were lined with canvas or made of canvas or corduroy. Buckskin was the choice of the dandy. Evidence of rank, other than an occasional shoulder strap, was rare.

Although the army did experiment with some types of clothing and equipment designed for the heat of summer or the cold of winter, the soldiers improvised as necessary. Buffalo skins were the choice for winter use and had become standard by the 1870s. In 1880, cork helmets were approved for summer use but never replaced the straw hats soldiers purchased from stores. White cotton uniforms were issued in 1886 but never replaced the informal clothing that the army had found to be suitable for the frontier.

—*Patrick H. Butler, III*

SUGGESTED READING:

Butler, David F. *United States Firearms: The First Century, 1776–1775.* New York, 1971.

Flayderman, Norm. *Flayderman's Guide to Antique American Firearms . . . and Their Values.* Northfield, Ill., multiple editions.

Steffen, Randy. *The Horse Soldier, 1776–1943: The United States Cavalryman, His Uniforms, Arms, Accouterments, and Equipment.* 4 vols. Norman, Okla., 1977–1979.

Utley, Robert M. *Frontier Regulars: The United States Army and the Indian, 1866–1891.* New York, 1973.

SUPPLIES AND LOGISITCS

The efficiency of the frontier army depended upon logistics: the procuring and transporting of troops and supplies to areas of military activity. Expansion into the trans-Mississippi West following the UNITED STATES–MEXICAN WAR from 1846 to 1848 enormously increased logistical problems, due to the vast new areas open to settlement and exploitation. Previously, the army had established most of its frontier posts close to navigable waters to provide comparatively easy access to centers of supply. But the new military FORTS established after 1846 often were located in isolated and inhospitable environs. To supply these posts, the army had to use overland wagon trains or ocean- and river-going vessels.

Although the size of the frontier army varied during the four decades after the war with Mexico, problems of supply remained much the same. Because of the distances involved and the ruggedness of Western terrain and CLIMATE, outfitting this army proved to be an enormous drain on the country's finances. Military transportation costs rose from $130,000 in 1845 to more than $2 million in 1851. General WILLIAM TECUMSEH SHERMAN noted in 1869 that the cost for maintaining a soldier in areas such as Texas, New Mexico, Idaho, and Montana was "two and three times as great as on the Kansas and Nebraska frontier." Despite the army's vastly increased Western responsibilities, congressional leaders persistently called for reductions in military expenditures.

The army purchased clothing, blankets, camp equipage, and other quartermaster and commissary supplies in the East and dispatched them by land and water to interior depots and posts. Ocean-going vessels were chartered to transport troops and supplies via Cape Horn or the Isthmus of Panama to the Pacific Coast. San Francisco and FORT VANCOUVER on the Columbia River became major distribution points. In the 1860s, for example, the army shipped supplies destined for Arizona in privately owned vessels that sailed from San Francisco around Lower California to the mouth of the Colorado River. There, the supplies were reshipped on small steamers that ascended the river to Forts Yuma and Mojave. Wagon trains then carried the supplies overland to their final destination. In times of low water on the Colorado, however, that system broke down, and some garrisons ran dangerously short of supplies.

A sea and land route also served Texas, with ocean-going vessels depositing stores at Indianola and wagon trains hauling them overland to the depot at San Antonio or directly to the inland posts. In the north, steamers were used to supply posts on the upper Missouri, but low water and freezing temperatures limited the navigation season to about seven months of the year.

Costly mule- and oxen-drawn wagon trains hauled vast amounts of supplies overland from Fort Leavenworth, Kansas, to posts situated in the great arid regions between the Missouri River and the Pacific slope. The government soon learned that it was more efficient and economical to contract for freighting than to operate its own wagon trains. Thus, in the mid-1850s, the firm later known as RUSSELL, MAJORS AND WADDELL gained a short-lived monopoly of army freight west of the Missouri. During the Civil War, the Kansas firm of Irwin, Jackman and Company similarly monopolized the hauling of government supplies over the Santa Fe Trail to a supply depot at Fort Union, New Mexico, a distance of 728 miles. The company received between $1.30 and $1.50 per hundred pounds of freight per hundred miles, depending on the season of the year.

Freighting for the military, in fact, became big business, and competing firms scrambled for contracts. Brigadier General Montgomery C. Meigs, quartermaster general of the army, reported that for the fiscal year ending June 30, 1865, contractors carrying mili-

The acquisition of new lands following the United States–Mexican War complicated logistical problems for the U.S. Army in the West as it tried to supply an increasing number of isolated outposts. A camp of George Armstrong Custer's 1874 campaign into the Black Hills of the Dakota Territory suggests the difficulties in keeping an army on the move supplied with food, ammunition, and other necessities. *Courtesy National Archives.*

tary stores to Fort Union and the interior posts of New Mexico had received $1,439, 578—about a third of the total cost of maintaining troops in that territory. Profits in carrying army supplies were high, but so, too, were the risks involved. Freighters everywhere faced similar problems: long distances, primitive roads, uncertain weather, and the threat of Indian attacks. In 1868, Apaches attacked the wagon train of military contractors Pinckney R. Tully and ESTEBAN OCHOA, about twenty miles southeast of Tucson, Arizona; two men were killed, four were wounded, and thirty-eight mules were captured. Apaches again struck their train the following year, this time killing three men, wounding two, and capturing eighty mules. The firm's losses in the second attack amounted to about $12,000.

Storms, bad roads, floods, drought, and Indian scares could all delay contract trains en route to Western posts. When the posts experienced shortages, some officers demanded that the army operate its own transportation. In fact, the army maintained significant numbers of teams and wagons for routine post duties and to accompany troops on campaign. But both government and contract transportation proved inadequate during the Red River War of 1874 to 1875, and field commanders often were forced to break off pursuit when their supplies ran out.

When preparing for campaigns, commanders typically stockpiled supplies at the most advanced army posts and then created temporary supply camps further into the interior. Still, the supply trains accompanying the marching columns impeded their mobility and made it difficult to close with the enemy. Sometimes pack trains, instead of slow-moving wagon trains, were used for a quick strike. Yet forage (feed for animals) requirements also placed limits on the radius of their operations, and troops sometimes suffered when commanders pushed beyond those limits. General GEORGE CROOK's 1876 Bighorn and Yellowstone Expedition, for example, turned into a race for survival when supplies ran out; soldiers warded off starvation by eating their horses and pack mules.

To reduce transportation costs, the army tried to purchase supplies close to the Western forts, although initially the subsistence department had to rely on Eastern markets for the main articles in the soldier's ration: beef, pork, bacon, flour, beans, coffee, sugar, and salt. By providing both markets and protection, however, the army's presence soon stimulated Western settlement, and, in many areas, local producers came to supply most of the ration requirements.

Except for commissary, medical, and ordnance stores, the quartermaster's department purchased all other military supplies, including forage, fuel, clothing, camp and garrison equipage, horses, wagons, harnesses, tools, and so forth. Most of the clothing and equipment required at the Western posts was shipped in from the large Eastern army depots, but local residents often used resources close at hand, such as grama grass, mesquite roots, and adobes, to satisfy the army's need for forage, fuel, and construction materials.

The subsistence and quartermaster's departments procured supplies through the contract system in which they advertised for bids and awarded contracts to the lowest bidder. Most advertisements carried the statement that the army reserved the right to reject any bid deemed unsatisfactory. On occasion, purchasing agents rejected all bids as being too high and thereafter resorted to purchases on the open market. Many army officers, farmers, and ranchers, in fact, wanted to abolish the contract system altogether; they argued that the army could obtain supplies at a lower cost by purchasing directly from producers rather than through contractors. But the contract system prevailed, since government officials believed that open-market purchases increased opportunity for fraud and favoritism. Successful bidders were required to provide surety bonds, with cosignatures of at least two men of recognized means, making them equally responsible for satisfactory completion of the contract. If neither contractor nor bondsmen delivered the required commodities, the government purchased supplies on open market and charged the contractor the difference between the contract price and the open-market price.

Throughout the trans-Mississippi West, military spending stimulated local economies by encouraging farmers to raise more crops and cattle to satisfy the military market. Even though most contracts were held by merchants and large capitalists, small producers also reaped benefits by selling their surplus to contractors. When the army purchased on the open market, even the poorest citizen had opportunity to sell small amounts of forage and fuel to the quartermaster. Many residents found employment helping to build and maintain the frontier posts, especially following the Civil War, when the government often issued contracts for the construction of barracks and other buildings. Military expenditures, then, played a pivotal role in the Western economy and conditioned residents to rely on federal money for survival and expansion. Indeed, army contracts provided capitalists with funds to invest in mining, ranching, and other enterprises, thus speeding economic development and exploitation.

Reducing costs of supplying its Western posts remained an elusive goal for the army until RAILROADS provided the West with rapid and inexpensive transportation. The completion of transcontinental railroads, however, fundamentally changed subsistence and quartermaster operations, allowing for quicker and less expensive movement of troops and supplies. Ironically, cheaper commodities now would be purchased outside the frontier zone and sent to replace higher priced local products. But this new means of transportation ensured that perishable supplies would be shipped more frequently and arrive in better condition, an improvement that helped elevate the morale of the frontier soldier.

—*Darlis A. Miller*

SEE ALSO: Federal Government; Overland Freight

SUGGESTED READING:

Frazer, Robert W. *Forts and Supplies: The Role of the Army in the Economy of the Southwest, 1846–1861.* Albuquerque, N. Mex., 1983.

Huston, James A. *The Sinews of War: Army Logistics, 1775–1953.* Washington, D.C., 1966.

Miller, Darlis A. *Soldiers and Settlers: Military Supply in the Southwest, 1861–1885.* Albuquerque, N. Mex., 1989.

Risch, Erna. *Quartermaster Support of the Army: A History of the Corps, 1775–1939.* Washington, D.C., 1962.

Utley, Robert M. *Frontier Regulars: The United States Army and the Indian, 1866–1891.* New York, 1973.

WOMEN AND THE WESTERN ARMY

Although the nineteenth-century army normally conjures up images of men without women, the reality was quite different. Women always accompanied soldiers to Western outposts, some as wives of officers, others as laundresses and camp followers. Further, army personnel stationed in the American West came into contact with Native American women around the post or on the battlefield. Only the laundresses merited official recognition from the United States Army, in the form of regulations regarding their quarters, rations, and medical care. The other women's presence was tolerated but not officially sanctioned. Since most women had no official role, what we know about their lives stems mostly from personal accounts.

An 1802 law allowed four laundresses per one hundred men. Eventually that was altered to one washerwoman for every nineteen and a half men. Each company's captain retained the authority to hire laundresses, and the post's Council of Administration established the rate of pay. Subject to military law, laundresses could even be court-martialed. Most commonly, laundresses were married to noncommissioned officers or enlisted men. Those who came to the job as single women rarely remained unattached for long. Housing for the laundresses varied from dugouts and rude adobe or log huts to tents or even houses in more established posts. After railroads linked Western posts with the rest of the nation, housing improved considerably.

Housing for wives on army outposts was no better than the structures their husbands occupied. These crude quarters were homes to the officers' wives at Fort Rawlins, Wyoming. *Courtesy National Archives.*

If the women working at army posts were literate, they rarely had the time to write about their lives. Officers or their wives occasionally commented on the laundresses. Most often women who appeared in documents attracted attention because they were in trouble. Characterizations ranged from boisterous, bawdy, and rowdy to quiet, hard-working, and maternal. The most notorious laundress was Mrs. Nash, a washerwoman who had a series of husbands before her death. On her deathbed, Mrs. Nash pleaded with the women in attendance to bury her quickly. Thinking this a strange request, they ignored it. As the women prepared the body for interment, Mrs. Nash's secret was at last revealed: she was a man. Her last husband committed suicide soon after the revelation was made public. The vast majority of laundress-soldier marriages proved far more conventional.

In the late 1870s, congressional committees investigated cost cutting measures for the military and concluded the government could save money by eliminating laundresses. The matter provoked some discussion among officers about their usefulness. Some argued the washerwomen served no useful purpose but, rather, proved disruptive and troublesome. Others claimed the presence of the women and their children had a salutary, even refining influence on the enlisted men. In 1878, the army issued orders that no new laundresses would be enrolled, while those presently at work and married to soldiers could remain until their husbands' enlistment expired. While laundresses as an official institution gradually faded, soldiers' wives continued to take in laundry to supplement family income.

Although the government tried to discourage women on post by barring the enlistment of married men, recruiters sometimes ignored the regulation. Further, once in the military, some men found mates and, after obtaining permission from their commanding officer, married. Wives who could not work as laundresses often found other employment opportunities as cooks, maids, or servants of officers and their families. Since the government made no provision for these women, sometimes known as "camp followers," their housing was often very poor.

Prostitutes followed military camps, as well. They lived in nearby towns, on "hog ranches" just out of reach of the military reservation, or sometimes on posts. Authorities tolerated their presence and of course had no jurisdiction over those who plied their trade beyond the military reservation's boundary. Civilians often profited and even encouraged them, for along with PROSTITUTION came GAMBLING and whiskey selling—all lucrative activities for entrepreneurs.

Official accounts of prostitutes focused on the spread of venereal disease (it is noteworthy that reports limited commentary to disease among enlisted men and ignored its incidence among officers) and on the occasional breakdown in post order relating to problems with prostitutes. The women represented the ethnic diversity of the American West: Anglo, African American, Mexican, and Indian women all found employment as prostitutes catering to a military clientele. Since Victorian military people rarely wrote about sexual matters, it is difficult to assess the nature of these women's lives. Yet, more general studies on prostitution in the nineteenth century indicate it was of life of danger, drugs, and disease.

A huge social and economical gulf existed between prostitutes and army officers' wives. Like the prostitutes and other "camp followers," the officers' wives had no official status, but in joining their husbands at Western posts in order to keep marriages and families intact, they reinforced a "caste system" that placed officers and their families at the top of the social scale. Further, in 1866, General WILLIAM TECUMSEH SHERMAN encouraged officers' wives to accompany their husbands west in order to benefit from the healthful environment of a "newly opened country." To be sure, Sherman did not extend a similar invitation to prostitutes. Finally, all women linked to the military, regardless of status, shared the rigors and difficulties of Western travel and life. Yet officers' wives enjoyed the luxury of servants and strikers (soldiers assigned to domestic duty in an officer's home) to help them adjust to garrison existence. This kind of domestic help afforded officers' wives more leisure time to explore their surroundings on horseback; put on plays, theatricals, and balls for the post's enjoyment; and write letters and even books about their experiences in the Far West. As a result, officers' wives proved the best source of information concerning women in the frontier army, despite the fact that their view was a privileged one.

Elizabeth Custer is the most famous of these women. "Libbie" did not commence her writing until after GEORGE ARMSTRONG CUSTER's death on the Little Bighorn River in 1876. Vindicating her controversial husband, warding off his detractors, reinforcing an image of Custer as a "boy's hero," and earning a living all motivated Mrs. Custer's writing career. In recreating her life in the West, she emphasized its romantic qualities, yet her books also revealed some of life's strains, not the least of which was the possibility of widowhood. Other wives' accounts stressed different difficulties, including the travails of frequent moves,

Officers' wives enjoyed the luxury of servants and strikers, which afforded them some time for leisure activities. A group at Fort Keogh in Montana took time out for a skating party in 1890. *Courtesy National Archives.*

isolation of Western posts, and worry about children's health and education.

Indians too posed a concern for officers' wives, who initially feared the Native Americans they met. Having read or heard about captivity narratives, these Anglo, middle-class women assured their readers they preferred death to capture. None ever faced that choice. In time, some officers' wives put aside fiction-inspired fears and acknowledged Indian humanity, particularly that of children but occasionally that of adult men and women as well. Of course, outbreaks of hostilities between Indians and the army obscured such feelings, as the wives of officers' became preeminently concerned with their husbands' well-being. In moments of crisis, these women felt no hesitation to call for extermination of all Indians.

Indian women provoked commentary not only from officers' wives but also from their husbands. The Anglo women tended to emphasize the hardships Indian women faced as virtual "slaves and drudges." Officers occasionally repeated this stereotypical version of native women, but some emphasized the vitality and healthfulness of the Plains Indians' outdoor existence and urged white women to become more like native women. Some soldiers did more than admire Indian women from afar and engaged in relationships that ranged from the romantic to the sordid. On at least one occasion, in the aftermath of the Battle of the Washita, officers selected Cheyenne women captives as "spoils of war" for temporary mistresses. In other situations, Indian women apparently sought out liaisons with white men.

Women did not play a numerically significant role in the frontier army, yet their presence was important. Officers' wives and children provided a degree of domestic normality to isolated posts. Laundresses and enlisted men's wives who found work as cooks, servants, and maids in officers' households did the same while simultaneously providing essential services to the military community. Relations among the women were not always harmonious. Class differences as well as the inevitable conflicts of personalities in small, confined garrisons ensured some conflict. If not one happy family, however, women and men of the frontier army shared a good deal. In the face of civilian criticism, they forged a strong consensus about the value of their work and closed ranks in defense of the army's efforts to bring an end to the conquest of Indians—a national goal the vast majority of Americans embraced.

—*Sherry L. Smith*

SUGGESTED READING:

Coffman, Edward M. *The Old Army: A Portrait of the American Army in Peacetime, 1784–1898.* New York, 1986.

Knight, Oliver. *Life and Manners in the Frontier Army.* Norman, Okla., 1978.

Leckie, Shirley A. *Elizabeth Bacon Custer and the Making of a Myth.* Norman, Okla., 1993.

Leckie, William H., and Shirley A. Leckie. *Unlikely Warriors: General Benjamin H. Grierson and His Family.* Norman, Okla., 1984.

Myres, Sandra L. "Romance and Reality on the American Frontier: Views of Army Wives." *Western Historical Quarterly* 13 (1982): 409–427.

Smith, Sherry L. "A Window on Themselves: Perceptions of Indians by Military Officers and Their Wives." *New Mexico Historical Review* 64 (1989): 447–461.

Stallard, Patricia Y. *Glittering Misery: Dependents of the Indian Fighting Army.* Norman, Okla., 1992.

UNITED STATES ARMY CORPS OF ENGINEERS

Founded in 1802, the United States Army Corps of Engineers is the oldest of the federal agencies charged with developing an infrastructure for the nation. Its mandate includes construction projects, roads, surveys, and water-resource management. While always important in the West, in the nineteenth and early twentieth centuries, the corps was limited by jurisdictional disputes with other federal agencies as well as by its role in supporting exploration.

The early prominence of the Corps of Engineers stems from its unique position. In the early nineteenth century, the Army's academy at West Point offered the only training in engineering in the United States. As a result, the corps was an elite group, the only people in federal employ with the skills to undertake work such as road building, large-scale construction, and water-resource management, including dredging, clearing snags from rivers, surveying, and building piers and jetties.

Although the Corps of Engineers was responsible for the entire nation, the nature of much of its activity limited its role in the nineteenth-century West. Another entity carved from it in 1838, the CORPS OF TOPOGRAPHICAL ENGINEERS, played an important role in surveying the West until it was brought back into the Corps of Engineers during the Civil War. During that time, the Army Corps of Engineers remained in the background of Western exploration. Cases such as the attempt to clear the Little Colorado River from Austin, Texas, to the Gulf of Mexico in the early 1850s—a project that ended in failure—typified corps activities.

The corps played a more prominent role in the era of the great Western surveys that followed the Civil War. A new era, spurred by industrialization and the

Photographer Timothy H. O'Sullivan spent part of the 1860s accompanying the grand surveys of the West conducted by the United States Army Corps of Engineers. O'Sullivan photographed a glacier on one such expedition from 1868 to 1869. *Courtesy National Archives.*

increased need for specialized skill, had dawned for engineering. No longer were West Point graduates the only trained engineers; talented civilians such as CLARENCE KING learned engineering and applied it in the West. Sometimes the activities of the corps and those of civilians were fused; King's first major survey, the United States Geological and Geographical Survey of the Fortieth Parallel, was sponsored by the Corps of Engineers.

The King survey was a stunning success. Not only did it complete important work such as the mapping of a triangulation system across California, Nevada, Utah, and Wyoming, but King himself uncovered an effort to bilk investors by seeding remote Western land with uncut diamonds and other gems. With their extensive knowledge of the West, King and his surveyors uncovered the secret location where the diamonds had been "found," and what they saw there could not have occurred in nature. King became a hero as he exposed the fraud, known as the GREAT DIAMOND HOAX, and his actions helped the Corps of Engineers retain primacy in exploration against the claims of other federal agencies that sought to carry the mantle of lead exploration agency. These included the Department of the Interior, under whose auspices JOHN WESLEY POWELL carried out much of his activity throughout the late 1860s and 1870s. The work of FERDINAND VANDEVEER HAYDEN, another scientist-explorer attached to the Department of the Interior, accentuated an already competitive situation. To enhance its status, the Army Corps of Engineers turned to Lieutenant George Montague Wheeler.

Wheeler was the last of a breed, born a generation too late. He would have been more at home among the members of the Corps of Topographical Engineers before 1860, but by the time he graduated from West Point, it had been merged back into the Corps of Engineers. Yet Wheeler was able to fashion a place in exploration for himself; by 1873, he had become head of a survey of his own, the United States Geographical Surveys West of the 100th Meridian. With it, he was supposed to reclaim the honor of military science from civilian upstarts.

Wheeler's career was checkered. An avowed Indian-hater, he appears a cruel man who manipulated the press, only to find it turn against him. Although he recognized that the era of the pathfinders was ending, he persisted in that kind of endeavor. Between 1871 and 1879, Wheeler and his men mapped almost one-fourth of the region west of the 100th meridian, including 200 mining districts and 143 mountain ranges, but he ended his career in disgrace.

Wheeler's own conduct and the politics of the situation contributed to his demise. He went against the currents of his time and found himself pitted against the extremely influential Hayden. By 1874, "civilian science" had army science on the defensive. Although the Wheeler survey continued for five more years, its work was reminiscent of the great reconnaissance surveys of the pre–Civil War era. Out-of-date and anachronistic, Wheeler fell by the wayside as government science became consolidated in the new UNITED STATES GEOLOGICAL SURVEY, located in the Department of the Interior and headed by John Wesley Powell.

The end of a role for Army Corps of Engineers in exploration did not limit its effectiveness. As the West opened to Anglo-American settlement, the corps played an instrumental role in developing infrastructure. Although members of the corps, such as HIRAM MARTIN CHITTENDEN, advocated a federal role in the development of irrigation dams, the creation of the BUREAU OF RECLAMATION—itself an acquisitive and territorial agency—limited the role the corps could play in that area. The corps built roads and levees, dredged harbors and rivers, and generally supported activities of other federal agencies and the public.

One such notable instance of this role was during the World War II. The Corps of Engineers, through its Manhattan Engineering District, became the rubric under which the Los Alamos installation that developed the atomic bomb was cloaked. Not only did the corps build the roads to the isolated mesas that changed human history, it lent its name to the entire project. At the same time, the corps rushed the construction of the Alcan highway across Canada to Alaska, thus helping to avert a possible invasion. It is in this manner that the impact of the U.S. Army Corps of Engineers is most clear in the West: it is the agency through which necessary and, in some cases, unnecessary infrastructure develops.

—*Hal Rothman*

SEE ALSO: Exploration: United States Expeditions; Exploration and Science

SUGGESTED READING:
Goetzmann, William H. *Exploration and Empire: The Explorer and the Scientist in the Winning of the American West*. New York, 1966.

UNITED STATES BUREAU OF INDIAN AFFAIRS

SEE: Bureau of Indian Affairs

UNITED STATES BUREAU OF LAND MANAGEMENT

SEE: Bureau of Land Management

UNITED STATES BUREAU OF RECLAMATION

SEE: Bureau of Reclamation

UNITED STATES FOREST SERVICE

An agency in the Department of Agriculture, the United States Forest Service is responsible for managing almost 200 million acres of federally owned forests and grasslands. Throughout the nineteenth century, the Department of the Interior had jurisdiction over the public domain in the West. Federal LAND POLICY encouraged settlement, development, and exploitation. Timber barons, settlers, land speculators, and miners despised the few restrictions placed by the FEDERAL GOVERNMENT on development and often ignored or circumvented them. At the 1873 annual meeting of the American Association for the Advancement of Science, Franklin B. Hough, a physician, historian, and statistician, presented a paper that claimed timber supplies in the West were rapidly disappearing. He worked fever-

ishly throughout the 1870s to stop destructive practices and overcutting of forests by private loggers, particularly in Minnesota, Wisconsin, and Michigan. Largely as a result of his efforts, the Division of Forestry was created in the Department of Agriculture in 1881. Hough was named the chief of the division, an education and research agency without land-management responsibilities.

Hough's work, together with that of Bernhard Fernow, who became the first professional forester named chief of the division in 1886, kindled widespread fear of impending timber famines and ultimately led to corrective legislation. The General Revision Act of 1891 (or the FOREST RESERVE ACT OF 1891) granted the president authority to designate specific areas as forest reserves. On February 1, 1905, the Transfer Act shifted jurisdiction of the 63 million acres of forest reserves from the Department of the Interior to the Division of Forestry, which by that time was headed by Gifford PINCHOT, a professional forester. The division was renamed the United States Forest Service five months later. In 1907, the federal lands were renamed national forests—not reserves—a designation that reflected Pinchot's view that the lands were for use, not merely for preservation.

By 1990, the total acreage in the national forest system had risen to 191 million acres, including 22 million acres in Alaska and nearly 60 million acres east of the Mississippi purchased from private owners. In addition to managing the national forests, the United States Forest Service cooperated with the states to help

The United States Forest Service was established, in part, to prevent the disappearance of the nation's timber supply in the West. Loggers pictured here run a seemingly endless river of logs down a slough from the nineteenth-century Oregon forests. *Courtesy Oregon Historical Society.*

private landowners apply the techniques of good forest management on their lands. The service also conducted research to find better ways to manage and use natural resources. Policies of the service have evolved to reflect changing conditions and public attitudes. Two good examples of that evolution are FIRE protection and the policies that determine which, if any, forest resources would be given priority in management.

In the summer of 1910, a series of fires known as "The Big Blow Up" burned more than 5 million acres in the United States, including some 3 million acres in the northern Rockies alone. At that time, the service viewed fire as an unnatural and highly destructive force—an enemy to be conquered. Fire suppression became the moral equivalent of war. But because fire had been prevented for years, massive amounts of combustible fuel had built up in the national forests, and the longer fires were prevented, the greater the probability catastrophic fires would ultimately occur. In the 1970s, the service revised its policy by recognizing that fire is a natural and necessary part of forest growth and ecological succession. By 1990, fire, including those deliberately set by agency personnel, was an important tool of federal foresters.

The management policies of the service have always aimed at increasing the long-range output of forest commodities (timber, forage, and water). Conservationists, ranchers, timber companies, mill operators, small farmers, and other competing interests fought to establish priorities that favored one use or output over the others. People with particular interests in water and timber, for example, interpreted the Organic Administration Act of 1897 as establishing the principle of "dominant use," whereby priority was given to water and timber over other resources and uses of the forests. But legislation passed in the years before World War II made it clear that "multiple use"—including recreation, cattle and sheep grazing, maintenance of fish and wildlife habitat, protection of soil, water, environmental amenities, and ecological integrity—was to be the guiding principle. Nevertheless, the issue of priorities remained muddled, and timber management was emphasized.

The actual impact of the service's policies on timber harvests was of little significance before World War II, however, because there was very limited demand for timber from the national forests. After the war, increased construction activity led to increased demand for timber. While legislation such as the Multiple Use-Sustained Yield Act of 1960 reemphasized the mandate for multiple use and called for balanced forest management, increased timber harvesting emerged as the dominant objective of national forest management.

By 1970, the years of high timber harvests following World War II came under heavy fire. The public, led by environmentalists, revolted against clear cutting, a common practice that stripped all timber—not just the mature trees—from vast expanses in the national forests. The Wilderness Act (1964), the National Environmental Policy Act (1969), the Endangered Species Act (1973), and the National Forest Management Act (1976) further thwarted the United States Forest Service's emphasis on high timber harvests.

The service continued its timber program for twenty years after the onslaught of protest. But, in 1992, it attempted to adopt a new policy referred to as "new perspectives," "new forestry," "sustainable forestry," or "ecosystem-based forestry." While harvesting timber from the national forests was allowed under the new policy, timber and other consumptive uses became secondary to the primary purpose of preserving and enhancing the ecological stability, integrity, and biodiversity of the forests. Not surprisingly, the new policy was not popular with all forest users, including many within the service itself, and the debate continued throughout the 1990s as the United States Forest Service remained at the heart of federal policy in the American West.

—*Richard M. Alston*

SEE ALSO: Forestry; Multiple-Use Doctrine; Sustained Yield

SUGGESTED READING:
Frome, Michael. *The Forest Service.* Boulder, Colo., 1984.
Pinchot, Gifford. *Breaking New Ground.* New York, 1947.
Pyne, Stephen J. *Fire in America: A Cultural History of Wildland and Rural Fire.* Princeton, N.J., 1982.
Robinson, Glen O. *The Forest Service: A Study in Public Land Management.* Baltimore, 1975.
Steen, Harold K. *The U.S. Forest Service: A History.* Seattle, Wash., 1977.

UNITED STATES GEOLOGICAL SURVEY

In 1879, Congress established the United States Geological Survey (USGS) in order to consolidate the geological and geographical surveys then receiving government funds. Placed under the administration of the Department of the Interior, the USGS from its inception adhered to the highest standards of scientific research. Its directors, beginning with CLARENCE KING and followed by JOHN WESLEY POWELL, guided the survey with administrative skill, and over the years, the survey has been given more and more responsibility. Today, the USGS is in charge of determining radioactive age, conducting geothermal surveys, surveying by means of satellites, and predicting volcanic eruptions and earthquakes.

Initially, the USGS concerned itself with scientific investigations of the locations of precious and nonprecious minerals in the trans-Mississippi West. In the process, USGS scientists evolved theories on the origins of ore deposits and the probability of minerals in types of geologic structures. From its inception, the USGS released scientific papers, statistics, and annual reports.

King left the USGS after a year and was succeeded by Powell, who expanded the survey's activities into states east of the Mississippi. He also increased the USGS's topographical activities and encouraged research in paleontology. He inaugurated a survey of irrigable lands and reservoir sites and began stream measurements. These activities coincided with Powell's own concepts of how the lands of the arid regions should be dispensed with and put to use. Powell and the USGS came under heavy criticism when it became clear that enforcement of his policies meant withdrawing lands from sale to the public, closing land offices, and curtailing development. The irrigation survey was abandoned, and Powell resigned.

His successor, Charles Doolittle Walcott, pacified Congress by returning the USGS to its basic interests in geology, coal reserves, and mapping. Under Walcott, the USGS also surveyed the geological resources of Alaska.

In the twentieth century, the USGS manifested increased interest in the nation's petroleum reserves. The USGS aided other federal agencies as well as states in formulating methods of royalty payments, lease arrangements, and other matters associated with the allocation and management of minerals and water resources. During World War I and World War II, the survey identified sources of such rare but essential minerals as tungsten, bauxite, and molybdenum.

Although the USGS has been engaged in the practical aspects of science throughout its history, it has allotted more of its resources to pure research in recent years. The American public is most aware of USGS investigations of earthquakes and volcanoes and survey efforts to predict such occurrences with increasing accuracy.

—*Richard A. Bartlett*

SEE ALSO: *Report on the Lands of Arid Regions*

SUGGESTED READING:
Manning, Thomas A. *Government in Science: The U.S. Geological Survey, 1867–1894.* Lexington, Ky., 1967.
———. "United States Geological Survey (USGS)." In *Government Agencies.* Edited by Donald R. Whitnah. Westport, Conn., 1983.
Rabbitt, Mary C. *The United States Geological Survey, 1879–1989.* Reston, Va., 1989.

UNITED STATES INDIAN POLICY

Indian Treaties
Alan Axelrod

Reservations
Robert A. Trennert

Reform Movement
Charles Phillips

Civilization Programs
Henry E. Fritz

Twentieth-Century Developments
Peter Iverson

INDIAN TREATIES

All of the European powers that colonized parts of the New World concluded treaties with the Native American peoples. That the first four centuries of contact between Euro-Americans and Indians in America produced almost continual warfare indicates just how tragically ineffectual the treaties generally were. Treaties between whites and Indians were violated sooner or later, and usually sooner rather than later. Often the violations could be ascribed to white perfidy; colonial or federal governments sometimes entered into treaties in bad faith. More often, however, white negotiators did have what they at least believed to be good intentions and fully expected that their side would abide by the terms of the agreement. The problem was that neither colonial nor federal governments always had the means to enforce the compliance of the people they governed. The best-known example is the case of the Proclamation of 1763, by which the British Crown, through a treaty concluded at Easton, Pennsylvania, sought to establish a western limit to white settlement. The so-called Proclamation Line was immediately violated by westering settlers, whom colonial authorities were powerless to restrain. Indeed, efforts to enforce the line led to the discontent on the frontier that helped bring about the American Revolution. In the nineteenth century, United States–Indian treaties often proved just as difficult to enforce, as states, territories, individual military commanders, militia forces, or vaguely organized bands of settlers typically took matters into their own hands and did as they pleased. Perhaps even more notoriously, federal Indian policy was administered with scandalous inconsistency, incompetence, and corruption. Policy also shifted with changes in administration.

The failures typical of United States–Indian treaties also resulted from characteristics of Native American tribal organization, which was customarily loose and democratic to a degree that Euro-Americans would consider anarchy. So-called chiefs were seldom if ever truly analogous to sovereigns in the Euro-American sense, so that even when a particular chief or group of chiefs assented to a treaty, the decision was not necessarily binding on anyone else in the tribe. Moreover, tribes often splintered into "peace" factions and "war" factions, usually with the older men (those with whom colonial or federal authorities customarily treated) constituting the former, and the young warriors belonging to the latter. Frequently, government negotiators deliberately exploited the ambiguity of authority to their advantage. For example, ANDREW JACKSON's administration chose to deal exclusively with the "Treaty party" among the Cherokees in drafting the Treaty of New Echota, the instrument by which the U.S. government justified removing the entire Cherokee tribe to the Indian Territory. Jackson unilaterally declared the Treaty party's agreements binding on all Cherokees, even though this faction of the tribe was outnumbered seventeen to one by the "National party."

Probably more often, the ambiguity that doomed so many treaties was unintentional, the product of profound cultural differences and of a stubborn federal policy to treat with the Indians as if the tribes were sovereign foreign powers. It was an approach destined to fail.

In many cases, Euro-American treaty-makers and Native Americans probably also had very different understandings of the significance of the treaty ceremonies themselves. Some of these events were relatively casual occasions, which were solemnized by the presentation of gifts. Indian leaders often signed a treaty primarily to obtain the accompanying gifts, which were not the beads and trinkets of cliché and folklore but, more often, sorely needed and immensely valuable items, including guns, ammunition, food, and clothing. Later, federal authorities offered annuities, schools, homes, and the like. For the Indian signatories, such tangible goods frequently loomed far larger than their agreement to cede land or to move to a reservation.

If some ceremonies were friendly and characterized by an atmosphere of gift giving and good will, others were tense and coercive military occasions, presided over by large forces of armed and uniformed soldiers. The message of these ceremonies was quite clear: sign the treaty or suffer destruction. Under duress, Indian leaders sometimes assented with little or no intention of abiding by the terms of the treaties they signed.

Finally, treaties, like all aspects of Indian-white relations, were strongly affected by a variety of cultural differences that are as varied and difficult to define as they are essential. Perhaps the widest cultural gulf separating many Indian communities from Euro-Americans was differing concepts of ownership and property. Many Indian cultures did not embrace concepts of private property and exclusive ownership; that is, no one "owned" for eternity a particular parcel of land that he or she could sell anymore than anyone "owned" forever any other aspect of the natural world. True, a given tribe or group might claim the right to hunt or live in a certain territory and might well defend that right by force of arms, but most tribes were willing to make agreements allowing other tribes or individuals to hunt on "their" land. Such an agreement did not convey ownership of the land to the other party. For example, folklore has made much of the so-called sale of Manhattan to the Dutch for twenty-four dollars, calling it a great bargain. (Taking into account modern exchange rates, recent economists figure that sixty gulden worth of goods was probably closer to several thousands of dollars in value.) Indeed, it was a bargain—less so for the Dutch, however, than for the Wappinger Indians who made the sale. The Wappingers accepted the goods but did not believe that they had any more power to convey exclusive title to the land than they had power to convey the right to breathe the air. Elements of the natural world could neither be bought nor sold. Well into the nineteenth century, treaties persistently ignored this profound cultural point.

The Euro-Americans' failure to appreciate the significance of the cultural differences between them and the Indians with whom they made treaties was probably caused by more than unconscious ethnocentrism. Colonial authorities sought from treaties not merely peace with the Indians, nor merely to acquire Indian lands for the sake of settlement, but also to establish their own legitimacy as political entities as they pressed westward. Many nations and factions within nations laid claim to pieces of the New World, and one way to assert the precedence of one's claim over that of another was to demonstrate that one had acquired the land from those who owned it by "primitive right." Therefore, it became crucially important for colonists to purchase land or otherwise obtain cession of it from the Indians. The acquisition, of course, assumed that the Indians owned the land to begin with. It was not an assumption most Indians shared, but it was nevertheless a key point in virtually all treaties. The tradition of treaty making was, therefore, fundamentally and profoundly flawed from its inception.

Key treaties of early Western expansion

The following are typical of the documents that laid the foundations and established the traditions of United States–Indian treaties intended primarily to acquire land.

The Treaty with the Six Nations, October 22, 1784, was typical of the spate of treaties concluded directly after the American Revolution. Signatories were U.S. Commissioners plenipotentiary (a term typically borrowed from international diplomacy) and sachems of the Seneca, Mohawk, Onondaga, and Cayuga tribes (who also represented the Oneida and Tuscarora, the two other members of the Six Iroquois Nations). Peace was concluded by means of the treaty, together with an agreement for the mutual release of prisoners. A new boundary to the lands of the Six Nations was established, and the tribes ceded to the United States all claims to territory west of the new line. In exchange for the cession, the United States agreed "in the execution of [its] humane and liberal views" to "order goods to be delivered to the said Six Nations for their use and comfort."

The Treaty of Fort McIntosh, January 21, 1785, a post-Revolutionary treaty between the United States and the northwestern tribes (Wyandots, Delawares, Ojibwas, and Ottawas), exchanged goods for land and obligated the Indians to "acknowledge themselves and all their tribes to be under the protection of the United States and of no other sovereign whatsoever." Despite the fact that the Indians were empowered to "punish . . . as they please" any "citizen of the United States, or other person not being an Indian" who might attempt to settle on Indian land, the treaty proved so ineffective that it had to be augmented by the Treaty of Fort Harmar (January 9, 1789), which made more specific provisions for payment for lands ceded.

The Treaty of Portage des Sioux, July 19, 1815, signed with the Sioux, was typical of the treaties signed after the conclusion of the WAR OF 1812 with tribes who had supported the British. The principal objective was the establishment of peace and the renunciation of vengeance for "every injury or act of hostility committed by one or either of the contracting parties against the other" during the war. The Sioux also acknowledged "themselves and their tribe to be under the protection of the United States, and of no other power, nation, or sovereign, whatsoever."

The Treaty of Prairie du Chien, August 19, 1825, was an attempt by the federal government to settle boundary questions among the Sioux, Ojibwa (Chippewa), Sac (Sauk) and Fox (Mesquakie), Menominee, Iowa, Winnebago, and "a portion of" the Ottawa and Potawatomi tribes. Periodically, the United States concluded treaties attempting to fix intertribal boundaries and, thereby, preclude intertribal disputes. Settlers saw such violence as a chronic threat to their own safety as well as to the general peace of the frontier.

The Treaty with the Choctaw Indians, September 27, 1830, was the first of the removal treaties concluded pursuant to the Indian Removal Act of 1830. It provided for "perpetual friendship" and guaranteed protection for the Indians as well as the cession of "the entire country they own and possess, east of the Mississippi River" and the Choctaws' agreement to "move beyond the Mississippi River, early as practicable" to a reservation in the Indian Territory. The government agreed to make cash payments and annuities and to "extend to [the Choctaw] . . . facilities and comforts . . . in conveying them to their new homes." Article XIV of the treaty provided "each Choctaw head of a family desirous to remain and become a citizen of the States . . . a reservation of [640] acres" in the Indian Territory.

Treaty of New Echota, December 29, 1835, the most infamous of the removal treaties, governed the removal of the Cherokees from their Eastern homeland. After a majority of the tribe rejected previous proposals as unfair, the federal government ordered the full Cherokee council to negotiate at New Echota. Government officials unilaterally declared that those who failed to appear would be counted as having voted in favor of the treaty. Key tribal leaders of the antitreaty "National party" were arrested, and the tribal newspaper was suppressed. Only a small minority of the Cherokee council signed the treaty, and 80 percent of the tribe was represented on protest resolutions submitted to officials in Washington. The Senate, however, ratified the document, and President Andrew Jackson enforced it. Under its authority, the Cherokees, over a three-year period, were evicted from their homelands and sent marching on the TRAIL OF TEARS to the Indian Territory. Not only was the treaty fundamentally illegal, but the removal process was particularly cruel and ineptly administered. Of the roughly fifteen thousand herded along the Trail of Tears, at least four thousand perished from the effects of exposure, privation, and disease.

The treaty provided for a payment of $5 million for the ceded lands and relocation along the Arkansas, Grand, and Canadian rivers, with additional lands available if necessary. The removal itself would be financed by the federal government, which would also provide subsistence funds for a year after the removal. Removal was to be completed within two years of signing the treaty.

The Treaty of Fort Laramie, September 17, 1851, was one of the most significant documents attempting to secure safe passage for pioneers crossing the plains. It established formal relations between the United States and the Northern Plains tribes (the Sioux, Cheyenne, Arapaho, Crow, Assiniboin, Gros Ventre, and Arikara tribes), set boundaries for the various tribes, authorized the federal construction of roads and forts, and

William Tecumseh Sherman and commissioners counsel with Indian chiefs at Fort Laramie, Wyoming, about 1867 or 1868. *Courtesy National Archives.*

bound the Indians to make restitution to white travelers for any damages they might suffer due to Indian hostility. In return, the government provided annuities and bound itself "to protect the aforesaid Indian nations against the commission of all depredations by the people of the said United States."

The Treaty with the Creeks, June 14, 1866, is typical of those made with the Five Civilized Tribes after the CIVIL WAR. The Five Civilized Tribes (the Creeks, Choctaws, Chickasaws, Cherokees, and Seminoles), who had moved from the East and resettled in the Indian Territory, generally and collectively supported the cause of the Confederacy during the Civil War. The Treaty with the Creeks reinstated relations between the United States and the tribe and abolished slavery within the tribe, effecting the emancipation of all slaves held by the Creeks. The treaty also stipulated the tribe's cession of portions of its western lands in the Indian Territory to accommodate other Indian tribes and "freedmen" (primarily slaves emancipated by the treaty). An annuity was established to compensate the tribes for the cessions.

The Treaty of Fort Laramie, April 29, 1868, was one of the few treaties between the federal government and Indians that was negotiated from a position of Indian strength. In 1866, the U.S. Army had built three forts to protect the BOZEMAN TRAIL. Indians, primarily led by the Oglala Chief RED CLOUD, fought a vigorous campaign to prevent emigrants from passing along the trail. After more than a year of fighting, in which the army was repeatedly defeated or frustrated, the Treaty of Fort Laramie was concluded. It recognized Indian hunting rights in the Powder River area, closed the Bozeman Trail, withdrew the garrisons from the forts

established to protect the trail, and established a Sioux reservation west of the Missouri River (in the present-day state of South Dakota). While the treaty represents an Indian triumph, its major concession—the closing of the Bozeman Trail—was vitiated by the fact that the transcontinental railroad was nearing completion, and the Bozeman Trail was becoming, in effect, obsolete.

The abolition of treaty making

On March 3, 1871, the U.S. Congress recognized the ineffectiveness, injustice, and outright brutality of the treaty system. Yielding to a combination of pressure from humanitarian groups and responding to what it felt was the Senate's undue concentration of power over Indian affairs (the Senate had the constitutional authority to make treaties), the House of Representatives attached to the Indian appropriating bill a rider outlawing further treaty making with the Indians. The legislation, although momentous, was conveyed in the most obscure of riders to an appropriation for the Yankton Sioux:

> . . . For insurance and transportation of goods for the Yanktons, one thousand five hundred dollars: *Provided,* That hereafter no Indian nation or tribe within the territory of the United States shall be acknowledged or recognized as an independent nation, tribe, or power with whom the United States may contract by treaty: *Provided, further,* That nothing herein contained shall be construed to invalidate or impair the obligation of any treaty heretofore lawfully made and ratified with any such Indian nation or tribe . . .

With this act, no further treaties were made with the Indian tribes, and relations between the United States and the tribes became the province of the military and the BUREAU OF INDIAN AFFAIRS, which characteristically fought over jurisdiction and thereby exacerbated the inconsistency of U.S. Indian policy.

—*Alan Axelrod*

SEE ALSO: Medicine Lodge Treaty of 1867

SUGGESTED READING:
Axelrod, Alan. *Chronicle of the Indian Wars: From Colonial Times to Wounded Knee.* New York, 1993.
Coupler, Charles J., ed. *Indian Treaties, 1778–1883.* New York, 1972.
Lazarus, Edward. *Black Hills, White Justice: The Sioux Nation versus the United States, 1775 to Present.* New York, 1991.
Prucha, Francis Paul. *The Great Father: The United States Government and the American Indian.* Lincoln, Nebr., 1984.

RESERVATIONS

Reservations are federally owned trust lands set aside for the Indians' benefit. They were created during the latter half of the nineteenth century as temporary holding areas where the native population, under controlled conditions, could undergo forced "Americanization." With the failure of the government's assimilation program, reservations became a permanent feature of Indian life. Since the 1930s, these native lands have formed an important symbolic and political component of Indian nationalism. Slightly less than half the native population of the United States, exclusive of Alaskan Indians, lived on reservations during the 1980s.

Historical background

The earliest European settlers listed the "civilization" of the native population among their justifications for colonization. Colonial leaders, especially the clergy, saw conversion to Christianity as a first step in "saving" the Indians and quickly concluded that success rested in isolating potential converts. Segregated from their "savage" kinsmen and the distractions of wilderness life, the Indians might be instilled more easily with the values of European civilization. In theory, the adoption of Christianity, the English language, Euro-American dress, and other non-Indian habits would transform the indigenous population into refined individuals ultimately capable of assimilating into a more advanced society. By European standards, bringing civilization to the natives satisfied a moral obligation.

Early Indian reservations were established in Puritan New England between 1651 and 1674. Placed in charge of devout missionaries such as John Eliot, "praying Indians" lived in villages apart from other tribesmen. Supported by their own labor, residents lived according to European standards, with the expectation of eventually becoming landowning farmers. By 1675, as many as twenty-five hundred New England natives resided in praying towns. The outbreak of King Philip's War in 1675, however, wiped out much of the native population, destroyed Eliot's work, and put an end to the first reservations.

The notion of separate Indian reserves languished during the remainder of the colonial period. Colonial leaders lost interest, few natives could be persuaded to submit, and continual warfare created bitter resentments. As a consequence, native groups refused to abandon their traditional ways, and the Europeans possessed little ability to force compliance.

The United States government pledged to bring "the gift of civilization" to the Indian after the Revolutionary War but, for decades, did little more than offer limited financial support to missionary efforts. With the LOUISIANA PURCHASE in 1803, national leaders such as THOMAS JEFFERSON saw the moving of Eastern tribes west of the Mississippi River as a solution to the problem created by Indians living within American society. Separated from the white population on lands thought to be undesirable, the relocated tribes could live in peace until ready to integrate into mainstream life. This philosophy went into effect with ANDREW JACKSON's removal policy, as Eastern tribal groups were forcibly relocated between 1828 and 1846. Although some vague tribal boundaries were drawn in the new Indian Country, the removals, with a few exceptions, did not establish true reservations. Residents remained free to come and go, agents and teachers exerted little influence, and no comprehensive civilization program existed. Moreover, the powerful Western tribes remained completely independent.

Establishing the reservation system

American expansion during the 1840s dramatically altered Indian policy. Events like the CALIFORNIA GOLD RUSH quickly made it necessary for citizens to travel across the heart of the West, directly through lands relegated to the Indians. The old Indian Country became obsolete as tribesmen could no longer be pushed out of the way. As a result, in the years following 1846, the government established a reservation system, intended to facilitate Western expansion while at the same time offering the native population an alternative to ultimate extinction.

The reservation program required that all tribal groups, whether friendly or hostile, be confined to defined sanctuaries located away from the path of white activity. Because such confinement restricted traditional means of livelihood (such as buffalo hunting), policy-

Nez Percé Agency, Idaho, 1879. *Courtesy National Archives.*

Top: Sioux policemen on horseback lined up in front of the buildings of the Pine Ridge Agency, Dakota Territory, 1884. *Courtesy National Archives.*

Bottom: Round Valley Agency, office and sutler store in California, 1876. *Courtesy National Archives.*

makers decided to instruct the Indians in farming and all other aspects of Euro-American Christian civilization. A protective setting thus seemed well designed to foster native self-sufficiency while simultaneously controlling the more belligerent groups. The proposed reservations therefore met both practical and humanitarian goals: removing the Indian as an obstacle to American expansion while simultaneously providing for their eventual civilization. Implicit in this concept was an obligation for the federal government to assume full trust responsibility for these wards of the state. The cost to the Indians of this experiment in colonialism, not considered by the whites, included total submission to economic, religious, and social transformations. Not surprisingly, most native groups looked on reservations as concentration camps.

Implementation of the reservation policy began in the 1850s. In California, where the native population faced extermination, small reservations were established as early as 1852. Problems surfaced immediately: whites objected to giving decent land to Indians; the reserves were small and unsuited for farming; corruption within the Indian Bureau ran rampant; and Indian residents continued to perish. The initial program fared little better elsewhere. In 1855, for instance, without understanding the implications, Navajo leaders signed a treaty accepting defined boundaries. In that case, the entire affair came to little. The undefeated Navajos ignored the restrictions and the cost-conscious U.S. Senate refused to ratify the agreement. Oregon, Kansas, and other regions also witnessed the establishment of reservations, most with limited success.

The American CIVIL WAR disrupted Indian policy, increased incidents of Indian-white violence, and sped nationwide implementation of the reservation system. During the conflict, the army abandoned its role as frontier peacekeeper just as thousands of unruly miners and settlers flooded the Indian Country, setting off hostilities from the High Plains to the Southwest. These bloody conflicts took hundreds of lives and prompted demands that the government chastise the hostile tribes and implement more effective controls.

In New Mexico, General JAMES H. CARLETON determined to put an end to raiding by sending an army against the Navajos and forcing them onto a miserable reservation located on the Pecos River in eastern New Mexico. There the Navajos suffered from 1864 to 1868, attempting to farm the alkaline soil. The government admitted failure and returned them to a small reservation created in their old homeland. Most tribes did not fare as well. In Colorado, the Cheyennes and Arapahos were forced onto a reservation. When they failed to abide by the new arrangement and fought back, the Colorado militia responded with the massacre at Sand Creek in 1864 and forced the two tribes to accept an even less desirable location. Such wartime events reinforced a public attitude that favored military action to establish reservations and end the threat of hostilities.

The number of reservations increased dramatically after the Civil War. Undesirable lands in the Far West were set aside as reservations by treaty or administrative order, and tribes were either persuaded or forced to accept their new homes. By 1877, almost every surviving tribe lived in confinement—mostly on the northern Great Plains, in Oklahoma (the Indian Territory), the Southwest, and along the Pacific Coast. An estimated 280,000 natives were incarcerated on dozens of formal reservations, ranging in size from a few hundred to several million acres. In most instances, the assigned lands, generally parched and barren, barely resembled traditional tribal homelands. Some tribes suffered through several relocations. By 1886, when the Indian Wars ended, Native Americans had no choice but to submit to a paternalistic government's assimilation program.

The assimilation era

The reservations established between 1860 and 1880 focused on "Americanizing" the Indians. The Indian Bureau strove to "detribalize" and transform its wards. The intensive effort contained a number of elements. Missionaries, intent on obliterating native religions and converting the "heathen" to Christianity, invaded the reservations. Schools, both on and off the reservation, took children away from the tribal environment and taught them to speak and act as whites and to scorn anything of native origin. Government agents prohibited traditional forms of government and substituted themselves for tribal leaders. Indians living on reservations suffered intense pressure to become like their Euro-American neighbors—capitalistic farmers imbued with a strong work ethic and a passion for private property. One advocate of the program wrote that America needed to "get the Indian out of the blanket and into trousers—and trousers with pockets in them, and with a pocket that aches to be filled with dollars."

During the last three decades of the nineteenth century, white optimism remained strong, despite indications that Indians living on reservations were not assimilating. Some reformers attempted to make reservation life more acceptable. Between 1869 and 1876, for example, President Ulysses S. Grant instituted a program to curb corruption on the reservations by placing church groups in charge. Indian resistance to change, political opposition, and a lack of adequate financial support doomed the effort. Nevertheless, reformers agitated for legislation to implement the next step towards assimilation—abolishing the reservations in favor of private property. As a consequence, Congress passed the General Allotment Act, or DAWES ACT, in 1887. The law authorized the Indian Bureau to divide reservation lands into individual allotments and to make surplus lands available to land-hungry whites.

The government held allotted lands in trust for twenty-five years, at which time the landholder received title, became eligible for citizenship, and came under state or territorial jurisdiction. The Dawes Act thus provided a formula for the liquidation of reservations.

Despite Indian opposition to the loss of their lands, allotments rapidly followed, and millions of acres of reservation land were lost. Tribes, especially those on the northern Great Plains, in the Rockies, and along the Pacific Coast, lost an estimated 102 million acres between 1887 and 1934. In a particularly intense effort, government commissioners forced all sixty-seven Oklahoma tribes to disband their reservations between 1893 and 1905. Although the dispersal of tribal lands successfully reduced the number of reservations, it failed to improve Indian life. Allotment created instead additional poverty and disillusionment. Fraud ran rampant; the Indians exhibited little enthusiasm for the program; and most allotted lands fell into the possession of Euro-Americans. The native population became even more demoralized; those living on the remaining reservations felt lucky to have a homeland, no matter how desolate.

Twentieth century reservations

Reservations languished during the first three decades of the twentieth century as federal officials did little to protect Indian lands. Allotments continued, although at a diminished rate, and pressure to end tribalism persisted. During that period, reservation life proved especially dismal. Although the Indian residents failed to blend into the American mainstream, the government succeeded in obliterating much of traditional culture. Language skills, religious practices, ceremonies, arts and crafts, and native government disappeared under the heavy government hand. The reservation population was left frustrated and angry. Few reservations were self-sufficient, poverty reigned, and the government appeared to have forgotten the Indians. Bitter at their shoddy treatment, many tribes withdrew from contact with the outside. Even where natural resources such as oil and gas existed, the profits ended up elsewhere. A blight on the landscape, reservations indeed embarrassed the public and dehumanized the native people.

During the 1920s, a reform movement led by John Collier argued that traditional Indian culture and society must be preserved. In 1928, the Meriam Report testified to the deplorable conditions on reservations and served to document the failure of the assimilation program. When Collier became commissioner of Indian affairs in 1933, he advocated a New Deal for the Indians, including the retention of traditional culture and an end to allotments. Consequently, the Indian

Reorganization Act (1934) halted the dismantling of reservations, by then only about one-third of their original area. The government's change in direction marked the adoption of a philosophy that reservation lands formed an important part of the native heritage and must be preserved. Protection of the land-based tribal estate as well as other New Deal reforms gave new life to Indian nationalism and spirit.

Since 1940, the amount of reservation land has increased, and reservations have become bastions of native culture. Nevertheless, native leaders continued to defend their lands from elements in American society that want to break up the reservations. The most serious threat came during the termination era of the 1950s. Arguing that New Deal reforms produced a permanent group of second-class citizens and that reservations must be abolished in order to free the native population from oppression and wardship, Congress adopted in 1952 a scheme to terminate federal services, divide reservation lands among the residents, and encourage relocation to urban areas. Although a few small reservations actually disappeared, Indian groups effectively protested the loss of tribal lands and their special status in American society. By 1960, the termination program had run its course. The Indians' success in defeating the program spurred a new commitment to the preservation of tribal lands as the basis of cultural survival.

Modern reservations are far different from their nineteenth-century predecessors. Although remaining under federal control, most have a democratic form of government; capitalize on natural resources such as gas and coal; offer their people health, educational, and social services; and encourage tourism. Because of the trust status, the lands remain free from state control and some taxation. Nonetheless, unemployment remains high, health problems continue, and alcoholism and suicide take a toll. In 1980, some 270 Indian reservations existed in the United States. They ranged in size from a few acres to thousands of square miles. The Navajo reservation, for example, occupies more than 14 million acres in the Southwest and provides homes for better than 160,000 individuals. Larger in land area than several states, the Navajo Nation offers a place of refuge where ceremonial life survives in a modernized community with its own police, courts, government, sophisticated business practices, and well-educated managers. As a consequence, as on many other reservations, the resident population is able to use the benefits of the modern world without losing its traditional identity.

Since World War II, Indian reservations have formed the center of Indian spirit. Tribes have demanded, and received, more control over their own lands. Although economic conditions seldom keep pace with the rest of the nation and severe poverty remains, reservations are the Indian homeland. With tribal self-determination advancing, there is little danger that reservations will be abolished. They are a permanent and vital feature of American diversity and are guarded zealously by tribal leaders.

—*Robert A. Trennert*

SEE ALSO: Indian Schools; Missions; Native American Culture; Navajo Stock-Reduction Program

SUGGESTED READING:
Castile, George P., and Robert L. Bee, eds. *State and Reservation: New Perspectives on Federal Indian Policy.* Tucson, Ariz., 1992.
Fixico, Donald L. *Termination and Relocation: Federal Indian Policy, 1945–1960.* Albuquerque, N. Mex., 1986.
McDonnell, Janet A. *The Dispossession of the American Indian, 1887–1934.* Bloomington, Ind., 1991.
Philip, Kenneth. *John Collier's Crusade for Indian Reform, 1920–1954.* Tucson, Ariz., 1977.
Prucha, Francis P. *American Indian Policy in Crisis: Christian Reformers and the Indian, 1865–1900.* Norman, Okla., 1976.
———.*The Great Father: The United States Government and the American Indians.* 2 vols. Lincoln, Nebr., 1984.
———. *The Indian in American Society: From the Revolutionary War to the Present.* Berkeley, Calif., 1985.
Trennert, Robert A. *Alternative to Extinction: Federal Indian Policy and the Beginnings of the Reservation System, 1846–51.* Philadelphia, 1975.
Utley, Robert M. *The Indian Frontier of the American West, 1846–1890.* Albuquerque, N. Mex., 1984.

REFORM MOVEMENT

The sense of an impending crisis in Indian affairs began to grow after the 1840s, when national expansion began to undercut earlier official policies that had called for the Indians to be isolated from white "civilization" out in the American West. After the CIVIL WAR, those seeking a reform to outdated policies and political corruption in the government agencies that dealt with Native Americans agreed that the treatment of Indians needed to be better, fairer, and more effective, although they argued over some finer points. Some thought immediate citizenship should be the goal; some argued that assimilation should come first, that the Indians needed to be "civilized"—that is, made into white farmers—before they could be enfranchised. Reformers also disagreed as to the timetable, with some taking an evolutionary approach and arguing that, first, the Indians should be counseled to develop toward the higher civilization of the whites in stages, and with others—especially in the military—arguing that they

Helen Hunt Jackson wrote *A Century of Dishonor* in response to the forced removal of the Ponca Indians from northeastern Nebraska to the Indian Territory. Her work brought the "Indian problem" to national attention and fueled the cause of reform. *Courtesy Library of Congress.*

needed to be whipped into submission and be "compelled to civilize." Some advised keeping the Indians apart from white society on reservations, where they could be slowly trained in the arts of civilizations; others—and their numbers were growing—argued that only when the reservations were subdivided and the Indians made individual property owners and fully incorporated in American society would there be progress toward solving the Indian "problem."

All reformers agreed that something had to be done to restore the integrity of the Indian Service, which its critics claimed was a sink of corruption in the wake of the scandals and rumors of scandals during the 1860s. Civilian reformers and army officers alike, regardless of their differences otherwise, assumed the existence, within the BUREAU OF INDIAN AFFAIRS, of an "Indian Ring" that robbed both the U.S. Treasury and the Indians blind. If nothing else, effective reform, they insisted, meant an end to the spoils system connected with official dealings with the Indians. In 1865, Congress appointed a special joint committee, headed by Senator James R. Doolittle of Wisconsin, to look into

reform; the committee spent time conducting investigations and compiling evidence but made little in the way of innovative recommendations. In fact, the 1860s and 1870s were times of confusion and false starts. Gradually, those reformers who called for allotment of Indian lands in severalty—giving individual tribal members fee-simple title to pieces of land—won over others. Allotment was the only hope of solving the problem, since it would lead, the reformers claimed, to citizenship and full assimilation.

Then in 1871, President Ulysses S. Grant signed into law an act that changed the way the government had dealt with Indians since the beginning of the republic. The U.S. House of Representatives, mainly because it resented footing the bill for all the new Indian treaties ratified by the Senate after the Civil War, had decided to do away with the treaty system altogether. Henceforth, Indians would no longer be considered members of sovereign nations, foreigners whose rights were protected by treaty, but members of dependent domestic nations, noncitizen wards of the federal government. In many ways, the new definition merely recognized the reality of the Indians' situation represented by the program for Indian "improvement" that Grant had initiated upon taking office in 1869. Grant's policy included elements of reform: it sought to isolate Indians on reservations not only to pacify them, but to concentrate them in locations where they could be trained in the ways of white civilization, with an eye toward eventual assimilation into American society at large.

Grant's policy appeased the reformers to a degree, especially as his administration cleaned up some of the corruption associated with the use of Indian agencies as a vehicle of congressional patronage. But the battle for control over Indian policy between the army and the philanthropists, brought into the Indian Bureau under Grant's "Quaker Policy," exacerbated the confusion and cross-purposes that had long plagued dealings with the Indians. Under Grant's policy, for administrative purposes, Indians fell into two categories: reservation Indians, "managed" by civilians, and hostile Indians, "controlled" by the military. That this was hardly a long-term solution was evident, but even its supposed short-term benefits fell out of favor when Francis A. Walker—a vocal Indian policy critic who based his authority on a short stint as commissioner of Indian affairs in the early 1870s—began calling for "removal" of all Indian tribes in the West to large reservations and for their "separation and seclusion" there "for the good of both races." To the reformers' ears, this sounded suspiciously like the shameful treatment of the Indian tribes east of the Mississippi back in the 1820s and 1830s. Mistreatment and bureaucratic blundering in the handling of both the "hostile" Cheyenne and the "peaceful" Poncas under Walker's policies led to an uproar among reformers, especially in Boston, and to federal promises to cease removing Indian tribes against their will.

For the reformers, the lessons of Grant's failed reservation policies were clear. Only when the Indians enjoyed the rights of citizenship, owned their own land, and held impeccable titles would they have any real protection against the abuses of trespass and usurpation of tribal reservation lands. Reform organizations such as the WOMEN'S NATIONAL INDIAN ASSOCIATION in Philadelphia, the Boston Indian Citizenship Committee, and especially the INDIAN RIGHTS ASSOCIATION sprang up in the late 1870s and the 1880s, committed to allotment and assimilation. To combat public apathy, always the most difficult hurdle for the Indian policy reformers, loud protests were organized to alert Congress to the need for comprehensive reform. A young Omaha woman named Bright Eyes (SUSETTE LAFLESCHE TIBBLES), an eloquent Ponca chief named Standing Bear, and a Paiute spokeswoman SARAH WINNEMUCCA were dragged into the public arena and egged on by a carefully orchestrated propaganda campaign. "Agitate! Agitate!" cried a Boston minister. "On the Indian question, Congress will go no further than it is forced to go by public opinion." Author George Monneypenny came out in 1880 with a book called *Our Indian Wards,* which catalogued historical abuses against the Native Americans and argued against demands that the Bureau of Indian Affairs be transferred back to the War Department. Then in 1881, HELEN HUNT JACKSON published her scathing indictment of American Indian policy, *A Century of Dishonor,* which remains, according to Brian Dippie, "a classic of muckraking polemic." An awakened nation grew indignant, and the reform movement was in full swing.

For the reformers, all reservations were, at best, necessary evils and temporary expedients. No law kept settlers from grabbing land on the borders of reservations or from taking over tracts that suddenly proved attractive because gold or oil had been discovered there. Safety for the quarter-million or so Native Americans in a nation of fifty million people could only be had "if the smaller people flow in the current of the life and the ways of the larger." The Indians would have to assimilate, said the reformers, and the way to get them to do so was to break up the reservations into individual allotments. When each Indian owned his own parcel of land "in fee simple," then his title to that land would be valid even to the white man and, more importantly, in the white man's court. Another beauty of allotment, as far as the reformers were concerned, was that it promised to accommodate both the hu-

manitarians in the East and the hard-nosed Westerners because, on the one hand, it would encourage the Indians to take up agriculture and become "civilized" (which meant that they could be welcomed as new citizens) and, on the other, it would break up and redistribute the large stretches of tribal holdings coveted by Westerners. From the beginning, those who wanted to subdivide the land made this clear to potential settlers: only so much acreage would go to each Indian family. What remained after allotment—in most cases, a huge portion—would be "opened" for white settlement. The reformers were interested in making individual Indians not into major real-estate barons but into modest homesteading citizens.

For that reason, Westerners, who had in the past been resentful of the influence of Eastern philanthropists and hostile to reform, warmed to the idea and the opportunities it promised. For that reason, too, the Indians themselves resisted the notion of allotment and the idea of becoming "civilized"—that is, hard-scrabble farmers in an arid land unsuited, as many homesteaders had discovered, to self-sufficient yeomanry. The 1887 General Allotment Act, also known as the DAWES ACT or the Dawes Severalty Act, was only the first step in the allotment-assimilation-citizenship scheme of the reformers, and it was followed by other laws that relentlessly accelerated the allotment process. The Indians tried to fight back. Kiowa Chief LONE WOLF took their case all the way to the U.S. Supreme Court by arguing that former treaty agreements made the allotment system illegal. In 1903, the court held in *LONE WOLF V. HITCHCOCK,* basically, that the government was under no obligation to continue honoring treaties that subsequent laws had made obsolete. After 1906, when the BURKE ACT gave the secretary of the interior the discretionary powers to shorten the twenty-five-year trust period during which, under the Dawes Act, Indian lands were inalienable, Secretary Francis E. Leupp gradually sped up the rate at which patents in fee simple were granted to "competent" Indians, often meaning any Indian who had attended one of the new Progressive boarding schools aimed at "civilizing" Indian children by alienating them from their parents and from tribal culture.

The results were sobering enough: in three years, 60 percent of the Indians receiving patents had been dispossessed of all their land and all their money. Between 1917 and 1921, when the former Iowa lawyer and Texas stock-raiser Cato Sells was commissioner of Indian affairs, the bureau urged every adult Indian with less than one-half native blood to assume full control of his property as soon as the law allowed. Sells immediately gave a fee patent to every Indian who had more than one-half native blood and whom he found to be "competent." Sells issued nearly eleven thousand such fees during his tenure and was proud of it, but his successor pointed out that more than two-thirds of the Indians who had received from Sells clear title to their allotments had been, in large measure, dispossessed. "Instead of land," says Dippie, "they owned Fords—and they would not own them for long." The Coeur d'Alene Indians came up with their own definition of competency: "The only competent Indian was the one who refused to accept a fee patent."

In many ways, the reform movement was part of the larger PROGRESSIVISM that swept the country at the end of the nineteenth century and the beginning of the twentieth century, and as such, it showed all the earmarks of Progressive upper- and middle-class reform. The Indians were not the only ones the Progressives arrogantly set out to homogenize and standardize; AMERICANIZATION PROGRAMS aimed at immigrant populations flourished during the same period. But for the Indians, who still had lands to take and who still lived in their homeland, however attenuated, acculturation—as a number of Native American and other scholars have pointed out—was more deculturation. As Senator HENRY M. TELLER, a Western critic of the reform movement and no friend of the Indian, charged in 1881, the assimilationists were attempting to "utterly annihilate" a people in the name of benevolence.

— *Charles Phillips*

SEE ALSO: Grant's Peace Policy; Indian Schools; Literature; Native American Literature; Missions; Native American Cultures: Acculturation

SUGGESTED READING:
Dippie, Brian W. *The Vanishing American: White Attitudes and U.S. Indian Policy.* Lawrence, Kans., 1982.
Milner, Clyde. *With Good Intentions: Quaker Work among the Pawnees, Otos, and Omahas in the 1870s.* Lincoln, Nebr., 1982.
Prucha, Francis Paul. *American Indian Policy in Crisis: Christian Reformers and the Indians, 1865–1900.* Norman, Okla., 1976.
———. *The Great Father: The United States Government and the American Indian.* Lincoln, Nebr., 1984.

CIVILIZATION PROGRAMS

The issue of whether the United States government should pursue a policy to incorporate Native Americans into the body politic of the American Republic became critical following the CIVIL WAR. Federal tax dollars had been appropriated for Indian education since 1819, and the money had been spent on mission schools, which operated largely among the Five Civilized Tribes of the southeastern United States and, af-

Nineteenth-century reformers believed that the Indians' only hope was in making themselves over into the white man's image by becoming farmers working their own little plots of land. A Navajo cornfield and hogan near Holbrook, Arizona, was something of what the reformers had in mind. Photograph by F. A. Ames, 1889. *Courtesy National Archives.*

ter forced removal, in the eastern Indian Territory. ANDREW JACKSON had urged missionaries to prepare Native Americans to become citizens of the Republic when he advocated their removal to the Indian Territory in the 1830s. By the late 1860s, it became clear that the government had to choose between assimilation and a war of extermination. Having just concluded a war to save the Union, the government could not afford to maintain a military establishment large enough to fight the Indians throughout the Great Plains where white settlers were rapidly overrunning the lands of the indigenous population.

The Board of Indian Commissioners, created by Congress on April 10, 1869, consisted of ten philanthropists who advocated educating young Native Americans and breaking up reservations into individually held homesteads. Indeed, the essence of the DAWES ACT of February 8, 1887, was found in the board's first annual report, which stated that the Indians "should be taught . . . the advantage of individual ownership of property, and should be given land in severalty, . . . and . . . the titles should be inalienable from the family of the holder for at least two or three generations." Because of public opposition, however, Congress was unprepared to draft a program for the civilization and assimilation of Native Americans in the 1860s and 1870s.

Moreover, before such a policy could be formulated, it was necessary to arrive at a compromise between two schools of thought about Indian civilization and assimilation. One of them was represented by General WILLIAM TECUMSEH SHERMAN, who thought that the War Department should take charge of Indian

To help Native Americans become more like white people, Indian children were sent away to schools to overcome the influence of families and tribes. At the schools, students wore uniforms, lived in a militarylike regime, and learned vocational skills. Top: The Phoenix Indian School conducted art class for its students. Photograph by Messinger, 1900. *Courtesy National Archives.* Left: The Carlisle Indian School Band poses on the steps of a school building, 1915. Photograph by Gustave Hensel. *Courtesy National Archives.*

affairs on the grounds that force must be used to subdue the Native Americans before they could be educated in the ways of the English-speaking white people. Commissioner of Indian Affairs Nathaniel G. Taylor represented the humanitarian school, whose proponents wanted to keep Indian affairs under the jurisdiction of the Department of the Interior while coaxing the Native Americans onto reservations and sending Christian teachers to prepare them for life in Anglo-American society. In 1870, the Board of Indian Commissioners proposed a compromise, which became known as GRANT'S PEACE POLICY. In essence the military was given jurisdiction over Indians who chose to

remain outside of reservations, while the churches of the United States assumed responsibility for naming Indian agents and took control of education programs at agencies.

By 1877, nearly all of the tribes of the southern and northern Great Plains had been rendered incapable of resisting the military forces of the United States. The Apaches of the American Southwest were an exception, and some of them would not be brought permanently to reservations until 1886.

As the wars for the subjugation of the indigenous population came to a close in the late 1870s, public opinion shifted in favor of a legislated civilization program. Several reform organizations, founded between 1879 and 1882, were instrumental in bringing about the shift. The most important of these were the

WOMEN'S NATIONAL INDIAN ASSOCIATION and the INDIAN RIGHTS ASSOCIATION. A wave of reform activity swept the Eastern seaboard. Much of the new interest in Indian affairs was sparked by the forced removal of the Ponca Indians from northeastern Nebraska to the Indian Territory in 1876 and the attempt of Chief Standing Bear, with about thirty followers, to return to his old reservation between the Niobrara and Missouri rivers. In 1879, Standing Bear was arrested at Omaha by General GEORGE CROOK, who incarcerated him and his entourage in the federal fort. There, an editorial writer for the *Omaha Herald,* Thomas H. Tibbles, took up the Ponca Indians' cause and got the United States District Court to hear their case. Judge ELMER SCIPIO DUNDY decided that General Crook lacked the authority to return them to the Indian Territory and that Standing Bear and his followers were wrongfully held and must be released. Tibbles then took Standing Bear and Susette LaFlesche, the daughter of an Omaha chief, on a tour of the Eastern seaboard where they promoted the reform of United States' Indian policy. Publicity concerning the plight of the Poncas also inspired HELEN HUNT JACKSON to write *A Century of Dishonor,* published in 1881 with a forward by Episcopal Bishop Henry B. Whipple of Minnesota. Whipple advocated making Indians over in the white man's image by compelling them to become self-supporting through agriculture. In 1883, advocates of reform began to meet annually at Lake Mohonk in upper New York State where a member of the Board of Indian Commissioners, Albert K. Smiley, owned and operated a resort hotel.

The assimilation or civilization program that took form in the 1880s had three parts. The first part was breaking up reservations by the process of land allotment. The theory was that reservations would disappear as Native Americans became owners of real estate held under individual titles rather than in common. Native Americans were supposed to learn how to farm and thus become self-supporting, making it unnecessary for Congress to make annual appropriations to feed, clothe, and shelter them.

The second part of the civilization program was academic and vocational education. The industrial arts of blacksmithing, harness repair, and carpentry together with farming techniques were emphasized in educating young Indian males; likewise young females were taught skills associated with homemaking.

The third part of the assimilation program was law and order on the reservations. An important step in this direction was taken with the passage in 1878 of the Indian police bill, which grew out of the need for a constabulary on reservations where the army lacked jurisdiction. Indian police forces existed on all reservations by the early 1880s, and their presence was in-

valuable to the agents who were responsible for seeing that young Native Americans attended day or boarding schools. The police forces were also the eyes and ears of the agents who were charged with quieting disturbances and with maintaining a semblance of decorum.

The civilization program that took shape by the 1880s should be viewed in the context of forced assimilation. CARL SCHURZ, secretary of the interior under President Rutherford B. Hayes, remarked: "We must not expect them . . . to evolve out of their own consciousness what is best for their salvation. We must in a great measure do the necessary thinking for them, and then in the most humane way possible induce them to accept our conclusions." The Lake Mohonk reformers agreed with Schurz. The civilization program forged at Lake Mohonk reflected the ethnocentric values of mainstream Anglo-American culture, which placed no value on preserving the cultural traits of the indigenous population.

Law and order on the reservations was established by creating Courts of Indian Offenses in 1883 and by passage of the Major Crimes Act in 1885. The Courts of Indian Offenses not only dealt with civil disputes and misdemeanors but also prohibited practices associated with cultures of the indigenous population. Rules for these courts adopted in 1892 prohibited Sun Dances, Scalp Dances, and War Dances and prescribed the withholding of rations and imprisonment for up to ten days as an appropriate punishment for a first offense. Plural or polygamous marriages were forbidden and were punishable by fines and hard labor for

The Courts of Indian Offenses prohibited some traditional Indian dances and punished the transgressors. Shoshone Indians at Fort Washakie, Wyoming, danced for spectators in 1892. *Courtesy National Archives.*

twenty to sixty days. Distribution and drinking of intoxicants, cohabitation outside of marriage, destroying property of other Indians, and influencing children not to attend schools were all offenses subject to the jurisdiction of the courts.

The Major Crimes Act of 1885 was an emergency measure passed to give federal courts jurisdiction over specific crimes committed by Indians against Indians on and off reservations within the territories of the United States. If the crimes were committed within states, they were under the jurisdiction of federal or state courts. The crimes specified were murder, manslaughter, rape, assault with intent to kill, arson, burglary, and larceny.

The allotment of reservation lands in individual homesteads began with treaties in 1854. Since the making of treaties was ended in 1871, it became clear that general legislation was necessary. On February 8, 1887, Congress passed the Dawes Act. According to the law, named for HENRY LAURENS DAWES, chairman of the Senate Indian Committee, the president of the United States could decide when any given tribe was ready for the allotment of their reservation lands in severalty. Each adult Indian on such a reservation was to have four years to select an allotment or have one

selected in his or her behalf. Heads of families could select allotments for their children, and no provision was made for children born after allotment rolls were closed. Heads of families were to receive 160 acres, and single adults over eighteen years of age were to receive 80 acres. Children under eighteen were entitled to 40 acres unless they were orphans, in which case they received 80 acres. If the reservation lands were suited to grazing rather than farming, the size of the allotment was doubled in all categories. Citizenship was conferred upon allotees when the government issued trust patents, which were protected under federal guardianship for twenty-five years. Within that time span, it was expected that allotees would learn to manage their own affairs and become eligible for a fee-simple patent. Thus citizenship was linked to a vested interest in land, but those Indians who separated themselves from a tribal relationship and lived in the manner of white people became citizens immediately without adversely affecting their rights to tribal property. The law was amended in 1891 to provide for allotments of 80 acres to all Indians on eligible reservations regardless of their age or marital status. The size of these allotments was to be doubled in the case of land suitable for grazing rather than farming. A further amendment in 1910 reduced the size of allotments to 40 acres if the land was irrigated.

In October 1889, Commissioner of Indian Affairs Thomas J. Morgan presented a detailed plan for a national system of Indian schools to the Lake Mohonk Conference. Morgan was dissatisfied with the heavy reliance upon Christian denominations for Indian education and was particularly upset that the Bureau of Catholic Indian Missions had managed to corner the largest share of the annual appropriations for school contracts. Indicative of Morgan's ethnocentric mindset was his emphasis upon teaching patriotism in the government schools. Young Native Americans were to revere the American flag, sing patriotic songs, and celebrate all national holidays.

That policy led to the tragic massacre of BIG FOOT's band of Minneconjou Lakota in December 1890. The Lakota had adopted the GHOST DANCE religion and believed that the dances would help bring about the disappearance of the white race and the return of abundant game to-

In reaction to the new reforms imposed upon them, some Sioux Indians led by Big Foot embraced the Ghost Dance as a means of making the white race disappear. When troops of the Seventh Cavalry tried to disarm Big Foot's followers, their actions precipitated the Wounded Knee Massacre in 1890. Big Foot, one of the casualties, lies frozen on the snow-covered battlefield where he died. *Courtesy National Archives.*

gether with their traditional way of life. Contrary to the prophet WOVOKA's teaching and the beliefs of Ghost Dancers elsewhere, the Lakota warriors also believed that wearing ghost shirts would protect them from white soldiers' bullets. Thus the stage was set for the WOUNDED KNEE MASSACRE where Colonel James W. Forsyth in command of the Seventh Cavalry attempted to disarm Big Foot's followers. Big Foot and many of his comrades along with numerous women and children were slaughtered, some as they fled toward safety in nearby ravines. The massacre was the last gasp of Indian resistance to United States authority.

The power of Congress to legislate in behalf of Indians even to the extent of abrogating treaty obligations was upheld in the case of LONE WOLF V. HITCHCOCK in 1903. This case involved the MEDICINE LODGE TREATY OF 1867, which required the consent of three-fourths of the adult males in order to cede any reservation land to the government. Under pressure from the white settlers, such cessions were common in the late nineteenth century. Congress authorized commissions to negotiate cessions without regard to treaty requirements. In defense of this policy, the United States Supreme Court declared: "The power exists to abrogate the provisions of an Indian treaty, though presumably such power will be exercised only when circumstances arise which will not only justify the government in disregarding the stipulations of the treaty, but may demand, in the interest of the country and the Indians themselves, that it should do so." This statement was an endorsement of the policy of forced assimilation at the highest level of federal authority. Under the theory of wardship, Native Americans were left with no basis for resisting the effort of white reformers to impose a "superior" culture upon them.

During the early decades of the twentieth century, there were signs that the government would eventually change its policy. While strongly endorsing forced assimilation in 1905, Commissioner Francis Leupp did not want to make the mistake "in the process of absorbing them, of washing out of them whatever is distinctly Indian." Beginning in 1914, the Board of Indian Commissioners recommended the protection of Indian property whether held individually or in common. The commissioners began to view tribalism in a much more positive light since tribal organizations could become the basis for corporate developments on reservations. Tribal councils could be reorganized as business committees, which could manage tribal enterprises such as the lumber industry on the Menominee reservation in Wisconsin and the cattle industry on the Apache reservations of the Southwest.

There were other indications that the policy begun in the late nineteenth century would soon change. In 1914, Congress provided a $600,000 revolving fund from which a single tribe could borrow up to $75,000 for various kinds of improvements. This was clearly a precedent for the $10 million revolving fund that was provided for in the Indian Reorganization Act of 1934. Perhaps most important, the Board of Indian Commissioners advocated that Native American health should be a high priority of the government. Because the reform of Indian administration was low on the list of federal priorities during World War I, there was no Indian health drive until 1923 when Hubert Work became secretary of the interior. In the middle twenties, the BUREAU OF INDIAN AFFAIRS called on the United States Public Health Service for assistance in treating diseases on reservations and in Indian schools. The USPHS became responsible for Indian health care in 1955.

Despite the efforts of the Board of Indian Commissioners to reform Indian affairs in the second decade of the twentieth century, much Indian real estate was lost during the administration of Cato Sells, commissioner of Indian affairs under President Woodrow Wilson. Using the BURKE ACT of 1906, which provided for certificates of competency as the basis for issuing fee patents to Indian landowners, Sells in 1917 declared all Indians who possessed more than 50 percent non-Indian blood competent to manage their own estates. On this basis, many Indians not only became citizens but received full legal title to their allotments with the right to dispose of them to any buyer. Sells's policy, together with numerous other amendments to the Dawes Act of 1887, goes far to explain why approximately two-thirds of the Native American land base was lost by 1934.

In 1922 and 1923, new reform organizations endorsed a philosophy known as "cultural pluralism" in response to Commissioner of Indian Affairs Charles Burke's policy of suppressing Indian dances that were considered pagan and which caused Native Americans to abandon their farm work. The other issue that motivated advocates of cultural pluralism to establish new reform organizations was the introduction of the Bursum Bill by Senator HOLM OLAF BURSUM of New Mexico. That bill would have enabled non-Indians who had encroached on lands of the Pueblo Indians to gain legal possession if they had lived on them for more than ten years prior to June 20, 1910. The first reform organization was the Eastern Association on Indian Affairs. Headquartered in New York City and under the direction of Amelia E. White, it included in its membership several prominent anthropologists. A second cultural-pluralist organization founded at this time was the American Indian Defense Association, led by John Collier. The founding of these new associations meant that a struggle over reform philosophy would be important in determining the direction of policy. The Republican administrations of the 1920s worked closely with the assimilation advocates whose views were reflected in the activities of the Indian Rights Association and the Board of Indian Commissioners. When Democratic Franklin D. Roosevelt was elected president in 1933, he appointed a cultural pluralist, John Collier, as commissioner of Indian affairs. Collier terminated the Board of Indian Commissioners.

The stage had already been set for a new era in United States Indian policy by a survey of conditions on reservations conducted under the direction of Lewis Meriam in 1926 and 1927. Published in 1928 under the title *The Problem of Indian Administration,* the report advocated giving Native Americans a voice in determining their destiny in American life. All Indians, regardless of their willingness to accept the values of the dominant mainstream culture, were entitled to conduct their lives according to their respective desires. The Meriam survey team "would not recommend the disastrous attempt to force individual Indians or groups of Indians to be what they do not want to be, to break their pride in themselves and their Indian race, or to deprive them of their Indian culture." The Meriam survey staff, however, recognized that the clock could not be turned back because white civilization had destroyed the economic foundation upon which traditional Native American cultures rested. Indians would have to come to terms with being in the presence of the white race, and the objective of government policy should be "to fit them either to merge into the social and economic life of the prevailing civilization as developed by the whites or to live in the presence of that civilization at least in accordance with a minimum standard of health and decency." The Meriam survey staff advocated more sympathy for the Indian point of view by noting much good was to be found in the economic and social life of Indians as well as in their religions and ethics. Certainly the Meriam Report was an important stepping stone to Collier's Indian New Deal.

Under the Indian Reorganization Act of 1934, tribes were allowed to vote to accept or reject the law. Collier did his best to bring about a favorable reception of the measure by holding Indian congresses in different sections of the country. The response was mixed: 181 tribes accepted the IRA, while 77 tribes rejected it. The constitutions adopted by the tribes that accepted the IRA were often foreign to their traditions. The government provided model constitutions and otherwise assisted in drafting bylaws to establish Indian self-government. Despite Collier's pronouncements in favor of allowing Indians to govern themselves in accord with their ancient traditions, his administration of their affairs was often heavy-handed and paternalistic. Moreover the

$2 million annual appropriation to purchase lands lost under the allotment program had a limited effect because the amount was inadequate and because Congress sometimes did not vote funds at that level. However, the allotment of reservations lands was ended, and no further fee patents were issued. Most allotted lands on reservations today are held under trust patents, which means that the government is the perpetual guardian of that Indian real estate.

The Indians of Oklahoma were excluded from the major provisions of the IRA, and many of its benefits were not extended to the Indians of Alaska. The passage of the Oklahoma Welfare Act and the Alaskan Indian Welfare Act in 1936 partially remedied that situation. The Indians of Oklahoma were reluctant to take advantage of the legislation because of opposition to Collier's program and because all of the reservations in Oklahoma had been allotted under the Curtis Act of 1898. However, eighteen Oklahoma tribes did write constitutions, and thirteen of them incorporated for business purposes between 1936 and 1945. The Alaskan Welfare Act authorized the creation of reservations for the indigenous population and allowed them to establish constitutions and to incorporate for business purposes. Six reservations were established in 1944, and forty-nine Alaskan villages drew up constitutions and charters of incorporation under this law.

A notable achievement of the Indian New Deal in 1935 was the creation of an Arts and Crafts Board. Warren K. Moorehead had encouraged government support of Indian crafts shortly after he became a member of the Board of Indian Commissioners in 1908, but bills drafted at that time did not pass. The economic imperatives of the Great Depression created a climate more favorable to such legislation. The Act of August 27, 1935, provided for a board of five commissioners who were "to promote the economic welfare of the Indian tribes . . . through the development of Indian arts and crafts and the expansion of the market for the products of Indian art and craftsmanship." While the purpose of the legislation was economic, the law encouraged Native Americans to learn the techniques of making pottery, weaving blankets, and smithing silver.

By the late 1940s, the government of the United States was once again ready to change its Indian policy. All Native Americans had been citizens since 1924, and many of them had given outstanding service to the nation during World War II on battlefields and in production plants. It seemed time to give them a first-class citizenship by bringing them into the cities where they could enjoy a standard of living not possible on reservations. It was also thought that the government could economize by terminating its special responsibility to be the guardian of Indian welfare. The first step was to pay off all claims of Indian tribes against the federal government. The Indian Claims Commission Act of 1946 created a special commission that operated as a court to hear such claims. Each tribe would have five years to make a claim, and another five-year period was provided to hold hearings and make an appropriate award if any were called for. So many claims were filed within the initial five-year period that the hearing process had to be extended until 1978. Even then, there were many dockets that had not been disposed of, and the remaining cases were turned over to the United States Court of Claims.

By the 1950s, the government had introduced the policy known as "termination," meaning that certain tribes identified in 1947 would cease to be recognized by the federal government. The House Concurrent Resolution 108 in 1953 proved a disaster as illustrated by the case of the Menominee tribe in Wisconsin. After the government ceased to recognize the Menominee tribe, conditions on the former Menominee reservation rapidly deteriorated, and the people of that tribe experienced grinding poverty and serious health problems. Consequently, it was necessary to declare an end to termination as a policy, and Menominee County once again became the Menominee reservation in 1973. The Voluntary Relocation and Adult Vocational Training programs of the 1950s were only slightly more successful. Of more than thirty-five thousand Native Americans who were relocated from reservations to cities between 1952 and 1960, about 30 percent returned to their respective reservations.

Indian organizations continued to influence the direction of federal Indian policy in the second half of the twentieth century. The National Congress of American Indians, formed in Denver in 1944, opposed termination from the beginning and viewed it as a new form of forced assimilation. In the 1960s, more activist Native American organizations were established: National Indian Youth Council (1961), United Native Americans (1968), and the American Indian Movement (1968). These organizations became militant in 1969 when they occupied Alcatraz, an abandoned federal prison in San Francisco Bay, in an attempt to focus public attention on Indian concerns. The incident at Alcatraz was followed by the Trail of Broken Treaties, in which militants from these organizations seized control of the Bureau of Indian Affairs in Washington, D.C., just before the November election in 1972. Finally, during the second Wounded Knee incident in February and March of 1973, members of American Indian Movement took control of Wounded Knee village on the Pine Ridge Reservation of South Dakota in an effort to oust the tribal chairman who was of mixed-blood descent. These events, widely publicized in the press and on television, prepared the public to accept the idea of an ongoing responsibility of the federal government for the well-being of Native Americans and for recognition that tribes are dependent but sovereign nations living within the American Republic.

Under the Self-Determination and Educational Assistance Act of 1975, tribes took considerable control of their own affairs with funds coming from the federal government. Under the law, they were able to make contracts to provide many of the services previously provided by the Bureau of Indian Affairs and other federal agencies. Offices of the Bureau of Indian Affairs were still found on every reservation but were there in an advisory capacity. The tribes were considered to be sovereign in much the same manner that states are sovereign. Indians were considered to have three rather than two citizenships—federal, state, and tribal. This was appropriate since, as Solicitor of the Indian Office Nathan Margold argued in a legal brief entitled "Powers of Indian Tribes" in 1934, "those powers which are lawfully vested in an Indian tribe are not, in general, delegated powers granted by express acts of Congress, but rather inherent powers of a limited sovereignty which has never been extinguished."

—*Henry E. Fritz*

SEE ALSO: Missions; Native American Culture; Tibbles, Susette LaFlesche

SUGGESTED READING:
Burt, Larry W. *Tribalism in Crisis.* Albuquerque, N. Mex., 1982.
Deloria, Vine, Jr., and Clifford M. Lytle. *The Nations Within: The Past and Future of American Indian Sovereignty.* New York, 1984.
Fixico, Donald L. *Termination and Relocation: Federal Indian Policy, 1945–1960.* Albuquerque, N. Mex., 1986.
Fritz, Henry E. "Ethnocentric Reform, 1878–1893." In *Indian-White Relations: A Persistent Paradox.* Edited by Jane F. Smith and Robert M. Kvasnicka. Washington, D.C., 1976.
———. "The Last Hurrah of Christian Humanitarian Indian Reform: The Board of Indian Commissioners, 1909–1918. *Western Historical Quarterly* 16 (April 1985): 147–162.
———. *The Movement for Indian Assimilation, 1860–1890.* Philadelphia, 1963.
Hagan, William T. *Indian Police and Judges: Experiments in Acculturation and Control.* New Haven, Conn., 1966.
Kelly, Lawrence C. *The Assault on Assimilation: John Collier and the Origins of Indian Policy Reform.* Albuquerque, N. Mex., 1983.
Mardock, Robert W. *The Reformers and the American Indian.* Columbia, Mo., 1971.

Olson, James S., and Raymond Wilson. *Native Americans in the Twentieth Century.* Urbana, Ill., 1984.

Philip, Kenneth R. *John Collier's Crusade for Indian Reform, 1920–1954.* Tucson, Ariz., 1981.

Prucha, Francis Paul. *American Indian Policy in Crisis: Christian Reformers and the Indian, 1865–1900.* Norman, Okla., 1976.

———. *The Great Father: The United States Government and the American Indians.* 2 vols., Lincoln, Nebr., 1984.

———, ed. *Documents of United States Indian Policy.* Lincoln., Nebr., 1975.

TWENTIETH-CENTURY DEVELOPMENTS

In the final two decades of the nineteenth century, federal policy toward Indian communities reflected the changing nature of the West and the position of Indian individuals and reservations within the region. Although Indian nations remained east of the Mississippi River, their comparatively small numbers and land holdings allowed policy-makers to focus most of their attention on the Western states and territories. With GERONIMO's surrender at Skeleton Canyon in southern Arizona in 1886 and the battle of Wounded Knee in western South Dakota four years later, the era of warfare drew to a close. Influenced by the ideal of assimilation, federal officials, missionaries, and philanthropists sought to change native patterns of landholding, languages, religious beliefs, and economies.

The General Allotment Act of 1887 represented a key component of this effort. Also known as the DAWES ACT, it encouraged the subdivision of a tribe's lands into 160-acre parcels, to be held in trust for twenty-five years, and then subject to sale. "Surplus" lands left over after allotment could be maintained as trust property or sold. Given the pressure in the West to make more lands available, federal agents frequently prompted Indians to lease or sell. The 160-acre plots usually were inadequate for farming purposes in the more arid regions, and inheritance in the next generation only compounded the problem. Coupled with subsequent legislation, decisions by the U.S. Supreme Court (such as *LONE WOLF v. HITCHCOCK* [1903]), and the relentless assault on the best lands held by tribes, about two-thirds of the Indian lands were lost by the 1930s. Allotment wreaked havoc in the plains region. The rush to statehood decimated the Indian lands of Oklahoma. By contrast, the Indians of the Southwest fared better because demographic pressures were lighter and, with some exceptions, their lands were less appealing to whites.

The American vision held that hard work went hand in hand with private property, and farming clung to its progressively more shaky place as the most appropriate form of rural enterprise. Unfortunately for the Indians, the forces behind the NEWLANDS RECLAMATION ACT OF 1902, a law that recognized the need for irrigation in modern farming, did not press equally for native access to dams and canals. Ranching often emerged as a more viable form of economic activity, despite the reluctance of the BUREAU OF INDIAN AFFAIRS (BIA) to acknowledge its potential. Indian men who balked at plowing usually proved more interested in herding and branding. On the Great Plains and in the Southwest, cattle ranching sometimes took hold, and the Navajos continued to expand their flocks of sheep.

Indian children became the prime targets for enforced acculturation. RICHARD HENRY PRATT's Carlisle Indian Industrial School, founded in 1879 in Pennsylvania, served as a model for the education of young boys and girls. Through the boarding school, children would learn English, have access to teachings about Christianity, learn about American history and culture, and, at the same time, be removed from the environment that policy-makers perceived to be holding them back from "progress." At the turn of the century, other large off-reservation boarding schools were established in the West—in Haskell, Kansas; Chilocco, Oklahoma; Chemawa, Oregon; Phoenix, Arizona; Albuquerque, New Mexico; Sherman, California; and Stewart, Nevada. Such INDIAN SCHOOLS stressed vocational-technical training, military drills, and strict discipline. Students had their hair cut, their names changed, and their old values challenged at every turn.

Federal officials in President Ulysses S. Grant's administration had divided up Indian country and allocated different reservations to various religious denominations. Pushing hard for converts, missionaries sometimes established schools as well as missions to further their cause. Occasionally, as with the Franciscan fathers at St. Michaels on the Navajo reservation, the missionaries also became authorities in the local language and culture, but this surely was atypical. Priests and ministers were far more likely to thunder against the "paganism" and "heathenism" they found in their midst. They helped inspire the BIA to outlaw such native institutions as the Sun Dance, and they lobbied actively against a permissive approach to the NATIVE AMERICAN CHURCH, which included the use of peyote.

Indians from the 1870s to the 1920s thus confronted enormous problems and transitions. While much of their culture and land was lost in that half century, many Indians made significant changes on their reservations to begin to make those imposed residences into home. National organizations such as the Society of American Indians and the Native American Church, writers such as CHARLES ALEXANDER EASTMAN and GERTRUDE SIMMONS BONNIN, and local leaders in many communities helped deny the image of the vanishing Indian.

In the 1930s, the problems created or exacerbated by Indian policies had reached such proportions that a reform movement began to alter the direction of federal emphases. The Meriam Report, published by the Brookings Institute in 1928, highlighted crucial failings in Indian economic development, health care, education, and other areas. Reformer John Collier, who had led attempts in New Mexico to maintain Pueblo lands, was appointed commissioner of Indian affairs by President Franklin D. Roosevelt in 1933. During Collier's Indian New Deal, the government moved toward a more pluralistic approach. Under the terms of the main piece of legislation passed in 1930s, the Indian Reorganization Act of 1934, the allotment of Indian land was halted officially. The IRA did not fully mirror Collier's bold hopes for greater self-governance and independence for Indian communities, but the commissioner generally did what he could to promote a bilingual, bicultural approach in Bureau of Indian Affairs schools, to support the evolution of Indian arts and crafts, to guarantee freedom of religion, and to add to the Indian land base. Collier made mistakes. In the name of soil conservation, he inflicted livestock reduction on native communities. And the new tribal governments called for by the IRA threatened the elders and the approach to consensus honored by many Indian tribes.

Nonetheless, in many realms, the Indian New Deal offered another transition before the onset of another conservative period. World War II ushered in the so-called termination era, when the federal government attempted to end its trust responsibilities. Some reservations, most notably the Menominee in Wisconsin and the Klamath in Oregon, were ended. Reservation residents were encouraged to move into the city. Although many children remained in BIA schools, the trend toward urbanization as well as the new support for public schools on the reservation began to shift an increasing percentage of Indian children into public schools.

The threats posed by termination, as the threats posed by the allotment era, cut in more than one direction. The 1950s witnessed a growth in Indian activism, which culminated in the 1960s in well-publicized protests at Alcatraz and elsewhere. The Reagan presidency brought a more assimilationist approach to federal Indian policy. By this time, however, the growth of national Indian organizations, the ability of Indian leaders and newspapers to articulate grievances and priorities, and the acceleration of Indian enrollment in colleges and universities all combined to publicize the limitations of enforced acculturation. Although the government, in the 1980s, cut back on badly needed programs of economic assistance, Indian communities found new ways to bolster local economies. Tourism, tribal enterprises, mineral resources, and, most recently, gambling made contributions to tribal coffers. More than two dozen Indian colleges offered new hopes and new opportunities to reservations residents. The Native American Church, powwows, rodeos, and other institutions provided forms of community and means to express identity. A little more than a century after the Dawes Act, the Indian population continued to expand. Urbanization and other forces promised that the nature of Indian life would not remain exactly the same. At the same time, there could be no doubt that the Indians themselves would remain.

—*Peter Iverson*

SEE ALSO: Navajo Stock-Reduction Program

SUGGESTED READING:
Hurtado, Albert, and Peter Iverson, eds. *Major Problems in American Indian History.* Lexington, Mass., 1994.

UNITED STATES MAIL STEAMSHIP COMPANY

The brainchild of shipping magnate Cornelius Vanderbilt, the United States Mail Steamship Company was incorporated in New York in 1848 to provide passenger service between the East Coast and the Isthmus of Panama—the first leg of an alternative to the overland route to the California gold fields. The company secured a contract for delivering mail to California, and in January 1851, Vanderbilt concluded a noncompetition agreement with the PACIFIC MAIL STEAMSHIP COMPANY, which provided service from the Pacific side of the isthmus to California. The agreement lasted until the termination of the mail contracts in 1859, and Vanderbilt replaced the company with his own through-route spanning both oceans.

While the United States Steamship Company performed a valuable service, transporting thousands to California, it was hardly loved by its passengers. Costs were cut to the bone, resulting in a fleet that was inadequate both in number and in quality. Vessels were poorly maintained, and amenities absent. Perhaps miraculously, the company suffered only a single major disaster, when the *Central America* sank in a hurricane on September 12, 1857, and 433 lives were lost. Another hardship for the California-bound passenger was the trek overland across the isthmus to a connection with the Pacific ships. Disease was a constant companion in the Panamanian jungle. In 1855, the overland phase of the journey was greatly improved by the construction of the Panama Railroad.

Despite the cost-cutting measures, the United States Mail Steamship Company was never profitable for shareholders. Dividends were erratic at best, and the stock consistently traded below par.

—*Alan Axelrod*

SUGGESTED READING:
Kemble, John H. *The Panama Route, 1848–1869.* Berkeley, Calif., 1943.

UNITED STATES–MEXICAN WAR

Declared in May 1846 and terminated by treaty in February 1848, the United States–Mexican War achieved the expansionist goals of the administration of President JAMES K. POLK. More than one million square miles—the present-day states of New Mexico, Arizona, and California and portions of Colorado, Nevada, Wyoming, and Utah—were added to the United States at the end of the war. Mexico's defeat plunged the nation into political and economic upheaval for the many of the remaining years of the nineteenth century.

Mexico and the United States had steered a collision course a decade before. Although the United States officially remained neutral during the TEXAS REVOLUTION, most Americans sympathized with the Texans' cause. When Texas won freedom from Mexican rule under President ANTONIO LÓPEZ DE SANTA ANNA in the Battle of San Jacinto on April 21, 1836, the United States and most European powers recognized the Republic of Texas, much to the consternation of Mexico City.

By the mid-1840s, many Americans firmly believed in MANIFEST DESTINY—the concept of American expansion to the Pacific rim. Obstructing the pathway to the West stood Mexico, which most Americans perceived as a weak, unorganized nation. Corruption, political turmoil, economic instability, and civil unrest forced a succession of Mexican officials to focus on internal struggles near Mexico City, thus preventing protection of Mexico's far-flung northern provinces of Texas, New Mexico, and California from Yankee invasion and economic and cultural dominance.

In 1845, expansion-minded President James K. Polk annexed Texas and sent John Slidell to Mexico City to negotiate a settlement over the boundary between Texas and Mexico and other issues. In return for cash and Mexican acceptance of the Rio Grande as the southern boundary of Texas, the United States would assume financial responsibilities for claims of U.S. citizens against Mexico. In addition, Slidell was to negotiate the acquisition of New Mexico for $5 million and to discuss the purchase of California.

Mexican President José Herrera refused to accept Slidell as "minister." When Herrera and his faction toppled from power, Mariano Paredes became president. Paredes, like Herrera before him, refused to meet with Slidell and insisted on the Nueces River as the boundary. Snubbed by the Mexican government, Slidell returned to Washington. President Polk, angered over Mexico's rebuff of Slidell and wanting to exert pressure on the Mexican government, ordered General ZACHARY TAYLOR to march his army from Corpus Christi, on the Nueces River, to the north bank of the Rio del Norte (Rio Grande).

Taylor's force, consisting of 3,000 U.S. regulars and a handful of Texas Rangers, departed Corpus Christi on March 8 and arrived at the Rio Grande opposite Matamoros on March 28. Taylor began construction of an earthen fortification, dubbed Fort Texas, at present-day Brownsville. Mexican General Mariano Arista arrived in Matamoros in late April with more than 8,000 Mexican troops poised to counter what they clearly perceived as American aggression.

Mexican lancers splashed across the turbid Rio Grande on April 24, 1846. The next day, an American patrol of 63 dragoons under Captain Seth Thornton collided with more than 1,600 lancers under General Anastasio Torrejón at Rancho de Carricitos, forty miles upstream from the mouth of the Rio Grande. In a matter of minutes, 16 American soldiers lay dead or wounded, and the remaining dragoons scattered or surrendered. This relatively insignificant skirmish served as a pretext for the United States to declare war. On May 13, 1846, President Polk signed the war bill formally beginning hostilities against the Republic of Mexico.

Meanwhile Torrejón's lancers moved to attack Taylor's rear and to cut communications with his supply base at Fort Polk (Point Isabel), located twenty miles northeast of Fort Texas at Brazos Santiago. Torrejón skirmished with Captain Samuel Walker's Texas Rangers before advancing downstream from Fort Texas to support Arista's army crossing the Rio Grande. Leaving five hundred infantry and artillery troops under Major Jacob Brown to defend Fort Texas, Taylor raced to Point Isabel on May 1 where he bolstered his defenses and gathered provisions and ammunition for the relief of Fort Texas.

Arista moved his main army astride the Matamoros-Point Isabel road and waited for Taylor. About midday on May 8, Taylor's army plodded into view along a series of water-filled ponds, dense chaparral, and mesquite entanglements, which locals referred to as Palo Alto (tall timber). Although Arista

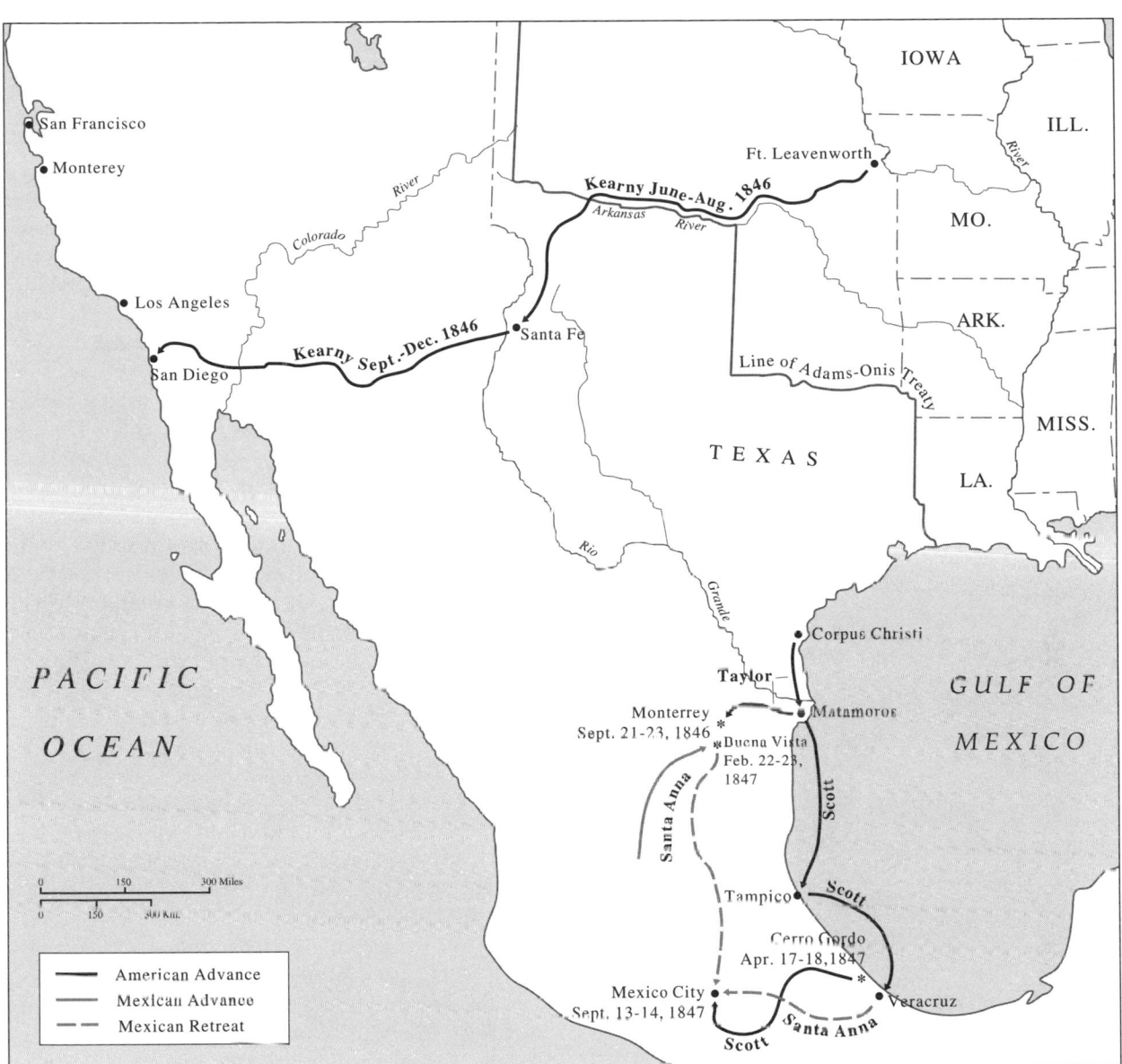

Campaigns of the United States–Mexican War, 1846 to 1848.

maintained superiority in numbers (5,700 troops to Taylor's 2,300), the Americans carried the day with their artillery. Arista's troops were shredded by the deadly accuracy of Taylor's long-range guns. By nightfall, the Mexicans retreated from Palo Alto. More than 200 Mexican soldiers had been killed and an unknown number wounded. Taylor's casualties numbered 53. Palo Alto, like other battles that followed, demonstrated U.S. artillery dominance over Mexico, an advantage that more than compensated for the numerical superiority of Mexican forces.

The next day, Taylor found Arista positioned behind several *resacas* (small ponds). At the Battle of Resaca de la Palma, Taylor used his infantry and cav-

alry to charge the stout Mexican lines. Resaca de la Palma proved catastrophic for Arista. The Mexicans abandoned their positions and left in their wake more than 600 casualties and eight pieces of artillery. A week later, Arista evacuated Matamoros and retreated toward Monterrey.

Taylor spent the remainder of the summer fortifying his position and receiving the first wave of volunteer enlistments, mostly from the Midwestern states. He marched up the Rio Grande to Camargo where he assembled his army for the push to Monterrey.

By mid-September, Taylor's forces reached the outskirts of heavily fortified Monterrey. Mexican cannon guarded the approach to the city. Taylor's infantry as-

Top: General Zachary Taylor led American forces in a decisive victory over Mexican troops at the city of Monterrey on September 24, 1846. *Courtesy Library of Congress.*

Bottom: Colonel Alexander William Doniphan's Missouri Volunteers routed Mexican forces on the banks of the Sacramento River in the Mexican province of Chihuahua on February 28, 1847. *Courtesy Library of Congress.*

saults bogged down in the face of stiff Mexican fire. While Taylor occupied the Mexicans to the front, he sent General William J. Worth's division on a circuitous route around the weakly defended Mexican left flank and rear. In a series of engagements, from September 20 to 24, Worth's men cut off the Mexican highway linking Saltillo and Monterrey. The Ameri-

cans captured in succession Federacion and Indendence hills, including the ridge-top defenses surrounding the unfinished Bishop's Palace. With Taylor pressuring the Mexicans from the northeast and Worth in their rear, the Americans entered the city amid street fighting. By September 24, the Mexicans under General Pedro Ampudia had surrendered.

Following his Monterrey success, Taylor entered into an eight-week armistice before resuming his march to occupy Saltillo, seventy miles south of Monterrey. President Polk, critical of Taylor's liberal truce terms to Ampudia and the war's stagnation, authorized General WINFIELD SCOTT to spearhead a second army-navy expeditionary force. Scott's build-up off the Mexican coastal-town of Tampico stripped Taylor of half his regulars. Taylor, however, received reinforcements from troops under General JOHN ELLIS WOOL marching from San Antonio.

In February 1847, Santa Anna, reestablished as president of Mexico, led a Mexican army of more than 20,000 soldiers northward from San Luis Potosí to Saltillo. On February 22 and 23, 1847, the combined forces of Taylor and Wool (4,800 men) fought stubbornly. On the second day, when it seemed that Santa Anna would turn to attack the American left flank, U.S. artillery and volunteer regiments from Indiana, Kentucky, Illinois, Mississippi, and Arkansas blunted the Mexican advance and forced Santa Anna to retreat. Known as the Battle of Buena Vista, this engagement would be Taylor's finest and last battle. Thereafter, fighting shifted elsewhere, and Taylor, by then a political enemy of the Polk administration, was only a spectator.

Polk's second objective in the war with Mexico was the conquest of California. During the summer of 1846, as Taylor prepared for his campaign to Monterrey, General STEPHEN WATTS KEARNY trekked westward from Fort Leavenworth, Kansas, along the Santa Fe Trail. More than 1,600 men—dragoons and Missouri Volunteers—composed Kearny's column. By August, Kearny reached Santa Fe, and all rumored threats of New Mexican defiance melted as his men plodded into the main plaza. Kearny's proclamation to the New Mexicans promised a democratic government, religious freedom, and military protection from Indian raids. Kearny installed Charles Bent as acting governor of the territory. Leaving Colonel ALEXANDER WILLIAM DONIPHAN's Missourians in New Mexico, Kearny proceeded to California to finish what had been to this point a peaceful expedition. He had scarcely left New Mexico when Indian raiders sacked New Mexican villages. Keeping his word to protect New Mexicans, Kearny detached Doniphan to quell the Indian attacks. With the arrival of Colonel STERLING PRICE's Second Missouri Mounted Volunteers, Doniphan departed Santa Fe for Chihuahua and a scheduled rendezvous with Wool's column. On Christmas Day, Doniphan's forces swept aside a small Mexican detachment north of El Paso at Brazitos. Resting in El Paso, Doniphan learned that Wool's men would not march on Chihuahua, because Taylor had diverted them to Saltillo to support his drive against Santa Anna.

Doniphan marched on Chihuahua. On February 28, 1847, fifteen miles north of Chihuahua, the Missourians ran into the Mexican defenses near the banks of the Sacramento River. General Garcia Conde, in command of 3,000 ill-trained troops, believed that the Missourians would attack along the road, which was heavily defended with artillery. Doniphan upset Conde's defensive scheme by detaching a portion of his command to the west and scaling the plateau. Approaching the Mexican left rear, the Missourians routed the Mexicans, captured all ten pieces of artillery, and killed or wounded more than 600 soldiers. Doniphan reported only 9 casualties. After occupying Chihuahua for two months, Doniphan turned east to link up with Wool at Saltillo in June. Meanwhile in Santa Fe, New Mexicans plotted to assassinate Bent and Price. Despite warnings that his life was in danger, Bent left Santa Fe in January to join his family in Taos. On the morning of January 19, 1847, an angry mob descended on Bent's home. They killed and beheaded the governor but spared his wife and female friends because of their Hispanic origins. The killing spree spread throughout the Taos region, including the villages of Mora and Arroyo Hondo where fifteen Americans perished.

In Santa Fe, Price organized a punitive expedition. On January 23, Price's Missourians and New Mexicans, about 380 troops, brushed aside 1,500 New Mexicans at La Cañada, fifteen miles north of Santa Fe. At Embudo Pass, Price repeated his La Cañada success. On February 2, he approached the outskirts of the Taos Pueblo where the rebels made their stand. Taos fell on February 5 after two days of artillery pounding that breached the soft adobe walls of the pueblo. With the surrender and execution of the ringleaders in April, peace was restored in New Mexico.

Initial American efforts to control California failed despite the efforts of Captain JOHN CHARLES FRÉMONT's Bear Flag supporters. American naval and land forces evacuated California's coastal communities of Los Angeles and Monterey. Meanwhile Kearny and his 100 dragoons marched west to participate in the pacification and conquest of California. On December 6, Kearny collided with a detachment of Californios under the command of Andrés Pico at San Pascual, east of San Diego. Pico's lancers killed 18 of Kearny's men and wounded 13. On December 11, 100 sailors and 80 marines from San Diego reached Kearny and lifted Pico's siege.

Combining his depleted detachment with Commodore ROBERT F. STOCKTON's sailors, Kearny set out on December 29 to reconquer Los Angeles. On January 8 and 9, 1847, the Americans captured Los Angeles after defeating Governor José María Flores's untrained army at San Gabriel and La Mesa. The triumph coincided with Frémont's successful conclusion of the Treaty of Cahuenga with the other leading Californio column under Andrés Pico. The treaty ended the war in California.

Despite American victories in Mexico's far-flung northern provinces, Mexican forces continued to mobilize in the interior. President Polk directed Winfield Scott to seize Mexico City and order the Mexican government to capitulate. On March 9, 1847, Scott, with cooperation from the U.S. Navy, landed troops south of the Mexican seaport of Veracruz. Scott quickly besieged the city, and on March 29, Veracruz surrendered. With a beachhead established, Scott turned his 12,000-man column westward. On April 18 and 19, Scott's forces routed Santa Anna's army at the battle of Cerro Gordo. In early May, the Americans occupied Puebla, fifty miles east of Mexico City. There Scott built up his army, gathered supplies, and prepared for the final campaign to Mexico City. In a series of sharp clashes south of Mexico City on August 19 and 20, Scott defeated the Mexicans at Contreras and Churubusco. Inching closer to the capital, Scott's attacking columns on September 8 hammered Mexican works at Molino del Rey. On September 13, Scott assaulted the Mexico City citadel at Chapultepec and marched into the Mexican capital the following day.

NICHOLAS TRIST concluded the Treaty of Guadalupe Hidalgo on February 2, 1848. It officially ended the two-year war with Mexico and created a festering wound between the nations. The trauma, humiliation, and damage to Mexican pride, to say nothing of Mexico's allegations of the American invasion and theft of Mexican land, left an indelible and lasting scar on Mexico's relations with the United States.

In the first year of the war, Americans strongly supported the Polk administration. But as the war dragged on into its second year, despite U.S. victories at every turn, the military failed to bring the Mexicans to the

A Currier and Ives lithograph depicts Mexican officers surrendering the city of Veracruz to U.S. Army General Winfield Scott on March 29, 1847. *Courtesy Library of Congress.*

negotiating table. American citizens became disillusioned and discontented as lists of dead and wounded lengthened. While U.S. casualties amounted to 1,700 battle deaths, more than 11,000 soldiers died of disease. More than 115,000 men fought in the conflict. Although America's expansionist goals were realized, the war fueled the sectional conflict in the United States. In less than two decades, the North and the South debated the issue of the expansion of slavery into the new territories gained by the war with Mexico. Militarily, the United States–Mexican War became the training ground for many Union and Confederate officers who served during the Civil War.

—*Neil C. Mangum*

SEE ALSO: National Expansion: The Election of 1844 and National Expansion

SUGGESTED READING:

Bauer, Jack. *The Mexican War, 1846–1848.* Lincoln, Nebr., 1974.

Brooks, Nathan C. *A Complete History of the Mexican War, 1846–1848.* Albuquerque, N. Mex., 1849. Reprint. Chicago, 1965.

Eisenhower, John S. D. *So Far from God: The U.S. War with Mexico, 1846–1848.* New York, 1989.

Ferrell, Robert H. *Monterrey is Ours! The Mexican War Letters of Lieutenant Dana, 1845–1847.* Lexington, Ky., 1990.

Lord, Walter. *A Time to Stand: The Epic of the Alamo.* Lincoln, Nebr., 1961.

Nevin, David. *The Mexican War.* Alexandria, Va., 1978.

Perry, Carmen, ed. *With Santa Anna in Texas: A Personal Narrative of the Revolution by José De La Pena.* College Station, Tex., 1975.

Smith, Justin. *The War with Mexico.* 2 vols. New York, 1919.

Weber, David J. *The Mexican Frontier, 1821–1846: The American Southwest under Mexico.* Albuquerque, N. Mex., 1982.

Weems, John E. *To Conquer a Peace.* College Station, Tex., 1974.

UNITED STATES V. REYNOLDS

After the passage of the Morrill Anti-Bigamy Act of 1862 and the Poland Act of 1874, the federal government began to prosecute MORMONS who practiced polygamy, a marriage system whereby a man takes more than one wife at a time. George Reynolds, private secretary to church leader BRIGHAM YOUNG, was convicted in the Utah territorial district court in 1876; he then appealed to the United States Supreme Court. In a decision read by Chief Justice Morrison R. Waite in January 1879, the court held that the First Amendment free-exercise clause did not protect religiously motivated plural marriages. Drawing a distinction between belief and conduct, the court held that people could believe anything they wished, but when people's actions violated social duties or subverted good order, the government could regulate or prohibit them.

—*Thomas G. Alexander*

SEE ALSO: Polygamy: Polygamy among Mormons

SUGGESTED READING:

Alexander, Thomas G. "The Utah Federal Courts and the Areas of Conflict, 1850–1896." M.S. thesis, Utah State University, 1961.

Baskin, Robert N. *Reminiscences of Early Utah.* Salt Lake City, 1914.

Firmage, Edwin Brown, and Richard Collin Mangrum. *Zion and the Courts: A Legal History of the Church of Jesus Christ of Latter-day Saints, 1830–1900.* Urbana, Ill., 1988.

UNIVERSITIES

SEE: Colleges and Universities

URBAN WEST

In the middle of the nineteenth century, brave prophets of urban destiny conjured up visions of a West of great cities. This took some doing. In 1850, the American West contained only one of the 126 cities considered "important places" by the U.S. Census Bureau. The bureau used the figure of 10,000 residents as its breaking point between "important" and "unimportant" places. The gold-rush city of San Francisco, with an 1850 population of 34,776, ranked fourteenth in size. Ten years later, SAN FRANCISCO, with 56,820 people, was still the only Western city with more than 10,000 people. The next largest communities in the West were SALT LAKE CITY and SAN ANTONIO, each with about 8,000 residents. Future "important" places, including DENVER, SEATTLE, and DALLAS, had no listed populations.

After the Civil War, advances in transportation—especially the railroad—new mineral rushes, agricultural development, and the willingness of the federal government to subdue and remove Native Americans facilitated town building. The 1880 census showed that the West had 23 cities with more than 10,000 people. San Francisco (233,959) was ninth nationally. KANSAS CITY (55,785) was second in the West. It was followed by Denver (35,629), OAKLAND (34,555), ST. JOSEPH (32,431), and OMAHA (30,518). Urban growth continued and increased markedly in the twentieth century. The coming of the railroads made LOS ANGELES and Seattle boom. With the removal of Indian tribes, cities grew overnight in Oklahoma. Oil strikes and a prosperous cattle industry led to rapid urban progress in Texas. World War I started a flow of federal monies into the West. A large movement of people from other parts of the country, especially from the Midwest, to California continued through the 1920s.

By 1930, while wide-open spaces still predominated, the West had achieved significant urban char-

When Native Americans were removed from land in the Indian Territory, towns like Guthrie, Oklahoma, grew up almost overnight. Guthrie's Harrison Avenue as it appeared in 1893. *Courtesy National Archives.*

acteristics. The region contained 21 of the 93 cities in the nation with more than 100,000 people and 45 of the 283 cities with more than 25,000 residents. Another 119 Western towns had at least 10,000 inhabitants. Nineteen of the 100 largest cities in the United States were in the West. Los Angeles (1,239,048) was fifth nationally, and San Francisco (634,394) eleventh. Six other places numbered in the top thirty: Kansas City (399,746), Seattle (365,583), PORTLAND (301,815), HOUSTON (292,352), Denver (287,861), and Oakland (284,063).

Almost all the successful cities developed after the initial settlement period. Speculators founded count-

The arrival of cattle for shipment to Eastern markets built Hays, Kansas, into a cow town. Many cattle towns prospered only for a few glorious years. *Courtesy Kansas State Historical Society.*

Although blessed with a natural harbor, San Diego was situated in a desert. Its deficient water supply was remedied by a network of flumes that brought distant waters to the city. *Courtesy San Diego Historical Society.*

less towns—6,000 alone in early Kansas—that had negligible chances of success. All a promoter needed was a piece of land, surveying equipment, and a stout heart. Railroads tried their luck at town building; sometimes, however, the railroads founded far more places than could possibly prosper, fostering a survival-of-the-fittest approach to urbanization. The military frontier spawned few permanent places, because planners of forts generally ignored civilian requirements. Other governmental efforts—the designation of county seats and even capital sites—sometimes succeeded. The Nebraska state government, for example, moved to Lincoln when it had only a few settlers. Mining camps and towns, especially those at bleak mountainous locations, had little chance. Once the mines played out, VIRGINIA CITY, Nevada, plunged from 25,000 people to only a few thousand. African American EXODUSTERS from the Reconstruction South founded on the central Great Plains a number of "black towns" that mostly failed to prosper. CATTLE TOWNS, too, had difficulties. After only a few years of glory, the famous Kansas cattle towns of ABILENE and DODGE CITY were relegated to the status of agricultural marketing points.

What sustained the pioneers of even the most uninviting sites was that some places did succeed. San Francisco generated enough money from the gold rush to sustain the momentum needed to become the "Monarch of the West." SACRAMENTO, situated in some of the best land in North America, swiftly made the transition from gold to agriculture. Denver persevered by following a railroad strategy. Of course, town promoters always claimed that success was inevitable, no matter how unfavorable the odds. In the mid-nineteenth century, WILLIAM GILPIN claimed to be able to predict the location of a gigantic "Centropolis" of 50 million people by postulating equations that combined a number of fallacious concepts—the Isothermal Zodiac, the Axis of Intensity, and doctrines of urban gravitation. First, he proclaimed Kansas City to be the future Centropolis. After moving to Denver, however, he announced that he had made an inadvertent mathematical error; Denver was the true Centropolis.

While promotional activities helped, especially in providing a rationale for growth and helping to sustain enthusiasm, other considerations seemed more substantive. Some places had undeniable natural advantages. Puget Sound, San Francisco Bay, and San Diego Bay afforded fine locations. Given problems of aridity, river locations obviously had more potential than deserts. Salt Lake City, however, was an exception. So were several Southwestern communities that eventually prospered, notably ALBUQUERQUE, TUCSON, and PHOENIX. A combination of "natural" and "artificial" channels of commerce sometimes held great promise. Kansas City quickly advanced to the status of a regional metropolis after obtaining the first permanent railroad bridge over the Missouri River. Omaha gained an advantage over seemingly more favored rivals when it became the eastern terminal of the Union Pacific Railroad. Omaha and Kansas City acquired large meatpacking industries, but the economies of most Western cities relied on commerce rather than manufacturing.

Western cities tended to mirror their counterparts in the East. Builders ignored Hispanic and Native American architectural forms. In early San Antonio, downtown looked much the same as in Indianapolis or Columbus. Street design showed little in the way of imagination. The traditional grid became even more pervasive as the city moved west. In San Francisco, authorities actually tried to level the massive hills of the San Francisco Peninsula to make a grid design easier to perfect. Sanitation services were neglected. As late as 1880, Los Angeles relied on municipally maintained pig herds to remove street garbage. Privies were all but universal. Few places had comprehensive systems of sewerage until the twentieth century. From their earliest days, most cities had organized police departments whose officers wore standard blue uniforms. Many cities abandoned volunteer fire brigades in favor of professional departments after their populations reached 10,000. Schools and religious institutions, just as elsewhere, acted as cultural influences. Regional literary traditions took hold, as did a sensational form of reporting called "yellow journalism." Theatrical entertainment flourished from the gold rush days onward, and in the early twentieth century, the new motion-picture industry, almost as a natural course of events, moved to southern California.

Urban convulsions left scars on Western cities. Ethnic riots against Chinese workers occurred from California to Wyoming. Labor violence was common. A general strike swept Seattle. Labor agitators apparently blew up the *Los Angeles Times* building. Natural disasters accompanied rapid growth. The GALVESTON tidal wave of 1900 killed more than 6,000 people, and the SAN FRANCISCO EARTHQUAKE OF 1906 destroyed almost all of the city. Although Galveston and Portland adopted an innovative commission form of government, which relied on experts to run city departments, most cities had a mayor and council. Many large cities had urban bosses who were frequently corrupt. In Kansas City, the Pendergast Machine ran the city in collaboration with criminal gambling elements. Apologists for political machines argued that their leaders

created a community consensus that prevented social disintegration. In a different way, the machines carried on the lawlessness associated with the wild, wild West.

The population characteristics of Western cities changed considerably over the years. The frontier settlements were very masculine. When Kansas City was a frontier camp, the almost exclusively male population was so rough that even prostitutes stayed away. In the formative days of Omaha, the few women living there were mainly the wives of the town promoters. The classic mineral towns had few females. The inhabitants of the California gold fields were almost entirely male. During an 1870s mining strike, Virginia City was roughly 80 percent male. In the Kansas cattle towns,

Top: Cheyenne, Wyoming, pictured here in 1876, began as a supply station on the Oregon Trail. *Courtesy National Archives.*

Bottom: Some communities had humble beginnings indeed. Photographer Burt L. Wheeler recorded the establishment of a tent town in an Idaho mountain valley in 1909. *Courtesy National Archives.*

The establishment of mercantile stores in a Western community assured the town folks of a variety of goods. The Clark and De Young general store in Dewey, Indian Territory, contained an impressive inventory. *Courtesy National Cowboy Hall of Fame and Western Heritage Center.*

the first women were prostitutes; they stayed only in summer. The leading cities at the end of the nineteenth century all had male majorities. San Francisco was 57 percent and Denver 60 percent male. The ratios gradually evened out and by 1930 had little significance.

In terms of race, Chinese composed 5 to 9 percent of all inhabitants of the major West Coast cities in 1880. By comparison, Japanese and Native American totals seemed infinitesimal. Native Americans shunned city life, and Japanese immigration had hardly started. Only a few cities, notably San Antonio, had a large number of Hispanics, a situation that changed in the twentieth century. In 1930, Los Angeles had 3,009 Chinese Americans and 21,081 Japanese Americans; San Francisco had 16,303 Chinese Americans and 6,250 Japanese Americans. In the late nineteenth century, the populations of most Western cities were less than 25 percent immigrant; Eastern cities generally had higher percentages. Except in Texas and some Missouri River towns, African American totals were small—less than 1 percent in San Francisco in 1880—well into the twentieth century. Despite considerable migration from the South in the World War I period, Los Angeles had only 38,894 African Americans in 1930, and San Francisco only 3,803. As for American-born inhabitants as a whole, Western cities always had large numbers of people who had been born elsewhere.

The leading Western cities that emerged by 1880 formed the urban fabric of the region well into the twentieth century. Given the intensity of urban competition, some places faded, especially in Kansas. New cities in Oklahoma and boom towns in Texas and California more than compensated for the losses. Despite oil, movies, and mineral wealth, the West remained dependent on Eastern capital until World War II ushered in a new stage in Western urban development.

—*Lawrence H. Larsen*

SEE ALSO: City Government; City Planning; Mining: Mining Camps and Towns

SUGGESTED READING:
Barth, Gunther. *Instant Cities: Urbanization and the Rise of San Francisco and Denver.* New York, 1975.
Larsen, Lawrence H. *The Urban West at the End of the Frontier.* Lawrence, Kans., 1978.
Nash, Gerald. *The American West in the Twentieth Century.* Albuquerque, N. Mex., 1977.
Quiett, Glenn. *They Built the West: An Epic of Rails and Cities.* New York, 1934.

Reps, John W. *Cities of the American West: A History of Frontier Urban Planning*. Princeton, N.J., 1979.

Wheeler, Kenneth. *To Wear a City's Crown: The Beginnings of Urban Growth in Texas, 1836–1865*. Cambridge, Mass., 1968.

U'REN, WILLIAM SIMON

William Simon U'Ren (1859–1959) was born in Lancaster, Wisconsin. He arrived in Oregon in 1889 and became the state's leading advocate of Progressivism.

U'Ren believed the people of Oregon needed new tools to allow them to rule without being dominated by political bosses and also to allow them to secure the single tax, a measure that would finance the government solely by a tax on land. After being elected to the state legislature in 1896 as a member of the Populist party, he worked to amend the state constitution to include the initiative and referendum, tools that would give people the means to pass legislation by plebiscite. A rupture within the dominant Republican party on a different issue enabled U'Ren to organize a coalition of Populists, Democrats, and some Republicans to prevent a quorum from being established in the lower house. The upheaval resulting from the "Hold-up Session" brought the issue of amending the constitution before the public. In a plebiscite held in 1902, the people voted to add the initiative and referendum amendments to the state constitution.

In 1905, U'Ren organized the People's Power League that successfully promoted Progressive legislation over the next few years. He managed the 1906 campaign of Jonathan Bourne, Jr., a Progressive Republican, to the United States Senate. After Woodrow Wilson won the election for governor of New Jersey in 1910, U'Ren persuaded Wilson that limited use of the initiative and referendum would be useful for political reform. Although the Progressives passed several reform measures, known as the "Oregon System," U'Ren failed to establish the single tax. His influence waned after the election of 1912.

—*Robert C. Woodward*

SUGGESTED READING:
Woodward, Robert C. "William Simon U'Ren: In an Age of Protest." M. A. thesis, University of Oregon, 1956.

URREA, TERESA

Called La Santa Niña de Cábora ("The Little Saint of Cábora"), faith healer and mystic Teresa Urrea (1873–1906) inspired a religious movement in politically volatile northern Mexico, especially among the Yaqui Indians, many of whom served under such rebel leaders as Alvaro Obregón and FRANCISCO ("PANCHO") VILLA during the Mexican Revolution. Born the bastard child of Tomás Urrea, a fairly well-to-do cattleman whose family had long been powerful in the region's politics and its military, and a Tehueco Indian woman in the Mexican state of Sinaloa, Teresa Urrea was taken as a child to her father's Cábora ranch in Sonora, where he had fled following the military coup that brought dictator Porfirio Díaz to power in 1876. At the age of sixteen, Urrea suffered a seizure some claim was epileptic and fell into a three-month-long coma. Although at several times near death, she finally emerged, talking of conversations she had had during her illness with the Virgin Mary. Practiced in the traditional folk medicine of the Yaqui and Mayo peoples, the youthful visionary undertook healings of the sick, deformed, and handicapped by using Christian prayers and Indian herbs and potions. She also began to predict, with some accuracy, events that lay in the future.

As news of her powers spread, "Santa" Teresa attracted to Cábora increasingly large crowds of true believers and the merely curious, most of them poor and powerless peasants and common people, but also some from among the wealthy and the influential. Newspaper reporters, too, came to the Sonoran village, some to denounce her as a fraud, others to wonder at her gifts. Authorities also suddenly started to pay attention, as sensational accounts of her miracles appeared in the press and the number of pilgrims swelled to as many as five thousand a week. Díaz's officials were troubled both by her following, which included some potentially rebellious Yaquis, and by her message. Influenced not only by her father, but also by one of her father's ranch hands, a former military engineer with revolutionary sentiments named Lauro Aguirre, Urrea—whose formal education had been limited, but who was purported to have taught herself to read and write—preached that the world's three great evils were priests, money, and doctors, that her followers need no longer follow the dictates of the Catholic church but could baptize and marry themselves, and that, indeed, the Antichrist had taken charge of the Roman clergy, including the pope. Not surprisingly, the area's archbishop railed against her, and *federales* scouted her father's rancho for signs of civil disobedience, disorder, and revolutionary fervor.

Although Urrea would later claim that her teachings carried no political message and that she herself did not believe in revolution, Mexicans found revolutionary inspiration in her calls for a better life and her visions of a different world. Eventually battle cries of

"Viva Santa Teresa!" would echo along a good deal of the U.S.–Mexican border, but in 1890, the religious movement inspired by her teachings—or by rebel interpretations of her teachings—had just begun to spread among Sonora's ethnically diverse population. By 1891, it had spilled over the Sierra Madre to the east into neighboring Chihuahua, where in December, in the small pueblo of Tomochic, the movement erupted into violence. A mostly mestizo village, led by a religiously intense thirty-four-year-old named Cruz Chávez, Tomochic had embraced Santa Teresa's message with a millennial fervor that led its *campesinos* to ridicule and expel a local priest. This, in turn, triggered government suppression of those "rebels" whom the authorities labeled *fanaticos*. After routing the Teresitas on December 8, *federales* found documents suggesting that Santa Teresa had armed her "warriors" with religious paraphernalia intended to shield them from enemy bullets and bayonets. On Christmas Day, 1891, a crowd estimated at ten thousand made the pilgrimage to Cábora. Meanwhile, thirty of the Tomochitecos who had escaped into the Sierra Madre were working their way toward the Urrea rancho, dogged throughout the journey by the Mexican army and local militia. Santa Teresa absented herself from Cábora to avoid trouble, and the Tomochitecos eventually returned to their own pueblo, where they would make a final stand against Mexican authorities and fight for their belief in Santa Teresa to the last man. By then Santa Teresa, Tomás Urrea, and Lauro Aguirre had been exiled to the United States.

Settling first in Nogales, Arizona, in May 1892, Teresa Urrea—accompanied by children from a failed marriage—soon attracted crowds similar in number to those who had sought her out at Cábora. Steadfastly maintaining that she was not involved in any political struggle, she had nevertheless become a symbol of the anti-Díaz resistance in Mexico. Paul Vanderwood points out that, during this period, she and her associates corresponded with the besieged Tomochitecos in Chihuahua and offered encouragement and spiritual advice. By the time she moved to El Paso, Texas, the spiritist movement she inspired was swirling on both sides of the border. At some point, she produced a letter that she claimed had been written by the Archangel Gabriel. The letter conveyed God's displeasure with the way people were living their lives, threatened punishment if they did not repent, and promised that those who revered the Virgin Mary and the Holy Cross, respected their superiors, gave to charity, and perpetrated no evil would be filled with prosperity and would "succeed in all their enterprises and business." Despite its ambiguous message, the letter's very existence contributed to the growing attraction of revolt for her followers. When an El Paso print shop duplicated several thousand copies of the letter, true believers eagerly acquired them because they believed no harm could come to them while they carried the message. For all she may have denied fomenting revolution, the faithful were determined to rebel in her name. Francisco Madera, one of the more important of Mexico's revolutionaries, advocated the kind of spiritism that animated Urrea's followers and organized spiritist groups throughout Mexico.

As the U.S.–Mexican border became a hotbed of unrest, Teresa Urrea moved again, this time to Clifton, Arizona, in part to avoid the role her presence played in the growing revolt in Mexico, which, in turn, was creating something of an international crisis. (Ultimately the confrontation between the United States and Mexico would lead to intervention by the Wilson administration in the Mexican Revolution). In 1900, she was in San Jose, California, where she began practicing her folk healing as part of a medicine show. In 1904, after she had come to understand the show's tawdry exploitation of her talents, she resigned in disgust. Two years later she died at age thirty-three.

—*Patricia Hogan*

SUGGESTED READING:

Holden, William C. *Teresita*. Owings Mills, Md., 1978.

Vanderwood, Paul. *Mexican Studies/Estudios Mexicanos*. 10 (Winter 1994) 1: 99–118.

UTAH

Utah's history has been closely associated with the MORMONS (CHURCH OF JESUS CHRIST OF LATTER-DAY SAINTS) and with mining, transportation, agriculture, and water development. Sometimes known as the "Beehive State," Utah encompasses 84,899 square miles. To the west, it borders on Nevada; to the north on Idaho and Wyoming; and to the east and south it forms the Four Corners with Colorado, New Mexico, and Arizona. In the early 1990s, some 1.8 million people lived in Utah, of whom the majority were of European extraction. Others included Native Americans, Asian Americans, and African Americans. Utah's population is concentrated in Wasatch Front cities, of which the most important is SALT LAKE CITY, the state capital.

Geography and climate

Along with striking beauty, Utah's dominant natural trait is aridity. Three distinct physiographic provinces bind it geographically to neighboring states. Its eastern half is on the Colorado Plateau, and its western third is in the inward draining Great Basin. The

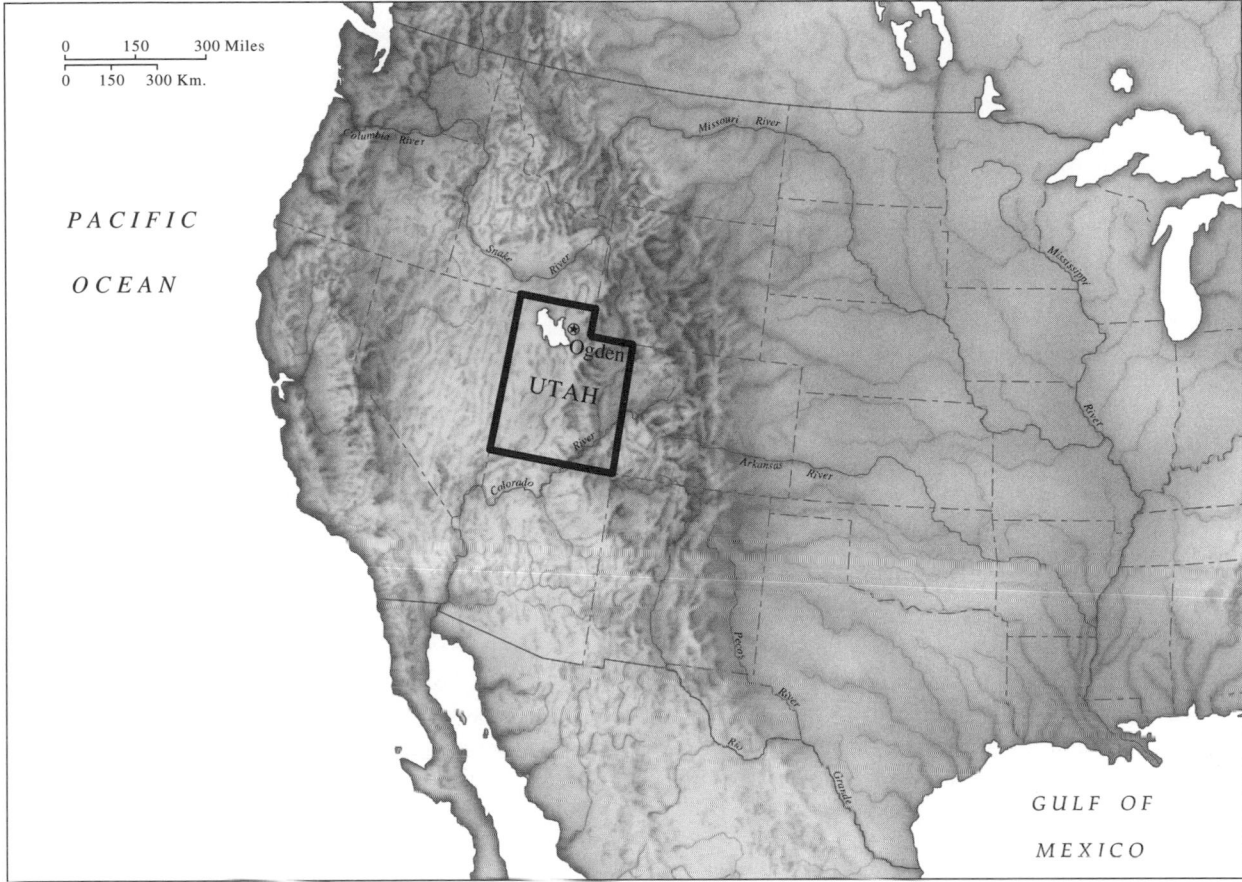

Wasatch Range of the Central Rocky Mountain province intrudes in north-central Utah, and the Uinta Range extends east along the Wyoming border. Other significant mountain ranges include the Wasatch Plateau extending south through central Utah, the high plateaus of southern Utah, and isolated ranges like the Henry, the La Sal, the Abajo, and the Pine Valley mountains.

The Great Salt Lake and the deserts of western Utah are remnants of prehistoric Lake Bonneville. Major watersheds include the Bear and Weber rivers, which flow from the Wasatch-Uinta elevations into the Great Salt Lake, and the Provo, which flows into the Salt Lake via Utah Lake and the Jordan River. Also rising in the Uintas is the Duschesne, which runs into the Green River and, in turn, into the Colorado. Other Colorado River waterways in Utah are the San Juan and the Virgin rivers. The Sevier River runs north from south-central Utah and loses itself in irrigation works and deserts.

Climate varies widely. The state has four distinct seasons. Temperatures fluctuate from winter lows of 50° F below zero, to summer highs of 115°. Rainfall averages about eleven inches annually, but the amount varies from less than five inches in the driest deserts to thirty or more in the loftiest mountains. Other natural resources include arable land (about 6.5 percent of the total area), summer and winter grazing, modest timber resources, extensive minerals and fossil fuels, and scenic and wildlife attractions.

Native Americans in Utah

Utah's Native American tradition is rich. Desert nomads were present as early as ten thousand years ago. By 300 A.D. more advanced cultures developed. In the far south, the Anasazi Indians progressed through stages of agriculture, basket weaving, and pueblo dwelling. The Sevier Fremont and the Fremont cultures emerged farther north. By 1250 A.D., all three peoples had died out or reverted to nomadic desert ways.

When European explorers first entered Utah, they encountered several Native American groups. To the north were Shoshones and Bannocks, to the west were Goshutes, and in the south were Paiutes. The Utes inhabited the Colorado Plateau and were found at Utah Lake and other central valleys. Both the Utes and the

Shoshones had begun to adapt to a horse culture and traded with the Spanish. The Goshutes and Paiutes were preyed upon by both Utes and whites. Navajos advanced into southern Utah, quarreled with the Utes, and traded with New Mexicans.

Mountain men viewed Utah's Indians with disdain but traded with them. Believing Native Americans to be descendants of *Book of Mormon* peoples, the Mormons tried to "redeem" them and adopted a feed-rather-than-fight policy. Nevertheless, the Mormons fought them in the Walker War (1852) and the Black Hawk War (1864 to 1868) and applauded when Colonel PATRICK E. CONNOR massacred Shoshones and Bannocks in 1863.

Mormon settlement forced the Indians out of the best country. By 1870, most of Indians lived on the Uintah Reservation, which was enlarged to nearly three million acres in 1882 to provide a home for the Uncompaghre Utes from Colorado. In the decade after 1897, the reservation was reduced by more than two-thirds when the Uinta Forest Reserve and homesteading districts were withdrawn from the Indian lands.

The twentieth century was also difficult for Utah Indians. Assimilationist policies cut away at the cultural values of the Utes as well as their land base. Extensions south of the San Juan River provided opportunity for increases in Navajo population. The Indian New Deal brought a degree of self-determination and appreciation, but then the "termination" policy of the 1950s deprived Paiutes and Goshutes of a variety of sustaining programs. In the early 1990s, Utes, Shoshones, Paiutes, and Goshutes were largely without opportunity or voice, and their numbers remained small. Utah Navajos lived below the poverty level but grew in number and played a role in local politics.

Exploration and settlement

Hispanic penetration of Utah was limited to the Dominguez Escalante expedition of 1776 and intermittent trade until the OLD SPANISH TRAIL opened between New Mexico and California after 1830. In the mid-1820s, Americans developed an interest in Utah when fur traders converged in the Great Salt Lake neighborhood. Mountain men explored much of Utah, opened trails, and established trading posts in the Uinta Basin and on the Weber River. A few married Indian wives and remained in neighboring regions. Some of those mountain men led the first emigrant groups across the Oregon and California trails and guided JOHN CHARLES FRÉMONT in expeditions that explored the Great Salt Lake, identified the Great Basin, and linked Utah to America.

Permanent settlement began in 1847 with the arrival of the Latter-day Saints, who, led by BRIGHAM YOUNG, located first at Salt Lake City. By 1869, when the transcontinental railway was completed, some seventy-five thousand Saints made Utah a gathering place. They located their settlements along the Wasatch Front and extended throughout Utah and neighboring localities. Forming agricultural communities, the Mormons hoped to create an independent economic commonwealth.

Territorial period

The Mexican government ceded Utah to the United States in the Treaty of Guadalupe Hidalgo in 1848. While Congress rejected applications for the Mormon State of Deseret, it did approve the formation of the Utah Territory as part of the Compromise of 1850. Church leader Brigham Young became the first territorial governor. Friction between Mormons and non-Mormons intensified when the church admitted to the practice of polygamy in 1852. An armed standoff occurred when the U.S. government sent the UTAH EXPEDITION to seat Alfred Cumming as governor in 1857. The Civil War diverted the nation's attention away from the Mormons, who were faint-hearted Unionists awaiting a collapse of government out of which their Kingdom of

Street view in Corinne, Boxelder County, Utah. Photograph by Jackson, 1869. *Courtesy National Archives.*

Utah boasts some of the West's rugged terrain. A group of riders and their horses make their way across the hot slick rocks west of Navajo Mountain on their way to Rainbow Bridge. Photograph by Neil M. Judd, August 13, 1909. *Courtesy National Archives.*

God would arise. Congress reduced the size of the territory when Colorado and Nevada were created, and in 1862, Congress passed the Morrill Anti-Bigamy Act, which proved to be more of an irritant to the Mormons than a deterrent.

As the Saints continued to mix church and state and defend polygamy, the "Mormon problem" persisted. With the coming of the railroad, influential commercial and mining populations moved to the region, and Utah divided politically over the Mormon issue into the People's and Liberal parties. Nationally, public opposition to polygamy ran high. Protestant mission schools and official initiatives were countered by the Mormons who controlled territorial courts and elections, gave women the vote, and established a system of tuition schools. The Mormons yielded only when the UNITED STATES V. REYNOLDS decision of 1879 upheld the constitutionality of antipolygamy legislation and the EDMUNDS ACT OF 1882 and the EDMUNDS-TUCKER ACT OF 1887 disfranchised poly-

gamist voters and provided laws under which polygamists could be prosecuted.

Statehood

In 1890, the Mormon church abandoned polygamy and moved towards partisan politics and free public schools. Utah achieved statehood in 1896. Its constitution outlawed polygamy, guaranteed women's suffrage, and set up the three conventional branches of government.

During a period of political, social, and economic development, old-line non-Mormons organized the American party and controlled Salt Lake City until about 1910. National opponents denied Mormon Democrat BRIGHAM HENRY ROBERTS a seat in Congress and pushed a long investigation into the propriety of seating Apostle REED SMOOT in the Senate. Supported by THEODORE ROOSEVELT, Smoot retained the seat, where as an advocate of Utah wool, sugar beets, and silver, he became a champion of protective tariffs, a friend of national forests and reclamation, and a pillar of party regularity. Non-Mormon GEORGE SUTHERLAND served first in the House of Representatives and then in the Senate and, in 1922, became an undeviating voice for conservative economics on the Supreme Court. Three Republican governors, Heber M. Wells, John Cutler, and William Spry were followed in 1916 by Democrat Simon Bamberger. Thereafter, the major parties divided political office about evenly for several decades.

MINING and smelting flourished. Park City silver mines funded the emergence of financial and political titans such as THOMAS KEARNS. Utah Copper (later Kennecott) under the leadership of Daniel Jackling developed great open pits and smelters developed at Bingham. Carbon and Emery counties provided coal for domestic heating and for the burgeoning railroad and smelting industries, all of which polluted the air of Salt Lake Valley.

Immediately after the completion of the transcontinental railroad, the Mormons began sponsoring the building of smaller lines throughout the region. In the 1880s, the Rio Grande and Western and the Oregon Short Line opened connections to Colorado and the Northwest. In the early twentieth century, interurban and streetcar systems tied the Wasatch Front together, while the Salt Lake, Los Angeles and San Pedro line promoted new farming districts, national parks, and TOURISM through southwestern Utah.

Agriculture too, expanded. The grazing industry grew dramatically. Some eight million acres of land were designated as national forests by 1908, and national monuments and parks concentrated in southern Utah continued to open until the 1960s. Under the TAYLOR GRAZING ACT of 1934, the remaining public domain came under the auspices of the BUREAU OF LAND MANAGEMENT, which left about two-thirds of Utah's land under federal control. After 1905, the BUREAU OF RECLAMATION's Strawberry Project brought water from the Colorado Plateau to Utah Valley, and water projects in the Weber and Bear River basins further enriched prosperous regions. Country-life movements, promotions of state and private land and water, and dryland farm projects resulted in a rush onto marginal lands and to a disastrous recession in the 1930s.

Education also advanced rapidly. Public schools came under increasing state regulation, and consolidated districts achieved efficiency. Normal schools trained teachers, including a large number of women who often taught for only a year or so and who earned substantially less than men. The University of Utah and Brigham Young University emerged as respectable institutions, and the Utah Agricultural College came into existence. Private colleges and academies flourished, including Salt Lake City's Westminster College

and a system of Mormon academies, most of which were phased out by 1926.

Populations grew and became more diverse and more urban. After 1870, transient Chinese and more stable Irish, German, Jewish, and African American groups responded to railroading, military needs, and industrial opportunity in Utah. After 1900, they were followed by Italians, Greeks, Serbs, Finns, Japanese, and Mexican Americans. Men from these various groups came first to Utah, followed by women and families. Together they broadened cultural traditions in Salt Lake City and at mining centers.

Twentieth-century Utah

Industrial accidents and labor discord were prevalent in the early 1900s. Mine explosions at the coalfield towns of Scofield (1900) and Castlegate (1924) were among the nation's most tragic industrial disasters. Labor unrest was common and sometimes expressed in radical terms. Festering tension resulted in strikes and open conflict in 1901, 1903, 1912, and 1922. A notorious labor incident involved Joe Hill, an INDUSTRIAL WORKERS OF THE WORLD balladeer who was executed for two Salt Lake City murders in a disputed case charged with antilabor sentiments. With the passage of favorable federal regulations, labor activists became more vocal in the early 1930s.

The 1920s and 1930s were difficult times. A postwar collapse in mining and agriculture was complicated by diminished rainfall during much of the 1920s, culminating in one of the region's worst droughts in the early 1930s. Education, public roads, and tourism all advanced, but the 1920s were depressed economically and complicated culturally as changing values and the implications of scientific learning challenged fundamentalist ideals, particularly among the Mormons.

Few states were harder hit by the Great Depression. With limited reserves, Utahns had speculated heavily and were badly injured by the stock market collapse of 1929. Mining, livestock, and agriculture suffered disastrous reverses, and by 1932, unemployment was widespread. Out-migration became significant, although it more often involved education and urban employment than the stream of itinerant agricultural labor that flowed from the Dust Bowl. In 1932, most Utahns endorsed the New Deal, were willing to accept federal aid, and voted for Franklin D. Roosevelt and rejected the previously unassailable Republican Senator Reed Smoot's bid for reelection. On the other hand, some business and church leaders cried out against Roosevelt and the New Deal and saw in them a serious constitutional breakdown.

World War II turned the sagging Utah economy around. The state was strategically located to serve national security needs. New industries, including Geneva Steel in Utah County, bolstered Utah's economy. Military installations and war material service depots were quickly built. More than 71,000 Utahns served in the armed forces, and the population became more mobile. Women worked out of the home in large numbers and found opportunities in offices, service industries, and manufacturing. Some eight thousand Japanese Americans were interned at the Topaz Relocation Center, and several thousand German and Italian prisoners of war spent time in the state.

After World War II, Utah was swept along by the Cold War and global tension. The population grew from 550,000 in 1940 to 1,460,000 in 1980. High birthrates and problems of distance and a limited tax base placed heavy burdens on state and local governments. Utahns increasingly voted Republican, although two popular governors and one long-term senator were conservative Democrats. In national politics, the Central Utah Project for water development loomed large. Flaming Gorge Reservoir on the Green River and Lake Powell on the Colorado were constructed in the 1960s. Environmental issues came to the fore as preservationists confronted traditional land users.

Officials and the society as a whole faced problems of urban growth including crime, drugs, gangs, and changing moral standards. Under special pressure was the Mormon church, which, until policy was changed in 1978, denied black males the priesthood. During the 1990s, the Mormon church grappled with the tensions surrounding the question of women's status in the church. Culturally, the performing arts had bright points in the development of the Utah Symphony, Ballet West, and the Shakespearean Festival at Cedar City. Per capita and family income lagged, and the state suffered periods when its economy stagnated at the rear of low national growth rates. With environmental issues among the most sensitive in the nation and growing urban problems, the 1980s and early 1990s, nevertheless, saw the Utah economy outperform the nation, enabling Utah's citizens to view the future with a measure of optimism.

—*Charles S. Peterson*

SEE ALSO: Deseret, State of; Japanese Internment; Labor Movement; People's Party of Utah; Polygamy: Polygamy among Mormons; Silver Mining

SUGGESTED READING:

Ellsworth, S. George. *Utah's Heritage*. Salt Lake City, 1972.

Greer, Deon C., et al. *Atlas of Utah*. Provo, Utah, 1981.

Peterson, Charles S. *Utah: A History*. New York, 1977. Reprint. 1984.

Poll, Richard D., et al. *Utah's History*. Provo, Utah, 1978.

UTAH EXPEDITION

In 1857, in response to growing public outrage over the Mormon practice of plural marriage in Utah, President JAMES BUCHANAN removed BRIGHAM YOUNG from the office of territorial governor and appointed in his stead a former mayor of Augusta, Georgia, Alfred Cumming. Buchanan then dispatched twenty-five hundred soldiers from Fort Leavenworth, Kansas, on an expedition to Utah to promote a smooth transition. Young responded by addressing a congregation in Temple Square: "Woe, woe to those men who came here to unlawfully meddle with me and this people. . . . I swore in Nauvoo, when my enemies were looking me in the face, that I would send them to hell . . . and I ask no more odds of all hell today." Young mobilized the Mormon militia even as he made plans for the evacuation and burning of Salt Lake City.

The inflammatory atmosphere was bound to breed tragedy. It came in September 1857, and it was called the MOUNTAIN MEADOWS MASSACRE, during which Mormon and Indian allies in a remote part of southern Utah, annihilated a band of 137 Gentile pioneers bound for California. The MORMONS spread the word that the band of pioneers had been the victims of Indian massacre, but the Gentile world laid the blame solely on the Mormons. President Buchanan labeled it a rebellion. During the fall of 1857, Mormons engaged in a guerrilla war against the column of troops Buchanan had dispatched to aid in the installation of the new governor. The soldiers were forced to hole up for the winter at Fort Bridger. Meanwhile, the Mormons made preparations to destroy all they had built in order "to disappoint our enemies."

By spring, in the face of repeated demonstrations of the strength of Mormon faith, public opinion was coming to favor the Saints. President Buchanan "forgave" the "rebellion," and Brigham Young, in turn, accepted Albert Cumming as territorial governor. Far more warily, Young agreed to allow Buchanan's twenty-five hundred soldiers to enter the Salt Lake valley, but on strict condition that they not stop in Salt Lake City itself. If they did so, Young warned, he would raze the city personally. To make his point, he ordered all thirty thousand Mormon residents to evacuate the city, save for those few who had the responsibility of applying the torches. When, on June 26, 1858, the soldiers marched into town, they found it eerily empty. The Saints waited in suspense, camped near Provo. Had the troops come to destroy the Mormon church? And would they, the Saints themselves, be forced to destroy the city they had built and move yet again—to Canada, to Mexico?

The troops marched through and set up camp, which they would occupy for the next three years, forty-four miles from the city. The Saints did not want the soldiers there, although they did manage to profit handsomely from supplying the garrison until the army, needed to fight the Civil War, left in 1861. When, during that war, T. B. H. Stenhouse, the Mormons' representative in Washington, asked President Lincoln what he intended to do with the Saints, the embattled chief executive told him a story:

> When I was a boy on the farm in Illinois, there was a great deal of timber which we had to clear away. Occasionally we would come to a log which had fallen down. It was too hard to split, too wet to burn, and too heavy to move, so we plowed around it. That's what I intend to do with the Mormons.

As for polygamy, Congress and the Supreme Court attempted now and then to act against it with such actions as the EDMUNDS ACT OF 1882 and the EDMUNDS-TUCKER ACT OF 1887. The issue became moot in 1890, when the Mormon church itself revoked its endorsement of the practice.

—Alan Axelrod

SEE ALSO: Mormon Manifesto; Polygamy: Polygamy among Mormons

UTE INDIANS

SEE: Native American Peoples: Peoples of the Great Basin, Peoples of the Southwest

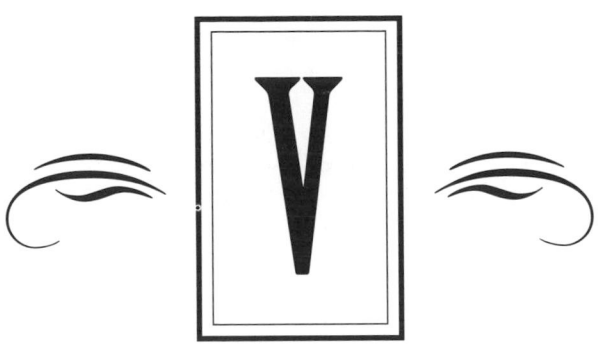

VALLEJO, MARIANO GUADALUPE

Landowner, colonizer, and military commander Mariano Guadalupe Vallejo (1808–1890) may have been the most powerful man in California at the time of American conquest during the UNITED STATES–MEXICAN WAR.

Born in the Spanish departmental capital of Monterey, Vallejo became a cadet in the Mexican army at the garrison of Monterey presidio when he was barely fifteen years old. In 1829, he won much prestige by defeating the Indian renegade Estanislao in battle.

In 1836, Juan B. Alvarado, the provisional governor, made Vallejo commandant general of all California. But Vallejo preferred the other of his dual roles: military commandant and director of colonization for the Frontera del Norte, a position he held by order of an earlier governor, JOSÉ FIGUEROA. The Northern Frontier extended from Marin County to the Carquinez Strait in a great defensive arc protecting San Francisco and San Pablo bays from incursions by the Americans, the British, and especially the Russians lodged in illegal enclaves at FORT ROSS and Bodega Bay.

Vallejo's major task was the pacification of the North Shore area, largely controlled by pagan Indians, who seemed ready to raid against Christianized Mission Indians and Californios (native-born Californians of Hispanic descent). Although his own pay (and that of his troops) was in arrears, Vallejo supported his small force of dragoons from his own pocket. He had grown rich from his land-grant ranchos at Petaluma and Suscol (Napa) and through his post as administrator of San Francisco Solano, the last of the Franciscan missions.

Nearly singlehandedly, Vallejo dealt with the Russians, Americans, Canadians, and raiding Indians. For a decade, he maintained a remarkable *tour de force* of military diplomacy. To do so, he established the presidial pueblo of Sonoma in 1835 adjacent to San Francisco Solano. He "held the fort" there from his Casa Grande headquarters, barracks, and medieval-like *torreón,* or "watch tower," and occasionally launched brutal punitive expeditions against such Indians as the Wappo tribe of the Russian River and Napa Valley.

In 1844, discouraged by years of unheeded applications to Monterey and Mexico City for support and reforms and tired of the near-anarchy of California's separatist politics, Vallejo disbanded his force and awaited the inevitable—the fall of California to the United States or Britain.

His own sympathies lay with the United States, so it was ironic that in California, the war with Mexico began with Vallejo's seizure (and rough captivity) by the Bear Flag republicans and JOHN CHARLES FRÉMONT. But Vallejo bore his new country no ill will and became a valuable link between the two regimes. He served in the California constitutional convention of 1849 and the first state senate in 1850 before retiring to his Sonoma estate, Lachryma Montis, to spend the remainder of his long life.

—*Richard H. Dillon*

SUGGESTED READING:
Bancroft, Hubert Howe. *History of California.* San Francisco, Calif., 1886–1890.

VAN DEVANTER, WILLIS

A U.S. Supreme Court Justice from Wyoming, Willis Van Devanter (1859–1941) was born in Marion, Indiana. He moved to Cheyenne, Wyoming, in 1884 and quickly established himself as a lawyer and an important Republican politician. After serving as Wyoming's last territorial chief justice from 1889 to 1890, he successfully defended the cattlemen responsible for the JOHNSON COUNTY WAR of 1892. In 1897, he became assistant attorney general of the United States and, six years later, a judge of the Eighth Circuit Court of Appeals. President William Howard Taft appointed him to the U.S. Supreme Court in December 1910, and he held that post until his retirement in 1937. He died in Washington, D.C.

Although most scholars today rank him among the weaker Supreme Court justices, Van Devanter's conservative contemporaries, especially in the 1920s, valued his legal craftsmanship. One important opinion, *Wyoming* v. *Colorado*, in 1922 affirmed the legal right of the state of Wyoming to the majority of the Laramie River's irrigation waters.

—*M. Paul Holsinger*

SUGGESTED READING:
Burner, David. "Willis Van Devanter." In *The Justices of the United States Supreme Court, 1789–1969: Their Lives and Major Opinions.* Edited by Leon Friedman and Fred L. Israel. New York, 1969.
Holsinger, M. Paul. "Willis Van Devanter: Wyoming Leader, 1884–1897." *Annals of Wyoming* 37 (October 1965): 170–206.

VAN WATERS, MIRIAM

Prison reformer Miriam Van Waters (1887–1974) grew up in Portland, Oregon, in the rectory of her father's Episcopal church. She graduated from the University of Oregon in 1908 and received a master's degree in 1910. She then enrolled at Clark University in Massachusetts, where she earned a Ph.D. in anthropology in 1913.

Van Waters began her career as a probation officer for the Boston Juvenile Court. In 1914, she returned to Portland as superintendent of the Frazer Detention Home, but a serious case of tuberculosis forced her to resign. After a long recuperation, she resumed work as director of Los Angeles County Juvenile Hall, where, from 1917 until 1920, she attempted to improve health and psychological services. In 1920, she became Juvenile Court "referee," hearing cases of girls and young boys. Near San Fernando, the El Retiro School for Girls, which she founded and helped run, became a showcase for student self-government, recreation, and rehabilitation.

Van Waters published two influential books about juvenile delinquency: *Youth in Conflict* (1925) and *Parents on Probation* (1928). In 1929, the National Conference on Social Work elected her president. After she left Los Angeles in 1931, she investigated

juvenile justice for the Harvard Crime Survey and the National Commission on Law Observance and Enforcement.

In 1932, Van Waters became superintendent of the Massachusetts Reformatory for Women in Framingham. Running the institution as though it were a progressive school, she emphasized education, counseling, spirituality, and paid work-release programs. Although political conservatives opposed her reforms, she enjoyed strong support among the clergy, women's groups, and powerful liberal reformers. In 1949, after the commissioner of corrections dismissed Van Waters from office for her day-work system and for allegedly tolerating homosexuality among inmates, a gubernatorial commission reinstated her. She retired in 1957 and pursued lifelong interests in the abolition of capital punishment and the rehabilitation of imprisoned men and women.

—*Estelle B. Freedman*

SUGGESTED READING:
Freedman, Estelle B. *Maternal Justice: Miriam Van Waters and the Female Reform Tradition, 1887–1974.* Chicago, 1996.

VARGAS, DIEGO DE

Diego de Vargas (1643–1704) is known as the "reconqueror of New Mexico." He first arrived in Mexico in 1673 from his native Spain, having been sent by the king to carry dispatches to the viceroy in Mexico City. After holding various minor posts in the Mexican government, he was named governor and captain general of New Mexico in 1688.

Before his appointment to the post, the province had witnessed extreme unrest. During the PUEBLO REVOLT in 1680, the Pueblo Indians had killed twenty-one Franciscans and more than four hundred colonists and had driven the survivors south to El Paso. The Mexican government made several attempts to regain control, but it was not until Vargas took up his duties at El Paso in 1691 that progress was made. In August 1692, he and a small army moved north. Reaching New Mexico, he was surprised to find that some of the Pueblo Indians were ready to negotiate. Many of their older, belligerent leaders had died, and the nearby nomadic tribes were constantly warring for Pueblo lands. Vargas reestablished a colonial government in Santa Fe and gained control of nearly the entire province. A year later, however, he found the Indians living in Santa Fe, San Ildefonso, and Cochiti had changed their minds, and he battled them into submission. In

1696, rebellion broke out again, but Vargas sternly regained control.

Don Pedro Cubero succeeded Vargas as governor of New Mexico in 1697. Cubero arrested Vargas on charges of misconduct, and the former governor spent three years in jail before his appeal reached Mexico City. Vargas was exonerated during the investigation and was restored to the governorship in 1703. He died the following year during battle with the Apaches.

—*Candace Floyd*

SUGGESTED READING:

Vargas, Diego de. *By Force of Arms: The Journals of don Diego de Vargas, New Mexico, 1691–93.* Edited by John L. Kessell, Rick Hendricks, and Meredith D. Dodge. Albuquerque, N. Mex., 1992.

VASQUEZ, PIERRE LOUIS

Mountain man and Indian trader Louis Vasquez (1798–1868) was born in St. Louis, the son of Benito Vasquez from Spain and Julie Papin, a French woman from St. Louis.

As early as 1823, Vasquez was engaged in trade with the Pawnees. He is generally believed to have accompanied JEDEDIAH STRONG SMITH's expedition in the winter of 1825 and 1826. In 1832, Vasquez was at Pierre's Hole with ROBERT CAMPBELL and Andrew Sublette. He returned with them in 1833 and stayed to trade with the Crow Indians until the 1834 caravan arrived.

The following year, Vasquez entered into a partnership with Andrew Sublette to build Fort Vasquez on the South Fork of the Platte River. After two competing posts were constructed, the two men sold out in 1841 to Lock and Randolph, a business that failed before it could pay Vasquez and Sublette the full amount owed them.

Vasquez joined JAMES (JIM) BRIDGER in a partnership in 1842 to build FORT BRIDGER on Black's Fork of the Green River for trading with the Utes, Shoshones, and white emigrants. The fort was a gathering spot for the trappers who remained in the field as the FUR TRADE declined, and Bridger used the fort as a starting point for leading parties to California.

In 1846, Vasquez returned to St. Louis and married a widow, Narcissa Land Ashcraft. Their son, Louis Vasquez, Jr., was born at Fort Bridger.

Vasquez frequently visited Salt Lake despite the Mormons' distrust of his partner, Jim Bridger. That distrust culminated in an unsuccessful attempt to arrest Bridger in 1853. In 1855, Vasquez sold at least his part of the fort to the Mormons for eight thousand dollars and returned to Missouri. He bought a brick house and a farm at Westport, where he died.

—*Charles E. Hanson, Jr.*

SEE ALSO: Mountain Men; Sublette Brothers

SUGGESTED READING:

Hafen, LeRoy R. "Louis Vasquez." In *The Mountain Men and the Far West.* Edited by LeRoy R. Hafen. Glendale, Calif., 1965.
Houck, Louis. *The Spanish Regime in Missouri.* Vol. 1. Chicago, 1909.
Missouri Historical Society. *Chouteau Accounts.* St. Louis, 1842.
Morgan, Dale L., ed. *The West of William H. Ashley, 1822–1838.* Denver, 1964.

VÁSQUEZ, TIBURCIO

Legendary bandit Tiburcio Vásquez (1835–1875) stated upon his final capture in 1874, "My career grew out of the circumstances by which I was surrounded as I grew to manhood." From the time his troubles began in 1851 until his execution, Vásquez excited the passions of all Californians. His compatriots saw him as an avenger of the injustices that the Americanos heaped upon the Californios (native-born Californians of Hispanic descent), while the Americans cited him as proof of the innate criminality of Mexican society and culture and as an example of how the West was successfully tamed. Surely, though, he acted in the context of the general lawlessness and racial animosity that prevailed in California in the decades following the United States–Mexican War.

A native of Monterey County, California, Vásquez alleged that his fights with the Americans began with their coveting of the Californio women and their rudeness toward the men. Vásquez took a herd of cattle inland from his comfortable home in Monterey, but "even here I was not permitted to remain in peace. . . . I went to my mother and told her I intended to commence a different life. I asked for and obtained her blessing, and at once commenced the life of a robber." From first reports in 1856, he and his companions rustled horses and cattle, shared a few with unfortunate Mexicans, and sold the rest to support Vasquez's expensive fondness for women and gambling. In and out of San Quentin prison for two decades, he organized a gang in 1873 that launched a crime spree, including a murderous episode at Tres Pinos, an incident that inflamed public opinion against him. His arrest in 1874 was brought about when one of his partners, whose wife he had seduced, betrayed him. Vásquez's arrest by a posse from Los Angeles, his trial, and execution in March 1875 attracted statewide attention.

—*Douglas Monroy*

SEE ALSO: Social Banditry

SUGGESTED READING:
Cleland, Robert Glass. *The Cattle on a Thousand Hills: Southern California, 1850–1880.* San Marino, Calif., 1975.
May, Ernest. "Tiburcio Vasquez." *Historical Society of Southern California Quarterly* 29 (1947): 122–135. Reprinted in Castillo, Pedro, and Albert Camarillo, eds. *Furia y Muerte: Los Bandidos Chicanos.* Los Angeles, 1973.

VEGETABLE GROWING

SEE: Fruit and Vegetable Growing

VELEZ, LUPE

One of the first Mexican movie actresses in Hollywood, Lupe Velez (1909–1944) was born Maria Guadalupe Villalobos in San Luis Potosi, Mexico. The daughter of a military colonel and opera singer, she attended an all-girls Catholic school in San Antonio, Texas. As a teen-ager, she worked in a department store and as a dancer in Mexico City.

In 1926, Velez moved to Hollywood and found work as an extra in several films. Douglas Fairbanks, Sr., chose her to costar with him in *The Gaucho* (1928), a movie in which she played a wild mountain girl. RKO then offered her a five-year contract. From her first publicity in Hollywood, Velez was cast as a "sex kitten," "hot tamale," and "Mexican spitfire," and she projected this image both on and off the screen, in films, interviews, and photo layouts. Historians and amateur film buffs have speculated that Velez internalized the spitfire image.

During the filming of *Wolf Song* (1928), she met Gary Cooper and began a relationship with him that lasted more than two years. Velez married Johnny Weismuller on October 8, 1933. Their relationship was a tumultuous one that every Hollywood magazine followed until their divorce in 1939. During that time, Velez made both English- and Spanish-language films and appeared on Broadway.

In 1939, working for RKO Studios, Velez began the "Mexican Spitfire" series, which included *Girl from Mexico* (1939), *Mexican Spitfire* (1939), *Mexican Spitfire out West* (1940), *Mexican Spitfire's Baby* (1941),

Mexican Spitfire at Sea (1942), *Mexican Spitfire Sees a Ghost* (1942), and *Mexican Spitfire's Elephant* (1942). The "Spitfire" series signaled the end of her career. Although she had made plans to go back to Mexico for film work, Velez, single and five months pregnant, committed suicide at her Beverly Hills home.

—*Alicia I. Rodríquez Estrada*

SEE ALSO: Film: Minority Images in Westerns; Stereotypes: Stereotypes of Mexicans

SUGGESTED READING:
Hadley-Garcia, George. *Hispanic Hollywood: The Latins in Motion Pictures.* New York, 1990.
López, Ana M. "Are All Latins from Manhattan? Hollywood, Ethnography, and Cultural Colonialism." In *Unspeakable Images: Ethnicity and the American Cinema.* Edited by Lester D. Friedman. Chicago, 1991.
Pinto, Alfonso. "Lupe Velez, 1909–1944." *Films in Review* 28 (November 1977): 513–524.
Rios-Bustamante, Antonio. "Lupe Velez: Tragic Prototype of the Latin Spitfire Stereotype." *Americas 2001* 1 (January 1988): 24–25.

VENARD, STEPHEN

A law officer in Nevada City, California, in lawless times, Stephen Venard (1824–1891) was born in a rural area southwest of Lebanon, Ohio. He received an education at the Waynesville Academy and afterwards moved to present-day Fountain City, Indiana. By day a schoolteacher, at night he became involved in the Underground Railroad, an activity that grew from his resolute commitment to abolition. When Southern slave owners put a price on his head, Venard headed west. By 1853, he was operating a grocery store in the gold-rush town of Nevada City. Two years later, he served as a deputy sheriff to W. W. ("Boss") Wright, but when Wright was killed the following year, Venard resigned rather than work for Wright's successor.

Venard ran for election to the office of city marshal in Nevada City in 1857 against WILLIAM HENRY PLUMMER, a man who knew both sides of the law. Venard lost the election but won the marshal's position seven years later after Plummer left town.

Northern California in the late 1860s was bedeviled by a notorious gang of "road agents," or stagecoach robbers, led by George Shanks. Venard pursued the outlaws and, in a confrontation in 1866, reportedly killed three of them with four bullets. Venard's reputation as an effective lawman was established when news of his exploits appeared in national magazines.

Venard became a deputy sheriff of Meadow Lake City, a mining town in the High Sierra, then a top guard for Wells, Fargo and Company in 1869, and a Nevada City police officer two years later. He held the latter position until 1886, and, on special assignment to Wells Fargo, he tracked a band of road agents headed by John L. Houx and Elisha William ("Big Foot") Ardus. Venard caught the gang and saw them prosecuted.

Following his retirement from law enforcement, Venard took up prospecting and named his stake the Detective Mine. More successful at finding outlaws than gold, Venard died penniless three years later.

—*Patricia Hogan*

SUGGESTED READING:

Axelrod, Alan, and Charles Phillips. *Cops, Crooks, and Criminologists: A International Biographical Dictionary of Law Enforcement.* New York, 1996.

VENIAMINOV, IVAN (POPOV, IOANN)

The first Russian Orthodox bishop of Alaska, Ivan Veniaminov (1797–1879) was a scholar, ethnographer, linguist, craftsman, and pastor. He is known for his piety and his commitment to the just treatment of Alaska's native people. He was glorified (canonized) as St. Innocent in 1977.

Born Ioann Popov near Irkutsk in southeastern Siberia, he was raised in a poor family that included several churchmen. For his superior scholarship, his teachers at Irkutsk Theological Seminary awarded him the name of a recently deceased, pious bishop there.

After his ordination in 1821, Ivan Veniaminov, accompanied by his wife and family, went as a missionary priest to Unalaska in the Aleutian Islands in Russian America. He immediately manifested a special pastoral dedication. He learned the Aleut language, developed an Aleut alphabet, and translated several Russian liturgical works. He opened an elementary school for boys and built a chapel, rectory, and other buildings while training native carpenters, stone masons, brick-makers, blacksmiths, and locksmiths.

As part of his pastoral commitment, Veniaminov traveled the difficult waters of the Aleutian Islands and the Bering Sea coast of Alaska by *baidarka* (kayak). Along the way, he established chapels and preached brotherhood and self-improvement. Studying the native culture, he kept meticulous notes, which he later published.

In 1834, the RUSSIAN-AMERICAN COMPANY transferred Veniaminov to Sitka. Despite translating liturgical works into the language of the Tlingit Indians there, he gained acceptance only when the Russians and Indians whom he had vaccinated survived a smallpox epidemic. In 1836, he visited the Russian post at FORT ROSS in California and stopped at the Spanish missions.

In 1839, Veniaminov returned with his family to Russia, where his wife died. He took monastic vows and was appointed bishop of a new episcopate created for Alaska and the far eastern region of Siberia; he took the name "Innokentii" (Innocent). For the next twenty-five years, he continued his pastoral work throughout Russian America, encouraged the translation of liturgical texts into aboriginal languages, taught natives to read and write, worked to protect native rights, and ministered to natives and colonists over a vast area from the Amur River to California.

In 1868, Czar Alexander II appointed him metropolitan of Moscow, the highest office in the Russian Orthodox Church. He inspired orthodoxy with work among the poor and his promotion of education. He died in Moscow.

—*Stephen Haycox*

SUGGESTED READING:

Chevigny, Hector. *Russian America: The Great Alaskan Venture, 1741–1867.* New York, 1967.

Nichols, Robert, and Robert Croskey. "'The Condition of the Orthodox Church in Russian America': Innokentii Veniaminov's History of the Russian Church in Alaska." *Pacific Northwest Quarterly* 63 (1972): 41–54.

Smith, Barbara. *Orthodoxy and Native Americans: The Alaska Mission.* Crestwood, N.Y., 1980.

Veniaminov, Ioann. *Notes on the Islands of the Unalashka District.* Translated and edited by Lydia T. Black, R. H. Geoghegan, and Richard Pierce. Kingston, Ont., 1984.

VIAL, PEDRO

Western trailblazer Pedro (or Pierre) Vial (?–1814) was born in Lyons, France. Little is known about his background before his arrival in the Southwest. He began trading with various Indian tribes from northern Texas to Louisiana, and in 1786, he was commissioned as a foreign agent to work for the Spanish government by Domingo Cabello, governor of Texas. In that role, Vial was responsible for opening a direct trail from San Antonio to Santa Fe. On October 4, 1786, he and his friend Cristobal de Los Santos began their journey toward New Mexico. Traveling up the Red River through Comanche country, Vial successfully completed the trip and arrived in Santa Fe on May 26, 1787.

A superior cartographer and crafty pathfinder, Vial traveled safely and unescorted among the Sioux, Arapahos, Kiowas, Utes, and Apaches and, over the next twenty years, opened new routes from Santa Fe to Natchitoches, Louisiana, and St. Louis, Missouri. He kept several journals that described in detail most of his travels.

Through Vial's successes, the Spanish government continued to legitimize its claims in the Southwest by consolidating outposts in Texas and New Mexico.

—*Fred L. Koestler*

SUGGESTED READING:
Loomis, Noel M., and Abraham P. Nasatir. *Pedro Vial and the Roads to Santa Fe.* Norman, Okla., 1967.

VICTOR, FRANCES FULLER

Writer Frances Fuller Victor (1826–1902) is best remembered for *The River of the West* (1870), a history of Oregon and the life of mountain man JOSEPH LAFAYETTE MEEK. Born Frances Fuller in Rome township, New York, she was educated at the Wooster Female Seminary in Ohio. She published her first literary work—a poem—in the *Wooster Democrat*. Early in her career, she and her sister Metta Victoria Fuller pooled their literary talents and gained national exposure as the "Sisters of the West" through a series of articles published in the *New York Home Journal*. They became editors of *The Monthly Hesperian* in Detroit, and published a collection of their verse, *Poems of Sentiment and Imagination* in 1851. In 1862, Frances Fuller produced two dime novels, divorced her first husband, and married Henry Victor, the brother of her sister's husband Orville J. Victor.

From 1863 to 1864, Frances Victor wrote a column for the *Golden Era* in San Francisco. After her husband resigned from the navy, the couple settled in Portland, Oregon. From then on, she plunged into the history of Oregon, Washington, and California by traveling throughout the Oregon countryside to collect firsthand material from settlers.

In 1868, her marriage to Henry Victor ended in separation. From 1868 to 1878, Frances Victor worked feverishly as a writer, struggling to earn a living and, in the process, creating a valuable body of Far Western histories and literature, including *The River of the West* (1870), *All over Oregon and Washington* (1872), *Women's War with Whiskey; or, Crusading in Portland* (1874), *Eleven Years in the Rocky Mountains and Life on the Frontier* (1877), and *The New Penelope and Other Stories and Poems* (1877). She also contributed to such Western periodicals as the *Overland Monthly, The West Shore,* the *Portland Oregonian,* the *San Francisco Call Bulletin,* and the *New Northwest,* a Portland-based journal on women's rights. In 1878, Victor accepted an offer from HUBERT HOWE BANCROFT to work in his library and to contribute to his series of histories of the Pacific states. She wrote Bancroft's *History of Oregon* and is credited with having substantially written the *History of Washington, Idaho, and Montana,* as well as most of the *History of Nevada, Colorado, and Wyoming.* In addition, she contributed chapters to Bancroft's *History of California, California Inter Pocula, History of the Northwest Coast,* and almost a volume of railroad history in the *Chronicles of the Builders of the Commonwealth.*

By 1889, Victor had earned sufficient money to resume her travels, and in 1891, she expanded her *All over Oregon and Washington* as *Atlantis Arisen.* Oregon's secretary of state commissioned her to write *Early Indian Wars of Oregon* in 1894. She then returned to San Francisco, where she supported herself by writing potboiler fiction. However, by this time, she had earned a reputation as a historian—gaining particular note for separating fact from legend in the life of Marcus Whitman, the missionary killed by Cayuse Indians in 1847. Her final book, *Poems,* was published in 1900. Victor died, in Portland, two years after its publication.

—*Alan Axelrod*

SEE ALSO: Literature: Dime Novels; Whitman, Marcus and Narcissa; Women Writers

SUGGESTED READING:
Caughey, John W. *Hubert Howe Bancroft: Historian of the West.* Berkeley, Calif., 1946.
Powers, Alfred. *History of Oregon Literature.* Portland, Oreg., 1955.

VICTORIO (APACHE)

A superb combat chieftain of the Mimbres Apaches and perhaps America's greatest guerrilla warrior, Victorio (ca. 1825–1880) was born probably in southwestern New Mexico, although some researchers have claimed he was a Mexican who was captured as a child by Indians. He first came to widespread attention when he signed a provisional compact with the United States in 1853. Two years later, he probably led a great raid into Chihuahua, returning with livestock and prisoners. He took part in the skirmishes surrounding the discovery of gold at Pinos Altos, New Mexico, near present-day Silver City and in the heart of Apache country. He may have participated in the Battle of Apache Pass in July 1862.

Victorio (Apache). *Courtesy Arizona Historical Society.*

After the Civil War, Victorio and Loco became joint chiefs of the Mimbres Apaches, who were based in the Black Range of New Mexico. An agency was established for the Mimbres at Canada Alamosa (present-day Monticello), and for two years, Victorio and his people were removed to Tularosa in western New Mexico.

In 1877, the U.S. government moved the Mimbres again, this time to San Carlos, Arizona. There they found themselves among their enemies, and they soon broke out. They surrendered in northwestern New Mexico and were returned briefly to Canada Alamosa. When threatened with another transfer to San Carlos, Loco agreed to the move, but Victorio broke out once more, committed minor depredations in order to survive, and settled at length on the Mescalero Reservation east of the Rio Grande.

Mistaking a visit by U.S. officials as an indication that he would once more be moved to San Carlos, Victorio broke out in August 1879 for the last time, defeated soldiers in various engagements, and took his people into the Black Range. There he was attacked several times, but he always triumphed over the army. At last, he and his followers escaped into Mexico. He committed a savage massacre of Mexicans in the Candelaria Range. After long maneuvering and many actions against the American and Mexican forces, he

at last surrendered on Tres Castillos, a rocky hill in Chihuahua. There he was killed along with seventy-eight members of his band. Lieutenant Colonel Joaquin Terrazas took sixty-eight women and children as prisoners. He was paid $17,250 for the scalps he had taken and $10,200 for his prisoners.

Victorio was considered by many to be the greatest Indian general. The self-disciplined chief abstained from alcohol, married only once, and was survived by a son and perhaps a daughter. His descendants live in New Mexico, Oklahoma, and New York City.

—*Dan L. Thrapp*

SUGGESTED READING:
Thrapp, Dan L. *Victorio and the Mimbres Apaches.* Norman, Okla., 1974. Reprint. 1991.

VIGILANTISM

Vigilantism is the assumption of law enforcement and judicial authority for some extended period of time by a formally organized, but extralegal, body of volunteers intent on punishing suspected wrongdoers. It should not be confused with a lynch mob or other spontaneous outbursts of retribution.

Vigilantism moved westward with American settlers, erupting first in the South Carolina backcountry in 1767, then in Illinois in 1816, in Indiana in 1820, in Alabama and Mississippi in 1830, and in Arkansas in 1839. Iowa and Texas experienced their first vigilantism in 1840, and Missouri in 1842. Vigilantism, like American settlers themselves, leapfrogged most of the West and landed in the ports and gold camps of California in 1849. From then through the turn of the twentieth century, there were some two hundred vigilante movements in the West.

"Committee of Vigilance" and "Committee of Safety" were the names that Western vigilantes most often used for their organizations. Occasionally, vigilantes used the older term "Regulators" or, following Virginia City's (Nevada) lead, the "601." They usually formed the organizations not because there were no institutions of law enforcement and justice, but because, in the eyes of the vigilantes, these institutions had failed to do their jobs. Vigilantes argued that they were forced to assert, in a phrase used repeatedly, their "right to self-preservation." Moreover, said vigilantes, they operated within the spirit, if not the letter, of the law.

The grand jury of Esmeralda County, Nevada, articulated such sentiments when it concluded in an 1864 report that the local vigilantes, who hanged four men and banished a dozen others, were simply asserting

An 1884 illustration from *Harper's Weekly* depicts a group of vigilantes guarding three captured horse thieves on the Texas-Oklahoma border. The telegraph pole, converted into a gallows, becomes the means of instant justice. *Courtesy Denver Public Library, Western History Department.*

"the right to self-preservation and the supremacy of natural law over defective statutory forms and tedious tribunals." Thomas J. Dimsdale in his classic contemporary account, *The Vigilantes of Montana* (1866), wrote that the vigilantes of the gold camps of western Montana rightly claimed that "self-preservation is the first law of nature." The *Territorial Enterprise* of Virginia City, Nevada, commenting on vigilantism in Bodie, California, in 1881, said "when the officers of the law persistently fail to do their duty, and the courts, established for the promotion of justice, prove themselves unequal to the task, it is time for the people to rise in their majesty and vindicate the first great law of self-preservation."

In the early days of settlement in the West, outlaws had at least one distinct advantage: local authorities rarely pursued them far from town or beyond the county line. The expense of a long-range pursuit was simply prohibitive. Once outlaws had eluded the town marshal or the county sheriff, they were usually gone for good. Detectives working for express companies or railroads were often the law officials who tracked down and captured stagecoach and train robbers.

If captured, all was not lost for the outlaws; the judicial system also worked in their favor. Then, as now, criminal defendants enjoyed the presumption of innocence. It was the job of the prosecutor to prove that defendants were not only guilty, but guilty beyond a reasonable doubt, and the verdict had to be unanimous. A guilty verdict was especially difficult to obtain in the early settlement days of the West. Because people moved about so often, witnesses to a crime were frequently long gone by the time a trial was held. For this and other reasons, defendants could many times expect verdicts of not guilty or mistrials. It did not disturb most citizens if one "badman" was being tried for the shooting death of another "badman," but if an innocent victim were killed, then a vigilante response was common.

The most prominent residents of a town or a region generally led the vigilance committees, which enjoyed widespread support. A grand jury report on the Citizens' Safety Committee of Aurora, Nevada, claimed that the committee was "composed of over six hundred of our best, most substantial and law-abiding citizens." A review of names of individual vigilantes who participated in various movements in the West suggests that Aurora's committee was typical. WILLIAM TELL COLEMAN, a wealthy merchant and importer, was president of San Francisco's 1856 vigilance committee. Another member of the committee was AMASA LELAND STANFORD, a successful merchant, who later became one of the "Big Four" of railroad fame as well as a governor of California and a U.S. senator. Wilbur Sanders, a young attorney, was the prosecutor for the vigilantes of Virginia City, Montana, in 1864; later, he was elected one of Montana's first two U.S. senators. GRANVILLE STUART, a cattle king, led the vigilantes of eastern Montana in 1884; he later became the American minister to Uruguay and the president of the Montana Historical Society. William J. McConnell, an Idaho vigilante during the early 1860s, later became one of Idaho's first two U.S. senators and then the governor of the state. Dr. John Osborne, a Rawlins physician, was a Wyoming vigilante in 1881; he later became the state's governor.

Typically, vigilantes formed an executive committee and adopted a constitution. They had a chain of command and were often organized into companies and squads. Although impassioned and violent, vigilantes were usually highly disciplined, orderly, and deliberate. This was not accidental. Many of them had military experience, and some were combat veterans, having served in the United States–Mexican War, the Civil War, or one or more of the Indian Wars. Officially constituted authorities, realizing that they would have to oppose hundreds, sometimes thousands, of well-organized and well-armed vigilantes, rarely attempted to interfere with their extralegal activities. Moreover, vigilantes generally represented the will of the majority of citizens in any particular community.

Most instances of vigilantism in the West can be categorized as, in the words of Richard Maxwell Brown, "socially constructive movements": the majority of the people either participated in the movement or approved of it; the vigilantes were well regulated; they dealt quickly and effectively with a specific criminal problem; they left the town or region in a more stable and orderly condition; they disbanded before substantial opposition developed.

Vigilantes usually gave those suspected of wrongdoing some kind of hearing or trial, and not all tried were found guilty and executed. Of ninety men taken into custody by the San Francisco vigilance committee of 1851, forty-one were exonerated and released, fifteen were remanded to the regular authorities, one was whipped, and twenty-eight were banished. Only four were executed. Although a popular theme in motion pictures and novels, the hanging of an innocent man at the direction of a vigilance committee occurred rarely and, in the case of the socially constructive movements, probably not at all. Unlike their modern counterparts, early Western novelists and historians, including HUBERT HOWE BANCROFT, Thomas J. Dimsdale, OWEN WISTER, and THEODORE ROOSEVELT, were often strong supporters of vigilantism.

Occasionally, though, vigilantes had ulterior motives in what was ostensibly an attack on criminals. The 1856 Committee of Vigilance in San Francisco, dominated by Protestants and Masons who supported the KNOW-NOTHING PARTY, seems to have been at least partly motivated by a fear of growing Irish Catholic political and economic power in the city. The Stranglers, a creation of the big Montana ranchers who depended on the open range for grazing their herds, may have driven out honest homesteaders along with cattle rustlers in 1884. This may also have been true of the Regulator movement in Wyoming, which culminated in the JOHNSON COUNTY WAR of 1892.

—*Roger D. McGrath*

SEE ALSO: San Francisco Vigilance Committee of 1856; Violence

SUGGESTED READING:

Bancroft, Hubert Howe. *Popular Tribunals*. San Francisco, 1887.

Brown, Richard Maxwell. *Strain of Violence: Historical Studies of American Violence and Vigilantism*. New York, 1975.

Dimsdale, Thomas J. *The Vigilantes of Montana*. Virginia City, Mont., 1866.

Gard, Wayne. *Frontier Justice*. Norman, Okla., 1949.

McGrath, Roger D. *Gunfighters, Highwaymen, and Vigilantes: Violence on the Frontier*. Berkeley, Calif., 1984.

Mercer, Asa. *The Banditti of the Plains*. Cheyenne, Wyo., 1894.

Nunis, Jr., Doyce B., ed. *The San Francisco Vigilance Committee of 1856: Three Views*. Los Angeles, 1971.

Senkewicz, Robert M. *Vigilantes in Gold Rush San Francisco*. Stanford, Calif., 1985.

Smith, Helena Huntington. *The War on the Powder River*. New York, 1966.

The vigilantes of Lake City, Colorado, printed this edict in the 1880s. The term *foot pads* refers to thieves who padded the soles of their shoes to allow them to sneak up on unsuspecting victims. *Courtesy Colorado Historical Society.*

VILLA, FRANCISCO ("PANCHO")

Mexican revolutionary Francisco "Pancho" Villa (1877 or 1878–1923) was born near San Juan del Rio in Durango and grew up as an orphan. He worked as a woodcutter, bricklayer, teamster, and vaquero (cowboy). His lack of education and family connections blocked his chances for social advancement, and following his shooting of a prominent landowner, he turned to banditry. When one of the leaders of his gang was killed by federal authorities, he gave up his baptismal name of Doroteo Arango to assume the deceased man's name—Francisco Villa. By 1905, he had become the leader of a group of cattle rustlers and had a sizeable price on his head.

Although Villa's sensitivities were with the peasants, his political views were neither philosophically sophisticated nor deeply rooted. Yet when Francisco Madero began his revolution against the autocratic government of President Porfirio Díaz in October 1910, Villa joined the crusade and played a crucial role in the capture of the border city of Juárez, a victory that hastened Díaz's resignation on May 25, 1911. Villa initially seemed content with ownership of a slaughterhouse in the northern state of Chihuahua, but Madero's failure to implement promised reforms undermined their alliance. After Madero was brutally assassinated by General Victoriano Huerta in February 1913, Villa actively reentered the second stage of the Mexican Revolution. In association with other rebels, especially Emiliano Zapata, leader of the anti-government forces in the south, Villa took control of Mexico City in December 1914 and briefly shared national power. During his extensive campaigns against the Huertistas, Villa demonstrated sound military tactics as well as personal daring and a character that attracted many eager sympathizers. He also enjoyed indirect support from United States President Woodrow Wilson, who allowed private shipments of weapons to be transported across the international border to the

Francisco ("Pancho") Villa, in the high-back chair, with other revolutionary leaders of Mexico. *Courtesy University of Texas at El Paso.*

Constitutionalists. Villa reciprocated with many acts of kindness to American property owners in northern Mexico.

After deposing President Huerta, the victorious Constitutionalists soon began quarreling among themselves over policies and desires for expansion of personal power. Villa found himself locked in battle with General Venustiano Carranza, who eventually established himself as president of Mexico. In 1915, Carranza's brilliant military commander General Alvaro Obregón defeated Villa at the battles of Celaya, Trinidad, and León. Equally important was Woodrow Wilson's de facto recognition of Carranza's government in October 1915 and his simultaneous closing of the border to additional weapons shipments to rebel armies. Villa felt betrayed by an American president whom he had always lauded and by a people who had long been among his most important supporters. Furthermore, he knew that the balance of power had turned against him; over the long run, his cause seemed doomed by the twin forces of domestic warfare and international diplomacy. Only a dramatic rupture between Carranza and the United States could revive his chances for success.

Amid this new wave of anti-Americanism and possibly because Villa wanted to spark an incident that could cause war between the two nations, members of his army attacked a train near Santa Ysabel, Chihuahua, on January 10, 1916. They singled out the seventeen American miners aboard the coaches and, amid cries of "Viva Villa," killed them all. Carranza's quick action against the raiders somewhat ameliorated the explosive situation.

On March 9, 1916, several hundred Villista soldiers attacked Columbus, New Mexico, killed seventeen Americans, and burned several buildings. Seven days later, the United States launched a forty-eight-hundred-man punitive expedition into the state of Chihuahua to drive the Villista forces away from the border. Amid the towering mountains and burning deserts and with almost no support from local civilians, General JOHN JOSEPH PERSHING's Punitive Expedition was locked in a cat-and-mouse game against an elusive army. Furthermore, President Carranza refused to cooperate with the American incursion, and he ordered federal commanders to resist the foreign troops if they moved farther south. On May 6, Villistas raided the small settlements of Glenn Springs and Boquillas in the Big Bend of southwestern Texas and killed four Americans. That attack prompted a smaller punitive expedition into Coahuila. After confrontations between American troops and Carranzista soldiers at Parral (April 12) and Carrizal (June 21) produced considerable bloodshed, the two governments moved toward reconciliation; on February 5, 1917, the last of Pershing's Punitive Expedition withdrew from Mexico. Not only had Villa's plan failed to produce war between the United States and Carranza's government, but further military reverses forced him to retire from political affairs.

On July 20, 1923, assassins killed Villa and three of his bodyguards while they were on a business trip to Parral. Many people felt that Villa had been considering a reentry into politics and that he was killed by General Obregón who, as the new president, feared Villa's revival as a competitor.

—*Michael L. Tate*

SUGGESTED READING:

Atkin, Ronald. *Revolution! Mexico 1910–1920.* New York, 1969.

Clendenen, Clarence C. *The United States and Pancho Villa.* Ithaca, N.Y., 1961.

Guzmán, Martín Luis. *Memoirs of Pancho Villa.* Austin, Tex., 1965.

VILLARD, HENRY

Journalist, financier, and railroad promoter Henry Villard (1835–1900) was born Ferdinand Heinrich Gustav Hilgard in Speyer, Bavaria, the son of a Bavarian supreme court justice. Due to his liberal sentiments in education and politics, Villard became estranged from his father and immigrated to the United States in 1853. After arriving in New York City, he moved to settle with relatives in Belleville, Illinois. He gained facility with the English language while engaging in various occupations, including law, book selling, real estate, teaching, and journalism. In 1858, he became a correspondent with the New York *Staats-Zeitung* and covered the Lincoln-Douglas debates.

Villard's ultimate goal was to work for the English-language press, and, in spring 1859, he traveled to Colorado to report on the Pikes Peak gold rush for the *Cincinnati Commercial.* Along with Horace Greeley of the *New York Tribune* and Albert D. Richardson of the *Boston Journal,* he composed a circular verifying the existence of gold in the Colorado gulches and later wrote a guidebook to the region.

Returning to the East, Villard covered the presidential campaign of 1860 and, when the Civil War broke out, worked as a war correspondent first for the *New York Herald* and then for the *New York Tribune.* In 1866, he married Helen Francis Garrison, the only daughter of abolitionist William Lloyd Garrison. Settling in Boston for a time after the war, Villard pioneered in civil-service reform and became secretary of the American Social Science Association in 1868, which familiarized him with public and corporate finance.

While traveling in Europe in 1871, Villard made contacts that led him into his most influential role as Western railroad financier and promoter. He met and eventually became the American representative for a group of bondholders for Oregon railroad and steamship interests and subsequently regularized the operation of transportation companies on the Columbia River. In 1876, Villard assumed similar responsibilities for the Kansas Pacific Railway. A wealthy man by 1879, he sought to provide a transcontinental connection to Portland for the Northern Pacific Railroad by constructing a railroad along the south bank of the Columbia River. When the Northern Pacific spurned his offer in favor of building to a better harbor on the Puget Sound, Villard organized a "blind pool" and raised, on the strength of his reputation alone, $8 million. He secured control of the Northern Pacific, and, realizing the superior qualities of a terminus farther to the north, he completed the Northern Pacific line to Tacoma in 1883. Soaring construction costs and financial problems with his other railroad interests forced Villard to resign from the Northern Pacific board in 1884.

Villard escaped a ruined reputation. A benevolent monopolist, he bought controlling interest in the *New York Post* in 1881 and promptly turned editorial control over to well-known associates. He was also a key organizer and investor in the Edison General Electric Company. He championed the rights of minorities all his life, a reformist view carried on by his son, Oswald Garrison Villard, who developed the *Nation* into one of American journalism's foremost liberal voices in the 1920s and 1930s.

—*Charles E. Rankin*

SEE ALSO: Magazines and Newspapers; Railroads

SUGGESTED READING:
Hedges, J. B. *Henry Villard and the Railways of the Northwest.* New Haven, Conn., 1930.
New York Times, November 13, 1900.

VIOLENCE

HISTORICAL OVERVIEW

The American past is replete with violence. Neither Puritan New England nor aristocratic Tidewater nor Tammany-dominated New York were models of safety and security, but the region of the United States most often and consistently identified as especially "violent" remains the American West. Partly as a result of traditional wisdom about the Western frontier and partly owing to the imaginative productions of America's publishing and film industries, the Western violence with which we are most familiar is a special brand of personal violence, one unquestionably appealing and even seductive. In the legendary Wild West at least, violence had purpose, a moral point with which to justify the attraction. Perhaps the violent expression of personality, of individual action, of a certain kind of masculinity was inherently fascinating; at any rate, such a near-conscious love of violence lay in the very structure and fabric of much popular and traditional Western history. Out in the Wild West, with its frontier morality play, killers and cads became legends. Shorn of politics, finances, and daily concerns, men such as JAMES BUTLER ("WILD BILL") HICKOK and Wyatt Earp became abstract, "authentic" Western heroes, battling equally abstract villains and triumphing in the name of civilization, rather than, say, the hirelings of Republican businessmen charged with destroying political and economic rivals in the name of greater profit. Faced with the fact of real social conflict, which Americans typically wanted to avoid, the story of the Western gunslinger may have been a pleasurable personal gloss on a violence they secretly feared was endemic to American society and wished to explain away.

Undeniably, lawlessness played a role in the history of every Western state. From the arrival of the MOUNTAIN MEN in the trans-Mississippi West, claim jumpers, miners, cowboys, cattle rustlers, Indian hunters, border ruffians, Mexican bandits, mule skinners, railroad workers, highwaymen, professional outlaws, and, indeed, hired gunslingers had more than a speaking acquaintance with violence. And they were joined by gentlemen of property and standing—ranchers, farmers, bankers, promoters, railroad magnates, lawyers, doctors, politicians, mine owners—who frequently took the law into their own hands and often considered themselves a law unto themselves. Operating as a mob of do-gooders, they beat, tarred-and-feathered, or hanged those they believed threats to the

James Butler ("Wild Bill") Hickok. *Courtesy National Cowboy Hall of Fame and Western Heritage Center.*

civil order, but their victims were as likely to be Chinese, African Americans, Mexicans, or Indians as they were bank robbers, horse thieves, and murderers. In fact, the evidence of violence in the West occasionally seems so extensive that it overshadows the causes of the violence. For the endemic social violence of the West was not simply a sideshow of shootouts and rough justice, not something the West put behind itself as its towns became "civilized," but an intrinsic part of Western culture, something intimately connected to Western communities as they established themselves in the larger social order. In short, Western violence was part not merely of a frontier process, but also of a region's entire history.

Roots of Anglo-American violence

The notion of a Western frontier had been around long before FREDERICK JACKSON TURNER announced in 1893 that it had just closed. In fact, the American West itself was a political and cultural construction before it was ever a landed reality. Invented in the late seventeenth century by Virginia planters as a political solution to Virginia's turbulent class problems, the American West began as a social construct that obscured common class interests. After Bacon's Rebellion had revealed the revolutionary potential of those the planters considered a rabble—many of them former debtors or indentured servants, or their descendents, whose position in the colonial economy had been assigned to African slaves—the landed elite hit upon the happy expedient of monopolizing good land in the East, forcing the landless whites into the wilderness, and making of them a buffer for the seaboard rich against Indian troubles. In 1705, the Virginia Assembly passed a law giving every freed indentured male ten bushels of corn, thirty shillings, and a gun (woman got fifteen bushels and forty shillings), and all freed servants fifty acres of land west of the Tidewater.

For poor Europeans so recently displaced from their homeland and their descendents, a plot of earth conferred dignity and distinguished them from the enslaved. Before the century was out, they were pressing beyond the Appalachians into the Ohio Valley, and the West had become the place where "shiftless" whites went to hack out a subsistence and fight "savages" while back East black slaves toiled endlessly to wrest profits for the planters from sprawling tobacco, rice, indigo, and cotton plantations. In the French and Indian War, in many ways a struggle between France and England for the American West, the French used Indians as instruments of deliberate terror and the British used their "beastly" backwoodsmen as a sacrificial advance guard. Much of the seemingly implacable hatred between Indian and pioneer lay in the mutual depredations of the long and bloody conflict. After it was over, King George issued his Proclamation of 1763, which declared a boundary line at the mountains beyond which the English colonists were not permitted to settle. In time the proclamation line both gave the word *frontier* a new American meaning as the advancing edge of white settlement and the march of civilization into the wilderness and led to a pioneer tradition of flouting authority. White settlers defiantly crossed the line, which made them subject to raids from resentful Indians, and which—since they were breaking the law—placed them beyond the king's protection. This lack of royal military support widened the gap between the frontier settlements and Tidewater civilization and between colonists and mother country. Troops, sent initially to patrol the frontier, were billeted in American homes, which caused more resentment; taxes passed to pay for increased troop strengths in America ultimately led to open rebellion.

During the American Revolution, Virginia gave birth to yet another historical phenomenon that would affect the subsequent history of the American West.

Since before the Norman Conquest, Saxon citizens had banded together for mutual protection in what early England called the "frankpledge." Under the private frankpledge, all adult males in a community became responsible for the good conduct of each community member. The frankpledge amounted to a social obligation, and when citizens observed a crime, they were expected to raise an alarm, form a posse, and chase down and capture the criminal. Those who refused to do so were themselves subject to punishment. Should no one actually witness a crime, it fell to the victim alone to investigate and identify the perpetrator to the satisfaction of his frankpledge peers. Perhaps it was no surprise then that—when citizens in Bedford County began stealing horses because both British and American troops were willing to pay high prices for fresh mounts—a Virginian would form an organization to punish horse thieves. His name was Charles Lynch, and when American rebels apprehended a suspected thief, they hauled him before Lynch and three of his neighbors for a summary trial. If the extralegal tribunal found the defendant guilty, he was immediately tied to a large walnut tree in Lynch's yard, hung by his thumbs, lashed across the back thirty-nine times, and banished from the country. During the war, Lynch's law spread throughout Virginia and spawned a VIGILANTISM that would become typical in both the South and the lands west of the mountains.

By then, the outlines of Western "character" had been formed. But it was not the frontier that had formed this character; indeed, the reverse was more true—the frontier was in many ways formed politically and culturally by and for the character of those who occupied the West. Descendants of landless Europeans, Westerners had made a fetish of the family-size plot of land, but in addition to free or cheap land from the government, they also espoused individual enterprise. Offered land belonging to Indians, many had become Indian haters and conquerors. Probably the first mass of poor people to be fully armed, they had come to believe that power emanated from the barrel of a gun. Cut off from the protection of governments housed in the East, they shifted for themselves following the private frankpledge tradition of personal redress. Understanding that in some ways they were social outcasts, they resented the rich planters and all Easterners.

Like others who lived hardscrabble lives and inhabited isolated and remote regions, many of them drank and gambled, which meant they argued and fought and soon had a reputation for hair-trigger violence. Most westerners, of course, like the majority in any society, lived quiet, mundane, hard-working, peaceful lives. And the well-springs of individual violence are frequently more immediate—and themselves more mundane—than some grandiose "frontier" tradition. Nevertheless, some societies are clearly more violent than others and for cultural as well as existential and psychological reasons. The American West was conceived as the place where *individuals seized* the wilderness and *held* it against another race. Such a notion, however well or ill it corresponded to reality, was bound to affect the people who held it, which in some ways was the point—or the point turned on its head—of the frontier historians, from Turner to THEODORE ROOSEVELT, whose *Winning of the West* (a frontier history more racist *and* more popular among the common reading public) indeed celebrated the Western culture of violence.

Culturally, then, it was no accident that the archetype of the "frontiersman" was the resourceful and adventuresome DANIEL BOONE; nor that he had a much undeserved reputation as an "Indian killer." In the same way, *politically* it should hardly be a surprise that the first man Westerners put in the White House was the willful and iconoclastic ANDREW JACKSON, nor that under his leadership, they removed the despised Indians west of the Mississippi and expanded south and west into Alabama, Mississippi, Louisiana, and Texas. By the nineteenth century, these Anglo-American frontiersmen were accustomed to brawling and knife fighting and to using firearms in personal disputes and frequent feuds as well as for hunting and defense against Native Americans or European enemies. When the development of the revolving pistol provided them with a repeating weapon, a lethal new dimension was added to saloon fights and private quarrels. The first systematic use of SAMUEL COLT's new revolvers during the 1840s by TEXAS RANGERS against Comanches and Kiowas introduced a decisive technology in the eventual defeat of Indians across the West. Indeed, Texas, according to historian Richard M. Brown, with its "explosive mixture of deep-southern and frontier-western characteristics," was considered the most violent of the territories in the new trans-Mississippi West.

Gunfighter ethics

American jurisprudence itself, as Brown has pointed out, came to reflect the influence of the pioneers. Since at least the thirteenth century, English common law had dealt harshly with homicide. Central to the common-law concept of self-defense was every citizen's duty to retreat. The law required that one retreat as far as possible from the face of a threat of violence, in fact, literally "to the wall" at one's

Two cavalrymen came to a violent end outside a Kansas dance hall. *Courtesy Historical Department, Archives of the Church of Jesus Christ of Latter-day Saints.*

back, before self-defense could result in excusable, not justifiable, homicide. As Anglo-Americans moved into the Ohio Valley and then across the Mississippi, state after state canceled the English duty to retreat in favor of the American right to stand one's ground. In 1876, Ohio landowner James W. Erwin, who had been convicted of killing his tenant son-in-law in a personal quarrel, was set free when a higher court judge ordered a new trial because a "true man" was not "obliged to fly" from an assailant as the jury had first been instructed. The following year, the Indiana Supreme Court followed *Erwin* v. *State* with a ruling in *Runyan* v. *State* concerning John Runyan's killing of his neighbor Charles Presnall in a personal political feud; the court stated: "The tendency of the American mind seems to be very strongly against the enforcement of any rule which requires a person to flee when assailed." In Minnesota in 1905, a judge ruling in appeal on *State* v. *Gardner* noted that Joseph Gardner, a homesteader and rural mailman who had killed William Garrison in an open field in 1904, was "a typical pioneer, industrious, courageous, and self-reliant." In that case, the judge declared that the old common-law

"doctrine of 'retreat to the wall' had its origins [in medieval England] before the general introductions of guns." While it made "good sense," he went on, "for the law to require, in many cases, an attempt to escape from a hand to hand encounter with fists, clubs, and even knives, as a condition of justification for killing in self defense," it was folly to do so "when experienced men, armed with repeating rifles, face each other in open space." In Missouri, the courts called self-defense a "divine right," and, in violence-prone Texas, the "brutal doctrine" of standing one's ground had been written into law, thus doing away with the need for police, judges, and jury so long as one could "convincingly establish that the killing was a response to a threat against person or property." The so-called Texas rule, which one Alabama judge objected to as promoting "hip-pocket ethics" (most gunmen carried their pistols not in holsters, but in their back pockets), became the basis for the landmark ruling of U.S. Supreme Court Justice Oliver Wendall Holmes, Jr., in the 1921 *Brown* v. *United States*, in which he declared that "a man is not born to walk away" and that, when threatened by violence, one had no duty to retreat but could instead stand one's ground.

Clearly, then, by the turn of the century, the American legal profession had clutched Frederick Jackson Turner's frontier thesis to its heart, and since laws generally reflect prevailing opinion, America had accepted what historian Brown has described as the cluster of beliefs—the values that Turner said were formed on the frontier—that "mentally programmed" Westerners to violence: the doctrine of no duty to retreat, the imperative of personal self-redress, the homestead ethic, the ethic of individual enterprise, an especially sensitive "somewhat primitive code of honor," and the ideology of vigilantism. It was in this atmosphere that the classic walk-down gunfight was born. By the 1850s, revolver duels were erupting regularly in the California gold camps and in Texas and other Western locales. In Texas and elsewhere, the belligerent BENJAMIN F. THOMPSON established himself as the first noted "pistoleer," engaging in at least fourteen shootouts between the 1850s and the 1870s. But the gunfight that first caught the imagination of the public and became the model for all those subsequently portrayed in Hollywood and television westerns occurred in July 1865 between "Wild Bill" Hickok and the luckless Dave Tutt in Springfield, Missouri. The bad blood between the two stemmed from the just-ended Civil War, in which Hickok, a Union spy and scout, had fought with Doc Jennison and his guerrilla JAYHAWKERS, and Tutt, scion of a respected family, had fought for the South. That summer, the two escalated their ideological rivalry by gambling and vying for the affections of the same women, Susanna Moore. Around sundown on July 21, they met, striding toward each other in the town square and opening fire almost simultaneously at seventy-five yards. Tutt's bullet whined over Hickok's head; Hickok's bullet penetrated Tutt's heart. In the subsequent trial, Hickok was found innocent of wrongdoing when a judge instructed the jury specifically that Hickok had no duty to retreat from the threat posed to his life by an armed and angry Tutt. In a feature on "Wild Bill" Hickok published in *Harper's Weekly*, the gunfight played center-stage, and Hickok was presented as a hero who stood his ground. As a result, Hickok became the first of a long list in the West of those Brown calls "glorified" GUNFIGHTERS—Wyatt Earp, JOHN HENRY ("DOC") HOLLIDAY, "BILLY THE KID", JOHN WESLEY HARDIN, and the like.

Now famous, Hickok's walk-down duel with Dave Tutt became the model for the classic shootout between the no-name hero and a badman named Trampas in OWEN WISTER's *Virginian*. In the novel, a fictional gloss on the JOHNSON COUNTY WAR between large cattle operators and alleged cattle rustlers and small ranchers, the hero slays the badman in a final shootout and wins the girl. This plot became the model for the formula

western and proved immensely popular with Americans already fed with tall tales about glorified gunfighters. One study of nearly 600 gunfights found that more than 160 occurred in Texas, with the next closest states being Kansas and New Mexico, which hosted about 80 shootouts apiece. Two-hundred-and-fifty-five professional gunslingers, the study found, killed some 181 men. Most historians, however, now believe those figures to be a drastic underestimate, since they included only the well-known glorified gunfighters. But the West was full of those not-so-famous, whom Brown calls "grassroots" gunfighters, local men good with a pistol or rifle who tended to resort to gunplay. They were the kind of men covered in John D. McGrath's study of the myth of the "Bad Men of Bodie," which he discovered was based on grim reality in the wild and woolly mining camps of Aurora, California, and Bodie, Nevada. Over the course of the booms years, some 70 shootings resulted in 30 deaths, which, translated into modern crime statistic, worked out to a homicide rate of 116 per 100,000 compared to, for example, 1980 Miami's figure of 32.7 per 100,000. At the same time, the most frequent criminal charge in Bodie was "drunk and disorderly," and the local courts convicted a grand total of one man on murder charges. Bodie's gunfighters were miners, teamsters, carpenters, attorneys, bartenders, and lawmen from every region of the country—none of them famous men. Bodie was "a shooter's town" and the home of "bad men," but it was also the home of "many average workingmen who used guns to resolve their differences." Brown estimates that there were thousands of Western gunmen, the vast majority of them grassroots gunfighters who earned neither national nor regional renown, and thus were ignored by the myth-makers, but whose violence constituted a significant social reality in the American West.

Political economy of Western violence

Those who imagine that the nineteenth-century American West was an especially violent place, where the only security was in an aptitude for gunplay and personal violence, usually have in mind such places as gunslinger-haunted mining camps and cow towns, where drunken and armed young men congregated, gambled, and fornicated. They do not have in mind, for example, Scandinavians in Minnesota or North Dakota squaring off in gunfights over milk cows, or Germans and Russians attacking each other in Kansas and Nebraska over the boundaries between wheat fields. But studies have shown that violent towns like Bodie boasted few famous gunmen, while the cow towns policed by the likes of Wyatt Earp and BARTHOLOMEW (BAT) MASTERSON were, relatively speaking, not all that violent. Part of the problem stems from the popular tendency to concentrate on glorified gunslingers as cultural heroes vanquishing evil in gunfights of mythic dimensions. Like most myths, the tales of Billy the Kid's search for revenge in the LINCOLN COUNTY WAR or Wyatt Earp's shootout at O.K. Corral tend to gloss over irreconcilable social differences by denuding history of all substantive content and producing attractive and universal simplicities. Western gunfighters, however, were not mere abstract heroes or villains, but men, and they were no more dedicated to cleaning up towns for the good of mankind than pioneers were committed to bringing civilization to the wilderness. Like the frontier, the Wild West was a mythologizing of concrete political, social, and economic forces, and gunfighters lived in the world shaped by these forces.

In a classic work, Charles and Mary Beard interpreted the Civil War as a "second American Revolution" during which the industrializing North overthrew the agrarian South's long-standing domination of national politics and economic policy. Certainly, after the war, America embarked on a rapid industrialization of the American West—a process that within a decade reduced the region to an economic dependency on the East. As businessmen invaded the West, they looked for capital from Eastern investors, who were hesitant to put their money into a region they imagined overly violent, even verging on anarchy. At the same time, the major industries of the West were extractive, which meant they lived by the gambler's rule of "get in, get rich, and get out" and were in some ways inherently destructive. In general, too, postwar America was as partisan as the country had ever been. Radical Republicans were determined to force social revolution on the South and industrialize the West, Southern Democrats to resist as best they could and perpetuate the agrarian ideals they had espoused since THOMAS JEFFERSON's day. The result was massive social conflict that historian Alan Trachtenburg has called a "Civil War of Incorporation." As rapidly as possible, business interests wished to move into the West and incorporate its wealth: cattlemen wanted to monopolize the range, mining magnates to lay claim to the West's mineral wealth, the railroads to enclose its lands for development and sale, and lumbermen to stake out and cut its forests—all with determined help from the federal government. Two of the basic Western "mind sets"—the homesteader ethic and the imperative to private enterprise—were set at odds in a region where all believed they had no duty to retreat and were inclined to stand their ground.

The postwar alliance between government and capital made the trans-Mississippi West not unlike certain parts of Britain and Ireland during the great enclosures, as corporate America moved into the West and pushed aside Indians, Hispanics, and homesteaders in order to realize profits and make returns to investors. Gunslingers were men of their times. Although gunfighters, as Paul Hutton has argued, like everyone else, had individual ambitions, personalities, and passions that guided their actions, those who came from the Northern Union states, claims Brown, tended to be Republicans and to hire on with the business interests in the mining camps, cow towns, and river valleys. Brown calls these men "incorporation" gunfighters, and like Wyatt Earp, "Wild Bill" Hickok, and Wyoming's FRANK M. CANTON, they most often got the glory. Grassroots gunmen usually from the former Confederacy tended to be Democrats in league with the West's rural interests, its small ranchers, homesteaders, and workingmen. Brown calls these men "resister" gunfighters, and they included such bandits as Jesse James and Billy the Kid whom the dime novels mythologized as "social outlaws." British historian Eric J. Hobsbawm defines these social outlaws as Robin Hood figures appearing in rural areas in times of massive social dislocations caused by distant forces and who enjoy the extralegal support of the rural areas from which they spring.

Whether glorified or grassroots, company hirelings or social bandits, gunfighters were merely the point men in a much broader social conflict that characterized the West in the second half of the nineteenth century and into the first quarter of the twentieth, a conflict fought on many fronts in almost all the Western territories and states. Incorporation led to the post–Civil War roundup of the Indians and the placing of them on reservations. It disfranchised Hispanics in the Southwest and led to such resistance movements as Las Gorras Blancas in New Mexico and the social-outlaw bandits who raided across the border in South Texas: GREGORIO CORTEZ, JUAN NEPOMUCENO CORTINA, and others. It pitted Republican Kansas cow town lawmen against Democratic Texas cowboys. It spawned conflicts between ranchers and homesteaders in Custer County, Nebraska, and between a large land company and local settlers in Colfax County, New Mexico. It sparked the Fence-cutters' War in central Texas, the Sand Hill War between cattlemen and homesteaders in Nebraska, and the Mussel Slough land war between the owners of the Southern Pacific Railroad, COLLIS P. HUNTINGTON, AMASA LELAND STANFORD, and CHARLES CROCKER, and small-farming settlers in California's Central Valley. It lay behind the complicated business and politics of the Lincoln County War and the intricate personal hatreds of the GRAHAM-TEWKESBURY FEUD. In Wyoming, it saw rich, arrogant cattle barons hire gunslinging thugs to kill Democratic small ranchers and cattle-rustling cowboys in the Johnson County War. And on what labor historian Carlos A. Schwantes calls the "wage-workers frontier," incorporation mining interests waged outright class warfare against miners and union members. The WESTERN FED-

ERATION OF MINERS took up the battle in conflicts at CRIPPLE CREEK, COLORADO, the LUDLOW MASSACRE, and the Coeur d'Alene War and was blamed for the assassination of Idaho's ex-governor FRANK STEUNENBERG in 1905. That year, the American West witnessed the birth of the INDUSTRIAL WORKERS OF THE WORLD (IWW), and the "Wobblies," too, joined the fight until World War I provided the federal government the excuse it needed to break the back of labor in the West.

Much more than the lone gunfighter, the regionwide conflict between big-money interests and local agrarians and workers that spilled over the normal political channels with which the nation usually handled its social problems came to characterize the American West. Such violence had damaging political effects, not the least being the long delay suffered by New Mexico and Arizona in achieving statehood. Long after their populations exceeded the required sixty thousand total, they were denied entry into the Union primarily because of Western lawlessness: labor wars, racial resistance, shootouts, rustling, and train and bank robberies. In 1901, Arizona's territorial assembly created the ARIZONA RANGERS, modeled on the Texas Rangers, with the express objective of halting outlawry so that Arizona could become a state. During the next eight years, there was a flurry of gunplay and horse chases that forced rustlers and "resister" gunfighters to flee into Mexico and New Mexico, which in turn saw the formation of the New Mexico Mounted Police in 1905. By 1909, outlawry had declined dramatically enough that the rangers were disbanded. Three years later, both Arizona and New Mexico became states.

Various historians have credited the causes of Western violence as owing to a frontier past, a gunfighter ethic, and a legacy of conquest, but few have doubted that the West was a major contributor to the nation's historically violent heritage. Through repeated portrayal in dime novels, Wild West shows, fiction, and motion pictures, the story of Western violence became deeply ingrained, and the simple solution of killing off a problem exerted a dangerous appeal to broad segments of American society. Perhaps an expression of self-reliance, even courage, the Western "tradition" of personal violence not only obscured the deeper conflicts in Western society but also left a hazardous legacy for contemporary America.

—*Charles Phillips and Bill O'Neal*

SEE ALSO: Cattle Rustling; Earp Brothers; Gorras Blancas, Las; Horse Theft and Horse Thieves; James Brothers; Lynching; O.K. Corral, Gunfight at; Social Banditry

SUGGESTED READING:

Brown, Richard Maxwell. *No Duty to Retreat: Violence and Values in American History and Society.* New York, 1991.

Bykrit, James W. *Forging the Copper Collar: Arizona's Labor-Management War of 1901–21.* Tucson, Ariz., 1982.

Daniel, Cletus E. *Bitter Harvest: A History of California Farmworkers, 1870–1941.* Berkeley, Calif., 1981.

Dedera, Don. *A Little War of Our Own: The Pleasant Valley Feud Revisited.* Flagstaff, Ariz., 1988.

Hobsbawm, Eric J. *Social Bandits and Primitive Rebels.* Glencoe, Ill., 1959.

Hollon, W. Eugene. *Frontier Violence: Another Look.* New York, 1974.

Lingenfelter, Richard E. *The Hardrock Miners: A History of the Mining Labor Movement in the American West, 1863–1893.* Berkeley, Calif., 1984.

Marks, Paula Mitchell. *And Die in the West: The Story of the O.K. Corral Gunfight.* New York, 1989.

McGrath, Roger D. *Gunfighters, Highwaymen, and Vigilantes: Violence on the Frontier.* Berkeley, Calif., 1984.

O'Neal, Bill. *The Arizona Rangers.* Austin, Tex., 1987.

———. *Cattlemen vs. Sheepherders.* Austin, Tex., 1989.

———. *Encyclopedia of Western Gunfighters.* Austin, Tex., 1979.

———. *Fighting Men of the Indian Wars.* Stillwater, Okla., 1991.

Rosa, Joseph G. *The Gunfighter: Man or Myth?* Norman, Okla., 1969.

———. *The West of Wild Bill Hickok.* Norman, Okla., 1989.

Slotkin, Richard. *The Fatal Environment: The Myth of the Frontier in the Age of Industrialism, 1800–1890.* New York, 1985.

———. *Gunfighter Nation: The Myth of the Frontier in Twentieth-Century America.* New York, 1992.

———. *Regeneration through Violence: The Mythology of the American Frontier, 1600–1860.* Middleton, Conn., 1973.

Trachtenberg, Alan. *The Incorporation of America: Culture and Society in the Gilded Age.* New York, 1982.

Tyler, Robert M. *Rebel of the Woods: The I.W.W. in the Pacific Northwest.* Eugene, Oreg., 1967.

Utley, Robert M. *Billy the Kid: A Short and Violent Life.* Lincoln, Nebr., 1989.

———. *High Noon in Lincoln: Violence on the Western Frontier.* Albuquerque, N. Mex., 1987.

Wellman, Paul I. *A Dynasty of Western Outlaws.* Lincoln, Nebr., 1986.

White, Richard. *"It's Your Misfortune and None of My Own": A New History of the American West.* Norman, Okla., 1991.

———. *"Outlaw Gangs of the Middle Border: American Social Bandits." Western Historical Quarterly* 12 (October 1981): 387–408.

RACIAL VIOLENCE

White Americans did not go west to kill the Indians and despoil a continent; they went to find jobs and make a living. Some were escaping the trials and burdens of life back East, as they were encouraged to do by policy-makers who repeatedly used the idea of the West as a mechanism for evading social problems. Much of what came to be thought of as Western optimism, as Patricia Nelson Limerick points out, was a faith in postponement, in deferring problems to the distant future. In general, Americans went west with high hopes for improved personal fortunes, but when those high hopes did not pan out, white Westerners frequently looked around for somebody to blame. And in the trans-Mississippi West, a crossroads for Europe, Asia, and Latin America, potential scapegoats abounded. Some Westerners were exuberantly racist; JOHN WESLEY HARDIN, for example, exulted in murdering African Americans, but more often Westerners were merely workingmen, who had roots in the old South and who felt threatened by the "cheap" labor of Asian and Mexican immigrants. Especially as American business began to incorporate the West and monopolize its land and wealth in a series of tumultuous post–Civil War market booms and busts, racial scapegoating became something of a Western tradition.

Closely allied to that tradition was the West's propensity toward VIGILANTISM. One historian has estimated that, excluding lynch mobs, there were some 210 vigilante movements—organized, extralegal groups meting out a violent "justice"—in the Far West between 1849 and 1902. Some historians have argued that vigilantes were a positive force in an unruly land, and vigilantes did indeed sometimes confront flagrant, even spectacular, breakdowns of law and order, as with the gang formed by WILLIAM HENRY PLUMMER in Virginia City, Montana, in the 1860s. More often than not, however, even these breakdowns had roots in social conflicts, and the role of the vigilantes was much more ambiguous and tended toward political and social oppression. The San Francisco Vigilance Committee did suppress some crime, but it was much more interested in taking political control of the city away from the Irish Catholic Democrats who dominated the town's government.

Farther south in California, the vigilantes turned on the Mexican American population that had long been prominent in the area. Between 1850 and 1856, Los Angeles was on the brink of race war. The social dislocations created by American challenges to Spanish land titles and by an economic downturn that severely depressed local Hispanic industry produced conditions that saw forty-four homicides a year in a village of only some two thousand residents. Anglo vigilantes brutally suppressed the Californios (native-born Californians of Hispanic descent) and lynched them almost at will. In Texas in the 1860s, the situation may well have been worse. TEXAS RANGERS intimidated, extorted, and "legally" plundered the Hispanics in the interests of an Anglo elite, and the TEJANOS despised them and their fellow "peace" officers in the local police. When the Tejanos, under the leadership of JUAN NEPOMUCENO CORTINA, struck back, the rangers—unable to capture the "bandit"—slaughtered Hispanics indiscriminately throughout the region. In El Paso, an Anglo judge tried to take possession of the traditionally public salt beds east of the city and charge Mexican-Americans a fee for hauling out salt that had previously been free for the taking. The judge's actions resulted in an anti-American riot and a brutal suppression known as the EL PASO SALT WAR.

Since the great boom in railroad building after the Civil War, white Westerners had engaged in racial violence against and intimidation of the Chinese. Anti-coolie clubs sprang up in California during the late 1860s, and by the 1870s, they were promoting the passage of laws against Chinese labor and organizing economic boycotts of Chinese-made goods. Club members physically attacked Chinese in the streets, and some claimed the clubs engaged in arson at factories that hired Chinese workers. The Chinese became major scapegoats in the economic troubles that hit California and the Pacific Coast in the early 1870s. Anti-Chinese riots left some nineteen Chinese dead in Los Angeles in 1871, and that year there were riots as well in Seattle and Tacoma. In San Francisco, first the Democrats then DENIS KEARNEY'S WORKINGMEN'S PARTY OF CALIFORNIA seized anti-Chinese sentiment as a road to political power, and in the countryside, the Caucasian League led a campaign of terror against the Chinese. Official exclusion set off something of an American pogrom against the Chinese in the mid-1880s. The wave of violence swept from the Pacific Northwest and northern California into Wyoming and Chinese communities across the West. All over the region, white mobs attacked the Chinese, driving them out of some cities—Eureka, California, Tacoma and Seattle, Washington—entirely. In Rock Springs, Wyoming, whites burned down Chinatown, killing twenty-five Chinese. "When I first came," Andrew Kan said of those days, "Chinese treated worse than dog. Oh, it was terrible, terrible. At that time all Chinese have queue and dress same as in China. The hoodlums, roughnecks, and young boys pull your queue, slap your face, throw all kind of old vegetables and rotten eggs at you." "The Chinese were in a pitiable condition in those days," recounted Huie Kin of San Francisco in the Gilded Age. "We were simply terrified; we kept indoors after dark for fear of being shot in the back. Children spit upon us as we passed and called us rats." For a Chinese man named Wan Lee, novelist BRET HARTE had written an obituary that might stand for

In Rufus E. Zogbaum's *Painting the Town Red,* done for an 1886 issue of *Harper's Weekly,* cowboys harass a Chinese man while people on the street only watch. *Courtesy Patrick H. Butler, III.*

many in this dark time: "Dead, my reverend friends, dead. Stoned to death in the streets of San Francisco . . . by a mob of halfgrown boys and Christian school children." As many of the migrants chose to return to China, the unofficial pogrom drastically reduced the total Chinese population of the United States; in California, their population was cut by at least a third between 1890 and 1900.

By then, there were signs that the race card did not work as well as it once had. In the late nineteenth century, racial violence tended to become thoroughly caught up in economic issues and class conflict. A bitter dispute broke out in San Miguel County, New Mexico, in 1889. Anglo cattle kings and merchants attempted to drive Hispanic villagers, or *campesinos,* off their communal grazing lands and to divide the lands into parcels and sell them off. The Knights of Labor supported the *campesinos.* After ranchers fenced off the lands, groups of masked and armed riders destroyed the fences, and as the violence toward Hispanics escalated, Las Gorras Blancas (the White Caps), in turn, broadened its attacks to include railroads, lumber operations, and Anglo businesses, until the authorities had on their hands a full-scale *campesino* resistance movement against capitalist institutions.

Especially in the West, where the work force consisted of unskilled or semiskilled labor employed in extractive industries, labor groups by the end of the century were organizing industrywide, unlike in many parts of the East, where skilled laborers seeking to protect their privileges joined trade unions that resembled the guilds of the Middle Ages as much as they did working-class institutions. And when workers organized industrywide, they tended sometimes to cross racial lines as their conflicts often spread to include broader social issues rather than merely working conditions and pay. But racial problems did not vanish in the West by any means, as the twentieth century would amply demonstrate. From the Zoot Suit riots in Los Angeles and the JAPANESE INTERNMENT in World War II to the Rodney King incident and the harsh antialien laws of the 1990s, racial scapegoating remained a hallmark of the West.

—*Charles Phillips*

SEE ALSO: Gorras Blancas, Las

SUGGESTED READING:
Brown, Richard Maxwell. *Strain of Violence: Historical Studies of American Violence and Vigilantism.* New York, 1975.

Bykrit, James W. *Forging the Copper Collar: Arizona's Labor-Management War of 1901–21.* Tucson, Ariz., 1982.

Daniel, Cletus E. *Bitter Harvest: A History of California Farmworkers, 1870–1941.* Berkeley, Calif., 1981.

Larson, Robert. "The White Caps of New Mexico: A Study in Ethnic Militancy in the Southwest." *Pacific Historical Quarterly* 44 (May 1975): 171–186.

Limerick, Patricia Nelson. *The Legacy of Conquest: The Unbroken Past of the American West.* New York, 1987.

Rosenbaum, Robert J. *Mexicano Resistance in the Southwest: The Sacred Right of Self-Preservation.* Austin, Tex., 1981.

Saxton, Alexander. *Indispensable Enemy: Labor and the Anti-Chinese Movement in California.* Berkeley, Calif., 1971.

Storti, Craig. *Incident at Bitter Creek: The Story of the Rock Springs Chinese Massacre.* Ames, Iowa, 1991.

Takaki, Ronald. *A Different Mirror: A History of Multicultural America.* Boston, 1993.

——. *Strangers from a Different Shore: A History of Asian Americans.* New York, 1989.

White, Richard. *"It's Your Misfortune and None of My Own": A New History of the American West.* Norman, Okla., 1991.

VIOLENCE AGAINST WOMEN

Although evidence of domestic violence against women is not hard to find, historians have only begun to explore the topic. Violence against women took different forms, including attacks against Indian women and Mexican women in the border towns, where women were commonly raped by soldiers and volunteers during raids and wars. It was also a common experience for prostitutes, who were routinely beaten by their procurers and by their customers, most often in the wretched "cribs" thrown up in mining camps and towns, but not infrequently in the higher-class brothels as well.

While historians have so far paid little attention to these forms of violence against women, they have recently noted that domestic violence was a prominent theme in literary memoirs and novels written by women in the trans-Mississippi West and have begun to wonder if there is a connection between the West's public celebration of male violence and a hidden tradition of domestic violence. Wife beating and sexual assault play prominently in such works as MARI SANDOZ's *Old Jules,* AGNES SMEDLY's *Daughter of Earth,* Meridel Le Sueur's *The Girl,* and Tillie Olsen's *Yonnodio,* where it is clear that in the nineteenth and early twentieth century, as today, such violence took place behind closed doors among people who were not likely to discuss it with outsiders.

The attidues of Westerners toward domestic violence is discernible in the September 1847 diary Elizabeth Greer kept of her trip west on the overland trails.

In the wagon trains, men typically were single-minded in keeping to the trail; women, often wrenched from communities they grew up in and unhappy with the move west, were expected to continue their domestic chores on the trail—cooking, cleaning, watching after children—and to give up the privacy to which most nineteenth-century married women were accustomed. These circumstances wore on domestic relations. Elizabeth Greer left an account of one of the domestic arguments she witnessed: "This morning one company moved on," she wrote, "except one family. The woman got mad and wouldn't budge, nor let the children go. He had his cattle hitched on for three hours and coaxing her to go but she would not stir." After some of the men came to his aid, taking the children from their mother and putting them in the wagon, "[the] husband drove off and left her sitting. She got up, took the back track and traveled out of sight. Cut across, overtook her husband. Meantime he sent his boy back to camp after a horse he had left and when she came up her husband says, 'Did you meet John?' 'Yes,' was the reply, 'and I picked up a stone and knocked out his brains.'" When her husband went to check out her story, she set fire to one of his wagons. "He saw the flames and came running and put it out, and then mustered up spunk enough to give her a good flogging."

In novels by Western women, it was more than spunk that drove their male characters to violence against their wives. As Melody Graulich points out, these writers present Western males as archetypal frontiersmen, whose desire for absolute free will and freedom of action not only made them romantic and heroic rugged individuals, but also brutal wife beaters. The pictures the women writers portray are of lonely females, isolated on the plains from their families and other female friends, trapped by an economic system that made them utterly dependent on their husbands and forced them to remain in violent marriages. If these works were at all indicative of actual social attitudes, then the West's male-centered violent ethic with its almost compulsive masculinity created an aggression toward women and led to widespread domestic violence, an institutionalized spousal abuse, commonly practiced, commonly accepted, rarely commented upon.

—*Patricia Hogan and Charles Phillips*

SUGGESTED READING:

Butler, Anne M. *Daughters of Joy, Sisters of Misery: Prostitution in the American West, 1865-1890.* Urbana, Ill., 1985.

Castaneda, Antonia. "Sexual Violence in the Politics of Conquest." In *Building with Our Hands: New Directions in Chicana Studies.* Edited by Adela de la Torre and Beatríz Pesquera. Berkeley, Calif., 1993.

Faragher, John Mack. *Men and Women on the Overland Trail.* New Haven, Conn., 1979.

Graulich, Melody. "Violence against Women: Power Dynamics in Literature of the Western Family." In *The Woman's West.* Edited by Susan Armitage and Elizabeth Jameson. Norman, Okla., 1987.

Le Sueur, Meridel. *The Girl.* Minneapolis, Minn., 1978.

Olsen, Tillie. *Yonnodio: From the Thirties.* New York, 1974.

Sandoz, Mari. *Old Jules.* Lincoln, Nebr., 1962.

Smedley, Agnes. *Daughter of Earth.* Old Westbury, N.Y., 1976.

White, Richard. *"It's Your Misfortune and None of My Own": A New History of the American West.* Norman, Okla. 1991.

MYTHS ABOUT VIOLENCE IN THE WEST

In the popular mind, the violent American West has always been as much a mythic space as a real land. The Wild West we all recognize from books and movies is the product of writers, showmen, and promoters who "packaged" a West for middle-class, mostly Eastern consumption: a fantastical place, ultimately peopled with brave and independent pioneers, carefree and fun-loving cowboys, strong and silent lawmen, hard-bitten and talented gunslingers, brave and pure horse soldiers, treacherous and bloodthirsty Indians, demure and faithful wives, dedicated and beautiful school marms, visionary and community-conscious businessmen, danger-loving and dedicated scouts, dashing and reckless gamblers. One of the early frontier mythologizers was Pennsylvania schoolteacher John Filson, who traveled to Kentucky in 1782 and wrote a wildly inaccurate and romantic piece of propaganda called *The Discovery, Settlement, and Present State of Kentucke,* which included a section subtitled "The Adventures of Col. Daniel Boone."

DANIEL BOONE was the first of the Western heroes, a Kentucky long hunter made over for the public into an Indian-fighting frontiersman who reclaimed the wilderness from the savages so that it could be settled by innocent and God-fearing Americans. Boone died in Missouri in 1819, the year before it became a state, and many—not the least being the upstate New York novelist JAMES FENIMORE COOPER—saw his death as symbolic of the closing of the frontier. By the end of the decade, certainly, Boone's deification as a frontiersman and an Indian fighter was complete. His family would long protest that the man was no Indian killer, not even an Indian hater, and that, in fact, outside combat perhaps in the French and Indian War and the American Revolution, the one time he actually shot a Native American he fell into a deep melancholy. Nevertheless his reputation as an Indian fighter had become proverbial, and the killing of Indians was proving not only central to frontier legends, but one of their appeals.

Cooper, whose central character was loosely modeled on Boone, began publishing his popular Leather-Stocking Tales with *The Pioneers* in 1823, followed by *The Last of the Mohicans*—based in part on the Indian kidnapping of Boone's daughter—in 1826 and *The Prairie* in 1827. Idyllic elegies for the vanishing frontier, the novels' focus was broad and sweeping and mythical in its dimensions. Their hero, a backwoodsman named Natty Bumppo, better known as Leatherstocking, Deerslayer, or Hawkeye, provided Americans with an enduring image of the ideal frontiersman: knowing, innocent, brave, self-reliant, perfectly at one with nature, a part of the very wilderness he was securing for civilization, a friend of the good Indians, an implacable foe to the bad. During the 1820s, Cooper built a lucrative literary reputation on his Leather-Stocking Tales. He touched a responsive chord in the hearts of American ideologues by pointing to what he saw as the redemptive potential of the frontier, where an American character was being defined in terms of the hardy lives and pure virtues of those who lived close to nature, giving Western civilization a new start by cleansing themselves, through violence, of the false values and artificial society of the Old World. Copper recognized that the racial opposition between whites and Indians was fundamental to Americans; he always portrayed the struggle as one between civilization and savagery; and his hero, Natty Bumppo, was, according to historian Richard Slotkin, always "American ideological ambivalence personified," making the "wilderness safe for a civilization [for] which he [was] unsuited. . . ."

Cooper published the last of his frontier romances, *The Deerslayer,* in 1841, and by then his formula had proved so successful that it became the mainstay of the dime novels that came into their own in the middle of the nineteenth century. Several types of heroes appeared in the dime-novel westerns. One was the backwoodsman of the Appalachian frontier often modeled on real characters such as Daniel Boone and DAVID (DAVEY) CROCKETT. Although the backwoods heroes employed their unique frontier skills to vanquish bloodthirsty Indians and save innocent heroines, their literary potential was limited in much the same way as Cooper's Natty Bumppo. While they represented the purer and more vital life of the frontier as opposed to the city, their lower-class origins made them ineligible for romantic matches with the genteel heroines, matches that would signal the development of a new American who embodied the best of both worlds. That union was not accomplished until men such as GEORGE ARMSTRONG CUSTER, WILLIAM F. ("BUFFALO BILL") CODY, and CHRISTOPHER HOUSTON ("KIT") CARSON inspired dime-novel heroes after the 1870s. The real life Custer, Cody, and Carson and their fictional counterparts functioned as well in the city as they did on the plains and were thus endowed with enough sophistication to be proper love matches for Eastern women.

The dime novels also included a new American cultural type, a cousin of the frontiersman and Plains Indian fighters: the civilizing gunfighter. Some of the dime novels elevated gunfighters to the level of cultural icons, though they did not call them "gunfighters." It would be BARTHOLOMEW (BAT) MASTERSON himself who used that sobriquet in a series of articles he wrote in 1907 for the magazine *Human Life* entitled "Famous Gun Fighters of the Western Frontier." At the time, and in the early dime novels, such men were called more prosaically if more accurately "man-killers" and occasionally "shootists." The cowboy, too, made his first literary appearance in the dime novels, but the authors at first seemed unable to free the cowboy enough from the drudgery of ranch work to develop his full potential as a romantic action hero. That development came later in the century when Buffalo Bill's Wild West show reached the apex of its popularity and early in the next century with the appearance of OWEN WISTER's *Virginian,* a novel that ended with the classic gunfight that became standard in every violent Western tale.

Outlaws, too, were the heroes of many dime novels. In order to be acceptable to a "civilized" audience—that is, in order to justify a certain kind of parlor-bound blood lust—their outlawry often was a reaction to a prior wrong done them that forced them outside the law to obtain justice. Many were Robin Hood–type figures—some historically based, such as Jesse James; others purely fictional, such as Deadwood Dick—who robbed from the rich to give to the poor and battled unjust laws and social institutions. As with most of the dime-novel social bandits, the fact that "BILLY THE KID," for example, was not much more than a urban street tough transplanted to the Wild West was beside the point. In newspaper accounts, in dime novels, in the popular imagination, he became the avenger, killing his first man before his sixteenth birthday for insulting his sainted mother and killing twenty-one more before it was over, one for each year of his short life, even shooting a man down while riding a rearing horse, a virtually impossible feat. A number of recent scholars have pointed out that the dime novel could be quite sensitive to social issues and that many used their Western setting "not only for escapist adventure but to state social conflicts through figures of bank and train robbers," wronged cowboys, and range wars. But if the secret attraction of the legend of Billy the Kid was a populist hatred of authority and a fantasy of individual rebellion, the legend operated as well to obscure the kind of social conflict that produced the violent young man. By concentrating on his personal story, making

him a Wild West Hawkeye rather than the tool and the victim of the powerful men who ran New Mexico and fought with each other to control it, the tales of daring and adventure also masked the true nature of social conflict and VIGILANTISM even when presenting them as subjects.

Perhaps even more than the novelists, Buffalo Bill Cody was the inventor the Wild West. By the 1890s, Cody had added to his wild west show—which began as a rodeolike display of cowboy skills framed by an elaborate parade—scenes "typical" of Western life. He publicized the show as "America's National Entertainment" and an emblematic telling of the entire course of American history. Its series of spectacles and "historical" reenactments were meant to unfurl for the spectator the different "epochs" of American history. Audiences were treated to displays of life on a cattle ranch, a buffalo hunt, and Indian attacks on a homesteader's cabin and a stagecoach. The show ended with "Custer's Last Fight," followed by Buffalo Bill standing in a tableau captioned by a transparency that read: "Too Late." Buffalo Bill was "the representative man of the frontiersman of the past . . . full of self-reliance. Young, sturdy, a remarkable specimen of manly beauty, with the brain to conceive and the nerve to execute, Buffalo Bill *par excellence* is the exemplar of the strong and unique traits that characterize a true American frontiersman" who believed in, as the title of one program essay put it, "The Rifle as an Aid to Civilization." Amazingly, the Wild West's performances were accepted not merely as good shows, which they were, but as exercises in public education. Brick Pomeroy, a journalist of the period, praised Buffalo

The stuff of American legend, *Gunfight at O.K. Corral,* as depicted by Nick Eggenhoffer. *Courtesy National Cowboy Hall of Fame and Western Heritage Center.*

Bill by wishing that "there were more progressive educators like William Cody in this world," and insisting that the show's conflation of wildly inaccurate history with widely accepted mythology be called "Wild West Reality."

Dramas like Cody's were the precursors to the Hollywood western. In fact, movies as a true narrative form and the western were born in the same film, Edwin S. Porter's *The Great Train Robbery* of 1903—made in New York. The medium and the genre proved extremely popular, and after the industry moved to southern California in the 1910s, a number of ex-cowhands and old roustabouts begin looking for work as extras, and the rest is history. William S. Hart, TOM MIX, Hopalong Cassidy, GENE AUTRY, Roy Rogers, Bob Steele, Gary Cooper, Jimmy Stewart, and JOHN WAYNE become the cowboy heroes of generations of Americans. In the hands of directors such as JOHN FORD, Howard Hawks, Anthony Mann, Sam Peckinpah, and Walter Hill, motion pictures, more than any other medium, perfected and perpetuated the myth of the violent American West. As the American West came to be portrayed in the movies, it was a wild land in need of "taming ." In this mythic Wild West, the hero mediates between civilization and savagery using his skills with a gun. The Western gunman, classically represented by John Wayne in *The Man Who Shot Liberty Valence,* is a transitional figure who employs violence in the frontier West to establish a peaceful society in its place. With a mixture of melodrama and hokum, the popular electronic media, film and television, continue to pass on the major legacy of Western mythology— the tradition of violent acts married to pure motives.

—*Charles Phillips*

SEE ALSO: Film; Rogers, Roy, and Dale Evans

SUGGESTED READING:

Bold, Christine. *Selling the Wild West: Popular Western Fiction, 1860 to 1960.* Bloomington, Ind., 1987.

Cawelti, John G. *The Six-Gun Mystique.* Bowling Green, Ohio, 1984.

Denning, Michael. *Mechanic Accents: Dime Novels and Working-Class Culture in America.* London, 1987.

Hamilton, Cynthia S. *Western and Hard-boiled Detective Fiction in America: From High Noon to Midnight.* Iowa City, Iowa, 1987.

Hobsbawm, Eric J. *Social Bandits and Primitive Rebels.* Glencoe, Ill., 1959.

Rosa, Joseph G. *The Gunfighter: Man or Myth?* Norman, Okla., 1969.

Slotkin, Richard. *The Fatal Environment: The Myth of the Frontier in the Age of Industrialism, 1800–1890.* New York, 1985.

———. *Gunfighter Nation: The Myth of the Frontier in Twentieth-Century America.* New York, 1992.

———. *Regeneration through Violence: The Mythology of the American Frontier, 1600–1860.* Middleton, Conn., 1973.

Smith, Henry Nash. *Virgin Land: The American West as Myth and Symbol.* Cambridge, Mass., 1950.

Steckmesser, Kent Ladd. *The Western Hero in History and Legend.* Norman, Okla., 1965.

Tompkins, Jane. *West of Everything: The Inner Life of the Western.* New York, 1992.

Utley, Robert M. *Billy the Kid: A Short and Violent Life.* Lincoln, Nebr., 1989.

VIRGINIA CITY, NEVADA

Virginia City and its neighbor Gold Hill served as an archetype for Western mining towns. Both towns are situated on the COMSTOCK LODE, an enormously wealthy silver- and gold-mining region that boomed in the 1860s and 1870s. Just as the Comstock combined wild speculation with practical industrial mining, so did Virginia City join a raucous spirit to an industrial social reality. Named for reprobate miner "Old Virginny" Fennimore, located in desolate northwest Nevada, halfway up the barren slopes of Mount Davidson, windswept, chronically short of water and timber, Virginia City was the richest place in the West by the mid-1870s.

In the summer of 1859, when the silver strike triggered a rush across the Sierra Nevada, Virginia City's residents lived in canvas and brush homes or burrowed directly into the side of the mountain for shelter. But the lode soon supported a town filled with brick and frame houses for its growing population (2,345 in 1860; 7,048 in 1870; and 25,000 during the "Big Bonanza" of the mid-1870s). Virginia City became famous for high living, a place where gambling—at cards or in mining stock—was pervasive, where illiterate miners such as Sandy Bowers suddenly became millionaires, where MARK TWAIN practiced irreverent journalism at the *Territorial Enterprise,* and where the most visible female, Julia Bulette, was a prostitute.

Yet the streets terraced into the side of Mount Davidson defined an industrial social structure based on class and ethnicity. "C" Street, the main business district, divided the town. The middle class and most married women and families lived above on "A" and "B" streets. The thriving red-light district, employing more than half the working women and catering to a population dominated by young, single miners, was below on "D" Street. Miners boarded or lived in barracks clustered around the mines, many farther down the slope in Gold Hill. Skilled Cornishmen, perhaps one-third of the hard-rock miners, had a separate community in Gold Hill. The equally numerous Irish miners concentrated in "Little Tipperary" in Virginia City.

Lingenfelter, Richard. *The Hardrock Miners*. Berkeley, Calif., 1974.

Main Street in Virginia City, Nevada, in 1878. When the gold and silver in nearby mines played out, Virginia City's population spiraled downward. *Courtesy Library of Congress.*

The Chinese, barred from mining and only marginally employed, lived in a segregated shantytown. And the native Paiutes lived as outcasts on the very edge of town.

Just as the technical innovations, corporate organization, and social structure of the Comstock mines were duplicated all over the West, the Miners' Unions of Virginia City and Gold Hill served as models for industrial unions elsewhere, including the WESTERN FEDERATION OF MINERS. Comstock miners' wages, four dollars for an eight-hour day, were high because of high living costs and labor shortages. The unions concentrated on maintaining these wages by organizing all men working underground into an industrial closed shop; promoting solidarity among Irish, Cornish, and American miners and prohibiting "cheap" Chinese labor; and translating miners' votes into political influence. During the bonanza of the 1870s, mine owners, unwilling to have production slowed, cooperated. But as the lode gave out, neither the millions of dollars invested by the companies nor the longer hours accepted by the unions could prevent Virginia City's population from plummeting to 10,917 in 1880. And although family life and legitimate businesses replaced gambling and prostitution, Virginia City continued to decline. It survives today as a tourist town. Its population in 1990 was 1,826.

—*Ralph Mann*

SUGGESTED READING:

Goldman, Marion C. *Gold Diggers and Silver Miners: Prostitution and Social Life on the Comstock Lode.* Ann Arbor, Mich., 1981.

Larson, Sarah. "The Census and Community History: A Reappraisal." *Prologue* 13 (1991): 209–220.

VOLCANOES

Volcanoes are generally found in the American West along the eastern rim of the Pacific tectonic plate, the "ring of fire" that is bordered by earthquake zones of New Zealand, New Guinea, the Mariana Islands, Japan, Kamchatka, the Aleutian Islands, western North America, the East Pacific Rise, and the Pacific Antarctic Ridge. As the Pacific plate pulls apart from the Nazca Plate (west of South America), rifting occurs, and magma rises into the gap between the diverging plates. Large shield volcanoes are formed as magma rises to the surface.

In the northwestern United States, the Cascade volcanoes are formed by the small Juan de Fuca and Cocos plates moving under the east side of the Pacific plate. That type of plate movement creates the more explosive Vulcanian-type volcanoes. Eight volcanoes in the Cascades have erupted violently in the last two hundred years. Between 1914 and 1915, Mount Lassen (10,457 feet) in northeastern California experienced massive mudflows and gaseous explosions, which destroyed large areas of forest. On May 18, 1980, Mount Saint Helens in Washington violently erupted, blowing 1,313 feet off the top of the mountain and sending up an 80,000-foot-high cloud of smoke and ash.

The most active volcanoes in the world, Mauna Loa and Kilauea, are found in the Hawaiian islands. Hawaii's volcanoes are examples of "hot-spot" volcanoes, which form as the Pacific plate moves over a deep vent in the earth's mantle. As the plate moves northwestward over the vent at the rate of eight to ten centimeters a year, new volcanoes are formed. Kauai and Niihau, the oldest of the inhabited Hawaiian islands, were formed by volcanic activity five million years ago. Oahu was formed by two large shield volcanoes, Waianae and Koolau. Haleakala, or "House of the Sun," is an extinct volcano on Maui that is today part of the Haleakala National Park. Hawaii is the youngest island of the chain; it was created by five volcanoes that are less than one million years old. A volcano called Loihi has recently been discovered more than 3,000 feet below sea level and 18 miles southeast of the island of Hawaii.

The five volcanoes of Hawaii are Kohala (5,480 feet), Mauna Kea, or "White Mountain" (13,796 feet), Hualalai (8,271 feet), Mauna Loa, or "Long Mountain" (13,677 feet), and Kilauea, or "The Spewing" (4,078 feet). Kohala and Mauna Kea are both extinct, while Hualalai, which last erupted in 1801, is now considered by the UNITED STATES GEOLOGICAL SURVEY as the fourth most dangerous volcano in the United States. Mauna Loa remains an active volcano composed of more than 10,000 cubic miles of lava extending 60 miles in length and 30 miles in width. Kilauea's most recent eruption began on January 3, 1983. Roads, homes, stores, and churches in the southeast Puna district were destroyed by the flow, which added more than one hundred acres of new land to the coastline of Hawaii.

The typical lava formations found in Hawaii consist of hot basalt *pahoehoe* flows (smooth to ropy surfaces) or the cooler *aa* (rough, broken surfaces). The topography is also marked by craters, calderas, cinder and tuff cones, and extensive volcanic fields. Fissure vents, common along the radial rift zones of Hawaiian volcanoes, cause "curtain-of-fire" eruptions.

Several varieties of native vegetation are found in the volcanic region—the leguminous tree mamane; the hardwood shrub aalii; the largest native tree, koa; and the gnarled ohia tree. Several species of native Hawaiian birds are also found—the flycatcher elepaio and the honey creeper apapane. The introduction of the wild pig, goat, and mongoose into the region greatly endangered the survival of the native flora and fauna.

Ancient native Hawaiians did not live in the uplands of the volcanoes although they traveled there to hunt birds, quarry stone adzes, or worship. The goddess Pele was believed to live at Halemaumau Crater within Kilauea caldera. Offerings and prayers to the goddess of the volcano are still offered at the crater's rim by native Hawaiian worshippers.

The first nonnative to visit Kilauea was the London missionary William Ellis in 1823. Other foreigners soon followed; the United States Exploring Expedition under Commander CHARLES WILKES made an extensive scientific study of the island's volcanoes in 1840 and 1841. As early the 1860s, the Volcano House was built on Kilauea's rim to offer overnight accommodations to visitors. The Hawaiian Volcano Observatory was established in 1911 at Kilauea by volcanologist Thomas A. Jaggar. Volcanological studies continue today at the observatory under the U.S. Geological Survey.

In 1916, a 358 square-mile area that includes Mauna Loa and Kilauea was set aside as Hawaii Volcanoes National Park. Designated an International Biosphere Reserve in 1986 and World Heritage Site in 1988, the park provides interpretive exhibits, hiking trails, and special programs for tourists who visit from around the world.

—*Glen Grant*

SUGGESTED READING:

Frierson, Pamela. *The Burning Island: A Journey through Myth and History in the Volcano Country, Hawaii.* San Francisco, Calif., 1991.

Macdonald, Gordon A., Agatin T. Abbott, and Frank L. Peterson. *Volcanoes in the Sea: The Geology of Hawaii.* Honolulu, Hawaii, 1983.

University of Hawaii at Manoa, Department of Geology. *Atlas of Hawaii.* Honolulu, Hawaii, 1983.

Wenkam, Robert. *The Edge of Fire: Volcano and Earthquake Country in Western North America and Hawaii.* San Francisco, 1987.

Wood, Charles A., and Jurgen Kienle. *Volcanoes of North America: United States and Canada.* New York, 1990.

WADDELL, WILLIAM BRADFORD

Businessman and freighter William Bradford Waddell (1807–1872) was born in Fauquier County, Virginia. At the age of eight, he moved with his family to Mason County, Kentucky. In 1824, he worked in the lead mines in Galena, Illinois, and then clerked briefly in a general store in St. Louis. He married Susan Byram in January 1829 and went into business on his own in Mayslick, Kentucky. He moved to Lexington, Missouri, in 1835, opened a general store, and became involved in the town's affairs by promoting real estate, organizing an insurance company, and founding a college for women. He formed a partnership known as Morehead and Waddell to engage in real-estate promotion. When WILLIAM HEPBURN RUSSELL purchased Morehead's interests in the company, it became known as Russell and Waddell.

Waddell became interested in railroads and helped organize and served on the board of directors of the Lexington and Booneville and the Lexington and Davies County railroads in 1853. The next year, he formed a partnership with Russell and ALEXANDER MAJORS to enter the freighting business. A cautious businessman, he tried unsuccessfully to restrain his partners from overextending their financial obligations. But with the failure of the firm in 1862, Waddell suffered general financial loss and gave up all business activity.
—*W. Turrentine Jackson*

SEE ALSO: Russell, Majors and Waddell

SUGGESTED READING:
Bloss, Roy. *Pony Express—The Great Gamble.* Berkeley, Calif., 1959.
Chapman, Arthur. *The Pony Express.* New York, 1932.
Harlow, Alvin. *Old Waybills: The Romance of the Express Companies.* New York, 1934.

Jackson, W. Turrentine. "A New Look at Wells Fargo, Stagecoaches, and the Pony Express." *California Historical Society Quarterly* 45 (1966): 291–324.
——. "Wells Fargo's Pony Expresses." *Journal of the West* 11 (1972): 405–436.
Settle, Raymond W., and Mary L. Settle. *Empire on Wheels.* Stanford, Calif., 1949.
——. *Saddles and Spurs: The Pony Express.* Harrisburg, Pa., 1955.
——. *War Drums and Wagon Wheels.* Lincoln, Nebr., 1966.
Walker, Henry Pickering. *The Wagonmasters.* Norman, Okla., 1966.

WAGGONER, DANIEL

Texas cattleman Daniel Waggoner (1828–1904) was born in Lincoln County, Tennessee. His family moved to Hopkins County, Texas, in the mid-1840s, and Waggoner married Nancy Moore in 1848. In 1850, he took a small herd of longhorns and established what became the Three D Ranch on Denton Creek in Wise County. In 1851, he attempted to settle west of Decatur, Texas, but was forced back to Denton Creek by Indian raiders.

In 1866, he modified his brand to a reverse "Three D" to prevent it from being altered by rustlers. In 1870, with his son William Thomas Waggoner, he drove a herd to the markets at Kansas City. As the frontier moved west, he settled in Clay County and then moved to Wichita County. His ranch territory included lands in parts of six counties. The ranch also leased land in Oklahoma during the mid-1880s, but with the end of the open range, he concentrated on acquiring land in Texas. By 1903, the ranch included more than one million acres. Waggoner had introduced shorthorns to upgrade his herd about 1885 and added Herefords in the 1890s.

Waggoner was a major figure in the development of the area around Decatur. He became president of the First National Bank of Decatur and the Decatur Oil Mill Company. After his death, the ranch grew and changed with the discovery of oil.

—*Patrick H. Butler, III*

SEE ALSO: Cattle Brands and Branding; Cattle Industry

SUGGESTED READING:
Halsell, H. H. *Cowboys and Cattleland.* Fort Worth, Tex., 1937. Reprint. 1983.
Webb, Walter Prescott, ed. *The Handbook of Texas.* Vol. 2. Austin, Tex., 1952.

WAILAKI INDIANS

See: Native American Peoples: Peoples of the Pacific Northwest

WAITE, DAVIS HANSON

Born in Jamestown, New York, Davis Hanson Waite (1825–1901) taught school, ranched, practiced law, sold goods, served in the Wisconsin and Kansas legislatures, and edited newspapers including the *Aspen Union Era.* A Republican-turned-Populist, he capped his career by serving as Colorado's governor from 1893 to 1895. Coloradans supported him not so much because they subscribed to all his Populist plans, but because they supported his view that the federal government should coin large amounts of silver, a commodity that undergirded the state's economy.

As governor, Waite proved to be much more than a silver bug. He sympathized with labor to the extent that, in 1894, he dispatched the state militia to protect strikers in Cripple Creek. To root out corruption in Denver, he demanded that police and fire commissioners resign. When they refused, he sent troops to eject them from City Hall. Federal intervention ended the bloodless one-day city hall War on March 15, 1894.

Waite once proclaimed, "It is better, infinitely better, that blood should flow to the horses' bridles than that our national liberties should be destroyed." Dubbed "Bloody Bridles" by enemies who turned his own rhetoric against him, he lost his bid for reelection in 1894 to a Republican, Albert W. McIntire. Among those who abandoned him were women voters, whose 1893 bid to gain equal suffrage in Colorado had been successful, in part because of Waite's support.

Waite returned to Aspen, where he died from a heart attack. Having been no luckier in business than in politics, he left his widow, Celia Crane Waite, in such reduced circumstances that she took in boarders. Waite is buried in Aspen's Red Butte Cemetery; his grave is marked by a monument donated by the WESTERN FEDERATION OF MINERS.

—*Stephen J. Leonard*

SUGGESTED READING:
Morris, John R. "Davis Hanson Waite: The Ideology of a Western Populist." Ph.D. diss., University of Colorado at Boulder, 1965.

WALKARA
(UTE)

One of the more powerful Indian leaders in the Great Basin region in the 1830s and 1840s, Walkara (ca. 1808–1855) was known for the daring raids he led on the horse herds owned by California's rancheros. Often called "Walker" by the whites, Walkara had been born in a Timpanogos village on the Spanish Fork River in present-day Utah, and he came to power by organizing a band of raiders and fighters from several tribes, including such traditional enemies of the Utes as the Paiutes and the Shoshones. Speaking not only several Indian languages but also Spanish and—to a limited extent—English, Walkara demanded unquestioning loyalty from his followers and ruthlessly exacted tributes from weaker tribes. In the 1830s, Walkara's band slipped through the Cajon Pass to raid the outlying ranchos in southern California. Aided by two mountain men, Thomas ("Pegleg") Smith and JAMES PIERSON (JIM) BECKWOURTH, Walkara succeeded in spiriting away some three thousand horses back to Utah, which led Californians to dub him the greatest horse thief in history. Targeting not only Californio settlements, Walkara also raided Digger and Paiute villages for women and children to sell into slavery in New Mexico and attacked wagon trains traveling the Old Spanish Trail between New Mexico and the coast. A compatriot of the mountain men, to whom he supplied Indian women for bedmates, Walkara grew friendly as well with the Mormons when they arrived in Utah in 1847. That year, the federal government closed off Walkara's access to fresh horses by stationing troops to guard the Cajon Pass, and the Mormons themselves put a stop to the traffic in slaves. Unsuccessful in his many attempts to add a Mormon woman to his large number of wives, Walkara nevertheless converted to Mormonism in 1850. It did not take Walkara long, however, to realize that he had, in effect, been outmaneuvered by the Latter-day Saints. As the herd diminished upon which his wealth and status depended and as his people fell prey to a measles epidemic, altercations broke out between Walkara's Utes and the Mormons. One such confrontation at Springfield left a number of Utes dead or wounded, and Walkara responded with attacks on Mormon towns and herds in what came to be called the Walker War of 1853. The Mormon defense was spirited, however, and the once powerful chief, surrounded by whites, his major sources of wealth denied him, sued for peace and died shortly afterward.

—*Charles Phillips*

WALKER, JAMES

Artist James Walker (1819–1889) was born in England and grew up in New York City. As a young man, he visited Mexico and was stranded in Mexico City at the beginning of the war between the United States and Mexico. Rescued by American forces, he served as an interpreter with the U.S. Army and remained in Mexico City during America's occupation. He returned to New York City in 1848 and subsequently visited South America before establishing a studio in New York in 1859. He worked there, except for brief periods spent in Washington, D.C., until 1884, when he moved to California to execute a large painting of a French battle for a private gallery in San Francisco.

Walker came to be noted for his large-scale battle scenes. His surviving works include *The Battle of Chapultepec* at the United States Capitol and several Civil War paintings. He also produced a number of paintings depicting the life of the vaquero or cowboy in Mexico and California. A collection of his cowboy paintings is owned today by the THOMAS GILCREASE INSTITUTE in Tulsa, Oklahoma.

—*David C. Hunt*

SUGGESTED READING:
Rossi, Paul A., and David C. Hunt. The Art of the Old West. 4th ed. New York, 1989.

WALKER, JOSEPH REDDEFORD

Western fur trapper and mountain man Joseph Reddeford Walker (1798–1876) was an explorer, expedition guide, gold-seeker, and pioneer California rancher. Born in the back country of Tennessee, Walker moved at the age of twenty to western Missouri with his family. In 1820, he joined a party of fur TRAPPERS headed for Santa Fe, where Spanish officials arrested

and briefly imprisoned him and his companions. After Mexico won its independence from Spain in 1821, Walker entered the Santa Fe trade, and in 1825, he guided the first U.S. government expedition to survey and mark the SANTA FE AND CHIHUAHUA TRAIL.

In western Missouri, Walker served a few years as sheriff for the town of Independence. Then in 1832, he joined the privately financed trapping and exploring expedition headed by Captain BENJAMIN LOUIS EULALIE DE BONNEVILLE. The next year, Walker led forty of Bonneville's men from the Green River fur-trade RENDEZVOUS to California by way of the Great Salt Lake, the Humboldt River, and the Yosemite region. After wintering in the San Joaquin Valley, the party returned in 1834, on a route that took them across Walker Pass, through the Owens Valley, northward to the Humboldt, and then eastward to rejoin Bonneville on the Bear River. That round-trip excursion added substantially to the geographical knowledge about the region and helped open the Great Basin and California to overland travel.

Subsequently, Walker served as a brigade leader for the AMERICAN FUR COMPANY and then engaged in various trading, trapping, and guiding activities in the Southwest. Among other notable exploits, he guided JOHN CHARLES FRÉMONT during his second expedition and part of his third, briefly mined gold in California, guided federal troops in an 1859 campaign against the Mojaves along the Colorado River, and led a major gold-hunting expedition in 1861 into southern Arizona. In 1867, at the age of sixty-nine, Walker returned to California. He lived quietly with a nephew on a ranch on the northwestern slopes of Mount Diablo, bordering San Francisco Bay, until his death.

—*Kenneth N. Owens*

SEE ALSO: Exploration: United States Expeditions; Fur Trade; Mountain Men

SUGGESTED READING:
Conner, Daniel Ellis. Joseph Reddeford Walker and the Arizona Adventure. Edited by Donald Berthrong and Odessa Davenport. Norman, Okla., 1970.
Gilbert, Bil. Westering Man: The Life of Joseph Walker. New York, 1983.

WALKER, SARAH BREEDLOVE

Sarah Breedlove Walker (1867–1919), born in the Louisiana Delta to former slaves, eventually became the first black female millionaire by perfecting hair conditioners for African American women. Orphaned at five and married at fourteen to Charles J. Walker, she was a widowed mother by her twenty-first birthday. Resolved to support her daughter, Walker worked as a washerwoman in Louisiana, Mississippi, and Missouri. In an effort to become self-employed, she decided to manufacture hair-care products and subsequently developed a formula called the "Walker System," which she sold door-to-door. Although the Walker System was usually described as a hair-straightening process, which suggested that her clients desired "Caucasian-type" hair, Walker claimed her products were designed to cure dry scalps, treat hair breakage, and encourage growth.

From 1905 to 1910, Walker lived in St. Louis, Denver, Pittsburgh, and finally Indianapolis. In each city, she developed a network of African American female commissioned agents to promote her products. By 1910, the Madame C. J. Walker Company, headquartered in Indianapolis, employed five thousand agents around the world and averaged revenues of $1,000 per day, making it one of the most successful and certainly the most famous black company.

Walker moved to New York City in 1913 and surrounded herself with the trappings of wealth. One of the first African Americans to reside in Harlem, she built a mansion on West 136th Street. Later, she called on Vertner W. Tandy, a young African American architect to design and build a $250,000 country estate, Villa Lewaro, in an exclusive New York suburb, Irvington-on-the-Hudson. Both residences became centers of numerous Harlem Renaissance social and cultural activities sponsored by her only daughter, A'Lelia. Walker's death in 1919 during a business trip to St. Louis, just as the Renaissance began, precluded her from seeing the artistic development that her fortune would help underwrite. Yet, even after her death, her fortune continued to assist African Americans. Her will stipulated that two-thirds of her estate be used to fund various black charities, educational institutions, and civil rights organizations.

—*Quintard Taylor*

Suggested reading:

Giddings, Paula. *When and Where I Enter: The Impact of Black Women on Race and Sex in America.* New York, 1984.

Lewis, David Levering. *When Harlem Was in Vogue.* New York, 1982.

WALKER, WILLIAM

Adventurer and revolutionary instigator William Walker (1824–1860) first practiced his filibustering schemes in an attempted takeover of Lower California. Born in Nashville, Tennessee, Walker headed to California in 1850. He plotted the colonization of Lower California for three years before launching his forces from San Francisco on October 15, 1853. Landing in La Paz, he declared Lower California and the province of Sonora an independent republic. Declaration, however, did not a republic make. Lacking supplies, Walker could not overcome Mexican opposition. He was forced to retreat to the United States in the following year.

In 1855, Walker sailed for Nicaragua at the invitation of Nicaraguan revolutionaries. Within months, Walker's military victories secured his control over the country, at the time a vital link in shipping between the Atlantic and Pacific oceans. Walker garnered financial support for his filibustering from two officials in Cornelius Vanderbilt's Accessory Transit Company. In exchange, Walker seized the company's property and turned it over to Vanderbilt's employees. Walker became president of Nicaragua on July 12, 1856; his presidency lasted less than a year against an alliance of Central American countries. Threatened by the coalition, he escaped to the United States and attempted two more forays to recapture Nicaragua. On his second attempt, he landed in Honduras in 1860. Walker was captured by the British navy who turned him over to the Honduran authorities for execution.

—*Patricia Hogan*

WALLACE, HENRY AGARD

Editor of the *Wallaces' Farmer,* secretary of agriculture (from 1933 to 1940), vice-president of the United States (from 1941 to 1945), and secretary of commerce (from 1945 to 1946), Henry A. Wallace (1888–1965) was born on a farm in Iowa, the son of May Broadhead and Henry Cantwell Wallace. He graduated from Iowa State College in 1910 and went to work for his family's farm journal. He became editor of *Wallaces' Farmer* in 1921, when his father was appointed secretary of agriculture. As editor, Wallace became acquainted with nationally known agricultural economists and joined in their efforts to develop a federally administered plan for cutting the nation's agricultural surpluses. He also played a role in the development of hybrid corn, a technological advance that greatly increased corn production.

Wallace's prominence as a spokesperson for the nation's farmers caused Franklin D. Roosevelt to seek his advice during the 1932 presidential campaign. After Roosevelt was elected, he selected Wallace as his secretary of agriculture. Agricultural policies of the

Henry Agard Wallace. *Editors' collection.*

College, Wallace went into the newspaper business with his father and brother in 1895. After his father's death in 1916, he assumed editorship of the family journal, *Wallaces' Farmer.* As his father had done, Wallace advocated scientific agriculture and conservation and extolled the virtues of rural life. He also covered national and international issues that affected American farmers.

Beginning in 1920, sharp decreases in demand for farm commodities plunged the agricultural sector of the economy into a severe depression. As secretary of agriculture from 1921 to 1925, Wallace sought to help the nation's farmers in several ways. He created the bureau of agricultural economics to provide information to farmers about the economic outlook for specific crops. To lower costs of production, he supported legislation to regulate stockyards, packers, warehouses, and railroads. However, surplus production was the nation's primary agricultural problem. Wallace asked farmers voluntarily to reduce their production but knew they were unlikely to do so. As an alternative, he joined farm leaders in advocating the establishment of a federal corporation to export surpluses. Although Congress considered several versions of the proposal during the 1920s, laissez-faire economic attitudes prevented its passage.

—*Judith Fabry*

SUGGESTED READING:
Lord, Russell. *The Wallaces of Iowa.* Boston, 1947.
Schapsmeier, Edward L., and Frederick H. Schapsmeier. *Henry A. Wallace of Iowa: The Agrarian Years, 1910–1940.* Ames, Iowa, 1968.

WALLA WALLA INDIANS

See: Native American Peoples: Peoples of the Pacific Northwest

WAPITI

SEE: Elk

WAR

SEE: Alamo; Apache Wars; Bozeman Trail; Buffalo Soldiers; Central Plains Indians Wars; Chinese Wars; Civil War; El Paso Salt War; Fetterman Massacre; Fredonia Rebellion; Gorras Blancas, Las; Graham-Tewksbury Feud; Grattan Massacre; Guerrillas; Hancock's Cam-

1930s reflected Wallace's desire to give farmers a fair share in the nation's economy, to sustain the family farm, and to use federal programs to reduce crop surpluses. Later, as vice-president and then as secretary of commerce, Wallace's liberal views about foreign policy alienated many Democrats and eventually forced him to resign from public office. His independent bid for the presidency in 1948, which was tainted by communist support, ended his political career.

—*Judith Fabry*

SUGGESTED READING:
Lord, Russell. *The Wallaces of Iowa.* Boston, 1947.
Schapsmeier, Edward L., and Frederick H. Schapsmeier. *Henry A. Wallace of Iowa: The Agrarian Years, 1910–1940.* Ames, Iowa, 1968.

WALLACE, HENRY CANTWELL

A prominent advocate of farmers and secretary of agriculture, Henry C. Wallace (1866–1925) was born in Illinois, the son of Nannie Cantwell and Henry Wallace. A graduate of the agricultural course at Iowa State

paign; Horrell-Higgins Feud; Jayhawkers; Johnson County War; Kansas-Nebraska Act; Kearny Code; Lincoln County War; Little Bighorn, Battle of; Mexican Border Conflicts; Mountain Meadows Massacre; National Expansion; Native American Cultures: Warfare; Navajo Wars; Pacific Northwest Indian Wars; Pueblo Revolt; Sand Creek Massacre; Scalping; Sioux Wars; Sutton-Taylor Feud; Texas Frontier Indian Wars; Texas Revolution; United States Army; Utah Expedition; Vigilantism; Violence; Wounded Knee Massacre; Yuma Revolt

WARNER, JONATHAN TRUMBULL

Connecticut-born Jonathan Trumbull Warner (1807–?) migrated west on the advice of his doctor. Arriving in St. Louis, Missouri, in his twenties, he hooked up with JEDEDIAH STRONG SMITH and accompanied the legendary mountain man on a trapping and trading expedition along the Santa Fe Trail. The expedition disintegrated when Smith died at the hands of Comanche Indians, but Warner followed Smith's partner on to Los Angeles in 1831. Warner trapped for furs in the interior reaches of CALIFORNIA for the next two years and then worked as a store clerk. Opening his own store by 1836, in the following year, Warner took as his wife a ward of the influential Pico family.

Warner, a well-educated man, became one of the Yankee adventurers who embraced the Mexican culture of California in the days before its American conquest. (In fact, at the time of the United States–Mexican War, Warner was arrested by U.S. Marines as an enemy sympathizer.) In 1843, Warner became a Mexican citizen and was baptized into the Roman Catholic church. Jonathan Trumbull became Juan José, and he acquired a large land grant, Rancho Valle de San Jose in San Diego County. Warner's Rancho, staffed with Yuma Indians, became a mercantile trading post along the southern trail to California. During the 1849 California gold rush, Warner's establishment served thousands of Forty-niners making their way to the gold fields. In the 1850s, the trading post became a stopover for the Butterfield Overland stage.

In spite of all the activity at Warner's Rancho, its owner never made much money from the land. Mostly, he kept body and soul together as a correspondent for Eastern and San Francisco newspapers. By 1855, he had moved back to Los Angeles and shortly thereafter began his own newspaper, the *Southern Vineyard*. The venture did not last long, but it gave Warner a vehicle

for the causes he advocated, the most prominent of which was a transcontinental railroad, which Warner saw as the key to California's agricultural prosperity. The prosperity, however, would belong to others. By the 1860s, Warner had lost all of his rancho lands.

—*Patricia Hogan*

SEE ALSO: California Gold Rushes; California Ranchos

SUGGESTED READING:
Hill, Joseph John. *The History of Warner's Ranch and Its Environs*. New York, 1927.
Morrison, Lorrin L. *Warner: The Man and the Ranch*. New York, 1962.

WAR OF 1812

In many respects, the War of 1812 set the stage for the United States's continental expansion across North America. The pressures leading to the declaration of war with Great Britain in 1812 were varied, but included elements that directly related to the Western vision of the United States. Many Congressmen, called "War Hawks"—HENRY CLAY, JOHN CALDWELL CALHOUN, Felix Grundy, Peter Porter, and others—shared a vision of expansion to the Spanish territories in the South and West, including Florida and Texas, as well as to the British territories, including the Oregon Country. Moreover, they feared the British would make use of Indian allies to harass settlements on the frontier. During the congressional session following the election of 1810, they became increasingly vocal in pressing for war, although it seems that the maritime and commercial issues driving Britain and the United States towards war were more important in the end.

Expansion into Indiana contributed to the coming of the war. Indian resistance to growing numbers of U.S. settlers in the Indiana Territory led to clashes between Indians and whites and, in the end, to the formation of an Indian confederation by TECUMSEH along the Wabash frontier. The hostilities culminated in the Battle of Tippecanoe on November 7, 1811, when troops under William Henry Harrison were attacked by Shawnee Indians. Harrison's forces stood off the assault and dispersed the Indians along the Upper Wabash.

When war was declared on June 18, 1812, the country and, in particular, the West, faced serious problems of organization, supply, and strategy. The military organization of the United States was small and ill equipped to carry on campaigns on the northern and southern frontiers, as well as to defend the coast. Despite hopes of gaining substantial support from

The Battle of New Orleans, a decisive victory for Andrew Jackson's forces, secured American control of the Mississippi River and made a hero of America's favorite Westerner, Old Hickory, himself. *Courtesy Library of Congress.*

Canadians, U.S. campaigns along the Northern frontier between Canada and the United States were fruitless. General William Hull moved north from Ohio toward Detroit in the summer of 1812 but was defeated. Other frontier outposts were taken, setting the Indians loose in the Illinois and Indiana settlements. Efforts in the fall and winter by Harrison to recover control led to defeat and massacre at Frenchtown and along the Raisin River. The shocked frontiersmen reorganized in the spring and summer of 1813, and the tide turned when Oliver Hazzard Perry, defeating the British at Put-in-Bay on September 10, 1813, gained control of the Western lakes. Perry's victory set the stage for American victory at the Battle of the Thames on October 5, which was marked by the death of Tecumseh.

Although 1812 saw little action in the South, the Creeks massacred whites at Fort Mims on the lower Alabama River on August 30, 1813. ANDREW JACKSON then led a campaign that climaxed with his victory at Horseshoe Bend on March 27, 1814. Jackson was given command of the Seventh Military District and the rank of major general. He proceeded to take Pensacola in West Florida and then sent forces to occupy Mobile, while he moved to New Orleans in what would be the successful defense of the city.

Events west of the Mississippi were on a more limited scale. Indians, seeing the difficulties that the whites were having in their campaigns, shut down the fur trade along the Upper Missouri. In 1813, the British captured the trading post established by JOHN JACOB ASTOR and the United States did not recover it during the war.

In 1814, diplomatic efforts to end the war included the British attempt to establish an Indian barrier territory north of the Ohio River, but the American delegation—including Albert Gallatin, John Quincy Adams, and Henry Clay—firmly opposed the effort, which was dropped by the British. The final draft of the treaty ending the war simply terminated the fighting and left other issues, including the British proposal of a right to navigate the Mississippi, for future discussion.

While the War of 1812 did little in terms of changing the territory of the United States, it set the stage for future expansion in the West and ended efforts by the British to block this expansion. The LOUISIANA PURCHASE was confirmed, and the Indian power was broken in Illinois and Indiana as well as in Alabama. The war made Americans more aware of the possibilities of western expansion and encouraged sentiments in favor of the acquisition of Texas. Moreover, it provided a base for the political careers of future presidents Andrew Jackson and William Henry Harrison as well as vice-president Richard Johnson and many other political figures on all levels. Finally, the war ended the efforts of the British to reincorporate the United States into its economic empire. The war set the stage for growth beyond the Mississippi and, in a sense, brought an end to the frontier east of the Mississippi.

—*Patrick H. Butler, III*

SUGGESTED READING:

Coles, Henry. *The War of 1812.* Chicago, 1965.

Hickey, Donald R. *The War of 1812: A Forgotten Conflict.* Chicago, 1990.

Horsman, Reginald. *The War of 1812.* New York, 1972.

Jacobs, James R., and Glenn Tucker. *The War of 1812: A Compact History.* New York 1969.

Mahon, John K. *War of 1812.* New York, 1972.

Tucker, Glenn. *Poltroons and Patriots: A Popular Account of the War of 1812.* New York, 1954.

WARREN, FRANCIS E.

The first governor of the state of Wyoming, Francis E. Warren (1844–1924) was born in Hinsdale, Massachusetts. Following distinguished service in the Civil War, he moved to Wyoming in 1868. Over the next fifteen years, he built an economic empire in the mercantile trade and the livestock business and became a major landowner in the new territory. He served as territorial treasurer for seven years and as mayor of Cheyenne for one term. President Chester Arthur appointed him territorial governor in 1885. A Democrat replaced him in 1886, but he regained the position two years later.

He worked closely with Territorial Delegate JOSEPH MAULL CAREY for Wyoming statehood, and when it was achieved in 1890, Warren was elected the first state governor. He resigned six weeks later when he was sent to the United States Senate for a two-year term. In April 1892, he was implicated in the JOHNSON COUNTY WAR. The legislature did not reelect him to the Senate, and the position remained vacant until the legislature chose C. D. Clark of Evanston for the seat in 1894. Warren then sought Carey's seat in the Senate, and his old ally was stunned when the legislature repudiated him in favor of Warren. The two Republicans feuded for two decades. Warren remained a senator until his death in 1929.

Warren built a personal political machine in Wyoming through efficient use of patronage and attention to the concerns of Wyoming's major economic interests—

the railroad and the livestock industry. He also promoted the careers of his son-in-law JOHN JOSEPH PERSHING and loyal aides such as WILLIS VAN DEVANTER who became a U.S. Supreme Court justice. He served as chairman of the Military Affairs Committee and the Appropriations Committee in the Senate.

During his campaigns for the Senate, opponents accused him of illegal fencing of public lands. Even though he remained largely unknown nationally, his power over Wyoming politics was considerable. After he died in 1929, Fort D. A. Russell near Cheyenne was renamed for him.

—*Phil Roberts*

SUGGESTED READING:

Bowen, Wesley D. "The Congressional Career of Francis E. Warren, 1912–1920." M.A. thesis, University of Wyoming, 1942

Erwin, Marie. *Wyoming Historical Blue Book.* Cheyenne, Wyo., 1943.

Gould, Lewis L. *Wyoming: A Political History, 1868–1896.* New Haven, Conn., 1968.

Hansen, Anne Carolyn. "The Congressional Career of Francis E. Warren from 1890 to 1902." M.A. thesis, University of Wyoming, 1942.

Jones, Robert F. "The Political Career of Francis E. Warren, 1902–1912." M.A. thesis, University of Wyoming, 1949.

Larson, T. A. *History of Wyoming.* Lincoln, Nebr., 1965. Reprint. 1978.

WASHAKIE (SHOSHONE)

Washakie (1804?–1900) was the most famous of the several names that the celebrated Eastern Shoshone chief bore. His father, Pasego, was a Flathead warrior of mixed stock. His mother reportedly was a Shoshone.

After the death of his father at the hands of Blackfoot raiders, Washakie, along with his mother and his four siblings, took refuge among the Lemhi people, a branch of the Shoshones living in central Idaho. A decade and a half later, Washakie left his adopted band to ride with Bannocks. During those years, he apparently traveled widely and came in contact with the mountaineers of the HUDSON'S BAY COMPANY and AMERICAN FUR COMPANY. From them and no doubt others, he learned many of the white man's ways.

In early adulthood, Washakie cast his lot with the Eastern Shoshone people of central Wyoming. An able craftsman, singer, orator, and fighter, the young man had the additional advantage of having a commanding presence. "Untutored though he is," said a white observer in the July 8, 1858, edition of the *New York*

Washakie. *Courtesy National Archives.*

accept his counsel. Normally that was enough, but during the late 1850s and early 1860s, many Eastern Shoshones, upset with the growing tide of white men, joined with other Native Americans to attack the overland trails. Washakie's influence returned after the raiders were defeated in punitive encounters, such as the "Battle" of Bear River in January 1863. Washakie's position was also strengthened by the consistent support of American officials.

In 1876, the chief enrolled more than one hundred of his men in General GEORGE CROOK's campaign against the Sioux. He and his warriors, however, arrived too late to take part in the Battle of the Rosebud and, like Crook himself, they had no role in the Battle of Little Bighorn.

Washakie spent his last years on the Wind River Reservation where he despaired over his people's decline; however, he succeeded better than he thought. Because of his leadership and his alliances with white men, the Eastern Shoshones were spared the military defeat and displacement of most Great Basin and Great Plains tribes. At his death, the federal government recognized his probity and friendship by according Washakie military honors; he was the only Western Native American chief so recognized.

—*Ronald W. Walker*

An animal skin with a pictorial history of Chief Washakie's battles. *Courtesy National Archives.*

Times, "his every word or step clearly marks the soul of a nobleman of nature's own commissioning." Such superlatives about the man's character and demeanor were common.

By 1840, the Eastern Shoshones accepted Washakie as one of their main leaders. Six years later, he dominated the tribe's affairs. With the Plains tribes pushing hard into Shoshone territory, Washakie allied his often outnumbered and retreating Eastern Shoshone bands with mountain men, Mormons, Wyoming settlers, and officials of the United States government. He offered peace in return for their trade, gifts, and annuities and, later, the prospect of securing a large, government-protected reserve of land in central Wyoming. The Fort Bridger Treaty of 1868 gave Washakie's people the Wind River Reservation. The cession, however, was reduced by several government-enforced negotiations. Worse, in 1878, American authorities gave the northern Arapahos, the Shoshones' frequent antagonists, "temporary" joint occupancy of the land. The arrangement became long lasting.

Washakie's control was never complete. With little power to enforce tribal discipline, his leadership depended on the willingness of his fellow tribesmen to

SUGGESTED READING:
Herbard, Grace Raymond. *Washakie*. Cleveland, Ohio, 1930.
Wright, Peter M. "Washakie." In *American Indian Leaders*. Edited by R. David Edmunds. Lincoln Nebr., 1980.

WASHINGTON

Washington, the "Evergreen State," is the most northwesterly of the forty-eight contiguous states and is bordered by the Pacific Ocean, Oregon, Idaho, and British Columbia, Canada. In 1994, 5,334,400 people resided in the state's sixty-eight thousand square miles.

Geographic regions

Washington has distinct geographic regions. A narrow Pacific coastal plain is punctuated with northern rock cliffs, sandy beaches, and two large inlets on the south. The hazardous mouth of the COLUMBIA RIVER marks the Oregon border. Folding processes and glacial action created the Olympic Mountains, a rugged cluster on a northwest peninsula. Fir, hemlock, and red cedar are thick, and abundant rainfall has created rain forests. Olympic National Park includes the 7,965-foot Mount Olympus. The Chehalis River valley separates the Olympics from the lower, rounded, thickly forested Willapa Hills to the south.

Just east, the Puget Sound trough extends from Canada to the Columbia River. Puget Sound is an inland sea joined to the Pacific by the Strait of Juan de Fuca. A maze of waterways, peninsulas, islands, isthmuses, harbors, and inlets, the sound extends over two thousand square miles. Freshwater lakes dot the area, and broad rivers create fertile wetlands.

Farther east, the Cascade Mountains are part of a range extending from Alaska to Mexico. Snow-covered year round, the Cascades have active volcanoes; Mount St. Helens was dramatically altered by its May 18, 1980, eruption. Several peaks rise spectacularly above the range, notably the 14,410-foot Mount Rainier. Mount Rainier and North Cascades national parks are in the region. The Columbia River cuts a deep gorge between the Washington and Oregon Cascades.

East of the Cascades, Washington is dominated by the great Columbia River basin. The river winds through in several great circles, the largest called the

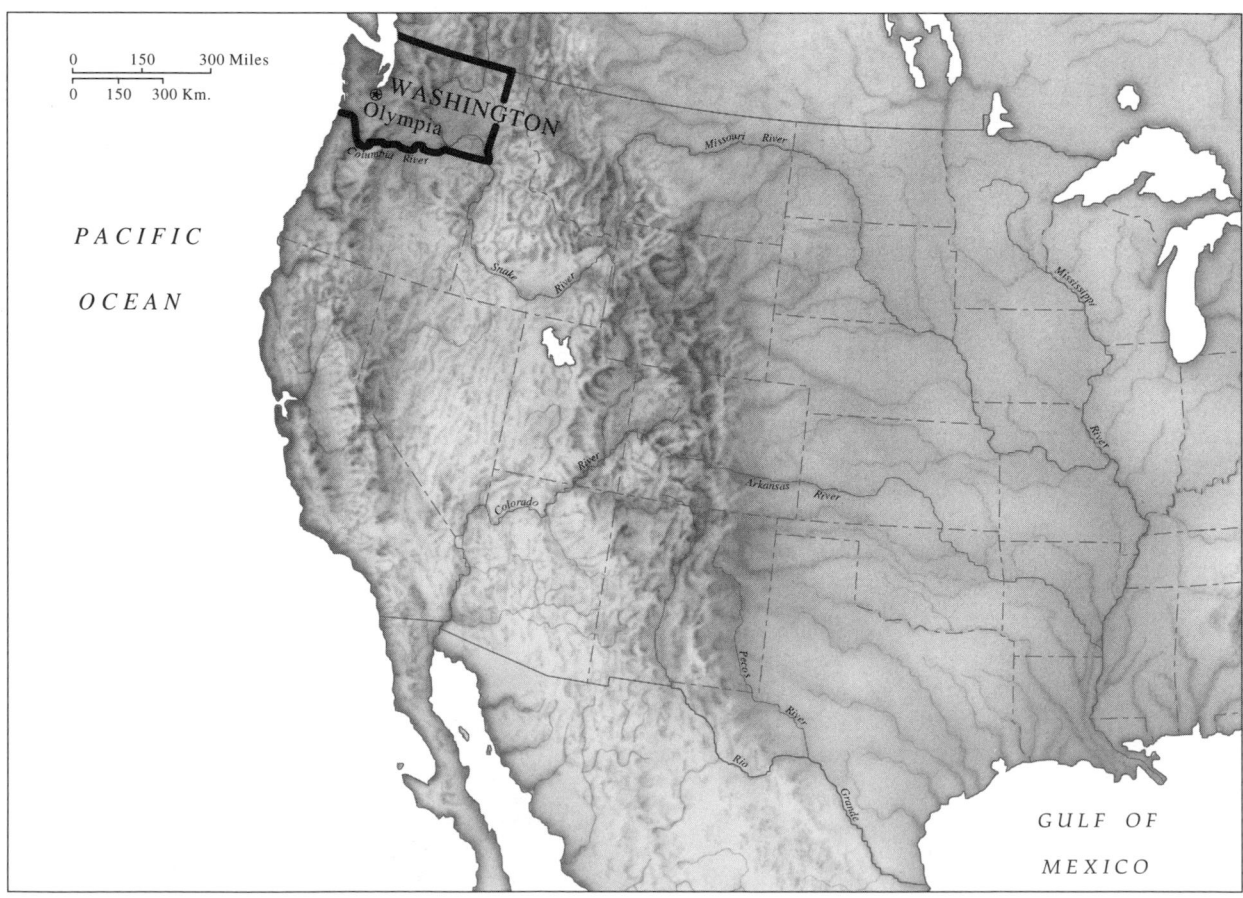

Big Bend. An ancient flood left channeled "scablands" when it subsided, and flat lands are scarred by former river beds. During glacial ages, a gigantic ice dam blocked the Columbia; when it broke, the river's course shifted to that known today.

The Yakima River valley stretches southeast from the Cascades toward the Columbia River. The large northeastern section of the state has a succession of rugged ridges and valleys cut through by snakelike Lake Roosevelt behind Grand Coulee Dam.

Climate differences result as ocean winds mount the Cascade range. On the west side, rising winds drop ocean moisture but foster dry, sunny spots in the rain shadow along the Strait of Juan de Fuca. Puget Sound enjoys a moist, moderate climate. The winds drop rain and snow in the Cascades, but east of the mountains the land is naturally dry with a wide temperature range.

Native Americans

Archaeologists have found human remains dating back twelve thousand years in widely separated locations in Washington. Humans, probably arriving over the Siberian land bridge as the glacial age ended, used tools and hunted large creatures. Possibly they were precursors of later Native American or Indian groups.

Indians acquired essentials easily, especially in western Washington. Staple foods were abundant: fish from the ocean, the region's sound, the lakes and streams; clams, oysters, and other shellfish on the beaches; small and large game; and easily gathered roots, vines, and berries. Coastal Indians captured whale and bestowed religious significance on salmon. Cedar was also important. Easily felled and split and having a fibrous bark, it provided material for houses, canoes, ocean-going whalers, baskets, house furnishings, and rain hats, capes, and shirts. Indians in western Washington had relatively permanent settlements, although they sometimes traveled short distances seasonally for berries, fish, and roots. There was little reason to develop agriculture.

East of the Cascades, salmon were abundant in rivers and roots plentiful. Yet, especially after the horse arrived, Indians traveled to obtain some necessities. Living in pit houses and caves, the Native Americans wore light clothing in the summer and animal skins in the winter.

The term *tribes* is barely applicable to the native people of Washington, where governmental organizations were loosely structured and leaders were often selected for particular skills. Trading was common around the Puget Sound and at the mouth of the Columbia River. A distinctive coastal ceremony was the potlatch, a festivity attended by guests coming great distances; a tribal leader ostentatiously disposed of belongings amid

The native peoples of Washington found abundant food on the state's shores, rivers, and lands. Makah Indians dried halibut fillets in the sun on towering racks at a summer encampment on Tatoosh Island. *Courtesy Special Collections Division, University of Washington Libraries.*

feasts and games. Generally peaceable, Coastal Indians suffered raids from warlike tribes to the north.

European and American exploration

By the late 1700s, the northwestern corner of North America remained unmapped, but explorers from Russia, Spain, Great Britain, and the United States were all active in the region. British seamen sought a water route through the continent. Merchants from the United States also sought routes and trade items; during the eighteenth century, few Americans desired land in the Northwest for expansion.

Spanish explorers noted the mouth of the Columbia River and touched the coast, but Spain was being challenged worldwide by Great Britain. Captain JAMES COOK had come in 1778, and his lieutenant George Vancouver returned in 1792. After resolving a dispute with Spaniards, Vancouver began searching for a transcontinental water route. This led him through the Strait of Juan de Fuca to the sea he named the Puget Sound. For three weeks, his men charted inland waters and named major features. He claimed the region for Britain. After Robert Gray, an American sent by Boston investors, entered the region and named the Columbia, Vancouver sent a crew upriver. The contest for the Northwest was under way.

Sea explorers soon found that North Pacific sea otter pelts were valued in Asia, and they developed a substantial trade. Sea exploration gave way to overland expeditions and trade centered on the mountain beaver. DAVID THOMPSON and others journeyed down the rivers to enhance British claims, but the scientific expedition of MERIWETHER LEWIS and WILLIAM CLARK in the opening years of the nineteenth century indelibly affixed American interests to the region.

Spain and Russia withdrew from the area between the 42° and the 54° 40' latitude. In 1818, Great Britain and the United States agreed to occupy jointly the region then called the Oregon Country. Conducting a fur trade and other activities from headquarters at FORT VANCOUVER on the Columbia's northern bank, the British HUDSON'S BAY COMPANY dominated the region and JOHN MCLOUGHLIN, the company's chief factor, governed it.

American settlement

During the early years of joint occupancy, the British dominated the region, but American fur traders, missionaries, and farmers began to arrive. Methodists Daniel and JASON LEE came to the Willamette Valley of present-day Oregon in 1834, and their enthusiasm for the agricultural potential attracted settlers. Several Protestant churches sent MARCUS AND NARCISSA WHITMAN, Elkanah and Mary Walker, and others into the eastern portion. The Whitmans and household members were murdered by disgruntled Cayuse Indians in 1847.

After 1843, more American settlers arrived annually over the OREGON TRAIL. As Americans filled the Willamette Valley, the United States decided to terminate joint occupancy. Although political rhetoric favored taking the entire area ("54° 40' or Fight!"), actual negotiations centered on where to divide the British and American territories in western Washington. An 1846 treaty placed the border on the forty-ninth parallel, but left Vancouver Island in British territory. Disputes over the intended border through the San Juan Islands resulted in the "Pig War" of the late 1850s; an arbitrated settlement gave the United States the islands.

In 1853, the Washington Territory was carved from the Oregon Territory. Walla Walla, on a spur of the Oregon Trail and near the old Whitman Mission, was the new territory's largest community. While conflicts between Euro-Americans and Indians inhibited settlement in eastern Washington during the 1850s, settlers moved north toward the Puget Sound. In 1845, Michael

T. Simmons and GEORGE WASHINGTON BUSH led an American group to claims near Olympia. Within a few years, several sawmill villages were scattered near inlets and river mouths about the sound.

Territorial years

U.S. Army engineer Isaac Stevens became the Washington Territory's first governor. Not only did Stevens tend to his administrative duties, he also surveyed the Cascades for a railroad route. He held councils with Native Americans and forced them onto reservations in return for other guarantees. The Stevens treaties resurfaced a century later as Euro-Americans and Indians disputed fishing rights on the Puget Sound. With a few exceptions, later territorial governors were mediocre political appointees.

Lumbermen in Washington found ready markets in a fast-growing northern California. In time, large lumber companies moved west from Maine and the northern Midwest, built large mills, and established company towns that resembled villages in the East. The arrival of the Weyerhaeuser Company from Minnesota in 1900 heralded a period of domination by a few huge firms. Meanwhile, steam sawmills, donkey engines, logging railroads, and improved technology in camps and plants transformed the LUMBER INDUSTRY. But workers suffered under poor living conditions in camps and mill towns, dangerous working conditions, and uncertain employment and benefits.

During the building of the transcontinental railroad, several towns competed for the Western terminus. Small local lines were constructed, but the region was largely in the grip of Eastern railroad magnates, and local prosperity rose or declined along with the capitalists' fortunes. When the Northern Pacific selected Tacoma as its terminus in 1873, the town burgeoned. Two decades later, JAMES J. HILL's Great Northern crossed the Cascades into Everett and turned south to Seattle. As the dominant city in the Northwest, SEATTLE was enhanced by rebuilding after a devastating fire, by trade across the Pacific, by the Alaska-Yukon gold rush, by the regrading of hills and filling in of tide flats, and by vigorous civic promoters.

As railroads crossed eastern Washington, connecting lines appeared, and railroad towns became distribution centers for wheat and other crops. In the late 1800s, Spokane burst ahead of rival towns with an economy based on pine lumbering, mining, and agriculture. Despite later setbacks, Spokane remained the center of an "Inland Empire" embracing neighboring states.

Statehood was delayed by Democratic fears that Washington would vote Republican, but the 1888 national election of a Republican administration accelerated the process, and Washington achieved statehood on November 11, 1889. Olympia remained the capital, and former territorial governor and Seattle capitalist Elisha Ferry was elected governor.

Statehood

Although conservative Republicans dominated early state politics, Washington emerged as a progressive state during the reform era. Crusaders both in and out of government promoted such reforms as women's suffrage, direct legislation, and industrial compensation. The radical INDUSTRIAL WORKERS OF THE WORLD gained followers and engaged in labor agitation in Spokane, Centralia, Everett, and other communities.

During the decade after World War I, Washington lost its pioneer characteristics and became more clearly amalgamated with the whole United States. As with the nation, the Great Depression engendered political change and a wave of Democratic officeholders. Yet, Governor Clarence D. Martin, while advocating a "little new deal," remained essentially conservative. Federal and state affairs became increasingly intertwined, as the construction of Grand Coulee Dam and various federal programs highlighted strong ties with the "other Washington."

Proximity to the Pacific theater created a sense of urgency during World War II, and the federal presence increased with military construction and troop movements. War contracts permanently altered old shipyards and benefited new companies; Boeing expanded as the B-17 and B-27 dominated the air war. The secret plutonium plant at Hanford in eastern Washington ushered in a nuclear industry, attracted highly skilled technicians, and created an urban center in the desert. New tides of workers altered the demography of the state. Meanwhile, several thousand Japanese Americans were removed to relocation camps; many returned to an unwelcome, hostile atmosphere.

The postwar era

The immediate postwar period brought further transformation to the state. Companies prosperous from wartime contracts continued, and Boeing turned to producing commercial jets. Population spread from cities into the suburbs, which attracted prospering young professionals and white-collar workers.

Washington's strides forward were marked by world's fairs in Seattle (1962) and Spokane (1974), the arrival of professional sports teams (1967), efforts to redefine downtown areas in large cities, new industries, facilities for container shipping in Seattle and Tacoma, a growing world view, and a reputation for "livability."

In the late 1960s, industrial growth slowed as the forestry and aircraft industries experienced reverses.

The economy rebounded as old industries diversified and new ones emerged, but uncertainties remained. Growing environmental issues seemed to run counter to economic needs, best illustrated when efforts to protect old-growth forests threatened timber harvests. Meanwhile, rapid population growth posed an array of problems. The region wrestled with issues concerning the economy, the environment, transportation, education, crime, and medical care. Increasingly, Washington joined neighboring states in regional undertakings.

With a weak traditional political party system, Washington voters have generally been nonpartisan. Three-term Republican governor and U.S. Senator Daniel J. Evans was politically successful alongside long-time Democratic senators, WARREN GRANT MAGNUSON and HENRY MARTIN ("SCOOP") JACKSON. Spokane representative Thomas Foley attended to local concerns while rising to become Speaker of the U.S. House of Representatives. Perhaps the most nationally influential Washingtonian was U.S. Supreme Court Justice William O. Douglas.

The population

Caucasians constitute 88 percent of the state's population, and they have clearly dominated political, economic, and social affairs. Since the 1970s, however, minority groups have gained influence.

The Native American population includes reservation and nonreservation Indians. Conflict between Euro Americans and Native Americans erupted during the 1960s over century-old treaty rights. Tribes and individuals have endeavored to retain and exhibit their cultural identity.

Asians have long constituted the largest minority group in Washington. Early Chinese laborers worked in railroad construction, mines, and fish canneries. Their expulsion from Seattle and Tacoma in the mid-1880s paralleled the 1940s removal of Japanese Americans during World War II. Both returned and were joined by Filipinos, Southeast Asians, and Koreans.

Many African Americans moved to Washington during and after World War II to take advantage of job opportunities. Civil rights disturbances during the 1960s were less frequent and violent than in many states. Spanish-speaking people worked seasonally in agricultural areas as part of migratory streams circling the West. Many put down roots, and in the 1990s, Hispanics constitute the fastest growing minority group. Minority residents have created an ethnic diversity, and many individuals have gained social influence and political and economic power.

—*Charles P. LeWarne*

SEE ALSO: Loggers; Native American Peoples: Peoples of the Pacific Northwest; Oregon Boundary Dispute

SUGGESTED READING:

Clark, Norman H. *Washington: A Bicentennial History.* The States and the Nation. New York and Nashville, Tenn., 1976.

Ficken, Robert E., and Charles P. LeWarne. *Washington: A Centennial History.* Seattle and London, 1988.

Schwantes, Carlos A. *The Pacific Northwest: An Interpretive History.* Lincoln, Nebr., and London, 1989.

WASHO INDIANS

SEE: Native American Peoples: Peoples of California

WATER

The windswept dry High Plains, the arid Rocky Mountains, and the blistering hot deserts of the West have always challenged people living in these regions to develop ways to use water that would not deplete sources. This fact has remained true for the people in aboriginal societies, in Hispanic pueblos, on irrigated farms, and in the modern tourist or high-tech cities of the West. The success or failure of human societies in the West has depended, in large part, on how well each developed a sustainable form of water use. Cultural values have determined how people have viewed water and, consequently, how they have used and developed it.

Generally, aboriginal peoples' uses of water centered around deep spiritual beliefs and practices. The Tohono O'odham people of southern Arizona practiced saguaro wine-drinking rituals and the *vitikita,* a religious observance, to evoke the rains for their irrigated fields. The Pueblo Indians, who grew cotton on irrigated fields, actively took part in the kachina cult; many of its rituals revolved around rainmaking. Around 1000 A.D., the Paiutes, who sang to their Mother Earth, developed a decentralized society around irrigation in the northern end of the Owens Valley in southern California. They practiced field rotation, lived in permanent villages, and dammed streams.

Still, some Indian people's practices failed them. Many anthropologists and archaeologists believe the elaborate Hohokam irrigation culture of southern Arizona collapsed with the build-up of salinity in its fields by 900 A.D. Some scholars believe the Anasazi, whose ruins are still apparent in Chaco Canyon in northwest New Mexico, adversely affected their flood irrigation practices by cutting down trees in the forests. Deforestation created deep arroyos, which hindered the surface diversion of stream flows.

When the Spanish colonized remote outposts in the Southwest, beginning with Santa Fe in 1610, they developed a community form of irrigation derived from a combination of Spanish and Indian practices. People shared in the governance and maintenance of the *acequia madre,* the "mother canal," which the community owned in common. Many Hispanics still practice community irrigation throughout northern New Mexico and southern Colorado.

After the United States–Mexican War, Anglos largely replaced the Hispanics' and Indian peoples' water-use practices. Anglo values stressed individual economic gain through a technological mastery of their environment, and most of the newcomers viewed water in economic rather than in communal or spiritual terms. A few utopian colonists and the Mormons of

Securing water rights was essential to any enterprise in the West. Hydraulic mining, for a time, provided a profitable means of extracting minerals from Western mines. *Courtesy National Cowboy Hall of Fame and Western Heritage Center.*

Utah, however, were possible exceptions to this rule; they developed their religious settlements around commonly owned irrigation systems. In general, however, Westerners transformed water into a marketable commodity to serve the needs of an economic system stressing individual gain.

Westerners first devised a legal system sympathetic to their social and economic ambitions in the gold fields of California. There, they originated the modern doctrine of prior appropriation. The person who first developed a use of water would receive his or her share before others who had later developed their use of water—"first in time, first in right." The prior-appropriation system sped the economic development of the West. Lawmakers recognized certain "beneficial uses," or economic uses, of water when they enacted their legal systems. Most Western states devised a hierarchy of uses—domestic, agricultural, and industrial. As developers planned cities, farms, and industries, they had to move quickly to secure their water rights. Failure to cement the rights could, and often did, guarantee the ruin of many projects when many Western water courses became "over-appropriated," meaning people had attached more rights to a stream than its flow could support. Regardless, between 1870 and 1900, private promoters built large irrigation systems throughout the West, and urban planners constructed increasingly complex conveyance systems to drain mountain watersheds. By 1900, a hydraulic infrastructure had taken shape in the West.

However, Westerners had overbuilt and, as a result, possessed worthless water rights for poorly designed systems. Congress passed the NEWLANDS RECLAMATION ACT OF 1902 to subsidize the hydraulic society in the West. The Reclamation Service (renamed the BUREAU OF RECLAMATION in 1927) bolstered and expanded water development with projects such as the Salt River in Arizona, the Truckee-Carson in Nevada, and, the most famous, Boulder Dam (now HOOVER DAM), along with hundreds of others in every major river basin. The UNITED STATES ARMY CORPS OF ENGINEERS added its flood-control projects after 1927 and cooperated at times with the Bureau of Reclamation in such sweeping undertakings as the Pick-Sloan Plan of the 1950s, which added hundreds of dams to the Missouri River basin.

The complexity of the Western hydraulic society spawned an intricate legal system to regulate the use, division, and development of water. Bureaucracies like the state engineers' offices regulated water rights and consumption, measured stream flows, and inspected and approved dams. In the 1930s, many states formed water boards to coordinate statewide planning with federal programs. A new specialty for lawyers emerged;

Top: Many of the activities of Westerners have involved moving water from where it was to where humans wanted it to be. Barrett Dam supplied the arid city of San Diego, California, with an essential resource. *Courtesy San Diego Historical Society.*

Bottom: Water development projects, often requiring cooperation among federal and state agencies and private enterprises, irrigated farms and built cities throughout the West. *Courtesy San Diego Historical Society.*

water lawyers dominated the litigation of water rights. A body of water law centered around the doctrine of equity—put forth in the Supreme Court decision of *KANSAS* v. *COLORADO*—and the doctrine of reserved rights, or the Winter's doctrine, which supposedly protected Indian water rights. Through interstate compacts, the first of which was the COLORADO RIVER COMPACT of 1922, Westerners allotted the benefits of interstate stream flows. All of the doctrines and the mechanisms, such as compacts, work simultaneously, but not necessarily harmoniously, to promote economic individualism, the subsidy of existent systems, and the development of new water projects. In this social milieu, water lawyers and consulting engineers thrived in the arid West.

The struggles over water uses have surely reflected the social and economic realities of the West. Undoubtedly, Westerners have enjoyed fabulous riches and growth due to their various water development projects. During the last decades of the twentieth century, however, river basins were degraded, and a rising environmental movement and tourism demanded the preservation of free-flowing streams. Contention blossomed among environmentalists, irrigation companies, ditch users in Hispanic communities, urban centers, and Indian tribes as the Western economy became more focused in cities. Many critics questioned a legal system that assigned to water only a commodity value subject to technological manipulation, yet water continued to flow uphill to money in the West.

—*James E. Sherow*

SEE ALSO: Agriculture; Arid-Lands Thesis; Arkansas River; *Arizona* v. *California;* Boulder Canyon Act of 1928; California Doctrine (of Water Rights); Central Valley Project; Climate; Colorado Doctrine (of Water Rights); Colorado River; Colorado River Storage Project; Columbia River; Desert Land Act of 1877; Desert Land Act of 1891; Echo Park; Erosion; Farming; Federal Government; Floods; Homesteading; Hoover Dam; Humboldt River and the Great Basin Streams; Irrigation; *Lux* v. *Haggin;* Missouri River; Multiple-Use Doctrine; Navajo Stock-Reduction Program; Ogallala Aquifer; Owens Valley War; Platte River; Reclamation; *Report on the Lands of Arid Regions;* Rocky Mountains; Snake River; Soil Conservation Service; Sustained Yield; West-as-Region School; Windmills; *Woodruff* v. *North Bloomfield;* Wright Irrigation Act of 1887

SUGGESTED READING:
Dunbar, Robert G. *Forging New Rights in Western Waters.* Lincoln, Nebr., 1983.
Lee, Lawrence B. *Reclaiming the American West: An Historiography and Guide.* Santa Barbara, Calif., 1980.
Pisani, Donald. *To Reclaim a Divided West: Water, Law, and Public Policy, 1848–1902.* Albuquerque, N. Mex., 1992.

Reisner, Marc. *Cadillac Desert: The American West and Its Disappearing Water.* New York, 1986.
Stegner, Wallace. *The American West as Living Space.* Ann Arbor, Mich., 1987.
Worster, Donald. *Rivers of Empire: Water, Aridity and The Growth of The American West.* New York, 1985.

WATIE, STAND (CHEROKEE)

Cherokee politician and soldier Stand Watie (1806–1871) was born into the Cherokee Nation east of the Mississippi River near Rome, Georgia, and grew to leadership as the founder and editor of the *Cherokee Phoenix,* a bilingual newspaper printed in Cherokee and English using SEQUOYAH's syllabary. Mission-educated and a member of the Cherokee "mixed-blood elite," Watie favored removal to the West in the face of the intense pressure the tribe faced from Georgia whites. Signing the controversial Treaty of New Echota in 1835—a treaty that cleared the way for western removal—Watie established a thriving plantation on Spavinaw Creek in the Indian Territory (present-day Oklahoma) and became a prosperous slave owner. During the Civil War, he led many Cherokees into the Confederacy and organized the First Cherokee Mounted Rifles, a regiment of cavalry. For his daring raids in Missouri, Kansas, Arkansas, and northern Oklahoma, Watie became a Confederate general, the last man of this rank, in fact, to surrender to the Union—on June 23, 1865, at Doaksville in the Choctaw Nation. After the war, Watie worked hard to rehabilitate the Cherokees and regain his personal fortune under a Reconstruction government bent on revenge and the annexation of Indian land. That Watie fared as well as he did had much to do with his achievement in combining the faction-ridden Cherokee tribe into a unified political community.

—*Charles Phillips*

WATSON, ELLA ("CATTLE KATE")

Ellen L. Watson (1861–1889), commonly known as "Ella" Watson, may have been born on a farm in Ontario, Canada. According to researcher George Hufsmith, her parents were of Scottish and Irish descent, and in 1877, they moved with their children to Lebanon, Kansas, where they farmed. At the age of eighteen, Ellen probably married William Pickell, an abusive husband from whom she was subsequently

divorced. She then took up work as a cook and domestic in a private residence near her parents' home
and later in hotels in Nebraska and, finally, Wyoming.
Many chroniclers identify this period of her life as the
start of her association with PROSTITUTION and CATTLE
RUSTLING. George Hufsmith, however, contends that
such chroniclers have confused Ellen Watson with two
Wyoming prostitutes—Ella Wilson, a mixed-blood
woman of Native American descent who worked in
Fetterman, and Kate Maxwell, a white woman from
Chicago who worked in Bessemer Bend and who first
earned the sobriquet "Cattle Kate." Yet all accounts
agree that someone named Ella Watson took up with
James Averell, a homesteader and store- and
saloonkeeper in Sweetwater Valley, Wyoming, sometime between 1886 and 1888. The two may or may
not have been married. Averell was known in the area
as one of the chief opponents of large landholders and
stock-raisers, often called the "Cattle Kings." Some
accounts portray Watson and Averell as innocent and
aggrieved homesteaders (both held homestead claims)
and small-business owners, hemmed in and harassed
at every turn by representatives of the powerful Wyoming Stock Growers' Association. Other accounts

James Averill, companion to "Cattle Kate" Watson, was
hanged with her for holding stolen cattle. *Courtesy
American Heritage Center, University of Wyoming.*

portray Averell as a cattle rustler and Watson as a common prostitute who took cattle in lieu of cash for sexual
favors. Watson did indeed acquire cattle, by whatever
means, which she marked with her own brand. The
ongoing tension between Watson and Averell, on one
hand, and the Cattle Kings, on the other, over both
land and cattle came to a dramatic conclusion on
July 20, 1889, just days after Watson's twenty-eighth
birthday, when men representing large stock-raisers
rode onto Watson's property and accused her of holding stolen cattle. Watson claimed innocence, to no avail;
both she and her partner Averell were hanged the same
day. In subsequent years, Ella Watson and the name
"Cattle Kate" became inextricably linked, and her alleged practice of trading sex for cattle became a fixture of Western historical memory.

—*Susan Lee Johnson*

SUGGESTED READING:
Aikman Duncan. *Calamity Jane and the Lady Wildcats.*
    1927. Reprint. Lincoln, Nebr., 1987.
Atherton, Lewis. *The Cattle Kings.* Bloomington, Ind., 1961.
Butler, Anne. *Daughters of Joy, Sisters of Misery: Prostitutes
    in the American West, 1865–90.* Urbana, Ill., 1987.
Hufsmith, George. *The Wyoming Lynching of Cattle Kate,
    1889.* Glendo, Wyo., 1993.

Ella Watson, known as "Cattle Kate." *Courtesy American
Heritage Center, University of Wyoming.*

WAYNE, JOHN

Noted star in nearly two hundred westerns and other movies and icon in American popular culture, John Wayne (Marion Robert Morrison, 1907–1979) was born in Winterset, Iowa. The man the world knew as John Wayne never legally changed his name, although he did substitute "Michael" for "Robert" when giving his name in later years.

Wayne grew up in Iowa only a generation or so removed from the Civil War and the outlaw Jesse James. His father's health forced the family to move to a farm near Palmdale, California, where Wayne learned to ride and shoot. The family then moved to Glendale, where Wayne attended public schools and was known as a good student.

Wayne wanted to attend the U.S. Naval Academy but enrolled in the University of Southern California on the insistence of his mother. He played football for two years until an off-season shoulder injury forced him to give up the sport. While still at the university, he obtained a summer job as a laborer at Fox Studios, where he met director John Ford. Although Wayne worked as a properties man, Ford occasionally cast him in small parts. He moved on to do stunt work because of the higher pay.

Raoul Walsh, seeking an unknown actor for the lead in a wagon-train adventure film titled *The Big Trail* (1930), saw Wayne working shirtless at the studio. He decided to cast him in the big-budget film, the first to use 70mm cameras. Because the film required special projection equipment that few exhibitors could afford during the Great Depression, it was not a success.

Wayne played in a series of "B-western" films and serials during the 1930s, some for Poverty Row filmmakers and some for Herbert B. Yates at Republic. Wayne's friendship with John Ford continued, and finally, Ford cast him as the Ringo Kid in *Stagecoach* (1938). From then until his death in 1979, John Wayne was a movie star of the first magnitude and the quintessential western star.

Noted westerns in which Wayne appeared with Ford as director included *Fort Apache* (1948), *Three Godfathers* (1948), *She Wore a Yellow Ribbon* (1949), and *The Searchers* (1956). He also appeared in *Red River* (1948), directed by Howard Hawks. Wayne played in as many movies with World War II settings as he did in westerns; his role in *Sands of Iwo Jima* (1949) earned him an Academy Award nomination. He finally won the award for playing the character Rooster Cogburn in *True Grit* (1969). In his final film, *The Shootist* (1976), he reprised the character of a driven, fanatic, unyielding man with a heart of gold who used his own death to straighten out an errant youth. Wayne's best-known personal film project was *The Alamo* (1960), in which he starred. Produced and directed by Wayne, *The Alamo* was thought by many to reflect his well-known conservative political views.

Long before his film career ended, Wayne had become an icon in American popular culture. Memorable lines from his films ("That'll be the day") became a part of American speech patterns, and the U.S. Marine Corps showed *Sands of Iwo Jima* to recruits to inspire them. Wayne did not serve in the Marines or any other branch of the service during World War II because of his age, his shoulder injury, and the four children born to him and his first wife.

Wayne had married Josephine Saenz on June 24, 1933. They divorced in 1945. On January 18, 1946, he married Mexican movie actress Esparanza (Chata) Baur; they divorced in 1953, and he married Peruvian actress Pilar Palette on November 1, 1953.

Wayne was diagnosed with lung cancer in 1964. He survived surgery to remove the diseased tissue and announced that he had beaten the "Big C." Wayne continued to make westerns and other action films until the mid-1970s despite growing health problems. Among the first actors to take public political positions, he supported the United States's efforts in Vietnam and campaigned for conservative political candidates until cancer returned in 1979. In Wayne's honor, the U.S. Congress authorized a special medal to be struck at the request of friends and admirers in politics and entertainment.

—*Archie P. McDonald*

SEE ALSO: Film: The Western

SUGGESTED READING:
Barbour, Alan G. *John Wayne*. New York, 1974.
McDonald, Archie P. "John Wayne: Hero of the Western." In *Shooting Stars, Heroes and Heroines of Western Film*. Edited by Archie P. McDonald. Bloomington, Ind., 1987.
Tuska, John. *The Filming of the West*. New York, 1976.

W-BAR RANCH, MONTANA

The prominent French mine owner Pierre Wibaux established the W-Bar Ranch in 1883 fifteen miles northeast of the Montana town bearing his name in Wibaux County. When the catastrophic winter of 1886 to 1887 wiped out vast numbers of the Western herds, Wibaux emerged a survivor and acquired what remained of herds owned by many other Montana ranchers. By the 1890s, the W-Bar had become one of the larger ranches in the nation. At its height, the ranch extended from eastern Montana to western North Dakota and maintained more than sixty-five thousand head of stock. Although Wibaux himself left ranching in the early twentieth century in order to resume mining, the ranch continued to operate well into the 1960s.

—*Alan Axelrod*

WEAVER, JAMES BAIRD

Iowa politician prominent in third-party movements of the late nineteenth century, James Baird Weaver (1833–1912) was born in Ohio but moved to Iowa with his family at a young age. The destitution of his boyhood on the hardscrabble farm his parents struggled to maintain probably colored the agrarian radicalism of his political career.

Bitten by gold fever, Weaver joined the California gold rush as a young man and worked as a bullwhacker. He attended law school in Cincinnati, Ohio, was admitted to the bar in 1856, practiced law in Bloomfield, Iowa, and entered politics. Until his mid-twenties, Weaver had embraced the Democratic party, but for a time, he became a Free-Soil advocate before casting his lot, by 1857, with Iowa's Republicans.

Weaver joined the Union Army at the outbreak of the Civil War and served with distinction, for which he was honored by a promotion to brevet brigadier general. He returned to his law practice at war's end.

Weaver's return to politics after the war was problematic. He antagonized his fellow Republicans with his criticism of the railroads, his advocacy of prohibition, and his call for easy money. Although elected as a Republican for the office of district attorney in 1866, he failed to secure his party's nomination for Congress in 1874 and for governor in 1875. Weaver broke with the Republicans in 1877 and moved into the Greenback party in time to become one of the fourteen Greenbackers elected to Congress in 1878 on the issue of expanding the supply of paper money in circulation. Weaver served six years in the House of Representatives and, in 1880, ran unsuccessfully for the presidency as the Greenback candidate.

Throughout the 1880s, Weaver played a significant role in the development of the People's party, the successor to the Farmers' Alliance, which took up the cause of soft money after the Greenback party dissolved. When the Populists fronted their own candidate for the presidential election of 1892, Weaver was their logical choice. Although he was defeated, he made an impressive showing. He garnered one million popular votes and was the first third-party candidate since the Civil War to secure votes in the electoral college. After the 1892 election, Weaver worked to join the Populist cause to the Democratic party, using his influence in 1896 to give the Populists' nomination to WILLIAM JENNINGS BRYAN, the Democrats' candidate for the presidency. The merger of the two parties signaled the dissolution of the Populists and the waning of Weaver's career. He served as a small-town mayor and local historian in his last years.

—*Charles Phillips*

SEE ALSO: Agrarianism; Currency and Silver as Western Political Issues; Greenback Party; Populism

SUGGESTED READING:
Haynes, Fred Emeroy. *James Baird Weaver*. Iowa City, Iowa, 1919.

WEAVERVILLE, CALIFORNIA

SEE: Ghost Towns

WEBB, WALTER PRESCOTT

One of the most influential historians of the American West, Walter Prescott Webb (1888–1963) was born in Panola County in eastern Texas. At the age of five, he moved with his family to a farm near Ranger, Texas, on the edge of the Great Plains; Webb later considered that move the start of his intellectual and emotional exploration of the West, its land, and its people. At the University of Texas, he was influenced by the multidisciplinary, holistic approach of the historian Lindley Miller Keasbey. Webb taught in public schools for a few years following his graduation in 1915 and then joined the faculty of the University of Texas. He briefly undertook graduate work at the University of Chicago and was later awarded a doctoral degree from the University of Texas.

Webb's first and most influential book was *The Great Plains* (1931), which was awarded the Loubat Prize. Writing history in the broadest sense, including the region's plant and animal life, literature, material culture, laws, and other human institutions, Webb argued that everything and everyone living on the plains had to adapt to its arid, flat, largely treeless environment. In a larger sense, Webb conceived the West as a distinctive region with enduring geographical and climatic features. This was in contrast to the approach of FREDERICK JACKSON TURNER, for whom the West had been the frontier, the expanding outer edge of Euro-American settlement, a process that had occurred everywhere in the nation but was completed by the

According to Walter Prescott Webb's arid-lands thesis, most of the West is a desert. Although most of the West's lands is not so dramatically arid as Death Valley, pictured here, Webb argued that the scarcity of rainfall would always limit the West's population, economic power, and cultural development. *Courtesy The Bettmann Archive.*

early twentieth century. Coming at a time when Turner's FRONTIER THESIS faced mounting criticism, *The Great Plains,* more than any other single work, recast the terms of Western history.

In an article in *Harper's Magazine* in 1957, Webb expanded his approach with his ARID-LANDS THESIS. Most of the West, he argued, is a desert. Its scarcity of rainfall would always limit its population, political and economic power, and cultural development. While many Westerners were not pleased by that opinion, the theme of aridity as a shaping and restricting factor in Western history has remained one of the field's most influential ideas.

In *Divided We Stand: The Crisis of a Frontierless Democracy* (1937), Webb wrote passionately about regional inequalities and argued that the West and the South in effect were economic colonies of the Northeast. He was editor of *The Handbook of Texas,* an essential reference work. His history of *The Texas*

Rangers (1935), although flawed by insensitivity toward Mexican Americans, remains the most complete work on the subject. Webb's last book, *The Great Frontier* (1952), advanced a sweeping thesis—that Europe's global expansion after 1492 had triggered a four-hundred year "boom," an era of prosperity that fostered political democracy and liberal individualism. Although some critics treated the work harshly, others considered it visionary, if somewhat simplistic.

Webb served as president of the Mississippi Valley Historical Association from 1954 to 1955 and of the American Historical Association from 1957 to 1958. He was named visiting professor at Harvard University and the University of London.

Webb was killed in an automobile accident near Austin, Texas, on March 8, 1963. His work remains a major influence on writers emphasizing the West as a geographically and historically distinct region.

—*Elliott West*

SUGGESTED READING:

Furman, Necah S. *Walter Prescott Webb.* Albuquerque, N. Mex., 1976.

Tobin, Gregory. *The Making of History.* Austin, Tex., 1976.

WEBSTER, DANIEL

One of the great orators of his age, Daniel Webster (1782–1852) was a statesman, lawyer, advocate of American nationalism, and opponent of Texas annexation and the UNITED STATES–MEXICAN WAR. Born in Salisbury, New Hampshire, he graduated from Dartmouth College in 1801. After gaining admission to the bar, he practiced law in Portsmouth, New Hampshire, in 1807. Achieving a strong local reputation, he was elected to the U.S. House of Representatives in 1812 on a platform of opposition to the WAR OF 1812, which was proving disastrous for New England's shipping trade. Webster left Congress in 1816 to resume private law practice in Boston. He successfully argued a number of high-profile constitutional cases before the Supreme Court—including *Dartmouth College* v. *Woodward, Gibbons* v. *Ogden,* and *McCulloch* v. *Maryland.* By 1823, when he was returned to Congress from Boston, Webster was regarded as the nation's greatest orator and a highly respected legal mind.

In 1827, Webster was elected senator from Massachusetts and became a champion of American nationalism. Leaving the defunct Federalist party, he joined the National Republicans and allied himself with Westerner HENRY CLAY in advocating strong federal aid for the development of roads in the West. However, in 1828, he backed high tariffs on manufactured goods (to nurture the burgeoning industries of New England), thus provoking South Carolina's JOHN CALDWELL CALHOUN to argue that his state had the right to nullify the law. In an 1830 Senate debate, Webster replied to South Carolina's Robert Hayne with a brilliant defense of the Union, and his exclamation of "Liberty and Union, now and forever, one and inseparable!" became one of the more famous phrases in American politics.

Webster unsuccessfully ran for the presidency in 1836. In 1841, President William Henry Harrison named him secretary of state. Harrison's death shortly after his inauguration brought John Tyler to the presidency, and in September 1841, all the Whigs except for Webster resigned from the cabinet. Webster felt duty-bound to settle the ongoing dispute with Great Britain over the Maine-Canada boundary. The matter was resolved by the Webster-Ashburton Treaty of 1842, and Webster left the cabinet in May 1843.

Webster opposed both the annexation of Texas and the war with Mexico because he felt that territorial expansion would either entail the expansion of slavery or intensify the dispute between North and South to the point of civil war. In a celebrated speech before the Senate on March 7, 1850, he supported the COMPROMISE OF 1850 by simultaneously denouncing Southern threats of secession and advocating Northern support for a stronger fugitive-slave law. After Webster was named secretary of state in July 1850 by President Millard Fillmore, he supervised the strict enforcement of the Fugitive Slave Act in an effort to preserve the union. His stance alienated abolitionist forces and badly divided the Whig party, but it did stave off civil war for another decade. Webster died in office.

—*Alan Axelrod*

SUGGESTED READING:

Bartlett, I. H. *Daniel Webster.* New York, 1978.

Dalzell, R. *Daniel Webster and the Trials of American Nationalism, 1843–52.* Boston, 1973.

Nathans, S. *Daniel Webster and Jacksonian Democracy.* Baltimore, 1953.

Peterson, Merrill D. *The Great Triumvirate: Webster, Clay, and Calhoun.* New York, 1987.

WELLS, EMMELINE BLANCHE WOODWARD

Emmeline B. Wells (1828–1921), ardent suffragist and women's advocate, used the *Woman's Exponent*, a bi-weekly newspaper she edited, as a champion of women's rights and a forum for Mormon women. Born in Petersham, Massachusetts, Wells briefly taught school. She converted to Mormonism, married, and followed the church to Utah in 1846. Deserted by her first husband and twice widowed after that, Wells learned to be self-reliant and developed her lifelong credo: "I am determined to do all in my power to elevate the condition of women."

An aspiring poet, Wells was a better journalist. She editorialized on diverse topics: her New England childhood, polygamy, and the rights of women in marriage and society. For thirty years, she represented Mormon women in national suffrage associations and the National Council of Women. She participated in the Women's Congress at the 1893 Columbia Exposition in Chicago and in the 1899 London Congress sponsored by the International Council of Women.

As president of the Utah Woman Suffrage Association, Wells was instrumental in making WOMEN'S SUFFRAGE a part of the state constitution in 1896. She ran unsuccessfully as a Republican for the state senate in 1898.

Wells devoted her last years to the Mormon women's RELIEF SOCIETY (LDS), an organization she served as general secretary for twenty years and as president from 1910 until her death. On the centenary of her birth, Utah women commissioned a bust of her for the state capitol; Wells is the only woman so honored. Its simple inscription acknowledged her efforts on behalf of women: "A Fine Soul Who Served Us."

—*Carol Cornwall Madsen*

SEE ALSO: Polygamy: Polygamy among Mormons

SUGGESTED READING:

DePillis, Mario S. "Emmeline B. Wells." *Notable American Women: A Biographical Dictionary.* 3 vols. Edited by Edward T. James, Janet Wilson James, and Paul S. Boyer. Cambridge, Mass., 1971.

Madsen, Carol Cornwall, and Mary Stovall Richards. "Emmeline B. Wells." *Encyclopedia of Mormonism.* 4 vols. Edited by Daniel H. Ludlow. New York, 1992.

WELLS, HENRY

Businessman and expressman, Henry Wells (1805–1878) was born in Thetford, Vermont, the son of a Presbyterian minister. In 1814, the family moved to central New York, where Wells attended school in Fayette and worked on a nearby farm. At the age of sixteen, he was apprenticed to a tanning and shoemaking firm in Palmyra. In 1836, he turned to transportation for a living and worked with companies operating on the Erie Canal and the Great Lakes

Henry Wells. *Courtesy Wells Fargo Bank.*

and then on railroad lines in Pennsylvania. With the beginning of the express business by William F. Herndon, Wells was employed as his agent for the express between Albany and New York City. Within two years, he formed a partnership with George E. Pomeroy and Crawford Livingston to operate between Albany and Buffalo and served as messenger, making the weekly trips via railroads and stages. He carried letters for six cents each or one dollar for twenty, while the United States Post Office charged two to four times as much. With James W. Hale, he also offered a through service to Bangor, Maine, via Boston and New York. Public support of his services forced the United States to pass legislation in 1845 authorizing five-cent postage.

In 1844, Wells and WILLIAM GEORGE FARGO formed a partnership known as the Western Express and extended their business first to Detroit and later to Cincinnati, Chicago, and St. Louis. In 1846, Wells sold his interest in the business and moved from Buffalo to New York to supervise the Eastern service then centered in New York with new offices in London and Paris. By 1850, competition on the important route between Albany and Buffalo was so keen that a merger of the three competing companies—Wells and Company, Butterfield and Wasson, and Livingston, Fargo and Company—was made under the name of the American Express Company. Wells served as president.

In 1852, Wells was instrumental in organizing another joint-stock company, Wells, Fargo and Company, to enter the express and banking business in California. By 1855, the firm established dominance in California, and through the purchase of the Pioneer Stage Company and investment in the OVERLAND MAIL COMPANY, Wells Fargo was heavily involved in all aspects of communication and transportation west of the Missouri River. With the completion of the transcontinental railroad in 1869, stagecoach operations quickly declined, but Wells Fargo's express business expanded throughout the West and ultimately reached the East Coast. East of the Missouri River, the Merchants Union Express Company challenged the dominance of Wells's American Express Company, and in 1868, the two companies merged to form the American Merchants Union Company. Wells then retired from the presidency, having made a fortune. In 1873, the company name again became the American Express Company.

The remaining years of Wells's life were spent in travel and in supporting favorite charities. He invested in the First National Bank of Aurora, his hometown, and in the Cayuga Lake Railroad, serving as president of both. In 1868, he founded Wells Seminary for young ladies, now known as Wells College. Because he had suffered from a speech impediment all his life, he became interested in various methods for alleviating stammering. He established schools in several cities for children thus afflicted. He died in Glasgow, Scotland.
—*W. Turrentine Jackson*

SEE ALSO: Overland Freight

SUGGESTED READING:
Harlow, Alvin. *Old Waybills: The Romance of the Express Companies.* New York, 1934..
Hungerford, Edward. *Wells Fargo: Advancing the American Frontier.* New York, 1949.
Loomis, Noel M. *Wells Fargo: An Illustrated History.* New York, 1968.
Stimson, A. L. *History of the Express Business.* New York, 1881.

WELLS, FARGO AND COMPANY

The express, banking, and freighting company of Wells, Fargo and Company was established as a joint-stock association in New York in March 1852 by a group expressmen, including Henry Wells and WILLIAM GEORGE FARGO. Organized to take advantage of express, banking, and other business opportunities in California, the company was prepared to deliver mails, papers, and packages from the East to San Francisco, then on to the mining camps of California. Business got under way in California in July 1852. A network of express lines, some purchased outright and others under contract, was established. Upon the failure of Adams and Company of California, Wells Fargo dominated the express field with 55 offices throughout the mining districts in California. The number steadily increased to 147 by 1860.

Wells Fargo also engaged in the BANKING business. The company purchased gold dust in the mining camps for fifteen or sixteen dollars an ounce and sold it to the U.S. Mint for eighteen dollars. The company also received deposits, made collections, extended credit, and issued bills of exchange. Banking headquarters were in San Francisco, with branches in Sacramento, Stockton, and Marysville.

In 1864, Wells Fargo purchased the Pioneer Stage Company, which had been organized by Louis McLane in 1855 to operate between Sacramento, California, and Virginia City and Carson City, Nevada. After 1862, the stage company had a contract to deliver the overland mail, and with the purchase of Pioneer Stage, Wells Fargo began carrying passengers, mails, and express on the trans-Sierra route. Wells Fargo also operated a fast freight and passenger service between 1864 and 1868 from the Nevada mining camps to the ever-changing head of railroad construction in California.

Wells Fargo agents transporting $250,000 in gold bullion from the Homestake Mine. *Courtesy Wells Fargo Bank.*

Wells Fargo used pony riders to deliver or pick up letters, packages, or treasure. Several routes were run in Placer County, California, as early as 1852. Periodically between 1861 and 1865, the company operated a pony-express service on the trans-Sierra route to assist businessmen interested in speed, particularly when rail or stagecoach communications were uncertain in winter months.

Agents of the Wells Fargo office in Reno. *Courtesy Wells Fargo Bank.*

Wells Fargo had a financial interest in the OVER-LAND MAIL COMPANY from its beginning in 1857. Some of Wells Fargo's directors served on the board of the Overland Mail, and Wells Fargo advanced funds to establish the mail route from El Paso, Texas, to San Francisco. Wells Fargo had great influence over the policy and personnel of the Overland Mail and, in 1861, obtained an exclusive subcontract to handle all express service west of Salt Lake City. Wells Fargo also assumed responsibility for administering and advertising the PONY EXPRESS, begun by RUSSELL, MAJORS AND WADDELL, during the last third of its existence.

In 1866, all the major express and stagecoach lines west of the Missouri River consolidated when BEN HOLLADAY sold his extensive interests. The Overland Mail Company, the Pioneer Stage Company, and several express companies merged under the name and control of Wells, Fargo and Company. At that juncture, the company established a stagecoach department, comparable to its express and banking departments. Wells Fargo maintained stagecoach service between the changing terminals of the Central Pacific and Union Pacific railroads until the two lines were joined in 1869. After that, the company maintained branch lines to carry passengers, express, and mail to and from the railroad in Montana and Idaho and the mining camps of Nevada, Utah, and Colorado.

In California, Wells Fargo maintained stagecoach connections over the Sierra Nevada as the railroad was constructed. When the transcontinental railroad was completed, three years earlier than anticipated, Wells Fargo reorganized its express business, which from that point was carried on the railroad network.

In 1901, the EDWARD HENRY HARRIMAN interests purchased Wells Fargo's express business and moved its headquarters to New York. During World War I, the company merged with other express companies into the American Railway Express Company, supervised by the United States government. Remaining in California, the Wells Fargo banking interests prospered, survived the great financial panic of 1873 and, in the twentieth century, became one of the nation's largest banks. Wells Fargo had been a highly successful business enterprise, earning sizable profits for its owners. At the same time, the company had made a significant contribution to business, banking, and transportation in the American West.

—*W. Turrentine Jackson*

SUGGESTED READING:

Beebe, Lucius, and Charles Clegg. *U.S. West: The Saga of Wells Fargo.* New York, 1949.

Hungerford, Edward. *Wells Fargo: Advancing the American Frontier.* New York, 1949.

Jackson, W. Turrentine. "A New Look at Wells Fargo, Stagecoaches, and the Pony Express." *California Historical Society Quarterly* 45 (1966): 291–324.

———. "Wells Fargo's Pony Expresses." *Journal of the West* 11 (1972): 405–436.

Loomis, Noel M. *Wells Fargo: An Illustrated History.* New York, 1968.

Winther, Oscar O. *Express and Stagecoach Days in California.* Stanford, Calif., 1935.

WELSH, HERBERT THOMAS

Herbert Welsh (1851–1941), the founder of the INDIAN RIGHTS ASSOCIATION, was the grandson of John Welsh, a Philadelphia merchant and minister to England. Welsh graduated from the University of Pennsylvania in 1871 and then studied art for two years in Paris. He returned to Philadelphia in 1874.

Supported by his family's fortune, Welsh became interested in Indian affairs and other reform movements. In 1882, he visited the Dakota Territory and wrote a pamphlet entitled *Four Weeks among Some of the Sioux Tribes,* in which he assessed the Native Americans' prospects for being fully assimilated into Euro-American culture. In December of that year, he formed the Indian Rights Association along with other prominent Philadelphians. He served as corresponding secretary for the group for thirty-four years, as president for eleven, and as president emeritus until his death.

In accordance with humanitarian thinking of the time, Welsh and his organization worked to assimilate Native Americans into American life. To gain that end, the Indian Rights Association concentrated on investigating and publicizing conditions on Indian reservations in order to arouse public concern and gain support for legislation related to reservations. Welsh promoted the passage of the DAWES ACT of 1887, which gave the president power to carve up Indian reservations for Native American farmers and to allot any unclaimed land for sale to Euro-American settlers. Despite the corruption and bureaucratic bungling that characterized enforcement, Welsh persisted in his belief that the law was the most effective means of assimilating Native Americans. While the law was never truly effective and was later criticized as being paternalistic and destructive to tribal heritage, Welsh's work aroused interest in the cause of Native Americans and cleaned up corruption on some reservations.

—*Candace Floyd*

SEE ALSO: United States Indian Policy: Civilization Programs, Reform Movement

Suggested reading:
Hagan, William Thomas. *The Indian Rights Association: The Herbert Welsh Years, 1882–1904.* Tucson, Ariz., 1985.

WEST-AS-REGION SCHOOL

Western history's founding father, Frederick Jackson Turner, in his famous essay "The Significance of the Frontier in American History" (1893), outlined the process of frontier settlement. The West, in Turner's thesis, was wherever the frontier was. Consequently, when the frontier process ended, the history of the West did too. This was somewhat ironic, because Turner, in founding the field of Western history, had implied that it was over in 1890 when the Census Bureau declared that there was no longer a distinctive frontier line. For Turner, it was the frontier process that was important, and not the West itself.

The New Western history, which emerged as a distinctive school of historical writing at the end of the 1980s, rejected Turner's notion of frontier process and, instead, viewed the West as a geographically definable and distinct place—a region. By discarding the notion of a closing frontier, these Western revisionists pointed to the importance of the twentieth-century West as a topic for study. They outlined a number of distinctive Western features that helped identify it as a separate region. First, they noted that their West was not the old frontier West, which could be anywhere in the country (even New England had once been the frontier). The revisionists generally agreed that the West was the area from the Mississippi River to the Pacific Coast, or the area west of the 100th meridian, where the land becomes semiarid.

Leading revisionist Patricia Nelson Limerick outlined ten distinctive Western characteristics, not all of which are evident in every part of the West, but which are common enough to most of the West that when taken together they characterize the region:

1) The Arid-West: The area west of the 100th meridian is largely arid or semiarid, receiving less than twenty inches of rainfall per year (the minimum level that is considered adequate for European-style farming methods). Heavy settlement in an area that lacks water required the building of dams, canals, reservoirs, and the redirecting of rivers to ensure a water supply.

2) The Indian West: Most American Indian reservations and the bulk of the American Indian population are located in the West.

3) The Borderland West: The West borders Mexico. Indeed, much of the present-day West was acquired by the United States after the United States–Mexican War from 1846 to 1848. This borderland has had a significant effect on the peoples living on both sides of it and has made the West home to large numbers of Spanish-speaking immigrants.

4) The Pacific West: The West borders the Pacific Ocean, which has made it the entry point for Asian immigrants and a key center of Pacific trade.

5) The Federal West: Most of the lands still under federal control are located in the West, including national parks, national forests, and military test sites.

6) The Colonized West: The West has been particularly subject to the control of the state. The federal government,

To some historians, the aridity of the West gives the region an important part of its peculiar character. Heavy settlement in areas of little rainfall required the construction of dams, canals, and reservoirs. Southern California's development required the redirection of rivers' natural water flow, as evidenced by the construction of a water flume. *Courtesy San Diego Historical Society.*

Top left: The West is unique for its numbers of Indian reservations and its large populations of Indian peoples. *Courtesy National Cowboy Hall of Fame and Western Heritage Center.*

Bottom left: The federal government's presence in the West has been a boon to settlement. Early military forts such as Fort Laramie, protected settlers from hostile peoples. *Courtesy National Cowboy Hall of Fame and Western Heritage Center.*

Right: The West of myth and romance bears little resemblance to the West of reality. Legends about such people as Billy the Kid paint a West far different from the West of the thousands of people who settled and lived there. *Courtesy Library of Congress.*

and in particular the Department of the Interior, has played a major role in governing the West. The federal government subsidized the railroads, controls the public lands, constructed irrigation systems, and legislated the fate of American Indians.

7) The Boom-and-Bust West: The prominence of extractive industries in the West—logging, mining, farming, oil drilling—has made it particularly prone to economic cycles of booms and busts.

8) The Mythic West: Romantic Western imagery has helped create a mythic West that bears little relation to the real West. This mythologizing, besides creating a gap between image and reality, has made the region quite dependent on the tourism industry.

9) The West as Dumping Ground: The West is the region where the nation's unwanted groups, such as Indians and Mormons, and unwanted materials, such as toxic and radioactive substances, have been dumped.

10) The Conquered West: The region contains the majority of the nation's conquered peoples. Furthermore, the West's aridity renders the effects of conquest of the land—abandoned mines, eroded soil—more visible.

In addition to outlining the key notions upon which the West-as-region school is based, Limerick, in her important book *The Legacy of Conquest: The Unbroken Past of the American West* (1987), provided good coverage of these various regional characteristics. She argued that by viewing the West as a distinct place with a distinct history, we are better able to see its racial and ethnic diversity and make connections between the nineteenth- and twentieth-century Wests.

New Western historian Donald Worster also viewed the West as a region in his influential work *Rivers of Empire: Water, Aridity, and the Growth of the American West* (1985). Worster focused on aridity as the key factor shaping the West's regional identity. The West's lack of water prompted the federal government to transform the Western landscape, damming and redirecting rivers to supply farmers and city dwellers with this essential resource. However, the transformation of a fragile, semiarid Western environment resulted in catastrophic ecological damage and in the dominance of the federal bureaucracy over the people of the West. Furthermore, in an important article entitled "Beyond the Agrarian Myth" (1989), Worster stressed that there was a moral urgency and a practical purpose in defining the West as a region. An important goal of the new Western history was "to discover a new regional identity and set of loyalties more inclusive and open to diversity than we have known and more compatible with a planetwide sense of ecological responsibility." So, for Worster, viewing the West as a region helps not only to explain its past, but to improve its present.

Richard White's important revisionist textbook, *"It's Your Misfortune and None of My Own": A New History of the American West* (1991) also rejected the frontier thesis (indeed, it doesn't even mention it) and focuses on the growth and development of the West as a region that stretches from the Missouri River to the Pacific Ocean. White emphasized the region's dependency on the federal government, its reliance on service-based and extractive economies, and its racial and ethnic diversity. These regional characteristics were also stressed by historian William G. Robbins in *Colony and Empire: The Capitalist Transformation of the American West* (1994). Robbins concentrated on how global capitalism has transformed the West. While admitting that "capitalism is a powerful, integrating, and homogenizing force [that] diffuses differences, erodes contrasts, and undermines regional identity," Robbins also argued that the American West can be viewed as a "prototype for modern capitalism"; that is, a region that is distinctive because the negative effects of capitalist development are very clearly evident there.

Critics of the new Western historians have questioned their claims for Western regional distinctiveness. Unlike the South—which was defeated in war and formed a distinct regional culture in the wake of that defeat—the West has not experienced any similarly significant circumstance that would produce a strong regional identity. While the Western revisionists stress "conquest" as a unifying theme of Western history, critics note that other areas of the North American continent have been conquered, too; so the West cannot claim any distinction on that ground. As for the West's aridity, or semiaridity, critics note that a significant portion of the Pacific Northwest, far from being arid, is a tropical rain forest. Indeed, the critics charge that the West is anything but a coherent region and

point to the tremendous diversity among Western subregions. What does the multicultural landscape of Los Angeles, California, have in common with the ethnic homogeneity of Boise, Idaho? Many citizens of an urbanized, racially and ethnically diverse Los Angeles, one suspects, would feel more at home in New York City, or Miami, Florida, than in Boise or Lincoln, Nebraska, or Topeka, Kansas. Furthermore, residents of the West are perhaps more likely to identify themselves according to subregional affiliation (such as Rocky Mountains, Pacific Northwest, Southwest, Great Plains) than they are to identify themselves as Westerners. Indeed, Western revisionists have had some trouble reaching a consensus on where the West is and what its geographical boundaries are, whether it includes cities such as Dallas, Texas, or states such as Hawaii, Alaska, Louisiana, and Arkansas. Western historians as a whole certainly do not agree on where the West's boundaries lie. This diversity of opinion was demonstrated in a fascinating study by historian Walter Nugent, entitled "Where is the American West?" (1992).

Limerick, responding quite effectively to these criticisms, noted that the whole of the West does not have to share every one of the distinctive Western features for it to be a part of the West. The Pacific Northwest, for example, even though it is considerably wetter than the rest of the West, does contain arid land; the interior lands of both Washington and Oregon are semideserts. Furthermore, many of the other "Western variables" are present in Washington: it has a significant Indian presence; much of its land is owned by the federal government; the state's logging industry has experienced painful boom-and-bust cycles; and the area is closely linked to the Pacific Rim.

Whether one chooses to emphasize place and view the West as a distinct and coherent region or play down the West's regional unity, it seems clear that the idea of the West as part of a frontier process no longer dominates the field of Western history. The West-as-region school has achieved preeminence. However, the new Western historians were not the first scholars to view the West as a region. In *Creating the West* (1991), Gerald Nash emphasized that scholars have been examining the West as a region for more than a century. Between 1890 and 1920, the West was viewed as a distinct place based on "climate, topography, and environmental factors." In the period from 1920 to 1945, a number of Western writers and historians, including the "old Spanish borderlands" specialist HERBERT EUGENE BOLTON, began to write about the Hispanic and Indian cultures of the West and their role in shaping the region. The great exception to the cultural regionalism of this period was WALTER PRESCOTT WEBB whose influential book *The Great Plains* (1931) emphasized the role of the environment in forming a unique region with a distinct way of life. World War II brought economic prosperity to the West and a massive population increase because of the availability of war-related jobs. This economic and demographic transformation prompted historians, in the period from 1945 to 1960, to view the West as an economic and political region. And, finally, Nash explains, by the 1960s, a new generation of historians, influenced by the social protests of that era, was beginning to examine the histories of racial and ethnic minorities and women. It was from this rich historiographical context, he suggests, that the West-as-region school emerged. It is worth remembering, too, the irony that Frederick Jackson Turner (whose frontier thesis is generally cited as the polar opposite of the West-as-region school) devoted most of his career to the analysis of regionalism.

—David M. Wrobel

SEE ALSO: Arid-Lands Thesis; Borderlands Theory; Frontier: Frontier Thesis

SUGGESTED READING:

Aron, Stephen. "Lessons in Conquest: Toward a Greater Western History." *Pacific Historical Review* 63 (1994): 125-147.

Limerick, Patricia Nelson. *The Legacy of Conquest: The Unbroken Past of the American West.* New York, 1987.

———, Clyde Milner, and Charles Rankin, eds. *Trails: Toward a New Western History.* Lawrence, Kans., 1991.

Nash, Gerald. *Creating the West: Historical Interpretations, 1890–1990.* Albuquerque, N. Mex., 1991.

Nugent, Walter. "Where Is the American West? A Survey Report." *Montana: The Magazine of Western History* 42 (1992): 2–23.

Robbins, William G. *Colony and Empire: The Capitalist Transformation of the West.* Lawrence, Kans., 1994.

Steiner, Michael. "Frederick Jackson Turner and Western Regionalism." In *Writing Western History: Essays on Major Western Historians.* Edited by Richard Etulain. Albuquerque, N. Mex., 1991.

Webb, Walter Prescott. *The Great Plains.* New York, 1931.

White, Richard. *"It's Your Misfortune and None of My Own": A New History of the American West.* Norman, Okla., 1991.

Worster, Donald. *Rivers of Empire: Water, Aridity, and the Growth of the American West.* New York, 1985.

———. *Under Western Skies: Nature and History in the American West.* New York, 1992.

WESTERN EMIGRANT SOCIETY

SEE: Bidwell, John

WESTERN FEDERATION OF MINERS

The Western Federation of Miners (WFM) was formed in 1892 to protect members from the large corporations that increasingly controlled the extractive industry. Following a disastrous miners' strike against the Bunker Hill and Sullivan Company in the Coeur d'Alene region of Idaho in 1892, the leaders of local miners' unions throughout the Rocky Mountain West decided to form the federation. In response to an invitation from J. L. Williams, president of the Butte Miners' Union, forty representatives of seventeen unions in Colorado, Montana, South Dakota, Utah, and Idaho, met in Butte, Montana, during May 1893 and organized the WFM. The new organization focused on issues of daily concern to miners: wages, hours, working conditions, mine safety, mine-inspection laws, and the preferential hiring of union miners. It also worked to eliminate private mine guards, child labor, the contract system, and conspiracy laws. John Gilligan of the Butte Miners' Union became the first president of the WFM.

In its early years, the WFM had no significant impact on the mining industry. Among the factors that contributed to its ineffectiveness were the severe industrial depression that followed its founding, the frequent turnover of incompetent leaders who (except for the secretary-treasurer) were unpaid, and the distance of its elected officials from the union's headquarters in Butte. With the election of Ed Boyce as president in 1896, leadership stabilized, and the WFM gradually became a significant force in industrial relations in most Western hard-rock mining camps.

Between 1896 and 1916, when the WFM became the International Union of Mine, Mill and Smelter Workers, the WFM had only two presidents—Ed Boyce (from 1896 to 1900) and Charles Moyer (from 1900 to 1916). Boyce was the more militant of the two. In 1897, he advised local unions to form rifle clubs and to provide each member with a modern rifle; from 1896 to 1897, he led the WFM in and out of the American Federation of Labor (AFL) and toward a more socialist and revolutionary orientation. Although less dynamic, Moyer presided over the calamitous "labor wars" in Colorado during 1903 and 1904, led the WFM in and out of the INDUSTRIAL WORKERS OF THE WORLD (IWW), and helped ensure the survival of the union in difficult times. In the public mind, however, the most important and most conspicuous official of the WFM was WILLIAM D. ("BIG BILL") HAYWOOD, secretary-treasurer from 1900 to 1907. A giant of a man who was blind in one eye, Haywood was militant, radical, and ready—

if necessary—to use VIOLENCE. To mine owners, he personified the heart and soul of the WFM until he opted in 1907 for exclusive membership in the more radical IWW, an organization he had earlier helped found.

The WFM was an industrial union. Although commonly known as the "miners' union," it attempted to include within its jurisdiction all workers—surface and underground—who labored in the nonferrous mines and mills of the West. The WFM eventually established locals in all but five states of the trans-Mississippi West, plus Wisconsin, Michigan, Alaska, and Canada. However, before the devastating Colorado strikes of 1903 and 1904, its principal stronghold was the Rocky Mountain hard-rock camps such as Cripple Creek, Colorado, where its power in industrial relations was enormous. WFM leaders had expansive ambitions. The union twice challenged the predominant position of the AFL in the LABOR MOVEMENT by launching short-lived alternatives—the Western Labor Union (1898) and the American Labor Union (1902), both of which the WFM dominated.

In its first decade, the strikes of the WFM were violent; the rhetoric of its principal leaders was militant; and its convention resolutions and agendas were increasingly socialist. With some justification, therefore, mine owners and the public perceived the WFM as a violent, radical, and socialist organization. The enemies of the WFM deliberately exaggerated and exploited that negative image to rally support for their opposition to the union. Little concrete evidence (for example, convictions for industrial violence) exists to support the widely held view that the WFM was a revolutionary organization intent on the forceful overthrow of the American capitalistic system.

Before changing its name to the International Union of Mine, Mill and Smelter Workers (IUMMSW) in 1916, the WFM made several significant contributions to the American labor movement. It was the first regional federation of miners' unions with sufficient power to challenge the mine and mill owners of the West; its Western Labor Union and American Labor Union offered important, if temporary, alternatives to the conservative AFL; its industrial unionism anticipated the organizational form adopted by mass-production workers of the future; its leaders (for example, Haywood) helped give birth to the IWW. The IUMMSW became a founding member of the Congress of Industrial Organizations (CIO), an industrial union, in 1938 but was expelled ten years later because of alleged communist leadership. In 1948, the IUMMSW merged with the United Steel Workers of America.

—*George G. Suggs, Jr.*

SEE ALSO: Cripple Creek Strikes; Mining; Socialism

SUGGESTED READING:
Jensen, Vernon H. *Heritage of Conflict: Labor Relations in Nonferrous Metals Industry up to 1930.* Ithaca N.Y., 1950.
Smith, Robert W. *The Coeur d'Alene Mining War of 1892: A Case Study of an Industrial Dispute.* Corvallis, Oreg., 1961.
Suggs, George G., Jr. *Colorado's War on Militant Unionism: James H. Peabody and the Western Federation of Miners.* Norman, Okla., 1991.

WESTERN PACIFIC RAILROAD

The Western Pacific was incorporated in 1903 to operate a route between Salt Lake City and San Francisco. It was essentially a subsidiary of the Denver and Rio Grande Western Railroad, which supplied its connections to the East. The Western Pacific did not become an independent, self-supporting company until 1916, when it was reorganized.

The Western Pacific nearly ceased operations during the Great Depression and entered into receivership. However, like many other Western railroads, it was revived by the demands of World War II, which also spurred a modernization program.

—*Alan Axelrod*

WESTERNS

SEE: Film: The Western; Literature: The Western Novel; Radio and Television Westerns

WESTERN TRAIL

SEE: Cattle Trails and Trail Driving

WESTPORT LANDING, MISSOURI

Westport Landing, Missouri, an important location on the Missouri River for shipping goods westward on the SANTA FE AND CHIHUAHUA TRAIL, was founded in the early 1830s by François Chouteau. Now within the boundaries of Kansas City, Westport Landing was the location of a trading post of the AMERICAN FUR COMPANY. In 1833, John C. McCoy established the town of Westport four miles south of the trading post. Supplies were unloaded from steamboats at Westport

Landing, hauled overland to the new town, and made ready for sale to Western travelers.

Since 1827, Independence, Missouri, had been the center of preparation for the journey between the Mississippi Valley and New Mexico, but after 1833, the leadership passed to Westport Landing. There, oxen and mule caravans were organized to cross the prairies and plains carrying the manufactured goods in great demand in New Mexico. The trade was so prosperous that Missouri became known as a mule-raising state and never lacked for specie. Westport later served as a gathering spot for pioneer settlers moving westward on overland trails, but it never was as important for migration as Independence or St. Joseph, Missouri.

During the 1840s, MORMONS used Westport as a gathering spot before heading to Utah. Mormon immigration agents in the East sent converts from overseas to Westport where they were provided with equipment and supplies for the Western journey. The Mormon presence brought about significant changes in the character and life styles of the community residents. The discovery of gold in California and later in Colorado brought another major change, when goldseekers overran the family-oriented community during their stops to purchase food and supplies for the westward trek. Shopkeepers took advantage of the newcomers by inflating prices for the limited quantity of goods, and saloon owners prospered.

The Civil War disrupted Westport's prosperity, and after the war, the railroads changed the pattern of transportation. Westport's prominence was diminished, but it remained an active trading center until it was annexed to Kansas City in 1899.

—*W. Turrentine Jackson*

SEE ALSO: Chouteau Family

SUGGESTED READING:

Gregg, Josiah. *Commerce of the Prairies*. Printed in *Early Western Travels*. Edited by Reuben Gold Thwaites. Cleveland, Ohio, 1904–1906. Vol. 19. and Vol. 20. Reprint, New York, 1968.

WHALING

The Inuits, or Eskimos, Aleuts, and other North American Indians probably hunted whales as early as 3000 B.C. They found in the sea mammals a plentiful source of food, fuel, and tools, but their quarries were often easily beached smaller whales or some larger specimens that swam close to shore during seasonal migrations from polar feeding grounds to the sheltered bays that served as breeding grounds. While the Japanese came to use nets, the Aleuts killed their prey with poisoned spears. The Inuits took to sea in skin boats and speared large whales with barbed harpoons tied by hide ropes to inflated sealskin buoys. The Eskimos used the harpoons to slow down the whale; when they had plunged enough of the toggle-headed spears into the animal to keep it from escaping, they finished the whale off—safely—with a long lance.

The Basques first began systematically hunting whales sometime in the late Middle Ages, perhaps as early as 1372, around the Bay of Biscay. They caught black-right whales as they gathered to breed. Using a rowboat to chase the docile, slow-moving, sleepy creatures, the Basques speared the whales with harpoons, played them like fish, and killed them with lances. The whalers towed the floating bodies to shore and then stripped them of their blubber and boiled it. The Basques also processed whale baleen. Once the Basques had developed seaworthy ocean-going ships, they set off, between the fourteenth and sixteenth centuries, in search of other whaling bays, and they found them along the shores of Newfoundland and Iceland.

When the English Muscovy Company began looking for whaling bays in 1610, it drafted experienced Basque whalers for its Arctic explorations. True commercial whaling had been launched, and the Dutch—England's seventeenth-century maritime rivals—quickly followed the English lead. There broke out a heated and violent competition—in one year the Dutch launched some 300 ships carrying perhaps eighteen thousand seamen—that lasted for decades before a miniature Ice Age sometime after mid-century brought Arctic-bay whaling to a halt. In the early decades of the eighteenth century, the English and Dutch fleets were forced to hunt in more distant waters near Greenland and the Davis Straits. Here appeared the first whaling vessels from Britain's North American colonies in the late eighteenth century.

Whale oil was used in colonial America for lubricating wagon axles, for medicine, and for burning in oil lamps. A large Atlantic Ocean whaling industry grew up headquartered in New England. With the New England fleets came a major innovation that changed the very nature of the whaling industry. On board their ships, the Yankees installed brick ovens, called "tryworks," which allowed whalers to boil and process whale blubber, or fat, into oil at sea and then to store it in barrels rather than hauling it to facilities on shore. With tryworks, whaling ships commonly remained at sea for as many as four years before returning to port with their cargoes, which not only vastly expanded the whaling business but captured the imagination of the public. Little wonder that New England produced

In 1910, photographer Asabel Curtis recorded the harpooning, beaching, and butchering of one of the last gray whales taken by Makah Indians at Neah Bay on Washington's Olympic Peninsula. In this image, the wounded whale is towed to the beach, laden by sealskin floats that exhaust the whale and, once killed near the shore, keep it afloat. *Courtesy Washington State Historical Society.*

the premier whaling adventure, Herman Melville's *Moby-Dick,* which many think to be nineteenth-century America's best work of fiction.

Since the 1790s, New Englanders, trafficking in beaver furs, sandalwood, and sea otters, had used HAWAII as a refueling stop in the CHINA TRADE en route to ALASKA. Then, in 1819, "new" whaling grounds were "discovered" off the coast of Japan, and Hawaii quickly became the major supply center for whaling vessels—European as well as American—in the Pacific. Twice a year, New England vessels stopped in the Sandwich Islands (as Hawaii was then called by English-speaking peoples) to gather provisions and take oil back to Atlantic Coast markets. As commerce in sea otters and sandalwood declined, whaling increasingly filled the commercial gap for America's maritime traders. In 1829, ten years after Pacific whaling began off Japan, more than 100 whaling ships called in at Hawaii, a number that increased some five times over the next two decades.

As happened with the Alaskan sea otters, the unencumbered slaughter of whales soon depleted the Japanese whaling grounds. American whaling ships began

exploring farther north around the Gulf of Alaska. There, they discovered, in 1835, the huge schools of whales who migrated annually to Alaska's plankton-rich waters. The hunting soon stretched into the Bering Sea, and the whaling industry expanded far beyond the old Atlantic and South Pacific trade. In 1848, the whaler *Superior* broached the Alaskan Arctic and came back with an enormous catch. By 1852, 278 American ships were whaling along Alaska's coast. Three years later, 154 American vessels passed through the Bering Strait looking for whales. The Russians, who held hegemony over Alaska, launched a whaling company, but it faltered against the American competition.

When Pacific whaling was in full boom, fishermen gave little thought to conservation; investors rushed abruptly into the industry; companies launched massive expansions of their fleets; and fortunes were made and lost overnight—all characteristic of the Pacific FISHING INDUSTRY in general. Although Alaskan whalers sought mainly the sperm whale, the blue whale and the North Pacific right whale also fell prey to the fleet's relentless slaughter. During the heyday of commercial whaling, the major means of catching whales was that described by Melville: a crew of six men set off from the mother ship in pursuit of the giant sperm whales in relatively light double-edged rowboats. (Americans commenced the chase in a thirty-foot boat made of one-half-inch cedar, but the British boats were sturdier.) Armed with hand harpoons and a coiled line to play the prey, they killed the whale with a lance after the harpooners had exhausted the beast.

From 1830 to 1850, the whaling industry generated between $6 million and $10 million worth of products annually. By 1857, the U.S. fleet had more than 700 vessels, with more than 400 registered in New Bedford, Massachusetts, alone. The traffic was immense for the time, and Hawaii's merchants and commercial farmers expanded their operations to meet the demands of the whaling vessels hauling into port. Americans on the island established some of the enterprises selling to the American fishing fleet and invested heavily in others, and they dominated the commercial expansion. Hawaiian chiefs, who in the past had controlled access to the source in the sandalwood trade, now played little role in the whaling commerce. Hawaii's very isolation increased its attractiveness as a wintering and resupply outpost for the Pacific fleet, since it had no real competition. As the local economy flourished, Hawaii's ties with New England grew stronger, and by 1845, two-thirds of the islands' foreign-born population were Americans, some four hundred merchants who ran the commerce in shipping. The growing wealth and power of the Americans over the islands' economy undercut the power of the native chiefs. Later, as the whale populations diminished and the whaling seasons grew irregular, it would be these American businessmen who turned to a more stable commerce—plantation-grown sugar.

In Alaska, because the RUSSIAN-AMERICAN COMPANY enjoyed a Russian-government monopoly, the fur trade continued to hold center place in the local commerce, despite the fact that profits were much higher in the whaling industry than in the sea-otter and beaver fur trade. Unable to compete at sea, the Russians tried to diversify on land, but since furs remained the only viable commercial product and since both sea otters and beaver were disappearing, their economic hold also began to slip in the face of the whaling industry's competitive onslaught. For a while, the Russian-American Company sold ice, a plentiful enough product in Alaska. The Russians paid the Aleuts, Tlingits, and Creoles to cut the ice and then shipped it to northern California, where demand was high because of the 1850s gold rush. When the rush died out and the demand dropped, the company experimented with coal mining before the United States bought Alaska in 1867.

By then, the whaling boom was on the wane. The decline came partly because the whalers were overfishing, and whales were much depleted during the first three-quarters of the nineteenth century. Mostly, however, the rapid decline was a result of the discovery of petroleum in Pennsylvania in 1859. When distilled as kerosene, the fossil fuel could be used in new "Austrian" lamps to light the homes and businesses of America. The Dutch fleet had collapsed earlier in the century, long before kerosene replaced sperm oil in the United States, and Britain's Arctic fleet had been devastated in the 1830s and 1840s by overfishing, by increasingly icy conditions, and by the introduction of vegetable oil, steel-boned corsets, and gas-fired lamps. Late in the nineteenth century, some whaling continued in the South Pacific and Davis Strait until the eve of World War I, and whalers launched a major attack on North Pacific right whales from San Francisco in the 1920s. But the industry, in general, was unable to stop the diminishing return on its investments. Whaling was all but moribund after World War I until the introduction of diesel-engined catchers, gun-fired harpoons, and standardized and highly efficient floating whale "factories" revived it. "Modern" whaling—now mostly Russian and Japanese—once again threatened to exterminate altogether the world's largest mammal.

—*Charles Phillips*

SEE ALSO: Honolulu, Hawaii; Native American Peoples: Peoples of Alaska

SUGGESTED READING:
Matthews, L. Harrison, et al. *The Whale.* New York, 1968.
Webb, Robert Lloyd. *On the Northwest: Commercial Whaling in the Pacific Northwest, 1790–1967.* Vancouver, B.C., 1988.

WHEAT FARMING

While wheat farming normally occurs in most regions of the United States, the Great Plains and the Pacific Northwest emerged as the leading areas for the crop's production early in the twentieth century. Of the five classes of the cereal grains grown in these regions, the hard red winter types raised in Kansas and its neighboring states of the Southern and Central Plains have traditionally surpassed in acreage and production both the hard red spring and durum types found in the Dakotas and Montana and the soft and white wheats of Washington and Idaho. By the 1980s, at least 70 percent of the 2.5 billion bushel average annual harvest from approximately seventy million acres came from these two regions.

The process for producing a wheat crop generally follows a basic pattern. First, the farmer plows the field with moldboard, sweep, or disk plows to turn under plant materials and to prepare a firm seed bed one to two inches below the surface. Farmers use grain drills to plant winter wheat in the fall. The machine places from 15 to 180 pounds of seed per acre at depths of one to three inches. The planting of spring wheat normally begins in March. After the plants surface, some winter-wheat farmers graze cattle on the crop during its dormant stage between late fall and late winter. When growth resumes, the crop may be fertilized and sprayed to control weeds, diseases, or insects using either tractor-mounted equipment or aircraft. Combines harvest the winter wheat between May and July and spring wheat in the fall. Once gathered, the grain may be placed in storage or sold at elevators for eventual delivery to flour mills. By the 1990s, approximately 40 percent of the nation's crop was exported to foreign markets.

Especially significant for Western wheat production was the ongoing search to find varieties adaptable to the environment. In 1898, the United States Department of Agriculture sent Mark Carleton to the Crimea and Turkey to collect seeds following the discovery that Mennonites who migrated to Kansas from Russia in the 1870s had brought with them wheat, called "Turkey Red," that produced well under adverse conditions. From Carleton's initial and later missions, common and durum wheats became available to geneticists, who developed variants that influenced breeding throughout most of the twentieth century. Winter-hardy varieties derived from Turkey Red and possessing disease-, insect-, and storm-resistant qualities include Kanred, Tenmarq, Quanah, Tascosa, and Triumph. These varieties became popular with farmers from the World War I–era until the 1960s with their normal yields ranging from ten to twenty bushels per dryland acre. Through continuous research, two other popular varieties became available by the 1970s: the semidwarf hard red winter wheats with average yields of seventy to ninety bushels per acre on the plains and the Gaines variety developed from the Japanese "Norin-10" gene plasm and often yielding more than one hundred bushels per acre in the Pacific Northwest.

Further achievements in science and technology enhanced wheat productivity while reducing labor requirements. The number of man-hours to produce one hundred bushels of wheat declined from 108 to 9 between 1900 and 1970 as wheat farming became fully mechanized with the replacement of draft animals with tractors and binders or headers and threshers with combines. In addition, after World War II, farmers began using fertilizers to stimulate yields and chemicals to eliminate or curb damage inflicted by insects (greenbugs, spider mites, aphids, or army worms) and diseases (rusts and smuts). Furthermore, both soil-conserving practices like summer fallowing, crop rotation, and minimum tillage and the application of irrigation in some areas brought greater yields.

—*Garry L. Nall*

SEE ALSO: Agriculture; Farming; Herbicides; Pesticides

SUGGESTED READING:

Ebeling, Walter. *The Fruited Plain: The Story of American Agriculture.* Berkeley, Calif., 1979.

Ham, George E., and Robin Higham, eds. *The Rise of the Wheat State: A History of Kansas Agriculture, 1861–1986.* Manhattan, Kans., 1987.

Texas Agricultural Experiment Station. *A History of Small Grain Crops in Texas.* College Station, Tex., 1980.

WHEELER, BENJAMIN IDE

President of the University of California, Benjamin Ide Wheeler (1854–1927) was born in Randolph, Massachusetts, the son of a Baptist minister. Wheeler, who showed no inclination to join the clergy, threw himself into all manner of other study. After graduating from Brown University in 1875, he first taught high school and then joined the faculty of Brown before studying in Germany for four years, where he received his Ph.D. in 1885. In 1887, he began teaching Greek and Latin at Cornell University and remained there for thirteen years. In 1899, he was offered the presidencies of several established Eastern universities, but he chose instead the University of California.

Although the school had been founded forty years earlier, it enrolled only two thousand students. Wheeler accepted the post at Berkeley on the condition that he would have free reign in hiring and firing professors and in setting their salaries. He presented to the regents a list of fifteen pressing items he felt the university needed to achieve if it were to establish itself as major center for scholarly education. The list included expanded seats on the faculty, new departments, new buildings, new colleges, greater laboratory facilities, and the rivalry with Stanford, which culminated in the annual football contest referred to as the "Big Game."

Although Wheeler's power was dictatorial, he used it carefully, giving plenty of space to faculty and students in matters of teaching and research and espousing a system of self-government for both the faculty and the students. Because of his evident concern for students, his advice on undergraduate activities—

particularly those of the football team—was frequently solicited, and he obliged as often as he was asked.

Outside the university, Wheeler developed close contacts with the Berkeley community, alumni, and state officials. These contacts helped turn the school into a well-supported university by attracting state tax dollars, alumni donations, and community support for local activities. By the time Wheeler stepped down as president in 1919, every item in his original list had either been fulfilled or was in the process of becoming so. After he retired as president, he continued to lecture in the Classics Department for another two years.

—*Kurt Edward Kemper*

SEE ALSO: Colleges and Universities

SUGGESTED READING:
Stadtman, Verne A. *The University of California, 1868–1968.* New York, 1970.
Wheeler, Benjamin Ide. *The Abundant Life.* Berkeley, Calif., 1926.

WHEELER, BURTON K.

A liberal reformer and vice-presidential candidate, Burton K. Wheeler (1882–1975) was born in Hudson, Massachusetts. Settling in Butte, Montana, Wheeler was elected to the state legislature in 1910 where he became a champion of labor interests. In 1922, he was elected to the U.S. Senate and continued to oppose the dominant "company interests." His work in labor reform gained him the 1924 vice-presidential nomination with Robert M. LaFollette on the Progressive ticket. The Progressives were defeated, but in the Senate, Wheeler continued to support isolationism and internal reform. Although Wheeler was an early supporter of Franklin D. Roosevelt for president, his later opposition to the president led to his defeat in 1946.

—*Kurt Edward Kemper*

SUGGESTED READING:
Southwick, Leslie. *Presidential Also-Rans and Running Mates, 1788–1980.* Jefferson, N.C., 1984.
Wheeler, Burton K. *Yankee from the West: The Candid, Turbulent Life Story of the Yankee-born U.S. Senator from Montana.* New York, 1962.

WHEELER EXPEDITION

SEE: Exploration: United States Expeditions; Exploration and Science; United States Army Corps of Engineers

WHITE, WILLIAM ALLEN

Influential Kansas newspaper editor, William Allen White (1868–1944) was born in Emporia, Kansas. He spent his youth in El Dorado, Kansas, where his father was a physician. He attended the College of Emporia and the University of Kansas and worked as a reporter for El Dorado newspapers and as an editorial writer for the *Kansas City* (Missouri) *Star.* In 1895, he purchased the *Emporia Gazette,* which he published until his death.

On August 20, 1896, White printed his scathing anti-Populist editorial, "What's the Matter with Kansas," which caught national attention. A decade later, as a leader of the Progressive Republicans, he promoted many of the social and political reforms called for by the Populists. He played a major role in the Progressive movement and supported THEODORE ROOSEVELT and the Bull Moose party ticket in 1912. While most of his political efforts were behind the scenes, he ran for governor of Kansas as an Independent in 1924, when he felt the regular party candidates did not stand firmly against the KU KLUX KLAN. He lost the election, but he made his point, and the Klan was dead in Kansas.

His editorials, one of which won a Pulitzer Prize in 1922, reflected life in Kansas and small-town America. In addition to writing editorials, he was a novelist, a poet, and a contributor to national periodicals. "Mary White," written on the death of his teen-aged daughter, was more lyric essay than editorial. It is still included in anthologies and, in 1977, was the basis for a television motion picture.

While he remained primarily concerned with Kansas and state issues, he did cover the Versailles peace conference in 1919 and the London economic conference in 1933. He headed the Committee to Defend America by Aiding the Allies in 1940 and was among the first to suggest the idea of lend-lease to President Franklin D. Roosevelt. His home, Red Rocks, still stands as a historic landmark in Emporia.

—*Robert W. Richmond*

SEE ALSO: Magazines and Newspapers; Progressivism

SUGGESTED READING:
Davis, Kenneth S. "The Sage of Emporia." *American Heritage* (October–November 1979): 81–96.
Johnson, Walter. *William Allen White's America.* New York, 1947.
Marvin, Burton W. "William Allen White, Senator-at-Large." In *Kansas: The First Century.* Vol 2. Edited by John D. Bright. New York, 1956.
White, William Allen. *The Autobiography of William Allen White.* Edited by Sally Foreman Griffith. Lawrence, Kans., 1990.

WHITE BIRD (NEZ PERCÉ)

A Nez Percé medicine man or shaman, White Bird (ca. 1807–1882) was one of the leaders of the Nez Percé War of 1877. His Indian name, Penpenhihi, may also be translated as "White Goose." White Bird was born along the Snake River in Idaho. Along with Old Joseph (Chief Joseph the Elder) and his son Young Joseph (CHIEF JOSEPH the Younger), White Bird was a nontreaty Nez Percé—one of a faction dispossessed of its land by a treaty revision of 1863. White Bird counseled peace with the white settlers, but when a series of incidents escalated tensions in 1877, he joined TOOHOOLHOOLZOTE and Young Joseph's bellicose brother OLLOKUT in calling for war.

White Bird distinguished himself at the Battle of Big Hole Valley, Montana, on August 9, 1877, helping the Nez Percés make a narrow escape from the forces of Colonel John Gibbon. By the conclusion of the battle at Bear Paw Mountain, Young Joseph and White Bird were the only surviving chiefs. On the night of October 5, as Joseph was preparing surrender terms, White Bird and others evaded the surrounding soldiers and escaped to Canada, where they joined the great Hunkpapa leader SITTING BULL. White Bird remained in Canada, even after Sitting Bull returned to the United States. He was killed by another Indian, who was grief-stricken and outraged because White Bird's magic had failed to save the life of his sick son.

Alan Axelrod

SEE ALSO: Pacific Northwest Indian Wars

WHITE CAPS, THE

SEE: Gorras Blancas, Las

WHITE HORSE (KIOWA)

A Southern Cheyenne active during the 1860s and 1870s, White Horse (whose birth and death dates are unknown) was one of the leaders of the militant Hotamitanio, or Dog Soldiers, the most elite of the "soldier societies" common to the Cheyenne and other Plains tribes beginning in the 1830s. The Dog Soldiers were leaders in the Cheyenne-Arapaho (Colorado) War of 1864 to 1865, in which White Horse distinguished himself.

White Horse signed the MEDICINE LODGE TREATY OF 1867 but continued to participate in major battles between the Cheyennes and white soldiers. After the death of Tall Bull in 1869, White Horse led his band north to join the Northern Cheyenne. Shortly thereafter, however, he returned to the reservation in the Indian Territory and became a member of the 1873 delegation sent to Washington, D.C., to negotiate a lasting peace. White Horse was unable to control the young warriors of his band, many of whom joined Comanche and Kiowa militants led by QUANAH PARKER and LONE WOLF during the Red River War in 1874. White Horse subsequently sunk into the obscurity of reservation life.

—Alan Axelrod

SEE ALSO: Central Plains Indian Wars

WHITETAIL DEER

The whitetail deer *(Odocileus virginianus),* named for its full, bushy tail with its characteristic white under hairs, is the most widely distributed and adaptable member of the deer family, *Cervidae.* There are seventeen subspecies found in the United States. Reaching up to 6 feet in length, standing up to 3 ³/₄ feet at the shoulders, and weighing up to three hundred pounds, these tawny, tan-colored deer are browsers who prefer the edges of mixed woodland or forest habitats. More than any other member of the deer family, whitetail deer have adapted to the development of agricultural settlement with its ranches and farms. They may be found throughout North America in Canada, Mexico, and in every state except Alaska and Hawaii.

Whitetail deer, mule deer, and blacktail deer were important food sources for both Native Americans and early Euro-American settlers. Settlers moving across the Mississippi River found large numbers of whitetail deer, and venison became one of the most commonly consumed meats of the period. Native Americans and Euro-American settlers used deer skins as material for clothing, moccasins, and caps. Deer skins were traded for other necessities—salt, flour, coffee, liquor, weapons, gunpowder, knives, and traps. Settlers hunted deer more extensively than did Native Americans. After the Civil War, market hunting led to a further reduction of whitetail populations; by 1900, their numbers were dramatically reduced in many areas. The growth of ranching and farming led to the reduction of the whitetail's predators in many Western states, and with these checks on their numbers reduced, with the decline of market hunting, and with the eradication of the screw worm in many areas, whitetail populations began to increase dramatically. By 1961 in the Llano

Basin of the Edwards Plateau in Central Texas, there were 121 deer per square mile. Malnutrition among the deer led to significant declines in size and health. Although agriculture, industrialization, and urbanization have fragmented and eliminated much of their historical habitat, their population in the last decade of the twentieth century was estimated at more than 13 million. Addressing growing whitetail deer populations in the West remains a significant game-management problem.

—*Phillip Drennon Thomas*

SUGGESTED READING:
Bauer, Erwin. *Horned and Antlered Game.* New York, 1986.
Rue, Leonard Lee, III. *The Deer of North America.* New York, 1978.

WHITMAN, MARCUS AND NARCISSA

Part of the first missionary group sent to the Oregon Country by the AMERICAN BOARD OF COMMISSIONERS FOR FOREIGN MISSIONS (ABCFM), Narcissa Whitman (1808–1847) and Marcus Whitman (1802–1847) spent eleven years working at their station at Waiilatpu. Their efforts to introduce the Cayuse Indians to evangelical Christianity and American culture contributed to the disintegration of the native way of life and to tribal division. In 1847, the Whitmans and several other whites were murdered by Cayuse Indians. While the "massacre" resulted in the termination of the ABCFM's work in Oregon, it also helped elevate the Whitmans to the status of Protestant martyrs during the nineteenth century.

Born in Prattsburg, New York, Narcissa Prentiss grew up in a comfortable, middle-class, rural household. She attended local schools and Franklin and Auburn academies before teaching school herself. Religiously precocious, she experienced conversion at the age of eleven and joined the Presbyterian church. Active in the religious revivals of the Second Great Awakening, she dreamed of a missionary life. As a single woman, however, her chances of being accepted for missionary work were slight.

Like other missionary candidates, Marcus Whitman needed a wife, and when he proposed marriage to Narcissa, whom he probably knew only slightly, she promptly agreed. Marcus had come to his vocation only with difficulty. Born in Rushville, New York, he spent much of his childhood living with relatives and attending school in Massachusetts, where he experienced conversion. Returning to New York at the age of eighteen, he worked in his stepfather's tannery and

shoe shop and taught school. He decided to pursue a medical career and practiced in Pennsylvania, Canada, and rural New York. Gradually, he concluded that he should become a medical missionary.

In 1835, Marcus set out with the Reverend Samuel Parker on his exploratory trip for the American Board of Commissioners for Foreign Missions. When Parker continued west to ascertain the readiness of the Western Indians for Christianity, Marcus returned home. Convinced that the overland trip was possible even for women, he gathered a missionary party that included his new wife, Narcissa; HENRY HARMON AND ELIZA HART SPALDING; and William Gray. The group arrived in Oregon in the fall of 1836.

The Whitmans settled in the eastern part of the Oregon Country among the Cayuse Indians, a small tribe culturally similar to the Nez Percés. Although Narcissa was taken aback by some of the realities of Indian life and disapproved of Indian culture, she and Marcus were initially optimistic about the possibility of converting the Cayuse Indians to both evangelical Christianity and a settled American way of life. Despite the willingness of the Indians to adopt some facets of white religion and life, the Whitmans gradually became disillusioned with missionary work. During eleven years, they made no Cayuse converts. Their teaching that without conversion the Indians were doomed to hell fed tribal hostility and division. The Whitmans confronted many threatening situations, indicative of Cayuses' displeasure with the missionaries.

Eventually the Whitmans retreated from their missionary goals. While Narcissa devoted herself to her large family of adopted children and to religious work with white emigrants, Marcus was busy with his medical practice. Both gave assistance to overland emigrants who stopped at the mission.

The Whitmans experienced difficulties with other members of the ABCFM mission, especially with the Spaldings. These problems almost resulted in the closing of the their mission. Relations between the missionaries improved somewhat but did not make the endeavor as a whole any more successful. A combination of factors—a measles epidemic, increasing white emigration to Oregon, and the growing realization on the part of the Cayuse Indians of the implications of the Whitmans' missionary program—led to the murder of the Whitmans and several other whites who were living at Waiilatpu. Their attack on the mission, however, did the Indians little good. In the 1860s, the Cayuse tribe was forced onto the Umatilla Reservation with members of the Walla Walla and Umatilla tribes.

With the Whitmans' deaths, the ABCFM closed down the Oregon missions. The Whitmans, however, became missionary heroes, a reputation that survived into the twentieth century. The reevaluation of American missionary work among Native Americans has prompted new interpretations of the Whitman mission in the 1980s and 1990s. Although early historians assumed that the Whitmans were heroic martyrs to Christian service, later historians have been more critical of the missionaries and more sensitive to the perspectives of the Cayuse Indians.

—*Julie Roy Jeffrey*

SEE ALSO: Evangelists; Protestants; Missions: Nineteenth-Century Missions to the Indians

SUGGESTED READING:

Drury, Clifford M. *Marcus and Narcissa Whitman and the Opening of Old Oregon.* Glendale, Calif., 1973.
Jeffrey, Julie Roy. *Converting the West: A Biography of Narcissa Whitman.* Norman, Okla., 1991.
———. "Narcissa Whitman: The Significance of a Missionary's Life." *Montana: The Magazine of Western History* 41 (Spring 1991): 2–15.

WHITNEY, ASA

A prominent merchant and a pioneer promoter of a transcontinental railroad to the Pacific, Asa Whitney (1797–1872) was born to a prosperous farmer in North Groton, Connecticut. Scion of an established New England family, Whitney moved to New York around 1817, went to work for a dry-goods merchant, and traveled extensively as a buyer in Europe. Upon his return to New York, Whitney launched his own firm but lost the business and some prime New York real estate during the panic of 1837. Discouraged not only by his financial reversals but also by emotional losses (his first wife, a French woman, died shortly after his return to America in 1833; his second wife, Sarah Jay Munro, the grandniece of John Jay, died in 1840), Whitney set out for China where he worked as an agent for several companies and on his own account. Profiting well in Asia, Whitney never again engaged directly in business but returned to the United States obsessed with the potential for a transcontinental railroad. Fascinated by railroading, Whitney had gathered statistical information in China to show that a line across country from Chicago to the Pacific would greatly enhance the lucrative China trade, and in 1844, he began pressing the U.S. Congress to charter such a railroad through the South Pass of the Rocky Mountains. Waging a massive publicity campaign against congressional and public indifference, Whitney argued that the immense cost of the transcontinental line could be defrayed by the sale of public lands along the route. Having personally inspected the first eight hundred miles of the route he proposed in 1845, Whitney kept

up his amazing newspaper and speaking-tour promotional campaign for seven years. He doggedly pursued individual congressmen and eventually found his personal motives called publicly into question. By 1851, he had given up on Congress and accepted an invitation to present his plan in England as a possibility for Canada. Although the English received Whitney favorably, they took a pass on his proposal. Thereafter, Whitney dropped the matter, married for a third time, and retired with his bride—Catherine Moore Campbell—to Locust Hill, an estate near Washington, D.C. There, he lived comfortably until his death from typhoid fever three years after the first transcontinental railroad had been completed.

—*Patricia Hogan*

WHITNEY, CHARLOTTE ANITA

A founder of the Communist party in California, Charlotte Anita Whitney (1867–1955) was one of the state's best-known radical activists from the Progressive era through the McCarthy era. Born in Oakland, California, Whitney was raised in comfortable circumstances; her father, whose ancestors came to America on the *Mayflower,* settled in California before the Civil War and became a prosperous lawyer and state senator. She received a teaching degree from San Jose State College and a B.A. from Wellesley College in Massachusetts in 1889. Like many of the first generation of college-educated women, she became involved in reform movements, including her work in the College Settlement house in New York before returning to Oakland. In 1901, she was hired as director of the Alameda County Association of Charities, a position she held for ten years. She served as Alameda County's first juvenile probation officer and helped organize relief efforts following the SAN FRANCISCO EARTHQUAKE OF 1906. During these years, she also served as head of the College Equal Suffrage League in the campaign to gain the vote for women in California.

In 1912, Whitney moved from reform movements to revolutionary politics when she became a supporter of the INDUSTRIAL WORKERS OF THE WORLD. The following year, she joined the Socialist party. When the Socialist party split into rival factions in 1919, she joined the newly formed Communist Labor party, a predecessor of the American Communist party. In November 1919, she was arrested and charged with violating California's criminal syndicalism law. Her crime consisted of advocating voting rights for African Americans in a speech to the Oakland chapter of the California Civic League. Tried and convicted in 1920, she was sentenced to one to fourteen years in San Quentin prison. The U.S. Supreme Court upheld Whitney's conviction, but she was pardoned by Governor Clement C. Young in 1927.

As chairman of the California Communist party from 1936 to 1944, Whitney was the party's leading vote-getter in the state; she polled one hundred thousand votes in races for state controller in 1934 and 1938 and for the U.S. Senate in 1940. She remained active in party affairs until shortly before her death.

—*Maurice Isserman*

SEE ALSO: Socialism

SUGGESTED READING:
Flynn, Elizabeth Gurley. *Daughters of America, Ella Reeve Bloor and Anita Whitney.* New York, 1942.
Richmond, Al. *Native Daughter: The Story of Anita Whitney.* San Francisco, 1942.
Rubens, Lisa. "The Patrician Radical: Charlotte Anita Whitney." *California History* 65 (September 1986): 158–171.
Whitten, Woodrow C. "The Trial of Charlotte Anita Whitney." *Pacific Historical Review* 15 (September 1946): 286–294.

WICHITA INDIANS

SEE: Native American Peoples: Peoples of the Great Plains

WICHITA, KANSAS

Situated at the confluence of the Arkansas and Little Arkansas rivers, the town of Wichita was founded as a trading post in 1864 by James R. Mead and Jesse Chisholm. Wichita's early growth resulted from sustained trading with Indians made possible by Mead's concerted attempts to maintain peaceful relations with his Wichita Indian neighbors. Chisholm, instrumental in the range CATTLE INDUSTRY, put Wichita on the map shortly after its founding when he established the CHISHOLM TRAIL by driving cattle north from Texas. The Chisholm Trail made Wichita a crossroads in the cattle industry, a designation that was cemented in 1872, when Wichita became the western terminus for the ATCHISON, TOPEKA AND SANTA FE RAILROAD.

Although Wichita remained a major center in the cattle business, the industry soon lost its dominance in the town's economy with the closing of the open range. As early as 1875, fences began to partition Wichita's rolling plains, and agriculture took hold on the local economy. Wichita adjusted to the change, however, when the price of grain exploded in the 1880s, providing a boom similar to what the cattle industry had brought a decade earlier.

As Wichita's economy expanded beyond its function as a cattle town, the composition of its population changed even as it grew. The bachelor town of cowboys and the saloons, GAMBLING halls, and brothels that served them gave way to merchants and retailers with wives and families. In a matter of a few years, Wichitans seeking a stable community life passed laws to suppress the town's vices. By late 1872, Wichita's city officials decreed the removal of the town's dance houses to the independent suburb of West Wichita on the far side of the Arkansas River. Restrictions on gambling and PROSTITUTION followed in 1876, but were short lived. Wichita's stability was well established, however, by 1880, when the Kansas constitution made prohibition a statewide law.

In 1872, the town's two newspapers, the *Beacon* and the *Eagle* were founded. Wichita expanded well beyond Mead's initial layout of the town. Along with the grain boom, which proved to be short lived, Wichita prospered from the discovery of nearby oil fields in the mid-1880s. The growth in population and the variety of enterprises in commerce and industry necessitated a city charter in 1886.

—*Kurt Edward Kemper*

SEE ALSO: Cattle Towns

SUGGESTED READING:
Dykstra, Robert R. *The Cattle Towns.* New York, 1976.
Miner, Craig. *West of Wichita: Settling the High Plains of Kansas, 1865–1890.* Lawrence, Kans., 1986.

WICKERSHAM, JAMES

Alaska politician James Wickersham (1857-1939) was born in Illinois and moved to the Washington Territory as a young man. In 1901, he traveled to Alaska to serve as a federal district county judge. His reputation led to his election, in 1908, as a Republican delegate to Congress, a position to which he was elected seven times. Wickersham supported "home rule" and was responsible for Alaska's Second Organic Act in 1912. Other significant legislation included the creation of the Alaska Railroad in 1914, the founding of Alaska's university system in 1915, and the establishment of Mount McKinley National Park in 1917. Upon his retirement from politics, he returned to Juneau and practiced law.

—*William R. Johnson, Jr.*

SUGGESTED READING:
Atwood, Evangeline. *Frontier Politics: Alaska's James Wickersham.* Portland, Oreg., 1979.

Wickersham, James. *Old Yukon, Tales, Trails, and Trials.* Washington, D.C., 1938.

WILBUR-CRUCE, EVA ANTONIA

Author and rancher Eva Wilbur-Cruce (1904–) was born on her family's ranch in Arivaca Valley in the Arizona Territory. Her father, Augustin Wilbur, had married Ramona Vilducea from Sonora, Mexico. Wilbur-Cruce grew up in a rich bicultural environment. In addition, she felt a deep kinship with the Sonoran Desert environment, which she shared with the Papago or Tohono O'odham Indians.

Since her father needed help on the ranch, Wilbur-Cruce's training began at an early age. A skillful rider at the age of four, she was herding and branding cattle by her fifth birthday. When she was ten years old, her father placed her in charge of the ranch hands.

Wilbur-Cruce and her brothers and sisters had little contact with the outside world and received their basic schooling at home. "We were confined," she said, "restrained by my father's ideas, no arguments or questions asked. His iron will kept us silent and hoping for the years to set us free." The longed-for release came in 1917, when she enrolled in the Guardian Angel School run by the Sisters of Mercy in Los Angeles. Later, she attended Woodbury College, also in Los Angeles.

Wilbur-Cruce returned to Arizona in April 1933 after her father's death and assumed control of the ranch. She met and married her husband, Marshall Cruce, the following November. The couple worked and lived in Tucson and spent weekends in Arivaca in order to keep and maintain the ranch. Ultimately, they sold the ranch to the Nature Conservancy in order to protect the land.

Wilbur-Cruce published her autobiography, entitled *A Beautiful, Cruel Country,* in 1987, not long after she celebrated her eighty-third birthday.

—*Patricia A. Etter*

SUGGESTED READING:

"Eva Antonia Wilbur-Cruce." In *Songs My Mother Sang to Me: An Oral History of Mexican American Women.* Edited by Patricia Preciado Martin. Tucson, 1992.

Wilbur-Cruce, Eva Antonia. *A Beautiful, Cruel Country.* Tucson, Ariz., 1987.

WILD BUNCH

SEE: Cassidy, Butch

WILDER, LAURA INGALLS

Laura Ingalls Wilder (1867–1957) was the author of the "Little House" books, seven award-winning children's novels based on her own late nineteenth-century childhood in the West. An eighth book drew on her husband's experiences growing up on an upstate New York farm, and a ninth book, which appeared posthumously, dealt with the first four years of her marriage. The public enthusiastically accepted the "Little House" series because of the books' fascinating details about everyday PIONEER LIFE and labor, vivid characterizations, and depiction of a tightly knit family. The series continues to be popular due to the books' artistry, to their use in thousands of language arts and social studies classrooms across the country, and to a long-lived television show, "Little House on the Prairie," based loosely on the books.

Propelled by her father's restlessness and persistent lack of success in prairie farming, young Laura Ingalls and her family moved from her birthplace in Pepin, Wisconsin, to Kansas, Minnesota, Iowa, and Dakota. In newly settled De Smet, (South) Dakota, the teenaged Laura met Almanzo Wilder who, like her father, had claimed a homestead. The two were married in 1885 and soon experienced a cycle of drought and series of personal tragedies that drove them and their surviving child off their land and into their own period of migration. In 1894, the family settled on a farm outside Mansfield, Missouri.

Making their Ozarks farm even marginally self-supporting took decades of farm and wage labor by husband and wife. To supplement the family's income, Wilder wrote for the *Missouri Ruralist,* and with the help of her journalist daughter, Rose Wilder Lane, who had editing skills and professional contacts, she published a few nonfiction articles in national magazines after World War I. In 1930, she completed something more ambitious: "Pioneer Girl," an adult-level first-person account of her childhood. The unpublished manuscript served as a resource for most of the "Little House" books. Thus, *Little House in the Big Woods* was not Wilder's first effort at writing, nor was it her effort alone. There is disagreement over the extent of Lane's contribution to it and the subsequent books, but there clearly was considerable collaboration between mother and daughter.

The "Little House" series includes: *Little House in the Big Woods* (1932); *Farmer Boy* (1933); *Little House on the Prairie* (1935); *On the Banks of Plum Creek* (1937); *By the Shores of Silver Lake* (1939); *The Long Winter* (1940); *Little Town on the Prairie* (1941); *These Happy Golden Years* (1943); and *The First Four Years* (1971).

Written mainly during the Great Depression, the "Little House" books gave the Wilders a dependable income. Through the books, Wilder and Lane reassessed both their own family history and that of the country. Recalling the many lean periods they had survived on their own, they rejected the enlarged role of government brought about by the New Deal. As a consequence, the "Little House" books are filled with incidents meant to illustrate the links between the Ingalls's warm and satisfying family life and their self-sufficiency and ingenuity in the face of pioneer hardships.

—*Anita Clair Fellman*

SUGGESTED READING:

Anderson, William. *Laura Ingalls Wilder: A Biography.* New York, 1992.

Fellman, Anita Clair. "Laura Ingalls Wilder and Rose Wilder Lane: The Politics of a Mother-Daughter Relationship." *Signs: Journal of Women in Culture and Society* 15 (1990): 535–561.

Hackett, Christine Olivieri. *Little House in the Classroom: A Guide to Using the Laura Ingalls Wilder Books.* Carthage, Ill., 1989.

Holtz, William. *The Ghost in the Little House: A Life of Rose Wilder Lane.* Columbia, Mo., 1993.

Miller, John E. *Laura Ingalls Wilder's Little Town: Where History and Literature Meet.* Lawrence, Kans., 1994.

Wilder, Laura Ingalls. "Little House" Series. New York, 1932–1971.

———. *On the Way Home: The Diary of a Trip from South Dakota to Mansfield, Missouri, in 1894.* New York, 1962.

———. *West From Home: Letters of Laura Ingalls Wilder to Almanzo Wilder—San Francisco 1915.* New York, 1974.

WILDLIFE

Embracing more than one-half of the nation's land mass, those lands that would ultimately constitute the American West contained the country's most varied topography and provided distinctive habitats for diverse wildlife species. Forests, prairies, mountains, and deserts were all home to specific fauna. On the prairies, bisons, or BUFFALOES, grazed in numbers that are impossible to calculate, although there is little question that in 1860 there were more bisons on the Great Plains than there were inhabitants of this nation. Wapiti, or ELK, were also found in substantial numbers on the

Buffaloes roamed the unsettled Western prairies in incalculable numbers before hunters and fur traders decimated their populations for hides and meat. *Courtesy National Archives.*

The West was home to an astounding variety of wildlife. Mountain goats plied the regions of the Cascade Mountains and the central and Northern Rockies. *Courtesy National Park Service.*

grasslands of the West as were the exceedingly numerous and uniquely American pronghorn antelopes. The numbers of PRONGHORNS may have rivaled those of buffaloes; and like buffaloes, by the end of the nineteenth century, their future was equally endangered.

Browsing WHITETAIL DEER and mule deer had substantial populations and were a favorite and common food for both Native Americans and Euro-Americans. MOOSE, the largest member of the deer family, browsed in the marshes and along the rivers and creeks of the northern mountains. Bighorn sheep grazed majestically not only on the verdant grasses of the open parks of the Rocky Mountains but also on the foothills and plains. Mountain goats were common in the alpine zone of the Cascades and the central and northern Rockies. In the northern Rocky Mountains, CARIBOU were found in large herds. BEAVERS, North America's largest rodent and its most prominent fur bearer, energetically built their dams and constructed their lodges along almost every drainage. Along the Pacific Coast, another important fur bearer, the sea otter was found in substantial populations. On countless prairie potholes and along Western rivers and creeks, thousands upon thousands of waterfowl nested, while the skies on both sides of the Mississippi River were often filled with vast flocks of passenger pigeons.

Both large and small predators were present in substantial numbers. GRIZZLY BEARS and BLACK BEARS could be found in all areas west of the Mississippi as could WOLVES and COYOTES. Almost equally ubiquitous were MOUNTAIN LIONS. The numbers and diversity of the fauna of the American West were equaled, if at all, in only a few areas of the world.

Providing Native Americans with food and the materials for tools, weapons, clothing and shelter, the wildlife of the American West was a valuable resource. Until the introduction of HORSES by the Spanish in the seventeenth century, hunting complemented the farming and food-gathering traditions of most tribes. Horses permitted Native Americans to pursue bisons with

The populations of pronghorn antelopes may have matched those of the buffaloes, but by the end of the nineteenth century, their very existence was threatened. *Courtesy National Cowboy Hall of Fame and Western Heritage Center.*

Railroad companies organized special hunting and fishing excursions into the West. The Northern Pacific Railroad offered such an excursion in 1876. *Courtesy F. J. Haynes, Minnesota Historical Society.*

greater effectiveness and allowed the tribes of the Great Plains to become dependent on them. While the Indians were effective hunters, their numbers and the HUNTING technology they used did not endanger bison populations. Deer, elk, moose, and bears were also valuable food resources, which were unharmed by Native American hunting pressures. Bears were highly esteemed by both Native Americans and Euro-Americans for their meat, hides, fat, and totemistic qualities.

The pursuit of fur-bearing animals in the nineteenth century led to the disappearance of the sea otter throughout most of its range from Alaska to California and the decimation of beaver populations throughout most major drainages in the mountains of the West. While the MOUNTAIN MEN played a significant role in the exploration of the West, their diligent pursuit of the beaver led to its dramatic and rapid decline. Restored to most of its former range in the twentieth century, beavers became a major wildlife-management problem as they sought to maintain millennia-old patterns of existence in an increasingly urban west.

The technological changes that transformed the nation in the latter half of the nineteenth century directly affected the wildlife of the West. The construction of Western railroads created a demand for game to feed work crews; provided convenient access to urban markets in the East for wild meat, hides, and robes; and carried more settlers into the West. These pressures, augmented by the development of more effective breech-loading, repeating FIREARMS and the increase in population due to mining and logging activities, led to the decline of many animal populations including

deer, moose, caribou, bighorn sheep, and grizzly and black bears. Requiring little capital, market hunting for wild game became an accepted Western vocation. With no closed seasons on hunting, big game of both sexes were pursued in the winter and spring when they were the most vulnerable. Fish were "harvested" with dynamite; birds were captured with nets, their feathers sold for the millinery trade, their meat sold for consumption, and their nests robbed so that their eggs could be sold for table use. Even the large and graceful trumpeter swan was nearly exterminated. By 1914, passenger pigeons, whose numbers were once counted in the millions, flew no more. Prairie chickens, doves, ducks, and pigeons were shipped by the barrel to the nation's larger cities. Needing passengers for their lines, Western railroads actively promoted hunting and fishing, and special trains with elaborate Pullman cars were organized for hunting excursions.

The development of intensive farming and ranching reduced the habitat of Western wildlife and defined some animals as the enemies of civilization. Plowed fields and fenced pastures ensured that the white man's buffalo was going to be a cow, and that the elk would be pushed farther west into inaccessible high mountain parks, which escaped encroaching civilization until the expansion of the mining frontier and the development of ski resorts after World War II. With the decline in the numbers of their natural prey as a result of settlement and new hunting technologies, wolves, coyotes, and bears began to kill cows, sheep, and hogs for food. Livestock losses inspired a war on predators, and individual, state, and federal efforts appeared to eliminate them. Professional trappers, or wolfers, were ultimately effective in destroying wolf populations, and the wolf became extinct throughout its Western range. In the last decade of the twentieth century, wolves were reintroduced in Yellowstone National Park in an attempt to reestablish their presence in the West. Coyotes were a more elusive and intractable foe, and attempts with poison, trap, and gun to eliminate them never met with lasting success. The most dangerous Western predator, the grizzly bear, was eliminated by the end of the nineteenth century from most Western states and, by the end of the twentieth century, existed almost exclusively in national parks where hunting was prohibited. Although not in danger of being eliminated, black bears and mountain lions also saw their numbers and range dramatically reduced. The reduction of predators in some ecosystems allowed populations of some animals to exceed the carrying capacity of their habitat. The thousands of mule deer that starved to death on the Kaibab Plateau in the mid-1920s demonstrated the importance of maintaining a balance between predators and prey.

By the last decades of the nineteenth century, the once abundant wildlife of the West was in visible decline. Populations of many species of Western fauna had been seriously reduced. The Bureau of Biological Survey, the forerunner of the U.S. Fish and Wildlife Service, prepared state surveys to chronicle the decline and status of wildlife in the West. States reacted to the decline of big-game animals in particular by passing legislation to reduce the hunting seasons and by establishing state fish and game wardens, supported initially with federal funds, to protect select species. To preserve declining populations of big-game animals, refuges and national parks were created as sanctuaries where animals could not be hunted. Created in 1872 to protect the natural wonders of the Yellowstone region, YELLOWSTONE NATIONAL PARK became a vast area where hunting was prohibited, but when poaching became a significant problem, the U.S. Cavalry was stationed there for more than two decades to prevent hunting.

Federal legislation developed to protect wildlife. By the terms of the LACEY ACT of 1900, it became illegal to transport wildlife across state lines if they had been taken in violation of state laws. Migratory birds were placed under federal protection when in 1913 the Weeks-McLean Act was passed, and the Migratory Bird Treaty of 1919 extended the protection of migratory birds throughout Canada and the United States. Wildlife came under greater protection when the National Wildlife Refuge System was authorized in 1929. The American Bison Society, the BOONE AND CROCKETT CLUB, and the American Game Protective Association became aggressive supporters of protecting and restoring Western wildlife. Passed in 1937, the Pittman-Robertson Act has played a significant role in providing funds for the restoration of wildlife and wildlife habitat by assessing an excise tax on firearms and ammunition. Since its inception, the program has provided more than two billion dollars in support for game, non-game, and endangered species. In the decades after World War II, state agencies recognized the economic importance of hunting and labored diligently to reintroduce both native species of big game that had disappeared or were in decline and exotic species from Africa and Asia.

While private environmental groups play important roles in maintaining appropriate habitat for Western wildlife and in seeking political support for wildlife protection, ultimate responsibility for managing wildlife in the West resides in the complex bureaucracies of state and federal agencies. All Western states have game agencies, but these agencies are generally superseded by federal agencies that have wildlife responsibilities. The UNITED STATES FOREST SERVICE, BUREAU OF LAND MANAGEMENT, SOIL CONSERVATION SERVICE, and United States Fish and Wildlife Service all have diverse, and often conflicting, obligations to protect Western wildlife and their habitats.

With no area in the American West more than seventeen miles from a road of some form, there remains no true wilderness. The habitat of the wildlife of the West is a managed habitat.

—*Phillip Drennon Thomas*

SEE ALSO: Fur Trade

SUGGESTED READING:

Allen, Durward. *Our Wildlife Legacy.* New York, 1962.

Borland, Hal. *The History of Wildlife in America.* Washington, D.C., 1975.

Hornaday, William Temple. *Thirty Years War for Wildlife.* Stamford, Conn., 1931.

———. *Wild Life Protection in Theory and Practice.* New Haven, Conn., 1914.

Kallman, Harmon. *Restoring America's Wildlife, 1937–1987.* Washington, D.C., 1987.

Matthiessen, Peter. *Wildlife in America.* New York, 1959.

Murray, John A. *Wildlife in Peril.* Boulder, Colo., 1987.

Tober, James A. *Who Owns the Wildlife? The Political Economy of Conservation in Nineteenth Century America.* Westport, Conn., 1981.

Trefethen, James B. *Crusade for Wildlife.* Harrisburg, Pa., and New York, 1961.

WILD WEST SHOWS

Historical Overview
  Paul Fees

Indians in Wild West Shows
  L. G. Moses

HISTORICAL OVERVIEW

WILLIAM F. ("BUFFALO BILL") CODY opened his Wild West show on May 19, 1883, at Omaha, Nebraska. His partner that first season was a dentist and exhibition shooter, Dr. W. F. Carver. Cody and Carver took the show, subtitled "Rocky Mountain and Prairie Exhibition," across the country to popular acclaim and favorable reviews, thereby launching a genre of outdoor entertainment that thrived for three decades and survived, in fits and starts, for almost three more.

The idea had been around for a long time. The earliest antecedent to the Wild West show may actually have been staged in France in the middle of the sixteenth century, when fifty Brazilian Indians were brought to Rouen to populate a replica of their village. Elevated walkways enabled royal visitors to watch the Indians play at real life. Exotic elements of Native

"Buffalo Bill" Cody's Wild West show was the most popular of the genre that entertained Americans for nearly sixty years. *Courtesy Patrick H. Butler, III.*

American life later became staples of European and American circuses.

Horse shows and menageries with exotic animals had been popular in America since the eighteenth century. The "Indian Gallery" of artist GEORGE CATLIN featured American Indians with native dress and accouterments to complement his paintings. Medicine shows employed frontiersmen and Indian people to help sell tonics and other "natural" cures.

In 1872, legendary plainsman JAMES BUTLER ("WILD BILL") HICKOK joined several cowboys and Indians in a "Grand Buffalo Hunt" staged at Niagara Falls. "Buffalo Bill" Cody himself had already been in show business for a decade, staging plays known as "border dramas," which actually were small-scale Wild West shows featuring genuine frontier characters, real Indians, fancy shooting, and sometimes horses.

The birth of the Wild West show as a successful genre was largely a product of personality, dramatic acumen, and good timing. The golden age of outdoor shows began in the 1880s, and with his theater experience, Cody already was skilled in the use of press agentry and poster advertising. His fame and credibility as a Westerner lent star appeal and an aura of authenticity. Most important, Cody gave the show a dramatic narrative structure.

Features such as the Pony Express, the wagon train, or the attack on a stagecoach recreated specific and well-known events. Spectacles such as "cowboy fun" or the "tableau" of American Indian life usually served as prelude to a dramatic event, such as a battle scene. Skill acts such as sharpshooting (with pistol and rifle), wing shooting (with shotgun), roping, and riding showcased star performers, and the show's narration linked these skills to survival in the frontier West. The script was boomed to the audience by an orator from an elevated platform in the arena. The circus band became the "Cowboy Band" and backed the arena action with appropriate mood-setting music. The same skits and music later were easily adapted to film and television westerns.

Cody once said that his favorite literary passage was Bishop George Berkeley's "Westward the course of empire takes its way." In New York's Madison Square Garden in 1886, Cody and his partners restaged the Wild West as "The Drama of Civilization." Theater and arena were now merged, and America's westward progress thus became an explicit theme in the show, even when it returned to its more familiar Wild West format.

Cody's success led other impresarios to organize their own versions. Doc Carver worked with a variety of partners, including the actor and "poet scout" Captain Jack Crawford and the great circus promoter W. C. Coup. GORDON W. LILLIE, an interpreter in Cody's show, adopted the name "Pawnee Bill" and, in 1888, started the first of his several shows.

One of the biggest names in American circus, Adam Forepaugh, jumped into the Wild West business in 1887. Forepaugh may have been first to stage a reenactment of "Custer's Last Fight" as a regular act. The Battle of Little Bighorn had been featured in many stage melodramas and was an obvious event for the Wild West both for its audience appeal and its narrative power. Cody did not reenact Custer's Last Stand until a year later, apparently in deference to the feelings of the martyr's widow, ELIZABETH CUSTER. She saw it performed in Cody's show in 1888 and wrote him appreciatively, describing her emotional reaction to its "terrible" realism. The Last Stand became a regular feature in Cody's and other shows, sometimes even employing actual battle participants from both sides.

The next twenty years saw the rise and fall of dozens of smaller scale Wild Wests. Some, such as Buck Taylor's Wild West, were started by alumni of Cody's show. Others such as the Cole Younger and Frank James Wild West attempted to capitalize on famous names or events. "Indian Congresses," usually in conjunction with major fairs or expositions, brought representatives of various tribes together with famous frontier characters. The most successful was Colonel Fred Cummins, whose congress at the Pan-American Exposition in Buffalo, New York, in 1901 included both CALAMITY JANE and the great Sioux leader RED CLOUD.

The role of Indian people was both essential and anomalous in the Wild West. At least in the big shows, they generally were treated and paid the same as other performers. They were able to travel with their families, and they earned a living not possible to them on their reservations. They were encouraged by Cody and others to retain their language and rituals. They gained access to political and economic leaders, and their causes were sometimes argued in the published show programs. Yet they were stereotyped as mounted, warbonneted warriors, the last impediment to civilization. Thus, they had to refight a losing war nightly; and their hollow victory in the Little Bighorn reenactments demonstrated over and over to their audiences the justification for American conquest.

Women also played several roles in the Wild West. ANNIE OAKLEY broke ground when she and her hus-band and manager, Frank Butler, joined Cody's show early in 1885. Not only could she outshoot most men, she did it while remaining entirely feminine, even girlish. Shooter Lillian Smith toured as a teen-ager with Cody, disappeared for awhile from public view, then resurfaced in Mexican Joe's and other Wild West shows as "Princess Wenona, the Indian Girl Shot." "Pawnee Bill" Lillie's wife, May Lillie, was a Smith College graduate from Philadelphia who earned fame as a sharpshooter in her husband's show.

Woman riders at first used sidesaddles, but by the 1890s, they were appearing as regular rancheras, or cowgirls. Lucille Mulhall gained fame in her father's show as a roper and rough rider. By the turn of the century, it was not uncommon for women such as Tad Lucas to ride bucking broncos in the arena. Women also played traditional dramatic roles as "prairie madonnas" or as Indian captives. Although there were fewer places for women in the shows, surviving records indicate that Cody, at least, paid women equally with the men.

Roles for persons of color changed subtly during the first decade of the Wild West. At first, they were well represented among the cowboys. Some attained minor fame; for example Voter Hall was facetiously billed in 1885 as "a Feejee Indian from Africa." As the popular image of the cowboy crystallized, black cowboys virtually disappeared from the arena, and others with dark skins were assigned different roles. The famous Esquivel brothers of San Antonio, for instance, were presented as vaqueros. However, contingents representing the all-black Ninth and Tenth U.S. Cavalry regiments appeared with Cody's and other Wild West shows, and the concert bands seem to have remained integrated. The most famous black cowboy, and perhaps the most famous of all Wild West show cowboys, was the 101 Ranch's bulldogger, BILL PICKETT.

During the tour of Europe in 1892, Cody's partner, Nate Salsbury, created "the Congress of Rough Riders of the World." Mounted military troops from many nations drilled in the arena alongside the American cowboys and Indians. Public interest in American military adventures abroad led to the addition of Hawaiian cowboys and Cuban, Philippine, and Japanese cavalry units.

The logistics of the show were formidable. The biggest of them all, Buffalo Bill's Wild West, in the late 1890s, carried as many as five hundred cast and staff members, including twenty-five cowboys, a dozen cowgirls, and one hundred Indian men, women, and children. They all were fed three hot meals a day cooked on twenty-foot-long ranges. The show generated its own electricity and staffed its own fire department. Performers lived in walled tents during long stands or slept in railroad sleeping cars when the show moved daily. Business on the back lot was carried on in what one reporter called "a Babel of languages." Expenses were as high as four thousand dollars per day.

Circus great James A. Bailey, of Barnum and Bailey, joined Cody and Salsbury in 1895 and revolutionized their travel arrangements. The show was loaded onto two trains totaling fifty or more cars. Strings of flat cars could be linked together with ramps for loading wagons from the back forward. Besides performers and staff, the trains transported hundreds of show and draft horses and as many as thirty buffaloes. The show carried grandstand seating for twenty thousand spectators along with the acres of canvas necessary to cover them. The arena itself remained open to the elements. Advance staff traveled ahead of the show to procure licenses and arrange for the ten to fifteen acres required for the show lot, preferably close to the railroad; to buy the tons of flour, meat, coffee, and other necessities; and to publicize and advertise.

In 1899, Buffalo Bill's Wild West covered more than eleven thousand miles in two hundred days giving 341 performances in 132 cities and towns across the United States. In most places, there would be a parade and two two-hour performances. Then the whole would be struck, loaded, and moved overnight to the next town. Europeans (and their armies) were often as fascinated by the ingenuity and efficiency behind the scenes as they were by the show itself. Not many shows could match Buffalo Bill's in scale, but all subscribed to similar regimens.

In the 1890s, Wild West shows began to add side shows and other circus elements. If the West seemed too familiar, "Far East" acts such as Arabian acrobats or dancing elephants and thrill acts such as bicyclists and high divers might inject sufficient novelty to draw new spectators.

For several reasons, the decade just before America's entry into World War I saw audiences decline. Motion pictures captivated public attention—the West could seem more real on the screen than in the arena. Shooting declined as a spectator sport, while the popularity of baseball and football soared. Riding and roping could be better showcased in rodeos, which were considerably less expensive to produce than Wild West shows. The old Western stars were fading as well—even Cody seemed a relic—and Indian people appeared to be quietly confined to reservations. The "old West" was no longer so exotic nor, at the same time, so relevant to a world of heavy industry and mechanized warfare.

Cody's show went bankrupt in July 1913. In a sign of the times, he immediately obtained backing to make a five-reel film, *The Indian Wars*. The Miller Brothers'

101 Ranch Real Wild West had the bad luck, in August 1914, to be in Great Britain, where it lost its horses to the war effort. The 101 continued to tour the United States intermittently through the 1920s. Western film stars such as TOM MIX started short-lived Wild West shows, and in 1938, Colonel Tim McCoy produced probably the last great traditional Wild West show. It folded after less than a month on the road.

Although occasional revivals and adaptations are staged in the United States and abroad, the era of the Wild West show can conveniently be said to have died in 1917 along with its greatest proponent, "Buffalo Bill" Cody. The most pervasive legacy of the Wild West shows has been the narrative vision of romance and conquest, based on real people and events, that they created and disseminated so successfully across boundaries of race, class, and geography.

—*Paul Fees*

SUGGESTED READING:

Blackstone, Sarah. *Buckskins, Bullets, and Business*. New York, 1986.

Bruce, Chris, ed. *The Myth of the West*. Seattle, Wash., 1990.

Fox, Charles P., and Tom Parkinson. *Billers, Banners and Bombast: The Story of Circus Advertising*. Boulder, Colo., 1985.

Grossman, James R., ed. *The Frontier in American Culture*. Berkeley, Calif., 1994.

Katzive, David, ed. *Buffalo Bill and the Wild West*. Pittsburgh, 1981.

Russell, Don. *The Wild West: A History of the Wild West Shows*. Fort Worth, Tex., 1970.

Slotkin, Richard. *Gunfighter Nation: The Myth of Frontier in Twentieth-Century America*. New York, 1992.

Wood-Clark, Sarah. *Beautiful Daring Western Girls: Women of the Wild West Shows*. Cody, Wyo., 1983. Reprint. 1992.

INDIANS IN WILD WEST SHOWS

In the late afternoon of May 17, 1883, WILLIAM F. ("BUFFALO BILL") CODY led a group of thirty-six Pawnees from the Indian Territory and locally recruited cowboys into the arena at the Omaha fairgrounds to begin a performance of "The Wild West, Rocky Mountain, and Prairie Exhibition." Between that time and 1938, the year in which Colonel Tim McCoy's Wild West show—the last of its kind—went bankrupt, perhaps as many as fifteen hundred American Indians traveled the nation and much of the world (all of Europe, including Russia; South America; South Africa; and Australia) performing in any of the fifty or so Wild West shows that imitated Cody's success. Within a decade of the first performance in Omaha, the Bureau of Indian Affairs began referring to Native American performers as "Show Indians."

Cody's program for the first season of the show included a grand introductory march; a bareback pony race; recreations of a Pony Express ride and an Indian attack on Deadwood Mail Coach; races by Indians on foot and on horseback; trick shooting by Cody and his partners; a horse race by cowboys; demonstrations of riding and roping, riding wild Texas steers, and roping and riding wild bison; and a "Grand Hunt" topped off by a "sham" battle with Indians.

Including the opening parade, Indians participated in six events, four of which had nothing to do with warfare. Later, when Cody added a feature called "The Drama of Civilization," he included Indian dances and ceremonies—demonstrations of skill and artistry that would later be found in modern powwows. All Wild West shows adopted variations on these themes.

SITTING BULL, the Hunkpapa Sioux spiritual leader, may be regarded as the first of the great Show Indians. Although he toured only briefly with Cody in the late summer of 1885, his employment established a course for all subsequent shows. His association with the Sioux victory at the Battle of Little Bighorn secured his exemplary status. The Sioux, or rather the Teton Lakota, became the most prized Show Indians. Their presence provided the necessary aura of authenticity for the shows in recreating scenes from the recent past. Their reputations as warriors confirmed the popular image of Indians in the minds of Americans and eventually Europeans who saw their performances.

In later years, other Sioux Indians—Red Shirt, American Horse the younger, Rocky Bear, Black Heart, SHORT BULL, KICKING BEAR, Luther Standing Bear, and Iron Tail—became leaders of the Show Indians.

Not much information is available about the thoughts and feelings of the Show Indians during the early years of the shows. An occasional quotation appears from the pen of a newspaper reporter. Much of the time, the reports about Indians are derogatory. This began to change, however, once the Show Indians toured Europe. In April 1887, Cody and his troupe arrived at Earl's Court outside London to participate in Queen Victoria's Golden Jubilee. The English and, in time, other Europeans were as interested in the "Red Indians" as they were in the other residents of wild America. The thoughts and commentary of Indians touring Europe are therefore more in evidence, if not always free of condescending asides. Later still, as Indians trained in the English language at government schools began to travel with the shows, the Show Indians would speak for themselves.

Indians joined the shows for the money, the opportunity to travel, and the adventure. They received each in abundance. BLACK ELK, the Oglala visionary, remembered that his enjoyment came in the adventure of it

"The Only Indians Ever in Venice," recorded in a photograph by Paolo Salvaiati, arrived there with Buffalo Bill's Wild West show. *Courtesy Buffalo Bill Historical Center.*

all, in performing recreations of brave deeds, and in getting paid for it. In addition, by traveling in the East and abroad, he and the other Show Indians enjoyed something they had never experienced before. For many, especially those who remembered a life before the reservations closed in, the Wild West shows offered a way out. Given the alternative of staying home where their cultures increasingly came under attack from government officials and religious groups determined to transform them, Indians continued to join Wild West shows and to travel the world in relative freedom. Although reformers and Indian bureau personnel maintained that the shows degraded the Indians, there is no question that Show Indians earned a good living, a singular feat in the difficult years of the late nineteenth and early twentieth centuries.

—*L. G. Moses*

SUGGESTED READING:

Deloria, Vine, Jr. "The Indians." In *Buffalo Bill and the Wild West.* Philadelphia, 1981.

DeMallie, Raymond J., ed. *The Sixth Grandfather: Black Elk's Teachings Given to John G. Neihardt.* Lincoln, Nebr., 1984.

Kasper, Shirl. *Annie Oakley.* Norman, Okla., 1992.

McCoy, Ron. *Tim McCoy Remembers the West.* New York, 1977.

Moses, L. G. "Interpreting the Wild West, 1883–1914." In *Between Indian and White Worlds: The Cultural Broker.* Edited by Margaret Connell Szasz. Norman, Okla., 1994.

———. "Wild West Shows, Reformers, and the Image of the American Indian." *South Dakota History* 14 (1984): 193–221.

Rosa, Joseph G., and Robin May. *Buffalo Bill and His Wild West.* Lawrence, Kans., 1989.
Russell, Don. *The Wild West.* Fort Worth, Tex., 1970.

WILKES, CHARLES

Leader of an important Western naval exploring expedition, Charles Wilkes (1798–1877) was born in New York City. He became a merchant marine at the age of seventeen. Three years later, he was appointed a midshipman in the United States Navy and served in the Mediterranean. In 1826, while back in Washington, D.C., to await orders, Wilkes studied under Ferdinand Hassler, founder of the United States Coast and Geodetic Survey. He sought scientific survey duty, and in 1830, he was assigned chief of the Depot of Charts and Instruments and began building what would become the U.S. Naval Observatory.

Wilkes's work at the depot and the observatory gained him a small measure of renown. When Congress sought to commission an exploration of the South Seas in 1837, Wilkes, then only a lieutenant, was offered the command. The South Seas Surveying and Exploring Expedition, later known as the Wilkes Expedition, set sail from Norfolk, Virginia, on August 18, 1838. The expedition contained members of the scientific community as well as military personnel and was designed to survey the regions from Cape Horn north and west.

The expedition spent the next four years gathering hundreds of plant, animal, and sea specimens, making maps and charts, and confirming or denying existing notions of passages and land masses in the Pacific and Antarctic oceans. In 1840, Wilkes's flagship, the *Vincennes,* skirted the Antarctic ice cap, and he identified this land mass for the first time as a separate continent. Other explorations were made in Australia, New Zealand, the Fiji Islands, and Hawaii. In Hawaii, Wilkes made extensive observations both from the summit of Mauna Loa, where he established an observatory, and from the rim of the Kilauea volcano.

From Hawaii, the expedition continued to the Northwest Coast of North America. In the vast Oregon Country, the expedition surveyed the Puget Sound and navigated the COLUMBIA RIVER inland to the mouth of the SNAKE RIVER. One of Wilkes's ships was lost when it ran aground on a sandbar at the mouth of the Columbia. The loss prompted Wilkes to suggest in his reports that the United States seek possession of the region north of 54° 40' in order to gain access to less hazardous routes inland. Parties were sent south down the WILLAMETTE RIVER to the SACRAMENTO RIVER

and Sutter's Fort in northern California before the expedition returned to New York on June 10, 1842. All told, the expedition gathered data on 280 islands in the Pacific and 800 miles of streams and rivers in Oregon and mapped for the first time 1,600 miles of the Antarctica coastline. Its detail was such that Wilkes's maps were still being used in World War II.

Wilkes gained more notoriety during the Civil War when he waylaid the British mail steamer *Trent* and captured the Confederate diplomats James Mason and John Slidell. This act almost sparked war with Britain, and the two were returned. Wilkes served in the navy until 1873 and died four years later.

—*Kurt Edward Kemper*

SEE ALSO: Alaskan Exploration; Exploration: United States Expeditions

SUGGESTED READING:
Morgan, James, et al., eds. *Autobiography of Rear Admiral Charles Wilkes, U.S. Navy, 1798–1877.* Washington, D.C., 1978.
Stanton, William. *The Great United States Exploring Expedition of 1838–1842.* Berkeley, Calif., 1975.

WILKINSON, JAMES

Soldier, land speculator, politician, and consummate double-dealer, James Wilkinson (1757–1825) was a native of Calvert Country, Maryland. The well-born, handsome son of a plantation owner, a big man of six feet, who in middle age would grow obese, Wilkinson at the age of seventeen took up the study of medicine in Philadelphia, where he married into the prominent Biddle family. After the battle of Concord launched the American Revolution, Wilkinson joined the rebel army forming around Boston and served under George Washington at Bunker Hill, under General Nathaniel Greene in New York, and with Benedict Arnold during the latter's failed Quebec campaign. Wilkinson might have been honored as a Revolutionary hero had he not participated in the "Conway Cabal," a 1777 attempt to unseat George Washington as commander of the Continental Army. Instead, Wilkinson was removed from the field and made clothier general, a safe sinecure offering ample opportunities for turning a private profit, opportunities of which he quickly took advantage.

Retiring to civilian life after the war, Wilkinson went into politics in Kentucky and business in New Orleans, both of which provided fertile ground for his seemingly natural perfidy. It was evidently in New Orleans in 1787 that he first offered secretly to "advise" the Spanish about their relations with the United States for an annuity. Wilkinson was by then already involved in the near treasonous "Spanish Conspiracy," in which a host of prominent Tennessee and Kentucky Westerners agreed to persuade frontier settlers to withdraw from the Union and swear allegiance to the Spanish crown. In return, the Spanish would offer the conspirators unlimited trade on the Spanish-controlled Mississippi, large land grants in Spain's trans-Mississippi territory, and favored status in the Indian fur trade. An explosive issue in local politics having almost no appreciable effect on the history of the West, the conspiracy did cost Wilkinson an election to office in the newly formed state of Kentucky.

In 1792, Wilkinson was appointed commander of Western military affairs and stationed at Fort Washington on the Ohio just as the Algonquin resistance, which had flared sporadically since the Revolution, heated up into open warfare. But he was passed over in favor of "Mad" Anthony Wayne to lead the army's successful campaign against the Old Northwest tribes. By 1794, Wilkinson had renewed his intrigues with the Spanish, offering not only to act as Madrid's agent in enticing Western settlers across the Mississippi, but also to tempt Kentucky itself to break from the United States and join the Spanish Empire—highly irregular conduct for an officer of the U.S. Army, if not bald treason. Anthony Wayne had never trusted his subordinate, and he had notified Secretary of War Thomas Pickering of his doubts. But when Wayne died in 1796, Wilkinson was confirmed as the commanding general of the United States Army early in March 1797. General Wilkinson was now in charge of enforcing the terms of the Treaty of San Lorenzo, which put him in constant contact with the Spanish of Louisiana, and he traveled all over the sprawling Western frontier with Spain during the years when Spain was threatening to close the Mississippi to American trade and Washington, hoping to avoid war, was negotiating for the purchase of New Orleans and parts of Florida. Following the Louisiana Purchase, President THOMAS JEFFERSON— probably with the urging of his vice-president, Aaron Burr—appointed Wilkinson governor of the Upper Louisiana Territory, also called the Missouri Territory.

In St. Louis, Wilkinson's cloak-and-dagger methods made the rivalries in the territory between long-time ethnic French residents and newly arrived land speculators immeasurably worse. At one point, he sent a secret message to the Spanish authorities in Santa Fe suggesting they might wish to arrest MERIWETHER LEWIS and WILLIAM CLARK, just then in the midst of their famous expedition. When Lewis and Clark returned to St. Louis in 1806, their hosts were the prominent French CHOUTEAU FAMILY, from whom perhaps the two explorers heard a description of Wilkinson's inauguration: a huge celebration, immensely enjoyed by St. Louis' citizens, during which the governor revealed his great fondness for the bottle. The Chouteaus might well have expressed their resentment at Wilkinson's attempts to elbow his way into their fur-trading business. And Lewis and Clark could hardly have missed the dark talk, especially among English-speaking residents, of a Western Conspiracy—a plan, gossip said, that Wilkinson had hatched to detach the West from the United States and make Aaron Burr its president—or its emperor.

Wilkinson was, in fact, deeply involved with Burr in some sort of scheme. Burr spent two weeks in the fall of 1805 consulting long into the night with the governor. The lawless conditions in the territory, created in large measure by the wide-open speculation resulting from disputed Spanish land-grants and the burgeoning mining business, made Upper Louisiana a perfect spot for such plots. Even while Wilkinson was—evidently—in the thick of the skullduggery, he negotiated, in 1806, the important Neutral Ground Treaty between the United States and Spain pertaining to the territory along the Sabine River—the very territory he and Burr supposedly planned to conquer for themselves. Ultimately, Wilkinson had second thoughts late in 1806 and betrayed Burr by informing Jefferson of the plot and by helping to engineer the arrest of Burr and his detainment in New Orleans. Wilkinson did not escape blame and public censure for his role in the BURR CONSPIRACY. When Burr was tried for treason in Virginia, ANDREW JACKSON, who liked Burr, labeled Wilkinson the true traitor. A sensational book entitled *Proofs of the Corruption of General James Wilkinson* (1809) by another of the conspirators further tarnished his reputation.

On March 3, 1807, much to the relief of almost everyone in the Missouri Territory, Thomas Jefferson removed Wilkinson from the governor's office and replaced him with Meriwether Lewis. When the War of 1812 broke out, however, Wilkinson was still commander of the U.S. Army. But failing health and the usual friction with his fellow officers, especially General Wade Hampton, brought Wilkinson's long, if undistinguished, military career to an end as well. The new president, James Madison, offered Wilkinson a sinecure as superintendent of Indian affairs, but he turned Madison down to write his memoirs and to run a Mississippi cotton plantation. When he failed at the latter, he tried to persuade the Spanish to grant him land in Mexican territory, but during an extended stay in Mexico City in 1825, James Wilkinson, if not an outright spy and traitor, certainly one of the American West's great scoundrels, contracted chronic diarrhea and died.

—*Charles Phillips*

SEE ALSO: Blount, William

WILLAMETTE RIVER

Draining an eleven-thousand-square-mile area south of the Columbia River, the Willamette River flows into a valley that forms the heartland of Oregon. Bounded on the east by the Cascades and on the west by the Pacific Coast Range, the Willamette Valley is home to the river after which it takes its name and such tributaries as the Middle Fork, McKenzie, Calapooya, Santiam, Molalla, and Clackamas rivers, all entering the valley from the east, and the Long Tom, Luckiamute, Yamhil, and Tualatin rivers from the west. Fed by melting mountain snows and a heavy annual rainfall averaging sixty-three inches a year, mostly coming in November to February, the Willamette and its tributaries carry about twenty-six million acre-feet of water a year, twice that of the Colorado River.

The first Europeans to visit the valley were MERIWETHER LEWIS and WILLIAM CLARK in 1806. These explorers predicted the valley would be the nucleus of the region's future settlement (as indeed it was), and they were followed by HUDSON'S BAY COMPANY trappers, who hunted beavers in the headwater streams and established a trading post at FORT VANCOUVER on the Columbia opposite the Willamette's delta. Mountain man JEDEDIAH STRONG SMITH traipsed the valley and wintered at Fort Vancouver on one of his epic explorations in 1828, after which he drafted a letter to the U.S. Congress on the potential for settlement. French trappers, granted land and supplied by Hudson's Bay, married into local Indian tribes and became the nucleus around which Protestant missionaries such as JASON LEE and Marcus Whitman, arriving after 1834 to minister to the Indians, built the settlements of what soon became the Oregon Territory. Beginning in the 1840s, pioneers arrived overland along the OREGON TRAIL, and by 1845, five thousand of them lived in the valley, sparking renewed disputes with Great Britain over the boundary between the two imperial-minded countries.

A negotiated settlement of the dispute and a growing stream of migrants might have made the valley the center of Far Western settlement had not the discovery of gold near Sacramento in 1848 caused California's population to leapfrog over that of the Oregon Territory. The gold rush diverted traffic from the overland trails and seduced settlers in the Willamette Valley

southward. When Washington and eastern Oregon were "opened" to settlers after the Native Americans were herded onto reservations in the late 1850s and the 1860s, many of those moving into the new areas came from the valley. Regardless, with a steadily growing population and an economy centered on agriculture and logging, the Willamette region thrived. Portland, located on the mouth of the Willamette, grew to be the major Columbia River port, while Eugene and Corvallis—home of major universities—served as supply posts for the farms around them. In the twentieth century, tourism became an important local industry as vacationers were increasingly attracted to the Willamette Valley's sparkling waters and thick, lush forests.

—*Charles Phillips*

SEE ALSO: Oregon Boundary Dispute; Whitman, Marcus and Narcissa

WILLIAMS, WILLIAM S. ("OLD BILL")

Trapper, guide, trader, and Indian fighter William S. Williams (1787–1849) was born in old Rutherford County, North Carolina. His family emigrated to Missouri around 1795, and he soon became an adopted warrior of the Osage Indians and often worked as an interpreter. Popularly known as "Old Bill," he was a skilled plainsman, distinguished by his ability to hide from danger, avoid enemies, trap beaver, and fight Indians. He was an expert tracker, a crack shot, and a good trader among the native peoples. He seldom lost his pelts to attacking warriors. "Old Bill" trapped all over the West: the Rio Grande; Salt Lake Valley; Wind River; the region north of the Gila River; the Green River; and South Park. He was noted for his gruff, determined manners and eccentric clothing.

—*Charles E. Hanson, Jr.*

SEE ALSO: Trappers

SUGGESTED READING:

Ceeland, Robert Glass. *This Reckless Breed of Men.* Albuquerque, N. Mex., 1976.

Voelker, Frederic E. "William Sherley (Old Bill) Williams." In *The Mountain Men and the Fur Trade of the Far West.* Vol. 8. Edited by LeRoy R. Hafen. Glendale, Calif., 1971.

WILLIAMSON, JAMES A.

A lawyer, Civil War major general, and later, president of the Atlantic and Pacific Railroad, General James A.

Williamson (1829–1902) served as commissioner of the GENERAL LAND OFFICE from 1876 to 1881. Williamson's tenure at the General Land Office revealed all the tensions that permeated the disposition of federal land. Selected by Secretary of the Interior CARL SCHURZ as a reformer for a corrupt department, Williamson embodied both reform impulses and the indiscretion and shady dealing for which the General Land Office was already famous. He lobbied for better support for the bureau so that its officials could do a more comprehensive job, helped pass the DESERT LAND ACT OF 1877 and the TIMBER AND STONE ACT OF 1878, served on the PUBLIC LANDS COMMISSION OF 1879, and is credited with starting the movement to codify land laws. But Williamson did not know how to avoid the appearance of conflict of interest. As commissioner, he reversed a seven-year old decision of a predecessor denying him a patent for lands he claimed in Utah. Becoming embroiled in the Maxwell Land Grant controversy, Williamson informed the secretary of the interior that a new Supreme Court ruling would allow the claimants of two million acres to keep that large amount instead of the ninety-seven thousand acres that the terms of their claim granted them. Rumors of his involvement with the owners of the grant persisted. During an 1880 visit to New Mexico, territorial newspapers alleged that he had a large interest in land there.

One of many leaders who sought to reform the General Land Office, Williamson, like many of his successors, could not keep clear of the practices that typified the time. He straddled two different views of how government operated; he saw it as both an avenue for personal aggrandizement and as a tool to reshape society.

—*Hal Rothman*

SEE ALSO: Land Policy; Maxwell Land Grant Company

SUGGESTED READING:
Peffer, E. Louise. *The Closing of the Public Domain.* Stanford, Calif., 1951.

WILMOT PROVISO

In 1846, David Wilmot, congressman from Pennsylvania, introduced an amendment to a bill appropriating $2 million to facilitate negotiations with Mexico for "territorial adjustments" as a way of bringing an end to the UNITED STATES–MEXICAN WAR. His amendment—the Wilmot Proviso, as it came to be called—would have prohibited slavery in any land acquired by the United States as a result of the war. Although it passed the House only to fail in the Senate, the Wilmot Proviso remained a source of sectional conflict until the COMPROMISE OF 1850, a legislative marker of the way in which expansion westward was rending the country north and south because the potential of vast new land was upsetting the volatile compromise over slavery upon which the nation had been founded and now upon which it threatened to founder. In response to the proviso, South Carolina senator JOHN CALDWELL CALHOUN proposed four resolutions in 1847: first, that the Western territories were the joint and common property of the states; second, that the Congress, as agent for the states, had no right to make laws discriminating between the states or depriving any state of its full and equal right in any Western territory acquired by the United States; third, that the enactment of any law pertaining to slavery would be a violation of the Constitution and of states' rights; and fourth, that the people had a right to form their state governments as they chose since the Constitution imposed no conditions for the admission of a state except that its government should be republican. In the 1850s, Calhoun's states' rights resolutions provided the Democrats and the South with their agenda; the Wilmot Proviso provided the new Republican party—and the North and much of the West—with a fundamental program. The Wilmot Proviso, the Compromise of 1850, and the KANSAS-NEBRASKA ACT revealed that, in many ways, expansion west was the precipitating factor that turned slavery from a political issue into a cause for civil war.

—*Charles Phillips*

WILSON, JAMES

Farmer, educator, and public official James Wilson (1835–1920) was born in Ayrshire, Scotland, and immigrated to the United States in 1851. Four years later, he began farming in Iowa. He held several public offices, including a seat in Congress from 1873 to 1877 and from 1883 to 1885. After directing the Iowa Agricultural Experiment Station from 1891 to 1897, he was named secretary of agriculture by President William McKinley in 1897. Wilson held this post until 1913. Strongly committed to education and science, Secretary Wilson championed meat-inspection and pure-food laws, agricultural-extension programs, scientific forestry, and the eradication of Texas fever and other cattle diseases.

—*David B. Danbom*

WIMAR, CARL (OR CHARLES) F.

The last artist to chronicle Native American culture on the Upper Missouri River before the mass settlement of the trans-Mississippi plains after the Civil War, Carl (or Charles) F. Wimar (1828–1862) was born in Sieburg, Germany. He immigrated to the United States with his family and settled in St. Louis in 1844. Shortly after opening his first studio, Wimar was inspired by Emanuel Leutze's monumental painting *Washington Crossing the Delaware* (1851) to travel to his homeland, study with Leutze, and create grand history paintings of the American West.

From 1852 to 1856, Wimar studied in Düsseldorf where he learned the German academic painting style. His paintings created there depicted confrontation and conflict between Euro-American settlers and Native Americans. His *Abduction of Daniel Boone's Daughter by the Indians* (1853) and *Attack on an Emigrant Train* (1856) were very popular in Germany and earned him the title "Indian painter." After his studies in Germany, Wimar returned to St. Louis and took two extensive expeditions in 1858 and 1859 up the Missouri River. He spent his time drawing and sketching and collecting Indian artifacts to use in his paintings. The panoramic paintings he created after the expeditions, such as *The Buffalo Dance* (1860) and *The Buffalo Hunt* (1860), portray romantic images of Upper Missouri Native American culture.

In 1861, the city of St. Louis commissioned Wimar to decorate its courthouse dome with murals depicting significant local history events: *DeSoto Discovering the Mississippi in 1541,* the founding of St. Louis in *The Landing of Laclede in 1763,* and a Revolutionary War victory in *The Year of the Blow.* The final mural, *Westward the Star of Empire,* represented the city's ambitions as the gateway to the West. Wimar's death in 1862 from tuberculosis marked the end of an era, the close of the first generation of artist-explorers who painted Native American cultures in the West.
—*Joseph D. Ketner*

SEE ALSO: Art: Surveys and Expeditions, Western Art

SUGGESTED READING:
Stewart, Rick, Joseph D. Ketner, and Angela L. Miller. *Carl Wimar: Chronicler of the Missouri River Frontier.* Fort Worth, Tex., 1991.

WINCHESTER RIFLES

SEE: Firearms

WINDMILLS

As typically used in the West, windmills are machines that pump water from underground sources to the surface for use by humans and their animals. The basic technology for using the wind to pump water came to the Americas from Europe as early as the seventeenth century, but the turbine-wheel wind machines common in the West had their origin in New England. In 1854, Daniel Halladay, a mechanic in Connecticut, invented and patented the first commercially successful American windmill. A wind machine fitted with paddle-shaped wooden blades, it was designed for either pumping water or grinding grain. It had two major design features, which soon made windmills successful in the American West: without human attention, the windmill turned to face changing wind directions, and it automatically controlled its own speed in varying wind velocities.

Daniel Halladay's windmill. *Courtesy The Bettmann Archive.*

Halladay's invention was manufactured in Connecticut, but its principal market was in the West and Midwest, where most water resources were underground and where the wind could be depended on to blow much of the time. In 1863, a firm purchased Halladay's company and shifted manufacturing operations to Batavia, Illinois, on the fringe of the Great Plains. From then on, the Midwest was the center for windmill manufacture in the United States.

Halladay's windmill typified one of the two major designs for North American windmills. Its wheel, originally composed of paddle-shaped blades, was later made from several sections of wooden, slatlike blades, pivoted to incline away from increasing winds and thus able to control speed. The other major pattern of windmill was made with a rigid wheel that pivoted to one side in increasing winds through the action of a governor vane parallel to the wheel; alternately, the wheel

itself was placed slightly to one side. In both major patterns, the windmills successfully regulated their speed of operation and thus avoided destruction from centrifugal force in high winds.

All of the pioneer windmills in the West were built from wood with some iron and steel parts holding them together and taking the greatest strain. By the 1870s, however, all-metal windmills were produced, and by the 1890s they were common. By World War I, most windmills in the West were made from steel, and many of them were erected on steel towers, which had supplanted the older wooden towers.

The major innovation in windmills during the twentieth century was the oil-bath or self-lubricating design, which appeared around 1912. Within two decades, nearly all windmills manufactured in the United States and Canada used this design feature, which made possible the lubrication of mechanical parts in a way similar to a crankcase of an automobile engine.

Although only a handful of windmill manufacturers are in operation today, tens of thousands of windmills remain throughout the West, many of them still pumping water for livestock and domestic consumers. The role of windmills in the history of the West, however, belies their decreasing numbers. Their provision of water from drilled wells made possible a comparatively even settlement, which never could have happened if Euro-Americans had been forced to locate only near springs, rivers, or other natural sources of water.

—*T. Lindsay Baker*

SUGGESTED READING:

Baker, T. Lindsay. *A Field Guide to American Windmills.* Norman, Okla., 1985.

Eide, A. Clyde. "Free as the Wind." *Nebraska History* 51: 1 (Spring 1970): 25–48.

Wolff, Alfred R. *The Windmill as a Prime Mover.* New York, 1885.

An advertisement for a Stover windmill. *Courtesy The Bettmann Archive.*

WINGFIELD, GEORGE

Nevada businessman and politician George Wingfield (1876–1959) was born near Cincinnati, Arkansas. He moved to Oregon and grew up on a cattle ranch. A professional gambler, he made a significant fortune in 1906 with the formation of Goldfield Consolidated Mines Company. From these beginnings, he went on to own a banking chain, hotels, ranches, and other extensive mining interests. He turned down an appointment to the U.S. Senate in 1912 but became a power in the Republican party in Nevada, although he was accused of operating a bipartisan political machine from his office in Reno. He was an avid promoter of

Nevada's embryonic tourism industry. In 1932, his banks failed, and by 1936, he had lost his fortune and political base. Through the Getchell Mine, he regained a second, smaller fortune during the 1940s.

—C. Elizabeth Raymond

SUGGESTED READING:

Nevada Historical Society Quarterly 32 (Summer 1989).
Raymond, C. Elizabeth. *George Wingfield: Owner and Operator of Nevada.* Reno, Nev., 1992.

WINNEMUCCA, SARAH (PAIUTE)

Born in western Nevada into a band of Paiutes led by her father, Chief Winnemucca, and centered around Humboldt and Pyramid lakes, Sarah Winnemucca (Tocmetone, or Shell Flower, 1844–1891) became a champion of Indian rights and the author of the influential *Life among the Paiutes: Their Wrongs and Claims* (1883). When her mother and sister were killed in 1865 during disturbances that followed the Paiutes' confinement to a reservation around Pyramid Lake, Winnemucca blamed Indian agents for causing the troubles. She served as an interpreter and messenger for General OLIVER OTIS HOWARD during the Paiute and Bannock hostilities of 1877 and 1878 when the general could find no man willing to negotiate with the Indians. Instrumental in persuading Chief Winnemucca to lead his band out of the war camp, she traveled with her father to Washington, D.C., in 1879 and 1880 to seek permission for the Paiutes to leave the Washington Territory and return to the Malhuer Reservation in Nevada. Although the secretary of the interior granted the request, the Yakima Indian agent thwarted the move, which only hardened Winnemucca's dislike of such men. Back East in 1881 and 1882, she lectured in Boston and other cities. Condemning the practices of Indian agents, she won sympathy for her people and the indignations visited upon them and converted many to the new Indian reform movement just then coming into full swing.

Winnemucca was married three times. The first marriage, to Lieutenant Edward Bartlett, lasted scarcely a year. When her second marriage to a Paiute also failed, she married Lieutenant Lambert H. Hopkins, probably an officer in the volunteers, who assisted her in the writing of her book. Her attacks on Indian agents led to savage countercharges that she was a liar and a "drunken prostitute," but these were refuted by General Howard and other distinguished officers, who praised her for the brave work she had done with them in the field. Money from her speaking tours allowed her to buy land in Nevada and to establish, near Lovelock, an Indian school, which she ran for three years. But in 1886, her husband died of tuberculosis, and Winnemucca—afflicted with psychological and emotional problems, her physical health failing—retired to Monida, Montana, to live with her sister. Hailed as "the most famous Indian woman on the Pacific Coast" by the whites, called "Mother" by her Paiute tribe, Sarah Winnemucca died in Montana of tuberculosis on October 16, 1891.

—Patricia Hogan

SEE ALSO: Literature: Native American Literature; United States Indian Policy: Reform Movement

Sarah Winnemucca. *Courtesy Nevada Historical Society.*

SUGGESTED READING:
Gaye, Canfield. *Sarah Winnemucca of the Northern Paiutes.* Norman, Okla., 1983.

WISTER, OWEN

There is a great irony in the career of Owen Wister (1860–1938): one of the most solid members of the Eastern aristocracy became one of the most important literary interpreters of the American cowboy and of the role of the West in American culture. Through several collections of short stories and a famous novel, *The Virginian: A Horseman of the Plains* (1902), Wister stands at the head of both serious and popular literary traditions.

Owen Wister was born to an aristocratic Philadelphia family that included in its lineage a signer of the Declaration of Independence and a famous actress and that often entertained the novelist Henry James as a dinner guest. Wister graduated from Harvard with a music major, earned the praise of composer and pianist Franz Liszt for one of his compositions, and became a close friend of future President THEODORE ROOSEVELT.

A Wyoming vacation in 1885 changed Wister's life by introducing him to the rigors of the frontier and to the cowboys who made it their home. Over the next six years, Wister revisited the West and deepened his understanding and admiration for Western life. He was inspired to write two stories featuring a cowboy character named Lin Maclean. Both stories were published in *Harper's Weekly* and were included in a larger collection of stories in 1897.

Lin Maclean was only a literary exercise in preparation for Wister's most famous and influential character, an anonymous cowboy called simply "the Virginian," hero of the 1902 novel of this name. The Virginian's mysterious identity, his colorful costume and speech, his competence in a difficult environment, and his tendency toward violence all became standard features of a multitude of popular western heroes developed by ZANE GREY, MAX BRAND, LUKE SHORT, and others. A vitally important difference between Wister's hero and his descendants in the popular western, though, is that the Virginian, in his gentility of manners and competence in settings in both the East and West, represents the best of Eastern as well as Western cultures.

The Virginian is, then, an American hero, not just a Western one. He represents a national culture that is a combination of the virtues of both regions (and no doubt of the South as well; he is, after all, a Virginian). He is a creative blend that Wister's literary predecessors, such as JAMES FENIMORE COOPER, never found possible to make. The popular writers who succeeded him found such a character unnecessary to make—Western local color and violence were enough to sell books.

Wister lived to see the end of the open range, the coming of technology, and the decline of what he saw as vital Western virtues. So the Virginian is a tragic figure, a vanishing resident of a fleeting time and place, and a reminder of the wholesome blend of the rough and the genteel that is no more.

—*Gary Topping*

SEE ALSO: Literature: The Western Novel

SUGGESTED READING:
Lambert, Neal. "Owen Wister." In *Fifty Western Writers.* Edited by Fred Erisman and Richard W. Etulain. Westport, Conn., 1982.
Wister, Owen. *Lin Maclean.* New York, 1897.
———. *The Virginian: A Horseman of the Plains.* New York, 1902.

WOBBLIES

SEE: Industrial Workers of the World

WOLFSKILL, WILLIAM

Fur trader and California pioneer William Wolfskill (1798–1866) was born in Kentucky where his parents had traveled via DANIEL BOONE's Wilderness Road. A long hunter by the age of fourteen, Wolfskill became one of the bold young men attracted by WILLIAM HENRY ASHLEY's advertisement in a St. Louis newspaper for independent trappers, and in the early 1820s he headed west to join the ranks of the MOUNTAIN MEN hunting and exploring the Southwest and California. Traveling the Sante Fe Trail with WILLIAM BECKNELL in 1822, Wolfskill went into business with EWING YOUNG and worked with all the great trappers, from William Sublette to CHRISTOPHER HOUSTON ("KIT") CARSON. Leading a veteran group over the Old Spanish Trail to join Young in California in 1830, Wolfskill became the first to demonstrate the trail's potential for pack trains. He helped launch the soon flourishing trade between New Mexico and California and pioneered major farming projects in California after 1836, including citrus production, grape growing, and wine making. Buying ranches and setting up cattle operations, Wolfskill financed the first private English-speaking schools in the area. His impact on the economic, political, and cultural life of early California was immense, and he was widely acclaimed as a founding father of the new state.

—*Charles Phillips*

SEE ALSO: Sublette Brothers

WOLVES

When the first Euro-American explorers arrived in the West, wolves roamed much of the region. By the end of the twentieth century, there were fewer than one hundred of these animals outside of Alaska and Minnesota. Due to a century of habitat destruction, hunting, and trapping, the northern gray wolf has been confined to remote pockets of the Far West. During the early 1970s, the U.S. Fish and Wildlife Service listed the animal as an endangered species.

Few wild creatures have evoked more fear and hatred than the wolf. Whites who settled in the West during the nineteenth century had inherited from Europe a long tradition of horror tales regarding the animal. Generations of children learned from the story of "Little Red Riding Hood" that wolves were deceitful, bloodthirsty fiends. Other stories advised children to avoid the "Big Bad Wolf." The fear of wolves found its way into highbrow literature as well. Published in 1918, Willa Cather's *My Ántonia* recounted a horrific attack on a Russian wedding party. As the wolf pack closed in, the doomed guests screamed "piteously" as the "little bride hid her face on the groom's shoulder and sobbed."

The gray wolf, an endangered species, was restored to Yellowstone National Park in the 1990s. *Editors' collection.*

Western adventure and hunting stories also portrayed wolves as dangerous animals. In these tales, the wolf typically appeared ready to attack, fangs bared in a snarl. Some popular accounts exaggerated the animal's ferocity in order to bolster sales of books and magazines. Yet even the *Encyclopaedia Britannica,* a publication not given to sensationalism, warned its readers in 1910 that wolves will attack children.

During the early twentieth century, conservationists and animal lovers supported this frightening image of wolf behavior. William T. Hornaday, director of the New York Zoological Park, claimed that wolves were mean, treacherous, and cruel. In 1914, he offered this advice: "Wherever found, the proper course with a wild gray wolf is to kill it as quickly as possible." As one of the nation's leading advocates for wildlife protection, Hornaday was a prominent figure whose ideas were taken seriously. President THEODORE ROOSEVELT, well known as a sportsman and respected as a naturalist, agreed with Hornaday. In his writings, he condemned the wolf as a "vicious, bloodthirsty" creature. While JOHN GRIFFITH (JACK) LONDON and a few other writers appreciated the wolf as a symbol of the wild, most Americans had little sympathy for the animal.

During the last half of the twentieth century, numerous studies confirmed that wolves are in general shy of humans and will attack only rarely. The *idea* of the predator, then, has been more terrifying than the animal's actual habits. More than any other creatures, wolves embody the essence of the wilderness: alien, disordered, and beyond the control of humans. There were also practical reasons for Americans to despise wolves: they killed game animals and livestock. By the early twentieth century, hatred of these animals erupted into a full-scale war against them. Much of the impetus for predator control came from Western ranchers whose lands were so extensive they could not provide constant protection for sheep and cattle. In response, the Bureau of Biological Survey, the precursor to the U.S. Fish and Wildlife Service, stepped in to eliminate offending predators. Established in 1905, the survey provided information on poisoning wolves and sent out trained hunters, trappers, and poisoners on private as well as public lands. Its goal, in the early years, was extermination of the wolf. So effective were these efforts that, by the 1930s, wolves were nearly wiped out in the West.

Reductions in populations of wolves and other predators resulted in an abundance of rodents and deer and other ungulates (hoofed mammals). In sections of the West, jackrabbits and deer became so numerous that they stripped the land of vegetation. Without predators to keep their numbers in check, these animals sometimes died of starvation. As biologists studied the problems caused by predator control, they developed an increasing appreciation for the role of wolves in natural systems. By the mid-twentieth century, the image of the wolf began to change.

Many Americans came to view wolves differently during the late twentieth century. Modern accounts endow wolves with the characteristics of admirable humans: loyalty, compassion, and courage. Some popular naturalists emphasize that wolves rarely attack humans and only under extreme provocation. They argue that wolves pair for life, adopt orphan cubs, educate their young, and even have a sense of humor. Naturalists now claim that wolves cooperate in "teams" rather than traveling in menacing, formidable packs. Far from being the bloodthirsty beasts of previous eras, wolves, as described by modern naturalists, are essentially peaceful creatures who kill mostly the sick and weak, thereby keeping deer populations strong. Wolves provide an excellent example of how changing perceptions affect portrayals of animals, even by scientists.

Some Americans have retained their hatred of wolves. Although the Endangered Species Act of 1973 requires that government agencies attempt to help populations recover, efforts to reintroduce wolves in sections of the West have been met with animosity. Ranchers especially worry that more wolves will result in a loss of livestock. To many Americans, however, wolves have become an important symbol of the remnants of wilderness in the West. To them, the effort to reintroduce the predators into their former ranges indicates a significant development in attitudes toward the natural world.

—*Lisa Mighetto*

SUGGESTED READING:
Bass, Rick. *The Ninemile Wolves.* Clark City, Mont., 1992.
DeBlieu, Jan. *Meant to Be Wild: The Struggle to Save Endangered Species through Captive Breeding.* Golden, Colo., 1991.
Dunlap, Thomas R. *Saving America's Wildlife.* Princeton, N.J., 1988.
Mech, L. David. *The Wolf: The Ecology and Behavior of an Endangered Species.* New York, 1970.
Mighetto, Lisa. *Wild Animals and American Environmental Ethics.* Tucson, Ariz., 1991.

WOMAN'S CHRISTIAN TEMPERANCE UNION

Founded in 1874, the Woman's Christian Temperance Union (WTCU) was the first mass organization for American women. Drawing on Protestant evangelicalism and the nineteenth-century view of women as domestic and moral arbiters, the organization appealed to Protestant women of different classes and regions. While the WCTU was initially strongest in the East and Midwest, major efforts were made to recruit Southern and Western women. In its first major Western campaign in 1883, about 1,000 new members were secured. Much of the growth between 1890 and 1910 (from 150,000 to almost 250,000 members) stemmed from gains in the West.

While interest in temperance (abstinence from alcoholic beverages) had risen during the first half of the nineteenth century, the WCTU's origin was prompted, in part, by the Women's Crusade from 1873 to 1874. During that effort, thousands of middle-class women in thirty-one states and territories prayed and sang hymns to pressure saloonkeepers and hoteliers to close their drinking establishments. In November 1874, some of these women recognized the need for a permanent organization and established the WCTU. The organization soon moved beyond moral persuasion to embrace political action.

Temperance was always an important focus of WCTU activities, but the group also attacked a wide range of other social problems. Frances Willard, president of the WCTU between 1879 and 1898, developed policies that attracted conservative as well as more progressive women into the organization. Insisting that women's nature and domestic responsibilities were the essential foundation of their work to improve society, Willard gave local chapters the flexibility to choose their specific agendas. This "Do Everything" policy, enunciated in 1882, allowed local chapters to avoid issues members found too threatening.

As early as 1876, however, Willard argued that women could not protect their homes or families from the deleterious influence of alcohol nor counter the powerful political influence of liquor interests without the vote. Prohibition, she said in 1884, "can never be accomplished until woman has the vote." (Later, the home protection argument for suffrage was joined by one emphasizing women's natural right to the ballot.) Western members took the suffrage message to heart and campaigned for the vote. In 1892, Wyoming gave women full suffrage; in other areas of the West, they won the right to vote in local or school board elections. In 1894, the WCTU adopted a formal position in favor of WOMEN'S SUFFRAGE.

Causes for which WCTU members worked ranged from prison reform to public kindergartens. The effort to have Scientific Temperance Instruction provided in all public schools was one of the WCTU's greatest successes. By 1900, nearly every state had passed legislation requiring schools to teach students that alcohol, in any amount, was poison.

In the 1890s, the Anti-Saloon League became the leading temperance organization, although the WCTU continued to grow, albeit more slowly than in its early years. During the Progressive era, both groups worked successfully for prohibition on the state and local levels. By 1905, four states (three of them—North Dakota, Nebraska and Kansas—west of the Mississippi) were dry. Fourteen years later, California was the only Western state that had not adopted prohibition.

Although other women's organizations reduced the influence of the WCTU in the twentieth century, the group's significance in the late nineteenth century is clear. Buttressed by the familiar views of female nature and female responsibilities, thousands of women entered the public arena as members of the WCTU and became political activists, lobbyists, and leaders. The WCTU legitimized women's work on a variety of issues and in various settings and even made the idea of the vote for women acceptable to those who found suffrage organizations far too radical for their support.

—*Julie Roy Jeffrey*

SEE ALSO: Temperance and Prohibition

SUGGESTED READING:

Bordin, Ruth. *Woman and Temperance, The Quest for Power and Liberty, 1873–1900.* Philadelphia, 1981.

Clark, Norman. *Deliver Us from Evil: An Interpretation of American Prohibition.* New York, 1976.

WOMAN'S COMMONWEALTH

A celibate utopian society, the Woman's Commonwealth evolved from the divine revelation of its founder, MARTHA WHITE McWHIRTER. Inspired in 1867 to "sanctify" herself through a commitment to celibacy and ecumenism (a unified Christian church), McWhirter attracted a small band of like-minded women, including Margaret Henry, Mary Johnson, Elizabeth Holtzclaw, and Rebecca Carter, along with a few of their daughters, in the town of Belton, Texas. The women first formed an informal prayer group, but they were eventually forced to withdraw into a separate community as their commitments to ecumenism, celibacy, and spiritual guidance through dreams alienated them from conventional social institutions and from their marriages. By the late 1870s, the "Sanctificationists," as they were called, had become an economic as well as a spiritual community.

With few economic alternatives, the twenty-odd followers of McWhirter decided to market the domestic skills they had acquired as wives. During the 1880s, when membership was reported at forty-two, the women established a commercial laundry and a series of boarding houses. In 1886, they remodeled a member's house to form the first Central Hotel. This business was so successful that they were able to replace it with a larger Central in 1894 and later to add boarding houses in New York City and Waco, Texas, to their business portfolio.

Despite a pleasant and profitable life in Belton, members began seeking a new home for the community in 1897. Their quest took them to New York City, Denver, Colorado Springs, and Mexico City. In the end, they relocated to Washington, D.C., in 1899. After the move, the members recommitted themselves to community life, codified group rules, and adopted a new name, The Woman's Commonwealth, which reflected the economic basis of the organization. The move to Washington also freed Commonwealth members from the tedium of hotel life. Some younger members sought outside jobs. In addition, the city introduced the group to suffrage and socialist organizations, in which many members became active in the first few years of the twentieth century. For a few years, the Commonwealth had its own chapter of the National American Woman's Suffrage Association.

Increased opportunities for work and social interaction gradually undermined younger members' commitment to the community. Mostly the daughters of founders, these young women began to drift away as their elders died. McWhirter died in 1904. By 1908, there were only nine members. By 1956, there were only two members, and thereafter, until her death in 1983, only one. Despite its gradual demise, however, the Commonwealth's survival as an active community for thirty-three years contrasts with the average four-year life span of utopian societies.

The Commonwealth was not designed to be an exclusively female organization. Several men joined, including the Dow Brothers in 1880, Joseph Barlow in 1884, and several former Shakers after the move to Washington. With the exception of Barlow, who had a troubled relationship with the group over a twenty-year period, most men found they could not endure "the rule of a woman" and left. Such reactions suggest how unusual female leadership was at the time, even among people seeking alternative social arrangements.

—*Sally L. Kitch*

SUGGESTED READING:

Kitch, Sally L. *Chaste Liberation: Celibacy and Female Cultural Status.* Urbana, Ill., 1989.

———. *This Strange Society of Women: Reading the Letters and Lives of the Woman's Commonwealth.* Columbus, Ohio, 1993.

Lamanna, Mary Ann, and Jayme Sokolow. "Women in Community: The Belton Woman's Commonwealth." *Texas Journal* 9 (Spring 1987): 10–15.

Werden, Frieda. "Martha White McWhirter and the Belton Sanctificationists." *Legendary Ladies of Texas.* Edited by Francis Edward Abernathy. Dallas, Tex., 1981.

WOMAN'S HOME MISSIONARY SOCIETY (METHODIST EPISCOPAL)

The Woman's Home Missionary Society was organized in Cincinnati, Ohio, on June 8, 1880. Under the leadership of figurehead Lucy Webb Hayes, wife of the U.S. President Rutherford B. Hayes, the society originally planned to devote itself to missionary work among the freedwomen of the South. Within a year, however, the group had begun work all over the West. Beginning with Indians in the Southwest, Mormons in Utah, and Chinese on the Pacific Coast, the society later added programs for Japanese and Latinos; its missionaries reached as far as Alaska and Hawaii. In the West and across the nation, for the six decades of its operation, the Woman's Home Missionary Society sponsored an ambitious program of mission schools, hospitals, and "industrial homes," which provided children and young adults with training in vocational and home-making skills. The society trained and provided its own deaconesses to staff these programs and published its own periodical, *Woman's Home Missions.* As early as 1890, the society claimed fifty-five thousand members, mostly in chapters in the Midwest. By 1940, when it lost its autonomy and was folded into a larger church missionary division, it turned over assets, including investments and buildings, worth more than $11 million. Although its missionary members prided themselves on dispensing a potent mixture of Christianity, charity, and American values, it was the society's social services, which ranged from English classes to maternity clinics and from kindergartens to homes for working girls, that seem to have been most important to recipients.

—*Peggy Pascoe*

SUGGESTED READING:

Meeker, Ruth Esther. *Six Decades of Service, 1880–1940: A History of The Woman's Home Missionary Society of the Methodist Episcopal Church.* Cincinnati, Ohio, 1969.

Ruiz, Vicki. "Dead Ends or Gold Mines?: Using Missionary Records in Mexican-American Women's History." *Frontiers* 12: 1 (1991): 33–56.

WOMEN ARTISTS

"Western art," writes Brian Dippie, "excludes women both as practitioners and subjects." What he means, of course, is that with the exception of GEORGIA O'KEEFFE, women artists are not commonly included in representative collections of Western art nor are they much covered in the scholarship about that art. When female Western artists are mentioned, such as illustrator and author MARY HALLOCK FOOTE, it is traditionally to note the exception that proves the rule rather than to include women artists. More recent studies of Western women artists most frequently deal with contemporaries working in Western traditions. None of which means there were no women in the arts in the trans-Mississippi West of the nineteenth and early twentieth centuries. Certainly there were Native American women practicing the crafts of their culture and Latinas working in folk-art traditions as well as Euro-American "pioneers" who exercised their creativity in the traditional female modes of quilts and costume, but there were also women painters, by 1890 some eleven hundred such female artists and teachers, according to one estimate. The problem is that they were, for the most part, invisible to the culture industry, as evidenced by the remarks of an art dealer in 1905 when faced with a painting he was exhibiting signed simply "Barchus" and told that the artist was a women: "No woman painted that picture," he asserted, "so impressive in scope, with such bold strokes."

The artist was Eliza Barchus; the work, a landscape of Mount Hood under an overcast sky, a subject she painted thousands of times. A widow who supported her family by painting and teaching, she earned such fame after 1885 that she was known as "the Oregon Artist." Many women in the West painted with a vigor and breadth of imagination to match Barchus's, but whether they created naive images with unschooled hands or applied the practiced techniques of formal training in art, they faced great odds that their work would never be noticed, much less exhibited and purchased. Not only was their work routinely belittled by the male-dominated art world, many of them were also wives, some pioneer women with housework and farm work to do and little time for indulging their creative urges. But a few braved the odds and followed their muses even into unexplored territory or subzero weather in search of subjects and inspiration.

Grace Carpenter Hunt, having studied at San Francisco's California School of Design, developed in the 1880s a passion for painting the Pomo Indians that would dominate her life, producing among her better known works *The Empty Basket,* depicting an Indian funeral procession, and *Little Mendocino,* a portrait

Mary Hallock Foote in her studio. *Courtesy The Bettmann Archive.*

of a crying Indian child strapped into a cradleboard. Mary Elizabeth Achey was probably the most prolific woman artist in the West from 1860 to 1885, when she died at age fifty-three. Her earliest works included sketches and oils of Colorado mining camps and various military scenes—works she executed while accompanying her husband to various miliary posts. She blamed him for the death of their only daughter from fever, and she left him to travel about the West and paint continuously. Folklore claimed that she carried her daughter's remains with her for a full year before finally consenting to the child's burial. Helen Tanner Brodt was a noted portraitist who moved, in 1863, from New York to California, where she immortalized, among others, Lily Langtry, the famous actress whose beauty Brodt captured in pastel sometime during the 1890s. Emma Green left Idaho to study art in New York but returned afterward to paint the West she loved and to design, in 1890, the state seal of Idaho, the first in the nation created by a woman. And, too, there was indeed Mary Hallock Foote, best known for

her novels about life in the rough mining camps and towns of the West. But before 1876, she enjoyed a sophisticated life style in New York City as a successful illustrator for such magazines as *Harper's Weekly* and *Scribner's Monthly* and for many books. She continued to produce illustrations for her own work after she married young civil engineer Arthur Foote and moved to raw towns in California, Colorado, and Idaho, where she grew homesick and took up writing short stories and articles as a way to keep in touch with the world of New York publishing.

Georgia O'Keeffe was not only the only woman usually included in collections and studies of Western art, she was also often the only Western artist usually included in collections and studies of modern art. A legendary figure, O'Keeffe first journeyed west in 1912 to teach in Amarillo, Texas, and fell in love with the wild forms, crazy colors, and eerie emptiness of the West's land. Hailed as a "visionary realist," in order—so Dippie says—to differentiate her from the run-of-the-mill realists who dominate Western art in general, she became a hero of modernism and of women's art. So ubiquitous is her work, writes Dippie, that "she is in danger of becoming a pinup girl for the 1990s and her strikingly original images the latest western clichés." Nevertheless, for most art scholars, the isolation that haunts her paintings—from skull and bones to wildflowers to geometric rocks—captures the West, and perhaps especially a woman's West, which was traditionally often defined by loneliness and isolation, as authentically as one of CHARLES MARION RUSSELL's romanticized memorials to horse soldiers and vanished Indian hunters ever did.

—*Patricia Hogan*

SEE ALSO: Art: Western Art

SUGGESTED READING:

Baird, Joseph Armstrong. *Grace Carpenter Hudson (1865–1937): Oil Paintings and Sketches.* San Francisco, 1962.

Barchus, Agnes. *Eliza R. Barchus: The Oregon Artist, 1857–1959.* Portland, Oreg., 1974.

Dippie, W. Brian. "The Visual West." *The Oxford History of the American West.* New York, 1994: 676-705.

Robinson, Roxana. *Georgia O'Keeffe: A Life.* New York, 1989.

WOMEN ON THE SPANISH AND MEXICAN FRONTIER

Mexican women have been survivors and innovators, important creative forces shaping the development of the area now known as the American Southwest. Beginning with the expedition of FRANCISCO VÁSQUEZ DE CORONADO in 1540, Spanish-speaking women migrated to the region decades, even centuries, before their Anglo counterparts. The Spanish colonial government, in efforts to secure its territorial claims, offered a number of inducements to those willing to undertake such an arduous and frequently perilous journey. Subsidies given to a band of settlers headed for Texas included not only food and livestock, but also petticoats and stockings.

Few women ventured to the Mexican North as widows or orphans; most arrived as the wives or daughters of soldiers, farmers, and artisans. Over the course of three centuries, women raised families on the frontier and, working alongside their fathers or husbands, herded cattle and tended crops. These pioneer women also participated in the day-to-day operation of area missions. Whether heralded as centers of civilization or condemned as "concentration camps," the missions, particularly in California, played instrumental roles in the region's economic development and in the acculturation (and decimation) of indigenous peoples.

The Franciscans recruited women into their service. As "housekeeper" of Mission San Gabriel (near Los Angeles), Eulalia Pérez was responsible for the preparation of meals, the allotment of rations, and the manufacture of soap, olive oil, and wine. She taught Indian women to sew in the Spanish fashion, practiced midwifery and folk medicine, and acted as a quartermaster. In her spare time, she dipped chocolates and bottled lemonade.

Women's networks based on ties of blood or fictive kinship proved central to the settlement of the Spanish-Mexican frontier. At times, women settlers acted as midwives to mission Indians, and they baptized sickly or stillborn babies. As godmothers, they established the bonds of *commadrazgo* between indigenous and Spanish and Mexican women. Acculturation was not a one-way street, however. Spanish-speaking women adopted many of the herbal remedies used by indigenous peoples. Eulalia Pérez, for instance, practiced the art of herbal medicine, which she learned from Indian women.

The importance of the *comadre* relationship lasted well beyond the mission era. In *We Fed Them Cactus,* New Mexico native FABIOLA CABEZA DE BACA recalled her grandmother's efforts to control smallpox by becoming a godmother to one child in each family in her village and then insisting on each child's vaccination.

Did a shared "sisterhood" exist between Spanish-Mexican and indigenous women? In her reminiscence, Señora Doña Juana Machado Alipáz de Ridington related how Cesarea, an Indian worker, warned her mistress of an impending attack on their rancho in 1838. Conversely, during the Bear Flag Revolt, a pregnant Rosalía Vallejo de Leese, under house arrest by JOHN CHARLES FRÉMONT and his men, refused to obey Frémont's orders that she turn over her servant for his officers' entertainment.

Historians such as Ramón Gutiérrez, Douglas Monroy, Antonia Castañeda, and Deena González also acknowledge the exploitation that took place *among* women. For women in DOMESTIC SERVICE, racial and class hierarchies undermined any pretense of sisterhood. In San Antonio, Anttonía Lusgardia Ernandes sued her former employer for custody of their son in 1735, Admitting paternity, the man claimed that his former servant had relinquished the child to his wife since his wife had baptized the child. The court, however, granted Ernandes custody. Under these circumstances, the sacrament of baptism did little to promote women's networks.

Indentured servitude was prevalent on the colonial frontier. Ramón Gutiérrez persuasively argues that captive Indians pressed into bondage by New Mexican colonists formed their own caste. After serving their time, these *genízaros* (detribalized peoples) created their own communities separate from the colonists. Bonded labor persisted well into the nineteenth century. California rancher Cave Couts and his wife Ysidora Bandini de Couts regularly appeared before the local courts to secure Indian children from their desperate, indigent parents. For example, a six-year-old child Sasaria became indentured to the Couts family for more than a decade. Indenturement and domestic service brought out the fissures marking colonial society. Bonded labor, however, cut both ways with the capture of Spanish and Mexican women and children during Indian raids. Historian James Brooks indicates that tribal adoption of captives and acculturation of children could soften the situation. "Captives" became "cousins" through the exchanges of women and children between colonists and indigenous peoples in New Mexico, and as a result, a "community of interests" developed between subsistence mestizo (mixed-blood) farmers and their Indian neighbors.

The *comadre* relationship, whether established through baptism or tribal adoption, could foster ties between mestizo colonists and Native Americans. Elites, in contrast, used *compadrazgo* as a venue of social control, whereas mestizos and Indians conferred more egalitarian meanings to the relation.

Spanish and Mexican settlement has been shrouded by myth. Walt Disney's *Zorro,* for example, epitomized the notion of romantic California controlled by fun-loving, swashbuckling rancheros. Scholars have even interpreted the rancho period largely in terms of entertainment. Certainly community rituals were important, but an emphasis on the fandango is akin to studying Anglo settlement within the context of a barn dance. In fairness, many elite Californios perpetuated a rose-colored image of a lost pastoral era. Guadalupe Vallejo, for instance, picturesquely described wash day as an enjoyable outing.

While ranch women, regardless of class, performed traditional female chores, some were accomplished vaqueras or cowgirls. Adventurer William Brewer recorded in his journal an embarrassing incident. In the midst of doing his laundry, Brewer spotted vaqueras herding cattle: "I straightened my aching back, drew a long breath . . . and reflected on the doctrine of woman's rights—I, a stout man, washing my shirt, and those ladies practicing the art of vaqueros."

Married women on the Spanish-Mexican frontier had certain legal advantages not afforded their Anglo peers. Under English common law, women, when they married, became *feme covert* (or dead in the eyes of the legal system), and, thus, they could not own property separate from their husbands. Conversely, Spanish and Mexican women retained control of their land after marriage and held one-half interest in the COMMUNITY PROPERTY they shared with their spouses. Interestingly, Rancho Rodeo de las Aguas, which María Rita Valdez operated well into the 1880s, is now better known as Beverly Hills.

As only 3 percent of California's Spanish and Mexican population could be considered rancheros in 1850, most women did not preside over large ranches but helped manage small family farms. Spanish-speaking women, like their Anglo counterparts, encountered a duality in frontier expectations. While placed on a pedestal as the delicate ladies of romantic verse, women had a variety of strenuous chores and responsibilities.

Life for those settlers changed dramatically in 1848 with the conclusion of the UNITED STATES–MEXICAN WAR, the discovery of gold in California, and the Treaty of Guadalupe Hidalgo. Their world turned upside down, Mexicans on the U.S. side of the border became second-class citizens, divested of their property, political power, and cultural entitlement. Segregated from the Anglo population, Mexican Americans in the BARRIOS of the Southwest sustained their sense of identity and cherished their traditions. With little opportunity for advancement, Mexicans were concentrated in lower-echelon industrial, service, and agricultural jobs. The period of conquest and marginalization, both physical and ideological, did not occur in a dispassionate environment. Stereotypes by which Mexicans were commonly described as lazy, sneaky, and greasy affected rich and poor alike. In Anglo journals, novels, and travelogues, Spanish-speaking women were frequently depicted as flashy, morally deficient sirens.

At times, these images had tragic results. On July 5, 1851, a Mexican woman swung from the gallows, the only woman lynched during the California gold rush. Josefa Segovia (also known as JUANITA OF DOWNIEVILLE) was tried, convicted, and hung the same day she had killed an Anglo miner, who the day before had assaulted her. Remembering his Texas youth, Gilbert Onderdonk mentioned the lynching of several Mexicans, and in recounting how he proposed to his sweetheart, he listed the qualities he felt set him apart from other suitors: "I told her . . . I did not use profane language, never drank whisky, never gambled, and never killed Mexicans."

Wealth and land provided no guarantees of future financial security. When her husband died, PATRICIA DE LEÓN ranked as one of the wealthiest women in the Southwest; yet she was among the first to lose her economic and social position. Although she contributed large sums to support the TEXAS REVOLUTION, she and her family were forced to flee their sprawling South Texas ranch in 1836.

Some historians have asserted that elite families believed they had a greater chance of retaining their land if they acquired an Anglo son-in-law. Intermarriage, however, was no insurance policy. Five years after their marriage in 1849, MARÍA AMPARO RUIZ DE BURTON and her husband Lieutenant Colonel Henry S. Burton purchased Rancho Jamul, a sprawling property of more than one-half million acres. When Henry Burton died in 1869, the ownership of Rancho Jamul came into question. After seven years of litigation, the court awarded Ruiz de Burton and her family only 8,926 acres. Even this amount was challenged by squatters, and she continued to lose acreage in the years that followed. Chronicling her experiences, Ruiz de Burton wrote *The Squatter and the Don* (1885), a fictionalized account of the decline of the ranching class.

Probably the first Spanish or Mexican woman writer in the Southwest, Ruiz de Burton published *Who Would Have Thought It?* her first novel, in 1872. The Cinderella-style romance novel detailed the life of Lola, a Spanish orphan who grew up in a New England household. Ruiz de Burton's maudlin style resembled that of novelist GERTRUDE ATHERTON. However, her not-so-thinly-veiled sexual imagery set her apart from most women writers of her day.

Regarding issues of sexual politics, nineteenth-century Spanish-language newspapers reveal ample information on social mores and expectations. Newspaper editors believed that women had to control the lusts of men. Women were to be cloistered and protected to the extent that some New Mexico residents protested the establishment of coeducational public schools. In 1877, Father Gasparri of *La revista católica* editorialized that women's suffrage would destroy the family. Despite prevailing conventions, Mexican women, due to economic circumstances wrought by political and social disfranchisement, sought employment for wages. Whether in cities or on farms, family members pooled their earnings to put food on the table. Some women worked at home taking in laundry, boarders, and sewing, while others worked in the fields, in restaurants and hotels, and in canneries and laundries.

Mexicans in the Southwest built their own community structures and took pride in their cultural traditions. Yet, the impact of U.S. consumer culture on Mexican American households had its beginnings during the late 1800s. Although advertising did not sweep through the barrios full-force until the 1920s, such items as newfangled household appliances and stylish furnishings and clothing found a receptive market among Mexican women, especially the elite. The Amador family papers, for example, contain photographs in which the Amador daughters proudly display their Gibson-girl hairdos and their bottles of Coca-Cola. Even those of modest means were not immune. A popular ballad, *"Las Caderas"* ("The Bustles"), decried the popularity of Anglo fashions among Mexican women.

Consumer goods and technology could prove advantageous. Labor-saving devices eased domestic and economic burdens. Portable sewing machines helped women support themselves and their families. Sewing by machine increased the productive capacities of seamstresses and could provide a small measure of economic security.

In 1900, more than four hundred thousand Mexicans lived in the Southwest; by 1930, that figure had increased dramatically as more than one million Mexicanos, pushed out by revolution and lured in by prospective jobs, came to the United States. Immigration, urbanization, and industrialization signaled the end of the frontier period. Fabiola Cabeza de Baca briefly summarized the daily experiences of earlier generations of Spanish and Mexican women. "The women . . . had to be resourceful in every way. They were their own doctors, dressmakers, tailors, and advisers." Historians have only begun to reclaim their voices within the legacy of the American West.

—*Vicki L. Ruiz*

SUGGESTED READING:

Brooks, James F. "Captives and Cousins: Bondage and Identity in New Mexico, 1700–1837." M.A. thesis, University of California, Davis, 1991.

Castañeda, Antonia I. "*Presidarias y Pobladoras:* Spanish-Mexican Women in Frontier Monterey, Alta California, 1770–1821." Ph.D. diss., Stanford University, 1990.

Cotera, Marta. *Diosa y Hembra: The History and Heritage of Chicanas in the U.S.* Austin, Tex., 1976.

Deutsch, Sarah. *No Separate Refuge: Culture, Class, and Gender on an Anglo-Hispanic Frontier in the American Southwest, 1880–1940.* New York, 1987.

González, Deena J. "Spanish-Mexican Women on the Santa Fe Frontier: Patters of Their Resistance and Accommodation." Ph.D. diss., University of California, Berkeley, 1985.

Griswold del Castillo, Richard. *La Familia: The Mexican American Family in the Urban Southwest.* Notre Dame, Ind., 1984.

Gutiérrez, Ramón. *When Jesus Came, The Corn Mothers Went Away: Marriage, Sexuality, and Power in New Mexico, 1500–1846.* Stanford, Calif., 1991.

Lara-Cea, Helen. "Notes on the Use of Parish Registers in the Reconstruction of Chicana History in California Prior to 1850." In *Between Borders: Essays on Mexicana/Chicana History.* Edited by Adelaida R. Del Castillo. Los Angeles, 1990.

Miranda, Gloria E. "Hispano-Mexican Childrearing Practices in Pre-American Santa Barbara." *Southern California Historical Quarterly* 65 (Winter 1983): 307–320.

Mirandé, Alfredo, and Evangelina Enríquez. *La Chicana: The Mexican-American Woman.* Chicago, 1979.

Monroy, Douglas. *Thrown among Strangers: The Making of Mexican Culture in Frontier California.* Berkeley, Calif., 1990.

Ruiz, Vicki L., and Susan Tiano, eds. *Women on the U.S.–Mexico Border: Responses to Change.* Boston, 1987.

Veyna, Angelina. "'It is My Last Wish That . . .': A Look at Colonial Nuevo Mexicanas through Their Testaments." In *Building with Our Hands: New Directions in Chicana Studies.* Edited by Adela de la Torre and Beatríz Pesquera. Berkeley, Calif., 1993.

WOMEN IN WAGE WORK

Wage work for women in the West began with the Spanish settlement of New Mexico in the sixteenth century and of California in the late eighteenth century. In New Mexico, between 1535 and 1680, some Pueblo Indian women worked for Spanish settlers as seamstresses, as construction workers to repair houses or churches, and as domestic servants. In California, some native women also became domestic servants for wealthy landowning Spanish elites. When the missions were secularized in the 1830s under the newly independent Mexican government, native women, in many cases left homeless, increased their reliance on wage work as domestic servants.

The participation of women in wage work greatly increased as a result of Euro-American conquest and settlement of the West from 1848 onward. As Euro-Americans sought to mine gold and silver, establish ranching, and build railroads, they both displaced many native, Mexican, and Spanish peoples from their land and drew them further into the wage-labor economy. In the late nineteenth century, in search of new economic opportunities, blacks moved to the West from the East and Chinese and Japanese arrived from Asia. While nonwhite men and many poor white men provided cheap labor for American entrepreneurs, their female counterparts engaged in work that was deemed more suitable to their gender.

In general, however, most women in the West, as in the nation at large, did not engage in wage labor at all. Instead they served as unpaid laborers in the home or on the family farm. For most racial groups, the majority of wage-earning females were single, divorced, or widowed. In California between 1850 and 1880, 20 percent of Mexican households were headed by women. By 1880, this figure climbed to 30 percent. In 1900, in Trinidad, Colorado, women headed 35 to 50 percent of Mexican households. It is likely that most of these women worked for wages. In 1920, about 21 percent of Japanese women in the West worked—a figure comparable to white women at the time. But unlike women of other races, virtually all Japanese women workers were married.

In the nineteenth-century West, the most common work for women of all races engaged in wage labor was DOMESTIC SERVICE—an occupation that did not challenge women's association with unpaid labor in the home. Even as late as 1900, 64 percent of women workers in the West still labored as domestics. In some cases, domestic service was a step down for women. For example, in Santa Fe, New Mexico, Spanish and Mexican women suffered a loss of independence as evidenced by statistics showing that in 1850, working Mexican women included midwives, confectioners, and farmers, but in the 1860 and 1870 censuses, almost all working Mexican women were listed as domestics and laundresses. Many women of all races also worked as personal service workers, including seamstresses, laundresses, and waitresses—occupations that reflected the unpaid labor done by women in their homes. While white women gradually moved out of domestic- and personal-service occupations, these low-paying jobs remained one of the few sources of employment for nonwhite women for the first half of the twentieth century.

Another major type of work for nonwhite women in the nineteenth and early twentieth centuries was seasonal agricultural field work, which edged out domestic service as the dominant occupation of Mexican and Japanese women in the West during the first half of the twentieth century. In Hawaii, women composed 7 percent of all field workers on sugar cane plantations in 1894 and 14 percent by 1920. Most of these women were Japanese immigrants. One-third of all Japanese women workers on the mainland in 1920 also engaged in agricultural work. Mexican women labored alongside their husbands in the summer in the sugar-beet fields of Colorado at the turn of the century. Native women also engaged in seasonal harvest work to eke out a subsistence life.

The canning and food-processing industry also offered another source of income for women in the late nineteenth and twentieth centuries. The food-processing industry, whose work force was 75 percent female, remained one of the top five industries in California from its beginning in the 1860s until 1963. Canneries first employed Irish, Italian, Greek, and Portuguese women and then began hiring Mexican women in the 1880s. In the twentieth century, canneries employed large numbers of foreign-born women.

Up until 1918, when it was criminalized in most states, PROSTITUTION served as another type of wage work for women of all races. In some mining towns such as Helena, Montana, prostitutes composed the largest group of white working women until 1900. In the Southwest, Mexican and native women who lived on the borders of army towns and forts sometimes also resorted to prostitution. When faced with limited options for earning a living, they voluntarily chose prostitution as a source of income. The case of Chinese prostitutes differs from that of other women. In 1871, 61 percent of Chinese women in California were prostitutes. Generally, Chinese women were sold into prostitution and forced to work off their indenture contracts in miserable conditions in San Francisco and many mining towns. But by 1880, only 24 percent of Chinese women in California practiced prostitution.

White Western women from middle-class backgrounds found other options for wage work in the West in the late nineteenth and early twentieth centuries. Some women who owned homes earned wages by operating boarding houses. In 1870 in Helena, Montana, for instance, 20 percent of women kept boarders; 27 percent did so in 1880. Other white, middle-class women entered the work force in the nineteenth century as teachers, missionaries, and nurses—jobs that were also traditionally associated with women but that held professional status. In this time period, too, new clerical jobs and department store clerking opened up as white-collar job opportunities for women.

Until 1930, most women in the West remained on the land as unpaid agricultural laborers for their family's farm operations. After 1930, however, due to a process of increased urbanization and trends toward larger, mechanized farms, many farm families moved from the land to urban areas, and more women entered the wage economy. The DUST BOWL and the Great Depression, too, caused severe hardship and encouraged more women to engage in wage labor. Unlike the predominant white middle-class model of the male breadwinner who provided for his family while his wife kept house, many nonwhite families and poorer white families instead practiced a family wage economy, in which most members of the family worked and pooled their income to earn a meager, subsistence living. For example, in the 1930s in San Diego, 50 percent of Mexican wives worked for wages, contributing 20 percent of the household income. Mexican children in San Diego earned 35 percent of their families' wages. In Albuquerque and Denver, 65 percent of Mexican American girls between the ages of fifteen and nineteen worked for wages—two-thirds of them in domestic service.

Although the exigencies of the Depression caused more women to enter the labor force, the New Deal actually reinforced old labor patterns and limited opportunities for women to earn money. In Albuquerque and Denver, for instance, the proportion of Mexican

women in domestic service rose in the 1930s. During this decade, the population of blacks in the West also grew. In 1930, forty thousand blacks lived in Los Angeles, the majority of them female. Of these, 50 percent worked—almost 87 percent of them in domestic service. Between 1910 and 1945, Sioux Indian women, too, turned to wage labor to supplement income earned from leasing their lands. Since most federal jobs such as farm labor and construction went to men, however, Sioux women resorted to domestic service.

Women increasingly entered wage work after the 1930s, but most female workers were still relegated to "women's" occupations. Only those jobs that could be seen as extensions of their jobs in the home or those jobs with technologies that became feminized (such as typewriting) were deemed suitable for women. Within this gender-stratified job market, women earned considerably lower wages than men. Even women's professional work in the fields of teaching and NURSING paid lower than men's professional—or men's unskilled—labor. Employers defended lower wages for women by arguing that women did not work as the sole breadwinners for their families or that they only worked for surplus income. Employers ignored statistics that showed that most working women were single, divorced, or widowed and often were the heads of household. Employers also overlooked the fact that, by the 1930s, many married women worked to supplement their husband's meager earnings. Although women did not relish their low wages, they nevertheless sometimes preferred the seasonal nature of canning or the flexible schedule of domestic work as they mixed family responsibilities with paid labor.

Nonwhite women suffered not only from gender stratification in the labor market but also from racial stratification. Nonwhite women routinely received lower wages than white women for the same work. Due to racial discrimination, employers also denied access to more prestigious professional and managerial white-collar jobs to all but a handful of nonwhite women. Many Mexican American women, for example, worked seasonally for low wages in canneries and found it difficult to break into full-time, more skilled jobs. Even second-generation Mexican American girls who sought higher education in hopes of securing white-collar jobs faced discrimination. In Colorado in 1930, only 5 percent of employed Chicanas worked as teachers, clerks, or other professionals.

With the advent of World War II and a sudden shortage of labor, gender and racial discrimination broke down, at least temporarily. No longer limited to traditional "women's work," Western women took jobs as welders, steamfitters, and electricians. The aircraft industry opened up jobs to women as never before.

Nationally, during the war, 30 percent of aircraft workers were women; in Los Angeles, this figure climbed to 42 percent. Racial stratification also relaxed as black women gained a foothold in new defense industries. Thousands of Southern black families went to the San Francisco area to take jobs in the defense industry.

After the war, the government mounted a campaign to return women to their homes. Some women did follow the dictates of social norms and governmental propaganda; still, the numbers of women in the work force rose throughout the 1950s, and women workers once again found themselves segregated into "women's" occupations.

Although racial discrimination remained a factor in determining the types of jobs nonwhite women could gain, some nonwhite women succeeded in breaking out of racially typed jobs to become secretaries, saleswomen, nurses, and teachers. For example, 47 percent of Japanese American women, segregated in domestic service and agricultural wage labor before the war, served in clerical, sales, and operative positions by 1950. Only 10 percent still labored in domestic service. In the Southwest, the percentage of Mexican American women employed in service occupations decreased from 38.4 percent in 1930 to 22.7 percent in 1980, in farm work from 20.7 percent in 1930 to 2.9 percent in 1980, while the proportion of Mexican American women in white-collar work climbed from 15.4 percent in 1930 to 48.8 percent in 1980. For native women, however, options for wage work did not generally improve. From 1945 to 1972, the only major source of employment for Sioux women was work in the potato and sugar-beet fields or continued domestic service. For California native women, the federal government's policy of encouraging urbanization resulted in low-paying, dead-end jobs, or unemployment.

From the 1960s through the 1980s, women's participation in the wage economy increased in the West as it did throughout the nation. In 1978 in California, 52 percent of all women over the age of sixteen worked, composing 42 percent of the work force. Mexican American women in particular, entered the work force in large numbers while white, black, and Asian women's participation in the work force increased more slowly or remained constant. In the 1970s and 1980s, new jobs in the Southwest, particularly in the electronics and apparel industries, contributed to the entrance of Mexican American women into the labor force. Some native women, such as the Sioux, now have greater options for professional work such as teaching and social service as well as clerical occupations. Nevertheless, a second wave of immigrant women from Southeast Asia who have settled in the West still work for low pay in garment factories, in the service sector,

and in agricultural field work. Professional women who immigrated from China, Korea, and the Philippines in the 1970s and 1980s have suffered occupational downgrading as a result of language difficulties and outright racial and gender discrimination.

—*Margaret D. Jacobs*

SEE ALSO: Teachers on the Frontier; Working-class Women

SUGGESTED READING:

Albers, Patricia. "Sioux Women in Transition: A Study of their Changing Status in Domestic and Capitalist Sectors of Production." In *The Hidden Half: Studies of Plains Indian Women.* Edited by Patricia Albers and Beatrice Medicine. New York, 1983.

Armitage, Susan, and Elizabeth Jameson, eds. *The Women's West.* Norman, Okla., 1987.

Deutsch, Sarah. *No Separate Refuge: Culture, Class, and Gender on an Anglo-Hispanic Frontier in the American Southwest, 1880–1940.* New York, 1987.

DuBois, Ellen Carol, and Vicki L. Ruiz, eds. *Unequal Sisters: A Multicultural Reader in U.S. Women's History.* New York, 1990.

Glenn, Evelyn Nakano. *Issei, Nisei, War Bride: Three Generations of Japanese American Women in Domestic Service.* Philadelphia, 1986.

Jensen, Joan, and Gloria Ricci Lothrop. *California Women: A History.* San Francisco, 1987.

Petrik, Paula. *No Step Backward: Women and Family on the Rocky Mountain Mining Frontier, Helena, Montana, 1865–1900.* Helena, Mont., 1987.

Ruiz, Vicki L. *Cannery Women, Cannery Lives: Mexican Women, Unionization, and the California Food Processing Industry, 1930-50.* Albuquerque, N. Mex., 1987.

———. "'And Miles to Go . . .': Mexican Women and Work, 1930–1985." In *Western Women: Their Land, Their Lives.* Edited by Lillian Schlissel, Vicki L. Ruiz, and Janice Monk. Albuquerque, N. Mex., 1988.

Takaki, Ronald. *Strangers from a Different Shore: A History of Asian Americans.* New York, 1989.

WOMEN'S CLUBS AND ORGANIZATIONS

Western women established a multitude of organizations for self-improvement, charitable work, and civic reform. From the mid-nineteenth century to the 1930s, these societies and clubs, like those that existed in the East, put members in touch with each other to discuss social problems and issues, devise strategies for change, and execute plans to create institutions, laws, and programs for the benefit of their communities. Traditionalists, who adhered to the belief that women's responsibilities should be limited to home and family, frowned on the idea of women having any impact on the public world; yet millions of club women defied the convention that a "woman's place is in the home" by uniting to voice opinions and engage in reform in the public world outside their households.

Women's organizations were plentiful in Western cities and towns, which offered state and local branches of national organizations of every type. Clubs and organizations for women in the West focused on benevolence (Red Cross, P. E. O., Florence Crittendon Homes for Fallen Women), religion (missions, ladies' aid societies, Ladies' Hebrew Benevolent Society, national Methodist, Lutheran, Presbyterian, and Episcopal women's groups), youth (Parent-Teachers Associations, Young Women's Christian Association, Girl Scouts, 4-H, Camp Fire Girls, Junior League), patriotism (Daughters of the American Revolution, National Society of Colonial Dames of America), community improvement (General Federation of Women's Clubs, National Association of Colored Women's Clubs, WOMAN'S CHRISTIAN TEMPERANCE UNION), work (National Federation of Business and Professional Women's Clubs, Altrusa, Soroptomist), education (American Association of University Women, sororities, alumnae associations), arts (National Federation of Music Clubs, Garden Clubs of America), politics (League of Women Voters, National Woman Suffrage Association, NATIONAL WOMAN'S PARTY, Women's Legislative Council, women's committees of the major political parties), and women's auxiliaries to men's secret societies and mutual-aid associations.

Although rural women faced the special obstacle of geographical isolation, they formed many of the groups mentioned above and became active in a net work for farmers, the Grange. In contrast with women in other parts of the United States, Western women created organizations that recognized and celebrated their pioneer ancestors in the West, including Daughters of the Pioneers of Utah. It is worth noting that women also played an important role in organizations dominated by male membership. For example, Nettie Asberry of Tacoma, Washington, founded one of the earliest branches of the National Association for the Advancement of Colored People. Women formed the bulk of the membership in the local circles or centers of the Drama League of America, although they were underrepresented in the leadership of the organization.

Most of the early clubs Western women founded were devoted to traditional concerns of women. In 1838, six wives of missionaries created the Columbia Maternal Association, near present-day Walla Walla, Washington, for the purpose of considering modern methods of child raising. In 1843, Mormon women

formed the RELIEF SOCIETY, which provided social welfare assistance for needy women and children of their faith. During the Civil War, Western women formed Sanitary Commissions to raise money for supplies for Union soldiers.

Late nineteenth-century women established several organizations to bring social services to their communities: orphanages, women's refuges, children's hospitals, public libraries, and settlement houses. For example, San Diego's Woman's Home Association established a haven for poor women in 1887, and Denver women organized in 1886 to maintain the Colorado Cottage Home for unmarried mothers. In Oregon, the Federation of Women's Clubs raised money for the children's hospital in Portland and aid for tubercular patients.

The rage in the East for literary clubs was reflected in the West. In 1875, CAROLINE MARIA SEYMOUR SEVERANCE moved to Los Angeles from Boston, where seven years before, she had founded one of the earliest American women's clubs for self-improvement and civic reform. On the Pacific Coast, she immediately moved to replicate her Massachusetts enterprise. After several false starts, the Friday Morning Club was founded in 1891. The Women's Board of Trade (later the Woman's Club of Santa Fe) was founded in 1892. In Washington State, the first woman's literary club was founded in the state's capitol; the Olympia Woman's Club, like many of its counterparts, celebrated its centennial in 1983. In Columbia Falls, Montana, the Clionic Circle was founded in 1893. The earliest black women's club in New Mexico was the Home Circle Club, founded in 1914 in Albuquerque to provide the library with materials about African Americans and to provide scholarships for students. Such organizations provided opportunities for members to read and discuss modern plays, poetry, essays, novels, and classic works of fiction and history. Sometimes the debates led members to investigate social problems and take action to effect change.

At the dawn of the twentieth century, women's organizations launched impressive campaigns for municipal reform. They lobbied for a wide range of state and local legislation, including conservation measures, civil-service programs, public-health measures, and educational improvements. The Woman's Club of Cheyenne, Wyoming, established the city's public library; club women of northern California rallied to save the redwoods; Colorado clubs preserved Mesa Verde; and Washington women lobbied for the registration of nurses.

Western women expressed early support for political activities, particularly for women's rights, and they had considerable success, winning the vote decades before their Eastern counterparts. Wyoming women voted in 1869, Utah in 1870, Colorado in 1893, Idaho in 1896, Washington in 1910, California in 1911, and Oregon in 1912. Not until 1920 did the federal constitutional amendment ensure the vote for women across the country.

By the 1920s, Western women enjoyed more opportunities for public activities than their grandmothers had. While club members were disappointed that their new right to vote did not grant them a major voice in the American political system, they continued to initiate and maintain social-welfare programs and lobby government to do the same. By the mid-twentieth century, mayors and governors recognized the influence of women's clubs by appointing club leaders to boards that directed the educational, social-welfare, and arts agencies of the Western states.

—*Karen J. Blair*

SEE ALSO: Women's Suffrage

SUGGESTED READING:

Blair, Karen J. *The History of American Women's Voluntary Organizations, 1810–1960: A Guide to Sources.* Boston, 1989.

Derr, Jill Mulvay, Janath Russell Cannon, and Maureen Ursenbach Beecher. *Women of Covenant: The Story of Relief Society.* Salt Lake City, 1992.

Pascoe, Peggy. *Relations of Rescue: The Search for Female Moral Authority in the American West, 1874–1939.* New York, 1990.

Schackel, Sandra. *Social Housekeepers: Women Shaping Public Policy in New Mexico, 1920–1940.* Albuquerque, N. Mex., 1992.

WOMEN'S NATIONAL INDIAN ASSOCIATION

The Women's National Indian Association, founded in 1884, was a reform-oriented organization of upper- and middle-class women who worked on behalf of the American Indian during the last quarter of the nineteenth century and the first half of the twentieth century. The WNIA had its beginnings in the spring of 1879 when Mary Lucinda Bonney, founder of the Chestnut Street Female Seminary, reported to the Women's Home Mission Circle of the First Baptist Church that railroads and settlers were entering the Indian Territory in direct violation of federal treaties. When the home mission circle took no action, Bonney sought help from Amelia Stone Quinton, a fellow reformer. In the time-honored feminist tradition of networking with those who shared similar values and

hopes, Bonney and Quinton, joined by like-minded women, began a petition drive to protest the invasion of the Indian Territory. To call attention to the mistreatment of the Indian, they established the Women's National Indian Association, formed a network of standing committees and departments, and published a monthly periodical, *The Indian's Friend*. To disseminate WNIA literature, leading members—including Quinton, who served as president for almost two decades—spoke before missionary and women's groups and toured the country to establish new branches and auxiliaries. By the end of the nineteenth century, almost forty states had WNIA branches or auxiliaries, and the WNIA, in league with the male-dominated INDIAN RIGHTS ASSOCIATION (1882) and the Lake Mohonk Conference of the Friends of the Indians (1883), exerted considerable influence over government Indian policy.

Seeing little value in preserving Indian culture and strongly influenced by evangelical Christianity, members of the Indian Rights Association sought to remold Indian males into Jeffersonian farmers, and members of the WNIA attempted to turn Indian women into Victorian homemakers. WNIA members vowed to raise Indian women from "pagan darkness, degradation, destitution and suffering into the light of Christian faith." The WNIA Missionary Department sponsored missionaries among such tribes as the Ponca, Oto, Sioux, Bannock, Shoshone, Omaha, Kiowa, Apache, Kickapoo, Seminole, Absentee Shawnee, Hopi, Piegan, Navajo, Mission Indians in southern California, and the Hoopa (Hupa) and Round Valley Indians of northern California. Their work, never intended to be permanent, served as a bridge until either a regular missionary society or the federal government assumed responsibility of the various missions. Besides underwriting the expenses of missionaries and constructing mission buildings and hospitals, the WNIA sponsored the medical education of Indian women, including that of SUSAN LAFLESCHE PICOTTE, an Omaha woman, who later became a WNIA medical missionary.

The WNIA's efforts are difficult to assess. Individual land allotment and forced assimilation policies failed because they were unrealistic. Nevertheless, the WNIA offered new homes, Christmas boxes, education, and medical care to individual tribal members. In the process, WNIA members, limited by the nineteenth-century concept of "woman's sphere" and therefore often confined to church-related activities, broadened their horizons by entering the Indian reform movement. This activity enabled them to bring their social housekeeping skills to a broader segment of society. The WNIA, known later as the National Indian Association, continued its operations until May 31, 1951.

—*Valerie Sherer Mathes*

SEE ALSO: United States Indian Policy: Reform Movement

SUGGESTED READING:

Mathes, Valerie Sherer. *Helen Hunt Jackson and Her Indian Reform Legacy*. Austin, Tex., 1990.

———. "Nineteenth Century Women and Reform: The Women's National Indian Association." *The American Indian Quarterly* 14 (Winter 1990): 1–18.

Wanken, Helen M. "Woman's Sphere and Indian Reform: The Women's National Indian Association 1879–1901." Ph.D. diss., Marquette University, 1981.

WOMEN'S RELIEF SOCIETY (LDS)

SEE: Relief Society (LDS)

WOMEN'S SUFFRAGE

A puzzle confronts historians when they study the role of the trans-Mississippi West in the women's suffrage movement. The campaign to grant women the right to vote began in the East, yet most states that enfranchised women before 1920, when the women's suffrage amendment to the United States Constitution was ratified, were in the West. By 1914, six years before the national amendment passed, women could vote in the following Western states: Wyoming (1869), Utah (1870), Colorado (1893), Idaho (1896), Washington (1910), California (1911), Arizona (1912), Kansas, (1912), Oregon (1912), Nevada (1914), and Montana (1914). In addition, the Alaska Territory granted women the vote in 1913. By contrast, Eastern states lagged behind. Illinois granted women the right to vote in presidential elections in 1913, but not until the New York victory of 1917 did any state east of the Mississippi grant women the right to vote in every election. As late as 1920, only one other state east of the Mississippi River, Michigan, had joined New York and fully enfranchised its female citizens.

Historians have long sought to explain why the West accepted women's suffrage so much earlier and to such a greater extent than any other region. Many explanations have been proposed only to be criticized. Initially, many people believed that the region's suffrage victories were due to a Western culture that was more democratic than Eastern culture, but few scholars today accept that argument.

In the late 1960s, social scientist Alan Grimes made the opposite argument. He hypothesized that white male community leaders saw women's suffrage as a means to empower themselves and that men hoped to use this power to impose their particular social values. Grimes's explanation makes sense of the early suffrage victories in Wyoming and Utah and, perhaps, Idaho. But his hypothesis fails to explain subsequent victories in other states—victories that occurred after an active women's movement had developed in the West.

Other explanations abound. The "newness" of the West might have played a role. Laws were technically easier to pass in territories, and new states might have been more willing to consider innovative legislation, such as women's suffrage. Yet if newness did play a role, it was not the only reason, because many Western territories and states repeatedly voted against giving women the ballot.

Perhaps a more important factor for women's suffrage victories in the West was their relationship to various social movements. The first suffrage victories in Wyoming (1869) and Utah (1870), for example, came during Reconstruction. The end of the Civil War

An 1888 weekly magazine recorded women of Cheyenne, Wyoming, exercising their right to vote. *Courtesy Library of Congress.*

prompted a debate about the nature of American citizenship, and although much of the discussion centered on newly freed African American men, women's rights advocates took the opportunity to raise the issue of women's citizenship and their ability to vote. The two suffrage victories of the 1890s, Colorado in 1893 and Idaho in 1896, were tied to the Populist movement, an uprising of Southern and Western farmers, who protested against an economic structure they believed favored corporate monopoly over the family farm. Later suffrage victories in the West, beginning with the 1910 victory in Washington State, were linked to the Progressive movement, a national movement of radicals and reformers who sought humane ways to hold together a nation that was being violently pulled apart by industrial capitalism.

But the connection to reform cannot answer the whole question either. Since these reform movements flourished in regions outside the West, historians have to explain why women's full voting rights failed to develop anywhere except the West until the 1917 New York State victory. So far, they have suggested that during Reconstruction, Wyoming and Utah enfranchised women for reasons unique to these states. They have also argued that the Populist movement failed to enfranchise women in the South because of white Southern racism; white Southerners denied African American men the right to vote in the late nineteenth century and feared that opening voting booths to white women would also open them to African Americans, men and women. But since many whites in the West also wanted suffrage reserved for themselves, the reasons for the suffrage victories linked to POPULISM in the West are not entirely clear either. And the question of why Eastern states, which contained cities that were often vibrant centers of Progressive reform, failed to give women the ballot before the 1917 New York victory remains baffling. Suffragists themselves often blamed the urban immigrant working class. Yet immigrant workers in New York City, mobilized mostly by socialists, made suffrage possible in the state. For whatever reason, women in the East were initially unable to build the necessary political coalitions to gain victories.

Clearly, traditional interpretations of women's suffrage in the West do not adequately explain its success. In order to understand the development of women's suffrage in the West, we must look to the women themselves and go back to when they first organized the suffrage movement. In 1848 at Seneca Falls, New York, a group of women, mostly white and active in abolitionism (the movement to free slaves), called a meeting in order to demand rights for women, including the right to vote. The demand for the vote almost failed

to pass the convention because it was considered so radical. Americans believed that when male heads of households voted, they spoke for all dependent members of their families. People feared that if women achieved the right to vote as individuals, first the family and then the social order would fall apart. Despite these fears, women's rights advocates accepted the demand for women's enfranchisement because they believed in the full humanity of women and thus in their full individual rights.

Until the end of the Civil War, the women's rights movement remained a small one, linked to abolitionism and based in a few Eastern states. When the war was over, activists tried to persuade the Republicans to grant universal adult suffrage, enfranchising both women and freed slaves. The Republican party chose, instead, to extend citizenship only to African American men. Advocates for women tried to change Republican policy by demonstrating, in various states, that it was possible to win political rights for both groups. In particular, suffragists devoted their resources to the 1867 Kansas election where voters were asked to enfranchise African American men and all women.

Because both suffrage measures lost, the Kansas campaign became a turning point for the movement. After witnessing the Republican attack on women's suffrage, women leaders knew that their hopes of winning universal adult suffrage through the Republican party—then or in the immediate future—had been dashed. Suffragists divided over the best response to the situation, and their divisions led, in 1869, to the formation of two separate suffrage organizations.

One of them, the American Woman Suffrage Association (AWSA), argued that the suffragists' best chance was to follow the Republican party, supporting its efforts to enfranchise African American men and trusting that Republicans would eventually support women's enfranchisement. New England Republicans and reformers, men and women, helped develop the AWSA, which remained largely an East Coast organization. The other organization, the National Woman Suffrage Association (NWSA), called for suffragists to leave the Republican party, to refuse to support the enfranchisement of only black men, and to make women's rights their first priority. The NWSA's call for women to develop their own movement meant searching for a larger constituency—a search that led it to the West where the NWSA began organizing women as early as 1869.

Political struggles after the Civil War, such as the 1867 Kansas election, made women's suffrage part of the postwar national news. Wyoming politicians enfranchised women in the territory in 1869 by arguing that the publicity of being the first to give women the vote would entice steady farm families to move into an area then renowned for its lawlessness. Although the documents show that pioneers did not come in record numbers, the territory announced itself pleased with the results and became a state in 1890 with women's suffrage.

Meanwhile, the Mormon community in the Utah territory worried that the federal government would respond to growing public opposition to the Mormon practice of polygamy by outlawing this Mormon marriage practice or refusing to allow Utah to become a state. Some Radical Republicans in Congress argued that women in Utah should be given the right to vote. The Radicals based their argument upon the belief that just as ex-slaves would use the ballot to maintain their freedom, so Mormon women would vote to end polygamy. Mormon leaders responded by giving Utah women the ballot in 1870. The leaders predicted, accurately, that Mormon women would vote to maintain the church and hoped that women's suffrage would dispel the popular images of "enslaved" Mormon women. When Utah women lost their right to vote in 1887 due to the national antipolygamy campaign, they responded by organizing a Utah Woman Suffrage Association; when Utah entered the Union in 1896, it did so with women's suffrage.

Women played only a small role in gaining the initial victories in Wyoming and Utah because an indigenous women's movement did not exist in either territory during Reconstruction. But during the last two decades of the nineteenth century, women throughout the trans-Mississippi West, indeed throughout the nation, transformed the suffrage movement as new organizations increased the movement's numbers and changed its objectives.

The WOMAN'S CHRISTIAN TEMPERANCE UNION (WCTU), the largest women's civic organization of the era, played a crucial role in the transformation. The WCTU spread throughout the trans-Mississippi West during the 1880s, initially calling for suffrage largely so that women could protect the home by prohibiting Americans, mostly men, from drinking alcohol. During the 1880s and 1890s, however, many temperance women came to believe they should vote because it was their right to do so. Some WCTU activists believed that, along with women's rights and temperance, they should develop the Cooperative Commonwealth, an America based on more just distribution of resources. Populist women (who were often temperance women) agreed; together they demanded votes for women. Some of these protesters also belonged to WOMEN'S CLUBS AND ORGANIZATIONS. Developed in the urban West during the 1880s first as places for women to study culture, women's clubs sometimes became bases from which

Caroline Nichols Churchill promoted the cause of women's suffrage in her *Colorado Antelope* and *Queen Bee. Courtesy Library of Congress.*

their members worked for social change, sometimes calling for women's suffrage. By the 1890s, an activist women's movement flourished in the West, and many of its members believed women should vote so they could change the country.

In Colorado, the women's movement, with support from the state's Populist movement, won women's suffrage in 1893. Populist government officials put the suffrage amendment before the male electorate, and the women persuaded male voters to pass it. The women built a coalition that stretched from the Populists, who were miners as well as farmers in Colorado, to Republican businessmen in Denver. The decisive number of votes came from Populist counties, but the Colorado women's movement—a mix of temperance women, socialist women, clubwomen, and women in the labor movement—could clearly claim they won the election themselves.

The 1896 suffrage victory in Idaho shares similarities with both the Colorado and Utah victories. As in Colorado, the Populist party placed the suffrage referendum before the voters, and the women built a broad coalition to support it. Unlike Colorado, however, Idaho had a number of Mormon settlers who favored women's suffrage, perhaps because they were familiar with it and perhaps because it would double the political clout of their community. Whatever the reason, Mormon settlers proved crucial to winning women's suffrage in Idaho.

That same year, voters in California rejected women's suffrage; for the next fourteen years, voters in every state refused to grant women full enfranchisement. An examination of the 1896 defeat in California illuminates why suffragists experienced such a long period of disappointment. In California, rural and Los Angeles voters, who were mostly native-born whites and Protestants, supported suffrage; San Francisco voters, who were more diverse, did not, and their opposition defeated the measure. Suffragists, who were themselves mostly affluent, white Protestants, blamed their defeat in San Francisco on liquor interests and the immigrant working class. Indeed, the alcohol industry, fearful that women would vote for prohibition, supported antisuffrage activity; and immigrants, who often accepted drinking as legitimate, worried about empowering a movement whose leaders publicly denigrated immigrants and the immigrant vote. Ultimately, suffrage would win despite the opposition of the liquor industry but only after suffragists built a coalition that included immigrant workers.

During the first decade of the twentieth century, a new suffrage strategy developed when elite women members of the women's movement began forming alliances with white working-class women wage earners. Both groups of women saw the alliance as a means to advance women's rights in the work place and the ballot as a necessary tool to secure those rights. Women who built these alliances were also building the Progressive movement; they hoped to create more social justice in America. By the 1910s, these efforts made the women's movement, for the first time, a mass movement that crossed class and, to a lesser extent, racial lines. Women now demanded the vote for a variety of reasons—to protect their class and racial interests, to bring women's values into the public arena, and to give women their full citizenship.

The revitalized movement enabled women to win the vote in Washington State in 1910 and in California the following year. In both cases, women won because they, like the Colorado women in 1893, built an inclusive coalition. In California, women Progressives successfully lobbied the male Progressives to place a suffrage referendum before the voters. Women with ties to the labor movement and the Socialist party helped provide the margin of victory by persuading enough working-class men to support women's suffrage.

In 1912, women gained three more suffrage victories—in Arizona, Oregon and Kansas—bringing the total number of suffrage states to nine. At this point, the West began once again to attract the attention of national suffrage leaders. The most militant of these was Alice Paul, leader of the newly organized Congressional Union (CU). Paul believed the nine Western states with women's suffrage could provide a power base strong enough to enable women to demand that the United States Congress pass a national suffrage amendment. In 1914, Paul and the CU launched a campaign; the CU called on Western women voters to "punish the party in power," the Democrats, for their failure to achieve a national suffrage amendment. When the Democrats lost twenty-three positions in a campaign for forty-three seats, the CU gained considerable attention and, even more important, attracted a growing number of militant young supporters, many from the West, who called themselves "feminists." The new members reveled in the CU tactic of using Western women's voting power to demand electoral power for all women because they believed it provided the best means for women to achieve full equality.

The CU believed that the necessary conditions to launch a national campaign for the women's suffrage amendment had been met. The Alaska Territory enfranchised women in 1913; both Nevada and Montana gave the ballot to women (thanks in large part to the socialists) in 1914. The CU planned three activities in 1915 to build on these gains: it launched an organizing drive in every state; it held the first national convention of women voters at the Panama-Pacific Exposition in San Francisco; and it sent President Woodrow Wilson, a Democrat, a massive suffrage petition, delivered by Sara Bard Field, who drove an automobile from San Francisco to Washington in a successful publicity stunt. Before Field arrived in Washington, Wilson committed himself to voting for women's suffrage in New Jersey, hoping to gain the support of Western women voters for his reelection in 1916. In the campaign, thanks to the Western suffrage states and the CU, the suffrage struggle entered the arena of national politics.

Wilson narrowly won the election. Since many attributed his victory to the votes of Western women, the campaign provided a vivid example of female electoral power on the national level. Only months after Wilson's second inauguration in 1917, the United States entered World War I. The suffrage campaign became part of the national debate about the nature of citizenship during a war, and the process of adopting the national suffrage amendment began in earnest. In 1920, the required two-thirds of the states ratified the Nineteenth Amendment to the Constitution guaranteeing women the right to vote.

Despite the adoption of the amendment, American women of color could not always exercise their right to vote. African American women had supported women's enfranchisement, and although their numbers were small in the West, they formed suffrage groups throughout the region. Yet African American women in Texas and Oklahoma had to launch separate political fights for their right to vote in 1920. (Black women in Texas subsequently transformed their suffrage groups into civil-rights organizations.) Other women of color also faced barriers either to gaining citizenship or, if citizens, to exercising the right to vote. In 1924, the United States Congress granted citizenship to all Native Americans, a departure from previous measures that had extended citizenship on a piecemeal basis, but Indians could not vote in every state until 1948. The first generation of Chinese and Japanese immigrants could not become American citizens, although their children born in this country were citizens. Mexican American women's voting rights varied, depending on where they lived and when. Hispanic women in New Mexico voted and held office; however, other Western states often found ways to disfranchise American citizens of Mexican descent.

In the end, women worked for more than seventy years to achieve the right to vote; their suffrage campaign took longer than any other kind of electoral reform. But women's suffrage was not simply an electoral reform. Women demanded the vote because they wanted full citizenship and equal political power. The women who struggled for the right to vote changed women's position in society and gained power and rights, and they did so through the women's movement. Women's ability to organize themselves, to speak for themselves, and to act for themselves made them powerful.

—*Gayle Gullett*

SEE ALSO: Progressivism; Socialism

SUGGESTED READING:

Beeton, Beverly. *Women Vote in the West: The Woman Suffrage Movement, 1869–1896.* New York, 1986.

Buhle, Mari Jo. *Women and American Socialism 1870–1920.* Urbana, Ill., 1981.

Deutsch, Sarah. *No Separate Refuge: Culture, Class, and Gender on an Anglo-Hispanic Frontier in the American Southwest, 1880–1940.* New York, 1987.

DuBois, Ellen. *Feminism and Suffrage: The Emergence of an Independent Women's Movement in America 1848–1869.* New York, 1978.

Lunardini, Christine A. *From Equal Suffrage to Equal Rights: Alice Paul and the National Woman's Party, 1910–1928.* New York, 1986.

Myres, Sandra L. *Westering Women and the Frontier Experience 1800–1915.* Albuquerque, N. Mex., 1982.

Stefanco, Carolyn. "Networking on the Frontier: The Colorado Women's Suffrage Movement, 1876–1893." *The Women's West.* Edited by Susan Armitage and Elizabeth Jameson. Norman, Okla., 1987.

Terborg-Penn, Rosalyn. "Nineteenth Century Black Women and Woman Suffrage." *Potomac Review* 7 (Spring-Summer 1977): 13–24.

———. "Discontented Black Feminists: Prelude and Postscript to the Passage of the Nineteenth Amendment." In *Decades of Discontent: The Women's Movement, 1920–1940.* Edited by Lois Scharf and Joan M. Jensen. Westport, Conn., 1983.

WOMEN, WORKING-CLASS

SEE: Working class Women

WOMEN WRITERS

Until the 1970s, women writers in general, much less Western women writers, were, with a few exceptions, usually excluded from the American literary canon and the scholarship about that canon. In 1940, William Forrest Sprague wrote of Western women writers in his *Women and the West: A Short Social History:* "While the amount of literature on the West produced by women may not be noteworthy for its volume, still such writings have often been definite contributions. . . . Since woman, more than man, is regarded as a civilizing agent, perhaps she is in the best position to analyze the forces which created the blend civilization of," in effect, the trans-Mississippi West. The growth later in the twentieth century of, first, women's studies programs and, then, gender studies as academic disciplines suggested that the reason the work of women writers was not noteworthy for its volume had less to do with the literature Western women produced than with the attention paid such work. At the same time, the idea that women had a unique perspective on the American West was reinforced. It was not so much that they were civilizers, however, that gave them this perspective, but that they were women, a gender whose social position—as Susan Armitage has pointed out—put them in a situation different from men, one which in many ways led them to a more realistic assessment of Western life.

One of the commonplaces of American literary history has become that regional writing in the late nineteenth and early twentieth century was significant not merely for its local color and its literary realism, but also because it gave women writers the opportunity to render the actual conditions of women in American society or to explore their perceptions of reality. In a region that—for Euro-Americans—was predominately male for many years, which took pride in its masculine culture even after Euro-American women began to arrive in some numbers, and whose myths and literature frequently centered around male codes of behavior, what female writers saw and wrote about could serve as a sober antidote to a long violent fantasy about the frontier. We are not dealing here with Native American literature, Mexican American literature, or Asian American literature, and generalizing even about Euro-American women writers, who were, after all, engaged in creating individual works of art, runs some risk of disservice to their particular accomplishments. Nevertheless, patterns and common concerns do emerge from the regional literature.

One common denominator among westering women writers, especially in California beginning with the gold-rush days, was simply a determination to write, to be heard, which in wide-open San Francisco soon became something like the *freedom* to write and be heard. In a society where the men outnumbered women twelve to one, just being there said something about the woman writer's robust nature and openness to change. Louisa Clapp, better known by her nom de plume "Dame Shirley," called herself "a regular Nomad" and admitted to a "passion for wandering." Georgianna Kirby came to California wanting to "share in the general prosperity." Helen Carpenter reported that she shouted enthusiastically "Ho to California!" to set her wagon train in motion. Again and again in the writings of California women, there appear images of the state's raw newness, its exciting promise, and its sometimes considerable challenges. Dame Shirley found herself struck by the hard work of Indian women harvesting seeds near Indian Bar mining camp and by the coarse and dangerous nature of the camps themselves. Sarah Royce and Helen Carpenter both describe the sometimes desperate hope and the true toil they engaged in so as to take advantage of the cheap land in California. Georgianna Kirby's diaries documented not only her fears of giving birth to a child alone and unaided but also the work involved in planting and harvesting potatoes on her ranch while she was pregnant.

In California, the emphasis of Western writers on regional realism became known as sagebrush realism, and the movement included among its ranks not only such celebrated male authors as MARK TWAIN and BRET HARTE, but also a number of women: INA COOLBRITH, Adah Menkin, FRANCIS FULLER VICTOR, Josephine Clifford McCrackin, and Ada Clare, in addition to those already mentioned. Centered in and around San Francisco, sagebrush realists were storytellers who mixed reality with a little Western mythology and a bonanza-style hyperbole for an audience who loved literature filled with picturesque characters, with pathos, with humor, and, occasionally, with a kind of abnormality peculiar to California. The school, according to Ida Rae Egli, lasted about twenty-five years before dying out with the frontier, when the transcontinental railroads had dumped enough Easterners in California that local tastes changed and began to reflect a more genteel literary tradition common to the late nineteenth century. Some—GERTRUDE ATHERTON, BENJAMIN FRANKLIN (FRANK) NORRIS, JR., JOHN GRIFFITH (JACK) LONDON—went on to have successful individual careers in later decades, but the collective spirit of the uniquely California "genre" had been lost. While a few turned to travel writing, many of the earlier writers, especially the women, fell into obscurity. "The world," wrote Josephine Clifford McCracken to Ina Coolbrith when both had grown old, "has not used us well, Ina; California has been ungrateful to us."

Realism was a hallmark of many women writers in the West, although at frontier outposts and out on the prairies, it was often a colder, more sober-eyed realism than that of the sagebrush school. For there, many came not of their own free will but to follow the dream of a husband or father, and they were ambivalent about the whole notion of westering. "No girl ever wanted less to 'go West' with any man, or paid a man a greater compliment by doing so," wrote MARY HALLOCK FOOTE, late of New York City and a sophisticated life as an illustrator for popular magazines and books. Once arriving in California in 1876, however, she became captivated by the physical and social landscapes of the mining camps and towns to which her civil engineer husband dragged her and determined to articulate in her writing and sketches the "real West." Such became the goal of many Western women writers. In novels and nonfiction, in notebooks and diaries, in poems and letters home, women writers painted pictures of the pioneering life as filled with insecurity and drudgery, absent—or dead—husbands and hungry mouths to feed. Since they were individuals, they responded differently to the circumstances, and the character of their work differs, although the circumstances they describe vary much less.

Some of their work was ignored or forgotten, such as that of Elinore Pruitt Stewart. In her *Letters of a Woman Homesteader* (1914), Stewart portrayed in letters written over a span of five years to her former employer, Juliet Coney, a woman facing poverty and tragedy with a kind of vitality and spirit of adventure not frequently associated with the traditional long-suffering, pinched-soul pioneer wife à la HAMLIN GARLAND. At the same time, women writers such as Dorothy Scarborough pulled no punches in their critiques of the frontier experience. Scarborough's *The Wind* (1925) sounds the notes of loneliness and hard work common to many of the prairie writers depicting the effect of the plains environment on women: "The wind is the worst thing. . . . The work out here is hard on women. Can't get any help, and can't have the conveniences they have in other sections." Attacked by the West Texas Chamber of Commerce for maligning Sweetwater, Texas, and exaggerating its climate in the book, Scarborough quipped that nothing required the novelist to be a booster of her setting and that she seemed to have been "convicted of realism in the first degree."

Realism in the first degree sometimes meant looking at hard truths few others wanted to face. "Somebody must say these things," wrote California author MARY HUNTER AUSTIN in 1932 as she prepared to give testimony in a domestic violence case, describing how a friend of her mother's showed up in the night "with a great bloody bruise on her face" and "the unwiped tears on mother's face while the two women kept up the pretence of a blameless accident." Austin was known for her philosophical nature and travel writing about the West, from *The Land of Little Rain* (1903) to *The Land of Journey's Ending* (1924), the latter which she called "a book of prophecy" that suggested the Western environment itself was working to create a new culture harmonious with the land, "the next great and fructifying world culture." For some, the culture of the West was more attuned to what Austin had seen that night at her mother's, a land where the male code of behavior sanctioned a stand-your-ground violence that not infrequently spilled over into the domestic world. MARI SANDOZ in *Old Jules* (1935) and AGNES SMEDLY in *Daughter of Earth* (1929) produced portraits of lonely females, isolated on the plains from their families and other female friends, trapped by an economic system that made them utterly dependent on their husbands and forced them to remain in violent marriages. Sometimes the dedication to a sober-eyed view of the real West led to moral outrage, as in HELEN HUNT JACKSON's great muckraking diatribe against the region's mistreatment of the Indians, *A Century of Dishonor* (1881). Sometimes it could also lead, to quote Thomas J. Lyon, "to a concern with the moral and spiritual dimensions of living in any certain landscape—indeed with the moral and spiritual dimensions of establishing and maintaining civilizations in general." Such concerns, says Lyon, characterized WILLA CATHER's mature fiction and her social Western works—*O Pioneers!* (1913), *My Ántonia* (1918), the *Professor's House* (1925), *Death Comes for the Archbishop* (1917)—and it lifted her work from the ranks of regional immigrant tales to a major spot in any truly American canon of literature.

—*Patricia Hogan*

SEE ALSO: Literature; Poetry; Violence: Violence against Women

SUGGESTED READING:

Armitage, Susan, and Elizabeth Jameson, eds. *The Woman's West*. Norman, Okla., 1987.

Egli, Ida Rae, ed. *No Rooms of Their Own: Women Writers of Early California*. Berkeley, Calif., 1992.

Fairbanks, Carol. *Prairie Women: Images in American and Canadian Fiction*. New Haven, Conn., 1986.

Lee, L. L., and Merill Lewis. *Women, Women Writers, and the West*. Troy, N.Y., 1980

Lyon, Thomas J. *A Literary History of the American West*. Fort Worth, Tex., 1987.

Riley, Glenda. *A Place to Grow: Women in the American West*. Arlington Heights, Ill., 1992.

Schlissel, Lillian. *Women's Diaries of the Westward Journey*. New York, 1982

Sprague, William Forrest. *Women and the West: A Short Social History*. Boston, 1940.

Stratton, Joanna. *Pioneer Women: Voices from the Kansas Frontier*. New York, 1981.

WONG KIM ARK V. THE UNITED STATES

The U.S. Supreme Court decision *Wong Kim Ark v. the United States* in 1898 involved an American-born son of Chinese immigrants. Wong Kim Ark had returned from a trip to China only to be refused permission to land in San Francisco on the grounds that he was not a U.S. citizen. As a result of the Chinese Exclusion Act of 1882 and related court decisions, Chinese immigrants were considered "ineligible" to become naturalized U.S. citizens. In deciding the *Wong* case, however, the Court drew a distinction between the tradition of denying naturalization to nonwhite immigrants (which continued to be U.S. policy into the mid-twentieth century) and the case of Wong Kim Ark. Holding that by virtue of the Fourteenth Amendment, anyone born in the U.S. was entitled to citizenship, the Court granted Wong entry, thus setting a rule that has governed U.S. citizenship policy ever since.

—*Peggy Pascoe*

SEE ALSO: Chinese Exclusion

WOODRUFF, WILFORD

A Mormon religious leader, Wilford Woodruff (1807–1898) was born in Farmington (now Avon), Connecticut. He received his early education in local schools and at the Farmington Academy. Although he grew up in a family of local leaders and pillars of the Congregational church, he and some of his family left the church.

Woodruff converted to the CHURCH OF JESUS CHRIST OF LATTER-DAY SAINTS (LDS church) in New York in 1833. A participant in the failed Zion's Camp expedition sent to recover Mormon property in Jackson County, Missouri, he later worked in proselytizing missions in Tennessee and Kentucky, Maine, England, and New England. On the first of his two missions to England, he converted hundreds of people, including several congregations of United Brethren.

Called in 1838 to the Quorum of the Twelve Apostles, the second governing body of the LDS church, he spent the remainder of his life in church service. In NAUVOO, ILLINOIS, he served as business manager for a church newspaper. After the murder of JOSEPH SMITH, JR., and a bloody civil war in Hancock County, the Quorum of the Twelve Apostles led the Mormons to Utah.

As a religious leader, farmer, horticulturist, rancher, educator, leader of voluntary organizations, and politician, Woodruff helped build communities and govern the LDS church. As church historian, he collected documents and established archives for Mormon records. Deeply spiritual, he received numerous revelations, which provided guidance for the community in their marriage relationships, personal salvation, and sacred ordinances, especially those performed in LDS temples.

First married to Phebe Whittemore Carter (1807–1885) in 1837, he subsequently married eight other women in plural marriages. He was divorced from four of them.

As a church leader, he played the role of facilitator and moderator, particularly in the Reformation of 1856 to 1857, in which church leaders promoted spirituality and conformity in the Latter-day Saints community. He served as president of the St. George Temple, the first completed temple in Utah.

Harried by the federal campaign to imprison polygamous church leaders, Woodruff and other church leaders hid from United States marshals during part of the 1880s. While in hiding, Woodruff lived in Arizona and southern Utah.

Leading the church as president of the Quorum of the Twelve Apostles after the death of John Taylor in 1887, he became president of the LDS church in 1889. Following the imprisonment of more than a thousand Latter-day Saints men and a number of women for practicing polygamy and the confiscation of much of the church's property, Woodruff received a revelation directing the abandonment of plural marriage; he presented his revelation to the church in September and October 1890. Throughout his presidency, he worked for accommodation with the remainder of American society by dividing the church membership into national political parties, renouncing offensive doctrines, and developing productive relationships with national business and political leaders. He died in San Francisco while visiting a non-Mormon friend.

Arguably the third most important LDS leader after Joseph Smith and BRIGHAM YOUNG, Woodruff helped build the LDS community in the nineteenth century, and he promoted accommodations that led the church to become one of the largest American churches in the twentieth century. Deeply spiritual, he was also well educated, intelligent, and personable. Establishing relationships with leaders outside the LDS community, he facilitated changes in Mormonism to retain its essential spiritual aspects, while compromising on matters not essential to maintaining a distinctive LDS life and religious tradition within Christianity.

—*Thomas G. Alexander*

SEE ALSO: Mormon Manifesto; Mormons; Polygamy: Polygamy among Mormons

SUGGESTED READING:

Alexander, Thomas G. *Things in Heaven and Earth: The Life and Times of Wilford Woodruff, a Mormon Prophet.* Salt Lake City, 1991.

Cowley, Matthias F. *Wilford Woodruff: History of His Life and Labors.* 1909. Reprint. Salt Lake City, 1964.

Gibbons, Francis M. *Wilford Woodruff: Wondrous Worker, Prophet of God.* Salt Lake City, 1988.

Woodruff, Wilford. *Wilford Woodruff's Journal, 1833–1898.* Typescript Edition. Edited by Scott G. Kenney. 9 vols. Midvale, Utah, 1983–1985.

WOODRUFF V. NORTH BLOOMFIELD, ET AL.

Woodruff v. North Bloomfield, et al. (1884) pitted California agriculture against MINING in the first major challenge to mining's use of the land and its resources.

The case came about when Edward Woodruff sued for a court injunction to stop hydraulic miners from leaving debris on his farm outside of Marysville. Woodruff argued that the accumulated debris raised the riverbed, caused flooding that ruined his fields, and disrupted river commerce. Northern California hydraulic miners countered that an injunction against them would cause direct economic loss to California and the United States.

On January 7, 1884, United States Circuit Court Judge Lorenzo Sawyer rejected the miners' claims and "perpetually enjoined and restrained" them from discharging or dumping into the rivers.

—*Duane A. Smith*

SUGGESTED READING:

Kelley, Robert L. *Gold vs. Grain: The Hydraulic Mining Controversy in California's Sacramento Valley.* Glendale, Calif., 1959.

Smith, Duane A. *Mining America: The Industry and the Environment, 1880–1980.* Lawrence, Kans., 1987.

WOOL, JOHN ELLIS

Army inspector general and celebrated military commander, John Ellis Wool (1784–1869) was born in Newburgh, New York. He attended common schools in Schaghticoke, New York, served an apprenticeship in neighboring Troy, ran a store, and became a militia officer. He entered the War of 1812 as a captain in the Thirteenth Infantry Regiment, won acclaim on the battlefield, and was brevetted a lieutenant colonel. For twenty-five years (from 1816 to 1841), Wool then served as an inspector general and focused his attention on improving personnel conditions and modernizing the artillery corps. He received numerous special assignments. He was sent to Europe in 1832 to purchase artillery weapons; he rounded up the Cherokees from 1836 to 1837 for removal to the West; and he curbed gunrunning to Canadian "patriots" on the New York–Vermont boundaries from 1837 to 1838. In 1841, he took command of the Eastern Department with the rank of brigadier general.

In 1846, Wool supervised the muster of twelve volunteer regiments for the service in the UNITED STATES–MEXICAN WAR and then led a division from San Antonio that joined ZACHARY TAYLOR's army at Saltillo. Wool selected the battlefield at Buena Vista and, as field commander, repulsed a larger Mexican force under General ANTONIO LÓPEZ DE SANTA ANNA. He headed the occupation in northeastern Mexico for six months and was brevetted a major general. From 1854 to 1857, he commanded the Division of the Pacific, where he tried to halt filibustering, update the military presence, and pacify Indians in the Oregon and Washington territories.

Wool played an active role in the Civil War. He took command of Fortress Monroe, Virginia, where he supervised civilian-mail traffic through the lines, created a work program for blacks, and captured Confederate Norfolk. Promoted to regular major general, Wool moved to Baltimore in June 1862 to command

John Ellis Wool. *Courtesy National Archives.*

the Middle Department and guard the Baltimore and Ohio Railroad line to Harper's Ferry. In January 1863, Wool arrived in New York City to head the Department of New York and New England and, in July, attempted to end the draft riots in the city. He retired on August 1, 1863.

—*Harwood P. Hinton*

SUGGESTED READING:

Bauer, K. Jack. *The Mexican War, 1846–1848.* New York, 1974.

WOOTEN, RICHENS LACY

Fur trapper, Indian fighter, and pioneer Richens Lacy Wooten (1816–1893) was the quintessential mountain man and trail-blazer. Covering much of the territory of the Far West in his exploits, Wooten made a living doing anything that would bring in profit. He trapped beavers, ran a buffalo ranch, and served in various military campaigns against the Indians. One of his most enterprising endeavors took place in 1852. Having settled in Taos in 1848 and married the first of his four wives, Wooten drove nine thousand sheep to California and sold them to the gold miners at a profit of forty thousand dollars.

When gold was discovered at Pikes Peak, Wooten set up a trading post, saloon, and hotel in Denver. Later he and his partners built a toll road at Raton Pass on the Santa Fe Trail. When the ATCHISON, TOPEKA AND SANTA FE RAILROAD claimed the right of way, Wooten negotiated a pension from the railroad as compensation for his loss of business.

—*Candace Floyd*

SUGGESTED READING:
Carter, H. L. "Richens Lacy Wootton." In *The Mountain Men and the Fur Trade of the Far West.* Vol. 3. Edited by LeRoy R. Hafen. Glendale, Calif., 1966.

WOO YEE-BEW

The first Chinese clergyman of the Episcopal church in Hawaii, Woo Yee-Bew (1864–1930) played a significant role in establishing the Chinese community on the islands. Born in Fat San, Woo converted to Christianity and attended the Lutheran Mission School in nearby Canton. His studies continued in Hong Kong, when he entered St. Stephen's College in 1880 to study theology. His graduate studies, begun three years later in San Francisco were cut short by the death of his benefactor. Unable to continue with school, he went to Hawaii and opened a camp for Chinese plantation workers in Kohala.

In 1887, Woo assumed his appointment as evangelist to Kohala's Chinese community, and during his tenure, he established the St. Paul Chinese Mission. The following year, he transferred to Honolulu to work with the Chinese of the city. Shortly after the turn of the century, Woo was appointed missionary to the Church of St. Paul, Makapala, Kohala; his appointment to the priesthood followed several months later. Woo continued his Christian ministry to the Chinese peoples of Hawaii until he moved back to Honolulu in 1915.

—*Patricia Hogan*

SEE ALSO: Missions: Missions to Hawaii

WORCESTER V. STATE OF GEORGIA

Brought before United States Supreme Court in 1832, *Worcester* v. *State of Georgia* resulted in a successful challenge to Georgia state laws that persecuted the Cherokee Indians. The suit was brought by Samuel A. Worcester, a white missionary to the Cherokees, who had defied an 1830 Georgia law forbidding any white man from residing in Cherokee country unless he took an oath of allegiance to the state and secured a license from the governor. Jailed for his refusal to obey the law, Worcester took his case to the Supreme Court. His attorney, William Wirt, brought suit under Section 25 of the Judiciary Act of 1789, which provided that the Supreme Court had jurisdiction in cases where federal treaties and state statutes conflicted.

Under the leadership of Chief Justice John Marshall, the court found that the United States had, by treaty, recognized the Cherokee Nation's right to self-government; that the United States was obligated to treat the Indians as a nation; and that since political intercourse with the Indians was to be carried out by the federal government, state laws could have no force over Indians. "The acts of Georgia," Marshall declared, were "repugnant to the Constitution, laws and treaties of the United States."

Although the decision was a legal triumph for Georgia's Cherokees, it had little practical effect. The state of Georgia defied the court by keeping Worcester locked up until the governor pardoned him. Furthermore, Georgia continued to persecute the Cherokees in order to obtain their lands. Siding with the state and refusing to enforce the Supreme Court's decision, President ANDREW JACKSON told the Indians that they must agree to be "removed" from their homes in Georgia to the Indian Territory in present-day Oklahoma. By 1838, the majority of the Cherokee Nation embarked westward along the so-called TRAIL OF TEARS.

—*Alan Axelrod*

SEE ALSO: *Cherokee Nation* v. *State of Georgia*

SUGGESTED READING:
Browder, Nathaniel C. *The Cherokee Indians and Those Who Came After.* Hayesville, N.C., 1973.
Cokran, David H. *The Cherokee Frontier.* Norman, Okla., 1969.
Finger, John R. *The Eastern Band of Cherokees, 1819–1900.* Knoxville, Tenn., 1984.
King, Duane. *The Cherokee Indian Nation: A Troubled History.* Knoxville, Tenn., 1979.

WORK AND WORKERS

SEE: Arizona Mining Strikes; Bullwhackers; Cattle Trails and Trail Driving; Cowboys; Cripple Creek Strikes; Domestic Service; Foreign Miners' Tax of 1850; Harvey Girls; Hawaii Laborer's Association; Homesteading; Industrial Workers of the World; Labor Movement; Loggers; Ludlow Massacre; Migrant Workers; Mining: Miners; Mountain Men; Nursing; Prostitution; Pony Express; Oxnard Agricultural Strike; Rivermen;

San Francisco Building Trades Council; Teachers on the Frontier; Trappers; Union Labor Party, San Francisco; United States Army: Composition, Military Life on the Frontier, Scouts; Western Federation of Miners; Women in Wage Work; Working-class Women; Workingmen's Party of California

WORKING-CLASS WOMEN

Social relationships of class and gender shaped women's options and opportunities in the West. Women's possibilities depended on particular Western regional economies, such as mining, lumber, cattle, and agriculture, and how they allocated work by gender. Work was also allocated by race, so women's options were further influenced by local racial-ethnic hierarchies. Thus, for instance, domestic work that might commonly be performed by African American or Irish immigrant women in the South or East would more commonly belong in the West to Chinese immigrant men, or to Mexican American or Native American women.

As this example indicates, the history of Western working-class women requires us to address the significance of class, race, gender, and region. The very category "working-class women" raises the questions of what class meant for women, and how gender was defined through divisions of labor. Traditional concepts of class, defined through people's relationships to the means of production, were formulated from the perspectives of wage work. In the West of the late nineteenth and early twentieth centuries, wage work was largely the province of men. It was inadequate to describe women's realities or class relationships. Wage labor excluded much of women's work, which occurred outside the wage system, and much of their participation in working-class organizing, which occurred through family and community ties rather than their own union membership. Women, like men, might be working-class because they worked for wages. But they could also be working class because they depended on someone else's wage work to help support their households, or because they participated in working-class institutions, like labor unions or mutual aid societies, from which they derived social identity and support.

Women's options were defined not only by class, but by gender, by race, and by who did what work in particular Western regional economies. Well into the twentieth century, much of the West held more men than women, partly because characteristic Western industries like railroad construction, mining, lumbering, and ranching all employed predominantly male work forces.

Demographically, frontier areas were marked by unbalanced sex ratios (the number of men per one hundred women). Just after the California gold rush, in 1850, men outnumbered women 123 to one. Colorado in 1860, a year after the Pikes Peak boom, counted 1,650 men per hundred women. Agricultural areas attracted more families and more women, but few Western states had equal numbers of men and women by 1930. Kansas had the lowest sex ratio of any state west of the Mississippi, with 101 men per hundred women, followed by Texas, with 104, and Utah, with 105. Oregon's sex ratio was 110; Montana's, 120; Nevada's, 139.

The shortage of women supported a romantic myth that women, because they were scarce, could achieve economic mobility in the West through advantageous marriages. Instead, however, women's options narrowed to

Dance-hall workers and their patrons in Cripple Creek, Colorado, in the 1890s. *Courtesy Denver Public Library, Western History Department.*

a variety of domestic work for pay, or to marriages where they did much the same work outside the wage system. Their labor and their options were rooted in the regional economies that supported such skewed sex ratios and were affected by whether they were single or married and by whether they worked in the "respectable" or "disreputable" marketplace. Where "masculine" industries predominated, the wage work available for women consisted largely of DOMESTIC SERVICE that supported the male work force. Working-class women might cook, sew, clean, do laundry, wait tables, or keep boarders—all occupations that provided domestic support for single male workers. Mining, cattle, and garrison towns offered the most stereotyped of jobs for many working-class women, the prostitutes and dance-hall workers who sold companionship as well as sex. Their work often paid better than "respectable" women's wage work, but it also carried particular risks, including venereal disease, violence, pregnancy, drug and alcohol abuse, and social and legal sanctions. It was, however, often the only way women could support themselves, and in many parts of the West it was the best-paying job available for women. Although a survey of wages, hours, and working conditions for women throughout the West is beyond the scope of this article, a few examples make the point. Domestic servants earned roughly $1 to $2 a week at the turn of the century. In the Cripple Creek, Colorado, mining district, where most working-class men earned at least $3 a day, women laundry workers earned from $7.50 to $9 for a week's work of fifty-four to sixty hours. The male drivers who delivered the laundry earned twice as much. Prostitutes who catered to a respectable working-class clientele might earn $1 a "date" and sell beer for $1 a bottle; women who worked in elite houses might make even more.

Both respectable and "non-respectable" wage work was stratified by race. African American and Mexican American women, and immigrants from China, Japan, and Mexico were all relegated to the bottom rungs of women's wage work, as domestic servants and as prostitutes. Very few Chinese women immigrated to the United States before the Chinese Exclusion Act of 1882 barred most Chinese; the best estimates suggest that the number of Chinese women fluctuated between 3.6 percent of the total CHINESE AMERICAN population in 1890 and 7.2 percent in 1870. Most were poor women with few options in China, imported to serve as prostitutes. In California in 1870, there were 2,163 prostitutes and 405 probable prostitutes out of a total Chinese female population of 3,797.

It is important to note that the proportions of prostitutes among Chinese women dropped quickly and that, within a decade, the stereotype of Chinese prostitutes, mobilized in arguments for CHINESE EXCLUSION, no longer fit the majority of Chinese immigrant women in California. At the same time, the status of Chinese prostitutes within the sexual marketplace illustrates how hierarchies of race and gender interacted to constrict working women's options. Chinese women's class status, like that of all prostitutes, depended partly on race and partly on the class of their customers. Prostitutes' work and working conditions varied by a number of factors, including whether they had one customer or many, by whether they sold forms of companionship other than sexual intercourse, by the length of time spent with each customer, and by their age and race, and how these affected the prices they could charge.

Established Western vice districts reflected class and racial hierarchies. Larger parlor houses offered younger, conventionally pretty women, usually white, for wealthier customers. Less affluent clients might frequent smaller houses, while working-class men patronized streetwalkers or hired women who operated out of their own "cribs." At the bottom of the hierarchy were African American and Mexican women, and Chinese prostitutes who were often virtual slaves to the companies that paid their passage to America. The best options available to them were in more elite houses that served an all-Chinese clientele in large West Coast cities, particularly San Francisco. Those who were rebellious, or who were considered less attractive because of their own peasant origins, might be sent to the mining camps of the Comstock, Coeur d'Alene, or Butte, where their degraded status was reinforced by the fact that they could choose neither their work, their work place, nor their customers and were required to sleep with Euro-American men.

The vastly skewed sex ratios among Japanese and Korean immigrants similarly restricted women's wage work to domestic labor. At the turn of the century, there were only 985 Japanese females in the United States; by 1930 there were 23,930 married Japanese women in a total JAPANESE AMERICAN population of 138,824. These women carried the dual responsibility of providing domestic support for many single men and managing families to ensure the survival of Japanese American communities in the West. As cooks and boarding-house keepers, they frequently provided for the domestic needs of Japanese contract laborers in mining and agriculture. The majority went into rural areas, where some entered labor camps their husbands operated to provide laborers for railroads, Wyoming coal mines, Idaho and Utah sugar-beet fields, lumber camps and mills in the Pacific Northwest, and salmon canneries in Alaska. Sometimes they worked as sharecroppers or labored in family businesses like bathhouses, laundries, restaurants, and boarding houses.

The work of feeding, clothing, and sheltering ethnic immigrant workers often fell to outnumbered immigrant women, who provided not only daily household support but the domestic space in which ethnic working-class communities took root. Whatever their ethnicity, most working-class women performed domestic labor outside the wage system. As wives, daughters, and mothers of working-class men, they cooked, cleaned, sewed, raised and processed vegetables, and hauled water and heated it for baths and laundry. They were, in economic terms, an essential part of the "infrastructure" of mines, mills, factories, farms, and ranches. But their pay was indirect, dependent on the earning power and the generosity of working-class men. Even daughters who worked for wages, or married women who kept lodgers or did laundry in their homes often contributed their earnings to the total family income and gained little autonomy from their labor.

The greatest economic opportunities for Western women were often associated with AGRICULTURE, where, either as family members or as independent homesteaders, they might benefit from the "free land" available through the HOMESTEAD ACT OF 1862 and subsequent laws that opened the public domain to farming. U.S. LAND POLICY was rooted in twin commitments to private property and nuclear families. The Homestead Act and related laws assumed that most farms would be worked by nuclear families headed by men. But it also, for the first time, allowed women an independent stake on the land if they were single or heads of households. All available evidence so far indicates that independent women homesteaders were always a significant presence on the agricultural frontier, ranging from approximately 5 percent of all homesteaders in the first agricultural settlements to some 20 percent after 1900. They appear to have been at least as successful as men in achieving final title to their claims. For some women, HOMESTEADING provided the opportunity to live independently, to escape abusive marriages, or, perhaps, to live with another woman. Most women homesteaders, however, continued to support the family ideal. Many postponed marriage and wed somewhat later than their peers. Some filed for land shortly before marriage to double family landholdings. And some added their land to extended family farm property. While most managed their own farms, in agriculture as in other economies, work was allocated by gender. Women homesteaders might hire men to do all or part of their field work or might trade domestic chores to single male homesteaders in exchange for plowing or other heavy labor. Some worked as teachers, journalists, seamstresses, or did other "women's" wage work to support their farms.

One study of North Dakota homesteaders suggests that women used their homesteads to support a variety of goals. Some continued to farm their land for extended periods; some sold it and used the money to buy new farms or to enlarge family holdings when they married. Others sold the land and used the money as a "stake" to establish small businesses, to pursue educations, or to provide similar opportunities for other family members. The variety of goals that homesteads supported should encourage us to reevaluate what homesteading promised and the ways that we measure success and failure in Western agriculture. Most homesteaders were forced out by weather, lack of capital, debts, low crop prices, and high freight rates before they received title to their claims. Others moved from farming as the nation industrialized and farms grew larger and more mechanized. But, like the women homesteaders, many people who left the land did not count their experience a failure. For some, the land did provide the means to economic improvement and modest class mobility.

Whether as independent homesteaders or as participants in family enterprises, women's agricultural labor was allocated by gender. They were most likely to do field work during emergencies or during the first few years of establishing a farm, when the land had to be cleared and plowed and the first home had to be erected. Subsequently, women's farm work might include keeping a garden, raising poultry, milking, processing food, making clothing, as well as the daily maintenance tasks of cooking, washing, and cleaning. These daily chores presented particular challenges in the small claim shanties, SOD HOUSES, and dugouts that were often the first shelters on Great Plains homesteads. The lack of timber meant that until families could buy coal, the women must learn to cook with the dried buffalo or cow dung that was the only available fuel.

In agriculture, too, class and ethnic distinctions affected women's work. The independent family homestead was, from the beginning, competing with larger commercial farms and ranches that were the forerunners of modern agribusiness, and that hired a variety of permanent and seasonal farm laborers. Small homesteaders sometimes cooperated to help one another with seasonally intensive work, like harvesting and threshing. Large bonanza farms in North Dakota's Red River Valley might hire work crews of more than one hundred men to plow, plant, harvest, and thresh hard winter wheat, while commercial farms in California hired temporary labor to pick fruit, vegetables, and hops. It fell to the women to preserve and manage food supplies to feed these agricultural laborers, whether they were hired "hands" or neighborhood volunteers who worked cooperatively. Domestic labor was particularly intensive for women during these peak seasons, where, in unmechanized kitchens, they labored over coal and wood stoves to provide food for large numbers of hungry men. Ironically, the larger and more prosperous a farm, the more intensive might be the woman's farm labor, with larger work forces to feed. On larger farms and ranches, foremen's wives were "part of the package," and it was their job to cook, clean, and wash for male workers, sometimes purchasing and managing food supplies for the entire business from their family wages.

The idealized picture of family farms excluded agricultural wage workers, many of them women and men of color, who occupied the "lowest rungs" of a wage system in much of Western agriculture. They were pulled in to do seasonal labor, like topping sugar beets or picking fruit and vegetables, and pushed out as work became scarce or during hard times, when Euro-American workers replaced them. Much of the land open to homesteading, of course, was taken from Indians, who, under the provisions of the DAWES ACT of 1887, lost their tribal lands and were instead allocated small family farms. The same commitments to nuclear families and private property that underlay the Homestead Act, in this instance, disrupted tribal economies, kinship systems, and gender relations. Similarly, Euro-American settlers in the Southwest used U.S. law and political influence to acquire lands held under Spanish land grants. As they lost the land, Mexican American men were forced into regional wage economies to support agricultural villages. At first, Mexican American women became responsible for managing families and village affairs during the men's absences. However, many women were ultimately drawn away from their villages to join the men who labored permanently in mining towns and agricultural wage work.

Throughout the West, working-class women performed domestic labor, both paid and unpaid, managed household consumption, and made and sold some commodities, like butter and eggs. Working-class women's organizing was as diverse as their work, rooted in the gendered division of labor and understandings of gender and race. The Western LABOR MOVEMENT was largely dominated by Euro-American men and was further divided by ethnicity in many areas. In mining, lumber, and railroad towns, women might participate in working-class organizing through women's auxiliaries. Most women worked in occupations that organized labor ignored; the labor movement focused instead primarily on jobs held by Euro-American men.

There were some exceptions. The Women's Protective Union of Butte, Montana, organized women janitors, dishwashers, cooks, and waitresses regardless of race. Elsewhere, women belonged to unions of laundry workers, clerks, restaurant and hotel employees, or retail clerks. In the 1910s, some women agricultural laborers joined the INDUSTRIAL WORKERS OF THE WORLD, the only union before the United Farm Workers in the 1960s and 1970s that successfully organized migrant agricultural labor.

Although often outnumbered by men, many women were staunch union members. In San Francisco in 1901, women members of Local No. 30 of the Hotel and Restaurant Employees International Alliance joined the men in a strike that closed 184 restaurants. Ultimately, however, court orders, violence, and the National Guard defeated their strike. The women later reorganized an all-women's local that won bargaining rights, higher wages (though still lower than waiters'), and better hours and working conditions. Seattle's Local No. 240 of the Hotel and Restaurant Employees, founded in 1900, was one of the most effective waitresses' unions in the country under the assertive leadership of Alice Lord. By 1904, the local had raised wages from $5 to $7 a week for a fourteen-hour day to a minimum of $8.50 a week for a ten-hour day. In 1908, Local 240 and its male counterpart struck eleven of the largest restaurants in town to end the seven-day work week.

Although Alice Lord was a respected union leader, most women found it difficult to achieve leadership and policy-making authority within organized labor. Their position in the Western labor movement derived from male union leaders' assumptions regarding masculine authority and female subordination, from the masculine social atmospheres of many union functions, and from women's own movements in and out of wage work. Many working-class women left wage work with marriage, shifting to unpaid domestic labor and to contributing to family incomes by keeping boarders or performing piece work from their homes, like sewing, laundry, or cooking. If they remained active in the union movement, they did so through women's auxiliaries. Some unions recognized that women's votes (in the Western states where women could vote before 1920) and their purchasing power could both be used to support organized labor. They encouraged working-class women to vote for pro-union candidates and to purchase union-label products. But the failure to organize many women wage workers or to recognize working-class women's unpaid domestic labor, some historians argue, weakened organized labor.

Women's support during strikes was more often recognized by the Western labor movement. In a number of dramatic instances—the WESTERN FEDERATION OF MINERS' strikes in CRIPPLE CREEK and the San Juans from 1903 to 1904, the IWW's 1917 Bisbee copper strike—women resisted state troops who deported male unionists, and supported families and the labor community in the men's absence. In the United Mine Workers' Strike against the Colorado Fuel and Iron Company (CF&I) from 1913 to 1914, women organized the domestic survival of strikers of some twenty-two different ethnicities who, evicted from company housing, maintained their struggle from tents. The women mobilized to confront the militia under the leadership of the legendary MARY HARRIS ("MOTHER") JONES, and were harassed and attacked in return. Before the UMW strike, the troops' reluctance to attack women allowed women to do things men could not—to distribute strike relief, cross militia lines, and harass soldiers sent to strike areas. The CF&I strike, however, ended with the LUDLOW MASSACRE, when the Colorado militia fired at strikers and burned their tents, suffocating eleven children and two women who huddled beneath in a cellar to escape the gunfire.

Women's direct and indirect participation in the labor movement reflected the direct and indirect ways they were linked to wage systems throughout the West. The complexity of working-class women's labor was also reflected in the many forms of organizing and resistance in which they participated to improve their status as workers, as women, and as persons of color. Prostitutes and dance-hall workers were generally excluded from organized labor and used more informal mechanisms to establish their wages or to try, often ineffectively, to protect themselves from violent customers and other hazards of their trade. Agricultural women, in common with all farmers, sought mutual support and political redress through the Grange, Farmers' Alliance, and the Populist party. The Grange and Farmers' Alliance were unusual among male-dominated organizations in admitting women members, officers, and convention delegates. The Grange responded to women's needs by establishing sewing-machine cooperatives and by fighting a new product, margarine, which undercut women's cash product, butter. It endorsed women's political rights. The Populist party supported women as organizers, theorists, delegates, and candidates for public office. Farm women participated in these organizations for much the same reasons that women wage workers and union men's wives participated in organized labor, out of the shared economic interests of working-class households. Their particular interests as women might also lead working-class women to fight for WOMEN'S SUFFRAGE, or to try to persuade legislators to expand the grounds for DIVORCE to include failure to support, as the women of Butte did. Women's organizing and resistance was as complex and varied as their relationships to Western economies and Western men. For the most part, however, effective union organizing did not reach most working-class women, particularly women of color, until the union drives of the 1930s and the much more recent organizing of women service and clerical workers in the 1970s and 1980s.

—*Elizabeth Jameson*

SEE ALSO: Migrant Workers; Populism; Prostitution; ; Violence: Violence against Women; Women in Wage Work

SUGGESTED READING:

Bush, Corlann Gee. "The Barn Is His, the House Is Mine: Agricultural Technology and Sex Roles." In *Energy and Transport*. Edited by George Daniels and Mark Rose. Berkeley, Calif., 1981.

Butler, Anne M. *Daughters of Joy, Sisters of Misery: Prostitution in the American West, 1865–90*. Urbana, Ill., 1985.

Chan, Sucheng. "The Exclusion of Chinese Women, 1870–1943." In *Entry Denied: Exclusion and the Chinese Community in America, 1882–1943*. Edited by Sucheng Chan. Philadelphia, 1991.

Deutsch, Sarah. *No Separate Refuge: Culture, Class, and Gender on an Anglo-Hispanic Frontier in the American Southwest, 1880–1940*. New York, 1984.

Frank, Dana. *Purchasing Power: Consumer Organizing, Gender, and the Seattle Labor Movement, 1919–1929*. New York, 1994.

Glenn, Evelyn Nakano. *Issei, Nisei, War Bride: Three Generations of Japanese American Women in Domestic Service*. Philadelphia, 1986.

Goldman, Marion S. *Gold Diggers and Silver Miners: Prostitutes and Social Life on the Comstock Lode*. Ann Arbor, Mich., 1981.

Hirata, Lucie Cheng. "Free, Indentured, and Enslaved: Chinese Prostitutes in Nineteenth-Century America." *Signs* 5:1 (Autumn 1979): 3–29.

Ichioka, Yuji. "Amerika Nadeshiko: Japanese Immigrant Women in the United States, 1900–1924." *Pacific Historical Review* 49 (1980): 539–557.

Jameson, Elizabeth. "Imperfect Unions: Class and Gender in Cripple Creek, 1894–1904." *Frontiers* 1 (Spring 1976): 85–117. Also in Cantor, Milton, and Bruce Laurie, eds. *Class, Sex, and the Woman Worker*. Westport, Conn., 1977.

Jameson, Elizabeth, and Susan Armitage, eds. *Writing the Range: Race, Class and Culture in the Women's West*. Norman, Okla., 1997.

Jensen, Joan M. *With These Hands: Women Working on the Land*. Old Woodbury, N.Y., 1981.

Lindgren, Elaine H. *Land in Her Own Name: Women as Homesteaders in North Dakota*. Fargo, N. Dak., 1991.

Long, Priscilla. *Where the Sun Never Shines: A History of America's Bloody Coal Industry*. New York, 1989.

Mora, Magdalena, and Adelaida R. Del Castillo, eds. *Mexican-American Women in the United States: Struggles Past and Present*. Los Angeles, 1980.

Murphy, Mary. "The Private Lives of Public Women: Prostitution in Butte, Montana, 1878–1917." In *The Women's West*. Edited by Susan Armitage and Elizabeth Jameson. Norman, Okla., 1987.

O'Neill, Colleen. "Domesticity Deployed Gender, Race, and the Construction of Class Struggle in the Bisbee Deportations." *Labor History* 34 (Spring-Summer 1993): 256–273.

Patterson-Black, Sheryll. "Women Homesteaders on the Great Plains Frontier." *Frontiers* 1 (Spring 1976): 67–88.

Petrik, Paula. *No Step Backward: Women and Family on the Rocky Mountain Mining Frontier, Helena, Montana, 1865–1900.* Helena, Mont., 1987.

Sanchez, George J. *Becoming Mexican American: Ethnicity, Culture and Identity in Chicano Los Angeles, 1900–1945.* New York, 1993.

Spence, Mary Lee. "Waitresses in the Trans-Mississippi West: 'Pretty Waiter Girls,' Harvey Girls, and Union Maids." In *The Women's West.* Edited by Susan Armitage and Elizabeth Jameson. Norman, Okla., 1987.

Tong, Benson. *Unsubmissive Women: Chinese Prostitutes in Nineteenth-Century San Francisco.* Norman, Okla., 1994.

Yung, Judy. *Unbound Feet: A Social History of Chinese Women in San Francisco.* Berkeley and Los Angeles, 1995.

WORKINGMEN'S PARTY OF CALIFORNIA

In 1877, DENIS KEARNEY, an Irish drayman who had gotten into politics to protest the potholes in the streets of San Francisco, began to work up local anti-Chinese sentiment into a full-fledged movement, which led him to found the Workingmen's Party of California (WPC). The city had already suffered anti-Chinese riots in July when blue-color workers and unskilled laborers began to flock in the tens of thousands to Kearney's WPC two months later. European, primarily Irish, immigrants, these men listened to Kearney when he argued that San Francisco's social and economic problems resulted from a monstrous conspiracy between the city's business elite and its Chinese immigrants. The city's wealthiest people, Kearney and other WPC leaders claimed, were plotting to overthrow the American republic, destroy the freedom of the workingman, and replace white American workingmen with Oriental slaves. Part political party, part mob, the WPC meant to foil the plot and save the country. By 1878, Kearney and the WPC had become a major political force not only in San Francisco but elsewhere in California as well. Recognizing that the WPC had solidified working-class and lower-middle-class immigrant voters against the Chinese, California's wealthy upper class, and the two traditional political parties, Republicans and Democrats, alike panicked and threw together a "nonpartisan" ticket for the upcoming election to California's new constitutional convention in 1878.

Since the WPC sent 51 and the nonpartisan slate 81 out of a possible 152 members to the convention, Kearney did have some say in drafting the new constitution. But since the party also had, according to Henry George, not even a "shadow of reform [that would] lessen social inequalities or purify politics," the WPC wound up merely promoting the bland notion that voters should "[e]lect honest men to office and have them cut down taxation." Being upright and making the life of Chinese immigrants miserable was hardly a program to transform society or to sustain a political movement, and the WPC fell quickly into decline. Never again did it achieve its electoral success of 1878, and by 1881, it had all but disappeared. Anti-Chinese sentiment, however, did not vanish but simply returned to more conventional channels and became something of a California tradition.

—*Charles Phillips*

SEE ALSO: Chinese Exclusion; Labor Movement; Violence: Racial Violence

SUGGESTED READING:
Shumsky, Neil Larry. *The Evolution of Political Protest and the Workingmen's Party of California.* Columbus, Ohio, 1991.

WOUNDED KNEE MASSACRE

During the 1880s, the GHOST DANCE religion spread through many Western Indian reservations. A fundamentally peaceful movement, it nevertheless took on militant overtones among the Teton Sioux; but, in any form, the Ghost Dance phenomenon frightened white authorities. Pine Ridge Reservation agent Daniel F. Royer telegraphed Washington, D.C., in November 1890: "Indians are dancing in the snow and are wild and crazy. We need protection and we need it now." On November 20, 1890, cavalry and infantry reinforcements arrived at Pine Ridge and at the Rosebud Reservation. When the soldiers arrived, some three thousand Indians gathered on a plateau at the northwest corner of Pine Ridge called the Stronghold. Brigadier General John R. Brooke, commander of the Pine Ridge area, sent emissaries to parley with the militants but to no avail. Brooke's commanding officer, General NELSON APPLETON MILES, decided to deal with the Ghost Dance situation himself and transferred his headquarters to Rapid City, South Dakota. In the meantime, SITTING BULL, the most influential of all Sioux leaders, began actively espousing the Ghost Dance doctrine at the Standing Rock Reservation. The agent in charge there, JAMES McLAUGHLIN, decided to arrest Sitting Bull. The operation went terribly wrong, and, on December 15, 1890, the arrest escalated into a riot, during which Sitting Bull was slain.

It was in this explosive atmosphere that Miles moved to arrest another Ghost Dance leader, BIG FOOT, chief of the Minneconjou Sioux, who lived on the Cheyenne River. What Miles did not know is that Big Foot, concluding that the Ghost Dance religion offered nothing but desperation and futility, had personally given it up. Miles was also unaware that Chief RED CLOUD, a Pine Ridge leader friendly to the whites, had invited Big Foot to come to the reservation in order to use his influence to persuade the Stronghold party to surrender. The only intelligence Miles had was that, with a reservation uprising in the offing and Sitting Bull martyred, Big Foot was headed for the Stronghold. Miles broadcast a dragnet across the prairies and Badlands to intercept all Minneconjous and, in particular, Big Foot.

On December 28, 1890, a squadron of the Seventh Cavalry located Big Foot (who was miserably ill with pneumonia) and about 350 Minneconjous camped near a stream called Wounded Knee Creek. That night, more troops arrived. By morning, five hundred soldiers under Colonel James W. Forsyth surrounded Big Foot's camp. Positioning four Hotchkiss guns—small howitzerlike cannon, capable of rapid fire—on the sur-

The total number of Sioux casualties at Wounded Knee was impossible to calculate. *Courtesy Denver Public Library, Western History Department.*

rounding hills, Forsyth ordered his men to disarm the Indians and take them to the railroad in order to "remove them from the zone of military operations." Despite tensions, it was seen as a routine operation, and the soldiers entered the camp to search for guns.

"Birds-eye" view of the Sioux camp at Pine Ridge, South Dakota, one week after the Wounded Knee massacre. *Courtesy National Archives.*

"Return of Casey's scouts from the fight at Wounded Knee, 1890–91." *Courtesy National Archives.*

Enraged by the intrusion, the medicine man Yellow Bird began dancing wildly, exhorting his people to resist. Yellow Bird reminded them all that they wore ghost shirts, which would protect them against white men's bullets. Next, Black Coyote, whom another Indian described as "a crazy man, a young man of very bad influence and in fact a nobody," defiantly raised his Winchester above his head as the troopers moved

about collecting weapons. He protested that the rifle had cost him dearly, that it was his, and that nobody was going to take it from him. The soldiers responded by crowding him, shoving him, then spinning him around.

At this point, a rifle discharged. It may have been Black Coyote's. It may have been deliberate. It may have been accidental. In any case, both sides now opened fire—although few of the Indians were armed. Hand-to-hand combat ensued, after which the Indians broke away and began to flee. The Hotchkiss guns opened fire—almost a shell a second—at men, women, and children.

Within less than an hour, Big Foot and 153 other Minneconjous were dead. But so many others staggered, limped, or crawled away that it was never determined precisely how many finally died. Most likely, 300 of the 350 who had been camped at Wounded Knee Creek perished. Casualties among the Seventh Cavalry were 25 killed and 39 wounded, mostly from errant Hotchkiss rounds.

Wounded Knee, which the army called a battle and the public immediately dubbed a massacre, prompted the union of so-called hostile and hitherto friendly Sioux factions in a December 30 ambush of the Seventh Cav-

Photographer John C. H. Grabill recorded the council of Sioux chiefs and leaders who settled the Indian wars, Pine Ridge, South Dakota, 1891. *Courtesy National Archives.*

alry near the Pine Ridge Agency. Elements of the Ninth Cavalry came to the rescue, and General Miles subsequently marshaled 3,500 troops (out of a total force of 5,000) around the Sioux who had assembled fifteen miles north of the Pine Ridge Agency along White Clay Creek. Dealing from a position of strength, Miles gradually contracted the ring of troops around the Indians, all the while urging their surrender and pledging good treatment.

That was sufficient; for it had become clear even to the most resolute among the Sioux leaders that the cause was lost. The union among the Sioux was short-lived, and a formal surrender on January 15, 1891, effectively brought to an end not only the series of conflicts the U.S. Army called the Indian Wars, but some four centuries of warfare between whites and Indians in North America. Miles condemned the cavalry's actions at Wounded Knee, summarily relieved Forsyth of command, and ordered a court of inquiry. To the commanding general's consternation, the inquiry exonerated the Seventh Cavalry's colonel, and over Miles's protests, Forsyth was reinstated to his command.

But Wounded Knee was not forgotten. In 1970, the popular Western historian Dee Brown incorporated it into the title of his best-selling critical history of white-Indian relations, *Bury My Heart at Wounded Knee: An Indian History of the American West.* On February 28, 1973, activists in the American Indian Movement once again drew the attention of the nation and the world to Wounded Knee when they seized the village there and defied federal authorities to repeat the massacre. After a siege of seventy-two days, resulting in the deaths of two Indians and the wounding of others, the protesters surrendered.

—*Alan Axelrod*

SUGGESTED READING:

Brown, Dee. *Bury My Heart at Wounded Knee.* New York, 1970.

Lazarus, Edward. *Black Hills, White Justice: The Sioux Nation Versus the United States, 1775 to the Present.* New York, 1991.

Utley, Robert M. *The Last Days of the Sioux Nation.* New Haven, Conn., 1963.

WOVOKA
(PAIUTE)

A Northern Paiute medicine man and prophet, Wovoka (ca. 1856–1932) founded the messianic GHOST DANCE religion, which heralded the end of warfare between Euro-Americans and Indians in North America.

Born in Mason Valley, Nevada, near the Walker River, Wovoka is believed to have been the son of Tavibo, a well-known medicine man and prophet, who preached the ultimate triumph of the Indian over the white man. Wovoka was influenced not only by the teachings of Tavibo and other reservation prophets, but also by the Christian traditions of the white ranching family with whom he lived for a time near Yerrington, Nevada. Among whites, Wovoka was known as Jack Wilson.

Late in 1888, Wovoka fell desperately ill with a fever. After his recovery, he told how he had been transported to the spirit world. There, the Supreme Being told him to broadcast the message that the end of the earth was near, but that it would be reborn pristine and would be inherited by all the Indians, dead and alive, who would exist forever, free from pain and heartbreak. To propitiate that event, Indians had to live in harmony with one another, to cleanse themselves often, and to reject all the ways of whites—in particular alcohol. Further, Wovoka advocated meditation, prayer, singing, and—especially—dancing, through which one might achieve a temporary deathlike state that afforded a glimpse of the dawning paradise. It was the latter aspect of the movement that most disturbed reservation authorities, for the so-called Ghost Dance was a demonstration of group ecstasy, which suggested the possibility of a collective uprising.

The Ghost Dance religion spread rapidly throughout the reservations, especially among the Shoshones, Arapahos, Cheyennes, and Sioux. Wovoka, whom some called the Red Man's Christ, enjoined his followers to walk in the ways of peace and, while eschewing white practices, to do no harm to whites. However, among militant Sioux bands led by KICKING BEAR, SHORT BULL, and nine others (all of whom had made a pilgrimage to Wovoka in Nevada in 1889 and 1890), the Ghost Dance was a way to eliminate the whites once and for all. These Sioux fashioned ghost shirts, which they claimed were impervious to bullets. The militants gathered in increasing numbers on the reservations and mounted the so-called Ghost Dance Uprising, which culminated in the botched arrest and killing of SITTING BULL, most revered of Sioux leaders, and, soon after, the massacre of BIG FOOT's Minneconjou band at Wounded Knee Creek in December 1890.

Wovoka was profoundly shocked by the violence his teachings had provoked, and he stressed his message of peace. But with the despair that followed Wounded Knee, the Ghost Dance religion quickly died out, except among the Arapahos and Cheyennes, who incorporated elements of the Ghost Dance into their traditional tribal dances. Wovoka lived the remainder of his life with his wife and four children on reservations and died at the Walker River Reservation near Schurz, Nevada.

—*Alan Axelrod*

SEE ALSO: Wounded Knee Massacre

SUGGESTED READING:

Bailey, Paul. *Wovoka, The Indian Messiah.* Los Angeles, 1957.
Mooney, James. *Ghost-Dance Religion and the Sioux Outbreak of 1890.* Westport, Conn., 1965.
Utley, Robert M. *Last Days of the Sioux Nation.* New Haven, Conn., 1963.

WRIGHT IRRIGATION ACT OF 1887

Passed in 1887 by the state of California, the Wright Irrigation Act created local IRRIGATION districts of fifty or more people or a majority of landowners. The act was sponsored by C. C. Wright from Modesto, and it was intended to help small farmers gain access to WATER rights often grabbed by "water monopolists." Set up like a local government, each district had the power to levy taxes, seize existing water works under eminent domain, and issue bonds for water projects. With the formation of the fiftieth district in 1911, the Wright Act was the basis for California's modern system of agriculture.

—*Kurt Edward Kemper*

SUGGESTED READING:

Bean, Walton. *California: An Interpretive History.* New York, 1968.
Miller, M. Catherine. *Flooding the Courtrooms: Law and Water in the Far West.* Lincoln, Nebr., 1993.

WYETH, N. C.

Artist-illustrator N. C. (Newell Convers) Wyeth (1882–1945) was born in Needham, Massachusetts. He received a basic art education in Boston before entering the Howard Pyle School of Art in Wilmington, Delaware, in 1902. Inspired by FREDERIC REMINGTON, Wyeth's early work brimmed with Western characters. His first published illustration, *Bronco Buster,* appeared in *The Saturday Evening Post* in 1903. The following year, Wyeth went to the West for the first time, sponsored by the *Post* and *Scribner's* magazine. *Outing Magazine* underwrote a second trip in 1906.

Back home, Wyeth translated his experiences with cowboys, Indians, teamsters, and sheepherders into articles and illustrations for several national publications. He also illustrated the works of some of the most important Western writers of the period including EMERSON HOUGH, Clarence Edward Mulford, Alfred Henry Lewis, and EDNA FERBER. In addition, Wyeth produced memorable advertisements with Western themes for cereal, firearms, and tobacco products.

Although Wyeth eventually emphasized other subjects, he continued to produce Western illustrations throughout his career. In time, he also became an accomplished easel painter and muralist. He was elected to the Society of Illustrators in 1912 and the National Academy in 1941.

Several of Wyeth's offspring also became distinguished artists as did his son-in-law, New Mexico painter Peter Hurd. Wyeth died at Chadds Ford, Pennsylvania, following a railroad-crossing accident.

—*B. Byron Price*

SUGGESTED READING:

Allen, Douglas, and Douglas Allen, Jr. *N. C. Wyeth.* New York, 1972.
Samuels, Howard, and Peggy Samuels. *The Illustrated Biographical Encyclopedia of Artists of the American West.* Garden City, N.Y., 1976.

WYETH, NATHANIEL JARVIS

Trapper, trader, and promoter of Oregon, Nathaniel Jarvis Wyeth (1802–1856) was born near Cambridge, Massachusetts. As a young man, he owned a pond and patented machinery to harvest ice. Seeking wider outlets for his ambitions, he devised a plan to establish a company to trade for furs on the Columbia River.

He planned a five-year expedition of fifty men and borrowed heavily to outfit his company. He set out with fewer than half that number of men to join the 1832 rendezvous. By the time he left the RENDEZVOUS, only eleven men remained in the party. The men trapped on their trek to the Columbia and hid their furs, but once they reached FORT VANCOUVER, they all resigned. Because the men lacked horses, they were unable to recover the buried furs.

Wyeth left the 1833 rendezvous after contracting with Milton Sublette and THOMAS FITZPATRICK to supply three thousand dollars in goods in exchange for beaver pelts. Wyeth returned to Boston in November of that year and organized the Columbia River Fishing and Trading Company. In April 1834, with a party of Methodist missionaries, he and Milton Sublette departed for the mountains with goods for the rendezvous participants.

When William Sublette passed their caravan bearing goods for trade, Wyeth learned that the ROCKY MOUNTAIN FUR COMPANY had dissolved and that it would not accept his goods. He then built FORT HALL and put his goods up for sale. His group spent the winter trapping, and after an unsuccessful attempt early in 1836 to make a trading agreement with the HUDSON'S BAY COMPANY, Wyeth returned to Boston. Hudson's Bay Company bought Fort Hall in 1837.

Wyeth was highly successful in the ice and refrigerated-produce business for the rest of his life. He also remained interested in the settlement of Oregon and promoted the OREGON TRAIL.

—*Charles E. Hanson, Jr.*

SEE ALSO: Sublette Brothers; Trappers

SUGGESTED READING:

Sampson, William R. "Nathaniel Jarvis Wyeth." In *The Mountain Men and the Fur Trade of the Far West*. Vol. 5. Edited by LeRoy R. Hafen. Glendale, Calif., 1968.

Young, F. G., ed. "The Correspondence and Journals of Captain Nathaniel J. Wyeth, 1831–1836." In *Sources of the History of Oregon*. Vol. 1, Parts 3–6. Eugene, Oreg., 1899.

WYOMING

The least populated of the fifty states, Wyoming, with 97,980 square miles, had a population of 453,528 in 1990. Only one city, the state capital of CHEYENNE, had a population in excess of 50,000. Most people live in the few towns separated by vast distances or on isolated ranches. Their daily lives are dictated by arid, semidesert, or mountainous land and harsh weather. As a result, Wyoming retains much of the flavor and character of the frontier in its culture, politics, and economy.

Because of the small and relatively homogenous population, the state has been characterized as "a small town with a very long main street." Casper, the second largest city and commercial center for much of central Wyoming, has the only statewide circulating daily newspaper. Shopping habits, cultural attractions,

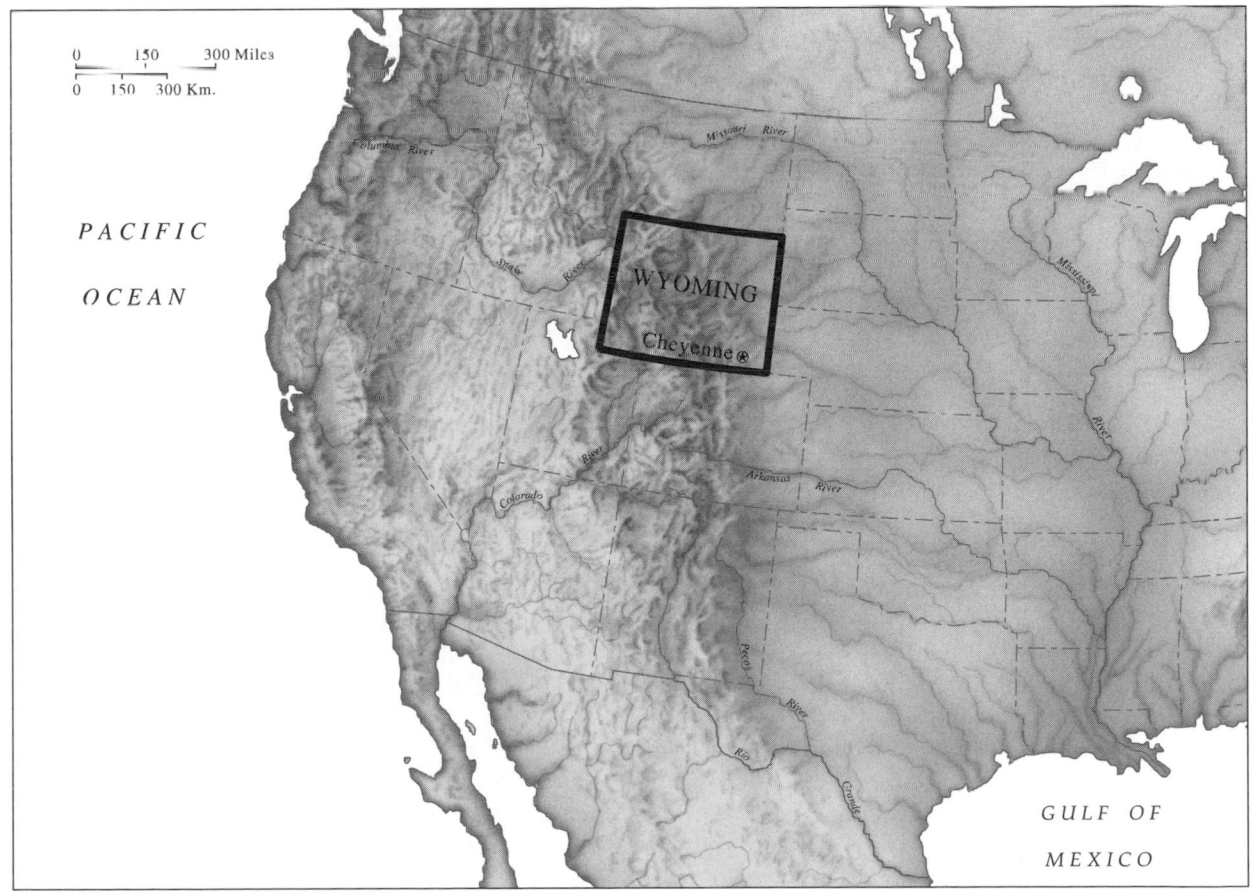

and media coverage pull Wyomingites in the four corners of the state toward Denver, Colorado; Salt Lake City, Utah; Billings, Montana; and Rapid City, South Dakota. Natural resource exploitation, livestock raising, irrigated farming, and TOURISM have been the main industries. Manufacturing is nearly nonexistent even in the larger towns.

Wyomingites generally take great pride in their state and its "cowboy heritage," apparent in its "bucking horse" license plate logo, the popularity of rodeos such as Cheyenne Frontier Days, and support for sports teams, especially the "Cowboys," from the state's only four-year college, the University of Wyoming. Most communities maintain local museums, many containing testimonials to the mythic West. The BUFFALO BILL HISTORICAL CENTER in Cody and the American Heritage Center in Laramie are nationally recognized. Casper and Cheyenne have supported civic orchestras since World War II. The Grand Teton Music Festival has been held annually in Jackson since the 1970s. Hunting, fishing, and hiking remain the most popular sports. Snow skiing, mountain climbing, and riding horses are popular hobbies for some residents and attract thousands of tourists.

The Great Plains extend into the eastern part of the state; the land rises to mountains and high plateaus in the western part. The highest point, Gannett Peak in the Wind River Range, is 13,804 feet, while the lowest point is 3,100 feet in northeastern Crook County. The state is second to Colorado in average highest elevation. Average precipitation is less than fourteen inches per year, much of it in the form of snow. Winter temperatures can fall as low as 60° F below zero. Average humidity is extremely low. The presence of brisk winds adds to the general harsh climate in many parts of the state. Wind speeds near Medicine Bow average 12.4 miles per hour, making it the third windiest location in the continental United States.

Native Americans in Wyoming

Wyoming was occupied as early as 7000 B.C., but little is known of the state's inhabitants before 1800. During the nineteenth century, Crow, Blackfoot, Shoshone, Cheyenne, Arapaho, and Sioux Indians hunted bisons (BUFFALOES) over various parts of Wyoming. The Indians were important partners in the FUR TRADE but became increasingly hostile as their hunting lands were destroyed by white settlers. Except for the Shoshone and Arapaho tribes, none remained in Wyoming after 1878. The American Indian population in the state in 1990 made up just 2.1 percent of the total population; most Native Americans lived on the Wind River Reservation established in west-central Wyoming by the Fort Bridger Treaty of 1865 for the Shoshones.

In 1877, the federal government sent a Northern Arapaho group to the reservation after promising the Shoshones that the move was only temporary until a reservation for the Arapahos was found. In 1939, the federal government finally conceded that the relocation was permanent. In 1993, the enrolled members of the Arapaho tribe living on the reservation numbered about 8,000 compared to 6,000 Shoshones. The most influential Shoshone leader in the nineteenth century was WASHAKIE who died in 1900 at the age of nearly one hundred.

Exploration period

François and Louis Joseph de La Verendrye are considered the first Europeans to explore Wyoming in 1742 and 1743. Through the 1803 LOUISIANA PURCHASE, Wyoming was transferred to the United States. JOHN COLTER was the first white American explorer in 1806 and 1807. Other early explorers included WILSON PRICE HUNT, who led the Overland Astorians through Wyoming in 1811, and Robert Stuart, who led the first party eastward across Wyoming in 1812 via South Pass. The fur trade brought WILLIAM HENRY ASHLEY and such colorful MOUNTAIN MEN as JAMES (JIM) BRIDGER, JEDEDIAH STRONG SMITH, William L. Sublette, and David E. Jackson to Wyoming. Declines in European markets and decreasing numbers of beavers brought an end to the fur trade in the 1840s.

Interest in the area as a route west grew following exploration by JOHN CHARLES FRÉMONT in 1842. The principal trail was the OREGON TRAIL, which followed the Platte and Sweetwater rivers and crossed the Continental Divide at South Pass. BRIGHAM YOUNG led the Mormon migration through Wyoming in 1847. Two years later, gold-seekers bound for California began using much of the same trail. The PONY EXPRESS crossed Wyoming in 1860 and 1861 before the completion of the transcontinental telegraph lines, which also passed through Wyoming. Treaties with the Indians and cavalry posts at FORT LARAMIE and FORT BRIDGER protected the early travelers, but attacks increased during the Civil War. The BOZEMAN TRAIL was blazed north through Indian lands in the Powder River region in 1863. Before the Fort Laramie Treaty of 1868 closed the Bozeman Trail, several white-Indian confrontations occurred, including the FETTERMAN MASSACRE in which Captain William J. Fetterman and eighty other men from Fort Phil Kearny were killed in 1866.

Territorial years

In 1868, the Wyoming Territory was created from the Dakota Territory after the UNION PACIFIC RAILROAD helped establish settlements across what is now southern Wyoming. Wyoming's government was the first in the world to provide full suffrage rights to women, when the first territorial legislature passed a bill giving women the right to vote. The state's nickname, "The Equality State," is derived from this distinction. On February 17, 1870, ESTHER HOBART MCQUIGG SLACK MORRIS was appointed justice of the peace in the mining town of South Pass City. She was the first woman judge in the United States, perhaps in the world. She served eight and a half months and presided over two dozen cases.

Wyoming's ethnic heritage

Most early pioneer settlers worked for the RAIL-ROADS, mined coal, or ran livestock. Members of numerous ethnic groups came to Wyoming primarily to work in the coal mines or for the railroad. The largest immigrant groups in the nineteenth century were Irish, Welsh, and English. In the early twentieth century, Italians, eastern Europeans, and Mexicans predominated. Early in the century, Rock Springs called itself the "International City" because it was home to people of almost every national background. Few African Americans lived in Wyoming although voters elected a black man to the legislature in 1879. The African American population in 1990 numbered fewer than three thousand. In 1990, Hispanics made up the largest ethnic group; many claimed ancestral roots in territorial days. Although their number remained small, Basques came to Wyoming in the early twentieth century and worked mostly as sheepherders. Germans from Russia established small colonies in eastern Wyoming and the Big Horn Basin in the early twentieth century.

Coal

Tensions between labor and management led to the Rock Springs massacre in September 1885 in which 28 Chinese were killed by whites, mostly European immigrants who feared the mine companies would replace them with cheaper labor. With the support of Territorial Governor FRANCIS E. WARREN, who furnished troops to restore order to the Union Pacific properties, the railroad's grip on COAL MINING remained strong. Numerous mine disasters marked the industry during the four decades after statehood, the worst occurring at Hanna in 1903, when 163 men died in a mine explosion. Twenty years later, 99 men died when coal gas ignited in a mine near Kemmerer.

Coal was mined underground until the mid-1920s when strip mining was first used in the Powder River basin. Although subbituminous coal underlies more than 40 percent of the state's land area, mining much of it has never been commercially feasible. The largest unbroken concentration of coal in the United States,

the Wyodak bed in the Powder River basin has a thickness of 25 to 150 feet and penetrates the surface along a 120-mile line. Geologists have estimated that it contains up to fifteen billion tons of usable coal, twenty times the entire annual output in the United States. Unlike underground mines, the open-pit mines are not labor intensive. The state led the nation in coal production in the late 1980s and 1990s.

Ranching

Livestock raising has been a major industry in Wyoming since territorial days. Although the first cattle were brought to a fur-trade RENDEZVOUS in 1830, cattle were not present in large numbers until after the Civil War. The first longhorns were trailed north from Texas to the Wyoming plains in 1865. The CATTLE INDUSTRY depended on the use of open range and accessibility to WATER courses. In the 1880s, ranching attracted many Eastern and foreign investors, most of whom remained absentee owners who gave operational authority to resident managers. In 1879, many of the territory's cattlemen formed the Wyoming Stock Growers' Association. Gradually, the organization gained a quasi-governmental control over roundups and the disposal of unbranded cattle. Few operators of large ranches bothered to purchase land; they preferred to use the land for free without having to make improvements on it or pay property taxes. Spectacular profits in the early 1880s diminished with increased competition later in the decade. Large losses of stock in the severe winter of 1886 to 1887 and increasing pressures on use of the open range led to violent confrontations between the remaining large operators and owners of smaller ranches. These conflicts culminated in the JOHNSON COUNTY WAR in 1892. Even though the Wyoming Stock Growers' Association was implicated in the incident, the organization remained a powerful force in the state's politics well into the twentieth century.

The first large herd of sheep was brought into Wyoming in 1870, and large bands were common, mostly in the central part of Wyoming, in the early 1880s. After 1900, sheep and cattle ranchers fought for grazing lands. One such incident was the Spring Creek raid in Washakie County in 1909. By the 1920s, however, many cattle ranchers diversified their operations to include sheep raising.

Agriculture

The state's aridity has hampered agricultural development and has made water issues important since territorial days. Under the state's constitution, the state owns all water within its borders, and the state engineer is responsible for apportioning it to users under the prior-appropriation doctrine, pioneered in Wyo-

The Indians of Fort Washakie, Wyoming Territory, gathered for a reception for President Chester A. Arthur in 1883. *Courtesy National Archives.*

ming largely through the influence of ELWOOD MEAD. Mexican Americans living near Fort Laramie pioneered irrigated FARMING in Wyoming in 1855. A few privately organized projects, many operated by MORMONS in western Wyoming, were established during the territorial period. After statehood, Wyoming profited from the CAREY ACT OF 1894, a federal law authored by Wyoming Senator JOSEPH MAULL CAREY to support RECLAMATION projects.

After Congress established the BUREAU OF RECLAMATION in 1902, its first significant project was the Buffalo Bill (Shoshone) Dam, completed in Wyoming in 1910. The bureau authorized six dams along the North Platte River from 1910 to 1958 (Pathfinder, Guernsey, Alcova, Seminoe, Kortes, and Glendo). The Riverton Reclamation Project, initiated in 1906, brought irrigated agriculture to Fremont County. Wyoming congressmen, particularly Senator JOHN B. KENDRICK and Representative Frank Mondell, were strong proponents of Bureau of Reclamation projects in the West. Dryland farming led to a boom in HOMESTEADING in the 1920s, mostly in eastern Wyoming. More homestead entries were made during the 1920s than in any other decade in Wyoming history.

Oil

Petroleum production has been an important industry since statehood. Indians first noticed petroleum seeping from the ground in Wyoming. A naturally occurring oil pool near Hilliard in southwestern Wyoming was well known by the 1830s. The first flowing well was drilled in Dallas Dome in Fremont County in 1883 by Mike Murphy, a former gold prospector who found oil at three hundred feet in the Chugwater formation. Since then, the most significant fields have been Salt Creek (Natrona County), Lance Creek (Niobrara County), and Oregon and Elk Basins (Park County). TEAPOT DOME, the petroleum oil reserve for which the infamous scandal during the Warren G. Harding administration was named, is located in Wyoming. By 1922, two major companies, Standard of Indiana and Ohio Oil Company, controlled 97 percent of all oil production in the state. Until a refinery was built in Casper in 1895, oil was used in its natural state as a lubricant or exported in small quantities by wagon and rail to refineries elsewhere. In the next half century, refineries were built in almost two dozen Wyoming towns. Several Wyoming communities, including Sinclair, Midwest, and Bairoil, began as oil-company towns. Casper, Glenrock, Evanston, Newcastle, Douglas, and Lusk owe much of their twentieth-century growth to nearby oil discoveries.

Booms and busts

The presence of oil and coal, along with other minerals such as trona (discovered in 1938) and uranium (discovered in 1918 but not mined until the 1950s), has made Wyoming susceptible to economic BOOMS and busts. The Great Depression struck in Wyoming in about 1924 and did not recede until World War II. Almost one hundred banks failed in the 1920s and early 1930s, including seventeen in 1924 alone. While all sectors of the economy suffered, AGRICULTURE was hardest hit. World War II brought an end to the Depression in Wyoming, but it did not lead to manufacturing or heavy industry in the state. Declines in the demand for coal in the 1930s continued through the 1950s and forced the closure of labor-intensive underground mines. Increases in automobile tourism offset the losses in many communities, but the economy remained heavily dependent on agriculture and mineral industries.

The Wyoming legislature passed a modest mineral severance-tax law in 1969. Five years later, fueled by the Arab oil embargo, the Wyoming economy entered another boom period. Communities that once lost population found themselves overcome with unimpeded growth. The mineral severance tax helped communities cope with the influx of population, but even with such help, many could not provide enough housing, utility services, recreational facilities, and law enforcement to deal with all of the new arrivals. In the 1970s, psychologists referred to the "Gillette syndrome," named for a Wyoming boom town, to describe the social malaise leading to alcoholism, drug abuse, family abuse, and depression that infected "impacted" communities. Several billions of dollars collected from the severance taxes were placed in a Permanent Mineral Trust Fund, the interest from which went to build infrastructure. Environmental activism gained many adherents among residents concerned about threats to the state's wilderness areas and wildlife. Ranchers, environmentalists, and railroad lobbyists teamed up to stop construction of a coal-slurry pipeline in the 1970s.

In the mid-1980s, steep declines in energy prices pushed the state into its worst economic depression. During the 1980s, the population fell 3.4 percent, after it had risen by more than 40 percent during the previous decade. By the early 1990s, the state's economy remained stagnant, and except for resort towns like Jackson, most places continued to lose population.

Federal-state relations

The FEDERAL GOVERNMENT controlled almost half of the land in the state in 1993, mostly through the BUREAU OF LAND MANAGEMENT, the UNITED STATES FOREST SERVICE, and the NATIONAL PARK SERVICE. Historically, Wyomingites have resented the federal presence, while, at the same time, many have relied on federal assistance, particularly in livestock, tourism, and mineral industries. With the exception of Warren Air Force Base, home of the "MX" missile system, the Department of Defense is not an important presence in the state even though Wyomingite Richard Cheney served as secretary of defense in George Bush's administration.

Politics

Republicans have dominated politics for much of the state's history, but much of the success of a typical Wyoming politician depends on strong personality and constituent service rather than party affiliation. The state legislatures have been dominated by Republicans, but the governors of Wyoming from 1974 to 1993 were Democrats. Prominent political figures from Wyoming have included Supreme Court Justice WILLIS VAN DEVANTER, Secretary of the Interior James Watt, lawyer and author Thurman Arnold, and Nellie Tayloe Ross, the first woman governor of any state following her election in 1924.

National parks

YELLOWSTONE NATIONAL PARK, the nation's oldest national park, was established in 1872. After World War II, when the park experienced huge gains in visitation, environmentalists and others expressed concerns that human pressures on the park would seriously erode its character. In 1988, a series of devastating forest fires blackened nearly a quarter of the land area within the park. Annual visitation continued to grow, however. GRAND TETON NATIONAL PARK was created in 1929 and expanded in the following decades, largely through land donations by John D. Rockefeller, Jr., whose intentions to keep the area free of annoying billboards and business development were met with significant local opposition. The state also contains the nation's oldest national monument, Devil's Tower National Monument, established in 1906.

—*Phil Roberts*

SEE ALSO: Farming: Dryland Farming; Oil and Gas Industry; Rodeo; Sheep and Sheep Ranching; Sublette Brothers; Women's Suffrage

SUGGESTED READING:
Adams, Randy, and Craig Sodaro. *Frontier Spirit: The Story of Wyoming.* Cheyenne, Wyo., 1986.

Brown, Robert H. *Wyoming: A Geography.* Boulder, Colo., 1980.

Cawley, Gregg, et al. *The Equality State: Government and Politics in Wyoming.* Dubuque, Iowa, 1988.

Erwin, Marie H., et al. *Wyoming Historical Blue Book.* 1946. Reprint. Cheyenne, Wyo., 1974.

Gould, Lewis L. *Wyoming: A Political History, 1868–1896.* New Haven, Conn., 1968.

Gressley, Gene M. *Bankers and Cattlemen.* New York, 1966.

Hendrickson, Gordon O., ed. *Peopling the High Plains: Wyoming's European Heritage.* Cheyenne, Wyo., 1977.

Larson, T. A. *History of Wyoming.* 2d ed., rev. Lincoln, Nebr., 1978.

——. *Wyoming: A History.* New York, 1977.

——. *Wyoming's War Years, 1941–1945.* 2d ed. Riverton, Wyo., 1993.

McPhee, John. *Rising from the Plains.* New York, 1986.

Phillips, Clynn, et al. *Wyoming Data Handbook.* Cheyenne, Wyo., 1992.

Righter, Robert. *Crucible for Conservation: The Struggle for Grand Teton National Park.* Boulder, Colo., 1982.

Roberts, Phil, et al. *Wyoming Almanac.* 3d ed., rev. Laramie, Wyo., 1993.

Smith, Helena Huntington. *The War on Powder River.* Lincoln, Nebr., 1966.

Starr, Eileen F. *Architecture in the Cowboy State.* Glendo, Wyo., 1992.

Tyler, Carolyn B., ed.. *Wyoming Newspapers: A Centennial History.* Cheyenne, Wyo., 1990.

Urbanek, Mae. *Wyoming Place Names.* 3d ed., rev. Boulder, Colo., 1974.

XIT RANCH, TEXAS

In 1885, the state of Texas tendered more than 3 million acres of public land, located in parts of nine counties on the western edge of the Texas Panhandle, to the Chicago corporation of Taylor, Babcock, and Company, in exchange for building a new state capitol building at Austin. Better known as the Capitol Syndicate, Abner Taylor and his associates A. C. Babcock and Chicago dry-goods merchants John V. Farwell and Charles B. Farwell established a cattle ranch on the property until they could attract sufficient settlers to warrant subdividing it into farms.

In order to secure the additional investment needed for livestock and improvements, the syndicate formed the Capitol Freehold Land and Investment Company, Limited, of London in 1885. By 1888, $10 million in capital had been raised through the sale of debenture bonds.

Kansas rancher B. H. Campbell was appointed the first general manager of the XIT. Campbell supervised the delivery of the first herds of stock cattle driven to the ranch from southern and western Texas in 1885. Drover Ab Blocker is credited with devising the easy to apply but difficult to alter XIT brand.

From 1887 onward, the ranch maintained an average herd size of 125,000 to 150,000 cattle. In the late 1880s, the XIT acquired a range near Miles City, Montana, where 20,000 to 30,000 steers fattened annually. During the same period, the ranch began to improve the quality of its herds with blooded Hereford, shorthorn, and Angus stock.

Some 335 windmills and one hundred reservoirs watered XIT herds while as many as 150 cowboys worked its ranges. The ranch was eventually divided into seven divisions with a general headquarters established in the town of Channing in 1890.

Fencing of the ranch perimeter began in 1885, took more than a year to complete and required more than three hundred carloads of barbed wire. By 1900, some fifteen hundred miles of fence had been erected using six thousand miles of wire. Cross fences divided the ranch into ninety-four separate pastures.

In order to demonstrate the agricultural potential of its land as well as raise forage crops for its cattle, the XIT was among the first and the most active ranches to experiment with farming. By the 1890s, the ranch had invested in farm machinery and was raising plots of prairie hay, maize, oats, alfalfa, millet, wheat, sorghum, and vegetables.

The Capitol Syndicate began to sell some of its lands in 1901. Cattleman George W. Littlefield bought the first large block consisting of 225,858 acres. Smaller tracts were sold to cattlemen, developers, and individual farmers into the 1950s. The ranch ceased operations in the fall of 1912 with the sale of its last herd.

—*B. Byron Price*

See also: Cattle Brands and Branding; Cattle Industry

Suggested reading:
Duke, Cardia Sloan, and Joe B. Frantz. *6000 Miles of Fence: Life on the XIT Ranch of Texas.* Austin, Tex., 1961.
Haley, J. Evetts. *The XIT Ranch of Texas and the Early Days of the Llano Estacado.* Chicago, 1929.
MacConnell, C. E. *XIT Buck.* Tucson, Ariz., 1968.
Nordyke, Lewis. *Cattle Empire: The Fabulous Story of the 3,000,000 Acre XIT.* New York, 1949.
XIT Ranch Papers. Panhandle Plains Historical Museum. Canyon, Tex.

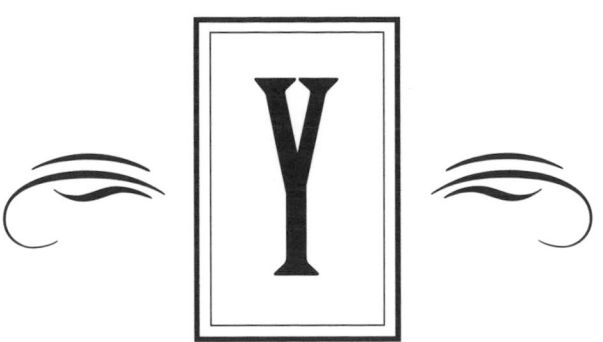

YAKIMA INDIANS

SEE: Native American Peoples: Peoples of the Pacific Northwest

YAKIMA WAR

SEE: Pacific Northwest Indian Wars

YELLOWSTONE NATIONAL PARK

Yellowstone National Park, established in 1872, was the nation's first national park. It covers an area of 3,468 square miles in eastern Idaho, southern Montana, and northwestern Wyoming. Most of the area occupies a volcanic plateau in the Rocky Mountains varying in elevation from 7,000 to 8,000 feet. The highest point within the park is Eagle Peak, at 11,358 feet, but the park is most famous for its spectacular geothermal features—some two hundred geysers, ten thousand hot springs, and many fumaroles. Best known among these features are the geyser Old Faithful and Mammoth Hot Springs. Old Faithful derived its name from the regularity with which it erupts—on average, every 65 minutes (actual intervals range from 33 to 148 minutes). Each eruption spouts some 1,400 cubic feet of water and steam about 150 feet in the air.

Most of the park is drained by the Yellowstone River. The park is richly forested by lodgepole pine, aspen, spruce, and fir. Indigenous wildlife includes elk, buffaloes, moose, deer, bighorn sheep, antelope, coyotes, and bears.

The first Euro-American visitor to the Yellowstone area was almost certainly the fur trader JOHN COLTER in 1807. In 1870, the federal government sponsored an expedition to study the area. Two years later, in part motivated by a popular resolve to protect the spectacular Western environment and in part encouraged by burgeoning railroads looking to increase tourist revenue, the government established Yellowstone as the first national park. Since then, frequent controversies have arisen over the preservation of nature and the encouragement of TOURISM. In 1988, devastating fires affected nearly 20 percent of the park area and resulted in the destruction of about 10 percent of Yellowstone's trees.

—*Alan Axelrod*

SEE ALSO: Albright, Horace Marden; National Park Service; Roosevelt, Theodore

Yellowstone Canyon and Lower Falls in Yellowstone National Park. *Courtesy National Park Service.*

SUGGESTED READING:
Chase, A. *Playing God in Yellowstone: The Destruction of America's National Parks.* Orlando, Fla., 1987.
Haines, Aubrey L. *The Yellowstone Story.* 2 vols. Niwot, Colo., 1977.
Keiter, Robert B., and Mark S. Boyce, eds. *The Greater Yellowstone Geosystem: Redefining America's Wilderness.* New Haven, Conn., 1991.
Reese, R. *Greater Yellowstone: The National Park and Adjoining Wildlands.* Helena, Mont., 1984.

YICK WO V. HOPKINS

The U.S. Supreme Court decision *Yick Wo* v. *Hopkins* in 1886 concerned a San Francisco ordinance that allowed the city board of supervisors to refuse laundries built of wood permission to operate. Although the law did not mention race, it was intended to target Chinese laundry owners. Seeing through this facade, the Supreme Court held that "equal protection of the laws is a pledge of the protection of equal laws" and applied the Fourteenth Amendment guarantee to Chinese immigrant aliens as well as to U.S. citizens; it rejected the ordinance as "illegal discrimination." Coming as it did from a court that would soon endorse

Conservationist John Muir in Yosemite National Park. *Courtesy National Park Service.*

racial segregation and allow the effective disfranchisement of African Americans, the *Yick Wo* decision was a remarkable defense of the principle of equal rights.

—*Peggy Pascoe*

SEE ALSO: Chinese Americans

YOSEMITE ACT OF 1864

By an act of Congress on June 30, 1864, the federal government granted the Yosemite Valley and the adjacent Mariposa Grove of redwoods to the state of California as a public park. The legislation came less than a decade after James M. Hutchings led the first party of tourists into the region in 1855 and publicized its magnificent beauty in the *Mariposa Gazette,* the *California Magazine,* and other periodicals. In 1868, the naturalist JOHN MUIR traveled to Yosemite for the first time and began agitating for the transfer of the park from state to federal jurisdiction, since, he felt, the federal government was most likely to provide the fullest degree of protection for it. YOSEMITE NATIONAL PARK was established on October 1, 1890, surrounding the valley. Muir then led a drive to persuade California to cede the valley back to the federal government for inclusion in the national park.

—*Alan Axelrod*

SEE ALSO: National Park Service

SUGGESTED READING:
Chase, Smeaton J. *Yosemite Trails.* Tahoe City, Calif., 1991.
Schaffer, Jeffrey P. *Yosemite National Park.* Berkeley, Calif., 1992.

YOSEMITE NATIONAL PARK

Yosemite National Park encompasses 1,189 square miles of land on the western edge of the Sierra Nevada in central California. At the center of the park is the spectacular Yosemite Valley of the Merced River. The valley descends to about 2,750 feet, and the Merced feeds a series of magnificent waterfalls along its route, most notably Yosemite Falls (2,425 feet), Ribbon Falls (612 feet), and Bridalveil Falls (620 feet). Around the valley, granite peaks and domes are prominent, including El Capitan (7,564 feet), Half Dome (8,852 feet), and Mount Lyell (13,095 feet). The park features three groves of ancient sequoias and is a sanctuary for mule deer and black bears.

Yosemite National Park. *Courtesy National Park Service.*

Although an expedition led by JOSEPH REDDEFORD WALKER in 1833 passed near the Yosemite Valley, the valley itself was unexplored by Euro-Americans until 1851 when the trader James Savage led a party into it in pursuit of Indians who had destroyed three of his trading posts. Indeed, the region contained twenty-two villages of the Yosemite (meaning "grizzly bear") Indians. Between 1851 and 1855—when James M. Hutchings led the first party of tourists into the valley—the Indians were driven out. After 1855, Yosemite became a tourist mecca, prompting passage of the Yosemite Act of 1864 by which the federal government ceded the land to the state of California for the creation of a state park. The naturalist JOHN MUIR, fearing the state lacked both the means and the resolve to protect Yosemite adequately, lobbied for the creation of a national park under federal jurisdiction, and on October 1, 1890, Yosemite National Park was created around the valley, which was still owned by the state of California. Still concerned about the valley,

Muir founded the SIERRA CLUB in 1892, which persuaded California legislators to cede the valley back to the federal government. In 1906, it was incorporated into the national park.

With its location near San Francisco—a situation that gave rise to the HETCH HETCHY CONTROVERSY in the early twentieth century, when the city wished to use a portion of Yosemite as a water reservoir—the park is one of the more heavily visited of America's national parks. Some 2.5 million people go to Yosemite each year.

—*Alan Axelrod*

SEE ALSO: National Park Service; Tourism

SUGGESTED READING:
Chase, Smeaton J. *Yosemite Trails.* Tahoe City, Calif., 1987.
Schaffer, Jeffrey P. *Yosemite National Park.* Berkeley, Calif., 1992.

YOUNG, ANN ELIZA WEBB

At one time a wife of Mormon church leader BRIGHAM YOUNG, Ann Eliza Webb Young (1844–?) became an ardent opponent of polygamy (the practice whereby a man is married to more than one wife at a time). Her Mormon father acquired another wife in 1846, although the practice of polygamy was not officially sanctioned by the church until 1852. By the time she was twelve years old, her father had married three other women. Acutely aware of her mother's bitterness, Webb became increasingly hostile to the system of polygamy. The Mormon leader Brigham Young, a friend of the Webb family, proposed marriage to her, but she spurned his offer, even though he had said he would help her become an actress at the Salt Lake City Theater and move her to the Lion House, where Young kept most of his wives and children. Instead, she married an abusive English plasterer in 1863.

When the marriage went bad, which was almost immediately, Young helped her get a divorce in 1865.

Ann Eliza Webb Young. *Courtesy Historical Department Archives of the Church of Jesus Christ of Latter-day Saints.*

Young persistently made offers of marriage, but she agreed only after he promised to take no more wives; the bride-groom was forty-eight years older than his twenty-seventh wife (this figure is debatable as some historians argue that Young took as many seventy wives). When she refused to live in the Lion House, Young rented her a small house and essentially ignored her; she was forced to take in boarders. Disgusted, she sold all the furniture and moved into a hotel; two weeks later she sued for a divorce, seeking a two-hundred-thousand-dollar settlement.

News of Young's divorce suit stirred a nation already leary of MORMONS. Ann Eliza Webb Young hit the lecture circuit, expounded on the evils of polygamy, and published her autobiography, *The 19th Wife, or Life in Mormon Bondage*. Her stops in Washington, D.C., were significant in the passage of the Poland Act, one of the federal government's early efforts to outlaw poly-gamy. Meanwhile, divorce proceedings raged on. Brigham Young argued that the two were never married, and he was eventually held liable for only court costs. Ann Eliza Webb Young disappeared from the historical record after 1908 following a third failed marriage.

—*Kurt Edward Kemper*

SEE ALSO: Polygamy: Polygamy among Mormons

SUGGESTED READING:
Brown, Dee. *The Gentle Tamers*. New York, 1958.
Wallace, Irving. *The Twenty-Seventh Wife*. New York, 1961.

YOUNG, BRIGHAM

Western colonizer, second president of the CHURCH OF JESUS CHRIST OF LATTER-DAY SAINTS (better known as the Mormon church), and Utah's first territorial governor, Brigham Young (1801–1877) was born in Whittingham, Vermont, the ninth of eleven children. He grew up in an unsettled environment characterized by frequent family moves throughout upstate New York. Despite the influences of a strict, moralistic family and exposure to the religious fervor that characterized the "burned-over district" of upstate New York, Young was slow to associate with a particular religion. At the age of twenty-three, he joined the Methodist church. With limited formal education, he held apprenticeships as a carpenter, painter, and glazier—trades he used to support himself, with minimal success. In 1824, he met and married his first wife, Miriam Works; they had two daughters.

Young first came into contact with the teachings of the then-fledgling Mormon church in 1830. He was drawn to Mormonism by its emphasis on Christian primitivism, its millennialist orientation (that is, the belief in the imminent Second Coming of Christ and end of the world), authoritarianism, and certain Puritan-like beliefs. Mormonism also offered Young an avenue to status and recognition through its lay priesthood. His commitment to the new faith was ensured by his initial meeting with Mormonism's founder and prophet, JOSEPH SMITH, JR. Impressed with Smith's charismatic, unpretentious demeanor, Young joined the new denomination in 1832, when other members of his immediate family joined.

From the moment of his conversion, Young threw his full energies into promoting Mormonism. He fulfilled several missions and various other church assignments. He rose quickly through church ranks, and in 1835, he was appointed to the church's ruling elite, the Council of the Twelve. In 1838, as the senior member of this body, he took charge of the Mormon exodus from Missouri to Illinois. In 1840, he gained further recognition through his missionary efforts in England, where he facilitated Mormonism's dynamic growth in that nation. Following his return to NAUVOO, ILLINOIS, in 1841, Young affirmed his complete loyalty to Mormonism by embracing the controversial and still-secret practice of polygamy (the practice whereby a man takes more than one wife), initially introduced by Smith to a small, select group of followers. Young eventually married a total of at least fifty-five women (some historians claim he married as many as seventy), by whom he fathered fifty-seven children.

Following Smith's assassination at the hands of an armed mob in June 1844, Young emerged as Mormonism's principal leader. Two years later, in response to continuing armed anti-Mormon violence in Illinois, he organized the mass migration to the Far West. Through careful planning and preparation, he presided over the largest and best-organized westward pioneer trek in American history. He personally led the first company into Utah's Great Salt Lake valley on July 24, 1847.

Over the next thirty years, he supervised the migration of thousands of MORMONS, who used varied modes of transportation including covered wagons, handcarts, church teams, and finally the railroad to travel to Utah. He oversaw the establishment of some 250 Mormon settlements, not just in Utah, but throughout the Far West—in Nevada, Idaho, Wyoming, Arizona, Colorado, and California.

Young was appointed Utah's first territorial governor in 1850, but his relations with the U.S. government became increasingly strained following the Mormons' public announcement of plural marriage in 1852. By 1857, Mormon-federal relations had deteriorated to the point that President JAMES BUCHANAN

Brigham Young. *Courtesy Utah State Historical Society.*

ordered a United States Army force to Utah, an action that precipitated a bloodless skirmish known as the UTAH EXPEDITION, or the Utah War. While Young was removed as territorial governor, tensions between him and the United States government remained high during the following years. In 1862, government authorities sent a second armed force to Utah to monitor Mormon behavior. Federal officials, moreover, sought to legislate polygamy out of existence through the Morrill Anti-Bigamy Act of 1862, the Poland Act of 1874, and subsequent congressional laws. Young, himself, was placed under house arrest for several weeks in 1872 and jailed briefly in March 1875.

As Mormon leader, Young stood in sharp contrast to his predecessor, the charismatic, idealistic, and theologically innovative Joseph Smith. Young inspired his followers through his down-to-earth demeanor and skills as a pragmatic organizer. He focused on the practical task of gathering his followers and building what he envisioned as the Kingdom of God; only rarely did he venture into the realm of theological innovation and then with mixed results. His pronouncements on the doctrines of blood atonement and the Adam-God theory were controversial and had minimal impact on the long-range course of Mormon theological development. More enduring was his 1847 pronouncement denying black men offices within the Mormon priesthood—a lay organization open to nearly all other Mormon males, regardless of race or ethnicity. Young's ban on the ordination of blacks remained in force until 1978.

Young's activities as a pioneer businessman were also noteworthy. His varied business enterprises included a wagon-express company, a ferryboat company, and a railroad. In the field of manufacturing, he owned businesses that processed lumber, wool, sugar beets, iron, and liquor. His greatest entrepreneurial success was in real estate. At the time of his death in 1877, his personal fortune was calculated at six hundred thousand dollars, making him the most successful Utah businessman up to that time.

During the later years of his life, Young tried to insulate his followers from an increasingly aggressive federal government seeking to eradicate Mormon polygamy and from non-Mormon social and economic influences. To fend off these influences and to maximize Mormon independence, he promoted a renewed program of colonization outside of Utah. He, in fact, hoped to establish Mormon colonies outside the boundaries of the United States itself, in Mexico, well beyond the reach of hostile federal officials. He also promoted economic self-sufficiency. He formed the ZION'S CO-OPERATIVE MERCANTILE INSTITUTION and established several self-sufficient cooperative communities—experiments in communitarian living, known collectively as the UNITED ORDER OF ENOCH.

In the end, however, his promotion of Mormon self-sufficiency was of limited success. Larger forces were gradually bringing the Mormons' economy and culture closer to the mainstream of American society. This trend, far beyond the ability of any one man to prevent, was clearly evident when the Mormon church officially renounced polygamy in 1890 and when Utah became a state in 1896. Young, himself, did not live to witness these remarkable developments; he died at the age of seventy-six of complications apparently resulting from acute appendicitis.

—*Newell G. Bringhurst*

SEE ALSO: Handcart Companies; Polygamy: Polygamy among Mormons

SUGGESTED READING:

Arrington, Leonard J. *Brigham Young: American Moses.* New York, 1985.

Bringhurst, Newell G. *Brigham Young and the Expanding American Frontier.* Boston, 1986.

Campbell, Eugene E. *Establishing Zion: The Mormon Church in the American West, 1847–1869.* Salt Lake City, 1988.

———, ed. *The Essential Brigham Young.* Salt Lake City, 1992.

Jessee, Dean C., ed. *Letters of Brigham Young to His Sons.* Salt Lake City, 1974.

West, Ray B. *Kingdom of the Saints: The Story of Brigham Young and the Mormons.* New York, 1957.

YOUNG, EWING

Southwestern trader, trapper, and early settler of Oregon, Ewing Young (ca. 1792–1841) was born near Jonesboro, Tennessee. After moving to Missouri where he bought a farm, he joined WILLIAM BECKNELL's second trip to Santa Fe in 1822. The party also included WILLIAM WOLFSKILL, who became Young's partner in a trading post in Taos.

Young led trapping parties in the Southwest and went to California from 1829 to 1831. Returning in 1832, he trapped and then took horses to Oregon, where he settled in 1834. He built a sawmill and gristmill and later bought a herd of cattle. Before his death of "dyspepsia," he had become a leader among the American settlers in Oregon.

—*Charles E. Hanson, Jr.*

SEE ALSO: Fur Trade; Mountain Men; Trappers

SUGGESTED READING:

Carter, Harvey L. "Ewing Young." In *The Mountain Men and the Fur Trade of the Far West.* Vol. 2. Edited by LeRoy R. Hafen. Glendale, Calif., 1965.

Holmes, Kenneth L. *Ewing Young, Master Trapper.* Portland, Oreg., 1967.

YOUNGER BROTHERS

The four outlaw Younger brothers—Thomas Coleman (Cole, 1844–1916); James (Jim, 1848–1902); John (1851-1874), and Robert (Bob, 1853–1889)—were born in Lees Summit, Missouri. Their primary occupations were farming and robbing.

Although they were the sons of a Unionist, Cole and Jim joined the Confederate guerrilla band of WILLIAM CLARKE QUANTRILL after Kansas JAYHAWKERS raided the family farm and killed their father. Cole may have later served in a Missouri volunteer unit, but Jim stayed with Quantrill throughout the war. Cole, at least, was with Quantrill when he sacked Lawrence, Kansas, on August 21, 1863.

Cole (left) and Jim Younger. *Courtesy State Historical Society of Missouri.*

The four brothers, out of a family of fourteen children, turned to outlawry shortly after the Civil War and associated themselves with the JAMES BROTHERS—Frank and Jesse—in committing bank and train robberies in and around Missouri.

It is impossible to tell which of many publicized robberies were actually committed by the Younger brothers. They did not write to local newspapers to proclaim their innocence when publicly accused, as Jesse James did.

Before joining his brothers, John got into a great deal of trouble all by himself. By the early 1870s, he was riding with his outlaw brothers. On March 16, 1874, he and Jim were involved in a gunfight with Pinkerton agents and local peace officers. John was shot in the throat and Jim in the thigh. Before he died, John shot Agent Louis J. Lull, who died the next day.

In the late summer of 1876, the remaining Younger outlaws accompanied Frank and Jesse James and three others to Northfield, Minnesota, where they planned to rob the First National Bank. Bank employees resisted, and local citizens began shooting at the outlaws, two of whom were killed; Bob and Cole Younger were wounded.

The remaining robbers escaped from the town, but after a gun battle with a pursuing posse two weeks later, another gang member was killed, and all three Youngers were wounded and captured. Frank and Jesse James escaped.

Cole, Bob, and Jim pleaded guilty to murder and were sentenced to the state prison in Stillwell. Bob contracted tuberculosis and died in prison in 1889, but Cole and Jim were paroled in 1901 under a new state law that required them to remain in Minnesota and which did not return their status as citizens.

Jim attempted to marry a local girl but, because of the legalities of the parole, could not. He became despondent and committed suicide.

Cole followed the terms of his parole and found occasional work selling tombstones or insurance. He was pardoned in 1903 and immediately returned to Missouri. He ran a Wild West show with Frank James for a while and then lectured on the evils of crime. He finally retired to Lee's Summit, where he died at the age of seventy-two.

—*Joseph W. Snell*

SEE ALSO: Guerrillas; Northfield Raid; Wild West Shows

SUGGESTED READING:
Horan, James D. *The Authentic Wild West: The Outlaws.* New York, 1976.

YOUNG-MAN-AFRAID-OF-HIS-HORSE (SIOUX)

An important leader of the Oglala Sioux reservation at Pine Ridge, Young-Man-Afraid-of-His-Horse (1839–1914), whose native name was actually translated "Young-Man-of-Whose-Horse-They-Are-Afraid," was born on the Northern Plains. He was a member of the Payabya band of Oglala Sioux, and his family traditionally held leadership positions in the band. His father, MAN-AFRAID-OF-HIS-HORSE, passed civil leadership to him at the time of the Sioux hostilities surrounding the opening of the BOZEMAN TRAIL; RED CLOUD was given military command.

The transition of power from father to son was made difficult by crucial military conflicts with the United States over the Bozeman Trail from 1866 to 1868. In addition, the youth of Young-Man-Afraid-of-His-Horse and Red Cloud's political ambition muddled the transition. After the conflict, Red Cloud broke Lakota tradition by refusing to relinquish his military authority, thus creating a rift between his followers and those of Young-Man-Afraid-of-His-Horse. The result of the feud between the two leaders was that Young-Man-Afraid-of-His-Horse appeared to be pro-American. His decisions and actions were not pro-American, however; instead they were aimed against Red Cloud.

During the early turbulent years at the reservation at Pine Ridge, Young-Man-Afraid-of-His-Horse used his influence and family prestige to maintain peace. He supported the Black Hills cession as a long-term solution for his people and created a tribal police force. The Oglalas responded favorably to his leadership and elected him to preside over the reservation council. In 1886, Red Cloud and Young-Man-Afraid-of-His-Horse ended their feud and used their combined forces at Pine Ridge to oppose the 1889 Sioux Bill, which would diminish the Great Sioux Reservation and allot the remaining lands. While the bill was defeated at the Pine Ridge Agency, it passed, due to the heavy vote in favor of the bill at other agencies, and the Sioux lands were diminished by nine million acres.

Young-Man-Afraid-of-His-Horse was visiting the Crow reservation at the time of the WOUNDED KNEE MASSACRE. Upon Young-Man-Afraid-of-His-Horse's return to Pine Ridge, General NELSON APPLETON MILES immediately asked him to use his influence to push for peace among the Sioux who were outraged by the army's killing of women and children at the massacre. Despite assisting in the peace process, he questioned American honor in the Wounded Knee disaster.

—*Richmond L. Clow*

SUGGESTED READING:
Grinnell, George Bird. *The Fighting Cheyennes.* Norman, Okla., 1956.
Hyde, George. *Red Cloud's Folk: A History of the Oglala Sioux.* Norman, Okla., 1937.

Young-Man-Afraid-of-His-Horse pictured here with Little Wound. *Courtesy Nebraska State Historical Society.*

———. *Spotted Tail's Folk: A History of the Brulé Sioux.* Norman, Okla., 1961.

McGillycuddy, Julia B. *McGillycuddy, Agent.* Palo Alto, Calif., 1941.

Olson, James C. *Red Cloud and the Sioux Problem.* Lincoln, Nebr., 1965.

YUKON RIVER

With a length of almost twenty-three hundred miles when its Canadian tributaries the Lewes and Teslin rivers are included, the Yukon River is not only the largest and most important river in Alaska but also North America's third longest river. Draining an area of approximately 330,000 square miles in Alaska, the Yukon Territory, and British Columbia, the Yukon flows north and west toward the Bering Sea within twenty miles of the tidal waters of the Lynn Canal near Dyea and Skagway in British Columbia. Receiving the waters from more than twenty other rivers, the Yukon is at the center of a complex water system in a land that is never more than a month away from winter. Temperatures throughout the Yukon Basin range from -70° F. in the winter to more than 90° F. in the fleeting summer. With the Brooks Range to the north and the Coast Range and Alaska Range to the south, moisture from the Pacific Ocean is blocked, and much of the area receives less than twelve inches of precipitation a year. Consequently, the Yukon drains a semiarid region, and its volume of flow is less than that of other rivers draining areas of similar size or smaller.

Evidence suggests that the early migrations from Eurasia to North America passed through the Yukon's glacier-free valleys. Native peoples used its abundant salmon runs for centuries. Eskimos living along its delta and Athabascan Indians living along its inner courses told Russian and other European explorers and traders about a great river that led into the interior, but it was not until the early 1790s that Aleksey Ivanov discovered it. The Yukon was the last major river system to be discovered, explored, and mapped by Euro-Americans on the North American continent.

Because overland travel was so difficult in the region, the Yukon became a major means of access to Alaska's interior. A unique feature of the river is that almost all of its course is open to navigation. Only three hundred miles are impassable. Along the banks of the Yukon, or near it, a number of native villages, towns, and small communities—Whitehorse, Fort Selkirk, Dawson, Fort Reliance, Forty Mile, Eagle, Circle, Fort Yukon, Rampart, Tanana, Nuklukayet, Nulato, Anvik, and Holy Cross—were nourished by the fish, fur, and mineral resources of the river and its basin. With the establishment of Fort Yukon in 1847, the FUR TRADE developed and reached its apex in the period between 1867 and 1885.

The discovery of gold along various tributaries of the Yukon River in 1875 and 1876 encouraged more prospecting, and as winter approached in 1896, a Canadian, an American, and two Indians made two discoveries of gold along the Klondike River—discoveries that would spark the West's last great gold rush. The rush to the Klondike began, and the majestic Yukon became a scene of both romance and history, the river of Sam McGee, Klondike Kate, and Robert Service. The Yukon was the artery on which most of the gold-seekers traveled as they made their way to the Klondike. As easily mined placer deposits disappeared, mining became more dependent on capital and technology. Techniques for thawing frozen gravel bars and permafrost allowed mining to become a year-round industry, and the development of hydraulic mining and dredging allowed low-grade deposits to be exploited. Until the beginning of World War II, mining was not only the principal economic activity along the Yukon River but also Alaska's leading industry.

In the 1960s, the world's largest dam and generating complex was proposed for the Yukon River. After much debate, the arguments for the project seemed specious, and the U.S. Congress did not support the construction of the dam that would have flooded more than 10,000 square miles, created a lake larger than Lake Erie, and generated five million kilowatts of electricity annually in a state with a small population, lacking major industries, and distant from other population centers. The Yukon remains a wilderness river.

—*Phillip Drennon Thomas*

SEE ALSO: Alaska Gold Rush; Alaskan Exploration; Klondike Gold Rush

SUGGESTED READING:

Brooks, Alfred Hulse. *Blazing Alaska's Trails.* Fairbanks, Alaska, and Washington, D.C., 1953.

Marks, Paula Mitchell. *Precious Dust: The American Gold Rush Era, 1848–1900.* New York, 1994.

Matthews, Richard. *The Yukon.* New York, 1968.

Webb, Melody. *The Last Frontier.* Albuquerque, N. Mex., 1985.

YUMA REVOLT

On July 17, 1781, the Quechan Indians, who occupied the land around the junction of the Gila and Colorado rivers, revolted against the Spanish and killed four Franciscan friars, thirty-one soldiers, and twenty settlers. Linguistically related to the Mojaves, Walapais, Havasupais, and Yavapais and called the Yumas by the Spanish after *fumo,* or "smoke," the tribe—perhaps four thousand strong—had long lived along the Colorado in present-day Arizona and California, at the time the far northern frontier of New Spain. The Spanish conquistador Hernando de Alarcón had first run across the tribe in 1540 as he was searching the area in vain for FRANCISCO VÁSQUEZ DE CORONADO. The Yuma soon discovered they were directly in the path of Spain's imperial ambitions to open overland routes to California, and by 1780, the Iberians had established two communities in Yuma territory, both half-mission half-colony and occupied by a handful of padres, troops, and settlers. Like the Spaniards, the Yumas were farmers, and they relied on water from the nearby rivers in order to grow their meager crops. When the missionaries proved unable to prevent depredations by the troops and by the settlers, who helped themselves to the Yumas' stores of food whenever they wished, the Indians attacked, utterly destroying the European outposts. Never again would Spain succeed in establishing new colonies among the Yumas. They continued to farm their homelands on into the American occupation and set up a ferry operation across the rivers during the United States–Mexican War and the gold rushes that followed. They were subdued by the Americans by the time of the GADSDEN PURCHASE in 1854, after which the United States built Fort Yuma on their territory. In 1884, the federal government established the Fort Yuma Indian Reservation, which today is home to some one thousand Yumas.

—*Charles Phillips*

SEE ALSO: Native American Peoples: Peoples of California

Y X COMPANY

A coalition of Mormon leaders and non-Mormon officeholders and businesspeople planned the Y X Company early in 1856 to conduct shipping operations between St. Joseph, Missouri, and Sacramento, California. Later in the year, the company was incorporated with Hiram Kimball, a Mormon convert living in Salt Lake City, as chief executive officer. Securing a contract for mail service between Independence, Missouri, and Salt Lake City, the Y X Company set up stations at fifty-mile intervals between the two cities. The company inaugurated mail service in February 1857. In June of that year, President JAMES BUCHANAN ordered the U.S. Army to march on Utah because of tense relations between BRIGHAM YOUNG, the territorial governor, and the federal government. During the UTAH EXPEDITION, the postmaster at Independence refused to turn the mail over to a company representative. The loss of the contract and other conditions related to the Utah Expedition forced the company to abandon its operations with a loss of perhaps two hundred thousand dollars.

—*Thomas G. Alexander*

SEE ALSO: Overland Freight

SUGGESTED READING:

Arrington, Leonard J. *Great Basin Kingdom: An Economic History of the Latter-Day Saints, 1830–1900.* Cambridge, Mass., 1958.

ZAVALA, LORENZO DE

Governor of the state of Mexico, minister to France, proponent of Texas independence, and vice-president of the Republic of Texas, Manuel Lorenzo Justiniano de Zavala y Saenz (1788–1836) was born in Tecoh, Mexico. Educated by priests, he embraced the liberal views of the Enlightenment and opposed Spanish colonialism. He was arrested and imprisoned in 1814.

Brilliant and ambitious, Zavala envisioned Mexico freed from the yoke of Spanish imperialism. After his release from prison, he was elected to the Yucatan Provincial Assembly and later served as a representative to the Spanish Cortes in Madrid. In 1821, he returned to Mexico and was appointed minister of the treasury and governor of the state of Mexico.

In 1829, Zavala obtained an empresario grant from the Mexican government to settle a number of families in Texas. In 1832, he was reelected governor of the state of Mexico and, a year later, was named minister to France.

While in Paris, he came to fear that abolishing the Constitution of 1824 would make President ANTONIO LÓPEZ DE SANTA ANNA dictator of Mexico. Opposing such a move, Zavala returned to Texas in 1835 and joined the Texan insurgents against the government of Santa Anna. Zavala was a representative of the Convention of 1836 and a signer of the Declaration of Independence of Texas. Elected vice-president of Texas in 1836, he was also a member of the mission that negotiated the terms of Texas's independence from Mexico.

—*Fred L. Koestler*

SEE ALSO: Empresarios; Texas Revolution

Lorenzo de Zavala. *Courtesy Texas State Library.*

ZION'S CO-OPERATIVE MERCANTILE INSTITUTION

Organized by Mormon leader BRIGHAM YOUNG when the transcontinental railroad reached Utah in 1869, Zion's Co-operative Mercantile Instiution (ZCMI) was a general retail firm that handled all the MORMONS' wholesale trade. Owned by WILLIAM JENNINGS, ZCMI established stores in 150 Mormon settlements. All members of the CHURCH OF JESUS CHRIST OF LATTER-DAY SAINTS were expected to patronize the stores exclusively. Each branch carried a sign over its door enscribed "Holiness of the Lord," and the ZCMI's considerable profits went to the church, its principal stockholder. When the anti-Mormon prosecutions of the 1880s began, private owners took over the stores, and none of the cooperatives was left by the time the panic of 1893 struck the American economy, after which ZCMI became primarily a Salt Lake City mercantile operation with a few retail outlets.

—*Charles Phillips*

ZOGBAUM, RUFUS FAIRCHILD

Illustrator and artist Rufus Fairchild Zogbaum (1849–1925) was born in Charleston, South Carolina, and grew up in New York City, where his father and uncle manufactured musical instruments. Although his parents discouraged his interest in art as a career, Zogbaum trained briefly at the Art Students League in New York City and with painter Leon J. F. Bonnat in Paris before becoming a professional illustrator.

Extended trips to Montana during the summer of 1884 and to Kansas and the Indian Territory four years later exposed Zogbaum to the West and provided grist for his sketchbooks and journals. He traveled by railroad, river boat, and stagecoach, accompanied cavalry in the field, visited mines and Indian reservations, and saw a cattle thief hung by vigilantes.

Beginning in 1885, Zogbaum's Western-based illustrations, many of them accompanied by articles he wrote himself, appeared with regularity in national magazines like *Harper's Weekly*. These contributions celebrated the frontier military and helped establish the cowboy as an American folk hero.

Although concentrating on naval illustration after about 1890, Zogbaum never completely abandoned Western subjects. He was awarded a medal at the Columbian Exposition in 1893 and covered the Spanish-American War for *Harper's Weekly*. He died in New York City.

—*B. Byron Price*

SEE ALSO: Art: Book and Magazine Illustration

SUGGESTED READING:
Alter, Judith MacBain. "Rufus Zogbaum and the Frontier West." *Montana* 23 (October 1973): 42–53.
Price, B. Byron. "Rufus Fairchild Zogbaum: A Champion of the West." *Persimmon Hill* 20 (Summer 1992): 38–41.
Taft, Robert. *Artists and Illustrators of the Old West, 1850–1900.* New York, 1953.

ZUNI INDIANS

SEE: Native American Peoples: Peoples of the Southwest

Biographical
Entries by Profession

ACTORS AND ENTERTAINERS

Anderson, "Bronco Billy"
Autry, Gene
Cody, William F. ("Buffalo Bill")
Crabtree, Lotta
Del Rio, Dolores
Hart, William S.
Lillie, Gordon William ("Pawnee Bill")
Middleton, "Doc" (Riley, James M.)
Mix, Tom
Montez, Lola
Oakley, Annie
Rogers, Roy, and Dale Evans
Rynning, Thomas H.
Velez, Lupe
Wayne, John

ARCHITECTS AND CITY PLANNERS

Bennett, Edward Herbert
Brown, Arthur Page
Bunham, Daniel Hudson
Huntington, Henry Edwards
Maybeck, Bernard Ralph
McFarland, John Horace
Morgan, Julia
Olmsted, Frederick Law
Speer, Robert Walker

ARTISTS

Audubon, John James
Bierstadt, Albert

Bingham, George Caleb
Bodmer, Karl (or Carl)
Borglum, Solon Hannibal
Cary, William de la Montagne
Catlin, George
Deas, Charles
Eastman, Seth
Farny, Henry F.
Hill, Thomas
Jackson, William Henry
Johnson, Frank Tenney
Kane, Paul
Kern, Edward Meyer
Kern, Richard Hovendon
King, Charles Bird
Leigh, William Robinson
Miller, Alfred Jacob
Moran, Thomas
O' Keeffe, Georgia
Proctor, Alexander Phimister (A.P.)
Remington, Frederic
Russell, Charles Marion
Schreyvogel, Charles
Seymour, Samuel
Stanley, John Mix
Tavernier, Jules
Walker, James
Wimar, Carl (or Charles) F.
Wyeth, N.C.
Zogbaum, Rufus Fairchild

BANKERS

Chaffee, Jerome Bonaparte
Cooke, Jay

BANKERS (CONT.)

Giannini, Amadeo Peter
Green, Joshua
Hauser, Samuel Thomas
Hill, James J.
Moffat, David Halliday
Ralston, William Chapman
Smoot, Reed

CARTOGRAPHERS

Emory, William Hemsley
Joliet, Louis
Kino, Eusebio Francisco
Marcy, Randolph Barnes
Preuss, Charles
Vial, Pedro

CATTLE RANCHERS

Altube, Pedro
Burnett, Samuel Burk
Chisum, John Simpson
Clay, John Henry
Cook, James Henry
Flake, William J.
French, Peter
Glenn, Hugh James
Goodnight, Charles
Hollister, William Wells
Hooker, Henry Clay
Iliff, John Wesley
Irvine, William C.
Kendrick, John Benjamin
Kenedy, Mifflin
Kino, Eusebio Francisco
Kohrs, Conrad
Loving, Oliver
Mackenzie, Murdo
Marsh, John
McCoy, Joseph G.
Miller, Henry
Mores, Antonio Marquis de
Mossman, Burton C.
Pierce, Abel Head ("Shanghai")
Prowers, John Wesley
Slaughter, Christopher Columbus
Slaughter, John Horton
Stuart, Granville
Sutter, John August
Swan, Alexander Hamilton (Alec)

Waggoner, Daniel
Wilbur-Cruce, Eva Antonia
Wolfskill, William

CONSERVATIONISTS AND ENVIRONMENTALISTS

Abbey, Edward
Albright, Horace Marden
Bennett, Hugh Hammond
Carson, Rachel Louise [and *Silent Spring*]
Edge, Rosalie Barrow
Grinnell, George Bird
Hill, James J.
Hough, Emerson
Johnson, Robert Underwood
Ickes, Harold L.
Kent, William
Lacey, John Fletcher
Leopold, Aldo
Marsh, George Perkins
Mather, Stephen Tyng
McFarland, John Horace
McGee, William John
Muir, John
Pinchot, Gifford
Pinkley, Frank ("Boss")
Roosevelt, Theodore

COWBOYS

Cook, James Henry
Olive, Isom Prentice ("Print")
Rynning, Thomas H.
Siringo, Charles Angelo

DETECTIVES

Burns, William J.
Canton, Frank
Horn, Tom
Hume, James B.
Siringo, Charles Angelo

DIPLOMATS

Butler, Anthony Wayne
Larkin, Thomas Oliver
Magoffin, James Wiley

Marsh, George Perkins
Natawista
Trist, Nicholas

ECONOMISTS

George, Henry

EDITORS

Bass, Charlotta Spears
Bausman, William
Boudinot, Elias (Cherokee)
Bush, Asahel
Byers, William Newton
Colman, Norman J.
Gilpin, William
Grimes, James Wilson
Gruening, Ernest
Hall, Frank
Hall, James
Harte, Bret
Johnson, Robert Underwood
Lummis, Charles Fletcher
Meeker, Nathan Cook
Miller, George
Montezuma, Carlos
Nelson, William Rockhill
Nye, Edgar Wilson (Bill)
Older, Fremont
Pratt, Orson
Sheldon, Charles Monroe
Smythe, William E.
Steffens, Joseph Lincoln
Wallace, Henry Agard
Wallace, Henry Cantwell
Wells, Emmeline Blanche Woodward
White, William Allen

EDUCATORS

Boone, William Judson
Cooper, Sarah Brown Ingersoll
Eastman, Elaine Goodale
Gates, Susa Amelia Young
George, Henry
Hewett, Edgar L.
Jordan, David Starr
Kennedy, Kate
Ladd, Edwin Fremont

Nelson, Aven
Pratt, Richard Henry
Robertson, Alice Mary
Royce, Josiah
Segale, Sister Blandina
Stegner, Wallace
Wheeler, Benjamin Ide

ENGINEERS

Abert, John James
Beeson, Desdemona Stott
Chittenden, Hiram Martin
Dodge, Grenville Mellen
Hoover, Herbert
Judah, Theodore Dehone
Long, Stephen Harriman
Mead, Elwood
Mulholland, William
Newell, Frederick Haynes
Sutro, Adolph

ENTREPRENEURS AND BUSINESS LEADERS

Ah Quin
Alvarez, Manuel
Armour, Philip Danforth
Ashley, William Henry
Assing, Norman
Beaubien, Carlos
Boeing, William E.
Brannan, Samuel
Briones, Juana
Broadwater, Charles Arthur
Burke, Thomas
Butterfield, John
Chandler, Alexander J.
Chapman, William S.
Chorpenning, George
Chouteau Family
Colt, Samuel
Culver, Henry
Dern, George Henry
Ficklin, Benjamin F.
Fung Ching
Gibson, Paris
Goldwater Family
Green, Joshua
Harvey, Ford Ferguson
Hauser, Samuel Thomas
Hearst, George

ENTREPRENEURS AND BUSINESS LEADERS (CONT.)

Hewett, Edgar L.
Hooker, Henry Clay
Hunt, George Wiley Paul
Huntington, Henry Edwards
Ilfeld, Charles
Jennings, William
Kaiser, Henry J.
Kearns, Thomas
King, Richard
Kinney, Henry Lawrence
Larkin, Thomas Oliver
Lathop, Austin E. ("Cap")
Lisa, Manuel
Lowe, Joseph and Kate
Magoffin, James Wiley
Mason, Biddy
Mears, Otto
Moffat, David Halliday
More, J. Marion
Mores, Antonio Marquis de
Ochoa, Esteban
Otero, Miguel Antonio, Sr.
Pleasant, Mary Ellen ("Mammy")
Prowers, John Wesley
Pullman, George Mortimer
Rath, Charles
Reed, Simeon Gannett
Ripley, Edward Payson
Ryan, John Dennis
St. Vrain, Ceran de Hault de Lassus
Spreckels, Claus
Stetson, John Batterson
Stillman, Charles
Strauss, Levi
Studebaker, John Mohler
Sutro, Adolph
Todd, John Blair Smith
Vasquez, Pierre Louis
Walker, Sarah Breedlove
Warner, Jonathan Trumbull
Whitney, Asa
Wingfield, George
Wolfskill, William
Wooten, Richens Lacy

ETHNOLOGISTS, ARCHAEOLOGISTS, AND ANTHROPOLOGISTS

Bandelier, Adolph Francis Alphonse
Bartlett, John Russell

Cushing, Frank Hamilton
Denig, Edwin Thompson
Fewkes, Jesse Walter
Fletcher, Alice Cunningham
Hewett, Edgar L.
Kern, Richard Hovendon
McGee, William John
Powell, John Wesley
Schoolcraft, Henry Roweí
Stevenson, Matilda Coxe

EXPLORERS

Allen, Henry T.
Anza, Juan Bautista de
Becknell, William
Bering, Vitus
Bonneville, Benjamin Louis Eulalie de
Cabeza de Vaca, Álvar Núñez
Cabrillo, Juan Rodríguez
Clark, William
Colter, John
Cook, James
Coronado, Francisco Vásquez de
Dorion, Marie
Ferris, Warren Angus
Fitzpatrick, Thomas
Frémont, John Charles
Gray, Robert
Gregg, Josiah
Joliet, Louis
Kino, Eusebio Francisco
La Salle, Sieur de (Cavelier René Robert)
Lewis, Meriwether
Long, Stephen Harriman
Marcos de Niza, Fray
Marcy, Randolph Barnes
Marquette, Jacques
Narváez, Pánfilo de
Nicolet, Jean
Ogden, Peter Skene
Oñate, Juan de
Pike, Zebulon Montgomery
Pond, Peter
Smith, Jedediah Strong
Thompson, David
Wilkes, Charles

FILMMAKERS

Anderson, "Bronco Billy"
Hart, William S.

FREIGHTERS

Carroll, Matthew
Fargo, William George
Holladay, Ben
Majors, Alexander
Ochoa, Esteban
Rath, Charles
Russell, William Hepburn
Waddell, William Bradford
Wells, Henry

FUR TRADERS AND TRAPPERS

Ashley, William Henry
Astor, John Jacob
Baker, James
Baranov, Aleksandr
Beckwourth, James Pierson (Jim)
Bent Brothers
Bonneville, Benjamin Louis Eulalie de
Bridger, James (Jim)
Campbell, Robert
Charbonneau, Jean Baptiste
Chouteau Family
Clyman, James
Denig, Edwin Thompson
Dubuque, Julien
Fitzpatrick, Thomas
Fraeb, Henry
Franchère, Gabriel
Glass, Hugh
Greenwood, Caleb
Henry, Andrew
Hunt, Wilson Price
Laclède, Pierre
Larpenteur, Charles
Lisa, Manuel
McKenzie, Donald
McKenzie, Kenneth
McLoughlin, John
Meek, Joseph Lafayette
Mitchell, David Dawson
Newell, Robert
Nicolet, Jean
Ogden, Peter Skene
Pond, Peter
Provost, Etienne
Robidoux Brothers
Ross, Alexander
St. Vrain, Ceran de Hault de Lassus
Smith, Jedediah Strong
Sublette Brothers

Walker, Joseph Reddeford
Williams, William S. ("Old Bill")
Wolfskill, William
Wooten, Richens Lacy
Wyeth, Nathaniel Jarvis
Young, Ewing

GUNFIGHTERS

Allison, [Robert] Clay
Brooks, William L. ("Buffalo Bill")
Courtright, Jim
Hardin, John Wesley
Hickok, James Butler ("Wild Bill")
Holliday, John Henry ("Doc")
Horn, Tom
Leslie, Nashville Franklin (Frank)
Longley, William Preston ("Wild Bill")
Mather, Dave
Miller, James B. ("Deacon Jim")
Olive, Isom Prentice ("Print")
Rockwell, Orrin Porter
Short, Luke
Stoudenmire, Dallas
Thompson, Benjamin F.

HISTORIANS

Bancroft, Hubert Howe
Billington, Ray A.
Bolton, Herbert Eugene
Brooks, Juanita Leavitt
Chittenden, Hiram Martin
Debo, Angie
Denig, Edwin Thompson
DeVoto, Bernard
Donaldson, Thomas Corwin
King, Charles
Malin, James Claude
Roberts, Brigham Henry
Turner, Frederick Jackson
Victor, Frances Fuller
Webb, Walter Prescott

ILLUSTRATORS

Borein, John Edward
Cary, William de la Montagne
Foote, Mary Hallock
Kern, Edward Meyer
Kern, Richard Hovenden

ILLUSTRATORS (CONT.)

Leigh, William Robinson
Moran, Thomas
Remington, Frederic
Tavernier, Jules
Wyeth, N.C.
Zogbaum, Rufus Fairchild

INDIAN AGENTS

Clark, William
Clum, John Philip
Jeffords, Thomas J.
McLaughlin, James
Meeker, Nathan Cook
Taliaferro, Lawrence

INVENTORS

Browning, John Moses
Colt, Samuel
Pullman, George Mortimer

JOURNALISTS

Adams, William Lysander
Bausman, William
Bierce, Ambrose Gwinett
Bush, Asahel
Derby, George Horatio
Diehl, Charles Sanford
Diggs, Annie La Porte
Flynn, Elizabeth Gurley
Gates, Susa Amelia Young
George, Henry
Hough, Emerson
Lane, Franklin Knight
Meeker, Nathan Cook
Older, Fremont
Rosewater, Edward
Villard, Henry
Wells, Emmeline Blanche Woodward

LAW ENFORCERS

Baca, Elfego
Brown, Henry Newton
Burns, William J.
Canton, Frank

Collins, Ben
Courtright, Jim
Cunningham, Tom
Dodge, Henry
Earp Brothers
Fisher, John King
Garrett, Patrick Floyd Jarvis ("Pat")
Hays, John Coffee (Jack)
Hickok, James Butler ("Wild Bill")
Leflors, Joe
Masterson, Bartholomew (Bat)
Mather, Dave
McNelly, Leander H.
Milton, Jeff Davis
Mossman, Burton C.
Owens, Commodore Perry
Plummer, William Henry
Rockwell, Orrin Porter
Rynning, Thomas H.
Selman, John Henry
Smith, Thomas James ("Bear River Tom")
Steele, Samuel Benfield
Stoudenmire, Dallas
Thomas, Henry Andrew ("Heck")
Thompson, Benjamin F.
Tilghman, William Matthew, Jr.
Venard, Stephen

LAWYERS AND JURISTS

Amidon, Charles Fremont
Bean, Roy
Cradlebaugh, John
Deady, Matthew Paul
Dole, Sanford B.
Donaldson, Thomas Corwin
Dundy, Elmer Scipio
Elkins, Stephen Benton
Field, Stephen J.
Fountain, Albert Jennings
Garland, Augustus Hill
Hallett, Moses
Hawley, James Henry
Heney, Francis Joseph
Hogg, James Stephen (Jim)
Kimball, Heber Chase
Lacey, John Fletcher
Lindsey, Benjamin Barr
Pike, Albert
Sutherland, George
Van Devanter, Willis
Webster, Daniel

MEDICINE

Eastman, Charles Alexander (Sioux)
Gregg, Josiah
Jones, Anson
Mosher, Clelia Duel
Owens-Adair, Bethenia Angelina
Picotte, Susan LaFlesche

MILITARY

Anza, Juan Bautista de
Atkinson, Henry
Banks, Nathaniel Prentiss
Baylor, John Robert
Beale, Edward Fitzgerald (Ned)
Bowie, James
Canby, Edward Richard Spring
Carleton, James H.
Castro, José
Chivington, John M.
Connor, Patrick E.
Cooke, Philip St. George
Crockett, David (Davey)
Crook, George
Curtis, Samuel Ryan
Custer, George Armstrong
Dodge, Henry
Doniphan, Alexander William
Emory, William Hemsley
Fannin, James Walker , Jr.
Figueroa, José
Geary, John White
Gibbon, John Oliver
Gillespie, Archibald H.
Grierson, Benjamin Henry
Harney, William Selby
Houston, Sam
Howard, Oliver Otis
Jackson, Andrew
Kearny, Philip
Kearny, Stephen Watts
King, Charles
Lane, Joseph
Leavenworth, Henry
Mackenzie, Ranald Slidell
Marcy, Randolph Barnes
Miles, Nelson Appleton
O' Neill, William Owen ("Buckey")
Pike, Albert
Pope, John
Price, Sterling
Santa Anna, Antonio López de

Scott, Winfield
Sheridan, Philip H.
Sherman, William Tecumseh
Sibley, Henry Hastings
Sibley, Henry Hopkins
Sloat, John Drake
Snively, Jacob
Stockton, Robert F.
Sully, Alfred
Sumner, Edwin V.
Taylor, Zachary
Terry, Alfred Howe
Todd, John Blair Smith
Travis, William Barret
Vallejo, Mariano Guadalupe
Wilkes, Charles
Wilkinson, James
Wool, John Ellis

MINING TYCOONS

Austin, Moses
Chaffee, Jerome Bonaparte
Clark, William Andrews
Daly, Marcus
Douglas Family
Dubuque, Julien
Fair, James Graham
Hauser, Samuel Thomas
Hearst, George
Heinze, Frederick Augustus
Kearns, Thomas
Mackay, John W.
More, J. Marion
Ryan, John Dennis
Tabor, Horace Austin Warner
Wingfield, George

MISSIONARIES

Bingham, Hiram and Sybil Moseley
Blake, Alice
Cabareaux, Sister Mary Catherine
Cameron, Donaldina Mackenzie
Corrigan, Sister Monica
Demers, Modeste P.
DeSmet, Pierre-Jean
Hare, William Hobart
Hyde, Orson
Jackson, Sheldon
Kino, Eusebio Francisco
Lee, Jason

MISSIONARIES (CONT.)

Marquette, Jacques
Mauer, Katherine R.
McBeth, Sue and Kate
Picotte, Susan LaFlesche
Pratt, Orson
Rich, Charles Coulson
Segale, Sister Blandina
Serra, Junípero
Spalding, Henry Harmon and Eliza Hart
Taylor, John
Tuttle, Daniel Sylvester
Veniaminov, Ivan (Popov, Ioann)
Whitman, Marcus and Narcissa
Woo Yee-Bew

NATIVE AMERICAN LEADERS

American Horse (Elder) (Sioux)
American Horse (Younger) (Sioux)
Barboncito (Navajo)
Big Foot (Spotted Elk) (Sioux)
Big Tree (Kiowa)
Black Elk (Sioux)
Black Kettle (Cheyenne)
Black Moon (Sioux)
Captain Jack (Modoc)
Chief Joseph (Nez Percé)
Cochise (Apache)
Crazy Horse (Sioux)
Crow Dog (Sioux)
Eastman, Charles Alexander (Sioux)
Eskiminzin (Apache)
Four Horns (Sioux)
Gall (Sioux)
Ganado Mucho (Navajo)
Geronimo (Apache)
Grass, John (Charging Bear) (Sioux)
Grey Beard (Cheyenne)
Hollow Horn Bear (Sioux)
Juh (Apache)
Kamiakin (Yakima)
Keokuk (Fox)
Kicking Bear (Sioux)
Kicking Bird (Kiowa)
Lawyer (Nez Percé)
Light, The (Assiniboine)
Lilioukalani, Queen
Little Crow (Sioux)
Little Raven (Arapaho)
Little Wolf (Northern Cheyenne)

Lone Wolf (Kiowa)
Looking Glass (Nez Percé)
Man-Afraid-of-His-Horse (Sioux)
Mangas Coloradas (Apache)
Manuelito (Navajo)
Minimic (Cheyenne)
Morning Star (Northern Cheyenne)
Naiche (Apache)
Nana (Apache)
Narbona (Navajo)
Ollokot (Nez Percé)
Opothleyahola (Creek)
Plenty Coups (Crow)
Quanah Parker (Comanche)
Rain in the Face (Sioux)
Red Cloud (Sioux)
Ridge, John
Riel, Louis David
Rose, Edward (Mixed Cherokee)
Ross, John (Cherokee)
Satank (Kiowa)
Satanta (Kiowa)
Sequoyah (Mixed Cherokee)
Short Bull (Sioux)
Sitting Bull (Sioux)
Spotted Tail (Sioux)
Struck by the Ree (Yankton)
Tecumseh (Shawnee)
Ten Bears (Comanche)
Toohoolhoolzote (Nez Percé)
Toypurina (Gabrielino)
Victorio (Apache)
Walkara (Ute)
Washakie (Shoshone)
Watie, Stand (Cherokee)
White Bird (Nez Percé)
White Horse (Kiowa)
Wovoka (Paiute)
Young-Man-Afraid-of-His-Horse (Sioux)

NATURALISTS

Audubon, John James
Bailey, Florence Augusta Merriam
Bessey, Charles Edwin
Bradbury, John
Burroughs, John
Coues, Elliott
James, Edwin
Maxwell, Martha Ann Dartt
Nelson, Aven
Thoreau, Henry David

OIL TYCOONS

Doheny, Edward Laurence
Kerr, Robert Samuel

OUTLAWS, GUERRILLAS, AND SOCIAL BANDITS

Anderson, William C. ("Bloody Bill")
Apache Kid
Bass, Sam
Brocius, "Curley" Bill
Brown, John
"Billy the Kid"
"Black Bart" (Boles, Charles E.)
Brocius, "Curly Bill"
Brooks, William L. ("Buffalo Bill")
Brown, Henry Newton
Brown, John
Cassidy, Butch (Parker, Robert Leroy)
Cortina, Juan Nepomuceno
Cortez, Gregorio
Doolin, William (Bill)
Fisher, John King
Hardin, John Wesley
Horn, Tom
James Brothers
Lane, James Henry
Longley, William Preston ("Wild Bill")
Middleton, "Doc" (Riley, James M.)
Miller, James B. ("Deacon Jim")
Murieta or Murrieta, Joaquin
Plummer, William Henry
Quantrill, William Clarke
Reavis, James Addison
Ringo, John Peters
Rose, Edward (Mixed Cherokee)
Selman, John Henry
Starr, Belle
Starr, Henry
Vásquez, Tiburcio
Villa, Francisco ("Pancho")
Younger Brothers

PHILANTHROPISTS

Bishop, Bernice Pauahi
Brown, Clara
Brunot, Felix Reville
Douglas Family

Elkins, Stephen Benton
Hearst, George
Hearst, Phoebe Apperson
Hollister, William Wells
Horton, Alonzo Erastus
Howard, Oliver Otis
Huntington, Collis P.
Huntington, Henry Edwards
Hutton, May Arkwright
Luhan, Mabel Dodge
Mackay, John W.
Reed, Simeon Gannett
Rockefeller, Winthrop
Slaughter, Christopher Columbus
Stanford, Jane Eliza Lathrop
Walker, Sarah Breedlove

PHILOSOPHERS

Royce, Josiah
Thoreau, Henry David

PHOTOGRAPHERS

Butcher, Solomon D.
Curtis, Edward Sheriff
Huffman, Laton Alton
Jackson, William Henry
O'Sullivan, Timothy H.
Smith, Erwin Evans

PIONEERS

Applegate, Jesse
Austin, Stephen Fuller
Bidwell, John
Boone, Daniel
Bridger, James (Jim)
Bush, George Washington
Greenwood, Caleb
Lee, Jason
Leon, Patricia de
Meek, Joseph Lafayette
Pratt, Orson
Rich, Charles Coulson
Rockwell, Orrin Porter
Warner, Jonathan Trumbull
Wolfskill, William

POLITICIANS

Alexander, Moses
Applegate, Jesse
Armijo, Manuel
Ashley, William Henry
Atchison, David Rice
Austin, Stephen Fuller
Banks, Nathaniel Prentiss
Baylor, John Robert
Benton, Thomas Hart
Bernhisel, John Milton
Blount, William
Borah, William E.
Bradley, Lewis R.
Brady, John Green
Broderick, David C.
Bryan, William Jennings
Buchanan, James
Buckley, Christopher Augustine
Burnet, David Gouverneur
Burns, John Anthony
Bursom, Holm Olaf
Calhoun, John Caldwell
Carey, Joseph Maull
Chaffee, Jerome Bonaparte
Chavez, Dennis
Church, Frank
Clark, James Beauchamp ("Champ")
Clark, William Andrews
Clay, Henry
Colman, Norman J.
Costigan, Edward Prentiss
Cradlebaugh, John
Crockett, David (Davey)
Cutting, Bronson
Dawes, Henry Laurens
Dern, George Henry
Dimond, Anthony J. (Tony)
Dodge, Grenville Mellen
Dodge, Henry
Dole, Sanford B.
Dole, William P.
Donnelly, Ignatius
Douglas, Stephen A.
Dundy, Elmer Scipio
Elkins, Stephen Benton
Evans, John
Fair, James Graham
Fall, Albert B.
Fargo, William George
Figueroa, José
Fountain, Albert Jennings
Frémont, John Charles

Gallegos, José Manuel
Garland, Augustus Hill
Garner, John Nance
Geary, John White
Gibson, Paris
Gilpin, William
Goldwater Family
Grimes, James Wilson
Gruening, Ernest
Gwin, William
Hall, Frank
Haskell, Charles Nathaniel
Hauser, Samuel Thomas
Hawley, James Henry
Hayden, Carl T.
Hearst, George
Heney, Francis Joseph
Hitchcock, Gilbert Monell
Hogg, James Stephen (Jim)
Hoover, Herbert
Houston, Sam
Huffman, Laton Alton (L.A.)
Hunt, George Wiley Paul
Ickes, Harold L.
Ingalls, John J.
Irvine, William C.
Jackson, Andrew
Jackson, Henry Martin ("Scoop")
Jefferson, Thomas
Johnson, Edwin Carl ("Big Ed")
Johnson, Hiram Warren
Johnson, Lyndon B.
Jones, Anson
Kearns, Thomas
Kendrick, John Benjamin
Kent, William
Kerr, Robert Samuel
Kinney, Henry Lawrence
Lacey, John Fletcher
Ladd, Edwin Fremont
Lamar, Mirabeau B.
Landon, Alfred Mossman
Lane, Franklin Knight
Lane, James Henry
Lane, Joseph
Lathrop, Austin E. ("Cap")
Magnuson, Warren Grant
Mansfield, Michael Joseph (Mike)
Marsh, George Perkins
Martin, Anne Henrietta
Mather, Stephen Tyng
McCarran, Patrick A.
McKenzie, Alexander ("Big Alex")
Mears, Otto

Medill, William
Mitchell, David Dawson
Montoya, Joseph
More, J. Marion
Morton, J. Sterling
Mundt, Karl E.
Murray, William ("Alfalfa Bill")
Navarro, José Antonio Baldomero
Newell, Frederick Haynes
Newell, Robert
Newlands, Francis G.
Norbeck, Peter
Norris, George W.
O' Hare, Kate Richards
Olson, Floyd Bjersterne
O' Neill, William Owen ("Buckey")
Otero, Miguel Antonio, Jr.
Otero, Miguel Antonio, Sr.
Otero-Warren, Maria Adelina Emilia (Nina)
Pico, Pío de Jesus
Pinchot, Gifford
Poindexter, Miles
Polk, James K.
Poston, Charles Debrille
Price, Sterling
Prowers, John Wesley
Rankin, Jeannette
Rayburn, Samuel Taliaferro (Sam)
Riel, Louis David
Roberts, Brigham Henry
Robertson, Alice Mary
Robinson, Charles
Robinson, Joseph Taylor
Roche, Josephine Aspinwall
Rockefeller, Winthrop
Rolph, James
Roosevelt, Theodore
Rosewater, Edward
Ruef, Abraham (Abe)
Santa Anna, Antonio López de
Schurz, Carl
Sibley, Henry Hastings
Simpson, Jerry
Smoot, Reed
Speer, Robert Walter
Stanford, Amasa Leland
Steunenberg, Frank
Stewart, William M.
Stuart, Granville
Sutro, Adolph
Tabor, Horace Austin Warner
Taylor, Glen Hearst
Taylor, Nathaniel G.
Taylor, Zachary

Teller, Henry M.
Thomas, Elbert D.
Tingley, Clyde
Todd, John Blair Smith
Townley, Arthur Charles (A.C.)
Truman, Harry S
Tyler, John
U' ren, William Simon
Vallejo, Mariano Guadalupe
Van Devanter, Willis
Vargas, Diego de
Villa, Francisco ("Pancho")
Waite, Davis Hanson
Wallace, Henry Agard
Wallace, Henry Cantwell
Warren, Francis E.
Weaver, James Baird
Webster, Daniel
Wheeler, Burton K.
Whitney, Charlotte Anita
Wickersham, James
Wilkinson, James
Williamson, James A.
Wilson, James
Zavala, Lorenzo de

POTTERS

Martinez, Maria Montoya

PROSPECTORS

Juneau, Joe

PROSTITUTES

Ah Toy
Bemis, Polly
Hensley, Josephine ("Chicago Joe")
Watson, Ella ("Cattle Kate")

PUBLISHERS

Abiko, Kyutaro
Adams, William Lysander
Bass, Charlotta Spears
Byers, William Newton
Cannon, George Quayle
Churchhill, Caroline Nichols
Cutting, Bronson

PUBLISHERS (CONT.)

Fountain, Albert Jennings
George, Henry
Godbe, William S.
Hearst, William Randolph
Hitchcock, Gilbert Monell
Nelson, William Rockhill
Hg Poon-Chew
Otis, Harrison Gray
Smythe, William E.
White, William Allen

RADICALS

Flynn, Elizabeth Gurley
Haywood, William D. ("Big Bill")
Jones, Mary Harris ("Mother")
Little, Frank
Magon, Ricardo Flores
Mooney, Thomas Joseph

RAILROAD TYCOONS

Ames, Oakes
Crocker, Charles
Dillon, Sidney
Durant, Thomas Clark
Forbes, John Murray
Gould, Jay
Harriman, Edward Henry
Hill, James J.
Holladay, Ben
Hopkins, Mark
Huntington, Collis P.
Kruttschnitt, Julius
Stanford, Amasa Leland
Villard, Henry

RELIGIOUS LEADERS

Alemany, Joseph Sadoc
Bernhisel, John Milton
Cannon, George Quayle
Cowdery, Oliver
Demers, Modeste P.
De Smet, Pierre-Jean
Gallegos, José Manuel
Godbe, William S.
Grant, Heber J.

Hare, William Hobart
Hyde, Orson
Jackson, Sheldon
Kimball, Heber Chase
Kimball, J. Golden
King, Thomas Starr
Lamy, Jean Baptiste
Lee, Jason
Martínez, Antonio José
McPherson, Aimee Semple
McWhirter, Martha White
Rich, Charles Coulson
Rigdon, Sidney
Roberts, Brigham Henry
Serra, Junípero
Severance, Carolina Maria Seymour
Sheldon, Charles Monroe
Smith, Joseph Fielding
Smith, Joseph, Jr.
Snow, Eliza Roxcy
Taylor, John
Toypurina (Gabrielino)
Urrea, Teresa
Woodruff, Wilford
Young, Brigham

SCOUTS, GUIDES, AND TRAILBLAZERS

Apache Kid
Baker, James
Beckwourth, James Pierson (Jim)
Boone, Daniel
Bridger, James (Jim)
Carson, Christopher Houston ("Kit")
Charbonneau, Jean Baptiste
Chatillon, Henri
Chisholm, Jesse
Cody, William F. ("Buffalo Bill")
Greenwood, Caleb
Hastings, Lansford Warren
Horn, Tom
Marcy, Randolph Barnes
Provost, Etienne
Robidoux Brothers
Rose, Edward (Mixed Cherokee)
Sacagawea (Shoshone)
Sieber, Al
Vial, Pedro
Walker, Joseph Reddeford
Williams, William S. ("Old Bill")
Wooten, Richens Lacy

SOCIAL REFORMERS

Allensworth, Josephine Leavell
Barnard, Catherine Ann (Kate)
Beardsley, Helen Marston
Bidwell, Annie Ellicott Kennedy
Bonnin, Gertrude Simmons (Zitkala-Sa) (Sioux)
Brown, John
Brunot, Felix Reville
Churchhill, Caroline Nichols
Daws, S.O.
Diggs, Annie La Porte
Donnelly, Ignatius
Duniway, Abigail Scott
Eastman, Charles Alexander (Sioux)
Edge, Rosalie Barrow
Edson, Katherine Philips
Farnham, Eliza Wood Burhans
Field, Sara Bard
Fletcher, Alice Cunningham
Gates, Susa Amelia Young
Gilman, Charlotte Perkins
Harriman, Job
Hoover, Lou Henry
Hutton, May Arkwright
Jackson, Helen Maria Fiske Hunt
Jordan, David Starr
Kane, Thomas Leiper
Kearney, Denis
Kelley, Oliver H.
Kennedy, Kate
Kent, William
Lane, Franklin Knight
Lease, Mary Elizabeth Clyens
Lindsey, Benjamin Barr
Luhan, Mabel Dodge
Martin, Anne Henrietta
McWhirter, Martha White
Montezuma, Carlos
Moreno, Luisa
Morris, Esther Hobart McQuigg Slack
Nation, Carrie Amelia Moore
Newman, Angie
O' Hare, Kate Richards
Older, Fremont
Otero-Warren, Maria Adelina Emilia (Nina)
Owens-Adair, Bethenia Angelina
Picotte, Susan LaFlesche
Rankin, Jeannette
Roche, Josephine Aspinwall
Salcido, Abrán
Schurz, Carl
Severance, Carolina Maria Seymour
Snow, Eliza Roxcy

Tibbles, Susette Laflesche
Tingley, Katherine Augusta
Van Waters, Miriam
Wells, Emmeline Blanche Woodward
Welsh, Herbert Thomas
Whitney, Charlotte Anita
Winnemucca, Sarah (Paiute)

SURVEYORS, TOPOGRAPHERS, AND SCIENTIFIC EXPLORERS

Abert, John James
Bartlett, John Russell
Beale, Edward Fitzgerald (Ned)
Derby, George Horatio
Emory, William Hemsley
Ferris, Warren Angus
Frémont, John Charles
Hayden, Ferdinand Vandeveer
James, Edwin
Kern, Edward Meyer
Kern, Richard Hovendon
King, Clarence
Long, Stephen Harriman
McGee, William John
Powell, John Wesley
Preuss, Charles
Snively, Jacob
Thompson, David
Wilkes, Charles

WRITERS

Abbey, Edward
Adams, Andy
Adams, Charles Francis, Jr.
Atherton, Gertrude
Austin, Mary Hunter
Bailey, Margaret Jewett
Bierce, Ambrose Gwinett
Bishop, Isabella Bird
Bonnin, Gertrude Simmons (Zitkala-Sa) (Sioux)
Brand, Max (Faust, Frederick Schiller)
Browne, John Ross
Buntline, Ned (Judson, Edward Zane Carroll)
Burroughs, John
Cabeza de Baca, Fabiola
Carlson, Rachel Louise
Cather, Willa

WRITERS (CONT.)

Clark, Charles ("Badger"), Jr.
Coolbrith, Ina
Cooper, James Fenimore
Custer, Elizabeth
Dame Shirley
Dana, Richard Henry, Jr.
Derby, George Horatio
DeVoto, Bernard
Donnelly, Ignatius
Eastman, Elaine Goodale
Farnham, Eliza Wood Burhans
Ferber, Edna
Field, Sara Bard
Fletcher, Alice Cunningham
Foote, Mary Hallock
Frémont, Jesse Ann Benton
Garland, Hamlin
Gates, Susa Amelia Young
George, Henry
Gibbon, John Oliver
Gilman, Charlotte Perkins
Gilpin, William
Gregg, Josiah
Grey, Zane
Grinnell, George Bird
Gruening, Ernest
Hall, James
Harte, Bret
Hastings, Lansford Warren
Hough, Emerson
Howard, Oliver Otis
Jackson, Helen Maria Fiske Hunt
Irving, Washington
Kelly, Fanny

King, Charles
Lacey, John Fletcher
Larpenteur, Charles
Lee, Mary Paik
London, John Griffith (Jack)
Lummis, Charles Fletcher
MacLane, Mary
Marsh, George Perkins
May, Karl Friedrich
Meeker, Nathan Cook
Miller, Joaquin (Heine [Hiner], Cincinnatus)
Mourning Dove
Norris, Benjamin Franklin, Jr. (Frank)
Nye, Edgar Wilson (Bill)
Pike, Albert
Rhodes, Eugene Manlove
Ross, Alexander
Ruiz de Burton, María Amparo
Ruxton, George Frederick
Sandoz, Mari
Sheldon, Charles Monroe
Sinclair, Upton
Siringo, Charles Angelo
Smedley, Agnes
Smythe, William E.
Snow, Eliza Roxcy
Steffens, Joseph Lincoln
Stegner, Wallace
Thompson, Era Bell
Thoreau, Henry David
Thorpe, Thomas Bangs
Twain, Mark (Clemens, Samuel Langhorne)
Victor, Frances Fuller
White, William Allen
Wilbur-Cruce, Eva Antonia
Wilder, Laura Ingalls
Wister, Owen

Index

Numbers in **boldface** refer to the main entry on the subject; numbers in *italics* refer to illustrations.

American Fur Company (cont.)
  and Henri Chatillon, 282
  and Chouteau family, 316
  and Edwin Thompson Denig, 439
  and Warren Angus Ferris, 525
  forts established by, 568-569, 570
  and Kenneth McKenzie, 952
  and the Métis people, 966
  and Alfred Jacob Miller, 978
  in Minnesota, 998
  and the mountain men, 1050, 1527
  and river transporation, 1378
  and Rocky Mountain Fur Company, 1385
  Upper Missouri Outfit, 38
  Western Department, 37-38
  in Westport Landing, Missouri, 1731
  see also Fur trade
American Fur Trade of the Far West (Chittenden), 313
American Horse (elder), **38-39**
American Horse (younger), **39**, *39*
American Humor: A Study of the National Character (Rourke), 710
American Indian Art League, 1089
American Indian Magazine, 165
American Indian Movement, 1657
American Indian Stories (Bonnin), 165
Americanization programs, **40-42**, 1651
  Americanization movement, 40-41
  goal of, 40
  government support for, 40-41
  historical background, 40
  impact on Mexican Americans, 41-42
  in the West, 41-42
  during World War I, 40-41
Americanization through Home-making (Ellis), 41
American Legion, 41
American Merchants' Union Express Company, 509
American Mercury, 927

American Naturalist, 141
American Ornithologists' Union, 398
American Ornithology (Wilson), 1275
American party. *See* Know-Nothing party
American Philosophical Society for the Promotion of Useful Knowledge, 503, 504, 866
American Potash Company, 30
American Protective Association, 1424
American Railway Express Company, 6
American Railway Union (ARU), 831
American River, **42-43**
  gold discovered at, 42
  as hydroelectric power source, 42-43
American Smelting and Refining Company, 388
American Socialist Party. *See* Socialism
American Society for Encouraging the Settlement of the Oregon Territory, 810
American System, **43**, 220, 221, 346
  and economic growth, 43
  see also Tariff policy
American Tobacco Company, 1081
American Tract Society, 927
"American West, The: Perpetual Mirage" (Webb), 676
American West in the Twentieth Century, The (Nash), 677
American Western and Frontier Issues (Nichols), 678
American Woman Suffrage Association, 1450, 1772
America's Frontier Heritage (Billington), 148
Ames, J. Judson, 925
Ames, Oakes, **43**, 469, 1350
  and Credit Mobilier scandal, 43, 413
Ames, Oliver, 43, 1330
Amidon, Charles Fremont, **44**
  as jurist, 44
Amish, in Iowa, 747-748
Amon Carter Museum, **44-45**, 87

  collections of, 44
  public programs, 45
Among the Birds in the Grand Canyon National Park (Bailey), 112
Amos Bad Heart Bull (Sioux), 1121
Ampudia, Pedro, 1662
Amundsen, Roald, 1206
Anaconda Mining Company, **45**, 214, 215, 387, 388, 518, 547, 665, 754, 758, 987, 1023, 1024, 1400-1401
Anaconda Standard, 387
Anadarko Agency, 147
Anaheim, California, 755
Anasazi, 70, 360-361, 1124, 1161, 1186-1187
Anchorage, Alaska, 22
Anderson, "Bronco Billy," **45**, 535, 1044
Anderson, G. M. *See* Anderson, "Bronco Billy"
Anderson, Marian, 720
Anderson, Maxwell, 1202
Anderson, Rufus, 37
Anderson, Sherwood, 637
Anderson, William C. ("Bloody Bill"), **46**, *46*, 335-336, 337, 768, 1346
Angel, Frank Warner, 872
Angel Island, California, 945, *1294*, 1440
Angell's Treaty of 1880, 310
Angle of Repose (Stegner), 560, 561
Anglo-Americans, tensions with Hispanics, 158-159
Angus cattle, 264
Angus, Red, 784
Anian, Strait of. *See* Northwest Passage
Animals
  armadillos, 80
  beavers, 131-132
  black bears, 153-154
  buffaloes, 195-197
  burros, 211
  camels, 237-238, *238*
  caribou, 245-246
  condors, 378-379
  coyotes, 410-411
  in Death Valley, 437
  elk, 479

Borglum, Solon Hannibal, 177-178
Cary, William de la Montagne, 252-253
Catlin, George, 261-263
Deas, Charles, 436
Eastman, Seth, 475-476
Farny, Henry F., 516
Hill, Thomas, 674
Johnson, Frank Tenney, 781
Kane, Paul, 796
Kern, Edward Meyer, 814
Kern, Richard Hovendon, 815
King, Charles Bird, 818
Leigh, William Robinson, 862-863
Miller, Alfred Jacob, 978
Moran, Thomas, 1029
O'Keeffe, Georgia, 1222
Paxson, Edgar Samuel, 1274
Peale, Titian Ramsey, 1275
Proctor, Alexander Phimister (A. P.), 1327
Remington, Frederic, 1064, 1365-1366, *1365*, 1397, 1439
Russell, Charles Marion, 1396-1398
Schreyvogel, Charles, 1438-1439
Stanley, John Mix, 1286, 1396, 1511-1512
Tavernier, Jules, 1539-1540
Walker, James, 1705
Wimar, Carl, 1754
Wyeth, N. C., 1790
Zogbaum, Rufus Fairchild, 1810
see also Taos School of Artists; Women artists
Asberry, Nettie, 1769
Ashcraft, Narcissa Land, 1679
Ashley, William Henry, **96**
  death of, 1392
  and the fur trade, 38, 96, 133, 183, 239, 351-352, 500, 556, 587, 612, 632, 669, 858, 1010, 1048, 1173, 1366, 1367, 1479, 1600
Asian American churches, **96-98**
  Buddhist, 97
  Protestant, 97-98
  see also East Indians; Chinese Americans; Japanese Americans

Asian American literature, 884-885
Asian Americans
  in Arizona, 68, 473
  child rearing, 293-294
  in films, 541
  in Idaho, 725
  marriage to Euro-Americans, 746
  marriage to Mexicans, 745-746
  newspapers and magazines of, 929
  restrictions on, 472-473
  stereotypes of, 1520-1521
  and vegetable growing, 582-583
  see also Chinese Americans; East Indians; Japanese Americans
Asian immigrants
  in Kansas, 801
  literature of, 885
  living conditions of, 860
  restrictions on, 728, 729
  see also Chinese exclusion; East Indians; Filipino immigrants; Japanese immigrants; Korean immigrants
Asiatic Exclusion League, **98-99**
Aspen, Colorado, 366, 994
Aspinwell, William H., 1259-1260
Assinboin Indians, 1021, 1134, 1137, 1140, 1141
  Light, The, 869
Assing, Norman, 17, **99**, 301
Associated Oil Company, 1219
Associated Press, 446
Association for Borderlands Scholars, 174
Astor, Henry, 99
Astor, John Jacob, 37-38, **99-100**, 316, 373, 374, 500, 568, 570, 572, 586, 632, 713, 757, 951, 1050, 1709
  and the Spanish-American War, 1080
Astoria, **100-101**, 374, 572-573, 708, 713
Astoria, or Anecdotes of an Enterprise beyond the Rocky Mountains (Irving), 757, 875
Atchison, David Rice, **101-102**, 805

Atchison, Topeka and Santa Fe Railroad, 32, 70, **102-103**, *102*, 441, 454, 455, 652, 1351, 1375, 1433
  building of, 102
  expansion of, 102-103
  nonrailroad assets, 103
  and Taos School of Artists, 1536
  and tourism, 1592
At the End of the Santa Fe Trail (Segale), 758
Athabasca River basin, 1312
Athapascan Indians, 24, 1127, 1137
Athearn, Robert, 677
Atherton, George Bowen, 103
Atherton, Gertrude, 103-104, 226
Atkinson, Henry, **104**, 647
Atlantic Monthly, 651, 1163
Atlantic and Pacific Railroad. *See* Atchison, Topeka and Santa Fe Railroad
Atlantic and Pacific Steamship Company, 1260
Atlantic Richfield, 215
Atlantis (Donnelly), 462
Atlas of Colorado, 663
Atomic energy. *See* Federal government
Atomic Energy Commission, 723
Atondo y Antillon, Isidro de, 821
Atwater, Caleb, 53
Auburn, California, 607
Auburn system (penal philosophy), 767
Audubon, Jean, 104
Audubon, John James, 44, **104-106**, *105*, 439, 570, 635, 714, 1063
Audubon, John Woodhouse, 106
Audubon, Lucy, 635
Audubon Society, 477, 636, 1387
Auerbach, Samuel H., 779
Auerbach, Theodore, 779
Augur, Christopher, C., 1262
Aurora (Illinois) Branch Railroad, 205
Aurora, Nevada, 608
Austin, Mary Hunter, **106-107**, 917, 1308, 1777
Austin, Moses, **107**, 487, 842, 1010, 1070, 1563

Austin, Stephen Fuller, **107-108,** *107, 158,* 485, 487, 508, 592, 842, 1070, 1170, 1414, 1569, 1573
  and colonization of Texas, 108, 1563
  in Texas Revolution, 1574, 1575, 1601
Austin, Wallace Stafford, 106
Austin, Texas, 1388, 1560
Authentic Life of Billy the Kid, The (Garrett), 149, 597
Autobiography of a Brown Buffalo (Acosta), 887
Automobiles. *See* Car culture
Autry, Gene, **108-109,** *108,* 536, 537, 1058, 1347, 1388
  and western films, 1515
Autry, Jackie, 109
Autry Museum of Western Heritage, 87, **109**
Avard, Sampson, 432
Averell, James, 1719, *1719*
Averell, Mary Williamson, 649
Aviation. *See* Aircraft industry
Awakening, The (Chopin), 1012
Axtel, Robert ("Spike"), 343
Axtell, Samuel, 872
Ayer, Edward, 1182
Ayrshire cattle, 265
Aztec Land and Cattle Company, 621, *621*
Aztecs, 1111, 1123
Azusa Street Revival, 7

B

Babbitt, Bruce, 111
Babbitt, David, 111
Babbitt, William, 111
Babbitt Ranch, Arizona, 111
Babcock, A. C., 1797
"Baby Doe." *See* Tabor, Baby Doe
Baca, Elfego, **111-112,** 855
Bacon, Daniel, 425
Bacon, Eleanor Sophia (Page), 425
Bacon, Francis, 462
Baer, John M., 1593
Bahapki, 142
Bailey, Florence Augusta Merriam, **112**

Bailey, James A., 1748
Bailey, Margaret Jewett, **112-113**
Bailey, William J., 112
Baird, Mary, 192
Baird, Spencer F., 398
Baker, Edward, 1238
Baker, George F., 1084
Baker, James, **113**
Baker, Melinda Harriet, 215
Bakewell, Lucy, 105
Balboa, Vasco Núñez de, 139
Baldwin, Thomas, 18
Baldwin, Tillie, 1388
Ballad of Baby Doe, The (Moore), 1234
Ballinger, Richard A., 113, 1085, 1297
Ballinger-Pinchot Controversy, **113-114,** 1297, 1392
Ballou's Pictorial Drawing Room Companion, 93
Baltimore and Ohio Railroad, 545
Bamberger, Simon, 780, 1674
Bancroft, Hubert Howe, 52, **114-115,** 159, 187, 281, 701, 1340, 1425, 1685
  and Frances Fuller Victor, 1682
Bancroft Library, 1289
Bancroft's Works, 114-115
Bancroft, George, 1074, 1075
Bandannas, 400
Bandelier, Adolph Francis Alphonse, 54, **115-116,** 917, 1321
Bandini, Ysidora, 1764
Bandit Makes Good, The, 45
Bangs, George H., 1298
Bank of America (California), 119, 609, 759, 794
Bank of California, 1354
Bank of Italy, 119, 608-609, 759
Bank of St. Louis, 107
Bank of the United States, 543
Bank robbers. *See* Outlaws
Banking Act of 1935, 609
Banking, **116-119**
  Biddle's role in, 116-117
  branch, 609
  Jay Cooke as banker, 383
  Deposit Act of 1836, 442
  in Dodge City, Kansas, 454
  federal bonds, 383
  historical background, 116-117

hostility toward, 116, 117, 118, 119
immigrants in, 118
and railroads, 118
in Texas, 1566
in the trans-Mississippi West, 117-119
and War of 1812, 116. *see also* Booms; Currency and silver as western political issues; Financial panics; Giannini, Amadeo Peter
Banks, Joseph, 382, 502-503
Banks, Nathaniel Prentiss, **119,** 242, 340
Bannack, Montana, 608
Bannock Indians, *1263,* 1132, 1334
  in Idaho, 724
Bannock War. *See* Pacific Northwest Indian Wars: Bannock War
Banvard, John, 93
Baptists. *See* Protestants
Barabbas (Field), 531
Baranov, Aleksandr, **120,** *120,* 498, 568, 1307, 1399
Barbarosa, 541
Barbed wire, **120-121**
  applications of, 121
  in cattle industry, 269
  development of, 120-121
  manufacturers of, 121
  market for, 121
  patents for, 121
Barber, Amos, 784
Barboncito (Navajo), **122,** 936
Barceló, Tules Gertrudes, 594
Barchus, Eliza, 1761
Barlow, Joseph, 1760
Barnard, Catherine Ann (Kate), **122-123,** 1226
Barnard, H. G., 281
Barnes, Jane, 708
Barnes, Johnny, 472
Barney, James, 692
Barrell, Joseph, 627-628
Barrett Dam, 1717
Barrio, Raymond, 887
Barrio Boy (Galarza), 887
Barrios, **123-125,** 1445, 1446, 1764
  anglicization of, 124
  in El Paso, 484

Black Hawk's War, 104, **155-156,** 345, 352, 384, 454, 749, 814, 820, 1158, 1542

Black Hills gold rush, **156-157,** *157,* 615, 665, 683
 and the Sioux Wars, 1469, 1473

Black Jack, Battle of, 190

Black Kettle (Cheyenne), **157- 158,** *158,* 278, 314, 426, 493, 1416-1417, 1591

Black Legend, **158-159,** *159,* 1003, 1518

Black Moon (Sioux), **159-160,** *572,* 590-591

Blackrobe. *See* De Smet, Pierre- Jean

Black Sun (Abbey), 1

Blacktail deer, 1737

Black-tailed jackrabbits, 761

Blacks. *See* African American churches; African Americans

Blaine, James G., 414, 480, 706

Blair, Francis P., Jr., 334, 810

Blake, Alice, **160,** 1336

Blake, William P., 1599

Blanchet, Francis Norbert, 438, 444

Blanchette, Louis, 1015

Bland, Richard Parks "Silver Dick," 160

Bland-Allison Act of 1878, **160- 161,** 423, 632, 1458

Blavatsky, Helen Petrovna, 1580- 1581

Bledsoe, Samuel T., 103

"Bleeding Kansas," 1078
 see also Atchison, David Rice; Brown, John; Kansas; Kansas-Nebraska Act

Blennerhasset, Harmon, 210

Blessingway, 281

Blevins, Mart, 621

Bliss, W. D. P., 317

Blocker, Ab, 1797

Blood Brother (Arnold), 354

Blood Indians
 Natawista, 1063

Bloody Knife, 1626

Blount, William, **161,** *161,* 761, 1555

Blue Corn Woman, 390

Blue Water, Battle of, 647

Blumenschein, Ernest L., 86, 1536

Blythe, Thomas, 369

Board of Indian Commissioners, 191, 192, 1651, 1655, 1656

Boatright, Mody, 711, 1275

"Bobby Benson's Adventures," 1347

Bodega y Quadra, Juan Francisco de la, 29

Bodie, California, 607

Bodmer, Karl, 44, 82, *82,* **162,** *162, 196,* 345, 476, 504, 570, 637, 788, 1016, 1396, 1591

Boeing, William E., 18, **162-163**

Boeing Airplane Company, 18- 19, 163, 1442

Boggs, Francis, 227, 1043

Boggs, Lilburn W., 1384

Bogy, Lewis, 1542

Boise, Idaho, *723, 724*
 Moses Alexander in, 33

Bold, Christine, 534

Bolduc House, *56*

Bolen, A. J., 1262

Boles, Charles E. *See* "Black Bart"

Bolon, Andrew J., 795-796

Bolton, Charles. *See* "Black Bart"

Bolton, Herbert Eugene, 159, **163,** 174, *175,* 676, 1729

"Bonanza" (television series), 1348

Bonanza farming, 15, **164,** 170, 206, 513

"Bonanza Kings," 921

Bonaparte, Napoleon, 210, 481

Bonifacio, Juan Giovanni, 758

Bonnat, Leon J. F., 1810

Bonneville, Benjamin Louis Eulalie de, **164-165,** *164,* 251, 500, 757, 1385, 1705

Bonneville Dam, 165, 375, 794

Bonney, Mary Lucinda, 1770

Bonney, William H. *See* "Billy the Kid"

Bonnin, Gertrude Simmons (Zitkala-Sa), **165,** 1027, 1658
 writings of, 165

Bonnin, Raymond, 165

Book illustration, 89-91, *89, 92*

Book and magazine illustration, **89-92**
 of Frederic Remington, 85, *91*

Book of Mormon, **166,** 242, 320, 409, 1033, 1373
 and state of Deseret, 443
 and Joseph Smith, Jr., 1480- 1481
 translation of, 1541
 see also Church of Jesus Christ of Latter-day Saints; Mor- mons

Boomers. *See* Oklahoma land rush; Payne, David L.

Booms, **166-171**
 in cattle industry, 266-267
 following Civil War, 166-168, 170-171
 in Houston, Texas, 706
 in lumber industry, 169
 in mining industry, *168, 169*
 in oil industry, 169-70, 706
 impact of railroads on, *167, 168,* 170

Boom towns. *See* Booms; Cattle towns; Gambling; Mining camps and towns; Prostitu- tion; Saloons; Urban West

Boone, Daniel, **171-172,** *171,* 385, 1010, 1690
 explorations of, 172
 as Western hero, 1698

Boone, James, 172

Boone, Jamima, 172

Boone, Rebecca Bryan, 172

Boone, William Judson, **172-173**

Boone and Crockett Club, **173,** *505,* 636, 714, 1745

Boonesborough, Fort, 172

Boorstin, Daniel, 880, 1227

Booth, Edwin, 608, 992, 1578

Booth, Junius Brutus, 992

Boots, 400

Boots and Saddles (Custer), 425

Borah, William E., **173,** 725, 1329, 1330, 1505

Borax mining, 437

Bordeaux, James, 1601

Border conflict. *See* Mexican border conflicts

Border Incident, 541

Borderlands, defined, 174

Borderlands theory, **174-176,** 1729
 and international conflict, 175
 and sense of otherness, 176
 separateness of, 176

Bronson, Charles, 1348
Brooke, John M., 814
Brooke, John R., 1786
Brooks, A. H., 30
Brooks, Garth, 1227
Brooks, J. A., 1571
Brooks, James, 1764
Brooks, Juanita Leavitt, **187**
Brooks, Nona, 1190
Brooks, Van Wyck, 578
Brooks, Will, 187
Brooks, William L. ("Buffalo Bill"), **187,** 700
Brooks, Winthrop, 467
Brooks-Scanlon Lumber Company, 912
Brothels. *See* Prostitution
Brotherhood of Penitents. *See* Penitentes
Brothers of Freedom, 78
Brougham, John, 411
Broughton, James, 374
Broughton, William, 1241
Brower, David, 476, 1368, 1461
Brown, Arthur Page, **188**
see also Architecture: urban; City planning
Brown, Ben, 342
Brown, Clara, **188-189,** *188*
Brown, Dee, 1789
Brown, Denise Scott, 333
Brown, Dutch Henry, 943
Brown, Edmund ("Pat"), 231
Brown, Elizabeth Gurley, 739
Brown, Eliza Jane, 189
Brown, Henry Newton, **189,** *189,* 700, 871
Brown, Jacob, 1615, 1660
Brown, James J., 857
Brown, John, **189-190,** 335, 799, 805, 932, 1078
Brown, John, Jr., 776
Brown, Johnny Mack, 536, 537
Brown, Milton, 407
Brown, "Unsinkable" Molly, 857
Brown, Orlando, 961
Brown, Richard Maxwell, 534, 831, 833, 1425, 1486, 1488, 1685, 1690, 1692
Brown, William, 691
Brown v. *Board of Education of Topeka,* 1055, 1447, 1590
Browne, John Ross, **190-191,** *190*

Browning, Edward, 191
Browning, George, 191
Browning, John Moses, **191**
Browning, Matthew, 191
Browning, Orville, 1542
Browning, Samuel, 191, 422
Browning Brothers Factory, 191
Brownson, Orestes A., 40
Brownson's Quarterly Review, 40
Brownsville, Texas: U.S.-Mexican conflict in, 396
Brown v. *United States,* 1691
Brué, A. H., 495
Bruff, J. Goldsborough, 716
Brûlé, Etienne, 584
Brulé Indians, 1135. *See also* Sioux Indians: federation of tribes
Brumble, H. David, III, 882
Brunot, Felix Reville, **191-192**
see also Temperance and Prohibition; United States Indian policy
Bryan, Mary Baird, 192
Bryan, Rebecca, 172
Bryan, William Jennings, 12, **192-194,** 366, 423, 632, 666, 858, 1721
as anti-imperalist, 1080
"Cross of Gold" speech, 419-420
and Nebraska politics, 1176
political rise of, 1458
presidential candidacy, 1082, 1084, 1317, 1539, 1566
Bryant, "Blackfaced Charley," 430
Bryant, Edward, 485
Bryant, Mary Hungerford, 921
Bryant, William Cullen, 805
Bryant, Sturgis and Company, **194,** 236
Bryce, James, *577,* 1406
Bryce Canyon National Park, 1086
Brynesen, John, 28
Bubonic plague, 1095
Bucareli, Antonio Maria, 758, 1503
Buchanan, James, 186, **194,** 797, *805,* 850, 1035, 1076, 1385, 1589
and Utah Expedition, 1675, 1808

Buck and the Preacher, 539
Buckley, Christopher Augustine, **194-195,** 1422
Buddhism, Japanese, 97
Buddhist Churches of America, 97
Buena Vista Vineyard, *228*
"Buffalo Bill." *See* Cody, William F.
Buffalo Bill and the Indians, 539
Buffalo Bill Historical Center, 87, **195,** 1289
Buffalo Bill Memorial Association, 195
Buffalo Bill's Wild West Show. *See* Cody, William F. ("Buffalo Bill"); Wild West Shows
Buffaloes, **195-197,** *195, 196, 549, 1742*
ancestors of, 195
demise of, 197, 505, 628, 1094, 1108
hunting of, 713-714, 965-966, 1138
Native American use of, 1106
population estimates, 196, 197
Buffalo grass. *See* Prairie
Buffalo Head (Cheyenne), 982
Buffalo Horn (Bannock), 1265, 1266
Buffalo Ship Channel Company, 705
Buffalo Soldiers, 10, **197-199,** *198,* 634
during Indian wars, 197-198
and John J. Pershing, 1283
Bugles in the Afternoon (Haycox), 880
Building Trades Council, San Francisco. *See* San Francisco Building Trades Council
Bukowski, Charles, 1308
Bulette, Julia, 1333, 1700
Bull Bear (Cheyenne), 634
Bull Bear (Sioux), 39, 283
Bull Moose party. *See* Progressive party
Bullis, John, 969
Bullwhackers, **199,** *199,* 219
Bulosan, Carlos, 885
Bumpers, Dale, 1384
Bunker Hill Mine, 1462
Bunny, John, 1044
Buntline, Ned, **199-200,** *200,* 355, 407, 877, 1486

Chouteau, Pierre, Sr., 315, 316, 586, 873, 1013, 1224, 1338

Chouteau, Pierre, Jr., 38, 316, 565, 566, 570, 572, 587, 1492, 1493-1494

Chouteau, René Auguste, 315, 837

Chouteau, Yvonne, 1227

Chouteau family, **315-316**, 803, 838, 847, 1751

Christensen, C. C. A., *321*

Christian Association of Washington (Pennsylvania), 240

Christian Baptist, The, 240

Christian Church, 240, 241

Christian Messenger, 240

Christian Socialism, **316-317**, 649

Christian System, The (Campbell), 240

Christie, Ned, 700, 1582

Christopher, Warren, 1202

Chronicles of the Builders of the Commonwealth, The (Bancroft), 281, 676

Chuck wagons, **318**, *318*

Chumash Indians, 1129

Chung Sai Yat Po, **318-319**, 885, 929, 1194

Chu Pak, **319**

Church, Frank, 319, 725

Church, Peggy Pond, 1308

Church of Divine Science, 1190

Church Divinity School of the Pacific, 1336

Churches. *See* African American churches; Asian American churches; Catholics; Church of Jesus Christ of Latter-day Saints; Mormons

Churches of Christ, 240, 241

Church of Jesus Christ of Latter-day Saints, **320-325**
  Oliver Cowdery as leader in, 409-410
  dissidents, 1281
  distinctiveness of, 325
  Doctrine and Covenants, 322, 327
  founding of, 320
  Heber J. Grant as leader in, 625
  Hebraic elements of, 320
  in Idaho, 724

missionary activity, 325
  and laws against polygamy, 477-478
  in the modern era, 325
  in Nauvoo, Illinois, 322
  Perpetual Emigrating Fund, 1282
  Relief Society, 1034-1035, 1364, 1485
  settlements of, 320-322
  John Taylor as leader in, 1541
  Brigham Young as president of, 323
  see also Church of Jesus Christ of Latter-Day Saints, Reorganized (RLDS); Mormons; Young, Brigham

Church of Jesus Christ of Latter-Day Saints, Reorganized (RLDS), 322, **326-328**
  Bible of, 327
  founding, 1481-1482
  leadership of, 326, 327-328
  under Joseph Smith, III, 326-327, 643, 1481-1482

Church of the Nazarene, 1337

Church of Religious Science, 1190

Churchill, Caroline Nichols, **319-320**, 928, *1773*

Churchill, Winston, 1080

Chy Lung v. Freeman, 308

Cibeque Indians, 1149

Cíbola, Seven Cities of, **328-329**, 368, 390, 499, 937, 1562

Cimarron, New Mexico, 947

Cimarron (film), 537

Cimarron Desert, 1432

"Cisco Kid, The," 1347, 1348

Cisneros, Sandra, 887

Cities. *See* City government; City planning; Urban West

Cities Service Company, 1218

Citizens Protective League, 11

City government, **329-331**
  in Denver, 330
  in Kansas City, 330-331
  and political machines, 329
  and public utilities, 330
  reform in, 329-330

City of Night (Rechy), 887

City planning, **331-333**
  and Edward Herbert Bennett, 134-135

and Daniel Hudson Burnham, 207
  and "city beautiful" movement, 332-333
  in Denver, Colorado, 440
  of early cities, 331-332
  of modern cities, 333

Civilian Conservation Corps, 71, 520

Civilization programs, 1118-1119, 1120. *See also* Native American cultures: assimilation; acculturation

Civil Rights Act of 1870, 305

Civil War, 4, 8, **333-341**, *338, 339*
  Albuquerque during, 32
  Clay Allison in, 36
  "Bloody Bill" Anderson in, 46, 639
  in Arizona, 338
  David Rice Atchison in, 101
  Nathaniel P. Banks in, 119
  John Robert Baylor in, 128
  Ambrose Bierce in, 143
  boom following, 166-168
  Felix Reville Brunot in, 192
  Buffalo Soldiers in, 197
  California during, 226
  use of camels during, 238
  Edward Richard Spring Canby in, 242, 246
  James H. Carleton in, 246
  Kit Carson in, 248
  Jesse Chisholm in, 312
  John M. Chivington in, 314
  Buffalo Bill Cody in, 355
  Philip St. George Cooke in, 384
  Jim Courtright in, 399
  John Cradlebaugh in, 412
  George Crook in, 418
  currency during, 632
  Samuel Ryan Curtis in, 424
  George Armstrong Custer in, 425-426
  deflation following, 422
  Grenville Mellen Dodge in, 453
  William Hemsley Emory in, 486
  federal-government expansion during, 518
  Benjamin F. Ficklin in, 530
  John Charles Frémont in, 334, 575

Cotton farming, 15, **396-398,** *397, 398*
  in Arkansas, 77
  production patterns, 397
  technological breakthroughs, 397-398, 515
  U.S. production of, 398
Couch, William L., 1228
Coues, Elliott, **398**
Cougars. *See* Mountain lions
Coughlin, "Bathhouse" John, 289
Coulee Dam, 794
Council Bluffs, Iowa, *749*
Council Grove, Kansas, 1432
Count of Monte Cristo, 227
Country music: cowboy image in, 407
Coup, W. C., 1747
Course of Empire, The (DeVoto), 446
Courtright, Jim, **399,** *399,* 1459
Couse, Eanger Irving, 86, 1536
Couts, Cave, 1764
Couzins, Phoebe W., 1301
Covered Wagon, The (Hough), 704
Covered Wagon, The (film), 536
Covered wagons. *See* Conestoga wagons
Cowboy outfits, **399-402,** *400, 401*
  boots, 400
  chaps, 401-402
  gloves, 402
  hats, 399-400
  pants, 400
  shirts, 400
  spurs, 400-401
  vests, 401
Cowboys, *265, 268, 273,* **402-406,** *403, 404, 405*
  Adams, Andy, 4
  Autry, Gene, 108-109, 1058, 1347, 1388, 1515
  African American, 8-9, *8,* 10
  Cook, James Henry, 383
  as depicted in film, 535-536
  as entertainers, 403-405, 407
  heroic image of, 403-404, 407, 535-536
  history of, 403
  humor of, 710-712
  Mix, Tom, 1017-1018

Pickett, Bill, 981, 1291-1292, 1388
  poetry of, 343
  Rogers, Roy, 1058, 1347, 1390, *1390*
  inging, 536
  vaqueros, 236
  see also Autry Museum of Western Heritage; Cattle driving; Cattle industry; Cowboy outfits; Cowboy songs; Cowboy tools and equipment
Cowboy songs, **406-407,** *559*
  instruments used in, 406
  printed collections of, 406-407
  recordings of, 407
  and Western music, 1058
Cowboys Turtle Association, 1388
Cowboy tools and equipment, **408-409**
  rope, 409
  saddles, 408-409
Cowdery, Oliver, 166, **409-410**
Cowlitz Indians, 1144
Cox, Joe, 917
Coyoteros, 48
Coyotes, **410-411**
  fur as commodity, 411
  as predators, 410, 411
Coyotes, 742
Crabtree, John, 411
Crabtree, Lotta, **411-412,** 992, 1026
Crabtree, Mary Ann, 411
Cradlebaugh, John, **412**
Cramer, Joseph, 1416
Cramer, Malina, 1190
Crandal, E. M., 121
Cranston, Susan Amelia, 1323
Crawford, Emmett, *969*
Crawford, Jack, 559, 1747
Crawford, Joan, 1515
Crawford, Samuel, 800
Crawford, T. Hartley, 961
Crawford, William H., 391
Crazy Horse (Sioux), 39, 154, 160, **412-413,** 426, 590, 591, 815, 888, 977, 1173
  as leader, 1497
  and the Sioux Wars, 1469, 1470
  and Sitting Bull, 1469, 1470

Crazy Horse: The Strange Man of the Oglalas (Sandoz), 1420
Creating the West (Nash), 678, 1729
Crédit Mobilier of America, **413-414,** 518, 1350
  Ames's role in, 43, 413, 469
  scandal involving, 5, 414, 447, 1569, 1611
Cree Indians, 1134, 1140, 1141
Creek Indians, 1155, 1224-1225; and Andrew Jackson, 761-762; treaty with, 1644
Creel, George, 330
Creighton, Donald, 581
Creighton, Edward, 1550
Crepusculo, El, 928
Crespi, Juan, 900, 901
Crèvecoeur, Hector St. John de, 674
Criminal syndicalism laws, 739, 740
Crimmins, Phil, 195
Criollos, 973, 1303
Cripple Creek, Colorado, 363, 366, **414-416,** *1781*
  as gold-mining town, 415, 616
  population of, 415
Cripple Creek strikes, **416-417,** 832, 908, 988
Critcher, Catherine C., 1536
Crocker, Charles, 188, 226, 276, **417,** 674, 695, 715, 789, 1404, 1498, 1510
Crocker, E. B., 91
Crocker, Samuel, 1228
Crocker, William H., 1268
Crocker Office Building, 188
Crockett, David (Davey), 21, **417-418,** 711, 1576
  and Mike Fink, 1376
  as folk hero, 417-418, 877, 1698
Croghan, George, 494
Croix, Teodoro de, 49, 1504
Croly, Herbert, 1329
Cronica, La, 928
Cronon, William, 290, 675, 677, 1191, 1193
Crook, George, 39, 48, 220, **418-419,** *419,* 452, 640, 1054, 1061, 1265, 1614, *1622,* 1634
  during Apache wars, 51-52, 418-419, 605, 707, 790,

of Western Heritage

General Allotment Act. *See* Dawes Act

General Circular to All Persons of Good Character Who Wish to Emigrate to the Oregon Territory (Kelley), 810

General Federation of Women's Clubs, 165

General Land Office, 203, 519, **599**, 684, 1339
  and Ballinger-Pinchot Controversy, 113-114
  and Desert Land Act of 1877, 444
  and Desert Land Act of 1891, 444
  and Timber Culture Act of 1873, 843
  and James A. Williamson, 1753

General Petroleum Company, 1219

General Revision Act, 893

Genesis of the Frontier Thesis, The: A Study in Historical Creativity (Billington), 148

Genizaros, 742

Genthe, Arnold, 1289

Gentlemen's Agreement, 99, **599-600**, *600,* 769, 771, 1294, 1424

Geological Report on the Yellowstone and Missouri Rivers (Raynolds), 1357

Geological Survey. *See* United States Geological Survey

George, Henry, **600-601**, 847, 1406

George B. Post and Sons, 134

George C. Page Museum of La Brea Discoveries, 904

Georgetown Courier, 927

Georgia gold rush, 614, 989, 991

Georgia-Pacific, 915

Gerdine, T. G., 30

German Americans, **601-604**
  and Americanization programs, 40
  architecture of, *56*
  after 1848, 603-604
  in Missouri, 1011
  newspapers and magazines of, 928

progressive politics of, 603

religious beliefs of, 603

Schurz, Carl, 1440-1441

Spreckels, Claus, 1507

in Texas, 602-603

see also Jewish Americans

Germania Gesellschaft, 602

Geronimo (Apache), 48, 51-52, *52,* 351, 418, **604-605,** *604,* 640
  as Apache leader, 1456, 1461
  family ties of, 1061, 1062
  and Tom Horn, 695-696
  and Indian scouts, 1627
  and Juh, 789
  surrender of, 969, 1061, 1151, 1189

Gervais, Jean Baptiste, 572, 1385

Ghadar party, 473

Ghent, Treaty of, 101

Ghost Dance religion, 145, 147, 154-155, 591, **605-606,** *606, 1654,* 1654-1655
  adherents, 1459
  Kicking Bear as leader of, 816
  and Nelson Appleton Miles, 977
  and Native American spiritualism, 1091, 1104, 1120, 1141, 1147-1148
  and Sitting Bull, 952, 1470-1471, 1474
  and Wounded Knee Massacre, 1786-1787
  Wovoka as founder of, 1789

Ghost Dance uprising, 420, 1789

Ghost towns, 169, **606-608,** *607,* 984, 994

Giannini, Amadeo Peter, 19, 119, 227, 228, 260, 521, **608-609,** *759,* 794

Giant, 541

Gibbon, John Oliver, **609-610,** 888, 1265, 1737

Gibbons, Cedric, 438

Gibson, Hoot, 536

Gibson, Mary Simons, 1341

Gibson, Paris, 346, **610**

Gibson, Walter Murray, 456, 1007

Gifford, Sanford R., 88

Gila City, Arizona, 606

Gila River, 589

Gila River Reservation, 69

Gilbert, Carlos, 217

Gilbert, Grove Karl, 252, 649-650

Gilbert, Humphrey, 494, 1206

Gilbert, W. J., 93

Gilcrease, Thomas, 356, 1582
  see also Thomas Gilcrease Institute

Gilcrease Institute. *See* Thomas Gilcrease Institute

Gilded Age, The (Twain), 1605

Gilder, Helena, 560

Gilder, Richard Watson, 783

Gildersleeve, Charles, 1435

Gilenos, 48

Gill, Irving, 62, 63, 64

Gill, Vince, 1227

Gillem, Alvin C., 1265

Gillespie, Archibald H., **611**

Gillespie, Richard Addison (Ad), 1570

Gilliam, Cornelius, 1261

Gilligan, John, 1730

Gilman, Charlotte Perkins, **611**

Gilman, Daniel Coit, 1394

Gilman, George G., 881

Gilpin County, Colorado, 280

Gilpin, William, **611-612,** 1666

Ginsberg, Allen, 1308

Girl of the Golden West, The (Puccini), 1234

Girl Scouts of America (GSA), 693, 694

Girls Rodeo Association, 1388-1389

Girty, George, 1625

Girty, James, 1625

Girty, Simon, 1625

Gish, Lillian, 1515

Gist, Christopher, 494

Glass, Hugh, 183, **612-613,** 1048, 1049

Glavis, Louis, 113-114

Glazunov, Andrei, 29

Glen Canyon Dam, 369, 371, 372, 624, 1360

Glenn, Edwin, 30

Glenn, Hugh (explorer), 613-614, *613*

Glenn, Hugh James (rancher), *575-576,* **613**

Glenn-Fowler Expedition, **613-614,** *613,* 1431

Glick, George W., 455, 801

558, 603, 683, **736-740,**
737, 894, 913, 919, 928,
1489, 1739
and class war, 739-740
culture of, 737-738; and free-
speech movement, 738-739
and William D. Haywood,
664-665, 736
and Mary Harris ("Mother")
Jones, 786
and Frank Little, 888
and the mining industry, 991,
994, 1730
violence among members, 739-
740, 832-834, 1674
women in, 1784
Ingalls, John J., **740,** 858
Ingalls, Laura. *See* Wilder, Laura
Ingalls
Inge, William, 803
Ingersoll, Sarah. *See* Cooper,
Sarah Brown Ingersoll
Ingraham, Prentiss, 403, 535
In His Steps (Sheldon), 1454-
1455
Inkpaduta (Sioux), 889, 1467,
1468, 1528
In the Land of the Headhunters,
424
Innis, Harold, 161, 581
In Old Arizona, 537
In Old Santa Fe, 108-109
Interior, Department of the, 30, 208
under Harold L. Ickes, 719-720
and Richard Wetherill, 54
Intermarriage, **741-746**
and antimiscegenation laws,
741
between Asian Americans and
Euro-Americans, 746
between Asian Americans and
Mexicans, 745-746
between Euro-Americans and
Native Americans, 742-743,
1601
between Euro-Americans and
Spanish/Mexicans, 743-745
political implications of, 744
between Spanish/Mexicans and
Native Americans, 741-742
tensions deriving from, 744-
745
International Church of the
Foursquare Gospel, 1337

International Congress of
Women, 598
International Fisheries Commis-
sion, 556
International Longshoreman's
and Warehouseman's Union
(ILWU), 660
International Longshoreman's
Association, 834
International Museum of Folk
Art (Santa Fe), 96
International Pacific Salmon
Fisheries Commission, 556
International Union of Mine, Mill
and Smelter Workers
(IUMMSW), 1731
Interstate Commerce Act of
1887, 746, **746-747**
and rail rates, 922
Interstate Commerce Commis-
sion, 103, 746, 848
Interstate Highway Act, 1352
Interstate Highway System, 522
Intertribal Bison Cooperative,
195
*Introduction to the Study of
Indian Languages, An*
(Powell), 1321
Inuits. *See* Eskimos
Invaders, The, 536
Invaders. *See* Johnson County
War
Iolani Palace, 656
Iowa, **747-751,** 749
during the Civil War, 750
climate of, 748
as corn-growing state, 390
cultural life of, 750
Dubuque, Julien (fur trader),
466, 749
ethnic groups in, 747-748, 750
farming in, 750
French heritage, 749
geography of, 748
Lacey, John Fletcher (congressman), 836-837
map of, 747
museums in, 750
native inhabitants of, 748
politics in, 751
population, 747, 748, 750
and school segregation, 1447
statehood, 750
territorial period, 749-750

Weaver, James Baird (politician), 1721
Iowa, University of, 358, 750
Iowa Farmer and Horticulturist,
635
Iowa Indians, 1139
Iowa State University of Science
and Technology, 750
Iowa Writers Workshop, 750
Irish Americans, **751-755,** 752,
753, 754
Kennedy, Kate, 812-813
and labor movement, 754-755
in Missouri, 1011
Mackay, John W. (mining
magnate), 921
Patricios, 752-753; and the
railroads, 1350
in Texas, 1415
and the Texas annexation, 1076
as Westerners, 753-755
in United States–Mexican War,
752 753
Irish immigrants, 458
Irkutsk Company, 498
Iron Horse, The, 536
Iron Jacket (Comanche), 1570
Iron Mountain Ranch Company,
696
Iron Shell, 682
Iron Shield. *See* American Horse
(elder)
Iroquois Indians, 1003, 1111,
1155-1156
Irrigation, **755-756,** 756
in California, 582, 1790
of crops, 512, 512-513, 514-
515
government's role in, 756
and Elwood Mead, 955
and the Ogallala Aquifer, 1213-
1214
and William E. Smythe, 1482
and the Soil Conservation
Service, 1492
and the United States Geological Survey, 1182
Wright Irrigation Act of 1887,
1790
see also Reclamation
Irrigation projects, 14, 67, 203-
204, 520, 756
in California, 227, 229, 279,
281

as domestic servants, 459, 460

and Gentlemen's Agreement, 599-600, 1294, 1424

language schools for, 849-850

literature of, 885

as workers, 829, 1766

Japanese internment, 226, **773-776**, 774, 1442-1443, 1521, 1675

Japanese Reform Association, 771

Japanese-Mexican Labor Association (JMLA), 771, 1257

Jaramillo, Maria Ignacia, 136

JA Ranch, 618, **776**

milk and meat cooler at, 57, 57

Jay, John, 1739

Jay Cooke and Company, 383

Jayhawkers, 335, 355, 639, **776-777**, 1804

and William Clarke Quantrill, 777, 1346

Jayne, William, 1496

J. B. Hunt (trucking firm), 78

Jeffers, Robinson, 911, 1307-1308

Jefferson, James, 9

Jefferson, Thomas, 11, 82, 100, 180, 316, 495, **777-778**, 777, 845, 1602, 1751

and Aaron Burr, 209

and Indian policy, 1096, 1165, 1547, 1645

and Lewis and Clark Expedition, 251, 344, 499-500, 503, 586, 778, 865, 866-867, 1236

and Louisiana Purchase, 905, 906, 1066, 1067-1068, 1408

and the Northwest Ordinance, 1204

Notes on the State of Virginia, 53, 504, 778

territorial ordinance of, 1555

view of West, 577, 674, 777-778

and Western expansion, 934, 935, 1406

Jefferson Barracks, 568, 1613, 1628

Jeffords, Thomas J., 354, **778**

Jeffrey, Julie Roy, 677

Jenner, Edward, 447

Jenney, Walter P., 156, 501, 1469

Jenney, William Le Baron, 288

Jennings, Francis, 1002, 1065

Jennings, Waylon, 405

Jennings, William, **778-779**, 1810

Jennison, Charles (Doc), 335, 336, 776, 1692

Jerome Agreement, 1345-1346

Jersey cattle, 265

Jesse James, 537

Jesuits, 256-257

and colonization, 974

De Smet, Pierre Jean, 1005, 1022, 1063

as explorers, 497, 503

Kino, Eusebio Francisco, 820-821

Marquette, Jacques 939, 1008, 1009, 1015

and parochial schools, 1271

see also Missions: early Franciscan and Jesuit

Jewish Americans, **779-781**, 779

Alexander, Moses, 33

as businessmen, 779-780

in motion picture industry, 780-781

role of in Western development, 780-781

Jewish immigrants, colony in Utah, 342-343

J. F. Shea, 794

Jicarilla Indians, 1149

Jimenez, Fortun, 1503

Jimenez, Luis, 94

Jiménez, Flaco, 381

Jiménez, Francisco, 887

Jiménez, Santiago, 381

Jinshan ge ji, 885

John Burroughs Society, 211

John Deere and Company, 751

John Muir Award, 764

Johnson, Albert (brother of Hiram Johnson), 782

Johnson, Albert (congressman), 1519

Johnson, Albert S. (army commander), 529

Johnson, Andrew, 122, 341, 635, 648, 707, 800, 849, 1542

Johnson, Arthur, 1044

Johnson, Carrie, 1401

Johnson, Claudia Taylor "Ladybird," 782

Johnson, Edwin Carl ("Big Ed"), 396, **781**

Johnson, Frank Tenney, 87, 109, **781-782**

Johnson, Hiram Warren, 34, 179, 230, 478, **782**, 1329, 1395, 1610

Johnson, J. Neely, 1425

Johnson, Jeremiah, 1049

Johnson, John J., 50

Johnson, L. B., 1040

Johnson, Luci Baines, 782

Johnson, Lynda Byrd, 782

Johnson, Lyndon B., 19, 319, **782-783**, 1566

Johnson, Mary, 1760

Johnson, Phil, 162

Johnson, Philip, 44

Johnson, Richard Mentor, 1074, 1548

Johnson, Robert Underwood, **783-784**

Johnson, W. T., 1388

Johnson County War, 243, 271, 347, **784-785**, 1678, 1685, 1710

Johnson-Reed Act of 1924, 729, 769

Johnson Space Center, 783

Johnston, Albert Sidney, 797, 938, 1385

Johnston, Henry S., 1226, 1227

Joliet, Louis, 77, 79, 256, 497, 585, 749, **785**, 939, 1009, 1015

Jones and Plummer Trail, 275

Jones, Anson, **785-786**

Jones, A. Quincy, 65

Jones, Buck, 536

Jones, Charles J. "Buffalo," 633

Jones, David, 53

Jones, Edwin, 54

Jones, Jennifer, 1515

Jones, Jesse, 119

Jones, John B., 1571

Jones, John, 1180

Jones, Margo, 1579

Jones, Mary Harris ("Mother"), 664, 736, **786-787**, 909, 1785

Jones, Nathaniel V., 1038

Jones, Pirkle, 44

Jones-Costigan Sugar Control Act, 396

Joplin, Scott, 1012

Jordan, David Starr, 357, **787-788**

Jordan, Tabitha, 840
Jornada del Muerto, 1595
José, Nicholas, 1594
Joseph, Chief. *See* Chief Joseph
(Nez Percé)
Joseph the Elder (Nez Percé),
291, 292, 855, 898, 1737
and Nez Percé War, 1230, 1265
Joseph, Antonio, 972
Joslyn, George A., 788
Joslyn, Sarah, 788
Joslyn Art Museum, **788**
Journal of Arizona History, The,
72
Journal of Borderlands Studies,
174
Journal of Forestry, 564
Journalism. *See* Newspapers and
magazines
Journals of Lewis and Clark, The
(DeVoto), 445
Journal of Travels into the
Arkansas Territory, during
the year 1819 (Nuthall), 874
Journey Home, The (Abbey), 1
Journey to California, A
(Bidwell), 485
Joutel, Henri, 77
J. P. Morgan and Company, 546
Juana Briones Beach, 185
Juanita of Downieville, **788**, 919,
994, 1764
Juárez, Benito, 183, 396, 968
Juárez, Mexico, 481, 483, 484
Judah, Theodore Dehone, 276,
674, 695, **789**, 1404
Judd, Gerrit P., 658-659
Judge, William Quan, 1588
Judicial system. *See* Legal system
Judson, Edward Zane Carroll.
See Buntline, Ned
Juh (Apache), 51, 604, **789-790**
Juneau, Joe, 27, **790-791**, *790,*
791
Juneau, Solomon, 790
Juneau, Alaska, 21, *24, 25,* 790,
791
during gold rush, 27
Jungle, The (Sinclair), 290, 317,
1464
Jurado, Katy, 1515
Justices of the peace, 1556
Juvenile Instructor, 242
J. W. Coop, 539

K

Kaahumanu, Queen, 151, 1006-
1007
Kachina carving, **793**, 1102,
1150
Kael, Pauline, 1516
Kafir corn, 510
Kahn, Florence Prag, 780
Kahn, Julius, 780
Kahoolawe, 656
Kaiser, Henry J., 19, 228, 521,
609, 660, 694, **794-795**,
794
damming of the Colorado and
Columbia rivers, 1360
and health-maintenance
organizations, 959
as shipbuilder, 794-795, 1239,
1319
Kaiser Aluminum Company, 795
Kalakaua, King David, 456, 659,
1540
Kalispel Indians, 1021
Kalloch, Isaac S., 808
Kalm, Peter, 53
Kamchatka Expedition, First, 497
Kamchatka Expedition, Second,
497
Kamehameha I, 151, 302, 658,
1006, 1143
Kamehameha II (Liholiho), King,
1006, 1143
Kamehameha III, 659, 1007,
1143
Kamehameha V, 151
Kamiakin (Yakima), **795-796**,
796, 1262, 1263, 1264
Kan, Andrew, 1695
Kanakas, 659
Kane, Elizabeth Wood, 797
Kane, Paul, 82, **796**
Kane, Thomas Leiper, **797**
Kansa Indians, 1014, 1134,
1135, 1136, 1139
Kansas, **797-803**, *799, 801, 802*
aircraft industry in, 802, 803
cattle industry in, 800-801
cattle towns in, 272, 273, 800
Civil War in, 335-336, 800
education in, 800
ethnic groups in, 801
Exodusters' migration to, 493-
494, 1465-1466

exploration of, 798-799
farming in, 14, 802
geographical features, 797
immigrants in, 801
Indian missions in, 799
Ingalls, John J. (politician), 740
Jayhawkers in, 776-777
Lane, James Henry (senator),
848-849
Malin, James Claude (historian), 932
map of, *798*
Native Americans in, 797-798,
800
political life of, 801-802
population of, 803
railroads in, 800
Robinson, Charles (governor),
1383
and school segregation, 1447
Simpson, Jerry (politician),
1464
slavery as political issue in,
799-800, 859
statehood, 800
territorial period, 799-800
in the twentieth century, 801-
803
White, William Allen (newspaper editor), 1736
after World War II, 802-803
see also Dodge City, Kansas;
Kansas-Nebraska Act;
Topeka, Kansas; Wichita,
Kansas
Kansas, University of, 358
Kansas Brigade, 776
Kansas City, Missouri, **803-804**
during the Civil War, 804
Missouri: growth, 1012
meat-packing industry in, 290
and the Pendergast machine,
1277-1278, 1667
politics in, 329, 330-331, 804
population, 804, 1665
Kansas City Evening Star, 1177
Kansas v. Colorado, **806**, 1717
Kansas Indians. *See* Native
American peoples: peoples of
the Great Plains
Kansas-Nebraska Act, 101, 194,
333, 464, 590, 799, **804-**
806, 824, 907, 1753
Kansas News, 925

in Hawaii, 658
Jackson, Sheldon, 764-765
in Kansas, 799
Kino, Eusebio Francisco, 820-821
Lee, Jason, 859
McBeth, Sue and Kate, 948-949
Maurer, Katherine R., 945
Spalding, Henry Harmon and Eliza Hart, 1072
Whitman, Marcus, 1003, 1004-1005, 1006, 1072, 1237, 1738-1739
Whitman, Narcissa, 1004-1005, 1006, 1072, 1237, 1738-1739
see also American Board of Commissioners for Foreign Missions
Mission Dolores, 63
Mission Indians, 764, *1131*
Mission of the North American People (Gilpin), 612
Missions
in Alaska, 1128
in Arizona, 821
in California, 1002
California ranchos as adjuncts to, 235-236
decline of, 257-258
early Franciscan and Jesuit, 974, 1000-1003, 1303, 1342, 1430, 1449-1450, 1502, 1503
in El Paso, 481
and the *encomienda* system, 1000, 1187, 1342, 1476
in Hawaii, 1006-1007, 1234-1235
to the Indians, 948-949, 1003-1006
Nuestra Señora de Guadalupe, 481
in the Oregon territory(see also Whitman, Marcus), 1072, 1237
Protestant, 1003-1006, 1335-1336, 1761
Woman's Home Missionary Society, 1761
Mississippi River, **1007-1009**
bridging of, 1012
exploration of, 1008-1009
navigation rights, 906

as transportation route, 1009
tributaries of, 1007, *1008*
Mississippi River Commission, 1009
Mississippi Valley mounds: archaeology of, 54
Mississippian culture, 77, 1009
Missouri, **1009-1013**
Ashley, William Henry (congressman), 96
Atchison, David Rice (senator), 101-102
Benton, Thomas Hart (senator), 137-138
during the Civil War, 333-337, 1011-1012
Civil War refugees in, 336-337
Clark, James Beauchamp ("Champ") (congressman), 343
Colman, Norman J. (lieutenant governor), 359
cultural life of, 1012
exploration and settlement by Europeans, 1009-1010
Italian immigrants in, 759
map of, *1010*
and mules, 1053, 1060
and Native Americans, 1009
and statehood, 1011
as U. S. territory, 1010-1011, 1751
James Wilkinson in, 1751
see also Kansas City, Missouri; St. Louis, Missouri; Westport, Missouri
Missouri and California Overland Mail and Transportation Company, 1017
Missouri Compromise, 101, 346, 377, 464, 465, 590, 799, 804, 907, 971, 1011, **1013**, 1077-1078
Missouri Equal Rights League, 1012
Missouri Fur Company, 135, 345, 372, 373, 500, 567, 624, **1013-1014**
Missouri Indians, 1009, 1139, 1172. *See also* Native American peoples: people of the Great Plains
Missouri River, **1014-1016**, *1015, 1016*

exploration of, 1014, 1015
and flood control, 1016
railroad bridge over, 804
tributaries of, 1014, 1021
Mitchell, Albert K., 134
Mitchell, David Dawson, **1016-1017**
Mitchell, John, 208
Mitla, Town of the Souls and other Zapoteco-Speaking Pueblos of Oaxaca, Mexico (Parsons), 1271
Miwok Indians. *See* Native American Peoples: Peoples of California
Mix, Tom, 407, 536, 537, **1017-1018**, *1017*, 1064, 1256, 1347, 1748
"Mixed-blood" people. *See* Métis people
Moby-Dick (Melville), 191, 1733, 1734
Mochilas, 408
Moczygemba, Leopold, 260
Modoc Indians, 1129, *1129*, 1145, 1147
Captain Jack, 241, *241*, 242, 243-244, *244*
Modoc War, 241-242, 243-244, 1264-1265
Moen Manufacturing Company, 121
Moffat, David Halliday, **1018**, *1018*
Mogollon, New Mexico, 608
Mogollon Indians, 48, 70, 933, 1124, 1186
Mojave Desert, 224, **1018-1019**
Mojave Indians, *1130*
captives of, 1211-1212
culture, 1114, 1116, 1129, 1149, 1153
Möllhausen, Heinrich B., 88, 1599
Molly Maguires, 755, 1298
Molokai, 656
Momaday, N. Scott, 844, 1308
Monadnock Building (Chicago), 207
Mondale, Walter, 999
Mondell, Frank W., 487
Monk, Hank, 1509
Monkey Wrench Gang, The (Abbey), 1

N

NAC. *See* Native American Church

NAFTA. *See* North American Free Trade Agreement

Nahl, Charles, 89-91

Nahl, Hugo, 91

Naiche (Apache), 604, **1061,** *1061*

Naked Spur, The, 538

Nakota Indians. *See* Sioux Indians: federation of tribes

Nampeyo (Hopi), 1159

Nana (Apache), 198, 640, **1061-1062,** *1062,* 1151

Napoleon, Emperor, 164

Narbona (Navajo), 936, **1062,** 1169

Narbona, Antonio, 1169

Nardroff, Ellen von, 1407

Narrative (Thompson), 502

Narrative of My Captivity Among the Sioux Indians (Kelly), 811-812, 876

Narrative of the United States Exploration Edition (Wilkes), 504

Narváez, Pánfilo de, 218, 328, 499, 592, **1062-1063,** 1187, 1562

NASA. *See* National Aeronautics and Space Administration

Nash, Gerald, 677, 678, 1192, 1729

Nash, Roderick, 677

Nashville Company, 1070

Natawista (Blood), **1063**

Natchez Indians, 1157

Nathoy, Lulu (Polly Bemis), 134

Nation, Carry, 801, *802,* 928, **1063-1064,** *1552*

Nation, The, 637, 638

National Aeronautics and Space Administration (NASA), 19-20, 706

National Airlines, 163

National Amateur Athletic Foundation (NAAF), 693

National American Woman Suffrage Organization, 1087

National Association for the Advancement of Colored People, 1769

National Banking Act, 117

National City Bank of New York, 1084

National Colored Colonization Society, 493

National Congress of American Indians, 1657

National Conservation Commission, 1297

National Consumer's League, 1383

National Council of American Indians, 165

National Cowboy Hall of Fame and Western Heritage Center, 87, **1064,** 1289

National Elk Refuge, 479

National Environmental Policy Act, 1640

National expansion, 517-518, **1064-1084**
  and colonial period, 1065-1066
  and imperialist policy, 1078-1084
  and the Louisiana Purchase, 1066-1069
  and the Mexican cession, 970
  and post-Revolutionary period, 1066
  and Texas, 1069-1072
  and the Polk administration, 1072-1077
  and slavery, 971, 1072, 1073, 1077
  Webster's view of, 1723
  see also Louisiana Purchase; Manifest Destiny; United States–Mexican War; War of 1812

National Farmers' Alliance and Industrial Union, 1315

National Farmers Organization (NFO), 12

National Forest Management Act of 1976, 562, 1640

National Good Roads Association, 1380

National Industrial Recovery Act of 1933, 910

National Land Company, 216

National Origins Act of 1924, 729, 759

National Parks. *See* Grand Canyon and Grand Canyon National Park; Grand Teton National Park; Great Smoky Mountains National Park; Mesa Verde National Park; National Park Service; Olympic National Park; Sequoia National Park; Yellowstone National Park; Yosemite National Park

National Parks Association, 476

National Park Service, 203, 253, 623, 624, 848, **1086-1087**
  Albright as director of, 30-31
  creation of, 813, 1052, 1085
  and John Horace McFarland, 950, 1085
  and Stephen Tyng Mather, 944-945, 1085-1086, 1592
  mission, 1085, 1087
  and multiple-use doctrine, 1055
  and Frank Pinkley, 1299
  and John Wesley Powell, 1321
  tourism at, 1592-1593

National Popular Education Board, **1086-1087**

National Recreation Areas, 319

National Security League, 41

National Wildlife Refuge System, 1745

National Woman's Party, 940, **1087**

National Woman Suffrage Association, 142, 598, 1772

National Women's Relief Society. *See* Relief Society (LDS)

National Wool Growers Association, 1454

National Youth Administration for Texas, 782

Native American basketry, **1087-1089,** *1088*
  decline of, 1089
  materials, 1087-1088
  revival of, 1089
  uses, 1088-1089;

Native American beadwork, **1089-1091,** *1089, 1090*
  materials, 1089-1090
  styles, 1090

Native American Church (NAC), **1091-1092**, 1104, 1141, 1346, 1658

Native American cultures, **1092-1121**

acculturation, 474, 1094, 1118-1121, 1134, 1141

assimilation, 433, 474-475, 732-733, 959-960, 1099-1100, 1104, 1108, 1165, 1647, 1653, 1672

importance of bears to, 637

impact of Catholicism on, 257, 444-445

child rearing, 296-298, 1097-1098

clan system, 1097

concept of property, 1642

creation myths, 280

deities, 1103

demography, 1092-1095

and disease, 582, 1093-1094; 1095-1097, 1119, 1128, 1135-1136, 1143, 1342

ecology, 1107-1108, 1009-1110

and Euro-American culture, 201-202, 731, 734, 1110, 1116

family life, 1097-1101

fertility among, 526-527

fire as viewed by, 548-549

importance of fish to, 553

gambling among, 593-594

gender roles, 297, 531-532, 1097-1098, 1112-1113, 1150, 1637

Ghost Dance religious movement, 605-606

homosexuality among, 138-140

kinship societies, 1097

political organization, 1111-1113, 1133

in prehistory, 1092-1093

and property rights, 1110

puberty rites, 298

relocations, 1094

recovery of, 1094-1095

spiritual life, 390, 793, 1101-1105, 1119-1120, 1133

subsistence patterns, 1094, 1005-1109, 1129, 1132, 1137-1141

view of death, 1103

warfare, 1094, 1113-1115

water as significant to, 1716

weapons, 1113-1114, 1116-1118, 1119

see also Native American peoples; United States Indian policy

Native American ledger drawing, **1121**, *1121*

Native American literature, 881-884

Native American peoples

activist groups, 1131, 1134

in Arizona, 68, 69-70

as army scouts, 1625-1627

and arrival of Spanish, 361

under Burke Act, 205

and California ranchos, 235-236

civilization programs, 1651-1675

in Colorado, 360-361

as Confederate allies, 337-338

under Dawes Act, 434-435

and William P. Dole, 457

education of, 202, 285, 474-475, 731-735, 1658

federal policy toward, 201-202, 205, 286, 434-435, 457, 518

and field matrons, 531-532

in films, 538, 539-541

in Grand Canyon area, 623

and Grant's Peace Policy, 625-626

healers, 958

health care, 1655

historians of, 437, 439

as homesteaders, 690-691

as horse breeders, 698

and Oliver Otis Howard, 707

in Idaho, 724

in Iowa, 748-749

and Helen Maria Fiske Hunt Jackson, 763-764

in Kansas, 797-798, 800

land concessions following Civil War, 340-341

language groups, 1132, 1137, 1144-1145, 1148-1149

legal status of, 285-286

legislation affecting, 433, 434-435

and Lewis and Clark Expedition, 865

marriage to Euro-Americans, 742-743

marriage to Spanish/Mexicans, 741-742

paintings of, 82, 162, 261-263, 436, 516, 818, 1754

peoples of Alaska, 1125-1129

peoples of California, 1116, 1129-1132

peoples of the Great Basin, 1106-1107, 1114, 1129, 1132-1134

peoples of the Great Plains, 1107, 1115, 1117-1118, 1121, 1161

peoples of Hawaii, 1142-1144

peoples of the Pacific Northwest, 1107, 1112, 1144-1148, 1161

peoples removed from the East, 961, 1153-1158

peoples of the Southwest, 1148-1153, 1158-1162

photographs of, 423-424

population of, 582

pre-Columbian peoples, 1122-1125

raids during the Civil War, 338-340

and reform movement, 1648-1651, 1652-1653

removed to Kansas, 798-799

reservation life, 1141-1142

stereotypes of, 1516-1517

in Texas, 1561-1562

treaties affecting, 1641-1644

and United States Army, 1628-1630

in Utah, 1671-1672

and warfare, 1113-1114

in Washington, 1713

in Wild West Shows, 1747, 1748-1749

in Wyoming, 1792

see also Bureau of Indian Affairs; Native American cultures; United States Indian policy; names of individual tribes

Native American pottery, Southwestern, **1158-1160**, *1158*, *1159*

and Maria Montoya Martinez, 941, 1152, 1159

New Echota, Treaty of, 1371, 1394, 1596, 1642, 1643, 1718

New England Workingmen's Association, 1076

New Madrid Earthquake of 1811, **1184-1185**

New Mexico, **1185-1190**
Agricultural Extension Service, 217
alien land laws in, 34
Alvarez, Manuel (trader/ lieutenant governor), 36
Anza, Juan Bautista de (soldier/ governor), 47-48
Armijo, Manuel (governor), 80-81
Bell Ranch, 133-134
Bent, Charles (governor), 136
Bursom, Holm Olaf (senator), 212
Chavez, Dennis (senator), 284
during the Civil War, 338-339, 1460
Cutting, Bronson (senator), 284, 427
and early settlement, 970, 973, 974, 1000, 1502-1503
economy, 1185, 1186, 1189-1190
Elkins, Stephen Benton (politician), 479-480
folk art of, 94
Fountain, Albert Jennings (politician), 571
furniture design in, 94-95, *95*
Gallegos, José Manuel (congressman), 591
geography, 1185
ghost towns in, 608
Las Gorras Blancas in, 619
Ilfeld, Charles (businessman), 726
laws of, 810
Martínez, Antonio José (priest), 940-941
mixing of Mexican and Anglo cultures, 972
Montoya, Joseph (politician), 1027
museums in, 672
Native Americans in, 1186-1187
Otero, Miguel Antonio, Jr. (territorial governor), 1246

Otero, Miguel Antonio, Sr. (businessman), 1245-1246
Otero-Warren, Maria Adelina Emilia (Nina) (activist), 1246-1247
and school segregation, 1447
Spanish colonial period, 1187-1188, 1502-1503
statehood, 1189
Tingley, Clyde (governor), 1588
as U.S. territory, 970, 1188-1189
see also Lincoln County War; Santa Fe, New Mexico; Taos, New Mexico

New Mexico Cattle Growers Association, 271

New Mexico Mounted Police, 853

New Mexico Museum of Fine Arts, 96

New Mexico Museum. *See* Palace of the Governors

New Mexico Rangers, 74

New Northwest, The, 468, 928

New Orleans, Louisiana, 1067
as center of Burr conspiracy, 209-210
gambling in, 594

New Orleans (steamboat), 1378

New Orleans, Battle of, 762, *1709*

New Thought movement, **1190-1191**

New Urban America, The: Growth and Politics in Sunbelt Cities (Abbott), 677

New West of Edward Abbey, The (Ronald), 1

New Western history, 438, **1191-1194**
as catalyst to study, 1193
contribution of, 1194
public reaction to, 1191-1192
revisionism, 1192-1194
and the "Trails" symposium, 1191
and West-as-Region School, 1727-1730

New York Journal, 1080

New York Public Library, 100

New York Times, 986

New York Tribune, 1076-1077

New York World, 1080

Newark Methodist Maternity Hospital (El Paso), 703

Newberry, Walter, 1182

Newberry Library, **1182**

Newcomb, George "Bitter Creek," 430, 431

Newell, Frederick Haynes, 203, 370, **1182-1183**, 1254

Newell, Martha, 836

Newell, Robert, 962, **1183**

Newlands, Francis G., 1180, **1183**, 1329, 1359

Newlands Reclamation Act of 1902, 14, 203-204, 227, 229, 520, 547, 558, **1183-1184**, 1658
and conservationists, 1359
effects of, 1184, 1485
passage of, 1180, 1182, 1183, 1392, 1717
and Progressivism, 1183-1184, 1329

Newman, Angie, 736, **1185**

Newman, John, 867

News Letter (San Francisco), 143

Newspaper publishing
Abiko, Kyutaro, 2-3, 97, 395
Adams, William Lysander, 5
Bass, Charlotta Spears, 126
Byers, William Newton, 216-217
Chung Sai Yat Po (Chinese-language newspaper), 318-319, 885
Clamor Público, El, 342
Diehl, Charles Sanford, 446
Duniway, Abigail Scott, 468
Hearst, William Randolph, 666-667
Hitchcock, Gilbert Monell, 678
White, William Allen, 1736
see also Magazines and newspapers

Newton, Henry, 88

Newton, Kansas, 267, 275

Nez Percé Agency, *1645*

Nez Percé campaign, 609-610

Nez Percé Indians
Chief Joseph as leader of, 291-293
in Idaho, 724
and Oliver Otis Howard, 707
Lawyer, 855-856

Polygamy, 242, 243, **1310-1312**
  laws against, 477-478, 1653,
    1664, 1673, 1676, 1802, 1803
  among Mormons, 322, 324-325,
    327, 381, 817, 1031-1032,
    1035, 1038-1039, 1185, 1302,
    1310-1312, *1311*, 1481, 1520,
    1541, 1803
  among Native Americans,
    1097, 1312, 1653
  opposition to, 736, 838, 1675-
    1676, 1773, 1802
  and*United States* v. *Reynolds*,
    1664, 1673
Polynesian people, *657*, 1142-
  1143
Polysophical Society, 1485
Pomarede, Leon, 93
Pomeroy, Earl, 676-677
Pomeroy, George E., 1724
Pomeroy, Samuel, 800
Ponca Indians, 763, 1134, 1135,
  1139, 1172, 1441, 1586
Ponce de León, Juan Maria, 483
Ponchos, 401
Pond, Peter, 495, 585-586, **1312-
1313**
Pontiac (Ottawa), 1155, 1157
Pony Express, 220, 530, *567*,
  800, **1313-1314**, 1726
  Buffalo Bill Cody's involvement
    with, 355
  investors, 931, 1398
  and the Mormon Trail, 1039
  riders, *1313*, *1314*
  route, 1011, 1313, 1404, 1408
  success of, 1314
Poole, David, 1346
Poole, William F., 1182
Poon-Chew, Ng, 929
Poor Man's Friend (Gunn), 452
Popé (Pueblo), 1342-1343
Pope, John, 336, **1314-1315**,
  1314, 1417, 1599, 1629
Popular prints and commercial
  art, **92-94**
  lithographs, 92-93, *93*, 94
  panoramic exhibits, 92-93
Popular Sovereignty. *See* Compromise of 1850; Kansas-
  Nebraska Act
Populism, 230, 446, 1082, **1315-
1318**
  coalitions, 1316-1317

  decline, 1317
  impact, 1317-1318
  and the National People's
    Party, 1316-1317
  origins, 1315
  and farmers, 1315-1316
  and labor groups, 1315-1316
  leaders, 1316
  legislation, 1316
  and Jerry Simpson, 1464
  and socialism, 1489
  successes, 1316
  and Adolph Sutro, 1530-1531
Populist Revolt, The (Hicks),
  1317
Populists, 12, 462
  Bryan as candidate for, 192-
    193, 423
  Diggs, Annie La Porte, 446
  and Las Gorras Blancas, 619
  in Idaho, 725
  in Kansas, 801
  Lease, Mary Elizabeth Clyens,
    857-858
  in Texas, 1566
  Waite, Davis Hanson, 1704
  Weaver, James Baird, 1721
P&O Ranch, 1022
Portage des Sioux, Treaty of,
  1643
Porter, Edwin S., 45, 1043, 1700
Porter, Kenneth, 803
Portland, Oregon, **1318-1320**
  development, 1238-1239.
    1242, 1318, *1319*
  ethnic groups, 1318, 1319
  founding, 1318
  Jewish Americans in, 779, 780
  neighborhoods, 1318-1319
  plans for city, 135
  in the twentieth century, 1319
Portland Oregonian, 5, 212, 925,
  926
Portolá, Gaspar de, 235, 899,
  1418, 1503
Posadas, Las, 974, **1320**
Post, Charles, 806
Post, George B., 134, 207
Post, W. S., 30
Postal service. *See* Mail service
Poston, Charles Debrille, **1320**
Potawatomi Indians, 1157-1158
Poteaux-en-terre construction,
  56, 56

Potlatch, 1107, 1110, 1147
Potosi, Missouri, 107
Pottery. *See* Native American
  pottery, Southwestern
Potts, Daniel, 1367
Potts, John, 586
Powatomi Indians, 444
Powder River campaign, 1315
Powder River Trail. *See* Bozeman
  Trail
Powell, John (evangelist), 492
Powell, John Wesley (explorer),
  54, 68, 88, 216, 252, 460,
  501, 504, 623, 663, **1320-
1321**, *1321*
  expeditions, 1029, 1321, *1368*
  influence, 1368
  and land use, 1339, 1358-
    1359, 1368, 1387
  and Native American ethnol-
    ogy, 1321
  *Report on the Lands of Arid
    Regions,* 67, 369, 630, 1358-
    1359, 1368
  and the United States Geologi-
    cal Survey, 950, 1182, 1321,
    1359, 1638, 1640, 1641
Powell, Lasarus, 797
Power, James, 487
Powers, John, 289
Prairie, **1321-1323**
Prairie, The (Cooper), 385
Prairie, looking-glass, 899
Prairie dogs, **1323**
Prairie du Chien, 345
Prairie du Chien, Treaty of, 1643
Prairie fires, 1322
Prairie Folks (Garland), 596
Prairie Land and Cattle Com-
  pany, 922, *922*
Prairie Oil and Gas Company,
  1218
Prairie schooners, 380; *see also*
  Conestoga wagon
Prairie Traveler, The (Marcy), 938
Prather, Ed, 1586
Pratt, John, 59
Pratt, Orson, **1323-1324**, 1412
Pratt, Parley, 718, 1373
Pratt, Richard Henry, 731, 883,
  1324, 1441, 1658
Pratte, Bernard, 587
Pratte, Chouteau and Company,
  38

Tallgrass Prairie Preserve, 281
Tallmadge, James, Jr., 1013
Tall Men, The, 537
*Tall Tales from Texas Cow
    Camps* (Boatright), 711
Tanaka, Michiko, **1534**
Tandy, Vertner W., 1706
Tanka, 885
Tanner, George, 861
Tano Indians, 1433
Taos, New Mexico, 928, 941,
    946, **1535**, *1535*
    artistic community in, 910-911,
        1535
Taos Indians, *1105*
Taos School of Artists, 86-87,
    1536
Taos Society of Artists, 1064
Tape, John and Mary, 1447
Tape, Joseph, 1536-1537
Tape, Mamie, 1536-1537
Tape, Mary, 1536-1537
Tape v. Hurley, **1536-1537**
Tapia, Isidore, 184
Targee, Thomas B., 1410
Tariff policy, **1537-1539**
    and the American West, 1538
    of John Calhoun, 220, 221
    of Henry Clay, 346-347, 1537
    during the Civil War, 1537-
        1538
    and the election of 1888, 1538-
        1539
    historical background, 1537-
        1538
    of Andrew Jackson, 762
Tasquienachi, Inclán, 49
Tatum, Lawrie, 1435-1436
Tau-Ankia, 895
Tavernier, Jules, **1539-1540**,
    1540
Taylor, Abner, 1797
Taylor, Carl, 1280
Taylor, Edward T., 1523, 1543
Taylor, Glen Hearst, **1541**
Taylor, Jim. *See* Sutton-Taylor
    feud
Taylor, John, 242, 243, 1033,
    1038, 1039, **1541-1542**
Taylor, Leonora, 242
Taylor, Nathaniel G., **1542**, 1652
Taylor, Richard, 242
Taylor, William Levi (Buck), 403,
    535, 1747

Taylor, William, 491
Taylor, Zachary, 133, 214, 377,
    424, 461, 753, 819, 840,
    1071, 1310, 1429, **1542-
    1543**
    in United States–Mexican War,
        1542-1543, 1563-1565,
        1570, 1586, 1660-1662,
        1662, 1779
Taylor Grazing Act, 203, 470,
    520, 629, **1543-1544**, 1674
TB. *See* Tuberculosis
Teachers on the frontier, 1086-
    1087, **1544-1545**, *1544,
    1545*
Teapot Dome, 456, **1545-1546**
    Albert Fall's role in, 507-508,
        1545-1546
"Teasing cousins," 1098
Teatro Villalongín (Companía
    Hernández-Villalongín),
    1546-1547
Tecumseh (Shawnee), 155, 345,
    567, 749, 1068, 1074, 1113,
    1185, **1547-1548**, 1708
Tejanos, 972, **1548-1549**
    conflicts with U.S. authorities,
        396, 1695
    Cortez, Gregorio, 394
    Leon, Patricia de, 863
Telegraph, **1549-1550**, *1550;* and
    Western expansion, 168
Television Westerns. *See* Radio
    and television Westerns
Teller, Henry M., 423, 1358,
    1359, **1551**, 1651
Teller Amendment, 1080
Telles, Raymond, 484
Temperance and prohibition,
    1551-1554, *1551, 1552,
    1553*
    and the press, 928
    and Progressivism, 1328
    women's involvement in, 420
    see also Saloons; Woman's
        Christian Temperance Union
Temple, Shirley, 1515
Ten Bears (Comanche), **1554-
    1555**, *1555*
Ten Elks. *See* Ten Bears
"Ten-gallon hat." *See* Cowboy
    outfits
Tenorio, Antonio, 1601
Tenskwatawa (Shawnee), 1547

Tenting on the Plains (Custer),
    425
Teotihuacan, 1123
Terrazas, Joaquin, 51, 1683
Territorial government, 518-519,
    520, **1555-1556**
    effectiveness of, 1556
    and federal marshals, 523, 524
    federal supervision of, 1556
    of Northwest Territory, 1555
    origin of, 1555
    admission to statehood, 1555-
        1556
Territorial law and courts, **1556-
    1558**, *1556*
*Territories and the United States,
    1861-1890, The* (Pomeroy),
    677
Terrónes, 61
Terry, Alfred Howe, 446, 888,
    1558-1559, 1631
Terry, Benjamin F., 1570
Terry, David S., 187, 1425
Teton Dam, 725
Teton Indians, 1111, 1173
    see also Sioux Indians
Tetrazzini, Luisa, 758
Tevis, Lloyd, 231, 683, 918
Tewa Indians, 1148, 1433
Tewksbury, Edward, 621, 622
Tewksbury, John D., 620-621
Texaco, 1218
Texas, **1559-1567**, *1560, 1564,
    1566*
    alien land laws in, 34
    annexation of, 785, 786, 1071-
        1072, 1078, 1309, 1310,
        1542, *1560,* 1563, 1606
    Baylor, John Robert (Indian
        agent), 127-128
    Burnet, David Gouverneur
        (vice-president), 206
    El Camino Real, 239
    colonization of, 108
    during the Civil War, 128, 206,
        337-338, 705, 1565-1566
    as Confederate state, 128, 206
    Declaration of Independence,
        704
    economic growth, 1565, 1566,
        1567
    empresarios in, 486-487, 1563
    ethnic groups in, 1560
    and Fredonia rebellion, 573

Utah Copper Company, 388
Utah Expedition, 1672, **1675-1676**, 1704, 1808
 as anti-Mormon action, 1035, 1038, 1384, 1385
 and logistics, 931, 938
Utah Indians, 1047
Utah Magazine, 614
Utah Southern Railroad, 779
Utah War, 1047
Ute Indian agency, 113
Ute Indians, 361, 368, 923, 962, *1098*, 1132
 culture, 1148, 1150-1151
 relocation, 1152
 Walkara, 1704-1705
Utley, Robert M., 1486
Utrecht, Treaty of, 585

V

Valdes, Luis, 1580
Valdez Is Coming, 541
Valera, Eamon de, 755
Vallejo, Mariano Guadalupe, 743, **1677**, 1764
Vallejo de Leese, Rosalía, 1763
Valley Farmer, 359
Valley Ranch, 467
Van Brunt and Howe, 207
Van Buren, Martin, 763, 1073-1074, 1548, 1596
Vance, Nina, 1579
Vance, Robert H.
Vancouver Island, 1037
Vancouver, George, 29, 250, 494, 1236, 1241, 1713-1714
Vanderbilt, Cornelius, 4, 620, 1260, 1659, 1706
Vanderwood, Paul, 1670
Vanishing American, The, 540, *540*
Van de Water, Frederic, 425
Van Devanter, Willis, 1557, **1677-1678**, 1710, 1796
Van Dorn, Earl, 278, 1629
Van Name, Willard, 477
Van Ness, James, 1425
Van Orsdel, William Wesley, 491
Vantage Point (Johnson), 783
Van Vechten, Carl, 911
Van Waters, Miriam, **1678**

Vaqueros, 236, 265, 401, 408, 697
Vargas, Diego de, 1187-1188, 1433, **1678**
Variennes, Pierre Gaultier de, 1015
Vasil'ev, M. N., 29
Vasilev, Ivan, 29, 498
Vasquez, Benito, 1679
Vasquez, Louis, Jr., 1679
Vasquez, Pierre Louis, 565, 1527, **1679**
Vásquez, Richard, 887
Vásquez, Tiburcio, 422, 700, 855, **1679-1680**
Vaux, Calvert, 1231
Vavazos, Lolo, 381
Vawter, Keith, 283
Vegetable growing. *See* Fruit and vegetable growing
Velez, Lupe, **1680**
Venard, Stephen, **1680-1681**
Veniaminov, Ivan (Popov, Ioann), **1681**
Venturi, Robert, 333
Vérendrye, François, 585, 1792
Vérendrye, Louis-Joseph, 585, 1792
Vérendrye, Pierre Gaultier de Varennes, Sieur de La, 585
Vérendrye, sieur de la, 1200
Vérendrye family, 250, 495, 497
Verity, Oliver, 682
Vernon, Mabel, 1087
Verrazzano, Giovanni da, 250
Via Industrial, La, 928
Vial, Pedro, **1681-1682**
Victor, Frances Fuller, 962, **1682**, 1776
Victor, Henry, 1682
Victor, Orville J., 1682
Victoria, Texas, 863
Victorio (Apache), 51, 198, 635, 640, 789, 1569, 1626-1627, **1682-1683**, *1683*
Vidor, King, 537, 538
Vigilantes of Montana, The (Dimsdale), 1684
Vigilantism, 226, 260, **1683-1685**, *1684*, *1685*, 1695
 and Graham-Tewksbury Feud, 622
 in Johnson County War, 784-785
 in nineteenth century, 855

 organization of vigilantes, 1684-1685
 see also Lynching; San Francisco Committee of Vigilance of 1856
Vignau, Nicolas, 584
Vilducea, Ramona, 1741
Villa, Francisco ("Pancho"), 112, 143, 198, 969-970, 1189, 1282, 1571, 1669, **1686-1687**, *1686*
 as social bandit, 1486, 1487
Villagrá, Gaspar Pérez de, 886
Villalobos, López de, 218
Villalongín, Carlos, 1547
Villard, Henry, 206, 431, **1687-1688**
Villard, Oswald Garrison, 1688
Villareal, José Antonio, 886
Villarreal, Bruno, 381
Villaseñor, Victor, 887
Villazur, Pedro de, 798, 1172
Vincent, John H., 283
Vincentians, 1271
Violence, **1688-1700**, *1689*, *1691*, *1696*, *1699*
 Anglo-American, roots of, 1689-1690
 during California gold rush, 854-855
 and concept of frontier, 1689-1690, *1692*
 historical overview, 1688-1694
 associated with labor movement, 739-740, 832-834, 888, 908-910, 1694
 as manifestation of social conflict, 1692-1694
 myths about, 1694, 1698-1700
 associated with racial tension, 855, 1694-1697
 against women, 1697-1698
 see also Lynching
Virginia City, Nevada, 608, 830, **1700-1701**
 fire of 1875, 985, 921, 992, 1666, 1700-1701, *1701*
Virginian, The (Wister), 403, 533, 535-536, 785, 878, 1514, 1699, 1757
"Virginian, The" (television series), 1348
Virgin Land: The American West as Symbol and Myth (Smith), 676